Gabriel Fauré:

The Songs and their Poets

Gabriel Fauré at the Hotel Métropole, Lugano, summer of 1912, working on his opera Pénélope

Gabriel Fauré:
The Songs
and their Poets

Graham Johnson

With translations of the song texts by Richard Stokes

ASHGATE   **Guildhall SCHOOL** of Music & Drama

Co-published in 2009 by:
The Guildhall School of Music & Drama
Barbican
Silk Street
London
EC2Y 8DT
Tel: 0044 (0) 207628 2571
Fax: 0044 (0) 20 7382 7212

www.gsmd.ac.uk

and

Ashgate Publishing Limited
Wey Court East
Union Road
Farnham
Surrey
GU9 7PT
England

www.ashgate.com

Ashgate Pulblishing Company
110 Cherry Street
Suite 3-1
Burlington, VT 05401-3818
USA

British Library Cataloguing in Publication Data

Johnson, Graham, 1950–

Gabriel Fauré : the songs and their poets. – (Guildhall research studies)

1. Fauré, Gabriel, 1845–1924 – Criticism and interpretation

2. Songs – History and criticism 3. French poetry – 19th century – History and criticism

I. Title

780.9'2

Reprinted 2014

ISBN 9780754659600 (hbk)

Library of Congress Cataloging-in-Publication Data

Johnson, Graham, 1950–

Gabriel Fauré: the songs and their poets / Graham Johnson, with translations of the song texts by Richard Stokes.

p. cm. – (Guildhall research studies)

Includes bibliographical references and index.

ISBN 978-0-7546-5960-0 (pbk. : alk. paper) 1. Fauré, Gabriel, 1845–1924. Songs. 2. Songs, French – France – History and criticism. 3. French poetry – History and criticism. 4. Music and literature. I. Stokes, Richard. II. Title.

ML410.F27J64 2008

782.42168092–dc22

2008039246

Printed in the United Kingdom by Henry Ling Limited, at the Dorset Press, Dorchester, DT1 1HD

For Pamela Lidiard

Contents

Foreword and Acknowledgements

This book is the outcome of a project I directed in 2005 at the Guildhall School of Music and Drama in London: the complete songs and duets of Fauré were performed by dozens of student singers and pianists. Before this I had recorded the songs on four CDs with an array of professional singers (as well as with Ronan O'Hora in piano duets) for Hyperion Records. The chance to work on this music with artists of different ages and levels of experience was extremely revealing and provided the impetus to write a study of this kind under the imprint of the school in which I am honoured to teach.

The full scope of Fauré's greatness as a composer cannot be appreciated by a study of his songs alone, and this is a book, first and foremost, about Fauré's songs. In the case of some composers such specialism comes at a higher cost than others; a comparison with Schubert in this regard is not inappropriate, for it is all too easy to write about that composer's lieder while conveniently ignoring his vast output in other spheres. I have endeavoured to incorporate as much information as I can to provide a more rounded picture of Fauré than as a mere composer of *mélodies* – not that there is anything 'mere' about this extraordinary repertoire. Throughout the book I have referred to his other works in the hope that readers will follow-up these signposts towards a greater understanding of the totality of the composer's achievement. Nevertheless it seems to me that the songs are as good a starting place as any in Fauré's œuvre to initiate in the student a deeper understanding of the composer's genius, and how he gradually changed from a salon composer of the 1860s and 1870s to take his rightful place as a great sage of early twentieth-century music.

Although *Gabriel Fauré: The Songs and their Poets* contains a certain amount of information not easily available elsewhere, particularly regarding the song texts and their authors, I lay no claim to having broken a great deal of new musicological ground. Like almost all practising musicians, whose writing about music must be fitted in between concert engagements, I have relied on established biographical sources and benefitted from the first-hand research of the experts acknowledged overleaf, the scholars who have sifted documents, studied manuscripts, and done all the research in the field which earns for them the admiration and gratitude of their performing colleagues. What comes at first hand, however, is my experience of the music itself. I have unearthed no new letters, and no brand new facts about Fauré's life, but the interpretation of those established facts, and of the music itself, is my own. I remain someone who has puzzled over and loved this composer at close quarters for three decades and more.

My first teacher of accompaniment at the Royal Academy of Music – John Streets – was also the first out-and-out Fauré enthusiast I had ever encountered. For him this composer's songs, to my initial astonishment, were automatically taken to be as important as Debussy's – or even Schubert's. My fellow-student Felicity Lott and I were coached in the *Cinq mélodies 'de Venise'* among other *mélodies*; the late cycle *Mirages* was spoken about, rightly, as a masterpiece with no room for dissent. It was some thirty-five years ago that Streets (also Head of Opera at the RAM) oversaw a fine student production of the opera *Pénélope*, the first in the UK. In 1999 the Guildhall School presented the same work to my rather less puzzled and more seasoned ears. My own students at the Guildhall, fascinated and sometimes perplexed, were on the beginning of their own journeys with Fauré, but that is as it should be; he is a composer of, and for, a lifetime – and it sometimes takes a lifetime to appreciate him fully.

As a pianist who encounters Fauré's songs, if not every day of the week, then almost every week of the year, I became aware of the need among English-speaking students and listeners for a song-oriented guide to the composer's life, or to put it another way, a book that places the vocal achievements of an exceptionally long musical career into a time-frame and a biographical context. The complete texts of the songs with translations by Richard Stokes can be read separately, skipping my commentaries, as a means of following this composer on his journey through the literature of his time. If this book enables singers and pianists to devise their recital programmes with anything like the fastidious taste that is the hallmark of this composer himself, and if the commentaries encourage potential performers to look at music that otherwise would have remained unexplored on the shelf, it will have fulfilled its purpose.

Everyone writing about Fauré in our time is in the debt of Jean-Michel Nectoux, who has dominated scholarship around this composer for decades. I am extremely grateful to him for his help via a correspondence that has been (at least for me) fascinating, and for his continuing devotion to every aspect of Fauréan detail. Despite the fact that his current musicological and art-historical interests have taken him into other areas (including the resplendent *Harmonie en bleu et or – Debussy, la musique et les arts*, Paris: Fayard, 2005), M. Nectoux has taken on board my various enquiries and requests regarding Fauré with punctual and good-humoured exactitude. For permission to quote frequently from his published writings I am very grateful, and also for permission to use some of the rare photographs in his possession. Some time ago it was his happy idea in one of his publications to link the endearing photograph of Fauré to be seen at the beginning of Chapter 10 of this book with the title of one of the composer's most haunting songs – *Dans la forêt de septembre*. The paradox inherent in the original French title of M. Nectoux's major book *Gabriel Fauré: Les Voix du clair-obscur* (translated by Roger Nichols as *Fauré: A Musical Life*, Cambridge: Cambridge University Press, 1991) encouraged me in turn to choose a cover design for my own book with the composer photographed standing at the piano in his apartment at boulevard Malesherbes, only partly lit by the afternoon sun, the 'demi-jour' of Verlaine's *En sourdine*. The caption's reference to the composer's *Dans la pénombre* alludes of course to the title of a song in *Le Jardin clos*.

Unfortunately the projected five-volume edition of the *mélodies* to be published by Leduc as part of the complete Fauré edition under M. Nectoux's aegis will not be available for some time, although the first volume of this series is now with the publishers. M. Nectoux's collaborator on this edition of songs is Mimi Daitz of New York City. I am grateful to Ms Daitz for her advice and help, and for an unforgettable evening spent with her and her husband Stephen, who recited Homer in ancient Greek for us with a mastery that would have fascinated the composer of *Lydia* and *Pénélope*. Also present on that convivial occasion was Susan Youens, the great Schubert scholar, whose expertise in the field of the *mélodie*, an earlier specialism as far as her career is concerned, has been one of the many things that enriches our friendship. That Fauré scholarship is in fine fettle in the United States is proved by the more recent work of Carlos Caballero, whose remarkable *Fauré and French Musical Aesthetics* (Cambridge: Cambridge University Press, 2001) was, and remains, an inspiration. A recent masterclass for Rosemary Hyler's *Songfest* in Malibu, California, presented me with a stunning array of young singers and pianists from all over the country, all enraptured (and coping wonderfully well – dare I say unexpectedly?) with *La Bonne chanson*. This was indeed heartening for the Fauréan future across the Atlantic. One can detect there a backlash against an era of emptiness and spin, and the youngsters' hunger for music of this depth seemed to me happily associated with a gradual shift of *Zeitgeist*. I am deeply grateful to my friend Dr Gerald Perman (President and Musical Director of the Vocal Arts Society of Washington DC as well as a distinguished psychiatrist, now retired) for our correspondence concerning Fauré's early childhood.

Scholars of the past will always have their august role to play in a book of this kind, and there is no greater debt than that to the philosopher and musicologist Vladimir Jankélévitch (1903–1985). The depth and eloquence of Jankélévitch's books on music in general, and on Fauré in particular (*Gabriel Fauré et ses mélodies* first appeared in the late 1930s and has since been reissued in various editions), is such as to discourage anyone else writing on the subject. Indeed it has long done so, and I am aware that I am one of the few to break, with some trepidation, this awed silence. Jankélévitch's study was the first to make a case for considering Fauré's song output as a chronicle of an artistic journey complete in itself, but it is written in a poetic, allusive style that renders it almost untranslatable from the original French. It is also a masterpiece by a great aesthetician, and it is little wonder that other writers, not to mention performers, should be wary of entering the same territory. However indispensable Jankélévitch's book remains, it is perhaps not the easiest starting point for the English reader and student, mainly because it contains none of the song texts themselves and it assumes an enormous background knowledge about the composer's music. If it were merely the purpose of my own volume to prepare the reader to embark on Jankélévitch's amazing study I should be satisfied.

English writers on Fauré have long continued the tradition of helpful enthusiasm for this composer established by the ever-hospitable (and rich) Frank Schuster in the London of the 1890s. After my studentship my first serious conversations about Fauré were with the late and much-missed critic Felix Aprahamian, doyen of musical Francophiles in London. When he masterminded a festival of Fauré's works during the Second World War at Wigmore Hall he spotted a tall elderly lady, up from the country for the day, waiting for return tickets. It was one of the triumphs of his life to be able to usher, with some ceremony, the Princesse de Polignac, into a seat; she had gone into exile in Devon during the hostilities and had been, over sixty years earlier, the 'onlie begetter' of some of the music soon to be heard.

Norman Suckling's book for the 'Master Musicians' series, *Fauré* (London: Dent, 1946), is also that of a philosopher, and it remains an underestimated source of trenchant observations on the Fauré style. Every scholar of French music in English-speaking countries is by now indebted to the work of Robert Orledge, who has marked out his own special niche in Fauré studies, especially in regard to his analysis of the composer's harmonic world, *Gabriel Fauré* (London: Eulenburg, 1979). Jessica Duchen's more recent and accessibly illustrated book on Fauré, *Gabriel Fauré* (London: Phaidon, 2000), has almost certainly won the composer many English-speaking friends. I continue to miss conversations on every aspect of the song repertoire with the late Eric Sams, despite his reluctance to appreciate the later songs of Fauré. This had always been a bone of contention between him and his son Jeremy, whose affection for, and knowledge of, these inscrutable cycles is second to none.

I must thank other people who have also helped me in the writing of this book. That great Poulenc expert and translator Sidney Buckland has come to my aid on more than one occasion. I am grateful to M. Thierry Bodin in Paris for giving me permission to perform and reproduce an unpublished song by Fauré – *Puisque j'ai mis ma lèvre* – of which he owns the autograph; he has also shared his encyclopaedic knowledge of nineteenth-century French musical life. For the open-hearted and almost casual (because so easily given) generosity of my collaborator Richard Stokes when it comes to projects such as these, I am only one of many to offer praise and gratitude. Dr Jonathan Katz kindly provided translations from Latin and Greek. Steven Isserlis made extremely helpful comments on one of the chapters, and Stephen Hough on another; my colleague François Le Roux has been a generous source of information. Robert White in New York, with an eagle's eye for detail, has been as always a source of support and perspicacity, and I am grateful to that great expert on all matters relating to the Polignac family, Sylvia Kahan, also of New York City, for her advice concerning certain aspects of this book's iconography. Michael Kennedy shared with me his thoughts on the Elgar–Fauré connection, and my former student, the pianist and musicologist Roger Moseley, discussed with me the writing of Roland Barthes. In connection with Frank Schuster, Jill Balcon relayed to me information from Lady Spender, Sir Stephen Spender's widow. Those great *doyens* of vocal recorded music, Vivian Liff and his partner the late and much missed George Stuart, were kind enough to put me in touch with Marc Matzner in Los Angeles. Mr Matzner, a hugely well-informed connoisseur of fine singing, enabled me to hear many of the records of artists (especially those of the unaccountably forgotten Noëmie Pérugia) that were not contained in my own collection. His willingness to make these and other recordings available to me with the aid of modern technology was kindness itself.

Heidi Bishop at Ashgate has spent a good deal of extra time and trouble in seeing this book through to publication. I must also acknowledge the efficiency and patience of Sarah Charters, and thank John Peacock for his splendid book design. Fiona Little's fine-tuning of the text was remarkably thorough, while always tactful. I wish to express my ongoing gratitude to my partner, Brandon Velarde, for his support for this project, as well as for his indulgence of the domestic vagaries of an author in the middle of a time-consuming project such as this. Geoffrey, Gerald and Harry also extended as much patience to me as is possible to expect of regally demanding cats when it came to impromptu adjustments (the author busy at his desk) to their morning and evening feeding times. It was not lost on me at the time that Emile Vuillermoz spoke of Fauré's 'cat-like flexibility' and Vladimir Jankélévitch referred to Fauré's music falling on its feet with the precision of a cat. Suckling expands this comparison to explain the admiration of a certain kind of animal owner, as well as certain kind of listener, for Fauré's art:

Strength without brutality; muscles which achieve grace all the more perfectly because they do not have to strain after it – these are essentially feline traits; and on the less tangible side a demand for understanding before it will yield you its companionship, and a distinction of character which prevents it from being degraded to the function of a mere toy or a mere stimulant.[1]

Gabriel Fauré: The Songs and their Poets is first and foremost a Guildhall School of Music production, so I wish to close these acknowledgements with thanks to my colleagues there. George Odam worked on an earlier version of the manuscript and Rebecca Heath was helpful during the later stages. Robin Bowman, Head of Vocal Studies (now retired), and Ronan O'Hora, Head of Keyboard Studies, were instrumental in crafting the concert series that led to the writing of this study. The support of the Guildhall School Principal for these concerts and for musical research has been a major factor in my attempting a work of this scope. Needless to say, without Dr Barry Ife's continuing support, both moral and material, a book of this size could never have been published under the school's auspices.

Without the enthusiasm of our Deputy Head of Keyboard Studies I cannot imagine that we could have undertaken the Britten, Fauré and Heine song projects in the first place. She is 'mother' of our very demanding accompaniment course and an indispensable part of the students' lives. Her calm and tenacity in the face of serious illness, and her refusal to be away from the school for a day, nay hour, more than necessary, have been more inspiring than is possible to describe. In the midst of everything else she has read the manuscript and made comments, and for lots of practical reasons this book could not have been written without her. She has always played the Fauré songs beautifully and teaches them with love. Her calm courage, a quality that recalls the stoicism of the composer himself, has been an example to us all.

On behalf of her colleagues at the Guildhall School of Music, and in gratitude for her tireless work on behalf of its pianists and singers this book is dedicated to Pamela Lidiard.

Graham Johnson
London

1   Norman Suckling, *Fauré* (London: Dent, 1946), p. 12.

Gabriel Fauré:
Songs through a Life

He belongs to that very rare breed of men who improve all the time as one gets to know them better ...
Camille Saint-Saëns in a letter to Pauline Viardot, 23 July 1877

1845   On 12 May at 4 o'clock in the morning, Gabriel Urbain Fauré is born in Pamiers, Ariège, sixth child of Toussaint-Honoré Fauré (1810–1885) and Marie-Antoinette-Hélène Fauré, née de Lalène-Laprade (1809–1887). The baby is christened the next day and consigned to a wet-nurse in nearby Verniolle. Fauré is fifteen years younger than his eldest sibling, his only sister, Rose-Élodie-Gabrielle, known as Victoire.

1849   The family moves to Montgauzy, near Foix, where Fauré *père* has been promoted to head the École Normale. From about 1850 Gabriel takes music lessons and improvises on the chapel harmonium. In 1853 Toussaint Fauré consults Monsieur Dufaur de Saubiac about the future course of his son's education.

1854   Gabriel is taken to Paris and entrusted to the care of the pedagogue and composer Louis Niedermeyer, who has recently opened (1853) a new school for young church musicians. Fauré wins various prizes (for both music and literary studies) at the École Niedermeyer from 1857 onwards.

1861   After the death of Niedermeyer (14 March), Camille Saint-Saëns (aged twenty-six) joins the staff of the school. Fauré composes (1) *Le Papillon et la fleur* (Hugo).

1862   Saint-Saëns is invited to holiday with the Fauré family in Tarbes in August. Three further Victor Hugo settings almost certainly date from this year: (2) *Mai*, the lost song *L'Aube naît* and *Puisqu'ici-bas*, a one-time solo setting that becomes a duet in 1873 (see below). The autograph of a fourth Hugo song, (3) *Puisque j'ai mis ma lèvre*, is clearly dated 8 December 1862. This third piece remains unpublished.

1863	Fauré passes his organ examination with distinction, just failing to obtain the first prize (it is never his favourite instrument). He writes a piano sonata for his niece that has never been published.
1864	(4) *Rêve d'amour* is composed on 5 May. Between May and August the publisher Choudens negotiates with Victor Hugo for the publishing rights for the six *romances* by Fauré (see above), with texts by the great poet; in that number are included two settings that remain unpublished.
1865	Fauré leaves the École Niedermeyer at the end of July after winning a first prize for the compostion of *Cantique de Jean Racine*. (5) *Tristesse d'Olympio* possibly dates from this time, as well as (6) *Dans les ruines d'une abbaye* (both Hugo). Both songs could equally well have been composed at the beginning of the Rennes period (see below).
1866–70	Having left school at last, and in need of regular employment, Fauré takes up a place in January 1866 as organist at Saint-Saveur in Rennes (Brittany), where his address is 4 rue de Nemours. He lives and works there, somewhat uneventfully, for the next four years. He holidays with Saint-Saëns in Britanny in August 1866. He accompanies the famous opera singer Madame Miolan-Carvalho on a recital tour of Brittany in the summer of 1868.
1869	He signs his first contract with the publisher Choudens to issue *Le Papillon et la fleur* and *Dans les ruines d'une abbaye*.
1870	Fauré moves back to Paris, where he is briefly organist at Notre-Dame-de-Clignancourt. He meets Lalo, Duparc and César Franck. With the declaration of the Franco-Prussian War in July Fauré enlists in the First Light Infantry Regiment of the Imperial Guard. He sees action in the battles of Champigny, Le Bourget and Créteil. It is also probably at some time during 1870 that he composes the Hugo setting (7) *L'Aurore*, as well as (8) *Les Matelots* (Gautier), (9) *Lydia* (Leconte de Lisle) and (10) *Hymne* (Baudelaire).
1871	With the Armistice at the end of January Fauré returns to Paris and lives with his brother Amand. In February he is a founder member of the Société Nationale de Musique (SNM). In March he flees the dangers of the Commune in June and takes up temporary exile in Switzerland; four months later he returns to Paris to take up the post of organist at St Sulpice (October). Fauré completes his last Hugo solo setting, (12) *L'Absent*, on 3 April. In December the publisher Georges Hartmann issues a volume of four songs: *Lydia*, *Hymne*, *Mai* and the more recently composed (11) *Seule!* (Gautier). (13) *La Rançon* and (14) *Chant d'automne* (both to Baudelaire texts) are probably composed in this year.

1872	Fauré is introduced to the circle of the celebrated singer and composer Pauline Viardot, where he meets Gounod, Flaubert and George Sand among many other celebrities. He also becomes friends with Camille Clerc and his wife Marie, serious music lovers who are hosts of many summer sojourns in Normandy. Marie takes on a mothering role in the composer's life, particularly in terms of encouraging the composition of chamber music. It is probably in this year that Fauré composes his Gautier setting (15) *Chanson du pêcheur (Lamento)*.
1873	It is probably at some point in 1873 that Fauré composes (16) *Aubade* (Pomey) as well as (17) *Tristesse* (Gautier). Madame Édouard Lalo sings *Chanson du pêcheur* at a concert of the SNM. On 19 October he finishes (18) *Barcarolle* (Monnier) and dedicates it to Pauline Viardot. At about this time he composes the duets (19) *Puisqu'ici-bas* (a Hugo setting that adapts musical material from a solo song written a decade earlier) and (20) *Tarentelle* (Monnier).
1874	Fauré leaves St Sulpice in order to deputise for Saint-Saëns at the Madeleine. (21) *Ici-bas!* (Sully Prudhomme) is probably composed at this time. He spends the summer with the Clercs in Sainte-Adresse in Normandy after installing himself at his new Parisian address, 7 rue de Parme, in the nineteenth *arrondissement*.
1875	On 10 April Claudie and Marianne Viardot give the first performances of the duets *Puisqu'ici-bas* and *Tarentelle*, which Fauré dedicates to them. He works on an ambitious violin sonata. He summers once again at Sainte-Adresse. In August he writes (22) *Au bord de l'eau* (Sully Prudhomme).
1876	In April Pauline Viardot sings *Chanson du pêcheur* and *Barcarolle* for the SNM. In May Georges Hartmann hands over the rights of four Fauré songs to the composer's new publisher, Choudens. The *Cantique de Jean Racine* is published by the firm of F. Schoen. Thanks to the negotiations of Camille Clerc, the Leipzig firm of Breitkopf & Härtel accepts Fauré's Violin Sonata in A major, Op. 13, for publication. He begins the Piano Quartet in C minor, Op. 15.
1877	The year begins with triumphant performances of the A major Violin Sonata, including one at the home of Benjamin Godard. In April Fauré becomes choirmaster (*maître de chapelle*) at the Madeleine; to make ends meet he has to give numerous piano and harmony lessons. In July he becomes engaged to Marianne Viardot, with whom he has been smitten for some time. She breaks off the engagement in October. In December Fauré travels with Saint-Saëns to Weimar for the première of the older composer's *Samson et Dalila*. The song (23) *Après un rêve* (Bussine) is composed. Choudens publishes five separate songs: *Lydia, Mai, Ici-bas!, Barcarolle* and *Au bord de l'eau*.

1878	(25) *Sylvie* (Choudens), the three songs of the cycle (26–28) *Poëme d'un jour* (Grandmougin), the celebrated (29) *Nell* (Leconte de Lisle) and the equally famous (31) *Automne* (Silvestre) are all composed in 1878. (30) *Le Voyageur* (Silvestre) and (24) *Sérénade toscane* (Bussine) probably date from this year. A performance at the end of June of *Les Djinns* in its version for choir and orchestra (conducted by Colonne, and repeated in February 1879) is the composer's definitive farewell to Hugo.
1879	In January Choudens publishes *Hymne*, *Chant d'automne*, *L'Absent* and *Sérénade toscane*. In April Fauré journeys to Cologne to see two Wagner productions. During the spring he composes (32) *Les Berceaux* (Sully Prudhomme). In September he goes to Munich with Messager to see Wagner's *Ring*. He finishes the solo piano version of the *Ballade*. In December Choudens publishes the first *recueil* of *Vingt mélodies*. The song (33) *Notre amour* (Silvestre) is probably written during this year.
1880	The celebrated *Élegie* for cello and piano is given its first performance at the home of Saint-Saëns. In November *Poëme d'un jour* appears as a single volume published by Durand.
1881	The song (34) *Le Secret* (Silvestre) is completed (6 July). Fauré visits Munich for the third time, on this occasion with his friends the Baugnies, to hear *Lohengrin*, *Tristan und Isolde* and *Die Meistersinger*. *Messe des pêcheurs de Villerville* is composed in collaboration with Messager, and it is more than likely that the vocal quartet (35) *Le Ruisseau* (to an anonymous text) for two-part female choir and piano also dates from this year; it receives its first performance on 14 January 1882.
1882	Fauré visits London for a performance of Wagner's *Ring*. Songs of this year are the two Silvestre settings (36) *Chanson d'amour* and (37) *La Fée aux chansons*. In September Fauré stays at Villerville with the Clercs for the last time. Camille Clerc dies in November.
1883	Fauré's cantata *La Naissance de Vénus* is performed. On 27 March he marries Marie Fremiet, daughter of a well-known sculptor, and he moves into a new home, 93 avenue Niel, in the seventeenth *arrondissement of* Paris. (38) *Madrigal* (Silvestre), for vocal quartet (or chorus) and piano, is dated 1 December 1883. On 29 December his first son, Emmanuel, is born. Marie will insist that their children add her birth name (and that of their grandfather, the sculptor) to their surname – thus Fauré-Fremiet.
1884	The first three nocturnes for piano are published. This is a year rich in songs – 20 May: (39) *Aurore* (Silvestre); 25 May: (40) *Fleur jetée* (Silvestre); 30 May: (41) *Le Pays des rêves* (Silvestre); 6 June: (42) *Les Roses d'Ispahan* (Leconte de Lisle, orchestrated in 1890). All four, as well as the part-song *Madrigal*, are performed at two concerts of the SNM in December.
1885	Fauré's Symphony in D minor receives a cool reception at the SNM. The composer later destroys this work. His father dies on 25 July. The *cantique* entitled (43) *Noël* (Wilder) dates from this time.

1886	Fauré meets the celebrated aesthete Robert de Montesquiou, who becomes his 'literary adviser'. (44) *Nocturne* (Villiers de L'Isle Adam) is composed in this year, as are the Second Piano Quartet Op. 45 and the Fourth Barcarolle for piano. During a visit to Paris in June, Tchaikovsky finds the First Piano Quartet 'excellent'. In October the Fauré family move to a bigger apartment at 154 boulevard Malesherbes in the seventeenth *arrondissement*, near the Madeleine.
1887	On 26 April a concert entitled 'Audition de mélodies de Fauré' is given at the home of Robert de Montesquiou. (45) *Les Présents* (Villiers de L'Isle Adam) dates from this year, as does (52) *Clair de lune*, the composer's first setting of Verlaine. Fauré's portrait is painted by Jacques-Emile Blanche. He stays in Dieppe as the guest of Élisabeth Greffulhe. The composer's mother dies on 31 December.
1888	The first performance of Fauré's *Requiem* is given at the Madeleine on 16 January; in May the work is performed non-liturgically with brass added to the string orchestra. Fauré plays the harmonium at a performance of Chabrier's opera *Gwendoline* at the home of Winnaretta Singer, Princesse de Scey-Montbéliard. He makes his first journey to Bayreuth, where he meets Debussy and is received cordially by Wagner's family. Three songs are composed in November: (46) *Au cimetière* (Richepin), (47) *Larmes* (Richepin) and (53) *Spleen* (Verlaine).
1889	Fauré's music for Dumas's play *Caligula* (first performed in November 1888 at the Odéon) is performed at the SNM. Tchaikovsky finds it 'adorable'. John Singer Sargent paints Fauré's portrait. The composer's second son, Philippe, is born on 28 July in Prunay, where Fauré regularly spends the summers at the home of his parents-in-law. He visits the Comtesse Greffulhe for a brief holiday at Bois-Boudran at the end of September. The incidental music for Haraucourt's play *Shylock* – including (48) *Chanson* and (49) *Madrigal* – is composed in the autumn and receives its first performance at the Odéon in December.
1890	Fauré is commissioned to write an opera by Winnaretta Singer to a text of his own choosing. This never-to-be-realised project gradually becomes a millstone around the composer's neck. In August he visits the Passion Play at Oberammergau and finishes (50) *La Rose* (Leconte de Lisle). In the autumn the firm of Hamelle republishes the first volume of *Vingt mélodies* (originally issued by Choudens) in two keys for soprano and mezzo. The *cantique* entitled (51) *En prière* (Bordèse) dates from this year and is given its first performance on 28 December in an orchestrally accompanied version.
1891	Fauré works at a piano quintet. He asks Paul Verlaine for an opera libretto. This collaboration comes to nothing, but Verlaine's poetry will nevertheless play an important part in the year's work. In May he is invited to stay as the guest of Winnaretta Singer at the Palazzo Wolkoff in Venice and begins the sketches for (54) *Mandoline*. He returns to Paris on 20 June, travelling via Florence and Genoa, and finishes (55) *En sourdine*. (56) *Green* is completed on 23 July; (57) *À Clymène* is written in August; in September he completes these (54–58) *Cinq mélodies 'de Venise'*, to Verlaine texts, with (58) *C'est l'extase*.

1892

(margin handwritten note: Emma Bardac)

The tenor Maurice Bagès gives the first public performance of the *Cinq mélodies 'de Venise'* in April. On 1 June Fauré succeeds Guiraud as inspector of instruction (*inspecteur de l'enseignement*), supervising the provincial conservatoires. In the summer at Prunay he meets and falls in love with a married woman, the amateur soprano, Emma Bardac. Inspired by her, (59) *Une Sainte en son auréole* – the first song in the cycle later published as *La Bonne chanson* – is written on 17 September. The first song from the cycle actually to be composed is (65) *Donc, ce sera par un clair jour d'été* on 9 August.

1893

(margin handwritten note: La Bonne chanson)

In February Fauré begins the incidental music for *Le Bourgeois gentilhomme* (Molière), a production that fails to reach the stage. The (69) *Sérénade* from that work will remain unpublished until 1957. On 27 October Fauré plays the organ for Gounod's funeral at the Madeleine. Between May and December he continues work on *La Bonne chanson*. The composer's passionate involvement with Emma Bardac is now at its height.

1894

In February Fauré completes (59–67) *La Bonne chanson*, and the nine-song cycle is published in April; its first public performance is given on the 25th of that month at the home of the Comte de Saussine, with the tenor Maurice Bagès accompanied by the composer. In the same month at the École des Beaux-Arts Fauré accompanies his arrangement of the dubiously transcribed *Hymne à Apollon* recently unearthed in Delphi. In the summer he resumes work on his piano quintet, and completes the famous Sixth Nocturne on 3 August and the *Tantum ergo* later in the same month. A festival of Fauré's works in Geneva in November is followed by a visit to London, where a concert is devoted to his chamber music at St James's Hall. He composes (68) *Prison* (Verlaine) on 4 December, and (70) *Soir* (Samain) on the 17th of the same month.

1895

The composer at fifty. A year without songs. Fauré makes an unsuccessful attempt to become the music critic of *Le Figaro*. The post goes to another composer, Alfred Bruneau. Fauré composes the *Thème et variations* for piano.

1896

(margin handwritten note: Prélude)

On 10 January Fauré plays the organ for Verlaine's funeral. On 21 April he completes the duet (71) *Pleurs d'or* (Samain), which is given its first performance in London. In June he relinquishes his position as choirmaster at the Madeleine and takes up the more senior post of organist. As a result of a temporary break with Hamelle, the two songs *Soir* and *Prison* are issued by the publisher Fromont. Fauré journeys for the second time to Bayreuth, this time in the company of Winnaretta Singer, now Princesse de Polignac. In October he succeeds Massenet as professor of composition at the Conservatoire. He makes another successful visit to London, where Metzler publishes six songs with English translations.

1897	In June Hamelle publishes the second *recueil*, a bigger collection this time of *Vingt-cinq mélodies*. This includes six songs that will later be transferred, against the composer's wishes, to the beginning of Hamelle's *troisième recueil* of 1908. In London Metzler publishes another twelve songs for the English-speaking market. On 22 August Fauré completes (72) *Le Parfum impérissable* (Leconte de Lisle), and on 6 September (73) *Arpège* (Samain).
1898	Maurice Ravel enters Fauré's composition class at the Conservatoire. During a visit to London in late March and early April Fauré is commissioned by Mrs Patrick Campbell to write the incidental music for the English production of Maeterlinck's *Pelléas et Mélisande*. On 1 April the tenor Maurice Bagès sings *La Bonne chanson* (the first performance of the version with piano and string quintet) at the home of Frank Schuster in Westminster. On 31 May Fauré sets (74) *Mélisande's Song* to the English translation of J.W. Mackail. This production (with its première on 21 June) is a great success, and Fauré himself conducts nine performances in the Prince of Wales Theatre, London. There is a revival in October of that year at the Lyceum.
1899–1901	After the success of *Déjanire* by Saint-Saëns at the open-air arena of Béziers in August 1899, the summer of 1900 sees the acclaimed performance of Fauré's outdoor drama with music, *Prométhée*. This is an important turning point in his career, opening important stylistic doors. At Béziers Fauré meets the young pianist Marguerite Hasselmans, who becomes his constant companion for the rest of his life, particularly when he is on his frequent travels. Nevertheless he continues to maintain the marital home in the rue des Vignes, and when he is away he corresponds assiduously with his wife, particularly on musical matters. *Prométhée* is revived in 1901. The Prince Edmond de Polignac dies in August. At the end of that year Ravel dedicates the piano piece *Jeux d'eau* to his teacher Fauré. This is another period when no songs are composed.
1902	In March Fauré accompanies Émilie Girette in a recital of his songs. It is for her that (75) *Accompagnement* (Samain) is written on 28 March. In April and May he attends several performances of Debussy's *Pelléas et Mélisande* at the Opéra-Comique. On 13 September he finishes (76) *La Fleur qui va sur l'eau* (Mendès), and on 29 September (77) *Dans la forêt de septembre* (to a text by the same poet).
1903	In March Fauré begins his work as music critic at *Le Figaro*, a position he will hold until 1921. In April he is appointed *officier* of the Légion d'Honneur. In the summer of this year he is troubled by the first signs of his loss of hearing. He enjoys a late summer holiday in Lausanne (the first of a long series of working sojourns in Switzerland) and returns to his piano quintet, first sketched in 1891. Ravel dedicates his String Quartet in F to Fauré.

1904	*Pelléas et Mélisande* with Fauré's music is revived in London with Sarah Bernhardt. Debussy attends a performance in the company of Mary Garden, his first Mélisande. Fauré returns to the poet Armand Silvestre for two settings: (78) *Le Plus doux chemin* and (79) *Le Ramier*.
1905	The composer turns sixty in May. On 15 June he is appointed director of the Paris Conservatoire. In July he signs a new contract with the publishing house of Heugel. In October he plays the organ for the last time at the Madeleine.
1906	In March the composer is made aware by Belgian friends of Charles Van Lerberghe's cycle of poems *La Chanson d'Ève*. At the beginning of June he finishes (91) *Crépuscule*, which will eventually be the ninth song in the cycle. In May there is a large Fauré festival at the SNM, where Jane Bathori sings *La Bonne chanson*. On 20 August Fauré finishes (80) *Le Don silencieux* (Dominique) during a stay in Vitznau, Lac des Quatres Cantons. On a holiday in Stresa he finishes (83) *Paradis* on 8 September. This is to be the first song in *La Chanson d'Ève*. On 28 September the second, (84) *Prima verba*, is completed in Lausanne. (81) *Chanson* (Régnier) and the (82) *Vocalise-étude* are also composed in this year.
1907	Edouard Risler's performances of Fauré's Fourth Impromptu and Eighth Barcarolle, as well as a performance of the First Piano Quintet, are given at the same SNM concert where Ravel's song cycle *Histoires naturelles* (performed by Jane Bathori) causes great controversy. (The same singer has given the first performance of *Le Don silencieux* in Brussels in March.) Fauré begins work on his opera *Pénélope*. No further songs from *La Chanson d'Ève* are written in this year, which also marks the death of the poet Van Lerberghe.
1908	In March a concert at Bechstein (Wigmore) Hall in London includes a performance of *La Bonne chanson* by Jeanne Raunay, as well as several items from *La Chanson d'Ève*. (85) *Roses ardentes* and (87) *L'Aube blanche* from this cycle are completed in June. Hamelle publishes the third *recueil* of Fauré's songs. The composer continues work on his opera, and he visits England at the end of the year.
1909	Fauré signs a new contract with the pubisher Heugel. He is elected to the Institut on 13 March while away in Barcelona. There is another recital by Jeanne Raunay, this time in the Salle Erard, with seven songs from the new cycle. Work on *La Chanson d'Ève* is continued in Lugano between July and October. From that cycle (86) *Comme Dieu rayonne*, (88) *Eau vivante* and (90) *Dans un parfum de roses blanches* are composed.
1910	In January, with the composition of (89) *Veilles-tu, ma senteur de soleil?* and the valedictory (92) *Ô mort, poussière d'étoiles*, the cycle (83–92) *La Chanson d'Ève* is complete at last. In April the ten songs are published as a cycle in a single volume. Fauré visits Russia and Finland in the most extensive foreign tour of his working life.

1911–13	In April 1911, after twenty-five years, the Fauré household leaves the Plaine Monceau and moves to a newly built luxury flat at Passy: 32 rue des Vignes, in the sixteenth *arrondissement*. This period of the composer's life is given over to the composition and preparation of the opera *Pénélope*, which receives its Paris première on 2 October 1913 at the Théâtre des Champs-Élysées with Lucienne Bréval in the title role. *Pénélope* is also performed on 1 December 1913 at the Théâtre de la Monnaie in Brussels, this time with Claire Croiza. During this period there are also opportunities for the composer to accompany song recitals by such artists as Germaine Sanderson and Jeanne Raunay.
1914	In February the first biography of Fauré (by Louis Vuillemin) appears. The pianist Robert Lortat gives cycles of complete performances of Fauré's piano music in both Paris and London. In the last week of July, on holiday in Bad Ems in Germany, the composer works on the opening songs of the cycle *Le Jardin clos*. The outbreak of the First World War disrupts Fauré's summer (his younger son Philippe joins up), but (93– 100) *Le Jardin clos*, a 'suite' of eight *mélodies*, is completed in the autumn.
1915	*Le Jardin clos* is given its first performance on 28 January by Claire Croiza accompanied by Alfred Casella. The work is published in May by Durand. Fauré composes his Twelfth Nocturne and his Twelfth Barcarolle. He edits the piano music of Schumann for his new publisher, and also prepares an edition of Bach's *48 Preludes and Fugues*.
1916–18	Fauré works on an edition of the organ works of Bach (thirteen volumes up to 1920). He writes two movements of the Second Violin Sonata, which is finished in May 1917. In May of that year he begins a cello sonata, a work which is completed some months later. In 1918 he suffers considerable ill-health, exacerbated by the deaths of his brothers Fernand and Amand.
1919	*Pénélope* returns to the repertoire of the Opéra-Comique. In April *Masques et bergamasques* (a Verlaine-inspired work that includes orchestrations of earlier songs) is very successful in Monaco. From mid-July to mid-September Fauré stays at the Villa Dunand, Annecy-le-Vieux, where he composes a song cycle of four *mélodies*, (101–104) *Mirages* (Brimont), as well as beginning the Second Piano Quintet. *Mirages* is given its first performance on 27 December at the SNM by Madeleine Grey; the first private performance of the work, with the same singer, was a month earlier in Fauré's office in the Conservatoire. On 8 December Fauré composes a song, (105) *C'est la paix*, to a prize-winning text by a reader of *Le Figaro* – the otherwise completely unknown Georgette Debladis.
1920	Fauré, seriously ill at the beginning of the year, continues work on the Second Piano Quintet, completing the second and third movements. He visits Venice again in the company of the Lortats. At the beginning of October he retires from the Conservatoire. In November he hears *Pénélope* again in Brussels, sung by Croiza.

1921   The release from Conservatoire duties initiates an Indian summer in the composer's life. He finishes the Second Piano Quintet, and writes the Thirteenth Barcarolle. He begins the Second Cello Sonata, which is finished by mid-November. In the autumn of the year he writes the four *mélodies* of (106–109) *L'Horizon chimérique* (Jean de La Ville de Mirmont). With the death of Saint-Saëns on 16 December, this period of prolific creativity comes to an end.

1922–24   On 13 May 1922 *L'Horizon chimérique* is given its first performance at the SNM. In June there is a concert of national homage at the Sorbonne with the singers Croiza, Panzéra and Raunay, the pianists Cortot and Lortat, the cellist Casals and the conductor–composers D'Indy and Messager. Fauré suffers from bronchial pneumonia, his shortness of breath exacerbated by a lifetime of smoking. In 1923 he is awarded the *Grand Croix* of the Légion d'Honneur, an unusual honour for a musician. The Piano Trio is performed, and he begins work on his last composition, the String Quartet. He sketches a song, *Ronsard à son âme*, in honour of the poet's 400th anniversary, but he destroys this on hearing that his student Ravel has set the same poem. Fauré turns seventy-nine on 12 May 1924, and enters his eightieth year. Despite serious illness he completes his String Quartet in September. He dies at his Paris home, 32 rue des Vignes, on 4 November. On 8 November he is accorded a state funeral at the Madeleine and buried in Passy cemetery. His wife survives him by less than eighteen months: Marie Fauré dies on 13 March 1926.

Chapter One

An Indifference to Success

I n the late 1890s Marcel Proust, peerless observer of human nature as well as discerning music lover, was often at concerts and gatherings where Gabriel Fauré performed his own works. He noticed that the composer's reaction to applause was different from that of most other artists: the revered musician seemed to take little pleasure in public approval, including Proust's own 'uproarious enthusiasm'. The great novelist of the future wrote to Fauré and admiringly described this response, or lack of response, as a 'disdainful indifference to success'.[1]

Only on very rare occasions do we catch a glimpse of Fauré being pleased by any expression of warmth from his audience: he wrote mischievously to his wife from Russia that his old rival Théodore Dubois would have been unsettled by the cheers of 'Fauré! Fauré!' in St Petersburg.[2] On the whole however we sense that after each public appearance he would have preferred to disappear entirely, if only to avoid the tiresome social obligations that went hand in hand with fame. When the time came for the final bow, his death in 1924, he made it quite clear to his sons that he was not at all worried about being forgotten for a while, and that indeed he seemed to think it was to be expected and inevitable. If he had been told that it was his fate to be written out of musical history altogether it would have been typical of Fauré to have greeted the news with perfect equanimity.

It would be all too easy, alarmingly easy, to imagine a world without him and his music. Gabriel Fauré is part of no inevitable musical lineage; instead he came as if from nowhere, like an unexpected blessing. He left the world inestimably richer as far as his listeners and admirers are concerned, but there was no successor in sight. That overused word 'inimitable' applies to him as it applies to few other artists. The composer was something of a loner all his life, but in terms of history he seems even more so; he slipped quietly into the narrative of musical France, and after decades of fruitful work he slipped quietly out again – honoured and admired, always respected, but hardly imitated. He was also much loved; Émile Vuillermoz wrote of Fauré at the time of the composer's death: 'Great geniuses of the past have been given more solemn tributes of admiration, have called forth more demonstrative enthusiasm; they have acted with more intensity on the crowd and known a more universal, and noisy fame; but none of them, in departing, have made hearts grieve more painfully.'[3]

1

It is a truism that the French are individualists and cut their cloth according to their own style. The passing of a mantle from one great composer to another is a German, rather than a French, notion; thus Haydn, Mozart, Beethoven and Schubert overlap each other in a solemn Viennese succession, making it difficult at times to disentangle some of the threads that bind together their histories, both personal and musical. This is despite the fact that these composers spent little time (sometimes none) in each other's company. In France – or, to be more specific, in Paris – there was more personal interaction between artistic personalities, but composers made way for each other politely in the street (as might those determinedly competitive automobiles, Renault and Citroën) without sacrificing a whit of their differently wired autonomy.

French composers had a much greater inclination than their German or British colleagues to dine and socialise with each other, though very seldom in their own homes. The boulevard and café culture of Paris played a huge part in the cross-pollination of the arts in France, a country where people seemed to bump into each other all the time. Thanks largely to that remarkable institution, the Société National de la Musique, formed shortly after the Franco-Prussian War, French composers of completely different sympathies sat side by side at many a function and developed a perfectly amicable means of getting on with each other with varying degrees of warmth. Fauré's relationship with his contemporaries runs the full gamut between his filial devotion to Saint-Saëns and his life-long aversion to Massenet. Somewhere between these two extremes were his relaxed, affectionate relationship with his *copain* Messager and his cool but always punctilious exchanges with Debussy.

If we were to remove any of the above-named composers – Saint-Saëns, Massenet, Messager, Debussy – from the annals of French musical history, there would be any number of knock-on effects. In his youth Saint-Saëns, a tireless participant in musical politics, built essential bridges between French and German music (although he attempted to destroy them in later years); there is scarcely anything to parallel the manner in which he played the role of Fauré's teacher, mentor and publicist and for so many years. Had Saint-Saëns not existed it is very possible that the subject of this book would hardly strike us now as being worthy of extended comment. Debussy relied on Messager, dedicatee and conductor of *Pelléas et Mélisande*, at crucial moments in his career, and French operetta continued to revolve around the influence of this master of light music well into modern times. Without Massenet an entire chapter in the history of French opera would have to be re-written; his example was crucial to the early Debussy, and without Debussy the whole of French music in the twentieth century would be entirely different, right up to Boulez and beyond.

Fauré's indispensability is more difficult to pin down. If he had been absent from the fabric of the story, as if in a French version of the James Stewart film *It's a Wonderful Life*, many details in other people's lives might have been different: Ravel might have suffered and rebelled in the hands of a less liberal composition teacher, the Conservatoire would have been less welcoming to twentieth-century talents in the hands of another director, and so on. Fauré was the type of man who made a personal difference to many musicians who were instructed and blessed by his wisdom and his *gentillesse*. But there was no single younger composer who was as dear to him, as indispensable, as he had been to Saint-Saëns, and it is hard to imagine what might have changed if he had never written the *Requiem*, much less *Pénélope* or *La Chanson d'Ève*. Of course our own lives would have been incomparably poorer in musical terms, but it would have been that kind of impoverishment that we would never know, unless the thing we had lost were before our eyes and ears; no school of musicians is undermined by the removal of these works, and with their disappearance we lose no other masterpieces by composers dependent on Fauré's example.

There are other composers of the period who seem equally 'one-off', but whose historical absence would be disruptive. What would have been the future of French song without the slender output of Duparc, whose influence extended to almost all his song-composing contemporaries? Emmanuel Chabrier seems to have been every bit as self-sufficient as Fauré and without musical issue – and yet, when we listen to the music of Francis Poulenc, we realise that without Chabrier's example Poulenc would have been a different composer. (As a younger man he vehemently disliked Fauré's music, although he was later to recant to an extent, and he accompanied some of the songs beautifully.) If we look very hard we may find a trace of Fauré in the early work of his young admirer, another, very different, member of 'Les Six', Arthur Honegger. The concision of Albert Roussel (though not his harmonic world) seems vaguely influenced by the self-discipline of Fauré's late style. The early and scarcely known songs of Nadia Boulanger have a Fauréan tinge, but we look in vain for it in the music of other pupils such as Charles Koechlin and Florent Schmitt. The pupil who was probably most influenced by the older teacher is now a sadly forgotten name – Jean Roger-Ducasse. Ravel strikes a Fauréan note very rarely; at the time when he wrote his earliest songs he was already under the spell of Erik Satie in his medievalist phase, a man whose impact on music in the twentieth century is literally incalculable. Ravel's 'ouverture de féerie' entitled *Shéhérazade*, composed when Fauré was still his teacher, looks beyond Paris to the inspiration of the Russian masters (whose country Fauré visited in physical terms, but whose influence never touched his music). If the *dépouillé* nature of Ravel's later songs and chamber music (*Ronsard à son âme*, for example, and *Rêves*) echo the minimalist character of Fauré's last period, this was probably more to do with Ravel's encroaching illness than with his desire to emulate the hermetic style of his former teacher.

From whatever angle we look at it, Fauré stands alone.

This sounds rather negative, as if no one quite admired Fauré enough to copy him, but the lack of imitators is surely because this composer is impossible to imitate convincingly. There is a complexity and subtlety in his harmonic language that puts it beyond emulation, facile or otherwise. Fauré's style is too elusive to fabricate as a party trick, and as a result is avoided by *pasticheurs*. It is hardly difficult to 'do a Debussy' via the whole-tone scale, just as the comedienne Anna Russell did with a spoof that shamelessly imitated the manner of the *Chansons de Bilitis*. Ravel found it disarmingly easy to write music *à la manière* of other composers, and Satie wrote *Le Chapelier*, a song about the mad-hatter's tea-party, in the style of Gounod, but Fauré was spared these affectionate ribbings. Although it was quite possible to write musical homages derived from the letters of his name, his own music might be better known if it were possible to encapsulate his style in a musical pastiche.

As a child pianist I found Schubert difficult to pin down; his music seemed to fall between the two schools of Mozart and Beethoven, while being neither. I understood the *galant* style of rococo music with an Alberti bass and classed this as 'Mozart'; I knew the *Sturm und Drang* of *Pathétique*-like fury and thought of this as 'Beethoven'. I was not yet ready for someone like Schubert who was purely of himself, someone who did not personify a school of music, and could not be reduced to a historical formula for the purposes of instant recognition, however instantly recognisable his music when he wrote it himself. Of course I only realised this much later. On hearing Fauré for the first time I was subject to the same kind of mystification: where on earth did this composer fit into musical history as I imagined it to be? His music, infinitely charming, was neither as catchy nor as virile as Bizet's *Carmen*, nor as hypnotically sensual as Debussy, who seemed to me as a teenager to be French music personified. Where does Fauré come from? This was my question, and the answer, if there is an answer at all, is more complicated than I could ever have realised.

∾   ∾   ∾   ∾

Fauré's provenance has nothing to do with the world of opera so dear to the French – it is true that at times his music can have the poise of Rameau, but Grétry, Monsigny and Philidor are not his ancestors, and neither is the Parisian visitor Gluck – although when we hear the strength and grandeur of the opera *Pénélope* for the first time we are tempted to revise this opinion. He was immune to the immensity of Berlioz, whose music meant little to him throughout his life. In his mid-twenties Fauré lost an organist's job by attending a performance of *Les Huguenots* instead of playing a service, but on the whole the great trundling operas of Meyerbeer passed the younger composer by, as did the lighter Offenbach. (An evocation of the latter may be glimpsed only in the spoof piano duet that Fauré wrote with Messager on themes from Wagner's operas). Of Wagner's music itself Fauré knew a great deal (only after he had left school and had travelled to Germany), but he was able to admire it without importing it into his own work (save a few *Siegfried*-inspired birdcalls in the *Ballade* for piano, a modulatory moment in the *Nocturne* from *Shylock*, and E♭ arpeggios at the beginning of *Le Ruisseau*, a musical stream that amusingly implies a watered-down opening of *Das Rheingold*).[4] This ability to confine himself to one or two rueful allusions as far as Wagner was concerned indicates Fauré's inoculated single-mindedness; if composers such as Chausson and D'Indy had been similarly impervious when writing their large stage works they might have written operas that held the stage. A cynic would here intervene to point out that Fauré's *Pénélope*, for all its greater originality, is hardly a work to be heard every day in the world's opera houses.

If Fauré was influenced by foreign composers at all, they were not theatre composers but rather composer–pianists. Saint-Saëns, his piano teacher at the École Niedermeyer, played Liszt and Schumann to his students despite the fact that these composers were not on the syllabus. There are echoes of Liszt's music to be found in some of the higher-lying passages of Fauré's solo piano works just as there are many discernible traces of Mendelssohn's urbane facility and charm. The first piano works of Fauré even have a Mendelssohnian title – *Trois romances sans paroles*, 'Three Songs without Words'. There is an even deeper link with Schumann, whose solo piano music, according to the Princesse de Polignac, Fauré played better than anyone else. The piano writing in the Baudelaire settings *Chant d'automne* and *La Rançon* has a Schumannesque flavour that recalls the arpeggiated accompaniment of Schumann's song *Der Nußbaum*, and Françoise Gervais has pointed out how Fauré might have been influenced by that composer's use of harmony in the sixth of his *Noveletten*.[5] (Fauré had the kind of musical mind that was influenced not only by the sound of another person's music, but also by how it was written down in terms of harmonic syntax.) Both composers, the German and the French, had dreamy, internalised natures that shielded a private world of fecund and highly personal harmonic invention, and Schumann was more famous in the French salons than any other German composer. Nevertheless, one has to go no further than Fauré's earlier nocturnes to see that his debt to Chopin is equally large. How moving it must have been for the young composer to encounter George Sand at the salon of Pauline Viardot! The easy, languid grace of the Polish expatriate, combined with an almost diabolical sophistication in the deployment of harmony, must have been addictively appealing to Fauré, and in the earlier of his works it shows. (Once again Chopin's complex orthography, and the way he 'spelled' his harmonic progressions. will have fascinated and influenced the young composer.) But all these are links to piano rather than vocal music, and nothing in the vocal lines of Fauré songs, only occasional passages in their accompaniments, refers back to Schumann or Chopin, Mendelssohn or Liszt. If we are to consider who influenced Fauré's *mélodies*, the subject of this book after all, we must search nearer to home.

∾   ∾   ∾   ∾

It is likely that he would have been at least aware of the female composers Pauline Duchambge and Loïsa Puget, who had cornered the *romance* market, where anodyne little songs were sumptuously published with beautiful accompanying engravings – the former composer at her height before he was born, and the latter in the years of his childhood.

Title-page of songs by Loïsa Puget (1810–1889) and the illustration for the Indian-inspired romance La Bayadère

Although Berlioz was scathing about the *romance* and its sentimental practitioners, Fauré was more likely to have encountered these harmless songs in his childhood than Berlioz's sophisticated and controversial settings of Thomas Moore's *Irish Melodies* in French translation, published as *Irlande*. There were almost certainly no volumes of *romances* to be found lying around Fauré's home, and his school concentrated religiously on the study of renaissance polyphony and church music. We must assume however that a certain number of songs, some old-fashioned, some less so, came his way somehow or other. Some of these by such composers as Hypolite Monpou (published in the 1830s and 1840s), Ernest Reyer, Félicien David and Henri Reber (all published between the 1840s and 1860s) and Edouard Lalo (*Six mélodies* to texts of Hugo, 1856) would have made some impression on Fauré if they had been available within the portals of the École Niedermeyer or during the school holidays. As we shall see, it may have been the success of this Lalo work that inspired the young composer to concentrate on assembling his own group of songs, also with Hugo texts, in the early 1860s.

We do know that Niedermeyer, head and founder of the school, encouraged the Fauré when still a little boy to sing folksongs from the Ariège for the delectation of visitors (the young Gabriel must have had a pretty singing voice), but the composer as an adult expressed absolutely no interest in folksong as a point of departure for his own music – although his contemporary D'Indy and Fauré's most famous pupil Ravel were to be of another mind entirely. Surprisingly, we know nothing of the secular vocal music Fauré admired as a teenager; it is much easier to discover the songs that influenced the young Schubert when he was still at school. Schubert's family, like Fauré's, was not in a position to furnish him with printed music by other composers, but some of his school friends were able to do so, thanks to their wealthier parents. Fauré's awareness of the contemporary *romance* and *mélodie* probably came from similar sources, and as a result of a similar curiosity. (And speaking of Schubert one must not forget that this composer's songs were published in France in the 1830s by Richault – Niedermeyer's publisher – and it is by no means impossible that Fauré came to know some of them at a relatively young age.[6]) As the students were permitted to sing secular music only when on walks, one can imagine pieces smuggled into the school after the holidays, and going the rounds.

Perhaps smuggling was not even necessary with the more lenient teachers; according to Fauré's testimony the pupils were permitted to study the operatic scores of Gluck, Mehul, Weber and Mozart, and the *mélodies* and lieder of the early to mid-nineteenth century were hardly seditious. The sternest musical guardian would have found these pieces preferable to the piano music of Liszt and operas by Wagner. Louis Niedermeyer was devoted to Fauré, whom he considered his most gifted pupil, and he is often credited with having written the first real *mélodie*. This was *Le Lac*, to a poem by Lamartine, written and published in the 1820s.

What is less known is that Niedermeyer also composed a number of more ambitious *mélodies* written shortly before his death and published by the Parisian firm of Pacini in 1862. These include a Hugo setting entitled *La Mer* (which seems an imitation of Gounod's Musset setting *Venise*, a famous song in the same key, dating from 1842) and *Ô ma belle rebelle* (again no doubt inspired by a setting of the same Baïf poem by Gounod, published in 1855). There was another Hugo setting in the Niedermeyer set published by Pacini in 1860 – this was *Puisqu'ici bas toute âme*, to a poem set as a solo song by Fauré later in the 1860s and subsequently rearranged as a duet for the Viardot sisters in the 1870s.[7]

The earlier songs of Gounod may well have been known to Fauré (perhaps via Niedermeyer – both older composers were avid setters of Lamartine). Ravel believed that the history of the *mélodie* began with Gounod, and Fauré was clearly also struck by this composer's astonishing gift for melody as well as the generosity of spirit and musical expansiveness that are the trademarks of his benign muse. In 1922 Fauré said in an interview that Gounod had brought something new to music; this admiration is to be heard here and there in some of Fauré's early Victor Hugo settings. He came to know the older composer personally through the Viardot family in the 1870s, directly after Gounod's return to Paris from temporary exile in London. During the period of the Commune Gounod had been accommodated by the impossibly bossy Mrs Georgina

Charles Gounod (1818–1893) in later life

Weldon in Tavistock Square, and sternly persuaded to compose English songs for the benefit of her orphanage. This episode when the embodiment of French *mélodie* was more or less taken hostage in London was an unhappy prelude to Fauré's less dramatic flirtations with the English capital some twenty years later.

Saint-Saëns, who took over from Niedermeyer as Fauré's teacher and protector, was a dab hand at setting the poetry of Hugo: *Rêverie* had been published in 1852, *Le Pas d'armes du roi Jean* in 1855, and *L'Attente* and *La Cloche* in 1856. There is something marvellously organised and neat about these songs; they all display remarkable craftsmanship, and they all became well known on the concert platform. There is something to be said for the theory that the perennially energetic Saint-Saëns was the ideal composer for Hugo's relentlessly energetic texts. The medieval-inspired *Le Pas d'armes du roi Jean*, bristling with plagal cadences, contains a passage where the composer has great fun creating a churchy, medieval atmosphere with modal harmonies. At the song's climax the body of a young page, killed at a joust, is handed over to an abbot and his monks for sombre burial. This is 'special effect' music, written in a succession of ancient-looking minims, and Saint-Saëns proves himself a racier composer than Gounod in terms of pastiche. It is the theatrical, one might say operatic, side of this kind of illustrative music that was not to Fauré's taste. He was never one for narrative songs, preferring always to describe a scene (or a state of mind) encapsulated in music, as if in a single wonderful photograph, rather than by a succession of flickering, cinematic images.

The very first of Fauré's songs, *Le Papillon et la fleur*, seems at first glance to be somewhat beholden to Saint-Saëns. In this little narrative Fauré manages a passable imitation of his teacher's scintillating style, especially in the glittering but heartless little waltz of the piano's *ritornello*; but he lacks the cynical nature of his mentor, and in the genuine emotion of the flower's entreaty, 'ne fuis pas', we hear more than a touch of Gounod's sincerity. In Fauré's *Dans les ruines d'une abbaye* we may possibly ascribe the song's A major tonality, and its vivacious verbal dexterity, to the example of *Enlèvement*, a Hugo setting by Saint-Saëns composed in 1865. But Fauré suffuses his own song with a geniality and affection, a teasing warmth and melodic grace, that is lacking from his teacher's galloping scherzo. There is some of Fauré's music for solo piano that adopts the manner of Saint-Saëns's sometimes dizzying virtuosity, but we must scour Fauré's mature *mélodies* carefully, and mostly in vain, in order to find deeper signs of Saint-Saëns's sheerly *musical* influence, notwithstanding the older composer's personal and professional impact on the life of the younger.

Camille Saint-Saëns (1835–1921) wearing the Légion d'Honneur

There is even some evidence of Saint-Saëns having set a *bad* example, and that is in the very careless prosody of the earlier Fauré songs. The performer who takes the trouble to compare the high-voice and medium-voice versions of the first *recueil* of the Hamelle edition will be puzzled to come across varied readings of the same phrase, with different accentuations on different words. As Mimi Daitz has pointed out,[8] a song such as *Rêve d'amour* is perplexingly rich in different readings, and Fauré, in making *post facto* adjustments to the vocal line, is not always able to resolve the central problem of having been too little concerned with prosody in the first place (it is an added drawback that, in the absence of a critical edition of the songs,[9] the singer is not always able to determine which of the two versions represented the composer's later thoughts).

Daitz notes that in the introduction to Saint-Saëns's collected songs in two volumes (issued by Durand in 1896) the composer confesses 'quelques négligences de style' in his own work, including faulty prosody; he excuses this on the grounds of youthful inexperience at the time of their composition. And he does not seem to have been over-fussy with his student Fauré, failing to correct the sometimes very awkward accentuations of the teenager's Hugo settings.

Sheerly in terms of harmony and texture it is the Niedermeyer songs of 1861 that seem to have struck an ongoing chord with Fauré, although none of them has the musical wit and brilliance of Saint-Saëns. Niedermeyer's *La Mer* seems prophetic of Fauré's *Automne* (with the strength of its basses in octaves, and a sense of the drama inherent in nature); the same composer's *Puisqu'ici-bas* looks forward to Fauré's Baudelaire setting *Chant d'automne* (in its organisation in two contrasting musical sections, the second charmingly lyrical), and there is also a prophecy of the almost academic part-writing of the opening of *La Rançon* (also Baudelaire). Niedermeyer's *Ô ma belle rebelle* points the way to the 'madrigal' style, with its quasi-lute accompaniment, that is initiated so elegantly in Fauré's early Hugo setting, still unpublished, *Puisque j'ai mis ma lèvre.*

In Niedermeyer's last songs there is a certain freedom in the use of harmony that is not to be found in Saint-Saëns's Hugo settings, which is not to say that Niedermeyer was as gifted or accomplished a composer as Saint-Saëns; there is nothing in his music that is as deftly effective as *Le Pas d'armes du roi Jean*. Nevertheless Niedermeyer's harmonic language shows here and there a subtly different way of considering how to move from one chord to the next. Even in this modest writing we have an indication of the divide between the vast majority of French composers on one hand, mostly educated at the Paris Conservatoire, and those who had the grounding in harmony enjoyed by the students at the École Niedermeyer – and this applied to Niedermeyer himself, of course. If this seems to imply two opposing schools lined up against each other in battle formation, it is very much how the establishments themselves viewed it at the time. And yet the Conservatoire produced dozens of composers, and the École Niedermeyer only two of international rank: Fauré, and André Messager. Of these, the latter was a composer of delicious operettas, so in terms of heavyweight musical achievement it is Gabriel Fauré who was left to play the role of the Niedermeyer 'David' against the 'Goliath' of the Conservatoire. Before we discuss their differences of harmonic outlook we have to go back into French musical history to find out how and why this curious rivalry came about.

⁓ ⁓ ⁓ ⁓

The middle of the nineteenth century found France as little better than a vassal state of Germany and Italy in terms of the musical language employed by its composers: to the east, German romanticism was triumphant; to the south, Italian opera. The work of Beethoven, Schubert, Weber, Schumann and Liszt (all of whose music was known and admired in France in varying degrees) seemed to lead ineluctably to that of Wagner, whose *Tannhäuser* was eulogised by Baudelaire in 1861 and then slowly assimilated by the rest of France in succeeding decades. One of the very few substantial composers who stands outside this tradition, admired by both German and French composers, was Frédéric Chopin. The role he played in the formation of the style of such composers as Fauré and Debussy is inestimable.

During the years of the Second Empire the musical tastes of Germany and France differed enormously, particularly when it came to the French public's preference for undemanding opera and ballet over symphonic or chamber music. But the language used by most French composers was one hardly different from that employed by all the famous Germans and Italians– that is to say, a diatonic system of harmony dominated by the tonic and dominant, ever in search of a perfect cadence. Even the use of the diminished seventh (encouraged by Weber) emphasised the dependence of harmony on a rather limited number of options. A great many musical thinkers of the time, including some in England, were becoming increasingly bored with the ubiquity of the sharpened leading note; the case against the status quo was eloquently put in England by Gerard Manley Hopkins, who, apart from being a visionary poet, was also a fine musician:

> What they [i.e. the harmony experts of the time] call the key of the dominant, viz. one in which the fourth of the tonic is sharpened, I say is not the key of the dominant (which is another mode than the key of the tonic and has no leading note) but the key of the tonic misplaced and transposed … . What he calls variety I call sameness, because modulation reduces all the rich diatonic keyboard with its six or seven authentic, not to speak of plagal, modes, to one dead level of major.[10]

This was an era when church music, and a nostalgia for the purities and certainties of medieval times, began to undermine (in France at least) the hegemony of the Germans in terms of harmony. The heart of this revolution was in Solesmes, a village between Le Mans and Angers, where a Benedictine abbey was the centre of a Gregorian revival. Under the guidance of Dom Prosper Guéranger (1805–1875) plainchant melodies were released from the tyranny and straitjacket of bar lines, and allowed a freedom and flexibility of performance that they had not known since the sixteenth century. Catholic churches the world over were the beneficiaries of this development, and modal harmony was once more on the agenda, once more something to be studied. This was eventually to lead to such institutions as the Chanteurs de St Gervais – from 1892 – devoted to the performance of early music under the direction of the composer Charles Bordes – and the establishment under Vincent d'Indy of the powerful Schola Cantorum in 1894.

If the study of plainchant was something relatively new, there had been a long tradition whereby church music was taken very seriously. A school founded in 1817 in Paris by Alexandre-Etienne Choron (1771–1834), the Conservatoire de Musique Classique et Religieuse, had specialised in the study and performance of the works of Palestrina and the Renaissance. This establishment was shut down in Louis-Philippe's reign, but was eventually replaced by the École Niedermeyer. In 1922 Fauré recalled his life at this school when he was a boy. The differences between his musical upbringing and that available at the Conservatoire were to shape his musical tastes for the rest of his life:

> The masterpieces of J.S. Bach that constituted our daily bread, had still not found their way into the organ class at the Conservatoire; and in the pianoforte classes at the same Conservatoire the students still laboured at the performance of Herz's concertos, while Adolphe Adam shed his brilliant light on the composition class.[11]

We must now briefly examine what Fauré learned at the École Niedermeyer and which Adolphe Adam at the Conservatoire could never have taught him. Most of the school's students went on to a life in church music, the kind of career that Fauré *père* had expected for his son when he brought his boy, aged nine, up to Paris in 1854. These organists and choirmasters had learned enough about modal harmony to accompany plainchant in a way that avoided placing it in the straitjacket of diatonic tonality (the fact that we now feel that plainchant is best left unaccompanied is beside the point). An important book for the development of a serious study of the church modes was *Traité théorique et pratique de l'accompagnement du plain-chant* by Joseph d'Ortigue (1857), but the harmony bible of the students at the École Niedermeyer was *Traité d'harmonie* by one of their own teachers, Gustave Lefèvre. Quite contrary to the most prevalent practices of the 1850s, this treatise returned to a system of figuring the harmony that went back to the famous theoretician Abbé Vogler (1749–1814). Vogler had taught Pierre de Maleden who had, in turn, taught Saint-Saëns. With this pedigree one understands why this particular composer–pianist had been invited to take up a teaching position at the École Niedermeyer after the founder's death.

Vogler's theory permitted chord roots on all degrees of the scale, assigning to them the Roman numerals I to VII, in large figures for a major chord, smaller figures for a minor. This system of numbering is primarily concerned with the degree of the scale on which the chord is placed. (The more familiar use of Arabic numbers in the figuring of a bass line was criticised by Lefèvre as being confusing.) Vogler's system also encompassed the enharmonic 'spellings' of diminished seventh and augmented sixth chords to illustrate tonal paths from a given centre to any other major or minor key. One of the first tasks for the student of Lefèvre's book was to study the different functions of a chord. An E minor triad was printed (E–G–B in the treble clef), and then this same chord was differently numbered according to its context: i in the key of E minor, iii in the key of C major, ii in the key of D major, and iv in the key of B minor. The students had then to practise with these chords in transpositions. All chords on all degrees of the minor and major scales (with only a handful of exceptions) were permitted as valid harmonies. Alteration of triads for modulatory purposes, using sharps and flats, was allowed not only on the fifth degree, but also on the third and firsts degree of the scale (see Example 1.1).

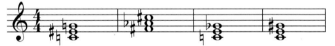

Example 1.1   Four triads from Gervais, Étude comparée des langues harmoniques, *p. 55*

In this way of teaching harmony, all these chords were permitted in themselves, but fascinating avenues opened up for movement *from* these triads via the altered notes; in the example printed above, E♮ (in a C major chord) has slid up to to E♯, and A♮ (in F♯ minor) has fallen to A♭; likewise G♮ (in C minor) to has fallen to G♭, and G♮ in a C major chord has been lifted to G♯. This is an an indication of how Fauré was encouraged to think about harmony in a completely different way from that of most of his contemporaries. The rule was that 'every consonant or dissonant chord can be modified by alterations to the notes that compose it'. Lefèvre's extraordinary liberality in relation to procedures that might be termed modulatory by others, but which he himself would have regarded as non-modulatory, opens a door for us on the whole of Fauré's harmonic outlook. Here is a crucial Lefèvre command: 'you must explore the directions in which every note of the chord can move, either diatonically, chromatically or enharmonically, so as to form a new aggregation. You can then assign this to a certain key depending on how you designate the notes that compose it.'[12] Nectoux spells out the implications of this way of thinking about harmony:

> In a C major chord the E can be considered as itself, the G as an F double sharp, an appoggiatura of G sharp, and the C as an appoggiatura of B natural. From here the chord can move either to B major, E major or G sharp major. According to this principle every chord can be thought of as consisting both of 'true' notes and 'artificial' notes.[13]

In this system one has simply to choose how to interpret any given chord and engineer a resolution that conforms with that interpretation. For the teachers of harmony at the Conservatoire, this Niedermeyer-approved system represented unacceptable anarchy. In the conventional dispensation every alteration to a chord implied a change of tonality, but the Lefèvre approach took into account how people heard music, not only how they read it or analysed it. The introduction to the song *Les Présents*, for example (see Chapter 7), rocks sensuously between F major (the opening bar) and A♭ major, with D♮s instead of D♭s (second bar). The pivotal note of C is the dominant of F major as well as the mediant of A♭ major. Lefèvre would have taught that the piece was simply in F major and the chord in the second bar was based on the flattened third.

As it turned out, Fauré was the only one of the Niedermeyer pupils to evolve a rich and rewarding idiom derived from a broadened knowledge of harmony that included the church and antique modes, combined with the liberal attitudes to diatonic harmony espoused by Lefèvre. He was not at all interested in using the modes as the basis of an entire piece; neither was he attracted by using them, like Saint-Saëns in his *Le Pas d'armes du roi Jean*, for the kind of illustrative colour that we now associate with film scores. Fauré was not principally drawn to modal harmony because it made his music sound atmospheric, or historically archaic; instead, he gradually drew the modes deep into his musical vocabulary because they broadened his options in moving inventively, ingeniously, from one harmony to the next. This also improved his capacity to invent melody, despite the fact that his melodic inventions were always linear.

'His tonalities, clear as they are, sometimes are established very quickly and for a passing moment only – a practice observed in the sixteenth century and favoured by familiarity with the ancient modes, because they allow greater flexibility in modulation.'[14] Thus wrote Charles Koechlin, but Fauré would probably not have labelled what he was doing as modulation – he could have demonstrated how he found his way to these so-called 'modulations' by viewing his progress within the home key through his own harmonic spectacles, a pathway rich in exploratory possibility and harmonic allusion. He had become accustomed to this richness early on; the flexibility of the modes was to open the doors of an Aladdin's cave of harmony to a youngster who remained in possession of this treasure for the rest of his life. By the very nature of the acquisition of this language, and in the absence of another genius within the École Niedermeyer who had been educated in the same way, Fauré's solution was bound to appear singular and unusual. It is no wonder that *pasticheurs*, past and present, lack the easy means to copy him, for despite its logicality his is an elusive language that no one else speaks, or has ever spoken, fluently or quite fluently enough.

If Louis Niedermeyer had been responsible for teaching Fauré that modern harmony could be expanded to accommodate the antique modes, it was Fauré, and only Fauré, who was responsible for the development of this idiosyncratic cause into great art. Saint-Saëns's lessons with his teacher Maladen might have yielded a similarly revolutionary response, but they failed to do so; it was only Fauré who was both willing and able to make the synthesis. From this stems much of the composer's uniqueness. For example, one must look at his harmonic progressions horizontally rather than vertically – this is because his very melodic sense is harmonic, and when he writes a melody it is so tied up with the harmonisation of that melody that it is virtually impossible to separate the strands of the composer's creative impulse. As Nadia Boulanger observes 'The harmony of Fauré and the harmony of Debussy are radically different. Harmony, for Fauré is an element of design, whereas Debussy tends to conceive it rather as a source of colour.'[15]

A person who comes to Fauré for the first time must learn that the twists and turns of this music are the result of the exercise of choice, as exquisite and refined a process of conscious deliberation as ever went into the making of a work of art. And the performer must realise that Fauré saw his songs as being all of a piece, that what may be regarded as modulations by other people are never red herrings which may be used to compartmentalise a piece of music and divide it into sections. This richness of harmony is the result of crystal-clear logic where the song progresses from the beginning to its end in a single *courbe* of thought and sound.

There are many signposts in the music that are noticeable without a deep knowledge of harmony. Even the neophyte singer and player will register the tritones in the melodic line of *Lydia*; they will note the refusal of the vocal line to rise to a sharpened leading note of the key in *La Lune blanche*, and that, in remaining flattened, this seventh gives the song a character that is unlike any other setting of those words; they may even notice that the *Prima verba* from *La Chanson d'Ève* is written entirely in modal style, without being able to identify this as Mixolydian, and that the left hand of the accompaniment of *Mandoline* is given vibrant life by a succession of unprepared chords of the major seventh. These are just a few of the thousands of such exquisite details in the songs. These never appear, or sound, as revolutionary as they actually are – the effect is of something subtly modified and enriched, and yet the whole Beethovenian system of harmony has been subverted. Proof of just how radically the composer's broom has swept through the fields of harmony is the fact that Fauré's music is almost impossible to sight-read. The unprepared pianist's fingers, after being used to playing the Viennese classics, go automatically into keyboard grooves that often prove to be the wrong ones. One can never second-guess where Fauré's harmonic imagination is taking him, any more than one can second-guess Bach. Nadia Boulanger described the fascination exerted by this composer's harmonic world:

Fauré etches in even the most subtle of his modulations with the sharp, fine lines of a pen. You never know to what key he is leading you, but when you reach your tonal destination, there is never any doubt as to its location. Indeed, you feel almost as though it would have been impossible to have gone elsewhere and you wonder only at the beauty of the voyage and the skill of your guide who, in coming, has led you so quickly and surely through so many lands. The subtlety of Fauré's transitory modulations, the ease and naturalness with which he alludes to the most remote keys, are the mind's sheerest delight.[16]

13

In the early songs there is less evidence of this feeling for a mode-enriched harmonic vocabulary. What Fauré had learned at the school was clearly stored at the back of his mind, and it began to be heard in earnest almost halfway through the songs of the first *recueil* (this word simply means 'collection' and refers to the publication of sixty of Fauré's songs – three *recueils* of twenty songs each – by the Parisian publishing house of Hamelle). As the years went by, he felt more confident in being able to draw on what he had understood about harmony and its possibilities since he was a teenager. At first it seemed more important to write songs to please other people – publishers such as Choudens and Hartmann, teachers such as Saint-Saëns and patrons such as Pauline Viardot. He was clever enough to understand the potential of his treasury of harmony, but he did not yet have the confidence to display those riches openly. But gradually he threw off the shackles of an imagined propriety to walk boldly into his destiny as a bringer of harmony in every sense; by the time he embarked on *La Bonne chanson* he was able to flex his chordal muscles in a way that was simply beyond the ability (and one must also say the inclination) of any other French composer. This success depended on another imponderable: the composer's response to words, and his increasing ability over a long career to inhabit a poem with rare sensibility and bring it to musical life. Without that extra talent, all the harmonic gifts in the world could not have turned Fauré into a great song composer. That this response was of a subtly different kind from that of the great lieder composers is discussed more fully in Chapter 15.

❧   ❧   ❧   ❧

Fauré's sarcasm about the quality of teaching at the old Conservatoire (Adam shedding 'his 'brilliant light') is a tiny indication of the barbed rivalry that existed between the two institutions. Fauré's education at the École Niedermeyer counted against him when his candidacy for the professorship of composition at the Conservatoire was blocked by its director, Ambroise Thomas, in 1892. But it is paradoxical that Fauré's eventual surprise appointment as director of the Conservatoire in 1905 was also, in part, thanks to his being an outsider. At the time the uncertainties of the political climate, including the possibility of anarchist revolt, and the shadow of *l'affaire Dreyfus*, made the men at the ministry look favourably on Fauré's independent background. He had kept his distance both from the internecine struggles for power at the Conservatoire and from the Schola Cantorum, the latter a stronghold of right-wing Catholic allegiance. This was at a time when the Third Republic was determined to keep the powers of Church and State separate. In 1905 Fauré's reputation for integrity promised a 'new broom' at the Conservatoire, which the composer duly provided. By then musicologists had begun to study composers whose music had scarcely been heard in modern times; attendance at the lectures given on music history at the Conservatoire by the famous scholar (and less famous composer) Louis-Albert Bourgault-Ducoudray (1840–1910) was made obligatory for all students by Fauré when he took up the directorship of the institution.

Looking back at the past was one source of renewal, and certainly the most important at the École Niedermeyer. But outside the walls of that institution there were other rejuvenating influences. If on one hand there was a growing interest in music from former times, in France there has always been an appetite for the new and the exotic; it was to be expected that composers would seek for some kind of release from what had become the boring sameness of the German-dominated musical landscape. The new field of ethnomusicology was awakened by music from far-away lands, not as yet a serious study of folksong, but as a fascination with local colour (one thinks of the scrupulously annotated artistic explorations of the Napoleonic age and the Empire style in clothes and furniture inspired by Egypt). More than half a century before Debussy was entranced by the music of the gamelan, Félicien David composed his *Mélodies orientales* (1835). The study of the music of the ancients also played its part: with *Lydia* (c.1870), Fauré chose a poem inspired by the purity of ancient Greece, and set it in a modal manner designed to evoke similarly ancient music. Saint-Saëns also deplored the ascendancy of the major and minor keys (while showing little sign of abandoning them in his own music); he welcomed the revival of the antique modes, and of the immense variety of the oriental ones. He felt assured that a new art would be born of this diversity. His cycle *Mélodies persanes* (1872) is not a truly innovative work in terms of harmony, but it does use effective splashes of oriental colour, as does his opera *La Princesse jaune* (also 1872) with its quasi-Japanese flavour. Bizet's one-act opera *Djamileh* is another oriental evocation from the same year. The cover of the first edition of Fauré's song *Seule!* (1871), with Istanbul's Hagia Sophia in the background, shows a contemporary fascination with a world of mosques and minarets. Ravel would compose his *Shéhérazade* in 1898 – a fairy-tale overture as a tribute to this enduring fad for orientalism – and of course his great song cycle with orchestral accompaniment of the same name in 1903. The single Fauré *mélodie* influenced by this passion for orientalism is *Les Roses d'Ispahan* of 1884 – a song that evokes Western delight in Eastern luxury from the first notes of its languorous introduction.

The Germans sought to escape the tyranny of dominant–tonic harmony by using an increasingly complex chromaticism – as in the works of Wagner, Strauss and later Schoenberg. A number of French composers followed this line of thought (many of them were disciples of Wagner, an influence that can be seen at some stage or other in their works), but there had been a long-established tradition of the study of modal harmony that gave to French music a flavour of its own. Berlioz in some of his music made use of the medieval modes, and these were also explored by Liszt and composers of the modern Russian school.

It was César Franck (1822–1890) who first attempted to combine modal writing with a quasi-Wagnerian chromaticism. He stayed more attached to the home key than Wagner, but he enlarged the field of his modulations with a fondness for *enchaînements* based on the common notes between two distant keys. His use of plagal cadences and passages of Gregorian-inspired modality bring a special, rather perfumed, colour to his style. Franckian disciples such as D'Indy and Chausson continued on this pathway in their own manner. If these had been the only examples for Fauré to follow he might have become an arch-conservative like his teacher Saint-Saëns, or another of the ardent Wagnerians.

There were at least two other composers, each of stunning individuality, whose music showed Fauré in his twenties that it was possible for a French composer to forge a style entirely of his own. The first of these was his older contemporary Georges Bizet (1838–1875), the majority of whose fine songs with piano were published between 1865 and 1868 when Fauré was employed as an organist in Rennes, in Brittany (see Chapter 3). *Carmen* was first performed in 1875 at a time when the younger composer was taken up with the Viardot family (see Chapter 4). The other composer was Emmanuel Chabrier (1841–1894), whose more important songs were published in Fauré's own maturity, but whose operetta, the almost universally admired *L'Étoile* (1877), must have made some impression on Fauré in a rather directionless period of his life. Both of these composers were capable of extreme harmonic audacity and refinement; Bizet and Chabrier were deeply serious, while being capable of humour; both were bold, and at the same time delicate.

Bizet was first and foremost a man of the theatre, as was Chabrier – temperamentally they were both a long way from Fauré with his penchant for piano music, songs and chamber music. But they belonged to no school, and they were both moderns without subscribing to the current

Georges Bizet (1838–1875)

Wagnerian mania (Chabrier and Fauré both knew and loved their Wagner through and through, and laughed at the music at the same time; both wrote piano duets parodying Wagnerian operatic themes). Bizet was a rebellious product of the Conservatoire; he died believing that his masterpiece, *Carmen*, was a failure, and that success had eluded him to the last. Chabrier, the lovable auto-didact from the Auvergne, had nothing to do with the Conservatoire: he had taken private lessons in Paris but evolved his own, strikingly individual, musical language. Much of his musical career ran parallel to that of Fauré's first period without the two composers influencing each other in the slightest. That two such great (and utterly different) composers should exist at the same time in Paris is no less remarkable, indeed no less a sign of the musical richness of the epoch, than the more famous later synchronicity of Fauré and Debussy, and of Debussy and Ravel.

It is all too easy to talk about Fauré as a composer 'apart' in sheerly musical or historical terms without considering aspects of his personality and private life. Great composers are by definition a 'success': because we would not wish their music to be different we would also refrain from changing details in their biography, had we the power to do so. It is clear that whatever shaped Fauré's life and mind we, the listeners, are the grateful beneficiaries. Nevertheless, even great composers are subject to crucial, and sometimes unfortunate, early experiences, where a different set of circumstances might have produced a different person, and thus arguably different music. This book will attempt such an hypothesis on behalf of Fauré only from the point of view

Emmanuel Chabrier (1841–1894)

of an observation that arises from reading the facts on the very first page of his biography, a reminder that the composer was born into a Dickensian age in terms of bringing up children.

Gabriel was the last of six, fifteen years younger than the eldest – possibly an unwanted child. His birth had not been planned, according to the pianist Marguerite Long.[17] She must have heard the composer refer to this when he reminisced about his childhood – he already in his sixties, and she still a student. Fauré's thirty-six-year-old mother, exhausted by childbearing, was simply unable to cope with the new arrival. Of the stresses and strains in her life we have no idea. The child was consigned to a wet-nurse in a neighbouring village of Verniolle, where he spent the first four years of his life with a foster family. After this he lived with his own mother and father during the school year, but as his siblings were older he remained a solitary child who spent enormous stretches of time on his own – he effectively brought himself up, it seems. In each of the summers of 1849 to 1854 he returned to live with his foster family, and he was dispatched to school far away in Paris at the age of nine.

Fauré himself never complained about this; indeed, he would have thought such a train of events completely unremarkable; in later years there were large stretches of time when he saw little of his own children, and yet he was extremely fond of them. In the twenty-first century we are more aware of the emotional damage unwittingly inflicted by busy or distracted parents. At the other end of the spectrum there is no doubt that the emotional development of Saint-Saëns was blighted by an obsessively controlling mother and aunt who fussed and worried over every aspect of the composer's life well into his middle age. With Fauré's parents there was no such danger, and the quality of affection he received from his stand-in mother (we know very little about her in contrast to Chabrier's beloved 'Nanine', a substitute that 'worked') would have been crucial to his development – it was perhaps from his nanny in Verniolle that he learned hope and patience. She was astounded to learn of his musical gifts – and deeply disappointed: 'There I was hoping he would be a bishop,' she groaned.[18]

We might wonder whether a failure of bonding between mother and son resulted in Gabriel's lifelong lack of self-esteem, as well as the early development of a self-protective shell (whereby 'nothing matters') to shield him from the pain of that rejection. Such a child often escapes from a low sense of self-worth by becoming someone else in his own mind, someone impervious to rejection, someone who falls back on any talents he may possess to explore his own fantasy world where he is a 'someone'. Fauré was thought to be a silent and self-contained little boy, and no wonder – but once his musical gift had emerged it was a matter of family discussion and approbation – he had proved himself very different from his elder brothers and sister. As Nicholas Spice has pointed out this can seem a saving grace for an otherwise unremarkable child, but it is not always healthy:

> To be good at music as a child is not always an unmixed blessing. It brings complications that may take a lifetime to smooth out … A child who is spoken to by music will quickly learn to speak through music. This is what adults call talent, and it entrances them … Musical ability draws down onto the child the approval of the adult world to an immoderate degree. This can be a source of deep ambiguity. On the one hand it's great for the child to feel valued and to have a way of establishing an identity with peers and siblings. On the other hand, the child may come partly to believe that he is only valued for his music and not for who he is.[19]

An 'indifference to success' and a disdain for praise can be the result of a childhood armoured against what the child perceives, rightly or wrongly, as an absence of love – and when love or success comes in later life it seems undeserved, not to be trusted, indistinguishable from blame. Fauré's lifelong obsession with a passing parade of amorous female companionship might be considered another consequence of this early deprivation; he loved women, everyone knew that, but whether he allowed them, or trusted them, to love him back is another matter. Did Fauré's wet-nurse have a rich and low speaking or singing voice? If so the composer's propensity for the mezzo-soprano timbre in composing his songs would be entirely understandable.

In some respects the way in which the infant Fauré was dispatched to the next village to grow up and develop apart was reflected in his position within the French family of musicians; his education at the École Niedermeyer, also a school very much apart, simply reinforced this sense of distance from his colleagues and rivals. If the badge of distance was initially painful the ingenious child had a way of adapting to pain – it became the badge of pride. He acquired a substantially new musical language from that of other composers, not merely as a hapless result of having gone to a different school, but because it was essential to his survival that he should remove himself from direct competition with his contemporaries and rivals – his musical siblings, if you like. In this we discern a conflict of self-evaluations: on one hand a feeling that he was unlovable, thus undeserving of success, indeed deserving of failure, and on the other a certainty of excellence within a long-built citadel of quiet defiance, a superiority so obvious to the composer himself that there was no need to have it put to the test. In this way the co-existence of a crushing lack of confidence and a lofty grandiosity is hardly surprising. 'Olympian' is an adjective that was applied to Fauré's demeanour more than once in his career, but at heart he was anything but that. In his emotive life we find a similar conflict: with very few exceptions he found it difficult to sustain relationships over any length of time that required him truly to share anything of his 'worthless' inner self while an outer facade of sexually persuasive charm ensured the conquering of pastures new, the latter leading to a succession of liaisons of self-defeating pointlessness. The fact that his relationship with his wife survived (although certainly not sexually) seems to have been thanks to her dysfunctional upbringing as much as his; both feared intimacy, although with time they developed a remarkable epistolary substitute at arms' length. Like two wounded birds they remained in the same coop without realising that (to adopt an old witticism) in their marrying, two people were made miserable instead of four.[20] It would seem that Fauré and his wife were, entirely by chance, rather well suited to each other; she called herself the 'zero of the family' – a phrase that sums up how the last and unwanted child of Toussaint and Hélène Fauré, whatever his fame, must have felt, even if only subconsciously, about his own position in his own family hierarchy – apart of course from his sovereign musical talent, and therein lies the conflict. A photograph taken in 1878 shows Fauré with his elder brothers Albert, Amand and Fernand; he was extremely fond of them but such family gatherings could scarcely make good the deprivations of a small boy thirty years earlier.

ᘒ ᘒ ᘒ ᘒ

His basic aim was not to become a public figure or get involved in being a revolutionary or a founding father; it was quite simply to develop his gifts and remain faithful to his own deeply held principles.
Jean-Michel Nectoux[21]

One can scarcely imagine what Fauré would have done, what he might have become, if he had not been able to live out his life in music. But if he had been able only to write music in the manner of Saint-Saëns, or even Massenet, one wonders whether he would have stayed the course. He needed the protection that the exclusivity of this musical language afforded him; it was his magic shield, the thing that ensured he was *hors de combat* in comparison with other composers, his own quiet way of removing himself from being compared with anyone else. Within the capsule of his own musical language he was, and remains, inviolate. He was one of those people who prefer to be ignored completely, rather than to find themselves demeaned by being ranked within a hierarchy. When viewed in this way, the composer's famous disinclination to push himself forward was not merely the result of a self-defeating humility; it may also be seen as a kind of inverse pride where he refused to plead for the merits of something that was self-evidently superior to the work of his rivals – or at least its superiority *should* have been self-evident if people only had the ears to comprehend.

At times it seems that the composer has made a posthumous breakthrough and that more and more people are recognising his greatness; at others one feels that his listeners will always be in the minority. That few people seem to have the necessary ears to understand him completely is perceived by some as the tragedy of Fauré's life and work, both when he was alive and even today, but the composer himself might not have seen it as such. His exclusivity, even inaccessibility, was something that became curiously positive and even necessary for his own comfort, his own self-image. It suited him to have appeared to come from nowhere, like a changeling, and when he died he went back into nowhere with the imperturbable shrug of the shoulders that reminds us of Thomas Hardy. who believed in the intervention of chance in human fate, and contended in one of his late poems that in never having asked for much he was not disappointed at the end of his days with not having received much.[22] For those who know and love both the poetry of Hardy and the music of Fauré there is an impervious doughtiness and self-sufficiency that link these two near-contemporaries. In the loneliness of their great art in old age they reached ineffable depths of expression through prodigious feats of concision: both were honoured, revered and (within four years of each other) given state funerals by so-called grateful governments that had little idea of the enduring scope of their achievements; both died without a successor in sight.

It seems part of some kind of sad inevitability in the Fauréan chronicle that both his sons should die childless, and that there has been no Wagnerian succession or a battle between heirs. He had no spiritual heirs either: grateful students and admirers a-plenty, all with different kinds of creative ideals, but no one who could continue the work of the Master where he had left off.[23]

ᘐ   ᘐ   ᘐ   ᘐ

Fauré remained completely uninvolved with the tide of music that was being composed in the year of his death – Janáček's *The Cunning little Vixen*, Gershwin's *Rhapsody in Blue*, Satie's *Relâche*, Ravel's *Tzigane*, Stravinsky's Piano Sonata – what did all this have to do with him, including the piece by Ravel, who had once been his pupil? Similarly it was no fault of his own that Wagner's *Lohengrin* and Berlioz's *La Damnation de Faust* were composed in the year of his birth. Even during his life he remained distant from Bizet's *Carmen* or Debussy's *Pelléas et Mélisande*; he must have known these works rather well, but they stand so far away from Fauré's own that they seem to exist merely in a kind of parallel universe, written not only without his having lifted a finger, but also without his scarcely having lent an ear. Stravinsky remembers seeing Fauré at a performance of *Le Sacre du printemps* in 1913 (the older composer possessed a copy of the work in its piano duet version) and the score of *Pierrot Lunaire*, lent to him by Émile Vuillermoz, gave him a sleepless night – as if he had consumed an indigestible meal.

None of the above-mentioned works, iconic as they are, had the power to touch and change a note of Fauré's legacy. Nothing by any composer since Fauré put down his pen has rendered anything he has written obsolete or old-fashioned; nothing has rendered it easier to understand either. No more recent music has made Fauré's appear more accessible than when it was first written, but nothing composed since he died has made it sound dated and passé either. As for listeners (or performers), the composer will do nothing, beyond the gift of his music, to beg or persuade them into loving or even admiring him; this was never his way.

ᘐ   ᘐ   ᘐ   ᘐ

J.-M. Nectoux prefaces his smaller volume on the composer, *Fauré*,[24] with a poem by Mallarmé (set by Ravel, not by Fauré) entitled 'Sainte'. These beautiful and evocative lines form a hymn to the patron saint of music, and Nectoux clearly intends that Mallarmé's words 'Musicien de silence' ('Musician of Silence') should be read with reference to Fauré himself, as well as St Cecilia.

In a similar way the reader of this book is asked to turn to page 290 and read the poem entitled 'Le Don silencieux' – 'The silent gift'. The quality of silence mentioned by Mallarmé is once again crucial here; it is strange perhaps that this attribute should be equated with a composer who gave the world so much sound, incomparably beautiful sound, but the silence of Fauré in terms of his disinclination to self-advertisement is deafening. 'Le Don silencieux' is the one song text in Fauré's whole output that seems applicable to his own work, music created during a lifetime of toil that was his gift to the world, his own 'don silencieux', where the adjective 'silencieux' describes the music in spiritual, rather than acoustical, terms.

During the ups and downs of a life full of disappointments Fauré displayed a remarkable outward calm and unruffled temperament, a kind of passive resistance that was heroic and positive in its own understated way. Similarly, the diffidence of the poem by the redoubtable Marie Closset (Jean Dominique) should not be misread as something weak and slavish – the proffered gift may, or may not be, welcomed, but it is offered irrespective of its reception, and the donor is steeled to rejection as if it were an inevitable price to pay for being the person she is. It is also this kind of hidden steel that protects Fauré's matchless gifts. His lifelong ability to appear less important than he really was strikes us as a complicated manoeuvre of survival, and it can sometimes seem disingenuous – like a canny countryman of the Ariège (and no one can deny this aspect of the composer's genealogy) who plays the Nobody while hiding his store of food and wine from the foreign invader. For 'foreign invader' read 'Wagner' or 'Debussy' or 'well-paid job', 'lavish praise' or 'self-satisfaction'. If 'a disdainful indifference to success'[25] was part of the complex psychological means by which he was able to achieve his creative goals – even if this meant less material comfort in his own lifetime – we can only be reminded of the sometimes unbearably heavy dues payable to St Cecilia by her faithful servants.

And of course there were earthly compensations for a composer renowned for his ability to fall in love time and time again, as if endlessly in search of something lost in his childhood and never rediscovered. The patron saint of music is always depicted as a beautiful woman, and 'Le Don silencieux' is certainly addressed to one such by its poet. On first reading, the poem may seem to show only abject humility, but it is a love poem that is both ardent and seductive, however obliquely expressed. For this composer there is always hope that the lover's answer will be 'yes' and that she will *understand*, that her ears will be open and receptive to Fauréan delight. And if not (and here comes the defensive shrug) there will always be someone else; perhaps someone from a new generation of music lovers who will understand where her elders had been uncomprehending. Whatever the time lag, the composer knew that his gift would be spurned by some, even after a hundred years (and what else would the child with his low self-esteem expect?) but that it would be taken up by others – and this was something that the great musician knew as a fact. When he was on his deathbed he assured his sons of this, reminding them that a composer falls out of fashion after his death, a 'moment d'oubli' to be expected and accepted … 'Tout cela n'a pas d'importance.'

Fauré may never experience a dramatic breakthrough, but there will always be a steady stream of new adherents, performing artists and listeners whose response to such a 'don silencieux' is gratitude and a vow of lifelong service – such devotion as demonstrated by the young pianist Robert Lortat, who learned all of Fauré's piano music and astounded Fauré in 1912 by playing it to him by heart. Of course Fauré would almost certainly have preferred Lortat to have been a beautiful woman, but he was deeply moved; in many cases he had never heard performances of piano pieces he had composed decades earlier. When the pianist gave complete Fauré recitals in London to disappointingly small houses it was the composer who said to him, gently, without the slightest sign of self-pity, and even with a touch of pride 'But Lortat, I'm not in the habit of attracting crowds.'

Fauré struggled to survive in the ordinary world while guarding his inner flame. This juggling act cost him endless energy (and cost us much music that he should have written instead of scrambling for monetary survival) but he managed somehow. His works continue to be loved by those who find them indispensable. Music such as this cannot be foisted on unwilling ears; it must patiently wait its turn with each generation and be 'gathered up' by those who choose to do so. Of course such trust, a kind of stoic passivity typical of the composer, is hardly likely to make money, but it is the sign of a man too proud to be a salesman of any kind. Had Fauré been a ruthless promoter of his own work, or if he had slavishly 'cut his cloth' according to the commercial demands of his time, would he be better

Marcel Proust (1871–1922) Pencil drawing by Jacques-Émile Blanche (1891)

known today? Massenet did all that to perfection, but for all the enthusiasm of his operatic public for some of his works, he failed to achieve Fauré's standing. As Proust wrote: 'The reason why a work of genius is not easily admired from the first is that the man who created it is extraordinary, that few other men resemble him. It is the work itself, that, by fertilising the rare minds capable of understanding it, will make them increase and multiply'[26]

It is a relatively small but determined audience of deeply musical people that has sought out Fauré, and continues to seek him out, and in so doing assured his immortality and continues to assure it. From the perspective of the twenty-first century that side of him with the patience and long-term confidence of a great master has triumphed at last over the doubts of the rejected child.

When he was seventy-four the old composer wrote to the aspiring young singer Madeleine Grey, assuring her that she would have a career, but only, he said, once she had experienced 'a large measure of *suffering* and *patience*'.[27] It is as if he is gently trying to persuade his starry-eyed protégée (a young diva very much on the way up, and suited to neither suffering nor patience) to adopt his own way of coping with life. He might have quoted her part of a famous Edwardian poem, had he known it, that also counselled a young person to stoic indifference: 'if you can meet with triumph and disaster / and treat those two imposters just the same'. Fauré's punch-line would have been different from Kipling's, however … 'you'll be an Artist'.[28]

Fauré's almost indiscernible shrug in the face of adversity was no doubt partly defence mechanism and safety net, but it took on a life of its own in eventually determining aspects of his aesthetic. Decades before he wrote to Madeleine Grey advising her to expect 'suffering' and practise 'patience', qualities such as these had been woven deep into the heart of his music.

∾   ∾   ∾   ∾

As he sat applauding in the concert audience, Marcel Proust watched and admired Fauré as he bowed from the platform; the composer smiled from the stage at the clearly enthusiastic Proust but was seemingly indifferent as to whether the public had liked what they had heard or not. And yet beneath his noble and restrained *sang-froid* lay a breadth and depth of emotion all the more astonishing in its protean capacity to resolve itself into smaller musical forms such as the *mélodie*. 'Indifference to success' in Gabriel Fauré goes hand in hand with an axiom he had taken for granted all his artistic life: one's feelings and emotions, no matter how turbulent, are interesting for other people only when contained within the boundaries of art and subject to the discipline of form. This Apollonian control incorporates a kind of indifference to the Self, and this is also crucial to the composer's creative profile. If his appetite for success and fame had been untouched by suffering, untempered by self-defeating patience and free of a self-protective carapace of indifference (thanks, let us say, to a miraculously happy childhood, or the help of the best psychiatrist from another time and place),[29] we the listeners would have paid a heavy price: the incomparable output of Gabriel Fauré (of which we would not wish to change a note) might well have sounded completely different from the music we have and hold, the music we know and love.

1   *Gabriel Fauré: A Life in Letters*, trans. and ed. Barrie Jones (London: B.T. Batsford, 1989), letter 75, p. 86.

2   Fauré on a visit to Russia, letter of 14 November 1910, in Gabriel Fauré, *Lettres intimes*, ed. Philippe Fauré-Fremiet (Paris: La Colombe, 1951), p. 192.

3   Quoted in a lecture given at the Rice Institute in 1925 by Nadia Boulanger, transcribed in Don G. Campbell, *Master Teacher – Nadia Boulanger* (Washington DC: The Pastoral Press,1984), p. 105.

4   Although Nadia Boulanger perceptively opined in 1925: 'Fauré, like Wagner, is one of the few composers who conceive tonality as a mobile and not a static state.' Quoted in a lecture given at the Rice Institute, transcribed in Campbell, *Master Teacher – Nadia Boulanger*, p. 105.

5   F. Gervais, *Étude comparée des langages harmoniques de Fauré et de Debussy* (doctoral thesis, Sorbonne, Paris, 1954), reprinted (Paris: Éditions de la Revue Musicale, Nos 272–3, 1971).

6   Pauline Viardot later edited *50 mélodies de Schubert* published by Hamelle, a collection that influenced Bizet among other composers.

7   Some of the Niedermeyer songs are reprinted in *Romantic French Song 1830–1870*, vol. 1, ed. D. Tunley (New York and London: Garland, 1994).

8   Mimi Segal Daitz, 'Les Manuscripts et les premières éditions de mélodies de Fauré: Étude préliminaire', *Études Fauréennes*, 20–21 (1983–84), 1–28.

9   At the time of writing, Mimi Daitz and Jean-Michel Nectoux are preparing such an edition, to be published in 2009.

10 Quoted in Norman Suckling, *Fauré* (London: Dent, 1946), p. 54.

11 Jean-Michel Nectoux, *Gabriel Fauré: A Musical Life*, trans. Roger Nichols (Cambridge: Cambridge University Press, 1991), p. 228.

12 Ibid., p. 228.

13 Ibid.

14 Charles Koechlin, *Gabriel Fauré (1845–1924)*, trans. Leslie Orry (London: Denis Dobson, 1946), p. 64.

15 Quoted in a lecture given at the Rice Institute in 1925 by Nadia Boulanger, transcribed in Campbell, *Master Teacher – Nadia Boulanger*, p. 107.

16 Ibid., p. 107.

17 Marguerite Long, *Au piano avec Gabriel Fauré* (Paris: Gérard Billandot, 1963), p. 19.

18 Philippe Fauré-Fremiet, *Gabriel Fauré* (Paris: Les Éditions Rieder, 1929), p. 28.

19 Nicholas Spice in a review of Ruth Railton's *Daring to Excel*, *London Review of Books*, 6 January 1994.

20 Samuel Butler: 'It was very good of God to let Carlyle and Mrs. Carlyle marry one another and so make only two people miserable instead of four.' Letter to E.M.A. Savage, 21 November 1884, in *Letters between Samuel Butler and Mrs E.M.A. Savage, 1871–1885* (London: Jonathan Cape, 1935).

21 Nectoux, *Gabriel Fauré: A Musical Life*, p. 312.

22 Thomas Hardy, 'He Never Expected Much – a Reflection on my 86th Birthday', from *Winter Words* (London: Macmillan, 1928), pp. 113–14.

23 Hardy had no children, but the sentences above applied as much to him at his death in 1928 as to Fauré in 1924.

24 2nd edition, Paris: Seuil, 1995.

25 See n. 1 above.

26 Marcel Proust, *Remembrance of Things Past: The Budding Grove* (*À l'ombre des jeunes filles en fleur*) translated by C. K. Scott Moncrieff and Terence Kilmartin, London, 1981, Volume 1 p. 572.

27 Unpublished letter from Fauré, 10 August 1919, quoted in Nectoux, *Gabriel Fauré: A Musical Life*, p. 443.

28 Rudyard Kipling, 'If' (1910), where the poem ends 'You'll be a Man, my son!' (London, Sydney, Auckland, Toronto: Definitive Edition, 1977, p. 576).

29 After a four-hour consultation with Gustav Mahler in the summer of 1910, Sigmund Freud observed: 'There are those that argue that a neurosis is useful to an artist! If Mahler had been analysed and cured of his neurosis, his works would probably have been quite different'. The psychoanalyst Erwin Ringel observed in 1997 'We must be very careful when we are dealing with artistic-creative people. These people too suffer in their unconscious, but they filter out their suffering in their great creative works'. Writing of her husband the poet Hermann Hesse, Nina Hesse wrote 'I became convinced that attempts by me to lessen his bad moods would lessen his urge to produce. In helping the man I endangered the poet'. Quoted in Henri-Louis de la Grange, *Gustav Mahler: A New Life Cut Short* (Oxford University Press, 2008), pp. 894–5.

Chapter Two

Second Empire and First Songs

Victor Hugo

The final defeat of Napoleon Bonaparte at Waterloo in 1815, thirty years before the birth of Gabriel Fauré, was less decisive than it seemed. The French had first chopped their rulers and then changed them with some regularity in over half a century of political vacillation. They finally settled for the Third Republic of 1870, which, after a violent birth in the wake of the Franco-Prussian War, held sway for seventy mostly peaceful and prosperous years. This was the state umbrella under which Fauré sheltered safely for more than two-thirds of his life – a haven of bourgeois stability disturbed only by the upheaval of the First World War. As an older man the composer took a keen interest in current affairs, although little in his maturity could match the colourful political vicissitudes of his childhood and adolescence.

The restoration in 1814 of the Bourbon monarchy and the reign of Louis XVIII had been interrupted by Napoleon's surprise return from Elba for the 'Hundred Days' in 1815, a comeback that turned out to be only a temporary storm in an ultra-conservative European political landscape where peace was preserved at all costs. The new King of France was a brother of the decapitated Louis XVI; his awkward and extravagant reign was an uneasy tussle with the unfamiliar concept of constitutional monarchy. When Louis died in 1824 his even more reactionary and intransigent brother Charles X took the throne, seemingly determined to wipe out all vestiges of the Revolution. To his regal surprise the uneasy truce between the people and this branch of the autocratic Bourbons was at an end. The July Revolution of 1830 swept Charles aside in favour of Louis-Philippe, Duc d'Orléans, the so-called Citizen King, whose relatively enlightened and liberal agenda became a rallying cry for European left. The German poet Heinrich Heine and other starry-eyed European intellectuals adopted Paris as their new home in what seemed like the dawning of a new age of equality.

As we shall see, it was in these heady 1830s that the poet, playwright and novelist Victor Hugo laid the foundations of his fame as an artist of the people and enjoyed some of his most important successes. But despite the fact that Louis-Philippe's reign had begun with the best of intentions, all was not well: as the *roi citoyen* attempted to steer a course between the royalists and an increasingly powerful middle class it became clear that a great deal of idealistic revolutionary fervour had been somewhat misplaced at the expense of the dissatisfied working class.

1848 was a year of revolution and political upheaval throughout Europe. After eighteen years in power and a worsening economic crisis Louis-Philippe's time was also up – he abdicated and a Second Republic was proclaimed in France. For the first time since 1830 the emancipation of the proletariat seemed a real possibility, but not for long. The left-leaning poet Alphonse de Lamartine became foreign minister, but he did not last in office. In June 1848 Paris was torn asunder by a brief left-wing revolt that was suppressed with great bloodshed. The stage was set for the election of a new leader, Louis-Napoleon, nephew of the great Bonaparte, who at first seemed an unlikely and unpromising candidate; he had twice failed to unseat Louis-Philippe in military coups, and had escaped to England to avoid life imprisonment.

At the outset, as 'Prince-Président' of the new republic, Louis-Napoleon was careful to abide by the constitution, but by the end of 1851 there was a *coup d'état*, and in 1852 a Second Empire was proclaimed, backed by an affirmative

Louis-Philippe de Bourbon (1773–1850), the Citizen King

plebiscite. France was now led by a brand-new Emperor, Napoleon III. Politics moved sharply to the right, not only in Paris of course but also in the provinces.

In the southern *département* of the Ariège, in the shadow of the Pyrenees and far away from the capital, the change of government, and its new educational policies, indirectly affected the future of the hero of this book, the sixth, and youngest child of Toussaint-Honoré-Toussaint and Marie-Antoinette-Hélène Fauré, née de Lalène-Laprade. Gabriel Urbain Fauré had been born towards the end of the reign of Louis-Philippe, on 12 May 1845, at 17 rue Major, Pamiers. He was almost immediately sent to the neighbouring town of Verniolle to live with a wet-nurse, who cared for him for a number of years. When Napoleon III proclaimed his new Empire in 1852 the child, already showing strong signs of an inexplicable musical gift, was seven years old. By this time Toussaint Fauré had conscientiously worked his way up through the local educational hierarchy to become director of the Montgauzy teacher-training college at Foix (in the same *département*); once Fauré *père* had been promoted to this new position, young Gabriel was permitted to return to live with his own family. A contemporary photograph (see p. 28) of the fortified town of Foix with its thirteenth-century buildings, 845 kilometres from Paris (the nearest big city is Toulouse), brings to mind the opening of that great Fauré cycle *La Bonne chanson*, with its medieval imagery: 'Une châtelaine en sa tour'.

The college headed by Fauré *père* shared the grounds of a ruined convent with a chapel and a beautiful walled garden that was a complete contrast to the austerity of the surrounding buildings. Gabriel's brothers and sisters were much older, so he was solitary lord of his new domain. The

26

Alphonse de Lamartine (1790–1869), portrait by François Gérard, 1831

child never forgot the sights and smells of this childhood paradise, resplendent with magnolia, pine, cypress and cedar; all his life he remembered the beguiling light of the Mediterranean region, although he returned to enjoy it only on family holidays early in his career, and in the summers of his old age when the Swiss lakes, and Lugano in particular, also reminded him of the landscapes of the Ariège.

There was also a rhythmic sound of a kind to be heard – that of the dull and distant reverberations of the Catalan metal forges at the foot of the mountains; in the midday heat of the region this gave the aural impression of a buzzing beehive.[1] From the age of four Gabriel played as well as he could on an old harmonium he discovered in the chapel at Montgauzy; he remembered an old blind woman who used to encourage his stumbling efforts by giving him rudimentary lessons, a scene that might have come out of a Maeterlinck play. This old lady, as if she were one of the Fates, made it clear to his parents that the boy would benefit from a musical education. Years later a music teacher called Bernard Delgay claimed to have given Fauré his first music lessons.

In the new political order of 1852 the Church, more influential in royalist and imperial epochs than in republican ones, had money to spare for the grooming of its future employees. Toussaint Fauré consulted the parliamentary deputy for the *département*, one Dufaur de Saubiac, concerning his youngest son's prospects, and he was advised to send Gabriel to a newly opened school in Paris for the education of church musicians. The subvention of the newly established ministry of Beaux Arts ensured that three-quarters of the boy's school fees would be paid.

It was a year before the cautious Toussaint Fauré followed the deputy's advice. In 1854 the nine-year-old Fauré was taken up to the capital city to enrol as a student at Louis Niedermeyer's École de Musique Classique et Religieuse. The journey from Foix to Paris took three days with alternating journeys by both carriage and train (this again according to Marguerite Long, who seems to have questioned Fauré in some detail concerning his early memories). Niedermeyer himself had apparently been on a concert tour in the south of France, had auditioned the boy, and decided to take him under his wing (presumably with an offer of a full scholarship) – all this before Gabriel even left home.[2] The boy's father was content, but somewhat mystified. In the distant past the Faurés had been an aristocratic family that had lost its money and status, but the composer's grandfather and great-

The hilly fortifications of the town of Foix in the Ariège

grandfather had worked as butchers. Madame Fauré had come from a military family, and there was little sign of musical talent in the parental genealogies. From the beginning of his life this composer had the mysterious attributes of a changeling, but he never forgot his roots. In his later years when he was bidden to visit a government minister he asked a friend to go with him for moral support: Fauré explained: 'I'm always a little intimidated … My father was only a schoolmaster.'[3]

The École Niedermeyer (at 10 rue Neuve-Fontaine-Saint-Georges – today, rue Fromentin – in the ninth *arrondissement*) had benefited from its proprietor's personal petition to the new Emperor. Napoleon III was keen to subsidise a closeness between the Church and the new Empire, and the school was only part of what promised to be an exciting mosaic of educational reforms. In this respect, as in many others, the regime promised more than it delivered. Opinion is still divided as to whether the Emperor was an untalented opportunist or a visionary statesman. The truth is probably somewhere between the two. His was the kind of political career, a pattern that repeats to this day, that began with quasi-socialist credentials and veered sharply to the right in search of personal aggrandisement. A clever and even charming communicator, Louis-Napoleon cannily negotiated his way between the notoriously fractious elements of French politics and displayed a flair for a kind of 'third way' compromise that set the country on course for a reversal of the economic slump of 1846–51. France's fat cats prospered in a new age of industrial technocracy, but unfortunately this wealth (accompanied by the demands of the *nouveaux riches* for vacuous entertainment) was coupled with a longing for glory, as if the new Emperor and his cohorts imagined they might surpass the military record of Napoleon I. Then as now, dynastic one-upmanship is a toxic ingredient when it comes to going to war, and this was the hubris that was to destroy the Second Empire. 'Napoléon le petit', as Victor Hugo scornfully dubbed him, soon acquired a taste for foreign adventure. One of his principal concerns was to ally himself with the greatest military power of the day: Napoleon III's participation on the British side in the Crimean conflict procured his friendship with Britain and Queen Victoria. England and France had been at war with Russia for seven months when Toussaint Fauré brought his son Gabriel to Paris in October 1854.

In the middle of a capital city that was soon to become renowned for its voluptuous worldliness, the École Niedermeyer must have appeared an austere refuge, a symbol of all the upright precepts that were the respectable garb of the Second Empire, a believable front perhaps if one ignored

Louis Niedermeyer (1802–1861)

the licentious undergarments soon to be on display in the *Can-can* from Offenbach's *Orphée aux Enfers*. Fauré was a boarder at Niedermeyer's school for eleven years, between the ages of nine and twenty – towards the end of his stint there he was more or less co-opted as a staff member. In some ways it was as if he had entered a monastery situated at the heart of a red-light district, but there were also aspects of the school that made it resemble a military academy. There was strict discipline (the students wore a kind of cadet's uniform with peaked cap) and meagre food; he remembered 'a hard life but a delightful one' – delightful because there was always the making of music – and the students were trained in the great choral repertoire of earlier centuries: Josquin, Palestrina, Bach, Vittoria – music mostly unknown elsewhere in France at the time. His ability to concentrate while composing, no matter what the distraction, doubtlessly went back to his having to practise the piano in a room where fourteen other pianists were playing their scales and arpeggios at the same time.

Louis Niedermeyer himself (1802–1861) was a man of an extraordinarily wide musical background; he had studied with Moscheles in Vienna and had been an assistant to Rossini in Naples, and was an acknowledged expert on early music. He was no modernist, however: he believed that a composer like Schumann was unsuitable for the young. When Niedermeyer suddenly died in 1861 the sixteen-year-old Fauré lost a staunch admirer and father figure, but he was already at the age that rebels against fatherly discipline. The new professor of harmony was the unsympathetic Louis Dietsch, but the replacement professor of piano, Camille Saint-Saëns (1835–1921), was thankfully another matter, and this appointment was to prove as important for Fauré's future as the precocious Benjamin Britten's meeting with Frank Bridge some sixty years later. Saint-Saëns played the music of Schumann and Liszt to his pupils, who otherwise would never have had the chance to encounter such modernity, and of course he took an interest in their compositions. 'He read them', Fauré later wrote, 'with a curiosity and care which only masterpieces would have deserved.'

In the mean time the Empire's ambitions grew alongside the rich middle classes' appetite for the Parisian high life. Napoleon III's victories against the Austrians at Magenta and Solferino (1859) contributed to the regime's optimism and self-confidence, and there were certain happy side-effects. A low-tariff treaty with Britain was negotiated; there was a liberalisation of press censorship; an amnesty was announced pardoning the regime's home-grown opponents and the political climate lightened. The 1860s seemed to be the 'good years' of Napoleon's rule, a *belle époque*, of sorts. The worlds of music and literature were exceptionally active at this time; there was a groundswell of innovative literary activity (Baudelaire, Gautier, Leconte de Lisle) that was hardly matched in the musical world where the grandiose operas of Meyerbeer on one hand, and the hedonistic and satirical operettas of Offenbach on the other, still held sway. The city of Paris took on its definitive outward shape at this time thanks to the tireless, if autocratic, building programme of Baron Haussmann.

ও   ও   ও   ও

At the École Niedermeyer the young Fauré won many musical accolades but he also showed a budding taste for literature; he was awarded two prizes in that subject in 1858 and 1862. Study was restricted to such writers as Racine, Corneille, Bossuet and La Fontaine – indeed in 1865 Fauré composed a *Cantique de Jean Racine* for mixed choir with accompaniment of harmonium and string quintet, his first masterpiece, which was later described as a work of 'simplicité, ampleur, clarté, gran-

Caricature by Fauré of Saint-Saëns as a soldier, taken from Gabriel Fauré *by Philippe Fauré-Fremiet*

deur, délicatesse d'expression'.[4] A seventeenth-century poet was a safe choice for a text of this kind but Racine was hardly a man of the moment. In terms of contemporary poets there was only one acknowledged giant, Victor Hugo, and this despite the fact (or perhaps because) he had been exiled for denouncing the new Emperor in 1853 and was *persona non grata* in imperial circles.

Victor-Marie Hugo was born on 26 February 1802 in Besançon, the son of a general in Napoleon's army; in his childhood the family was stationed in Elba and Corsica, Italy and Spain. He moved to Paris with his mother and brother (his parents had separated by this time) in 1819. In his youth he was an ardent royalist, and at first he supported the restored Bourbon monarchy. Hugo received a pension from Louis XVIII in recognition of his first collection of poems, *Odes et poésies diverses*, written in 1822 (which was also the year of his marriage to Adèle Foucher – the poet was a father for the first time by 1823). Charles X appointed Hugo, at the age of twenty-three, to the Légion d'Honneur, but the poet was thoroughly out of sympathy with the censorship imposed by the last of the Bourbons, and the wild success of Hugo's *Hernani* in February 1830 was an augury of the revolution that led to Charles's abdication in August of the same year and the reign of the Citizen King, Louis-Philippe. The poet now found himself in the right place and at the right time for the kind of epic successes that befitted his talent: in 1831 the publication of *Notre-Dame de Paris* (in English *The Hunchback of Notre Dame*) and the first performances of the

Victor Hugo as a young man

plays *Lucrèce Borgia* and *Marie Tudor* (both 1833) assured his prosperity. Hugo moved his family into the house that can be visited today as the 'Maison Victor Hugo' in the place des Vosges in Paris. His fellow romanticist the critic Sainte-Beuve and Adèle Hugo embarked on an affair that caused the poet anguish; in February 1833 he met the actress Juliette Drouet, who was to be his mistress for many years (see the commentary on the song *Tristesse d'Olympio* below), long after Adèle had broken the liaison with Saint-Beuve. During the reign of Louis-Philippe no fewer than four volumes of verse were published. His daughter Léopoldine drowned in a boating accident on the Seine in 1843, and the result was the poems published much later in *Les Contemplations*, where the two books of the collection are entitled *Autrefois* and *Aujourd'hui* (*Another time* and *Today*) and in which the poet's more carefree contemplations are contrasted with those darkened by family tragedy. Elected to the Chamber of Peers, Hugo dedicated himself increasingly to political work in the closing years of Louis-Phillippe's reign. In 1845 he embarked on a long affair with Léonie Biard, a liaison he managed to keep from the ever-faithful Juliette for seven years.

When the revolution of 1848 instigated a new republic, headed by the Prince-Président, Louis-Napoleon, Hugo – by this time almost as much of a politician as a writer – was elected to the *Assemblée*, and had hopes of high office under this new administration. He felt personally betrayed by Louis-Napoleon's *coup d'état* in 1851, and unsuccessfully attempted to rally opposition at the barricades. (He may not have recognised the younger Charles Baudelaire as a fellow protestor.) He was forced to flee the police, and he left Paris disguised as a workman. He first went to Brussels but was deported after denouncing the recently self-created Napoleon III in print. Hugo lived for nineteen years in the Channel Islands – first in Jersey and then in Guernsey – where he castigated the excesses and inanities of the Second Empire from the comfort of Hauteville House (another Hugo monument worthy of a visit). Occupying the moral high ground, he was taken by many to represent the old virtues of an incorruptible republican France. Another republican of the old school was Alphonse Lamartine, whose poem 'Le Lac' had been set to music by Louis Niedermeyer. As a teenager Fauré had entertained his parents with performances of this piece with his breaking voice. And yet how dated and cumbersome these verses must have seemed a few years later to the ambitious young composer; the poetry of the recently deceased Alfred de Musset was also already passé, whereas Charles Baudelaire, Théophile Gautier and Leconte de Lisle were, as yet, still in the composer's future. Hugo had been around for decades, and yet he was still very much of the present; only five years younger than Schubert, the poet died when Debussy was writing his first songs. In a similarly astonishing way, Fauré's own career embraces Berlioz and Bizet at one end and Stravinsky and Poulenc at the other.

Hugo had achieved his fame as a writer some twenty years before Napoleon III seized power, and there was nothing the new regime could do to alter the high regard in which he and his works were held by the nation at large. The poet remained in Jersey taking potshots at the regime; with leonine pride he ignored the amnesty of 1859. Nevertheless this official change of attitude permitted musicians in the employ of the Second Empire to return to his poems with a good conscience: the dutiful Niedermeyer composed his Hugo settings in 1861 (for a discussion of these see Chapter 1) shortly before Fauré wrote the first of his songs with a text by this poet.

Other composers realised that Hugo's poetic greatness lay beyond the censor's control: in 1856 Edouard Lalo had published a group of *Six mélodies* to this poet's texts that made quite a stir. Camille Saint-Saëns, an admirer of Hugo for at least a decade, had also composed a number of the poet's texts during Hugo's official disgrace; he would almost certainly have shown these to the young Fauré while expressing his enthusiasm for the poems, just as he vaunted the talents of Liszt – the most famous of whose settings of the same poet had first been published as early as 1844.

Hugo straddled all forms of literature, and was perceived by his contemporaries as the colossus of *romantisme* – he wrote poems, plays, novels, all with a dazzling and innovative command of technique and a daring versatility unrivalled in French letters. It has been said of him that no poet ever lived so much in the full light of day. Charles Dantzig, claiming that Hugo had ink where other men had blood, estimates his output at 4,000 pages of poems, the same number of pages of essays, 3,000 pages of novels, 2,000 pages of plays.[5] This is an output to rival the prolixity of Voltaire. Hugo's mastery of rhyme and metre can still take the breath away; he had an inexhaustible passion for hard work, but so compelling was the quantity of his daily industry that he sometimes failed to monitor the quality of his output. The English critic W.J. Robertson, a passionate admirer of Hugo's genius, was eloquent on the subject of the writer's faults:

When the flux of images and metaphors at the poet's command pours in almost ludicrous disproportion to the magnitude of the thought; when grotesque antithesis and superfluous analogy are piled up to disguise the occasional lack of intense passion or sustained imagination; when an apparently egregious conceit finds expression in familiar colloquy with the majestic forces of Nature until it verges on the burlesque; – what can the judicious do but grieve?[6]

Even those poets who bemoaned the inconsistency of the œuvre itself could not fail to wonder at the skill with which it was fashioned: even Leconte de Lisle, a fervent admirer of Hugo, admitted that the great man was 'as stupid [*bête*] as the Himalayas', an epithet that acknowledged the poet as an immovable and gigantic part of the literary landscape, an irony that might have amused Hugo had he looked down from his promontory to read it. Even in his earlier writings there is scarcely a mention, even critical, of his contemporary authors. He was so sublimely egocentric that it had not occurred to him to compare himself with his *confrères*. This was, after all, the poet who without any irony compared the totality of his work to 'une Bible humaine', a book made up of many books that summed up the entire century. And yet he was unfailingly, almost systematically,

Victor Hugo in middle age

encouraging to younger writers. One cannot help but compare him to that other figure of towering romanticism, Franz Liszt, who always took the trouble to encourage young musicians, including Fauré. Both Hugo and Liszt can be condemned easily enough as self-promoting mountebanks, but the generosity and altruism in their large (and admittedly rather alarming) natures is beyond dispute.

When asked who was the greatest of the French poets, André Gide replied, 'Victor Hugo, hélas.' This 'hélas' from a twentieth-century master, judicious grieving if you like, perfectly conveys the mixture of admiration for, and a certain wearied indifference to, Hugo's achievements from the point of view of the French literary establishment after about 1860: his output is vast and uneven, and he is so towering a figure that he seems too much of an icon, too little a real person. Nevertheless Hugo's genius has always stubbornly (and successfully) resisted all attempts at dismissal. He was perhaps above all a poet for disturbed times: a masterly painter of war, havoc and confusion – in Napoleonic Spain his father had been in the confidence of Joseph Bonaparte no less. He was also, among many other things, the poet of terror both earthly and supernatural, the poet of the sea in its most imposing moods. The bourgeois mind-set of the Third Republic's citizens may have required literary art of a less dramatic, digressive and emphatic nature, but it would be foolish to underestimate the extent of Hugo's ongoing fame, and the size of his enthusiastic readership.

∾   ∾   ∾   ∾

As Fauré, still in his teens, embarked on settings of Hugo's poetry, the great poet was in late middle age, beginning to grow his famous beard and preparing to publish, after a long genesis, one of the greatest, and most successful, of his works, *Les Misérables* (1862). By this time Baudelaire had already published *Les Fleurs du mal* (1857), and Verlaine's first poems would soon appear; there were indeed already poets in France who could more than rival Hugo in terms of innovation and significance, but the teenaged Fauré seems to have looked to Hugo for his first song texts without any hesitation. This may have been largely to do with the influence of Niedermeyer's works, and those of Lalo and Saint-Saëns, but we should not assume that the young composer (even if he really was as dull and unmotivated as he later claimed to be at this stage of his life) was lacking in opinions and allegiances. Many an idealist of Fauré's age would have been inspired by the expatriate tirades of a poet who set out to discredit the increasingly disreputable, and seedy, political status quo. But even if we might wish to imagine Fauré was a strong supporter of Hugo in his self-imposed exile, one can pour cold water on such a theory by pointing out that the École Niedermeyer owed its existence to the support of Napoleon III, and its inmates had little chance to experience at first hand either the pleasurable or the undesirable aspects of the Second Empire.

Later, in 1864, when the publication of six Hugo songs by the firm of Georges Hartmann was a possibility, the poet was approached by his factotum Paul Meurice regarding Fauré's request for permission to set his texts to music. Declining to take any money for himself, the great man, ever the supporter of noble causes, told Meurice that Fauré's copyright fees should be sent on to Garibaldi to help buy rifles for the Italians, who were fighting to free themselves from foreign domination. Later, when informed of the small amount of money involved, and of the young composer's limited funds, Hugo, in typically kindly fashion, waived his rights entirely.

Hugo's wife died in 1868, and the death of two of their sons followed soon after his fêted return to Paris in 1870 with the defeat of Napoleon III at Sedan (see Chapter 3). The young Sarah Bernhardt mounted a special production of *Ruy Blas* in the poet's honour at the Odéon, but in the world of literature he had already been overtaken by younger men. Although he was appointed to the Senate he served there only briefly. He was honoured as a national figure and officially remained a symbol of the noble republican struggle, but the magic of the earlier years of exile inexorably faded. French poetry had moved on, and after the Franco-Prussian War even the composers of the *mélodie*, hardly the first to react to the latest literary fashions, were in the mood to turn their back on Hugo. Fauré's song *L'Absent*, composed in 1871, sounds remarkably like a farewell to a great man, rather than an ode to welcome him back to France. Fauré returned once more to this poet in the middle 1870s for a choral piece with piano (or orchestra) entitled *Les Djinns*; but this was a strange postlude to his earlier relationship to Victor Hugo's poems, and of no great significance to the poet's reputation among musicians.

Hugo was stricken by illness in 1878 and died on 22 May 1885; the street in which he lived had been named after him (and nearly every town in France has an avenue Victor Hugo). He was accorded a state funeral. Who would have believed that the same honour would one day be accorded to Gabriel Fauré?

∾   ∾   ∾   ∾

There is no one in all nineteenth-century literature who influenced more composers, and specifically opera composers, than this poet. Johann Wolfgang von Goethe, rightly deified by lieder enthusiasts, was certainly a more universal figure in small-scale vocal music, but his *Faust*, cheekily adapted for the theatre by Barbier and Carré in 1859 (Fauré and his schoolfriends mounted a forbidden nocturnal expedition to see Gounod's opera), hardly invited responsible musical setting *in toto*. Writing in 1831, the year before he died, Goethe claimed that Hugo's *Notre Dame de Paris* was 'the most ghastly book ever written',[7] but he had recognised the considerable talent of the *Odes et ballades* in 1827. In any case the great German poet turned out to be far less of an influence on composers of opera than Hugo; the only comparable literary figure in terms of providing stories and plots for dramatic musical works was Friedrich Schiller, whose life-span was as short as Hugo's was long. Schiller's earlier controversial successes in the theatre, and brushes with the authorities, had something in common with Hugo's struggles against oppression in his earlier career. (An opera composer like Verdi was to look to both Hugo and Schiller for inspiration.)

Victor Hugo photographed by Nadar

Below are listed some of the Hugo publications with some of the more important music they inspired in nineteenth-century song and opera – it would be a very much larger task to broaden this survey to the twentieth century. Although Hugo's writings inspired many a cinematic response (one thinks of *The Hunchback of Notre Dame* with Charles Laughton in 1939), his populist return to the English-speaking theatre had to wait for 1985, the centenary year of the poet's death, when Claude-Michel Schönberg's *Les Misérables* was first produced in London.

For his last setting of Hugo, the choral work *Les Djinns*, Fauré turned to the earliest of the poet's collections from which he was to take a text, *Les Orientales* (1829). As far as his *mélodies* were concerned, however, Fauré disregarded the famous Hugo publications from the 1820s; he found his texts in books that appeared between 1835 and 1870. It would be fair to conjecture that he had a copy of *Les Chants du crépuscule* somehow to hand at the École Niedermeyer (perhaps Niedermeyer himself lent him this volume), that Saint-Saëns lent him his copies of *Les Voix intérieures* and *Les Rayons et les ombres*, and that the composer acquired his own editions of *Chansons des rues et des bois* and *Les Châtiments* hot off the press in 1865 and 1870 respectively – finding only one poem in each that suited his musical purposes. One of the most famous of all Hugo collections, *Les Contemplations* (1856), seems to have passed Fauré by – probably precisely because this work was published at the height of the Second Empire's displeasure with the poet. Because Hugo was so often set by song composers there is always the possibility that the younger Fauré, instead of having the poetic source to hand, simply copied texts from songs already in print; Schubert certainly did this in his earlier years.

Collections by Victor Hugo and their Musical Settings

Odes et ballades (first collection of poetry, 1828): *La Fiancée du timbalier* (*ballades* by Saint-Saëns, Donizetti); *Le Pas d'armes de roi Jean* (*mélodies* by Saint-Saëns, Chabrier); *La Lyre et la harpe* (work for solo voices and orchestra by Saint-Saëns)

Les Orientales (second collection of poetry, 1829): *Chanson de pirates* (choral work by Berlioz); *La Captive* (*mélodies* with orchestra by Berlioz); *Vœu* ('Si j'étais la feuille') (*mélodie* by Reber); *Sara la baigneuse* (*mélodie* with orchestra by Berlioz); *Mazeppa* (symphonic poem by Liszt); *Attente* or *L'Attente* (*mélodies* by Wagner, Saint-Saëns, Lacombe, d'Indy); *Adieux de l'hôtesse arabe* (*mélodie* by Bizet); *La Ville prise* (*mélodie* by Lacombe); *Clair de lune* (*mélodie* by Lacombe); *Les Djinns* (work for chorus and orchestra by Fauré, Op. 12, 1875–76; symphonic poem with piano by César Franck, 1884)

OEUVRES COMPLÈTES

DE

VICTOR HUGO.

—

POÉSIE.

—

V.

LES CHANTS DU CRÉPUSCULE.

PARIS.

EUGÈNE RENDUEL,

ÉDITEUR-LIBRAIRE,

RUE DES GRANDS-AUGUSTINS, N° 22.

1835.

Title-page of first edition of Hugo's Les Chants du crépuscule *(1835)*

Hernani (play, 1830): Operas by Bellini, Verdi (*Ernani*) and at least eight other composers

Notre-Dame de Paris (novel, 1831): At least thirty stage works, invariably entitled *Esmeralda* or *La Esmeralda*, including works by Bizet, Massenet, Chausson

Les Feuilles d'automne (third collection of poetry, 1831): *Enfant si j'étais roi* (*mélodie* by Liszt)

Le Roi s'amuse (play, 1832): *Rigoletto* (opera, Verdi)

Lucrèce Borgia (play, 1833): *Chanson à boire* ('Amis, vive l'orgié') Lalo; *Lucrezia Borgia* (opera, Donizetti)

Marie Tudor (play, 1833): *Sérénade* (*mélodie* by Gounod)

Les Chants du crépuscule (fourth collection of poetry, 1835): *S'il est un charmant gazon* (*mélodies* by Liszt, Reber, Franck, Saint-Saëns, Fauré [under the title *Rêve d'amour*]); *Le Papillon et la fleur* (*mélodies* by Reber, Gounod [unpublished], Fauré, Franck, Cui); *Puisque j'ai mis ma lèvre* (*mélodies* by Reber, Franck, Saint-Saëns [*Extase*], Fauré, Hahn); *Mai* (*mélodie* by Fauré); *L'aurore* (*mélodie* by Fauré)

Les Voix intérieures (fifth collection of poetry, 1837): *La Tombe dit à la rose* (*mélodie* by Liszt); *Puisqu'ici-bas toute âme* (*mélodies* by Fauré, Saint-Saëns, Lalo, Niedermeyer); *Soirée en mer* (*mélodie* by Saint-Saëns); *La Mer* ('Quel sont ces bruits sourds?') (*mélodie* by Niedermeyer)

OEUVRES

COMPLÈTES

DE

VICTOR HUGO.

POËSIE.

VII

LES RAYONS ET LES OMBRES.

PARIS.

DELLOYE, LIBRAIRE,

PLACE DE LA BOURSE, 13.

1840.

VICTOR HUGO

LES

CHÂTIMENTS

SEULE ÉDITION COMPLÈTE

Quatrième Édition.

PARIS

J. HETZEL ET Cⁱᵉ, ÉDITEURS

18, RUE JACOB, 18

Droits de traduction et de reproduction réservés.

Title-page of first edition of Hugo's Les Rayons et les ombres *(1840)*

Title-page of Hugo's Les Châtiments *(1870)*

Ruy Blas (play, 1838): Incidental music or settings of the famous 'Sérénade' by Delibes, Mendelssohn (in German translation), Donizetti, Chabrier, Saint-Saëns, Massenet, Godard

Les Rayons et les ombres (sixth collection of poetry, 1840): *Gastibelza* (*mélodie* by Liszt); *Oh! Quand je dors …* (*mélodies* by Liszt, Lalo, Bizet); *Comment, disaient-ils* (*mélodies* by Liszt, Saint-Saëns, Reber, Lalo, Bizet, Lacombe, Massenet, Lecocq); *A Marie* ('Dieu qui sourit') (*mélodies* by Reber, Lalo, Massé); *Tristesse d'Olympio* (*mélodie* by Fauré)

Châtiments (seventh collection of poetry, 1853): Hugo's diatribe against Napoleon III, a true chastisement, earned him expulsion from his temporary refuge in Brussels. The fall of the Second Empire in 1870 prompted a new and complete edition of the work, this time *Les Châtiments*, a kind of poetic 'I told you so' and probably Fauré's source for *L'Absent*. Hugo prefaced the new edition rather melodramatically with a poem entitled 'Au moment de rentrer en France'.

Les Contemplations (eighth collection of poetry, 1856): *Viens! – une flûte invisible* (*mélodies* by Saint-Saëns, Delibes, Reber, Pierné, Caplet); *Vieille chanson du jeune temps* (*mélodies* by Reyer, Reber); *Après l'hiver* (*mélodie* by Bizet); *Si mes vers avaient des ailes* (*mélodies* by Hahn, Reber, Godard); *La Coccinelle* (*mélodies* by Bizet and Saint-Saëns)

Chansons des rues et des bois (ninth collection of poetry, 1865): *Sommation irrespectueuse* (*mélodie* by Chabrier); *Dans les ruines d'une abbaye* (*mélodie* by Fauré)

(1) *Le Papillon et la fleur* (*The butterfly and the flower*)[8]

1861, Op. 1 No. 1, C major, 'À Mme Miolan-Carvalho', 6/8, *Allegretto* or *Allegro non troppo*

La pauvre fleur disait au papillon céleste:
      Ne fuis pas!
Vois comme nos destins sont différents. Je reste,
      Tu t'en vas!
	The humble flower said to the heavenly butterfly:
	      Do not flee!
	See how our destinies differ. Fixed to earth am I,
	      You fly away!

Pourtant nous nous aimons, nous vivons sans les hommes
      Et loin d'eux,
Et nous nous ressemblons, et l'on dit que nous sommes
      Fleurs tous deux!
	Yet we love each other, we live without men
	      And far from them,
	And we are so alike, it's said that both of us
	      Are flowers!

Mais, hélas! l'air t'emporte et la terre m'enchaîne.
      Sort cruel!
Je voudrais embaumer ton vol de mon haleine
      Dans le ciel!
	But alas! The breeze bears you away, the earth holds me fast
	      Cruel fate!
	I would perfume your flight with my fragrant breath
	      In the sky!

Mais non, tu vas trop loin! – Parmi des fleurs sans nombre
      Vous fuyez,
Et moi je reste seule à voir tourner mon ombre
      À mes pieds.
	But no, you flit too far! Among countless flowers
	      You fly away,
	While I remain alone, and watch my shadow circle
	      Round my feet.

Tu fuis, puis tu reviens; puis tu t'en vas encore
      Luire ailleurs.
Aussi me trouves-tu toujours à chaque aurore
      Toute en pleurs!
	You fly away, then return; then take flight again
	      To shimmer elsewhere.
	And so you always find me at each dawn
	      Bathed in tears!

Oh! pour que notre amour coule des jours fidèles,
      Ô mon roi,
Prends comme moi racine, ou donne-moi des ailes
      Comme à toi!
	Ah, that our love might flow through faithful days,
	      O my king,
	Take root like me, or give me wings
	      Like yours!

Victor Hugo (1802–1885)

Fauré begins his career as a composer with an ornate flourish, a pianistic *carte de visite* that reminds us that throughout his life he would lavish just as much attention on the piano as a solo instrument as on the *mélodie*. This opening *ritornello* is launched with élan (one ascending scale, then another – a musical commonplace adapted for lepidopteran aerobatics) and is followed by sequences that spiral downwards in waltz rhythm making pleasing musical patterns that unfold gracefully, if somewhat trickily, under the fingers. It is somewhat alarming for pianists to discover that the key for this song in the young composer's autograph was D♭ major, a choice that was no doubt vetoed by the publishers, or perhaps even by Saint-Saëns, on account of the almost perversely awkward nature of the song's accompaniment when essayed in this tonality.

The coquetry of the opening, somewhat in the manner of Saint-Saëns, sets the mood for the entire song. But the influence of Gounod's *mélodie Venise* (1842) is also perhaps evident here, with its combination of strophic form with recurring *ritornelli* that challenge and flatter the pianist's fingers. All this showing-off vanishes immediately the voice enters and the piano writing is reduced to dutiful quavers of pure accompaniment. The introduction notwithstanding, the pianist is responsible for the flight of a butterfly, not that of a bumble bee: this music should be gracious rather than hectic. The adolescent Fauré was capable of irony and word-play, a kind of superficial sophistication, and he certainly drew amusing caricatures, but for him music was almost always a serious matter. There are those who see this song as pure knockabout fun but, it also encompasses, surely, the frustrating paradox of the composer's strict and sheltered upbringing within the walls of the most *mondaine* city in the world. In the flower's plight we can discern how Fauré must have felt as a sixteen-year-old rooted to the spot

Title-page of Fauré's autograph for La Fleur et le papillon (sic). *The comic drawing on the cover is by Saint-Saëns*

and cloistered at the École Niedermeyer. He was certainly not yet permitted to enjoy the freedoms that would have allowed him to go in search of adventure with flower maidens of his own choosing.

The cover of Fauré's autograph (where the composer takes more pains in the penmanship of the title, initially *La Fleur et le papillon*, than in the setting's prosody) contains an amusing sketch of a flower with tiny arms looking up to a hovering butterfly wearing a crown. This outsize butterfly brings to mind the scene in Offenbach's *Orphée aux enfers* when Jupiter turns into a fly so that he can enter Eurydice's room through a keyhole in order to woo her.

This little sketch on the title-page was not drawn by Fauré himself. It was the work of Saint-Saëns, who was clearly bemused by his talented pupil's achievement, and who was apparently the first person to sing the composition, with his nasal voice. The older composer was almost certainly cynical about the sentimentality of the poem (Saint-Saëns, unlike his pupil, always took delight in writing music to humorous effect). The ten-year difference between the ages of the older composer, already a sophisticated man of the world, and his younger protégé is especially evident here.

The poem, No. XXVII in Hugo's *Chants du crépuscule*, has no title in the first edition. Perhaps the composer knew the text from Henri Reber's modest setting of 1847, and eventually followed Reber's choice of title. Philippe Fauré-Fremiet points out that in faithfully following Hugo's unusual metre for this poem (a heavy alexandrine following by a tri-syllabic foot) his father was unusually brave by the standards of the time. Most of the poem's early *romance* composers solved this inconsistency by repeating the short line (for example 'Ne fuis pas!') to fill in the metric hiatus, but not Reber significantly – and not Fauré – an innovation that might have made Niedermeyer raise his eyebrows.

In 1922 the manuscript of this song came into the possession of the composer Reynaldo Hahn, who immediately sent it to Fauré as a gift in the hope that it would awaken pleasant memories of the past (nothing could better illustrate Hahn's devotion to the older composer). In a letter to his wife (14 July 1922) the seventy-five-year-old Fauré reminisced about this, his first song:

> composed in the school dining-hall amid the smells from the kitchen … and my first interpreter was Saint-Saëns. It was also in connection with this first song that my name found itself in Victor Hugo's correspondence over the permission that was needed before it could be published. What an encounter between minor and major personalities, between things great and small! The peerless poet concerned with the most minuscule composer's rights![9]

Even at the end of his life, when he was covered in musical glory, the composer failed to pat his younger self on the back as a great man of the future, and his description of Hugo as 'peerless' is surely without irony. All those years later Fauré, like Leconte de Lisle, still perceived Hugo to be as solidly immovable as the Himalayas; despite the vicissitudes of the literary stock market the poet's position in French letters has remained more or less the same – defiantly gilt-edged.

(2) *Mai* (May)[10]
1862?, Op. 1 No. 2, 'À Madame Henri Garnier', first Hamelle collection p. 5, F major, 3/4, *Allegretto*

Puisque mai tout en fleurs dans les prés nous réclame,	*Since full-flowering May calls us to the meadows,*
Viens! ne te lasse pas de mêler à ton âme	*Come! do not tire of mingling with your soul*
La campagne, les bois, les ombrages charmants,	*The countryside, the woods, the charming shade,*
Les larges clairs de lune au bord des flots dormants,	*Vast moonlights on the banks of sleeping waters,*
Le sentier qui finit où le chemin commence,	*The path ending where the road begins,*
Et l'air et le printemps et l'horizon immense,	*And the air, the spring and the huge horizon,*
L'horizon que ce monde attache humble et joyeux	*The horizon which this world fastens, humble and joyous,*
Comme une lèvre au bas de la robe des cieux!	*Like a lip to the hem of heaven's robe!*
Viens! et que le regard des pudiques étoiles	*Come! and may the gaze of the chaste stars,*
Qui tombe sur la terre à travers tant de voiles,	*Falling to earth through so many veils,*
Que l'arbre pénétré de parfums et de chants,	*May the tree steeped in scent and song,*
Que le souffle embrasé de midi dans les champs,	*May the burning breath of noon in the fields,*
Et l'ombre et le soleil et l'onde et la verdure,	*And the shade and the sun, and the tide and verdure,*
Et le rayonnement de toute la nature	*And the radiance of all nature –*
Fassent épanouir, comme une double fleur,	*May they cause to blossom, like a double flower,*
La beauté sur ton front et l'amour dans ton cœur!	*Beauty on your brow and love in your heart!*

Victor Hugo (1802–1885)

This was one of the six songs that Fauré, while still enrolled as a pupil at the École Niedermeyer under the tutelage of Saint-Saëns, offered to the publisher Choudens as early as 1864. These were all to Hugo texts: *Le Papillon et la fleur*, *Mai*, *S'il est un charmant gazon* (which later acquired the title *Rêve d'amour*), *Puisqu'ici-bas* (originally a solo song that was turned into the duet of later years), *L'Aube naît* and *Puisque j'ai mis ma lèvre*. Only *L'Aube naît*, despite the promise of its name, never saw the light of day, and not even a sketch remains of it. This publishing venture came to nothing, although, as we have mentioned earlier, the great poet (still very much in exile) was consulted over his financial expectations regarding prospective royalties. The accompaniment of *Mai*, rather conventional in its combination of strummed left-hand basses and right-hand quavers, has no important role to play, but the melody has an appealing freshness and sincerity, and for this it may seem a higher key is more suitable than a lower. The key of the autograph is A♭ major (admittedly rather squeak-inducing for the soprano voice), and the composer was obviously persuaded to transpose the song a minor third down for its first publication. Interestingly enough the higher of the two printed keys (G major) is nearer his original thoughts. In whatever tonality, the song has a special intimacy of expression: Fauré, still small beer in the age of the greater Meyerbeer, starts his career in the way he means to continue. The cadence first heard at 'et l'horizon immense' is rueful and tender; this is no match for the intended breadth of the poet's imagery, but in sheerly musical terms it is a delightfully turned phrase. In 1910 Fauré averred that he had never set Hugo successfully. This little song is a charmer, but the question, as the much older composer well understood, is whether charm is enough.

The problem faced by the interpreter of this song is that Hugo's over-the-top romantic enthusiasm (whereby he seems to embrace the whole of nature) is ill-suited to Fauré's less extrovert temperament. A modest performance in an equally modest *allegretto* can sound sweetly melancholic and little more. Nevertheless, this slightly forced marriage of Fauré and Hugo can be made to work when performed with a beautiful legato and a smile in the voice. As we shall discover in *La Bonne chanson*, unalloyed happiness is a good deal harder to convey than the darker emotions of anguish – particularly for male performers.

If the countours of *Mai* are anything to go by, elegantly melodic phrases that rise and fall with seraphic grace, the young composer's sympathies at the time lay almost certainly with that great tunesmith Gounod, whose music often unfolds in a disarmingly similar way while negotiating, with varying degrees of success, the danger of sugary complacency. If Fauré successfully avoided the influence of Wagner at a slightly later stage of his life, he already seems immune to Berlioz, a composer dear to Saint-Saëns. Fauré's lack of enthusiasm for this fiery pioneer of romanticism was to be a bone of contention between him and Saint-Saëns for the rest of their lives but a touch of Berliozian extroversion might have suited this poem somewhat better.

(3) *Puisque j'ai mis ma lèvre* (Since I've pressed my lips)[11]
8 December 1862, C major, 2/4, no tempo marking in the manuscript

Puisque j'ai mis ma lèvre à ta coupe encore pleine;	*Since I've pressed my lips to your still brimming cup;*
Puisque j'ai dans tes mains posé mon front pâli;	*Since on your hands I've laid my pale brow;*
Puisque j'ai respiré parfois la douce haleine	*Since at times I have caught the sweet breath*
De ton âme, parfum dans l'ombre enseveli;	*Of your soul, fragrance shrouded in the shade;*

Autograph of the opening of
Puisque j'ai mis ma lèvre

Puisqu'il me fut donné de t'entendre me dire
Les mots où se répand le cœur mystérieux;
Puisque j'ai vu pleurer, puisque j'ai vu sourire
Ta bouche sur ma bouche et tes yeux sur mes yeux;

Puisque j'ai vu briller sur ma tête ravie
Un rayon de ton astre, hélas! voilé toujours;
Puisque j'ai vu tomber dans l'onde de ma vie
Une feuille de rose arrachée à tes jours;

Je puis maintenant dire aux rapides années:
– Passez! passez toujours! je n'ai plus à vieillir!
Allez-vous-en avec vos fleurs toutes fanées;
J'ai dans l'âme une fleur que nul ne peut cueillir!

Votre aile en le heurtant ne fera rien répandre
Du vase où je m'abreuve et que j'ai bien rempli.
Mon âme a plus de feu que vous n'avez de cendre!
Mon cœur a plus d'amour que vous n'avez d'oubli!

Since I've been favoured to hear you utter
Words poured from a mysterious heart;
Since I've seen tears, since I've seen smiles,
Your mouth on my mouth, your eyes on mine;

Since catching on my delighted face
A ray of light from your star, still veiled alas!
Since watching fall into the stream of my life
A rose leaf snatched from your days;

I can now say to the swift years:
Roll on, roll ever on! I can age no more!
Away with you and your withered flowers;
In my soul I've a flower that none can gather!

Should your wing jolt it, nothing will spill
From the vessel where I drink and which I have filled.
My soul has more fire than you have ashes!
My heart has more love than you oblivion!

Victor Hugo (1802–1885)

The poem in Hugo's autograph has the added title 'À ma Juliette'. The song, still virtually unknown because still unpublished, was among the six Hugo settings that Fauré offered unsuccessfully to the publisher Choudens in 1864. *Puisque j'ai mis ma lèvre* has survived in a particularly handsome autograph, a testament to Fauré's fastidious penmanship at the age of seventeen. I was extremely grateful to M. Thierry Bodin for allowing me access to the manuscript in his possession for the complete Hyperion recording of the composer's songs.

The heading of the autograph is 'Poésie de Victor Hugo, mise en musique par Gabriel Fauré'. The poet himself gave this lyric no title (it was published simply as No. XXV of Hugo's *Les Chants du crépuscule*, 1835); perhaps the young composer thought it inappropriate or cheeky to adopt the rather risqué first line of the poem as his title. It is difficult to see why the composer thought that *Puisque j'ai mis ma lèvre* was less worth publishing than, say, his *Mai*, apart from a certain embarrassment concerning the erotic nature of the text. In the middle of the song one might point out a slightly awkward corner or two (at the end of the music for verse 3, and the first few lines of verse 4); but if the musical transitions here are less than ideally smooth, these small flaws are surely outweighed by the elegance of the accompaniment (left-hand staccatos suggest a plucked lute) and the graceful vocal line, which encourages a tenor to charm the ear with his *mezza voce*. The surprisingly mature poise of Fauré's song announces a deliberately contained madrigal style that was to be revisited regularly during the course of his long career. The swooning eroticism of Reynaldo Hahn's more Wagnerian (or Wolfian) late setting of the same words (in that composer's second *recueil*) suggests a lover almost drunk with rapture. This approach may be closer to the mood of Hugo's lyric, but Fauré's youthful temperament was incapable of such depth; even if the music for this song is truly charming it is also rather perfunctory as a setting of the poet's text. As the composer got older he realised how much happier he was with poetic collaborators who were less demonstrative and less overtly passionate.

(4) *Rêve d'amour* (A dream of love)[12]
5 May 1864, Op. 5 No. 2, 'À Madame C. de Gomiecourt', E♭ major, 3/4, *Allegretto*

S'il est un charmant gazon	*If there be a lovely lawn*
Que le ciel arrose,	*Watered by the sky,*
Où naisse en toute saison	*Where each new season*
Quelque fleur éclose,	*Blossoming flowers spring up,*
Où l'on cueille à pleine main	*Where lily, woodbine, and jasmine*
Lys, chèvrefeuille et jasmin,	*Can be gathered liberally,*
J'en veux faire le chemin	*I would strew the way with them*
Où ton pied se pose!	*Where your feet will settle!*
S'il est un sein bien aimant	*If there be a loving breast*
Dont l'honneur dispose,	*Wherein honour dwells,*
Dont le tendre dévouement	*Whose tender devotion*
N'ait rien de morose,	*Never is morose,*
Si toujours ce noble sein	*If this noble breast always*
Bat pour un digne dessein,	*Beats with worthy intent,*
J'en veux faire le coussin	*I would make of it a pillow*
Où ton front se pose!	*Where your head will settle!*

S'il est un rêve d'amour
    Parfumé de rose,
Où l'on trouve chaque jour
    Quelque douce chose,
Un rêve que Dieu bénit,
    Où l'âme à l'âme s'unit,
Oh! j'en veux faire le nid
    Où ton cœur se pose!
	If there be a dream of love
	    With the scent of roses,
	Where each day may be found
	    Some sweet new delight,
	A dream blessed by the Lord
	    Where soul unites with soul,
	Oh! I shall make of it the nest
	    Where your heart will settle!

Victor Hugo (1802–1885)

Hugo's title is 'Nouvelle chanson sur un vieil air', suggesting that the poet had fitted new words to a tune he already knew (just as Robert Louis Stevenson was later to write 'The Vagabond' to fit the tune and rhythm to that of a Schubert song that was playing in his mind, *Mut* from *Winterreise*). Hugo wrote the lyric for his mistress Juliette Drouet. The poem was first set by Liszt in 1844 (with an impossibly florid piano part; a revised version with a more playable accompaniment dates from 1859), then by César Franck in 1847, and soon afterwards by the adolescent Saint-Saëns, as his first song, an Offenbachian *galop*. Saint-Saëns's title is *Nouvelle chanson* but other composers adopt the poem's first line – 'S'il est un charmant gazon'. Fauré's setting, the celebrated poem disguised by its title, is one of the least performed of his songs. It is more four-square than his later work, and like *Mai* it has a certain affinity with Gounod – who had a special gift for combining sensuality with *pudeur*.

The style of the accompaniment seems somewhat Schumannian. The prosody is anything but perfect; for example, the dotted crotchet on the word 'Que' in the third bar of the vocal line is questionable, and is only the first of several such instances, some of which (though not this particular one) were corrected in later editions and printings. The composer would treat such matters of verbal emphasis very differently later in his career. It is worth noting that although the song was first published in the key of E♭ major, the composer's autograph was in F major, later the high-voice key in the Hamelle edition.

Already typical of Fauré are the fluidity and independence of the bass line, and the delicacy of the syncopated quavers that shadow the voice in the accompaniment and trace the ghost of a counter-melody. The whole song has an unforced, felicitous mood that already seems typical of the composer, whose desire to please avoids any slavish courting of popularity, even at this early stage of his career. Fauré directs that the third verse should be sung more slowly than the others ('beaucoup plus lente-ment'), a modification that mirrors the composer's

Title-page of Choudens's edition of Rêve d'amour

request that the third strophe of *Le Papillon et la fleur* should be sung faster. In later songs we will no longer encounter such facile means of providing variety. Fauré gives the impression – like Hugo himself – that he has squeezed the text, particularly as far as later strophes in the poem are concerned, to fit a tune already in his head. This is a more *laissez-faire* attitude to song composing than Fauré would allow himself later in his career.

What he disliked most about this piece was its title. In June 1870 he wrote to his former schoolfriend Julien Koszul complaining that his publisher Choudens ('who seems to be a man of considerable wit') had given the song the title *Rêve d'amour*. 'Not something that would ever have occurred to me,' added Fauré wryly.[13] We should be grateful at least that Choudens went to the trouble to extract this title from the third strophe of the poem itself; in terms of taking liberties with the composer's music he was rather less impudent than Fauré's later publisher Julien Hamelle.

(5) *Tristesse d'Olympio* (The sadness of Olympio)[14]
*c.*1865, 'À mon ami Adam Laussel', E minor, 2/4, *Grave* – ¢, *alla breve Allegro non troppo*

Les champs n'étaient point noirs, les cieux n'étaient pas mornes;	*The fields were not black, the skies were not bleak;*
Non, le jour rayonnait dans un azur sans bornes	*No, daylight blazed in infinite blueness*
Sur la terre étendu,	*Above the earth,*
L'air était plein d'encens et les prés de verdures	*The air was filled with incense, the meadows with greenness,*
Quand il revit ces lieux où par tant de blessures	*When he set eyes on those places again where through*
Son cœur s'est répandu!	*So many wounds his heart poured forth!*
Hélas! se rappelant ses douces aventures,	*Alas! recalling his sweet adventure,*
Regardant, sans entrer, par-dessus les clôtures,	*Gazing, without entering, over the fences*
Ainsi qu'un paria,	*Like an outcast,*
Il erra tout le jour. À l'heure où la nuit tombe,	*He wandered all day long. Towards nightfall,*
Il se sentit le cœur triste comme une tombe,	*His heart felt as heavy as a tomb,*
Alors il s'écria:	*Then he cried out:*
«Ô douleur! j'ai voulu, moi dont l'âme est troublée,	*'O grief! I, whose soul is troubled, wished*
Savoir si l'urne encor conservait la liqueur,	*To know if the urn still contained the liquor,*
Et voir ce qu'avait fait cette heureuse vallée	*And to see what this happy vale had made*
De tout ce que j'avais laissé là de mon cœur!	*Of all I had left there of my heart!*
«Que peu de temps suffit pour changer toutes choses!	*'How quickly everything can change!*
Nature au front serein, comme vous oubliez!	*O nature, how you forget with your unfurrowed brow!*
Et comme vous brisez dans vos métamorphoses	*And how you and your metamorphoses sever*
Les fils mystérieux où nos cœurs sont liés!	*The mysterious threads whereby our hearts are bound!*
«Eh bien! oubliez-nous, maison, jardin, ombrages!	*'So then! let house, garden and shade forget us!*
Herbe, use notre seuil! ronce, cache nos pas!	*Grasses, wear out our threshold! Brambles, hide our steps!*
Chantez, oiseaux! ruisseaux, coulez! croissez, feuillages!	*Sing, O birds; stream, O brooklets! Grow, O leaves!*
Ceux que vous oubliez ne vous oublieront pas.	*Those you forget shall not forget you.*

45

«Car vous êtes pour nous l'ombre de l'amour même!   *'Because you are for us the shadow of love itself!*
Vous êtes l'oasis qu'on rencontre en chemin!   *You are the oasis we encountered on the way!*
Vous êtes, ô vallon, la retraite suprême   *You are, O valley, the dearest shelter*
Où nous avons pleuré nous tenant par la main!»   *Where we wept and held hands!'*

Victor Hugo (1802–1885)

The poem, one of Hugo's most celebrated lyrics, appears in the collection entitled *Les Rayons et les ombres* (1840) as No. XXXIV, an extended structure of thirty-eight strophes. Of these Fauré (probably when he was working as an organist in Rennes in Britanny) selected verses 1 and 8 for the opening *Grave*, and then verses 9, 10, 31 and 32 for the *Allegro non troppo*. Victor Hugo is 'Olympio' (his contemporaries subsequently used this name as a nickname for him), and the background of the poem is the poet's love for his mistress Juliette Drouet. In 1834 and 1835 the couple had dallied in the woods that lay between their respective holiday lodgings in the valley of the Bièvre river, not far from Paris. (Hugo was a guest at the Château des Roches with his wife and young family.) After this secret idyll, which occasioned some of his greatest love poetry, Hugo revisited the region on his own in 1837, when, as 'Olympio', he castigated nature for being impervious to the former presence of the lovers; he realised that a landscape, however evocative, can never retain the imprint of human memories. *Tristesse d'Olympio* is also a lament for the cooling of the ardent passion that Hugo had known with Juliette, although she remained devoted to her beloved 'Toto' until the end of her life. (The fame of the relationship between Hugo and Drouet may account for the fact that 'Toto' was also the pet-name that Marianne Viardot used for Fauré when the two were a courting couple: see Chapter 4.)

The composer cut the poem so that it made some kind of narrative sense in its truncated version, but Fauré's song completely fails to encompass Hugo's philosophical scope; it is no surprise the composer withheld it from publication. The music, however, such as it is, aspires to something of the poem's grandeur: the modal feel of the opening slow section is typical of Fauré in elegiac mood, a spaciousness that suits the ornate rhyming structure (AABCCB) of the opening pair of six-line strophes. The solemnity of this music is prophetic of such later songs as *Seule!*, *L'Absent* and *Au cimetière*. This section ends with the words 'Alors il s'écria:'. After this colon Hugo places the poem's remaining thirty strophes – all quatrains – in inverted commas as Olympio speaks in the first person. This change of voice ushers in a new, faster tempo in Fauré's song – restless accompanying quavers supporting a terse and desperate vocal line where the ABAB rhymes tumble out across the stave – a certain forward drive and *alla breve* impetus are the only things that make this rather awkward music really singable. If the performers treat this section as a *moto perpetuo*, where the piano writing carries the voice ineluctably forward, we hear certain auguries of the passion of *Toujours* (from the *Poëme d'un jour* cycle), and the intensity of *J'ai presque peur, en vérité* from *La Bonne chanson*. Even the *Air romantique* from Poulenc's deliberately exaggerated settings of Moréas, the cycle *Airs chantés*, comes to mind. This, however, is unduly to flatter the musical quality of *Tristesse d'Olympio*, a song which sounds unwieldy in performance thanks to a complicated poem that is singularly unsuited to musical setting.

(6) *Dans les ruines d'une abbaye* (In the ruins of an abbey)[15]

c.1865, Op. 2 No. 1, 'À Mme Henriette Escalier', first Hamelle collection p. 10, A major, 6/8, *Allegretto*

Seuls tous deux, ravis, chantants!
    Comme on s'aime!
Comme on cueille le printemps
    Que Dieu sème!

Quels rires étincelants
    Dans ces ombres
Jadis pleines de fronts blancs,
    De cœurs sombres!

On est tout frais mariés.
    On s'envoie
Les charmants cris variés
    De la joie.

Frais échos mêlés au vent
    Qui frissonne!
Gaîté que le noir couvent
    Assaisonne!

On effeuille des jasmins
    Sur la pierre
Où l'abbesse joint les mains
    En prière.

On se cherche, on se poursuit,
    On sent croître
Ton aube, amour, dans la nuit
    Du vieux cloître.

On s'en va se becquetant,
    On s'adore,
On s'embrasse à chaque instant,
    Puis encore,

Sous les piliers, les arceaux,
    Et les marbres.
C'est l'histoire des oiseaux
    Dans les arbres.

Alone, together, enraptured, singing!
    How we love each other!
How we reap the springtime
    That God sows!

What sparkling laughter
    In these shadows
Once full of pale faces
    And sombre hearts!

We are newly married.
    We send each other
Charming and varied
    Cries of joy.

Fresh echoes mingling with
    The shivering wind!
Gaiety that the black convent
    Heightens!

We pluck the jasmine flowers
    On the stone
Where the abbess joins her hands
    In prayer.

We seek each other, chase each other,
    We feel your dawn
Grow in the night, O love,
    Of the old cloister.

On we go, kissing and cuddling,
    Adoring one another,
Embracing each other every moment,
    Then again,

Beneath the pillars, beneath the vault,
    And the marbles;
Just like all the birds
    In the trees.

Victor Hugo (1802–1885)

It is quite possible that this song was composed when Fauré was organist in Rennes (see Chapter 3). If, as seems likely, it was influenced by Saint-Saëns's *Enlèvement* in the same key, it was probably composed at some time following the appearance of that song in January 1865. Fauré had cut the text of Hugo's *Tristesse d'Olympio* short, but this extended paean to conjugal happiness is not long enough for the composer's purposes. The enthusiasm of this tempo requires so many words that he must re-employ the first two strophes of the poem as his six and seventh verses before going on to finish the song.

The newly-weds, joyfully 'Seuls tous deux' and unchaperoned at last, are outdoors in springtime and in the grounds of an old abbey. Their vivacious peals of joy and laughter seem almost sacrilegious in contrast to the sombre shadows cast by clerical history, but the poet remains defiantly irreverent on behalf of his frolicking lovers. A strophe not set by Fauré, the sixth, tells us that even the tombstones inscribed with crosses, and thoughts of the praying nuns of yore, fail to dampen their high spirits. There is a marked contrast between the imposing religiosity of the ruined abbey and the present-day joy of a modern young couple who have grown up in less pious times. The poem is a relatively late one, from *Les Chansons des rues et des bois* of 1865, and there is no mood of reverence. The great Fauré commentator the philosopher Vladimir Jankélévitch was hardly religious in any conventional sense, but he termed such flippancy 'décourageante stupidité'.[16]

Whatever the merits of the poem, we are treated to a simple *moto perpetuo* of high spirits. As in *Mai* the rippling accompaniment facilitates a catchy little tune that skips with considerable élan and with scarcely a pause for breath. Like *Mai*, another *mélodie* that has to be brought to life by the singer, this is a giddily elated song where the interpreters have to impose happiness on music that could very easily be pallid and uninteresting. I remember a masterclass at Aldeburgh in the 1980s when Hugues Cuenod (who, as I write this commentary in 2008, is only months away from his 106th birthday) snatched the score from a student who had plodded through the music with a well-meaning reverence. Cuenod, still singing marvellously, strolled through 'les ruines' with a *joie de vivre* that had all the onlookers applauding – Sir Peter Pears on his feet and calling for an encore. A much earlier masterclass on this song was demanded of Fauré himself by that beautiful amateur singer Mrs George Swinton, at Llandough Castle in Cowbridge, Wales, in August 1898. The obliging house guest agreed, providing that Mrs Swinton gave him a photographic copy of the stunning portrait of herself by John Singer Sargent.

It is understandable that the serious Mrs Swinton might have needed a little help in unlocking the song's secrets. There are only a few Fauré *mélodies*, and this is one of them, where the *gravitas* of the form must be thrown aside in favour of something more like *chanson* (although the singer must still observe the composer's markings). But Fauré did not dash off even a light-hearted song like this without considerable thought. As J.-M. Nectoux has pointed out, he was already ultra-sensitive to the avoidance of alliteration that he found ugly, as well as any preponderance of sibilants or repeated 'd's. Thus in the second verse of Hugo's poem the line containing 'Pleines jadis de front blancs' is changed to 'Jadis pleines de fronts blancs'. The poem was set most attractively some thirty years after Fauré by Ravel's other composition teacher, André Gédalge, who, less fastidious in these matters, or perhaps simply more faithful to the poet, accepts Hugo's 'Pleines jadis'.

The dedicatee of the song, the gifted amateur singer Henriette Escalier, known as 'Marraine', was the second wife of Alexandre Dumas *fils* and a neighbour and close friend of Marguerite de Saint-Marceaux – a major patron of Fauré whom we will encounter at close quarters later in this narrative.

(7) *L'Aurore* (*The dawn*)[17]

c.1870, 'A Mlle Anne Dufresne', A♭ major, 3/4, *Allegretto*, first published in 1954

L'aurore s'allume,	*The dawn lights up,*
L'ombre épaisse fuit;	*Thick shadows flee;*
Le rêve et la brume	*Dream and mist*
Vont où va la nuit;	*Go where night goes;*
Paupières et roses	*Eyelids and roses*
S'ouvrent demi-closes;	*Open half-closed;*
Du réveil des choses;	*The sound of things wakening*
On entend le bruit.	*Can be heard.*
Tout chante et murmure,	*All things sing and murmur,*
Tout parle à la fois,	*All things speak at once,*
Fumée et verdure,	*Smoke and verdure,*
Les nids et les toits;	*Nests and roofs;*
Le vent parle aux chênes,	*The wind speaks to the oaks,*
L'eau parle aux fontaines;	*Water speaks to the springs;*
Toutes les haleines	*The breath of all things*
Deviennent des voix!	*Becomes voice!*
Tout reprend son âme,	*All things recapture their soul,*
L'enfant son hochet,	*The child finds its rattle,*
Le foyer sa flamme,	*The hearth its flame,*
Le luth son archet;	*The lute its bow;*
Folie ou démence,	*Madness or lunacy*
Dans ce monde immense,	*In this vast world,*
Chacun recommence	*Everyone begins afresh*
Ce qu'il ébauchait.	*What he was sketching out.*

Victor Hugo (1802–1885)

This was a late discovery for the public; it appeared in print (a photograph of the manuscript) in 1954 in Frits Noske's indispensable *La Mélodie française de Berlioz à Duparc*.[18] A further two Hugo songs (*Puisque j'ai mis ma lèvre* and *Tristesse d'Olympio*) remain unpublished. Of these three Hugo orphans, *L'Aurore* is the most memorable in melodic terms – indeed the tune, an unfurling of conjoined sequences, has an adorable simplicity; this is music as fresh and fragrant as the time of day it describes. In the A section of the song the vocal line is steadfastly doubled by the piano – indeed the accompaniment could be played as a piano piece without sacrificing a note. The presence of a B section (instead of a strophic repetition) is an important attribute of the *mélodie*, as opposed to the old-fashioned *romance* in strict strophic style. (We will soon encounter this musical architecture again in *Lydia*.) In this middle section there is a welcome divergence between voice and piano where the accompaniment in throbbing mezzo-staccato quavers remains in the treble clef for both hands. At the return of the main melody there is a hint of canonic imitation that is not followed through.

If this is not the most sophisticated of songs (the composer himself, in not publishing it, was clearly less than satisfied), it has a classical poise that prepares the way for later song settings of ancient Greek and Roman inspiration.

The poem is No. XX of Hugo's *Chants du crépuscule*. Fauré's song is a simple ABA construction, which provides a good excuse for his decision to set only three of the poet's seventeen strophes in three large subsections. The conclusion to Hugo's fourth strophe, not set by Fauré, is particularly bombastic, ending with the words 'Moi, la vérité' – the truth, and only the truth, the poet says, is his ultimate goal when facing the dawn. Fauré, who hated getting up in the mornings throughout his life, would no doubt have settled for a strong cup of black coffee. Perhaps this banal comparison illustrates rather well the difference in temperament between poet and unawakened composer. At this point of his life Fauré's motto might have been 'anything for a quiet life', and he later admitted as much.

∾　　　∾　　　∾　　　∾

In the seven songs considered in this chapter the creative characteristics of the mature Fauré are to be noticed only in the bud, and with the benefit of hindsight. And yet if by some misfortune the composer had never published anything else, it is still quite possible that these Hugo settings would be affectionately remembered. Their appearance in a resourceful concert programme would naturally have occasioned delight, like the occasional revival of the songs of Alexis de Castillon (1838–1873), a composer whose first *mélodies* were much admired but who did not live long enough to fulfil his promise. The little-known Fauré's name might still have been confused with that of Jean-Baptise Faure (1830–1914), the opera singer and sometime composer, whose lack of an *accent aigu* at the end of his name did nothing to prevent his work being ascribed to his younger contemporary for many years (and vice versa).

Fauré's Hugo songs are incomparably superior to the simple, and sometimes vapid, *romances* of Loïsa Puget and Pauline Duchambge, but they are not yet as suavely graceful and persuasive as the spacious songs of Gounod at his best – the real pioneer of the *mélodie* according to Fauré's pupil Ravel – and not as worldly as the ever-resourceful Saint-Saëns. This largely conventional material is child's play in comparison to the songs of Berlioz, whose *mélodies* form an entirely separate chapter in song – an aspect of French musical history from which Fauré always kept his distance. These Hugo settings also remain entirely distinct from the rather more daring contemporary achievements of Chabrier and Bizet, not to mention Duparc – although it is fair to say that in the 1860s all these composers were also feeling their way towards their own styles. If the Hugo songs had been composed by an unfamiliar name, they would have fitted comfortably in a programme featuring such *petits maîtres* as Jules Cressonois, Henri Reber, Félicien David and Émile Paladilhe, and in this company they would undoubtedly shine. In an interview with *Le Petit Parisien* (18 April, 1922) the ageing composer stated that the early songs had been over-performed: 'Not enough to make my fortune, but too much even so.' By that time there were any number of singers who sang these songs not only because of their intrinsic merits but because they were by the director of the Conservatoire and relatively undemanding; on recital programmes early Fauré was, after all, still Fauré. This line of least resistance has persisted to this day.

The first *recueil* of Hamelle in which these songs have long been available to the public also] contains such uncontested masterpieces as *Lydia* (Leconte de Lisle), *Après un rêve* (Bussine) and *Au bord de l'eau* (Sully Prudhomme), not to mention the last Hugo setting, *L'Absent*, discussed in Chapter 3;

in these works we can begin to detect traces of the special training in harmony that Fauré received at the École Niedermeyer. In the earlier Hugo settings however Fauré seems to have been much less inclined to air his individuality.

If segments at least of *Le Papillon et la fleur* and *Rêve d'amour* might have come from the pen of Saint-Saëns, they are still charming valentines, and there is a colour and a touch of involuntary and gentle mournfulness in *Mai*, something imitated from Schumann via Gounod, where the pupil already shows greater, and more subtle, emotional depth than his teacher. The plucked lute of *Puisque j'ai mis ma lèvre* contains the premonitory ghost of Fauré's many songs in the madrigal style, and of *Mandoline* in particular. *Dans les ruines d'une abbaye* shows an ability to entertain and charm an audience that was always to be part of this composer's gift, at least up to the point where he felt he could remain true to himself; he was never over-concerned to curry favour with those who did not understand him in the first place. *L'Aurore* is an early prophecy of the quiet radiance we will encounter again in such slow songs as *Le Secret* and *Aurore*, where the music unfolds magically, as if petal by petal.

On the other hand, *Tristesse d'Olympio*, admittedly unearthed from the archives without the benefit of a revision by the composer himself, is an indication of a young man, admirably passionate and more ambitious than he would give himself credit for, but tackling a huge poem that was above his punching weight.

There is much promise here, gracefulness and delight, but greatness is not yet discernible in the music's own terms. If Fauré enthusiasts are inclined to love this undemanding, pleasantly melodious music (particularly in persuasive performances), it is surely because the child (or in this case the teenager) is father to the man. There are listeners who would prefer all French songs to be as effortlessly accessible as these, but, thank heavens, they are not. The Hugo settings represent one of the outer pillars of the composer's creative achievement while the other is the music of *L'Horizon chimérique* composed nearly sixty years later. We value the later masterpieces ever more dearly when we measure the astonishing distance travelled between these two widely spaced poles of the composer's creative journey. The first lesson that Fauré would learn as a song composer was that there was a huge, and unbridgeable, gap between Hugo's fervent larger-than-life poems, many of them already a quarter of a century old, and his own infinitely more introverted – and somehow more modern – creative impulses.

CH REUTLINGER PHOT

Fauré at the age of eighteen, wearing the uniform of the École Niedermeyer. © Bibliothèque nationale de France

Victor Hugo towards the end of his life (c.1884) by Auguste Rodin

1   Philippe Fauré-Fremiet, *Gabriel Fauré* (Paris: Les Éditions Rieder, 1929), p. 19. See also the commentary on *Veilles-tu, ma senteur de soleil?* from *La Chanson d'Ève* in Chapter 12.

2   Marguerite Long, *Au piano avec Gabriel Fauré* (Paris: Gérard Billandot, 1963), p. 19.

3   Ibid., pp. 46–7.

4   Claude Rostand, *L'Œuvre de Gabriel Fauré* (Paris: J.B. Janin, 'La Flûte de Pan', 1945), p. 44.

5   Charles Dantzig, *Dictionnaire égoiste de la langue française* (Paris: Grasset, 2005), p. 376.

6   W.J. Robertson, *A Century of French Verse* (London: A.D. Innes & Co., 1895), p. 23.

7   In a letter to Frédéric Jacob Soret, 27 June 1831, in *Sophiensausgabe: Goethes Werke*, part IV: *Goethes Briefe*, vol. 48 (Weimar: Hermann Böhlaus Nachfolger, 1909).

8   *La Papillon et la fleur:* Aspects of this song's interpretation are discussed in Chapter 16, p. 399.

9   *Gabriel Fauré: A Life in Letters*, trans. and ed. Barrie Jones (London: B.T. Batsford, 1989), letter 294, p. 200.

10   *Mai:* Aspects of this song's interpretation are discussed in Chapter 16, p. 400.

11   *Pusiqu'ici-bas toute âme:* Aspects of this song's interpretation are discussed in Chapter 16, p. 400.

12   *Rêve d'amour:* Aspects of this song's interpretation are discussed in Chapter 16, p. 400.

13   Gabriel Fauré, *Correspondance*, ed. Jean-Michel Nectoux (Paris: Flammarion, 1980), letter 5.

14   *Tristesse:* Aspects of this song's interpretation are discussed in Chapter 16, p. 400.

15   *Dans les ruines d'une abbaye:* Aspects of this song's interpretation are discussed in Chapter 16, p. 401.

16   Vladimir Jankélévitch, *De la musique au silence: Fauré et l'inexprimable* (Paris: Plon, 1974), p. 44.

17   *Aurore:* Aspects of this song's interpretation are discussed in Chapter 16, p. 401.

18   Frits Noske, *French Song from Berlioz to Duparc*, trans. Rita Benton (New York: Dover, 1988).

Chapter Three

War and Peace on Parnassus

Théophile Gautier,
Charles Marie René Leconte de Lisle, Charles Baudelaire

I n the mid-1860s it seemed unlikely that Fauré, an impecunious music student of provincial origin, would ever become a famous musical figure in Paris; it is true that he had already composed a successful *Cantique* and some charming songs and piano pieces, but he lacked ambition. He did not seem to be 'going places'. The wily and perceptive Saint-Saëns privately nursed great hopes for his protégé's future on account of the youngster's sheer talent; Saint-Saëns lived to see his faith vindicated and Fauré saluted as a great composer, but in the meantime he must have despaired of young Gabriel's complacency. Fauré's connection to the École Niedermeyer, rather than the Conservatoire where the majority of France's establishment musicians were trained, was always a sticking point with officialdom. It was Fauré's saving grace in the world of musical politics that he enjoyed the support of the powerful Saint-Saëns, who frequently worked behind the scenes to secure advantages for his unworldly and slightly wayward pupil.

When Fauré left the École Niedermeyer in 1866 he needed to make his living, and Gustave Lefèvre, the new director of the school, recommended him for an organist's position at the church of St Saveur in Rennes, Brittany. It seemed an easy enough way of making regular money for someone who had

Fauré during the Rennes period

The celebrated soprano Caroline Miolan-Carvalho (1827–1895). Portrait by Nadar

just completed a rather over-extended stint at school, and the composer remained in Rennes for four years. This period in the provinces during the last years of the Second Empire is the least documented of Fauré's life, although we can piece together a few salient details: we know that he looked back on his sojourn in Rennes with little affection, and that he took rooms with a family who insisted that he should be in bed by 8 o'clock in the evening. He seems to have had moderate success with the young ladies of the town, although they were all strictly chaperoned when he arrived to give them piano lessons (travelling to students' houses in order to teach was a drudgery that he would have to endure later on for many of his Parisian years). In 1868, in the middle of his Rennes period, he replaced Saint-Saëns as the accompanist of the famous Madame Miolan-Carvalho, who had created the role of Marguerite in Gounod's *Faust*. Her recital tour that year encompassed Brittany, and she graciously took *Le Papillon et la fleur* into her repertoire; this song was later dedicated to her in gratitude.

Looking back at this time in 1896, Fauré wrote that he had a mediocre view of himself and a huge indifference to everything except beautiful things (and beautiful women no doubt).[1] Fauré's departure from Rennes in 1870 was not even the result of his own decision to leave – it was precipitated by the censure of the rigidly pious *curé* and the tight-lipped congregation: the composer had a habit of smoking on the church porch during the Sunday sermons, and then on one occasion he accompanied a Sunday morning service still wearing evening dress from the previous night's party. In this respect he amply demonstrated what Harvey Grace described as 'the traditional organist's impatience of the pulpit'.[2]

If there is nothing very dramatic about this stage of the composer's life, historical events were moving far more quickly. By the 1860s it was clear that the prosperity and success of Germany had catastrophically altered the balance of power in Europe. France and Germany had never been good friends; the bad feeling engendered by the dispute over the Rhineland territories had been simmering for decades. The open-ended time-scale of this squabble is illustrated by the fact that Nikolaus Becker's poem 'Der deutsche Rhein' was set to music by Schumann in 1840, and Alfred de Musset's withering response, 'Nous l'avons eu, votre Rhin allemand, served Albéric Magnard as a *mélodie* text during the First World War. The French, and Napoleon III in particular, were spoiling for a fight with their German neighbours. In March 1870 Fauré left Rennes (under a cloud, but no doubt relieved and happy) and returned to Paris. Saint-Saëns came to the rescue and arranged for his former pupil to take up the appointment of organist at Notre-Dame-de-Clignancourt, in a northern suburb of the capital. As in Rennes, Fauré soon fell foul of the church authorities; he absented himself from a service in order to hear *Les Huguenots* by Meyerbeer. He also attended a performance of that old favourite, Gounod's *Faust*, and heard Saint-Saëns give the second performance of his E♭ major Piano Concerto. At about this time he met César Franck, Lalo, D'Indy and Duparc, who accepted the young Fauré into their ranks as an equal. The young composer would have been a guest at Henri Duparc's Tuesday gatherings as well as at the famous 'Mondays' of Saint-Saëns. But time was running out for the Second Empire: in that very July the French Emperor declared war on Prussia.

The Franco-Prussian War did not last long but it was a military disaster for France and for Napoleon III in particular. With the failure of General MacMahon's attempts to relieve Metz at the battle of Sedan in the Ardennes, the

Louis-Napoléon Bonaparte (Napoléon III) (1808–1873)

Emperor was taken prisoner by the enemy on 2 September 1870. This victory precipitated exactly what the rest of Europe feared – the unification of the German states into a single Reich, an imperial superpower, in 1871. Two days after the French defeat at Sedan there was a bloodless revolution in Paris, and the Third Republic was proclaimed. In the suddenly abandoned apartment at the Tuileries that had belonged to the Empress Eugénie (who fled to England), a bust of Marie Antoinette was found, and the complete works of Victor Hugo, the officially despised poet of the ever-hypocritical Second Empire.

By 23 September the Germans surrounded Paris, which was now under siege. In August Fauré had enlisted in the First Light Infantry Regiment of the Imperial Guard and found himself in uniform for the rest of the year; he saw action at Champigny in October, Le Bourget in November and December, and Créteil – all battles that attempted, and failed, to deliver Paris from the stranglehold of the enemy. If there was a piano to be found in any of the abandoned villas on the outskirts of the capital, Fauré enchanted his regimental colleagues with improvised recitals. In February 1871 the monarchists under Adolphe Thiers, who favoured *rapprochement* with the Germans, won a new election, and Thiers negotiated an armistice between France and Germany which included the

Louis-Adolphe Thiers (1797–1877)

payment of an indemnity of five billion francs. The citizens of Paris, more bloody-minded than their provincial confrères, had voted for the republicans led by Gambetta, who favoured continuing the war. Many working-class Parisians loathed Thiers for agreeing to a treaty that was so punitive to France – Alsace and much of Lorraine were ceded to the Germans, and the victors reserved the right to stage a victory parade through the Arc de Triomphe.

Just as the new national government shifted its headquarters from Bordeaux to Versailles, Paris rebelled and established a Commune. This left-wing response to the rural monarchists, and what was considered their dishonourable peace with Germany, was reminiscent of the June Days in Paris of 1848. The result was a civil war between Paris and the rest of the country, although there were also short-lived communes established in other French cities that were quickly suppressed. Fauré had been demobilised from the army in March, and after a very brief spell as organist at St Honoré-d'Eylau in Paris,

he left the increasingly turbulent capital, where it was becoming impossible to find anything to eat and where he was in danger, like other able-bodied young men, of being forcibly enlisted as a Communard. He crossed the federate lines with a forged passport, and reached the relative calm of Rambouillet, not far from Versailles, on foot (this was where his brother was stationed). He went on from there to Switzerland, where the students from the École Niedermeyer had found temporary refuge at the appropriately named 'Champs-asile' in Cours-sous-Lausanne. Niedermeyer, of blessed memory, was a typically providential Swiss, and 'Champs-asile' was his property. During his four-month exile in Switzerland, Fauré was appointed a teacher at the school; it was at this time that he met his lifelong friend, initially his pupil, the composer André Messager (1853–1929). The two men were later to share a flat in Paris before Fauré was married. Apart from being one of France's greatest composers of operetta, Messager was to bridge the seemingly unbridgeable chasm between Fauré and Debussy by being an indispensable friend and colleague to both composers.

During the siege of Paris and its aftermath, most people with the means to do so fled the capital, which had become increasingly lawless and dangerous. The situation was soon to become even uglier with the lynching of two army generals by the mob in Montmartre. For two months, between the end of March and the end of May 1871, Paris experienced a new and chaotic experiment in municipal government. Karl Marx was later to hail this, rather simplistically, as the first great uprising of the proletariat. In the 'bloody week', 21–28 May, Thiers retaliated, and the Communards (as they were known) were beaten back through the city to make a last stand at Père-Lachaise. As they retreated they set the Tuileries and the Hôtel de Ville on fire, and a hostage, the Archbishop of Paris, was killed. Thiers's revenge was terrible and unflinching: some 20,000 Communards were shot, and thousands were transported to penal colonies. The poet Paul Verlaine had stayed in the city during the Commune, and had flirted with the Communard cause. The ambivalence of his situation at the time was a blot against him in official terms for the rest of his life; he was never able to resume his career as a civil servant (see Chapters 8 and 9). Fauré returned to Paris in October 1871. By now he had found the third of his organist posts in a year, this time at St Sulpice, where he was assistant to Charles-Marie Widor.

This musical *rentrée*, a re-gathering in Paris of composers from various points of the compass, was a significant time. From the point of view of the creative artist, it was as if the boil of imperialism, with its attendant hyper-frivolity, had been finally lanced. For younger musicians the notorious failure of Wagner's *Tannhäuser* in Paris in 1861 was ancient history, and Baudelaire's pro-Wagner stance, howled down at the time, now seemed increasingly revelatory and prophetic; the anti-German jingoism felt by many French people in 1870 was later placed into a different perspective by the home-grown violence of the Commune and a sense of tragedy regarding the losses of a pointless war. French musical nationalism was unbowed, but it was now something infinitely healthier – a new generation of composers was willing to keep an open mind regarding the best of German music while declining to be swamped by it.

This was a watershed and a new beginning, one of the most exciting periods in French cultural history; for the next sixty years or so Paris was to become a world capital of the arts, and there was no more exciting place to be in Europe as a painter or a writer. The position of musicians was perhaps more equivocal, but Vienna's days as the city of Haydn, Beethoven and Schubert were long over, and *bel canto* Italian opera was also past its heyday. The foundation of the Third Republic initiated what would gradually turn into a golden age of French music; that the Paris of the 1890s was not seen as the musical capital of Europe by most of the English-speaking world of the time was the result of a long-established, and difficult to shift, German-centred hegemony that encompassed a rivalry between Brahms and Wagner that temporarily eclipsed all other creative endeavours.

An indispensable manifestation of this new French nationalism with an open mind was the formation of the Société Nationale de la Musique (known as the SNM), an organisation founded on 25 February 1871; as happy as many of the composers might have been to make their pilgrimages to Germany to hear Wagner's works, the concerts of the SNM were reserved for the performance of French music mostly by composers of the younger generation. Among the founding fathers of this vitally important body (with the motto of *Ars gallica*) were César Franck, Camille Saint-Saëns, Jules Massenet, Alexis Castillon, Henri Duparc, Théodore Dubois and Fauré himself.

Many of the concerts (where the members and their friends comprised the majority of the audience) were held at the Salle Pleyel. Some of the high points of Fauré's association with the SNM in its first quarter-century were as follows: the performance of the Hugo songs published by Hartmann in February 1871; the premières in January 1877 of the A major Violin Sonata, in February 1880 of his First Piano Quartet, Op. 15, in March 1885 of his Symphony in D minor (although this work was never published), in 1887 of his Second Piano Quartet, Op. 45; the first performances in April 1892 of *Cinq mélodies 'de Vénise'*, and in April 1895 of *La Bonne chanson*. Fauré's low point with the SNM was in 1874 when, as the organisation's inefficient and unpunctual secretary, he was censured by the committee. Over the years the rules that governed the organisation (active for nearly forty years until 1910) were changed, and music by foreign composers, as well as composers of the past, was gradually admitted.

∾ ∾ ∾ ∾

The study of song necessitates some understanding of history, especially in turbulent times such as these, but political events play an even more important part in the study of literature. Composers generally take a little time to catch up with the latest literary developments; the process of adding music to words, and then seeing the resulting songs through to publication, is hardly instantaneous. While the young Fauré was busy composing his first Hugo settings in the early 1860s, there was a literary revolution underway in Paris, a precursor to the war that changed French society entirely in 1870. Despite the fact that Victor Hugo was still in noble exile, some aspects of his vast personality – his self-appointed roles as educator, philanthropist, humanitarian and socialist – had long seemed absurdly self-conscious to a younger generation of poets. One could admire Hugo's technical prowess as a writer, but his highly engaged romanticism had lost its appeal.

The younger poets – Charles Cros, François Coppée and Léon Dierx among them – had met at the home of the highly musical Nina de Callias, 17 rue Chaptal, where she maintained a famous salon. It was here, in the early 1860s, that the young Emmanuel Chabrier was to be heard at the piano; many years later his friend Paul Verlaine would write a sonnet about him in memory of these halcyon days. Verlaine was fresh from the success of his first collection, a mixture of dramatic poetry in the manner of Hugo, and verses that refrained from earthly passions in favour of the ivory tower and artistic isolation. It was this latter aspect of Verlaine's *Poèmes saturniens* (1866) that was to signify the immediate future. The desire to change or reform the world with the pen now seemed fatuous, the roaring political challenges of the 1830s only a distant memory. There were other luminaries *chez* Callias whose names will mean something to the lovers of Fauré's *mélodies*: Catulle Mendès nearly forty years before Fauré would belatedly set two of his poems to music, Sully Prudhomme and August Villiers de L'Isle-Adam. Mendès (1841–1909) had in 1861 founded the influential *Revue fantaisiste*, which had published the work of Gautier, his future father-in-law. Two important people in the world of books were also very much part of this circle: the editor Louis Xavier de Ricard and Alphonse Lemerre, whose name is known to all those who read French poetry, and whose publishing firm survived until 1965. Fauré himself, still more or less walled in at the École Niedermeyer, was not of course part of these literary gatherings, but like all the song composers of France he was soon to benefit from them.

These poets somehow coalesced into a group of sorts. The French have a habit, as in that assembly of composers known as 'Les Six', of arranging their creators into named categories, even if the affinities between them are short-lived and of limited validity. The poets of the time regarded themselves as *Parnassiens*, a name taken from a succession of eighteen pamphlets of sixteen pages each that were published by Lemerre, weekly on Saturdays, between March and July 1866. This series appeared under the title *Le Parnasse contemporain*, with second and third collections published in 1871 and 1876, all edited by the young but indefatigable Catulle Mendès. The first issue contained poems by Théophile Gautier, Théodore de Banville and José Maria de Heredia. Gautier, the proponent of 'l'art pour art' in his novel *Mademoiselle de Maupin* (1835), was extremely famous and hardly an emerging talent; he had been set to music by Berlioz in the 1840s (*Les Nuits d'été*), but his appearance in *Le Parnasse contemporain* gave this venerable poet in his mid-fifties a new lease of life, despite the

58

fact that he disapproved of the relationship between its editor and his daughter. Composers like Fauré suddenly perceived Gautier as a man of the moment and were drawn to his poems of whatever epoch, not simply the more modern publications. Although the acid critic Barbey d'Aurevilly made merciless fun of Gautier's participation in a project of this kind with much younger writers, it did the older man no harm with emerging composers like Fauré. (Banville had to wait for his musical apotheosis until the rediscovery of his *Les Cariatides* by Debussy more than a decade later.) The second fascicle of *Le Parnasse contemporain* featured Leconte de Lisle; once again this was a poet who had published volumes of verse more than a decade earlier. Berlioz may have been the pioneer of Gautier composers, but it was Fauré who discovered the musical qualities of Leconte de Lisle, as we shall see. The third instalment included François Coppée, whose 'La Vague et la cloche' was later set to music by Duparc. The fifth fascicle, perhaps the most exciting of all in terms of sheer poetry if not texts for music, was given over to the posthumous appearance of Baudelaire's *Nouvelles fleurs du mal*. This preceded the third edition of the *Fleurs du mal* (1868), which would incorporate new material that had not appeared in

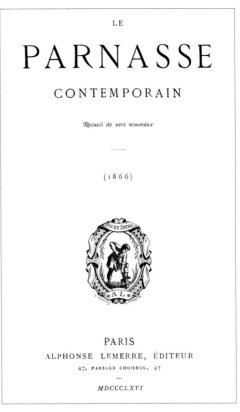

Frontispiece of Le Parnasse contemporain *(1866)*

the first two editions of this seminal collection (1857 and 1861). It is possible that Fauré discovered the texts for two of his Baudelaire settings in this celebrated issue of *Le Parnasse contemporain*. Sully Prudhomme, Paul Verlaine, Henri Cazalis (alias Jean Lahor, poet of Duparc's *Chanson triste*), Armand Renaud (poet of Saint-Saëns's *Mélodies persanes*) and Villiers de L'Isle-Adam were all featured in this remarkable assemblage of poets old and new. Alphonse de Musset had recently died, but the absence in these pages of Hugo, Lamartine and many of the old guard was eloquent enough; figures in French literature who had once seemed indispensable were now yesterday's men.

(8) *Les Matelots* (The sailors)[3]

*c.*1870, Op. 2 No. 2, 'À Madame Edouard Lalo', first Hamelle collection p. 15, E♭ major, 3/4, *Tempo animato quasi Allegro*

Sur l'eau bleue et profonde,	*We journey*
Nous allons voyageant,	*On the deep blue sea,*
Environnant le monde	*Encircling the world*
D'un sillage d'argent,	*With a silver wake,*
Des îles de la Sonde,	*From the Sunda Islands,*
De l'Inde au ciel brûlé,	*From India's burning sky,*
Jusqu'au pôle gelé …	*As far as the frozen pole …*

Nous pensons à la terre	*We think of the land*
Que nous fuyons toujours,	*We are leaving behind,*
À notre vieille mère,	*Of our old mother,*
À nos jeunes amours;	*Of our young loves;*
Mais la vague légère	*But the light wave*
Avec son doux refrain	*With its sweet refrain*
Endort notre chagrin!	*Lulls our sorrow to sleep!*

Existence sublime!	*Sublime existence!*
Bercés par notre nid,	*Rocked in our crow's-nest,*
Nous vivons sur l'abîme	*We live on the abyss*
Au sein de l'infini;	*At the heart of the infinite;*
Des flots rasant la cîme,	*Skimming the crests of waves,*
Dans le grand désert bleu	*In the great blue desert*
Nous marchons avec Dieu!	*We go with God!*

Théophile Gautier (1811–1872)

This is a song of transition, probably composed when Fauré was living and working in Rennes in Britanny. The composer's early *romance* style is now beginning to turn into something more interesting as certain aspects of the lied contribute a certain added depth to the newly minted *mélodie*. Perhaps the most useful lesson for Fauré to draw from German song at this stage was that an accompaniment of some character animated by a single, yet adaptable, pianistic motif was a means of binding a song together and making it greater than a sum of its parts. Almost certainly, Fauré mastered this knack thanks to his teacher, Camille Saint-Saëns. The musical treatment of *Les Matelots* seems influenced by the spacious grandeur of *Soirée en mer* (1862), one of the best Victor Hugo settings by the older composer.

Les Matelots is more vigorous than *Soirée en mer*, but both songs are powered by undulating triplets which reflect the fathomless motion of the sea. The subtle, and sometimes unexpected, harmonic shadings of Fauré's non-stop quavers enliven the potential monotony of the accompaniment; in this roving harmony we can savour the sailors' love of adventurous exploration. As each strophe progresses towards its vocal climax the bass line falls in steps, widening the distance between the piano's left hand and the vocal line. This depicts the breadth of vast nautical horizons with a musical grandeur that effectively counterbalances the sentimentality of the text.

The style of the poem belongs to an earlier era, but in one important way Fauré's music now displays a characteristic unknown to the old-fashioned *romance*: once his mature songs are set in motion they never flag or sag in the middle – they move forward as if drawn on a single unbroken thread, a musical unfurling where the composer seems absolutely sure of where he is going, and how. We hear this seamless and organic continuity for the first time in *Les Matelots*; although it is a strophic song it seems all of a piece. Fauré was never to lose his ability to create music that progresses ineluctably from first bar to last. This seriousness of intent is the mark of a new epoch in song composition in France, but, as in all art that conceals art, the composer's sure-footed and calm control of his musical materials makes for a result that sounds natural, but also deceptively easy.

The poem is from Théophile Gautier's *Poésies nouvelles*, the last subsection of the *Poésies complètes*

(1845). This was a famous old book of poems, and it would not have been hard to find a second-hand copy in Rennes. The composer, already merciless in terms of adapting poetry to his musical needs, cuts the second and fourth of Gautier's five strophes: we are thus spared the imagery of the labourer breaking the hard soil ('Le laboureur déchire / Un sol avare et dur') when Fauré's accompaniment has already launched us on the undulating ocean wave with no sight of dry land. The triplets that depict the movement of the water have not yet quite acquired their Fauréan trademark status. We shall encounter them again, in a more developed form in later songs in the barcarolles for piano, and they reach their apotheosis in the cycle *L'Horizon chimérique*.

The song's dedicatee was the well-to-do amateur singer Julie Bernier de Maligny, who became the second wife of the composer Edouard Lalo.

Théophile Gautier photographed by Nadar

∾   ∾   ∾   ∾

Théophile Gautier was a southerner like Fauré, born on 31 August 1811 (the year of Liszt's birth) in Tarbes at the foot of the Pyrenees, although he counted himself a Parisian from early childhood. Victor Hugo, only nine years older, was his idol. This capacity for enthusiastic friendship was one of Gautier's most attractive qualities: in later life he was to number Gustave Flaubert, Théodore de Banville and Charles Baudelaire (who dedicated *Les Fleurs du mal* to him[4]) among the intimates of his circle. As a young man Gautier was a fan of Byron and ardently embraced the cause of *romantisme*; dressed in green silk and a waistcoat of crimson velvet, he was leader of the student claque that ensured a *succès fou* for Hugo's play *Hernani* in 1830. In this earlier part of his career this young man with his long black hair and sallow countenance was a prolific and daring author and critic while always preserving a certain judicious detachment; he was as capable of writing *Mademoiselle de Maupin* (a novel with an androgynous subject that scandalised the middle classes of the time) as scholarly studies of such then-forgotten poets as François Villon and Théophile de Viau (whose 'À Chloris' was set to music years later by Reynaldo Hahn). Gothic horror stories were to Gautier's taste, and in *Fortunio* (1837) he combined the fantasy of the Arabian-nights with Parisian modernity. *La Comédie de la mort* was a long narrative poem that lent its name to a compendious (and beautifully produced) volume of poetry (1838), which also contained some of Gautier's immortal shorter lyrics – those set by Berlioz for example in *Les Nuits d'été*. The phrase 'art for art's sake' ('l'art pour l'art') was his invention, and it was to be a theme for philosophical discussion to the end of the century (among the decadents, for example) and well beyond.

The second string to Gautier's career as a highly regarded journalist, *feuilletoniste* and art – and even music – critic was initiated in 1835 by Balzac, who helped him obtain a post on the *Chronique de Paris*. Work of this kind was unworthy of Gautier's genius, but he lived a life of constant financial

Judith Gautier (1845–1917) and the autograph of Théophile Gautier's poem 'Fatuité'

restraints and crises, and writing for newspapers suited someone who was unfailingly disciplined when it came to deadlines and who was able to write copious copy with scarcely any need for revision. In his hands hack-work became literature; no one wrote prefaces like those of Gautier, whose output, including reprints of his journalism, was enormous: it is rare indeed that a poet should write multi-volume histories of the dramatic and visual arts. He was knowledgeable about ballet: he collaborated in the creation of Adolphe Adam's *Giselle* in 1841 and numbered dancers among his lovers, including Ernesta Grisi, sister of the great soprano Giuditta Grisi, and the mother of Gautier's famous daughter, Judith. Early on, the poet placed Bellini's *Norma* (rightly) above Meyerbeer's *Les Huguenots*, and he was a partisan of Berlioz's *Benvenuto Cellini*; he was won over to the Wagnerian cause by the enthusiasm of Judith and her husband Catulle Mendès. It must be admitted that he was not a natural musician (he once described music as 'the least disagreeable and most expensive of noises'), but he applied himself to the subject with his innate taste and sense of judgement. Among his composer-contemporaries he was closest to Ernest Reyer and Félicien David, who both wrote songs to Gautier texts that reflected the contemporary taste for orientalism. This in turn brings to mind Gautier's achievements as a first-class travel writer, who visited Spain (1840), the Levant (1850–52 – the poem for Fauré's song *Seule!* was written by no mere armchair traveller) and Russia (1860). His observations about the music of the Bedouins during a visit to Algeria in 1845 show him to have been something of an unintentional pioneer in the modern field of ethnomusicology.

Over the years Gautier's poetry became less romantic and increasingly in tune with the restraint and formal perfections of the much younger Parnassians; for this reason, and also because there was so little of the ageing grandee about him, he was invited to participate in *Le Parnasse contemporain* in 1866. This may have been an indication of Gautier's ongoing need to make money under any and every circumstance, but it is also a reproach to those less flexible artists who retreat to the grandeur of their past rather than seizing the chance to reinvent themselves among the young. Nevertheless, it has always been the earlier Gautier lyrics that appealed to musicians. While he was celebrated among the literati for the perfection of his collection of poetic 'enamels and cameos' – *Emaux et camées* (1852) – this work has all but been ignored by composers, who have always preferred to return to the earlier poems, especially those first published in *La Comédie de la mort*. Gautier died of heart disease in Neuilly on 23 October 1872; he had been devastated by the disastrous events of the Franco-Prussian War and the Commune, events that are said to have hastened his demise.

He was scarcely past sixty, and he had burned himself out with too much hard work undertaken for too little financial reward. Gautier is one of those writers who is indispensable to the history of literature but who, unlike Hugo, has been denied the destiny of becoming a household name in France, if only narrowly. It is significant that he was never elected to be a member of the Académie Française. His beautiful and wilful daughter Judith Gautier was married for a short time to Catulle Mendès (against the wishes of her father). She became a prominent advocate of the music of Wagner and had an affair with the Master of Bayreuth between 1876 and 1878; long before the première of *Parsifal* (an opera which reflects her influence on the composer) she was at work on the French translation of Wagner's text and she wrote a book about his work – *Richard Wagner et son œuvre poètique* (1882). The sympathy of Gautier and his daughter for the Wagnerian cause was one of the reasons why the composers of Fauré's generation regarded this poet as one of their almost-contemporaries.

(9) *Lydia* (*Lydia*)[5]
c.1870, Op. 4 No. 2, 'À Mme Marie Trélat', first Hamelle collection p. 32, F major, **c**, *Andante*

Lydia, sur tes roses joues,	*Lydia, onto your rosy cheeks*
Et sur ton col frais et si blanc,	*And your neck so fresh and pale,*
Roule étincelant	*The liquid gold that you unbind*
L'or fluide que tu dénoues.	*Cascades glittering down.*
Le jour qui luit est le meilleur:	*The day that dawns is the best;*
Oublions l'éternelle tombe.	*Let us forget the eternal tomb.*
Laisse tes baisers de colombe	*Let your dove-like kisses*
Chanter sur ta lèvre en fleur.	*Sing on your flowering lips.*
Un lys caché répand sans cesse	*A hidden lily unceasingly sheds*
Une odeur divine en ton sein:	*A heavenly fragrance in your breast;*
Les délices, comme un essaim,	*Delights without number*
Sortent de toi, jeune déesse!	*Stream from you, young goddess!*
Je t'aime et meurs, ô mes amours!	*I love you and die, O my love!*
Mon âme en baisers m'est ravie.	*My soul is ravished by kisses.*
Ô Lydia, rends-moi la vie,	*O Lydia, give me back my life again,*
Que je puisse mourir toujours!	*That I may ever die!*

Charles Marie René Leconte de Lisle (1818–1894)

Henri Duparc, a deeply hospitable soul, was known for his Tuesday evening gatherings, although these musical soirées were neither as famous nor as long running as the 'Mondays' of Saint-Saëns – a tradition among Parisian musicians already venerable by 1870. On Fauré's return to Paris after the upheavals of the Commune he heard Duparc's new masterpiece *L'Invitation au voyage*. He was bowled over by this song as were all of that composer's contemporaries. He would have liked to set this Baudelaire text himself, but Duparc's song was definitive; Chabrier withdrew his own *L'Invitation au voyage* (an attractive work with bassoon obbligato) for the same reason. The Duparc setting is a turning point in French song in that it confirmed once and for all that the *mélodie* in terms of depth and seriousness could match anything to be found in German lieder; it also served as Fauré's introduction to Baudelaire's work and encouraged him to abandon his youthful penchant for the poems of Hugo. Instead, he began to tackle shorter lyrics by somewhat younger poets who had the power to inspire him to a more intense musical response. Leconte de Lisle's 'Lydia' (No. XVII of the *Etudes latines* section of his *Poèmes antiques* of 1852) was an ideal match with the composer's new espousal of the *mélodie*. He confessed much later in his life that 'pagan antiquity has always held an enormous attraction for me'.[6] As Jankélévitch observes: 'What composers demand from Ancient Greece is neither dance rhythms nor popular songs, but a geographical dissolution compounded equally of ubiquity and Utopia.'[7] In *Lydia*, Fauré was thus composing his own *L'Invitation au voyage*.

This song was nothing less than a breakthrough. The simplicity of the music on the page belies a stunning new sophistication in the young composer's approach. The ravishing vocal line is discreetly shadowed by the piano, attenuated support that avoids anything unseemly or immodest and adds to the Attic purity of the evocation. An ancient Greek atmosphere is created partly by use of the Lydian mode with its sharpened fourth of the scale. The gentle exoticism of this tritone adds to the music's rarefied charm; the marvellous postlude dissolves into those ethereal regions even more convincingly than the ascension into heavenly heights depicted at the end of Schubert's *Ganymed* – it is as if we are breathing the very air of Parnassus. At 'tes baisers de colombe' the undulating vocal line, accompanied by gently fluting thirds, is one of the most haunting evocations of cooing doves in all song. (Fauré was later to depict birdsong more explicitly in *La Bonne chanson* and *Le Ramier*.)

Leconte de Lisle's description of Lydia's neck being as 'fresh and pale as milk' is more awkward. Confronted with the poet's 'Et sur ton col frais, et plus blanc / Que le lait', Fauré, with devilish cunning, changes 'plus' to 'si' and simply leaves out 'Que le lait', allowing 'blanc' to link with the next verb, 'roule'. A piano interlude (bars 6 to 7) papers over the cracks in this judicious textual cut. This is a bigger change than a tiny adaption at the end of the second strophe: Fauré clearly disliked two 'è' vowels one after the other: accordingly he changes the poet's 'tes lèvres' to 'ta lèvre'. The 'little death' of a kiss is a familiar sexual metaphor chastely expressed in the poem; it also appears in Chausson's *Le Colibri*, another Leconte de Lisle poem in one of the poet's several exotic guises. If Fauré's *Lydia* owes its existence to Duparc in 1870, it inspired, in a circular reciprocity of influences, the same composer's *Phidylé* of 1882. Duparc owed to Fauré those tranquil mezzo-staccato crotchet chords, seemingly suspended in the midday heat, that had announced *Lydia*, and which also open 'Duparc's song'. Both these demure Leconte de Lisle characters are neo-Grecian nymphs to be found within the pages of his *Poèmes antiques* – another classic collection (1852) that was influential in shaping the modernity of the Parnassians. The mode for this kind of writing is further illustrated by the Chausson song *Hébé*, where the poem is by Louise Ackermann, also a contributor to *Le Parnasse contemporain*. Fauré's shy masterpiece continued to be influential for many years – indeed, it had opened a new stylistic door as far as the *mélodie* was concerned. It is said that Massenet was present when

MÉLODIES
Chant et Piano
DE
GABRIEL FAURÉ

	PRIX			PRIX
1 · Le Papillon et la Fleur	5 fr ·	7 · Mai	5 fr ·
1 Mezzo-Soprano ou Baryton		*1 Mezzo-Soprano ou Baryton*	
2 Soprano ou Ténor		*2 Soprano ou Ténor*	
2 · Dans les Ruines d'une Abbaye	5 · ·	8 · Ici - Bas !	3 · ·
3 · Tristesse	5 · ·	9 · Barcarolle	3 · ·
1 Mezzo-Soprano ou Baryton		10 · Chanson du Pêcheur	5 · ·
2 Soprano ou Ténor		11 · Hymne	5 · ·
4 · Rêve d'Amour	5 · ·	12 · Seule !	5 · ·
1 Contralto ou Baryton		*1 Contralto ou Baryton*	
2 Soprano ou Ténor		*2 Mezzo-Soprano ou Ténor*	
5 · Les Matelots	3 · ·	13 · Au Bord de l'Eau	3 · ·
6 · Lydia	3 · ·	14 · Après un Rêve	3 · ·
1 · 1 Mezzo-Soprano ou Baryton			
2 Soprano ou Ténor			

Paris, CHOUDENS, Père et Fils, Éditeurs,
265, Rue St. Honoré (près l'Assomption)

*Title-page of the songs available singly from Choudens (*Lydia *among them)*
before the publication of the first recueil

Fauré played the song through for the publisher Hamelle and exclaimed: 'I wish I had written that!' Thirty years later Massenet's pupil Reynaldo Hahn in his *Etudes latines* (1900) would still be tilling Leconte de Lisle's (by then rather over-cultivated) Graeco-Roman terrain.

The dedicatee of *Lydia*, the mezzo-soprano Marie Trélat (1837–1914), daughter of Napoleon III's surgeon, was an amateur singer of considerable distinction. Massenet dedicated a number of songs to her (and also complimented her cuisine), as did César Franck and Bizet who regarded her as his ideal singer.[8] Her home in the rue Jacob, a precursor of the Saint-Marceaux and Polignac salons, was an important centre for the *mélodie* in the 1860s and 70s. Her appearances at concerts for the SNM were significant, and her position as a singing teacher in later years was equally important.

Lydia inspired other composers, but it was a sufficiently emblematic work to inspire Fauré himself to repeated self-quotation. He was acutely aware that it was this music that had first announced his individuality to the world; the sinuous musical shape, rising a third and then snaking back on itself to rise a further major third from the second degree of the scale, became a kind of musical signature or motto. The outline of a melody that depends on the tonic's relationship to the sharpened (or Lydian) fourth of the scale is another characteristic to be heard in the later Fauré. The works that contain references to *Lydia* include: *Adieu*, Op. 23 No. 3; *La Lune blanche*, Op. 61 No. 3 (*La Bonne chanson*); *J'ai presque peur, en vérité*, Op. 61 No. 5 (*La Bonne chanson*); the aria from Act 1 of the opera *Pénélope* beginning 'Vous n'avez fait qu'éveiller dans mon sein', where there is a *Lydia* quotation –at the line 'Maître à qui j'ai donné les trésors de ma grâce'; *Cygne sur l'eau*, Op. 113 No. 1 (*Mirages*); and the Second Piano Quintet, Op. 115, at the beginning of the slow movement.

Leconte de Lisle reappears regularly in Fauré's song writing. Most of the composer's other poets, from Hugo and Baudelaire through to Verlaine and Van Lerberghe, belong firmly in a certain phase of the composer's life; not so Leconte de Lisle, whose influence is well distributed, a leavening of a modest quantity of Parnassian yeast through almost the entire oeuvre. *Lydia* dates from c.1870, *Nell* was written in 1878 and *Les Roses d'Ispahan* in 1884, *La Rose* is from 1890 and *Le Parfum impérissable* from 1897. There are thus only five Leconte de Lisle settings (and sketches for a sixth, *Dans le ciel clair*, from 1902), but they are all marvellous songs, so special in fact that one must ascribe the success of each to a deep and continuing aesthetical affinity between poet and composer. It must surely be the reticence and technical mastery of the poet, his disinclination to unveil too much about himself and his own feelings, in short his disdain for any easy access to the emotions, which drew the sympathetic attention of Fauré's muse. Nevertheless, very much later in his career, in response to a questionnaire from the magazine *Musica*, Fauré was to lump this poet together with Hugo and explain why his settings had been so infrequent: 'the poetry is too full, too rich, too self-sufficient for the music to adapt to it successfully'. This remark from the sanctuary and refuge of *Le Jardin clos* was made with the benefit of hindsight; when Fauré set *Lydia* he could have been in no doubt that thanks to the exciting discovery of Leconte de Lisle he was already light years away from the overflowing ebullience of the Hugo poems.

Charles Marie René Leconte de Lisle was born in 1818 on Réunion island, in those days known as the Île Bourbon, in the Indian Ocean. His

POEMES

ANTIQUES

PAR

LECONTE DE LISLE.

PARIS
LIBRAIRIE DE MARC DUCLOUX, EDITEUR
RUE TRONCHET, 2
—
1852

Frontispiece of Poemes Antiques *by Leconte de Lisle (1852), the poet's first publication*

Breton father had been a surgeon in the Napoleonic wars and had gone there from Normandy to become a planter; his mother was a Creole (as those colonials of European stock born on the island were labelled) and was the cousin of the poet Evariste Parny (1753–1814), some of whose remarkable *Chansons madécasses traduites en français* were set to music by Ravel more than a century after the death of their poet. Leconte de Lisle never forgot his childhood in this exotic part of the world. Was it the pagan aspect of Réunion's history, or perhaps his visits to India and Madagascar as a young man, that pricked his desire to evoke the lush literary vegetation of lost civilisations and their gods? Some of his most notable work describes the stillness and the menace of the jungle with panthers in a state of repose, always ready to spring and wreak havoc. He writes of Druids and Syrian sages, of polar bears and Malay pirates, of Zeus and Brahma. He was drawn to religions that flourished in the heat: Shiva and Buddha were favourite topics. Indeed, Fauré's handful of Leconte de Lisle musical settings singularly fail to encompass the much wider range of the poet's philosophical, historical and religious interests. In terms of his range of subject-matter the poet seems to be every bit as extravagant as Hugo, in terms of far-flung geography even more so; the huge difference between the poets lies in the treatment of their material.

The critic Barbey D'Aurevilly remarked acidly that the poet's nose was buried so deep in the blue lotus (a flower that figures frequently in Leconte de Lisle's work) that he had asphyxiated himself. The exotic was his speciality: his imagination ranged far over the mountains of Greece ('Lydia' and 'Phidylé'), tarried in the exotic deserts and souks of Asia Minor ('Les Roses d'Ispahan' and 'Le Parfum impérissable') and luxuriated in the jungles of his native Réunion, where the humming-bird, Chausson's *Le Colibri*, may be seen in its natural habitat. Leconte de Lisle loved exotic names and exotic spellings – in his hands Clytemnestre changes into Klytaimnestra and Cain becomes Kaïn, or even Quaïn. One of the few

Leconte de Lisle

influential poems in the *mélodie* literature that seems to have influenced him is Gautier's 'La Fuite' (with its characters of Kadidja and Ahmed), set by both Duparc and Paladilhe as a duet. Animals such as elephants and hippopotamuses were also a speciality, all of them described with the gravity of Corneille. It was actually Racine who was Leconte de Lisle's favourite poet (apart from his revered Victor Hugo, whose chair he eventually inherited at the Académie Française in 1885); in the same way John Keats admired his virtuosic predecessor John Dryden.

The poet had made France his home from 1837, settling in Paris a decade later. The prosperous plantation on which he had been brought up became bankrupt after the revolution in France in 1848, largely because of the abolition of slavery following the fall of Louis-Philippe. Leconte de Lisle, who had written an anti-slavery pamphlet, was a supporter of that revolution (and like Victor Hugo he felt betrayed by Louis Napoleon's perversion of its ideals), but he lived in straitened circumstances for the rest of his life as the result of the loss of his family's money. It is perhaps significant that all his important work came after this change of fortune.

For some literary historians Leconte de Lisle's *Poèmes antiques* (1852), with its sweepingly audacious (and later suppressed) preface, is almost as significant in French literary history as Hugo's

Les Orientales and Baudelaire's *Les Fleurs du mal*. The poet believed that the corruption of the Second Empire could be somehow held at bay by evoking civilisations of ancient times that were nobler than the tawdry present ('the entire Christian cycle is barbarous. Dante, Shakespeare and Milton have only the force and grandeur of their individual genius; their speech and conceptions are barbarous').[9] The ancient Greece of Anacreon and Theocritus was an exemplary civilisation, the first to engage Leconte de Lisle's attentions, but Rome was also grist to the mill – Fauré's song *Lydia* was part of the subsection of the book, *Etudes latines*, that was inspired by the Roman poet Horace. *Nell* on the other hand belonged to a sequence of *Chansons écossaises*, a tribute to the folkloric purity of Robert Burns's Scotland, a nation of would-be republicans that had struggled against an oppressive English overlord. An early review from Sainte-Beuve for *Poèmes antiques* both patronised and praised the poet: Leconte de Lisle, said the critic, came from a 'race of créoles … born for dreams and for song', but added that (unlike others of his background) he had been 'nourished by his study of the ancients and readings of the ancient Greeks'.[10]

Autograph of a poem ('L'étendue est immense, et les champs n'ont point d'ombre') by Leconte de Lisle

If Sainte-Beuve ascribed indolence to his background and this 'race de créoles', Leconte de Lisle could claim to be more hard-working than most other poets; instead of exhibiting louche sensuality (as in the poems by Parny for example) he was the model of self-censoring restraint in sexual matters – he was married without children. If he was a 'colonial', and thus different from the Parisian literary establishment, it was because he did not share its politicised networking – he allowed followers to come to him. We can see much in common with Fauré in aspects of his personality, retiring and lofty at the same time. The poet was a pessimistic and rather embittered atheist but, like Fauré (who had also been transplanted in Parisian soil from earthier southern climes), he was irreproachable in terms of his professional integrity and dignity. In some ways he appeared to be a sage from another epoch; his only concessions to modernity were a monocle and a perpetual cigarette.

Leconte de Lisle's second book, *Poèmes et poésies* (1855, later to be the source of Fauré's *La Rose*), had continued the trend of *Poèmes antiques* but expanded on the Indian theme to be found only in the closing pages of the first collection. His explorations of different cultures and their faiths now strike the reader as pioneering sorties into the as yet uncharted study of comparative religion. He had also drawn to himself a number of disciples – he was the kind of person with *gravitas* who easily assumed the mantle of a *maître*. For his young followers in the newly established school of Parnassus he emanated a kind of sacerdotal grandeur, as if a high priest of a new religion. His home was a regular meeting place for the Parnassian poets at the time of the publication of *Le Parnasse contemporain* in 1866. By this time he had begun an extended series of translations from Latin and Greek (the last appearing in 1885) that would encompass the works of Homer, Theocritus, Hesiod, Aeschylus, Horace, Sophocles and Euripides. The advent of the Third Republic rewarded Leconte de Lisle for remaining distant from the Second Empire, at least in his writings; in fact his straitened circumstances had forced him to accept a pension from Napoleon III's officials (a seeming conflict of interest that prompted a minor scandal at the time among republicans). Nevertheless, perhaps as a recognition of his *Histoire populaire de la Révolution française* (1871) he was rewarded by the new order with the sinecure post of librarian to the Senate in 1872.

With greater financial security he published less frequently, preferring to return to such classical subjects as the *Oresteia* – his *tragédie antique* entitled *Les Erynnies* was performed in 1873 with music by Massenet. Continuing his interest in cultures of the past, he proved himself a medievalist with his *Histoire du moyen âge* in 1876. Leconte de Lisle died in 1894 a largely forgotten man. Edmond Gosse points out his similarities with the English poet, Walter Savage Landor, also almost forgotten;[11] Landor's descriptions of the pagan beauty of farthermost antiquity in a work like *Gebir* make a striking parallel with the French poet's *Kaïn*. Fauré returned to the *Poèmes tragiques* in 1897, three years after Leconte de Lisle's death, for one of his most exquisite settings, *Le Parfum impérissable*; this return to the literary realms of his younger years was admittedly at the behest of a beautiful actress, Julia Bartet, clearly a woman of considerable literary taste.

Elegance and beauty can seem an indication of coldness and lack of involvement in this poet's work– as if Baudelaire's 'ordre' and 'calme' had been drained of their 'luxe' and 'volupté'. Alexandre Dumas *fils* voiced the objections of the naturalists and realists to Leconte de Lisle's work in a hostile open letter to the poet.[12] 'You do not wish to entertain us with intimate or vulgar aspects of the soul … no more emotions, no more ideas, no more faith, no more heartbeats, no more tears … love is no part of life for you, science and philosophy suffice.' On the other hand, the poet's adherents, and one must number Fauré among these, perceived a passionate personality beneath the icy technical perfection mistrusted by some critics. After all, there are also *mélomanes* who unaccountably find Fauré's music similarly lacking in passion and human engagement.

Dumas had almost certainly read the *Poèmes barbares* (1862) and the *Poèmes tragiques* (1884), where Leconte de Lisle's calm evocations of Grecian purity are complemented by bloodthirsty epic poems littered with headless bodies; these show the poet's fascination with the savagery and violence of ancient times. In this vein Leconte de Lisle's writing resembles that of Flaubert's *Salammbô*. Dumas would probably have said of this writing that despite all the brilliant colour of these poems of mass slaughter, Leconte de Lisle's 'polished silver mirror of antiquity' ('l'antique miroir d'argent poli') always favoured the factual at the expense of the emotive. This is a quality with which Fauré clearly felt comfortable, and his less successful settings of the very different Baudelaire reinforce this impression. Leconte de Lisle was the kind of poet who could write a barbaric poem in a form that retained an aura of civilised tranquillity; the subject was separate from its treatment. It is this sense of containment that found an echo in Fauré's creative personality.

(10) *Hymne* (Hymn)[13]

*c.*1870, Op. 7 No. 2, 'À M. Félix Lévy', first Hamelle collection p. 71, G major, 6/8, *Allegretto vivo*

À la très-chère, à la très-belle	*To the dearest one, the fairest one,*
Qui remplit mon cœur de clarté,	*Who fills my heart with light,*
À l'ange, à l'idole immortelle,	*To the angel, the immortal idol –*
Salut en immortalité!	*I pledge undying love!*
Elle se répand dans ma vie	*She permeates my life*
Comme un air imprégné de sel,	*Like a briny breeze,*
Et dans mon âme inassouvie	*And into my unsated soul*
Verse le goût de l'éternel.	*Pours the taste of the eternal.*
Comment, amour incorruptible,	*How, incorruptible love,*
T'exprimer avec vérité?	*Can I express you faithfully?*
Grain de musc qui gis, invisible,	*Grain of musk lying unseen*
Au fond de mon éternité!	*In the depths of my eternity!*

Charles Baudelaire (1821–1867)

The work of Baudelaire was published in dribs and drabs: the notorious first edition of the *Fleurs du mal* appeared in 1857, and the second, augmented, edition 1861. But it was only after the death of the poet that a third 'definitive' edition was published that included the *Nouvelles fleurs du mal* and a collection entitled *Les Épaves*. It is in the latter, in the subsection *Galanteries*, that 'Hymne' and 'La Rançon' (also set by Fauré) are to be found. If Fauré had not seen the Baudelaire fascicle in *Le Parnasse contemporain*, it must have been the appearance of this volume in 1868 that excited him into musical action, at more or less the same time as Duparc and Chabrier set 'L'Invitation au voyage'. The poet's work, already some years old, must have seemed to be hot off the press as far as Fauré and many of the younger composers were concerned. Unfortunately it is also clear that Fauré creates a musical context for his Baudelaire settings that suggests the salon, a milieu that is too cosily bourgeois for the poet's passionate sentiments. It is a bold, or inexperienced, song composer who will tussle with a musical setting of phrases such as 'un air imprégné de sel', not to mention 'amour incorruptible' or 'mon éternité'. The gentle tremolos of the piano writing here are too soft-grained to launch or support such grand concepts, and the composer's natural charm is rendered leaden by a lyric that seems to embarrass him in its intensity.

In this instance Fauré, who was nearer to the Parnassians in terms of his innate reserve, seems to have encountered a hugely romantic poem in a literary context where he least expected to find it. Jean-Michel Nectoux also sternly notes in this setting a 'lack of discretion or variety in the accentuation of the words';[14] the two evenly stressed dotted crotchets of bar 9 ('À l'ange') are a case in point. The composer leaves out the poet's third verse and opts simply to repeat the first verse at the end of the song instead of setting Baudelaire's fifth strophe, which modifies the first. The form of the song – ABCA – is unusual for Fauré. Jankélévitch claimed to hear in this music a trace of the melodic *élan* that we find in full measure in the A major Violin Sonata,[15] Op. 13, but the remarkable muscular energy of the sonata never descends to the anodyne prettiness of *Hymne*. Baudelaire is simply too large in every way for Fauré to cope with in a song, particularly at this stage; the epic nature of the sonata, a work to take the breath away, might have provided a better musical portrait of the affirmative and optimistic side of the great poet.

The dedicatee of *Hymne*, Félix Lévy, was a well-known amateur tenor and a close friend of Saint-Saëns. He gave the song's first performance (together with the Hugo setting *Mai*) in a concert for the SNM in March 1873. Lévy had a small voice (Gabriel Astruc called him a 'tenorino') but he sang into his eighties.[16] Fauré dedicated the first of his *Trois romances sans paroles* for piano to Lévy's wife, Sarah. The Lévys' salon was one of the most lively of the time where some of the most famous musical personalities appeared, always expressing affection for their kindly hosts.

Charles Baudelaire was a greater literary figure than Leconte de Lisle, but his work was far less suited to the composer's purpose. There are three Fauré settings of Baudelaire, and of these it is only *Chant d'automne* that may be counted anything like a suc-

Charles Baudelaire, photographed by Nadar

cess. Nevertheless, the bare outlines of a famous life may be useful here in order to put these three songs in context. The greatest (though perhaps not the most personally admirable) French poet of the age, whose importance has seemed indisputable to each new generation of French letters, was born on 9 April 1821. He lost his father, a self-made man of letters and an artist, at the age of six; his mother, whom he adored to an almost unhealthy degree, remarried. This brought the unwelcome addition into his life of a stepfather, Jacques Aupick by name, a military man, who opposed the boy's ambitions to become a poet. In 1841, at Aupick's disciplinary insistence, the young Baudelaire made a journey to the East, setting off for Calcutta; once he had reached Mauritius he spent forty-five days on Île Bourbon, where Leconte de Lisle grew up, and then decided to turn back for Paris. This short time away was to be hugely influential in the poet's future evocations of the exotic realms of 'Luxe, calme et volupté' as described in 'L'Invitation au voyage'. The journey dazzled and hypnotised his senses but singularly failed to ignite in the writer an enthusiasm for the commercial possibilities of trade with the East as his stepfather had hoped.

Charles Baudelaire. Self-portrait (1863–1864)

In 1842, at the age of twenty-one, Baudelaire came into family money and was able to achieve his independence; he became a member of the Banville and Gautier circles, read Swedenborg and led a reckless and dissolute life founded on the celebration of every excess including the consumption of hashish and opium. He had earlier contracted syphilis from a Jewish prostitute named Sarah La Louchette. It was this exploration of the dark side of the Parisian *demi-monde* that was to lend such savage force to his poetic imagery which encompasses an ongoing battle between evil and good (the opposing worlds of 'Spleen' and 'L'Idéal', both titles of poems) or, more subtly, between appetite and apathy. The language employed in some of these texts seemed lewd and blasphemous to many of his contemporaries. In 1844 his family withdrew their financial support and he was cut off from his money. His relationship with his mulatto mistress Jeanne Duval – the 'Vénus noire' of the poems, and the inspiration behind 'Le Balcon', set by Debussy in 1889 – was especially painful; an unstable alcoholic, she became repulsive in his eyes, yet she remained somehow emotionally indispensable to him. He supplemented his work as a poet with art criticism, and his translations of the stories of the American novelist and poet Edgar Allan Poe were saluted as classics.

He is said to have taken part in the riots that displaced Louis-Philippe in 1848 and to have briefly resisted the Bonapartist *coup* of December 1851.

Baudelaire was convinced of his genius, and failed to realise that the conservative forces of society were capable of bringing him down and ruining his life. (One may compare his arrogance in this respect to that of another brilliant extrovert, Oscar Wilde.) The publication of *Les Fleurs du mal* in 1857 led to a prosecution for offences to public morals and blasphemy. The same hypocritical imperial concern for propriety had led to Flaubert's prosecution for his *Madame Bovary* at the end of 1857. Baudelaire's one-day trial resulted in a fine, but there were other consequences disastrous to the poet's finances. Six of the poems with Sapphic subject-matter were banned, which meant that the 1857 edition could not be sold without their deletion. The second and third editions (1861 and 1868) did not include these forbidden poems (which were published legally again in France only after the banning order was lifted in 1949). Leconte de Lisle admiringly reviewed the second edition of 1861, which contained much new material: 'maledictions et des plaintes, des chants extatiques, des blasphèmes, des cris d'angoisse. Les tortures de la passion … les âpres sanglots du désespoir, l'ironie et le dédain, tout se mêle avec force et harmonie dans ce cauchemar dantesque' ('a mixture of curses and groans, ecstatic songs, cries of blasphemy and anguish. All the torture of passion … the bitter sobs of despair, irony and disdain – all mingling powerfully and harmoniously in this Dante-like nightmare').[17]

Despite the towering literary significance of his great book, the setback to Baudelaire's standing represented by the criminal charges, and the curbing of his ability to reach a reading public, could not have been more catastrophic to his mental equilibrium. He became more or less an outcast from the high society he had once frequented with insouciance; the first symptoms of the tertiary stage of syphilis became apparent in 1862; at about the same time as his publisher Poulet-Malassis went bankrupt. In 1864 the poet moved to the Grand Miroir hotel in Brussels in a futile attempt to make a living as a lecturer. By this time he had written much else, including the work that would distinguish him as a pioneer of musical criticism – *Richard Wagner et Tannhäuser* (1861), one of the first works to appreciate the significance of Wagner, and certainly the first to do so in France.

Baudelaire lived in miserable squalor in Brussels, and his health gave way completely in 1866. In the same year his *Nouvelles fleurs du mal* was issued as part of *Le Parnasse contemporain*. The poet was brought back to Paris suffering from the general paralysis caused by his terrible illness. The last phase of his life – fifteen months in an institution – was as pitiable as those of Robert Schumann and Hugo Wolf, who were tormented by the same malady. He died on 31 August 1867.

(11) *Seule!* (Alone!)[18]
1871, Op. 3 No. 1, 'À Monsieur E. Fernier', first Hamelle collection p. 19, E minor, **c**, *Andante*

Dans un baiser, l'onde au rivage	*In a kiss, the wave to the shore*
Dit ses douleurs;	*Voices its grief;*
Pour consoler la fleur sauvage,	*To console the wild flower*
L'aube a des pleurs;	*Dawn has its tears;*
Le vent du soir conte sa plainte	*The evening breeze tells its sorrow*
Aux vieux cyprès;	*To the ancient cypress;*
La tourterelle au térébinthe	*The turtle-dove to the terebinth*
Ses longs regrets.	*Its endless regrets.*
Aux flots dormants, quand tout repose,	*To the sleeping waves, when all is quiet*
Hors la douleur,	*But pain,*
La lune parle, et dit la cause	*The moon speaks, explaining why*
De sa pâleur.	*It is pale.*
Ton dôme blanc, Sainte-Sophie,	*Your white dome, Santa Sophia,*
Parle au ciel bleu,	*Speaks to the blue sky*
Et, tout rêveur, le ciel confie	*And, lost in dreams, the sky confides*
Son rêve à Dieu.	*Its dream to God.*
Arbre ou tombeau, colombe ou rose,	*Tree or tomb, dove or rose,*
Onde ou rocher,	*Wave or rock,*
Tout, ici-bas, a quelque chose	*Everything here below*
Pour s'épancher …	*Has something to pour out …*
Moi, je suis seule, et rien au monde	*But I am alone, and nothing on earth*
Ne me répond,	*Ever responds to me,*
Rien que ta voix morne et profonde,	*Nothing but your deep and gloomy voice,*
Sombre Hellespont!	*Sombre Hellespont!*

Théophile Gautier (1811–1872)

THÉOPHILE GAUTIER.

Théophile Gautier in oriental dress. Caricature by Nadar

This poem finds the intrepid Gautier (the *Poésies nouvelles* again) in the Dardanelles. It has no heading, but Fauré changes the poet's own adjectival 'seul' in the third strophe to the feminine 'seule' and uses this, together with an exclamation mark (an addition, perhaps, of the publisher), as his title. The form of the poem (octosyllabic feminine lines alternating with four-syllable masculine ones) dictates the shape of the composer's musical response: it is as if the story is being told to us in alternation by two characters of different temperament, one excitable, the other more grave. The imposing classical economy and severity of the music bring to mind that most famous of mourners who waited in vain for a sign of life from the Hellespont – Hero, priestess of Aphrodite, whose lover Leander had drowned there. In order to visit Hero, Leander had nightly swum the four miles (Byron measured the distance by setting himself the same challenge) between Sestos and Abydos. Before committing suicide Hero lamented Leander's death – perhaps in words like these.

Gautier visited Constantinople in 1852 and saw for himself the Hagia Sophia to which he refers in his second strophe. The poet had not intended this poem specifically for the Hero of antiquity, if this had been the case mention of the basilica would of course have been an anachronism. But the lyric set Fauré thinking of Greek mythology and continued the classical inspiration inaugurated by *Lydia*. The contemporary example of Duparc's *L'Invitation au voyage* seems to have given the composer a new confidence to write songs in the grand manner. This is his first *mélodie* in the minor key, and he eschews a salon-pleasing charm. The music gives the impression of being an obsessive passacaglia (without being one); right-hand octaves suggest the tolling of death knells. There is more chromatic colouring than has been usual so far, an anguished dialogue of sorts between treble and bass, all played out against a background of a recurrent tonic pedal. This noble and little performed song is distantly prophetic of *Inscription sur le sable*, the final song of the cycle *Le Jardin clos* and in the same key of E minor.

Reynaldo Hahn paid tribute to Fauré by setting the same poem in 1892, albeit in a much more turbulent way, including an ominous 'Sombre Hellespont' declaimed in chest voice: Hahn's accompaniment recalls the impassioned triplet accompaniment of Fauré's *Toujours* from the *Poëme d'un jour*. The change from 'seul' to 'seule' is also adopted by the younger composer. In a gesture that possibly demonstrated a degree of historical awareness, typical of Hahn, he dedicated his setting to Georges Hartmann, who had published Fauré's *Seule!* with three other songs, twenty-oneyears earlier, in 1871. Debussy was to dedicate the score of *Pelléas et Mélisande* to the memory of this same publisher and friend.

74

(12) *L'Absent* (The absent one)[19]

3 April 1871, Op. 5 No. 3, 'À M. Romain Bussine', first Hamelle collection p. 47, A minor, **c**,
Andante sostenuto

– Sentiers où l'herbe se balance,	*– Paths of swaying grass,*
Vallons, coteaux, bois chevelus,	*Valleys, hillsides, leafy woods,*
Pourquoi ce deuil et ce silence?	*Why this mourning and this silence?*
– Celui qui venait ne vient plus.	*– He who came here comes no more.*
– Pourquoi personne à ta fenêtre,	*– Why is no one at your window,*
Et pourquoi ton jardin sans fleurs,	*And why is your garden without flowers,*
Ô maison! où donc est ton maître?	*O house, where is your master?*
– Je ne sais pas, il est ailleurs.	*– I do not know: he is elsewhere.*
– Chien, veille au logis. – Pourquoi faire?	*– Dog, guard the home. – For what reason?*
La maison est vide à présent.	*The house is empty now.*
– Enfant, qui pleures-tu? – Mon père.	*– Child, who is it you mourn? – My father.*
– Femme, qui pleures-tu? – L'absent.	*– Woman, who is it you mourn? – The absent one.*
– Où donc est-il allé? – Dans l'ombre.	*– Where has he gone? – Into the shadow.*
– Flots qui gémissez sur l'écueil,	*– Waves that moan against the reefs,*
D'où venez-vous? – Du bagne sombre.	*From where do you come? – The dark convict prison.*
– Et qu'apportez-vous? – Un cercueil.	*– And what do you carry? – A coffin.*

Victor Hugo (1802–1885)

Like *Tristesse d'Olympio* this is one of Hugo's many autobiographical fragments. As we have seen, he was an inexorable opponent of the 'little' Napoleon's regime. The poem was written in 1853 at the beginning of Hugo's exile in the Channel Islands. Fauré set these words eighteen years later in the wake of the Franco-Prussian War, and when he himself had run away from Paris to escape the Commune. Hugo's opposition to Napoleon III had been vindicated, if belatedly, by events, and in the grandeur of this music we feel that Fauré is paying tribute to the great republican's historic stand as a fellow-exile. The composer almost certainly came to know the poem from the Parisian edition of *Les Châtiments* that appeared in 1870 (*chez* Hetzel), where it is without title: poem No. XI of Livre III. The collection of poems had been initially printed in Brussels in truncated form in 1853, and soon after appeared in an imprint from St Helier in Jersey with publication in Geneva and New York. Was it the dramatic return of Hugo to Paris that made the composer revisit his erstwhile poet? It is typical of Fauré (who invented the song's title) that his tribute to Hugo's bravery is a retrospective one; it is equally typical of Hugo that he had overestimated the gravity of his fate: instead of finding the prison and shroud that he melodramatically predicted for himself in *L'Absent*, he had returned to Paris as the most celebrated French writer of all time.

The image of swaying grass of the poem's opening line inspires a bare accompaniment of undulating suspensions where minims toll like melancholy bells, as if mourning a living death. The vocal line, an elegiac pronouncement with the spoken immediacy of recitative, is supported by this rocking harmonic movement; the mood is one of emptiness. At 'Chien, veille au logis' the accompaniment quickens into triplets; pets, even guard dogs, are dangerously sentimental participants in songs of this seriousness (another dog appears in *Tristesse*), and Fauré would have exiled them from lyrics at a later stage of his career. The marking is *Un poco più mosso*, and the image of the child weeping for his absent father releases the floodgates of emotion. That this passage should be among the most heartfelt outbursts in the songs is food for thought for the composer's biographers, especially when remembering that Fauré was himself separated from his parents at a very early age. The plaintive cry of *L'Absent*, the highest note of the piece, speaks for the pity of war and the panic of the displaced and dispossessed. In a wild interlude for piano Fauré abandons his customary restraint; this kind of interlude is scarcely to be found elsewhere in his songs.

After these eight bars the return to the original tempo is precisely engineered; in the perfectly planned manner of this recapitulation shedding the storm-like character of the middle section with astonishing deftness, we are reminded of songs like *Le Voyageur* and *Au cimetière*, and in this music Robert Orledge finds a prophecy of the Thirteenth Nocturne, a work composed sixty years later.[20] The image of the 'bagne sombre' thickens the texture of the accompaniment, which now seems as impenetrable as prison walls, the vocal line fatally hesitant, the final left-hand triplets bathed in Stygian gloom. Here there is a link with Fauré's Ninth Barcarolle. This is also a song that is nearer than most to Duparc's musical style.

(13) *La Rançon* (The ransom)[21]
1871?, Op. 8 No. 2, 'À Mme Henri Duparc', first Hamelle collection p. 82, C minor – C major, 3/4, *Andante non troppo*

L'homme a, pour payer sa rançon,	*Man, that his ransom may be paid,*
Deux champs au tuf profond et riche,	*Has two fields of soil, rich and deep,*
Qu'il faut qu'il remue et défriche	*Which he must till and rake*
Avec le fer de la raison;	*With the blade of reason;*
Pour obtenir la moindre rose,	*To grow the merest rose,*
Pour extorquer quelques épis,	*To reap but meagre ears of corn,*
Des pleurs salés de son front gris	*He must water them night and morn*
Sans cesse il faut qu'il les arrose.	*With salt tears from his ashen brow.*
L'un est l'Art, et l'autre l'Amour.	*One field is Art, the other Love.*
– Pour rendre le juge propice,	*To propitiate the judge,*
Lorsque de la stricte justice	*When the terrible day*
Paraîtra le terrible jour,	*Of strict justice dawns,*
Il faudra lui montrer des granges	*He will have to show him barns abrim*
Pleines de moissons, et des fleurs	*With harvested crops and flowers,*
Dont les formes et les couleurs	*Whose forms and colours gain*
Gagnent le suffrage des Anges.	*The approval of the seraphim.*

Charles Baudelaire (1821–1867)

LES

FLEURS DU MAL

PAR

CHARLES BAUDELAIRE

PRÉCÉDÉES D'UNE NOTICE

PAR

THÉOPHILE GAUTIER

TROISIÈME ÉDITION

PARIS
MICHEL LÉVY FRÈRES, ÉDITEURS
RUE VIVIENNE 2 BIS, ET BOULEVARD DES ITALIENS, 15
A LA LIBRAIRIE NOUVELLE
1869
Droits de reproduction et de traduction réservés

The title-page of the third (1869) edition of Les Fleurs du mal, *and the portrait of Baudelaire printed as its frontispiece*

The first thing we notice is that this and the following Baudelaire setting are through-composed, as opposed to strophic, songs. This is surely part of Fauré's attempt to find a style that is suitably profound for these very serious poems; musical material repeated in the manner of a *romance* seems unworthy of such a poet. The composer had high hopes for this setting, as is shown by its dedication to Ellie Mac Swiney, the Scottish-born wife of the composer Henri Duparc and a singer and pianist of some ability. Only Duparc among the great French song composers can boast of complete success with Baudelaire, and then only on two occasions when he set poems that were chosen with the greatest care and perspicacity – qualities less evident in Fauré's dealings with the poet.

The first two strophes are set in his recently acquired solemn style (the song these two verses most resemble is *Seule!*), as if the words are engraved on stone like a classical pronouncement, with just a hint of contrapuntal commentary in the piano. After twenty-eight bars in this mood it is the verb 'arrose' that waters and revivifies this parched music: static crotchets turn into quavers, and flats dissolve into the naturals of the major key. This is only the first stage of resuscitation; after the word 'Amour' the tempo quickens (*un poco più mosso*); the accompaniment takes on a ruminative, lieder-like quality, as if the song were by César Franck, or Schumann–Brahms at one remove. This pianistic style – rambling arpeggios decorated with uncharacteristic acciaccaturas – attempts to plumb new depths, but in vain. The music is not without interest or beauty (at the mention of the seraphim at the end of the song we hear a distant prophecy of *La Bonne chanson*) but it never achieves unity with Baudelaire's text.

(14) *Chant d'automne* (Autumn song)[22]

1871?, Op. 5 No. 1, 'À Mme Camille Clerc', first Hamelle collection p. 35, A minor, 12/8, *Andante* – 9/8, *Lento ma non troppo*

Bientôt nous plongerons dans les froides ténèbres;	*Soon we shall plunge into cold shadows;*
Adieu, vive clarté de nos étés trop courts!	*Farewell, vivid light of our too-short summers!*
J'entends déjà tomber avec un choc funèbre	*Already I hear the funereal thud*
Le bois retentissant sur le pavé des cours.	*Of echoing logs on the courtyard floor.*
J'écoute en frémissant chaque bûche qui tombe;	*I listen, trembling, to the fall of each log;*
L'échafaud qu'on bâtit n'a pas d'écho plus sourd.	*A gallows being built makes no duller sound.*
Mon esprit est pareil à la tour qui succombe	*My spirit is like the tower that falls*
Sous les coups du bélier infatigable et lourd.	*To the remorseless blows of the battering-ram.*
Il me semble, bercé par ce choc monotone,	*Rocked by those monotone blows, it seems*
Qu'on cloue en grande hâte un cercueil quelque part.	*Somewhere in haste they are nailing a coffin.*
Pour qui? – C'était hier l'été; voici l'automne!	*But whose? Yesterday summer; autumn now!*
Ce bruit mystérieux sonne comme un départ.	*This eerie sound rings like some farewell.*
J'aime de vos longs yeux la lumière verdâtre,	*I love the emerald glow of your wide eyes,*
Douce beauté, mais aujourd'hui tout m'est amer,	*My sweet, but all today is bitter for me,*
Et rien, ni votre amour, ni le boudoir, ni l'âtre,	*And nothing, not your love, the boudoir, or the hearth*
Ne me vaut le soleil rayonnant sur la mer.	*Can compare with the sunlight on the sea.*

Charles Baudelaire (1821–1867)

In a ten-bar introduction for piano (one of his longest preludes – and prophetic of the Brahms intermezzi, says Nectoux)[23] Fauré attempts to set up a dark and brooding atmosphere that will match the poet's horror of encroaching autumn; the music encompasses weighty depression without quite managing to capture Baudelaire's panic and revulsion. The *sforzato* basses of the twelve-bar prelude are inspired by the 'choc funèbre' of the poem (which appeared in the second edition of *Les Fleurs du mal*, 1861, as well as the third edition, 1868, the composer's probable source). The imagery of 'bercé par ce choc monotone' prompts the *sforzato* dotted minims in the left hand of the accompaniment; these are surrounded, as if in a haze of reverberation, by quaver triplets that pervade the entire first section of the song and cradle the voice in their gentle undulations.

The clarity of summer has yielded to mist and darkness, both admirably suggested by the atmospheric accompaniment and the mournfully inflected vocal line. Baudelaire's virulent second verse with its 'hatred, ague and horror' was suppressed by Fauré. In an effort to provide an element of musical contrast, the song's fourth verse (the poet's fifth and sixth are also omitted) is made to change into the major key and triple time. As Nectoux notes, in the third line of the first verse Fauré changes Baudelaire's 'J'entends *déjà* tomber avec *des* chocs funèbres' to 'J'entends *déjà* tomber avec *un* choc funèbre'. This avoids a pile-up of 'd's ('déjà' and 'des') that clearly offended the composer's ear.

This is perhaps the most lyrical, certainly the most suave, music for voice and piano Fauré had written up to this time. Many years later Marcel Proust was famously enchanted by the long sinuous lines of the music for this second section – 'J'aime de vos longs yeux la lumière verdâtre'. According to Fernand Gregh, when Proust was enamoured with Marie Finaly in 1892 he used to hum this music ecstatically, 'with half-closed eyes, and head thrown back' – although this is scarcely the reaction Baudelaire might have expected from a phrase where the key words are 'tout m'est amer' – 'everything is bitter to me' – and where even the word 'verdâtre' glints with a certain menace. For a moment, despite the poet's unhappy statement, we have strayed into the lyrical territory more familiar to this composer; we realise (did Fauré before it was too late?) that this declaration of love has been made only to be cruelly knocked down – the emerald light of the beloved eyes *is no match* for the sunlight stolen by autumn. Fauré's setting manfully contrives to make of this downhearted comparison the triumphant peroration (the radiant 'rayonnant sur la mer') of a conventional love song.

This *mélodie* is a magnificent failure – magnificent because it contains much beautiful music (the dedication to Marie Clerc, someone whose good opinion was very important to the composer, shows a certain pride on his part), a failure because the wilfully contradictory Baudelaire was an unsuitable partner for Fauré's ordered musical temperament. Time has shown that the poet could never be the ideal muse for a *mélodie* composer, no matter how talented. Even Debussy struggled; perhaps only two of his *Cinq Poèmes de Baudelaire* join the two inimitable settings of Duparc in a rather short list of truly successful exceptions.

(15) *Chanson du pêcheur* (Lamento) (Song of the fisherman (lament))[24]
1872?, Op. 4 No. 1, 'À Madame Pauline Viardot', first Hamelle collection p. 27, E♭ minor, **c**, *Moderato*

Ma belle amie est morte,	*My dearest love is dead:*
Je pleurerai toujours;	*I shall weep for evermore;*
Sous la tombe elle emporte	*To the tomb she takes with her*
Mon âme et mes amours.	*My soul and all my love.*
Dans le ciel, sans m'attendre,	*Without waiting for me*
Elle s'en retourna;	*She has returned to Heaven;*
L'ange qui l'emmena	*The angel who took her away*
Ne voulut pas me prendre.	*Did not wish to take me.*
Que mon sort est amer;	*How bitter is my fate;*
Ah! sans amour, s'en aller sur la mer!	*Alas! to set sail loveless across the sea!*
La blanche créature	*The pure white soul*
Est couchée au cercueil;	*Lies in her coffin.*
Comme dans la nature	*How everything in nature*
Tout me paraît en deuil!	*Seems to mourn!*
La colombe oubliée	*The forsaken dove*
Pleure et songe à l'absent,	*Weeps, dreaming of its absent mate,*
Mon âme pleure et sent	*My soul weeps and feels*
Qu'elle est dépareillée.	*Itself bereft.*
Que mon sort est amer;	*How bitter is my fate;*
Ah! sans amour, s'en aller sur la mer!	*Alas! to set sail loveless across the sea!*

Sur moi la nuit immense	*The immense night above me*
Plane comme un linceul;	*Is spread like a shroud;*
Je chante ma romance	*I sing my song*
Que le ciel entend seul.	*Which heaven alone can hear.*
Ah! comme elle était belle	*Ah! how beautiful she was*
Et combien je l'aimais!	*And how I loved her!*
Je n'aimerai jamais	*I shall never love a woman*
Une femme autant qu'elle.	*As I loved her.*
Que mon sort est amer;	*How bitter is my fate;*
Ah! sans amour, s'en aller sur la mer!	*Alas! to set sail loveless across the sea!*

Théophile Gautier (1811–1872)

This poem is entitled 'Lamento' in Gautier's *La Comédie de la mort* (1838), and Gounod's setting of these words in 1841 seems to have been among the first. He re-used the music for the aria 'O my lyre immortelle' from the opera *Sapho* commissioned from him by Pauline Viardot in 1851; Offenbach composed a setting of the words in 1850 as part of his cycle *Les Voix mystérieuses*; Berlioz's famous *Sur les lagunes* (from *Les Nuits d'été*) dates from 1856. By the 1870s Gautier was enjoying a renaissance as a newly fashionable poet among musicians. Fauré first came into contact with Gounod in 1872, and both composers (who at this stage shared a publisher in Choudens) set this poem in that year, Gounod for the second time and under the title *Ma belle amie est morte*. Apart from repetitions of the phrase 'sans amour' Fauré avoids the verbal meanderings of the older Gounod, who shamelessly cuts Gautier's text. Idols when encountered in the flesh prove to have feet of clay, and personal contact with Gounod, whose *mélodie* style influenced Fauré's earliest songs to an extent, seems to have released the younger composer from his senior's thrall. In this setting Fauré fails to match the anguish of Berlioz at his height, but he writes an extremely effective song in the Italian manner, far removed from the style of Gounod's *romance*. This is most evident in the form of the song, which follows Gautier's poem and combines a strophic repetition with a refrain (R) and coda: thus ARARB.

On the printed page the opening gives the impression of an unaccompanied recitative *senza misura*, but it is evident, even at this early stage, that exactness of rhythm is a vital component of the composer's musical planning. Though the singer might be tempted to consider the lack of accompaniment in the song's opening two lines an excuse for a recitative-like freedom, he or she should reconsider. There are no *ad libitum* stretches in the rest of Fauré's songs, and there is no justification for them here. The composer reflects the narrator's solitary grief in harmonies that suggest the emptiness of bereavement and an unsettled state of mind; the tightness of the rhythm, and the way the song is propelled forward, are part of its power. At its opening the intermittent triplets of the accompaniment suggest the despondent plying of a fisherman's oar in the lagoons rather than the dipping and plunging of a larger vessel. As the song gets into its stride, the words tumble more readily from the singer's lips and an initially compressed emotional horizon broadens into a grieving seascape.

Mention of the words tumbling from the singers lips reminds us of how Fauré was unique among the *mélodie* composers for ever so slightly modifiying a poet's words to facilitate what he thought would make a more legato vocal flow for the singer. This tendency was first noticed and carefully researched by J-M Nectoux. From the beginning of his career, Fauré seems to have worried less about the finer points of prosody and more about what he considered an unattractive pile-up of sibilants or dental consonants (or a succession of 'e' vowels). Thus in a song such as this we find the composer in the penultimate verse changing a single word: Gautier's 'Sur moi la nuit immense / S'étend comme un linceul', is changed to 'Sur moi la nuit immense / Plane comme un linceul', thus reducing a relentless succession of four sibilants to three. The effect is less hectic as far as a singer is concerned, but we cannot deny that the disturbing, even sinister, effect of these repeated 's's was probably intentional on the poet's part. Fauré took pains here to avoid an effect that might have seemed perfectly acceptable, indeed attractive, to a grittier composer like Berlioz.

Chanson du pêcheur was immediately performed by the contralto Julie Bernier de Maligny, the second Madame Edouard Lalo, although its dedicatee, the more celebrated singer Pauline Viardot, took some time to include it in her repertoire. Fauré orchestrated this song a quarter of a century later, and his fondness for it is indicated by the musical character of the First Nocturne in E♭ minor (*c*.1875), which can be heard as a kind of meditation on this *lamento*: on its final page, by way of a coda, there is an eloquent solo piano variation on Fauré's vocal line for 'Sur moi, la nuit immense / Plane comme un linceul'.

❧   ❧   ❧   ❧

The two years covered by this chapter (1870–1871) were the most turbulent, and certainly the most physically dangerous, of Fauré's life: times were changing fast – for France, as well as for the young composer. The sleepy sojourn in Rennes, following his departure from the École Niedermeyer, had been a rather boring prelude to a tempestuous period during which he saw the collapse of the Second Empire, active military service, the rise and fall of the Commune and the creation of the SNM. The establishment of this institution also meant a broadening of his circle of musical friends. At the end of 1869 Choudens, perhaps impressed by the composer's links with the celebrated Madame Miolan-Cavalho, had published two of Fauré's songs – *Le Papillon et la fleur* and *Dans les ruines d'une abbaye*. The end of 1871 had seen the publication of four further songs by the firm of Georges Hartmann (these were *Lydia*, *Hymne*, *Mai* and *Seule!* – a mixed bag of settings by four different poets), which gave an entirely different, and more mature, public profile to Fauré the composer of *mélodies*. The first of these four songs seems to have been the one of which the composer was proudest, and with justification.

Leconte de Lisle wrote poetry that suited Fauré marvellously, largely because it demands that 'expression' should be resolved into form. The fact that Fauré had grasped this nettle also accounts for the effectiveness of the Gautier setting *Seule!*, probably the most completely successful song of 1871 – there is a musical rigour here that represents a real break from the style of the 1860s. (We detect a similarly grave and hieratic quality at the beginning of *La Rançon*, but the second section of the poem leads Fauré up the Schumannian garden path, and the song was not published by Hartmann.) *Hymne* was a well-meaning failure, and we suspect that Fauré may not yet have read, and assimilated, the texts of *Les Fleurs du mal* in their totality (the poet's own requirement of his readers); if he had they would almost certainly not have been to his taste. The selection of *Mai* for the Hartmann *recueil* suggests that Fauré was already aware that, in terms of composing *mélodies* at least, Gounod was a better role model than Saint-Saëns – not that he would ever have expressed any such opinion that might have seemed to denigrate his beloved teacher and mentor.

The other songs of this period, none of them out-and-out masterpieces, all have admirable features, and all are experimental in a way that one would expect from a young composer: *Les*

Frontispiece by Louis Duveau for Poésies complètes *by Leconte de Lisle (Paris, 1858)*

Matelots has a restless yet subtle accompaniment of a kind that will become a feature of the songs of the second *recueil*; *L'Absent* and *Chant d'automne*, with their suspended and anticipated harmonies, are ambitious attempts to break away from strophic song, where passages of memorable beauty jostle with material that can easily seem unwieldy. *L'Absent* was the last Hugo setting by Fauré; as Norman Suckling puts it, 'he [Hugo] was no encouragement to a composer whose best qualities lay in the direction of containing and resolving his emotions, rather than allowing them to overflow'.[25] Nevertheless, in *Chanson du pêcheur* Fauré abandons his reserve in favour of an intense, almost operatic outpouring – perhaps a necessary readjustment for a composer whose natural reticence threatened to inform every aspect of his life to an almost self-defeating extent. All in all, these years of dramatic change and renewal in French history had been a period of rather more subtle reorientation in Fauré's musical development. The rise of successful French opera composers of his own generation, liberated at last from the Scylla and Charybdis of Meyerbeer and Offenbach, partially encouraged him to a new openness and a new daring, a newly awakened interest and trust in a long-debased medium. But Fauré is already simply Fauré and, as we shall see, despite the best efforts of one of the most operatically oriented personalities in French music (enter Pauline Viardot, Chapter 4), his response to outside advice or pressure was always more polite than profound. Contact with the Viardot family would render some of his songs more accessible and less interior than they otherwise might have been, but the essential musical power of the man himself, still dormant in many aspects of its creativity, is already pure and more or less 'incorruptible' (to use Baudelaire's adjective in 'Hymne'). And as proof of this we have the perfection of the immortal *Lydia*.

1   Gabriel Fauré, *Lettres intimes*, ed. Philippe Fauré-Fremiet (Paris: La Colombe, 1951), p. 23.

2   Harvey Grace, writing of English church musicians in *The Organ Works of Bach* and quoted in Norman Suckling, *Fauré* (London: Dent, 1946), p. 14.

3   *Les Matelots:* Aspects of this song's interpretation are discussed in Chapter 16, p. 401.

4   The full dedication is 'Au poète impeccable, au parfait magicien ès lettres françaises, à mon très-cher et très-vénéré maître et ami Théophile Gautier'.

5   *Lydia:* Aspects of this song's interpretation are discussed in Chapter 16, p. 401.

6   Interview with François Crucy in *Le petit Parisien*, 28 April 1922.

7   Vladimir Jankélévitch, *Music and the Ineffable* (1961, rev. 1981), trans. Caroline Abbate (Princeton, NJ: Princeton University Press, 2003), p. 104.

8   Myriam Chimènes, *Mécènes et musiciens* (Paris: Fayard, 2004), pp. 285–6.

9   From the preface to *Poèmes antiques* (Paris: Librairie de Marc Ducloux, 1852).

10 C.-A. Sainte-Beuve, *Causeries du lundi*, vol. 5 (Paris: Garnier Frères, 1852).

11 Edmond Gosse, *Aspects and Impressions* (London: Cassell, 1922), p. 195.

12 A. Dumas fils, *Réponse au discours de la réception de M. Leconte de Lisle* à l'Académie (Paris, 1885).

13 *Hymne:* Aspects of this song's interpretation are discussed in Chapter 16, p. 402.

14 Jean-Nectoux, *Gabriel Fauré: A Musical Life*, trans. Roger Nichols (Cambridge: Cambridge University Press, 1991), p. 68.

15 Vladimir Jankélévitch, *De la musique au silence: Fauré et l'inexprimable* (Paris: Plon, 1974), p. 48.

16 Gabriel Astruc, *Le Pavillon des fantômes: Souvenirs*, new edition (Paris: Pierre Balfond, 1987), pp. 294, 296.

17 Leconte de Lisle, *Révue européenne* (1861), quoted in Catulle Mendès, *Le Mouvement poétique français de 1867* à *1900* (Paris: Imprimerie Nationale, E. Fasquelle, Editeur, 1903), p. 23.

18 *Seule!:* Aspects of this song's interpretation are discussed in Chapter 16, p. 402.

19 *L'Absent:* Aspects of this song's interpretation are discussed in Chapter 16, p. 402.

20 Robert Orledge, *Gabriel Fauré* (London: Eulenburg, 1979), p. 50.

21 *La Rançon:* Aspects of this song's interpretation are discussed in Chapter 16, p. 402.

22 *Chante d'automne:* Aspects of this song's interpretation are discussed in Chapter 16, p. 403.

23 Nectoux, *Gabriel Fauré: A Musical Life*, p. 69.

24 *Chanson du pêcheur:* Aspects of this song's interpretation are discussed in Chapter 16, p. 403.

25 Suckling, *Fauré*, pp. 63–4.

Chapter Four

Chez Mme P. Viardot-Garcia[1]

Louis Pomey, Marc Monnier,

Sully Prudhomme, Romain Bussine

The previous chapter ended with the Gautier song *Chanson du pêcheur*, and its distinguished dedicatee merits a chapter of her own in the story of Fauré's songs. In 1872 Camille Saint-Saëns introduced his twenty-seven-year-old protégé into the salon of Pauline Viardot (1821–1910), one of the most renowned singers and musical personalities of the nineteenth century. She was born Michelle Ferdinande Pauline Garcia, daughter of Manuel Garcia, the famed singing teacher, and younger sister of that incandescent soprano Maria Malibran, the Callas of her epoch, who had died tragically young and whose life has been recently chronicled in a programme presented and sung by Cecilia Bartoli. Although Pauline was married to the French critic Louis Viardot (who wrote among many other things an exhaustive series of books on the museums of Europe), she became the muse and mistress of Ivan Turgenev, whom she had met on a Russian tour in 1843. The novelist and playwright soon afterwards attached himself to her household, and she composed four operettas to his libretti. Fifty years later, in an interview with Roger Valbelle, Fauré reminisced fondly about the great Russian writer: 'he was the big shot, a fine looking man, and of a gentleness that was even more appealing. I have kept the memory of the sound of his voice to the extent that whenever I read one of his books, it seems that I can actually hear him.'[2]

Viardot had been the protégée of George Sand (whom Fauré also encountered as a venerable old lady at Pauline's salons) and had spent a great deal of time at Nohant, where she met, and studied with, Chopin. In her honour Berlioz had restored the title role of Gluck's *Orféo ed Euridice* to the alto voice (for which it was originally written – high tenors had taken over the role), and in 1859 this proved to be Pauline's most celebrated theatrical success. She also excelled as the same composer's *Alceste*, and in operas by Meyerbeer (above all as Fidès in *Le Prophète*), Rossini, Bellini and Mozart. At her request Charles Gounod wrote his opera *Sapho* for her in 1851. On Viardot's retirement from the Parisian stage at the early age of forty-two (she had begun her career when very young, and was opposed to Napoleon III's regime) she moved to Germany, making her base in Baden-Baden between 1859 and 1870 and concentrating on the song and oratorio repertoires. She was revered by Clara Schumann, who also lived in Baden-Baden (1863–73) and who regarded Pauline as the greatest woman genius she had ever met; Robert Schumann had dedicated his Heine *Liederkreis* Op. 24 to the astonishingly precocious Mademoiselle Garcia in 1840, when she was just nineteen (the year of her marriage to Louis Viardot), and Clara Schumann regularly accompanied Pauline in recitals between 1843 and 1867. During the Franco-Prussian War Viardot was obliged, as the wife of an enemy alien, to leave German territory; she sang the first performance of Brahms's *Alto Rhapsody* (1870) shortly before her return to France.

In Pauline Viardot the young and impressionable Fauré encountered someone utterly different from the strait-laced matrons of Rennes. She was a famously vivacious woman of just over fifty; in 1872 she was busy re-convening her circle of Parisian friends and encouraging new talents. Her salon (48 rue de Douai) had been a gathering point for musicians, artists, actors and writers since 1840, and now that she was back in Paris she quickly re-established her considerable presence. Her main salon, for which formal invitations were issued, was on Thursday evenings; a much smaller circle of intimate friends was invited for Sundays, and this hand-picked group soon included Fauré (the presence of Saint-Saëns was also a given). Her son Paul Viardot, a fine violinist, quickly became a close

Pauline Viardot (1821–1910) as a younger woman

friend of Fauré and was the dedicatee of the Violin Sonata in A major, Op. 13, composed in 1875–76. Pauline's two daughters, Claudie and Marianne, were both reasonably talented singers, although one cannot imagine that they aspired to the peaks of virtuosity and depths of feeling for which their mother was famous. Fauré seems to have found the second of these two girls extremely attractive.

Pauline Viardot herself was anything but beautiful. On the contrary, she was thought by her contemporaries to be extremely ugly, yet compellingly charismatic (like George Eliot, who was judged to be hideous at first glance, yet acquired ardent admirers after they had spent time in her company). Viardot spoke French with a Spanish accent (according to Reynaldo Hahn, who met her when she was a very old lady), but her English, after she had lived in England and the United States, was as fluent as her German. She was a citizen of the world and by far the most glamorous female musical personality that the young Fauré had ever encountered. Her collection of musical treasures included the autographs of Mozart's *Don Giovanni* and a Bach cantata, and Fauré must have thrilled to hear her talk of all the great personalities she had known.

Viardot was an excellent pianist and fluent composer (drawing was another of her seemingly endless accomplishments), but her style and to an extent her taste in vocal music were those of the very Second Empire she politically detested (she added words to the Chopin mazurkas, arranging them in almost comical versions for voice and piano, albeit with the composer's permission). Like Meyerbeer and Liszt, she composed songs in both French and German; her lieder, including charming settings of Mörike, took Mendelssohn and Schumann as their models; her *mélodies* looked to such composers as Gounod and Lalo for inspiration – she was a dab hand at the *pièce caractéristique*. Viardot was a forceful personality, not unaware of the latest cultural currents, but she could scarcely guess the direction soon to be taken in the *mélodie* by a whole range of younger composers; what could she have been expected to make of Duparc, for instance, who rated Wagner, not Brahms, as the most exciting contemporary composer? Viardot's thoughts on Fauré's *La Bonne chanson* or *La Chanson d'Ève* – both works that were composed within her long lifetime – would be even more difficult to imagine.

At more or less the same time as he was drawn into the Viardot circle, Fauré became friendly with Camille Clerc, a well-to-do engineer ('ingénieur des Ponts-et-Chaussées') from Le Havre, and his wife Marie (née Depret). These sensitive music lovers and their children became a second family for the composer. The Clercs' Paris home, 62 rue de Monceau, was always full of artists, a salon that was not exactly 'Celebrity Hall' like Viardot's, but profoundly musical nevertheless. During the summers the Clercs took their holidays in Normandy, where they had a house in Sainte-Adresse, a fashionable resort at the time not far from Le Havre – a town that will always be associated with the paintings of Monet, who was born nearby.

With five sons in the family, it is hardly surprising that there was no room to lodge Fauré at the Clercs' summer home; instead he took a room in a neighbouring restaurant and was able to work hard on major pieces under the eye of the motherly Marie. Later in the 1870s the Clercs took their summer holidays at Villerville. The social life on the Normandy coast was lively, and Fauré made a number of important contacts. It was there, for example, that he first met a rich young American, Winnaretta Singer, later Princesse de Polignac, only fifteen years old at the time and a guest at nearby Blosseville. It would be some years before she began to play an important role in the composer's life. In the meantime, Marie Clerc had realised that Fauré was supremely gifted, but also that there was an apathetic streak in his nature. As Saint-Saëns had noted, he lacked ambition. He needed to be galvanised by admonishments and support, specifically from a woman, and Marie Clerc was one of the people in Fauré's life who gladly took on that duty.

The famous and successful Violin Sonata in A major was dedicated to Paul Viardot, as we have noted, but it had owed its existence to the Clercs' hospitality. When no French publisher would touch the new work (it was considered far too demanding) Camille, a sophisticated businessman, negotiated with the German firm of Breitkopf & Härtel. After the sonata was published, Fauré had to forgo any remuneration in exchange for the privilege of beginning his career with such a famous house. At the time this seemed a reasonable *quid pro quo*. Emmanuel Chabrier wrote to Clerc when he needed to find volumes of Schumann songs – how better to find them than at Breitkopf & Härtel, a firm with whom Camille Clerc was in contact? Among the small *cardre* of composers news travelled fast. Fauré's Piano Quartet, Op. 15, also owed its existence to Normandy, and to the sustained periods of concentration of which the composer was capable when under Marie's affectionate supervision.

In 1874 Fauré had acquired an important though fairly tedious job as choirmaster and second organist (*maître de chapelle*) at the Madeleine; Saint-Saëns had abandoned his position there because he was perpetually touring as a pianist. The older composer once remarked, rather pointedly, that

Fauré could be a fine pianist and organist *whenever he wanted to be*. This appointment gave Fauré a certain amount of financial security, but it was desperately time-consuming (it took away almost all his mornings) and the church job was never well enough paid to enable the composer to abandon the peripatetic teaching that he found so burdensome.

Pauline Viardot provided a more glamorous kind of energy in Fauré's life than Marie Clerc. Like most celebrity performers she had travelled incessantly, and it is little wonder that when under her spell Fauré wrote some of his more worldly *mélodies*. Viardot was an international musician in the same way as Meyerbeer and Offenbach – in connection with whom one is tempted to think of Andrew Lloyd Webber today, with his works running in every capital city of Europe in different productions and languages. It was also almost inevitable that Fauré would eventually tire of this milieu inspired by the glories of a multicultural past that took little account of the oncoming tides of musical nationalism.

One cannot blame a great opera singer for believing that every young composer should aspire to the theatre and its *bel canto* requirements and for encouraging her young friend accordingly. Under Pauline's watchful eye Fauré flirted unsuccessfully with potential librettists time and again (above all with the famous Louis Gallet until as late as 1880), but it would be forty years before he felt ready to compose an opera, and he met this challenge very much in his own way.

In the meantime the songs he composed during this period seem somewhat commercial, as if designed for sophisticated professionals who would take them up and sing them without further ado. The Viardot household was attuned to the market forces of the time – exemplified by the rise of that most successful of younger composers, Fauré's *bête noire* Jules Massenet. It is likely that Fauré was encouraged to adopt something of Massenet's exquisitely conciliatory manner when it came to providing famous opera singers with music for salon performance. As a result, the poems the chose to set at this time, some of them almost comically downmarket from Hugo and Baudelaire, seem curiously unambitious from the literary point of view. Louis Pomey was a painter as well as an unpublished and not very distinguished wordsmith, but he had the rather dubious distinction of having provided Pauline Viardot with the words for all her vocal arrangements of the Chopin mazurkas – transcriptions, according to Saint-Saëns, where the singer's dramatic and chesty singing voice made Chopin's music appear 'the banter of a giant'. He had also provided fifty translations from the German for Viardot-Garcia's edition of fifty Schubert songs published by Hamelle, where, for example, Schubert's duet setting of Goethe's 'Nur wer die Sehnsucht kennt / Weiss was ich leide' ('Mignon et le Harpiste') is rendered as 'L'âme saignant d'amour / Seule peut dire / Quel long martyre j'endure nuit et jour' with a very awkward four-note melisma on the 'me' of 'âme'. Pomey's connection to Viardot as a kind of house poet (he was also a painter) must have seemed recommendation enough for Fauré to set his 'Aubade' to music, even if the composer did not spot in proof that the song's publishers had misspelled his name as Pommey.

(16) *Aubade* (Aubade)[3]

*c.*1873, Op. 6 No. 1, 'À Madame Amélie Duez', F major, 12/8, *Allegretto moderato quasi andante*

L'oiseau dans le buisson	*The bird in the thicket*
A salué l'aurore,	*Has greeted the dawn,*
Et d'un pâle rayon	*And the horizon is tinged*
L'horizon se colore,	*With a pale ray –*

Voici le frais matin!	*A fresh morning has broken!*
Pour voir les fleurs à la lumière,	*To see the flowers all around*
S'ouvrir de toute part,	*Opening to the light,*
Entr'ouvre ta paupière,	*Open your eyes a little,*
Ô vierge au doux regard!	*O maiden with the gentle look.*
La voix de ton amant	*Your lover's voice*
A dissipé ton rêve;	*Has dispersed your dream;*
Je vois ton rideau blanc	*I see your white veil*
Qui tremble et se soulève,	*Tremble and lift –*
D'amour signal charmant!	*That charming sign of love!*
Descends sur ce tapis de mousse,	*Come down to this mossy carpet,*
La brise est tiède encor,	*The breeze is still balmy*
Et la lumière est douce,	*And the light is soft,*
Accours, ô mon trésor!	*Make haste, my precious love!*

Louis Pomey (1831–1891)

This is the second of several songs apostrophising the dawn in Fauré's output (the first was *L'Aurore* (Hugo), and the others are the infinitely greater *Aurore*, *Paradis* and *L'Aube blanche*, the last two from the cycle *La Chanson d'Ève*). There are certain poets who can seldom resist describing the flowers that are first to experience the day's awakening, and Fauré was always strongly attracted to garden imagery – a part of him forever remained the delighted child who had ruled over the flowery domain of the convent at Montgauzy. The minimalist accompaniment of the song is fashioned in mezzo-staccato triplets and evokes pinpricks of light; as the strophe progresses, the distant brilliance of the morning star gradually gives way to legato phrasing and warmer sunlight. All this is in Fauré's best Italian style – similar to the two Romain Bussine settings – where the simplest of accompaniments supports a melodic curve that is independently eloquent. The seemingly static anonymity of such piano writing is graced with an ardent vocal serenade that evokes Massenet – compare this song with that composer's duet *Rêvons, c'est l'heure* of 1872, the first of all Verlaine settings by a major composer, with its similar quavers in pulsating duplets, or some of the better *canzone* of Tosti.

Fauré had the common touch when he chose to use it. If he had pushed himself into writing more songs of this kind, he might have made himself as rich as some of his more canny colleagues. And yet even this instantly accessible music remains typical of Fauré in his distinctive use of harmony: it is extraordinary how daring he is in returning to, and recovering, the tonic, F major, when he has strayed a long distance away from the home key. In these cadences the dominant is replaced by the third degree of the scale. An unusual touch of this kind stealthily rescues the song from being commonplace.

The song's dedicatee, Amélie Duez, was the wife of the painter Ernst-Ange Duez. She was a gifted amateur singer who gave the impromptu first performances of the immortal Fauré songs *Mandoline* and *En sourdine* in Venice soon after they were composed in that city in 1891 (see Chapter 8).

(17) *Tristesse* (Sadness)[4]

*c.*1873, Op 6, No. 2, 'À Mme Edouard Lalo', first Hamelle collection p. 56, C minor, 6/8, *Andante*

Avril est de retour.	*April has returned.*
La première des roses,	*The first of the roses*
De ses lèvres mi-closes,	*From half-open lips,*
Rit au premier beau jour;	*Smiles at the first fine day;*
La terre bienheureuse	*The happy earth*
S'ouvre et s'épanouit;	*Opens and blooms:*
Tout aime, tout jouit.	*All is love and ecstasy.*
Hélas! j'ai dans le cœur une tristesse affreuse.	*Alas! a dreadful sadness afflicts my heart.*
Les buveurs en gaîté,	*The merry drinkers*
Dans leurs chansons vermeilles,	*With their crimson songs*
Célèbrent sous les treilles	*Drink, beneath trellises,*
Le vin et la beauté;	*To wine and beauty;*
La musique joyeuse,	*The joyous music*
Avec leur rire clair,	*With their bright laughter,*
S'éparpille dans l'air.	*Scatters in the air.*
Hélas! j'ai dans le cœur une tristesse affreuse.	*Alas! a dreadful sadness afflicts my heart.*
En déshabillé blanc,	*In scanty white dresses*
Les jeunes demoiselles	*Young girls*
S'en vont sous les tonnelles,	*Pass beneath the arbours,*
Au bras de leur galants;	*On their lovers' arms;*
La lune langoureuse	*The languishing moon*
Argente leurs baisers	*Silvers their long*
Longuement appuyés.	*Insistent kisses.*
Hélas! j'ai dans le cœur une tristesse affreuse.	*Alas! a dreadful sadness afflicts my heart.*
Moi, je n'aime plus rien,	*But I love nothing any more,*
Ni l'homme, ni la femme,	*Neither man nor woman,*
Ni mon corps, ni mon âme,	*Neither my body nor my soul,*
Pas même mon vieux chien.	*Nor even my old dog;*
Allez dire qu'on creuse,	*Send for them to dig*
Sous le pâle gazon,	*Beneath the pallid turf*
Une fosse sans nom.	*A nameless grave.*
Hélas! j'ai dans le cœur une tristesse affreuse.	*Alas! a dreadful sadness afflicts my heart.*

Théophile Gautier (1811–1872)

This 6/8 rhythm sounds like a waltz to the innocent ear, although on paper it is nothing of the kind. There is a catchiness to this music and a very Parisian atmosphere, yet it is reviled by many of the commentators, and Noske regards it as foursquare – something that perhaps tells us more about the performances he heard than about the song itself. Of all Fauré's *mélodies* it is this and *Dans les ruines*

Title-page of the first edition of Tristesse, *published by Choudens*

d'une abbaye that most suggest popular song. There is a touch of Poulencian cross-over here (one thinks of that composer's Apollinaire setting *La Grenouillère* with its nostalgia for the Paris of Maupassant and Renoir), but *Tristesse* was written some twenty, or even thirty, years too early for any link with accordion-accompanied cabaret to be intentional. And yet, the refrain which ends each strophe ('Hélas! j'ai dans le coeur une tristesse affreuse') would not sound out of place sung by Edith Piaf, the guttural 'r' in 'affreuse' rolled deep in the throat. Nectoux refers to the 'painful melodrama' of this phrase, and it is true that music like this, relentlessly accented by the downbeats of the accompaniment, falls short of the Fauréan ideal of understatement and restraint. The poem's literary provenance is curiously exalted – Gautier's seminal *La Comédie de la mort* (1838), also the source of Berlioz's *Les Nuits d'été*.

For this passing parade of lovers and drinkers the composer treats the prosody with a casualness that one might term Parisian: one need go no further than the very first word ('Avril') to encounter the musical emphasis on the first, rather than the second, syllable. This displacement suggests a Parisian accent incorporating the swagger of a nonchalant *boulevardier* (Bernac pointed this out in Poulenc's *Montparnasse*, another setting of Apollinaire, where there is a slight emphasis on the first syllable of '*Paris*'). In Fauré's *Tristesse* this cabaret effect is reinforced by references to 'chansons vermeilles', and girls in 'déshabillé blanc'.

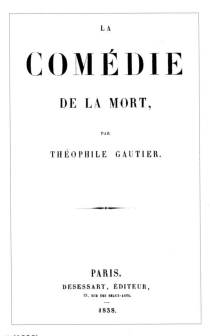

Frontispiece and title-page from the first edition of Gautier's La Comédie de la mort *(1838)*

Such earthy imagery is unusual in Fauré's songs, and his attraction to lyrics of this kind was to be short-lived. Everyday banalities are permitted here that would have been ruthlessly shunned by the older composer: the appearance of the word 'chien' in a *mélodie* seems rather curious, although, as we have seen, there is a guard dog in the Hugo setting *L'Absent*. The 'vieux chien' is an important feature of the engraving on the cover of the first edition pictured above. The dispirited lover is depicted in the dress of the early nineteenth century, and the publisher has added a spurious exclamation mark to the poem's title, as if believing that this touch of melodrama would shift more copies of a song which he clearly hoped would have commercial possibilities.

(18) *Barcarolle* (*Barcarolle*)[5]
19 October 1873, Op. 7 No. 3, 'À Madame Pauline Viardot', second Hamelle collection p. 82, G minor, 6/8, *Andante con moto*

Gondolier du Rialto,   *Gondolier of the Rialto,*
Mon château   *My castle*
   C'est la lagune,   *is the lagoon,*
Mon jardin c'est le Lido,   *My garden is the Lido,*
Mon rideau,   *My curtain,*
   Le clair de lune.   *the moonlight.*

Gondolier du Grand Canal,   *Gondolier of the Grand Canal,*
Pour fanal   *My beacon*
   J'ai la croisée   *Is the casement,*
Où s'allument tous les soirs   *Where every night*
Tes yeux noirs,   *Your dark eyes shine anew,*
   Mon épousée!   *My bride!*

Ma gondole est aux heureux: *My gondola is for the happy:*
Deux à deux   *I take them out*
   Je les promène,   *Two by two,*
Et les vents légers et frais   *And the fresh, light breezes*
Sont discrets   *Are discreet*
   Sur mon domaine.   *In my domain.*

J'ai passé dans les amours   *I have spent more days*
Plus de jours   *And intoxicated nights*
   Et de nuits folles,   *In loving,*
Que Venise n'a d'îlots,   *Than Venice has islands,*
Que ses flots   *Than its waves*
   N'ont de gondoles.   *Have gondolas.*

[As his fifth strophe Monnier repeats the first, not set by Fauré]

Marc Monnier (1829–1885)

92

Marc Monnier

Some eighteen years before his first visit to Venice in 1891 and eight years before composing his First Barcarolle for solo piano, Fauré here evokes the haunting bittersweet mood of 'Serenissima', with its gondolier calls resounding across the lagoons. The song's protagonist is hardly a cheery character, and one is reminded of Aschenbach's encounter with a surly gondolier in the opening pages of Thomas Mann's *Death in Venice*. There was an established tradition of Venetian stylisation, some of it very distinguished: the vocal *bel canto* seems inspired by the piano-writing in Chopin's great Barcarolle for piano Op. 60 (and perhaps this is a hidden tribute to Pauline Viardot's association with that composer). The singer's line, ornamented with Italianate *acciaccature*, is launched high in the stave and topples down in conjunct harmonic steps. This procedure is a feature of Fauré's songs of the early period, and Nectoux has identified it as a 'Viardot motif'.[6] In other songs this is usually launched by a leap of an octave or a fifth or sixth in the vocal line; in this case this leap is implied when the singer begins an octave higher than the top note of the dotted minim chords of the piano's introduction.

The accompaniment is merely an echo of this quasi-improvised vocal flowering; the piano, bereft of any independent motif, here temporarily withdraws as a driving force behind the singer's line. The anonymity of its accompanying role seems tailored to the musical style of the dedicatee, Madame Viardot, whose piano-writing in her own songs was never allowed to upstage the voice. The music is evocative in a way that suggests an aria in an operetta, or film music. The *Chanson* from Haraoucourt's *Shylock*, a re-working of Shakespeare's *Merchant of Venice*, is a younger relative of this *Barcarolle*.

The inclusion of the song in Fauré's second *recueil,* rather than the first, where it truly belongs, needs some explanation. In 1908 the publisher Hamelle wished to equalise the number of songs in each of the *mélodie* collections to a round figure of twenty. The results of this redistribution made nonsense of chronology: this song from 1873 appears to post-date the masterpiece *Clair de lune* from 1887. Fauré pleaded with him not to issue the songs in this way, but to no avail – by then the composer had defected to Henri Heugel, and 'Père' Hamelle (who, according to Marguerite Long, had never understood Fauré's greatness until he had heard her perform the piano pieces) could afford to disregard the composer's wishes entirely.

In the 1872 edition of *Poésies* by Monnier (where his name is hyphenated as Marc-Monnier by the publisher, Lemerre) we learn that his 'Barcarolle' had been set to music by his countryman Franz Gratz (or, according to the Fétis *Biographie*, Grast), a Swiss composer and music theorist resident in Paris who died in 1871. Monnier was born in Florence, and his knowledge of sixteenth- and seventeenth-century poetry was admired in his lifetime. Much of his own poetry was of Italian inspiration (as in the two poems Fauré set to music), but it had a serious side that championed the liberation of Italy from Austrian rule (as was the case with Musset's poem 'Venise', a lyric seized on by Gounod). From 1871 Monnier occupied a chair of comparative literature at Geneva University, and his translation of Goethe's *Faust* was once famous. The poet had the distinction of being a proscribed author under Napoleon III alongside Hugo: his most famous work, *Comédies de mari-onettes* (1871), is a political satire with imagined conversations between the potentates of Europe, prophetic of Thomas Hardy's *The Dynasts*. Monnier's high standing in the history of Swiss literature is scarcely reflected in the two settings made by Fauré of the poet's less challenging texts, but to regard him as a poet of no importance is clearly unfair. Monnier must have been an honoured guest in the Viardot home, where Fauré probably encountered him personally.

(19) *Puisqu'ici-bas toute âme* (*Since here on earth each soul*)[7]
*c.*1863–73, Op. 10 No. 1, 'À Mme Claudie Chamerot et Mlle Marianne Viardot', C major, 2/4,
Allegretto moderato

Puisqu'ici-bas toute âme	Since here on earth each soul
Donne à quelqu'un	Gives someone
Sa musique, sa flamme,	Its music, its ardour,
Ou son parfum;	Or its perfume;
Puisqu'ici toute chose	Since here all things
Donne toujours	Will always give
Son épine ou sa rose	Their thorns or roses
À ses amours;	To those they love;
Puisqu'avril donne aux chênes	Since April gives the oaks
Un bruit charmant;	A sound that charms,
Que la nuit donne aux peines	And night gives suffering
L'oubli dormant;	Drowsy oblivion;
Puisque, lorsqu'elle arrive	Since when they come
S'y reposer,	To settle there,
L'onde amère à la rive	The briny waves
Donne un baiser;	Give the shore a kiss;
Je te donne, à cette heure,	I give you, at this hour,
Penché sur toi,	Inclining over you,
La chose la meilleure	The finest things
Que j'aie en moi!	I have in me!
Reçois donc ma pensée,	Accept, then, my thoughts,
Triste d'ailleurs,	Sad though they be,
Qui, comme une rosée,	Which like drops of dew
T'arrive en pleurs!	Come to you as tears!
Reçois mes vœux sans nombre,	Accept my countless vows,
Ô mes amours!	O my loves!
Reçois la flamme ou l'ombre	Accept the flame and the shade
De tous mes jours!	Of all my days!
Mes transports pleins d'ivresses,	My frenzied rapture,
Purs de soupçons,	Devoid of all distrust,
Et toutes les caresses	And all the caresses
De mes chansons!	Of my songs!

Mon esprit qui sans voile	*My spirit that floats at random*
Vogue au hasard,	*Without a sail,*
Et qui n'a pour étoile	*And has no lodestar*
Que ton regard!	*But your gaze!*
Reçois, mon bien céleste,	*Take all my celestial qualities,*
Ô ma beauté,	*O my beauty,*
Mon cœur, dont rien ne reste,	*My heart, of which nothing remains,*
L'amour ôté!	*When there's no love!*

Victor Hugo (1802–1885)

This duet derives from a solo setting of the same words (composed at the École Niedermeyer in 1864) that was almost certainly destroyed after the creation of its adapted reincarnation. The poem was written in 1836 in the form of a letter to Juliette Drouet. Of Hugo's twelve strophes Fauré sets ten, omitting the fourth (where a thirsty bird profits from the dawn dew) and the eleventh referring to the poet's weeping muse. Niedermeyer in his song of 1862 had also omitted strophe 4 while retaining strophe 9 – an indication perhaps of both Fauré's willingness to learn from his elders and his own independent spirit. This ostensibly new work was specially prepared for the Viardot sisters, Claudie and Marianne; from the dedications of many works of this period we gather that a large number of duets by French composers owed their existence to this partnership, a Parisian Fiordiligi and Dorabella. The intensity of the words (phrases like 'mes transports pleins d'ivresses') better matches what we know of the composer's turbulent feelings for Marianne better than it does Fauré's emollient music. The melody is ingratiating and anxious to please rather than passionate – a similar musical atmosphere to that created by a song to the same text, *Rêverie*, one of Reynaldo Hahn's earliest and most successful songs.

This is a hybrid creation where the spontaneity of the teenager composer's original sketches for a solo song is checked and revised by the suave manners and more mature mastery of the twenty-eight-year-old. The music comes across like an exquisitely delivered calling-card, a veritable *compliment galant*. The piano writing is typical of the young master's flawless weave – a silken carpet of sound. Semiquaver arpeggios in both hands waft up and down the keyboard. These seem effortless except for the pianist who has to play them; as always with Fauré, this music contains countless harmonic shifts to catch out the unwary performer. This composer can always take us anywhere he likes, and on any degree of the scale; here he does just that.

The mezzo-soprano makes her entrance after a nine-bar solo for the soprano. When the two voices first coalesce, it is in a falling line of seductive thirds (at 'Puisque, lorsqu'elle arrive / S'y reposer'). This is another example of the 'Viardot motif' in Fauré's music – 'the formula of a rising sixth or octave followed by a descent through conjunct steps'.[8] There is a masterly interplay between the voices – one can hear the fruits of years of assiduous study of fugue and counterpoint. But high learning is disguised by a sweetness of diction and gentleness of intent. Even when in love, perhaps especially when in love, Fauré is a master of self-effacement.

(20) *Tarentelle* (*Tarantella*)[9]
1873, Op. 10 No. 2, 'À Mme Claudie Chamerot et Mlle Marianne Viardot', Choudens, 1879,
F minor, 6/8

Aux cieux la lune monte et luit.
Il fait grand jour en plein minuit.
Viens avec moi, me disait-elle,
Viens sur le sable grésillant
Où saute et glisse en frétillant
      La tarentelle.

The moon rises bright in the sky.
Turning midnight into day.
Come with me, she said,
Come to the whirling sands
And the leaping, wriggling and gliding
      Tarantella.

Sus, les danseurs! En voilà deux;
Foule sur l'eau, foule autour d'eux;
L'homme est bien fait, la fille est belle;
Mais gare à vous! Sans y penser,
C'est jeu d'amour que de danser
      La tarentelle.

Come, you dancers! Here's a pair;
Thronged around in the water;
The man is well-built, the girl beautiful;
But look out! Before you are aware,
You'll be playing with love if you dance
      The tarantella.

Doux est le bruit du tambourin!
Si j'étais fille de marin
Et toi pêcheur, me disait-elle,
Toutes les nuits joyeusement
Nous danserions en nous aimant
      La tarentelle.

Sweet is the sound of the drum!
If I were a sailor's daughter
And you a fisherman, she said,
Every night, full of joy,
We'd love each other and dance
      The tarantella.

Marc Monnier (1827–1885)

Faure's *Barcarolle* is to his *Tarentelle* as Liszt's languid *Venezia* is to that virtuoso's energetic *Napoli* (in the *Années de pèlerinage* for piano), or as Mendelssohn's brooding *Gondellied* to the joyful *Saltarella* of his 'Italian' Symphony. These are different sides of the same coin as well as different sides of the Italian coast. This four-strophe poem (Fauré omits the third) has a sequel in Marc Monnier's *Poésies* that reveals the whole scene is set in Naples. We glimpse here the devilish side of Fauré, that ostensibly charming note-spinner, by whom solo pianists are so often challenged; there are many of his virtuoso piano pieces that make the hair stand on end, but fewer songs or song accompaniments. This duet, however, is first and foremost a comprehensive work-out for singers, a very demanding *moto perpetuo* with all the runs and melismas that mimic the hurdles of instrumental chamber music, and it is not easy for the pianist either. The menace of the minor-key tonality adds a glittering erotic undertone to the proceedings.

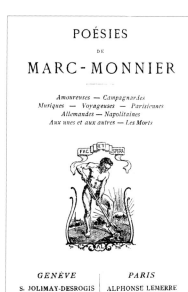

POÉSIES
DE
MARC-MONNIER

Amoureuses — Campagnardes
Musiques — Voyageuses — Parisiennes
Allemandes — Napolitaines
Aux unes et aux autres — Les Morts

GENÈVE   PARIS
S. JOLIMAY-DESROGIS   ALPHONSE LEMERRE
Rue du Rhône, 13   Passage Choiseul, 47

M.DCCC.LXXII.

Title-page of Poésies *by Marc Monnier (1872)*

Once again Fauré conceived the arrangement, if not the music, for Claudie and Marianne Viardot, and Naples seems an appropriately operatic setting for this Fiordiligi and Dorabella of the Third Republic. His being in love with Marianne at the time may account for the infinite trouble the composer seems to have taken to lavish truly sophisticated music on a bagatelle of a lyric, as well as his obvious delight in providing the musical prelude for what promises, on paper at least, to become a Neapolitan debauch – *Tarantelle* is as much of an erotic song as the times allowed. The first performance of both the duets of Op. 10 was given at a concert of the Société Nationale de la Musique (SNM) on 10 April 1875. With the help of Messager, Fauré orchestrated this duet later in the same year.

(21) *Ici-bas!* (*In this world!*)[10]

1874?, Op. 8 No. 3, 'À Madame Georges Lecoq, née Mac-Brid', F♯ minor, 2/4, *Andantino*

Ici-bas tous les lilas meurent,	*In this world every lily withers,*
Tous les chants des oiseaux sont courts;	*The songs of every bird are brief;*
Je rêve aux étés qui demeurent	*I dream of summers that will last*
Toujours …	*Ever more …*
Ici-bas les lèvres effleurent	*In this world lips touch but lightly,*
Sans rien laisser de leur velours;	*No taste of velvet sweetness remains;*
Je rêve aux baisers qui demeurent	*I dream of kisses that will last*
Toujours …	*Ever more …*
Ici-bas, tous les hommes pleurent	*In this world every man mourns*
Leurs amitiés ou leurs amours;	*His lost friendship or his lost love;*
Je rêve aux couples qui demeurent	*I dream of fond lovers abiding*
Toujours …	*Ever more …*

René François Armand Prudhomme, 'Sully Prudhomme' (1839–1907)

At this time the public could not get enough of the songs of Massenet. His 'affected listlessness' (as Fritz Noske puts it) is here briefly emulated by Fauré, as it was to be artfully incorporated into Debussy's early style (above all in the songs from the 1880s). A languid little vocal melody, almost *parlando*, is borne along by gently undulating semiquavers; these, in true Massenet fashion, look back to Schumann's *Dichterliebe*. The first two strophes are identical, but the vocal line of the third is tinged by the major key and becomes gradually animated with throbbing syncopations in the bass. There is a *forte* climax on the third page (more suited to the musical structure than to the words) where the singer's desperation and her top register are simultaneously revealed. A decrescendo and coda return us to gentle *ennui*.

Years later, Reynaldo Hahn, pupil of Massenet, excelled in songs like this, where a change in the final strophe (an unexpectedly floated high note, as in *L'Heure exquise*, or a rueful change of harmony as in *L'Infidélité*) crowns an expanse of murmured *parlando* inactivity with a fermata of ravishing, if self-conscious pathos. Such an over-exquisite mannerism, *fin-de-siècle* before its time, was inimical to Fauré; but he allowed himself temporarily to toy with its fashionable languidity. It is possible that the choice of poem was dictated by an optimistic idealism on the composer's part concerning his love for Marianne Viardot. If he had imagined that his relationship to her would last for ever, and that the two of them would be destined to be one of those couples who 'demeurent / Toujours', he was to be disabused by the events of 1877.

      ∾   ∾   ∾   ∾

Sully Prudhomme (the pen-name of René François Armand Prudhomme), a significant contributor to *Le Parnasse contemporain*, was a somewhat ponderous poet whose usually lightweight contributions to the song repertoire are often surprisingly successful; outside this realm the rest of his oeuvre is deeply influenced by philosophical considerations. It has been said of him that he was capable of 'versifying a body of thought that would have claimed attention even in prose', and he has been praised by the same critic for work that is 'lucid, precise, orderly and original'.[11] Unfortunately solid doctrine and exquisite poetic forms seem ill-matched, and this disparity is the flaw in much of Sully Prudhomme's work. Of the three Fauré settings of this poet, two of them – *Au bord de l'eau* (see p. 99) and *Les Berceaux* (see p. 130) – are acknowledged masterpieces. *Ici-bas* is the most slender and least performed of the three Sully Prudhomme poems that Fauré set to music. The text is typical of the lyrical, slightly effusive nature of the poet's earlier work and appeared in the *Stances et poëmes* published in 1865. Sully Prudhomme was popular and esteemed in his time (his most anthologised poem is 'Le Vase brisé', set by César Franck). In Jules Lemaître's words he is the 'least sensuous and the most precise of poets', someone who 'thinks and defines instead of feeling and singing'.[12] In his later work, avoided by composers, Sully Prudhomme attempted to turn the theory of science and philosophy into epic verse. This won him a place in the Académie Française in 1881 and the Nobel Prize for literature in 1901 (Paul Heyse, the German poet, was honoured in similar fashion in 1914). Both these writers figure honourably in the history of song, although the Nobel judges now seem to have over-estimated the literary importance of two rather middle-ranking figures.

Ici-bas

Ici-bas tous les lilas meurent,
Tous les chants des oiseaux sont courts,
Je rêve aux étés qui demeurent
Toujours ...

Ici-bas les lèvres effleurent
Sans rien laisser de leur velours,
Je rêve aux baisers qui demeurent
Toujours ...

Ici-bas tous les hommes pleurent
Leurs amitiés ou leurs amours;
Je rêve aux couples qui demeurent
Toujours ...

Sully Prudhomme

Autograph of Ici-bas! *The poet himself did not add an exclamation mark to the title, but Fauré's publisher did!*

(22) *Au bord de l'eau* (*At the water's edge*)[13]

August 1875, Op. 8 No. 1, 'À Madame Claudie Chamerot', first Hamelle collection p. 78, C♯ minor, 6/8, *Andante quasi allegretto*

S'asseoir tous deux au bord du flot qui passe, [d'un]	To sit together on the bank of a flowing stream,
Le voir passer;	To watch it flow;
Tous deux, s'il glisse un nuage en l'espace,	Together, if a cloud glides by,
Le voir glisser;	To watch it glide;
À l'horizon, s'il fume un toit de chaume,	On the horizon, if smoke rises from thatch,
Le voir fumer;	To watch it rise;
Aux alentours si quelque fleur embaume,	If nearby a flower smells sweet,
S'en embaumer;	To savour its sweetness;
Entendre au pied du saule où l'eau murmure	To listen at the foot of the willow, where water murmurs,
L'eau murmurer;	To the murmuring water;
Ne pas sentir, tant que ce rêve dure,	Not to feel, while this dream passes,
Le temps durer;	The passing of time;
Mais n'apportant de passion profonde	But feeling no deep passion,
Qu'à s'adorer,	Except to adore each other,
Sans nul souci des querelles du monde,	With no cares for the quarrels of the world,
Les ignorer;	To know nothing of them;
Et seuls, tous deux devant tout ce qui lasse,	And alone together, seeing all that tires,
Sans se lasser,	Not to tire of each other,
Sentir l'amour, devant tout ce qui passe,	To feel that love, in the face of all that passes,
Ne point passer!	Shall never pass!

Sully Prudhomme (1839–1907)

The poem was discovered by the composer in a newspaper or journal, and he immediately set it – a wise choice, because Fauré was now beginning to be more consistent in selecting texts suitable for his own unique musical purposes. The lyric subsequently appeared in Sully Prudhomme's 1875 collection entitled *Les Vaines tendresses*. The musical result is quintessential Fauré, attractive to those who do not admire the later songs of the composer, and equally attractive to those who do. This is music of gentle drift – the nonchalant flowing of water is seemingly uneventful, but it invisibly marks the melancholy passing of time. Each seductively inconsequential triplet gliding between voice and finger seems to prolong a summer idyll at the same time as effacing it. Fauré was already thirty when he wrote this, so it is not the work of a teenager or *Wunderkind*. It takes a certain maturity to be aware of water passing under the bridge, but one must be a master to comment on it in a musical language that conveys this degree of philosophical calm.

The poet's contention that his affections will uniquely survive time's passing seems quietly refuted by the flow of Fauré's music, graceful and curvaceous phrases that are tinged with an almost Schubertian air of resignation and acceptance. As in Schubert's *Frühlingsglaube*, where an optimistic text is clothed in music that conveys, almost despite itself, melancholy and pathos, Fauré allows his music wordlessly to contradict the poem's verbal message. This immeasurably deepens the impact of the song by creating a poignant gap between a hopeful fantasy, where love lasts for ever, and painful

reality, where every relationship must end, some sooner than later. Behind the serenity of this music lies the awful inevitability of 'tout passe, tout casse'.[14]

As in several other Fauré songs of this period, the vocal line launches itself with what Nectoux identifies as the 'Viardot motif', an upward leap followed by a spiralling descent of ingratiating melody, here rich in harmonic implications – the use of consecutive sevenths looks forward to later works. Fauré then interleaves this principal idea with two ascending themes that make the subsequent falling phrases ever more evocative of watery ebb and flow. It is a sign of the composer's skill that the song appears the most natural commentary on nature, that all these musical means have been conjured with what seems like the minimum of effort. He also demonstrates how he can create a smoother vocal line by slightly altering the poet's text: thus Sully Prudhomme's opening line 'au bord *d'un* flot qui passe' is modified to 'au bord *du* flot qui passe'. A comparison of these two versions confirms that the composer has indeed found a succession of vowels that are smoother for the singer; there is less need to alter the position of the mouth and lips than in the poet's original. Fauré's treatment of a poem where the alternating lines have ten and four syllables also shows considerable skill. When hearing the song we are not aware of a change of metre: any inequalities are skilfully disguised by melisma and the use of piano interludes. The song is dedicated to the woman who was almost to become Fauré's sister-in-law, Claudie Viardot, daughter of Pauline and sister of Marianne, under her married name.

The subtle growth in Fauré's stature represented by this song was well understood by the composer's friend Henri Duparc. For that creator of *mélodies*, *Au bord de l'eau* seemed so completely to encapsulate Fauré's genius for *mélodie* that we find Duparc addressing his colleague in a letter of March 1883 as 'My dear, old "au bord de l'eau"'.[15]

(23) *Après un rêve* (After a dream)[16]

1877, Op. 7 No. 1, 'À Mme Marguerite Baugnies' [in later editions 'À Mme de Saint-Marceaux'], first Hamelle collection p. 67, C minor, 3/4, *Andantino*

Dans un sommeil que charmait ton image	*In sleep made sweet by a vision of you*
Je rêvais le bonheur, ardent mirage,	*I dreamed of happiness, fervent illusion,*
Tes yeux étaient plus doux, ta voix pure et sonore,	*Your eyes were softer, your voice pure and ringing,*
Tu rayonnais comme un ciel éclairé par l'aurore;	*You shone like a sky that was lit by the dawn;*
Tu m'appelais et je quittais la terre	*You called me and I departed the earth*
Pour m'enfuir avec toi vers la lumière,	*To flee with you toward the light,*
Les cieux pour nous entr'ouvraient leurs nues,	*The heavens parted their clouds for us,*
Splendeurs inconnues, lueurs divines entrevues.	*We glimpsed unknown splendours, celestial fires.*
Hélas! hélas, triste réveil des songes,	*Alas! alas, sad awakening from dreams,*
Je t'appelle, ô nuit, rends-moi tes mensonges;	*I summon you, O night, give me back your delusions;*
Reviens, reviens, radieuse,	*Return, return in radiance,*
Reviens, ô nuit mystérieuse!	*Return, O mysterious night!*

Romain Bussine (1830–1899), after an anonymous Tuscan poet

The inspiration for this song, and for *Sérénade toscane* (See Chapter 5), probably came from Pauline Viardot's own settings of Tuscan folk poetry. The translator of the Italian texts that inspired Fauré's songs was Romain Bussine, a baritone friend of the composer, and a singing teacher at the Paris Conservatoire from 1872. We know that Bussine's more distinguished older brother, the operatic baritone Prosper-Alphonse Bussine (1821–1881), was a pupil of Manuel Garcia, Pauline Viardot's father; Romain Bussine also taught the Garcia method of singing at the Conservatoire. Bussine was a friend of the Clercs, and of Saint-Saëns, as well as a member of the extended musical family of pupils that surrounded the Garcias. He was thus an important link between the two separate and contrasting worlds that constituted the composer's private life at the time. Fauré was very attached to this cheery collaborator, who was neither quite a poet in his own right nor quite a librettist: he refers to him on more than one occasion in the letters as 'good old Bussine' or 'dear old Bussine'. In these poems Bussine is more than a mere translator – he has written free French paraphrases of the Italian that are not just dutiful renditions of the Tuscan originals.

One is tempted to wonder whether Fauré composed the Italian original of this song before the French words were appended. The original source of the poetry is the first book of Niccolò Tommaseo's *Canti popolari* (Venice, 1841), an anthology devoted in part to the poems of Tuscany: No. XI of the section entitled *Fine della Serenata* begins thus, with the first quatrain of an eight-line poem:

Levati, sol, che la luna è levata;	*Rise, O sun, because the moon has risen;*
Leva dagli occhi miei tanto dormire.	*Remove from my eyes so much sleep.*
Il traditor del sonno m'ha ingannata;	*Sleep's traitor has betrayed me;*
Il meglio [bello] amante m'ha fatto sparire.	*He has whisked the best [handsome] lover away.*

Neither Italian nor French version is convincing in terms of prosody, probably as a result of the compromises involved in making a bilingual edition of the song. If Bussine made the French version *before* Fauré began to compose, and the composer conceived his music for the French text alone, it is a miracle that the Italian, included in the song's first edition, also fitted the music. (Fauré apparently had the opportunity to study rudimentary Italian at the École Niedermeyer.) In translating the lyric into French, Bussine seems to have relied more on Tommaseo's footnote to 'Levati, sol' than on the Tuscan poem itself. This reads: 'Par ch'ella vegga in sogno il suo vago: e, desta, si dolga dell'averlo perduto: o che, avutolo accanto, e addormentatasi, nol trovi più.'[17] The Italian poem 'Levati, sol, che la luna', quoted in part above, nevertheless remains as the song's underlay in print.

Fauré's famous cantilena is a cornucopia of melodic plenty: the music unfolds organically from beginning to end, each phrase leading ineluctably to the next, an endless flowering. This in turn is supported by seemingly inevitable harmonies where the imponderable appears easy and masks the greatest subtlety. Pau Casals's instantly famous version of the piece for cello and piano (1910) proved that a tune of this quality can effortlessly become a song without words. Even when performed without a text this melody has a kind of culminative power, indeed in this case it must be admitted that the text contributes little to the moving impact of the song. Marcel Proust was an avid admirer of some very difficult Fauré songs, but it was perhaps this absence of real literary motivation that made the famous writer say that *Après un rêve* was 'a real dud'.[18] It certainly gives us an insight into the writer's taste for vocal music; he seems to have been infinitely less susceptible to a good tune when it was unsupported by an interesting poem.

One is reminded that Schumann was one of Pauline Viardot's favourite composers, and that there is something here of the manner of *Ich grolle nicht* from *Dichterliebe*, with its impassioned melody accompanied by throbbing quavers. The Fauré song is different from the essentially strophic Schumann lied in that, despite its own strophic components, it never finds a moment of repose until its final destination at the closing cadence. This seamless unity, from the first note to the last, became an identifying mark of Fauré's songs, and of his music in general. That *Après un rêve* was meant to be performed in an ongoing, non-sentimental way was the subject, in later years, of a conversation between Claire Croiza and the composer (see Chapter 15).

In later years the publishing house of Hamelle lost no opportunity to capitalise on its copyright. *Après un rêve* was arranged for every conceivable instrumental combination: as late as 1954 *One Golden Dream* by 'Fauré and Lou Shuk' was dedicated to Frank Sinatra, a kind of pop variant of *Après un rêve* with the song's original identity revealed only in its new-fangled English title.

༄   ༄   ༄   ༄

The songs of the Viardot years are still very much of the 'first' period. The awkward experimentations of the Baudelaire settings are in the past, but the composer has not managed easily to recapture the inspiration of *Lydia*, where he was able to create something innovative that was entirely his own. Fauré was becoming more aware of what other ambitious song composers (like Massenet) were doing, and for the time being he seems to have been content that his vocal works were more or less shaped by the tastes of Madame Viardot's salon and her duetting daughters. There is a huge gap between the complexity and sophistication of the A major Violin Sonata (clearly designed to be an enduring musical statement) and the songs – these seem destined for more ephemeral consumption, even if, as it turns out, they have all survived in the repertoire. One has the impression that Madame Viardot was enthusiastic about songs that enabled her to take on something of a role and to interpret the music from an operatic viewpoint (as in the declamatory *Chanson du pêcheur*, dedicated to her) The dedication of the violin sonata to Paul Viardot possibly shows Fauré's desire to reconcile two musical worlds, an attempt at the unification of the musical values of the Clercs with those of the Viardots. The eventual failure of the engagement with Marianne meant at least that Fauré was not forced to live a life where he would have been regularly reminded of his failure to engage successfully with an operatic venture.

In this period his choices of poet seem haphazard and slightly wayward. The obliging Pomey and Monnier in untypically frivolous mood were perhaps the suggestions of Pauline Viardot, or at the very least these were collaborations designed to please her. Romain Bussine was also a member of this circle, and the Monnier lyrics set by Fauré would certainly have appealed to

Fauré in 1877 at the time of his engagement to Marianne Viardot.
© *Bibliothèque nationale de France*

his Italian sympathies. Gautier's *Tristesse* has some of the characteristics of an Italian *canzone*, as do *Barcarolle* and *Tarentelle*, with their stage-like Venetian and Neapolitan backdrops. They were all clearly meant to resonate well in a household where opera was considered the natural medium of the greatest musicians and where Italy was celebrated as the natural home of *bel canto*.

Après un rêve proved to be the kind of blockbuster success – in terms of its melody alone – that Fauré was able to pull out of his hat from time to time in his career. Even in an operatic context this tune would have been a hit – it has the memorability and inevitability of an aria by Gounod harmonised with a subtlety that equals that composer, and exceeds him in audacity.

The most individual *mélodie* of this period is also the quietest and least theatrical – *Au bord de l'eau*. In this Sully Prudhomme setting, Fauré conjured something of the intimacy and calm of *Lydia*. In every way – harmonically, melodically and rhythmically – this is the real Fauré: seemingly effortless, but completely inimitable.

ꙮ   ꙮ   ꙮ   ꙮ

It was one of the positive aspects of Fauré's link with the Viardot household that he found himself in the swim of artistic society where the *mondaine* world of music and musicians was a far cry from anything he had previously encountered. In later years this training would stand him in good stead when it came to surviving the jungle-like musical gatherings run by various formidable hostesses of high society. In 1902 Louis Aguettant would write of 'the Fauré of the salons, moving at his ease among the milling crowds, with a blissful smile on his face like some ancient Olympian deity who has had his fill of incense'.[19] Such seeming imperviousness was not easily learned or won; it required the acquisition of skin thick enough to survive the competitive mêlée of self-promotion, while remaining ever the guardian of fragile gifts vulnerable to the coarsening pursuit of worldly success. An enormous test of his resilience now unexpectedly faced the young composer.

The magnet that had drawn Fauré to the very heart of the Viardot circle was Pauline's daughter Marianne. After a protracted courtship the composer became engaged to her in July 1877. The young composer was deeply smitten by the young singer (a mezzo, a vocal tessitura that ever remained his favourite), and he was passionately impatient for their union and its consummation. Indeed, Fauré seems to have been beside himself with frustration. Marianne on the other hand was uncertain of her feelings for the young composer and vacillated, acquiescent one day, expressing doubt the next. She found Fauré amusing enough, and her powerful mother as well as Turgenev approved of the match, but from her side, and from the point of view of sheer physical chemistry she was not quite convinced that he was the right man for her.

Pauline Viardot in old age

She complained of his temper and the intensity of his moods, a darker side of Fauré more or less unfamiliar to us. Marianne had already asked Gounod to be her witness at the wedding that had been set for September 1877 when she postponed the event for the time being.

Fauré's almost frightening vehemence in reacting to her decision gave her an excuse to withdraw definitively from the engagement. According to the composer's son (writing about this episode after his father's death), he took a long time to get over this emotional setback. This sudden failure was certainly one of the low points of Fauré's life. It may be imagined that someone who had undergone an early separation from his mother would have reacted particularly badly to being sent away like this; he was almost certainly psychologically inclined to have taken this rejection to be a damning reflection of his worth, and to have believed that Marianne's verdict was somehow deserved. Singularly ill-equipped to face relegation of this kind from a woman whom he had allowed into his affections, Fauré reacted to the news with a desperation that was completely uncharacteristic of his normal ability to control or suppress emotion.

Marianne later married the minor composer and pianist Victor-Alphonse Duvernoy. Eventually cordial relations were re-established between the Viardot family and Fauré; the violinist Paul remained a friend, his mother continued to advise Fauré about his search for a libretto, and in later years the composer looked back on his Viardot period with affection and gratitude. His last contact with Pauline herself was in her eighty-sixth year, in a letter dated February 1907, three years before her death, and addressed to the recently appointed director of the Conservatoire. Fauré, though not yet a composer of an opera, was about to embark on just such a work. He had at last become a celebrity and achieved the fame that she had always hoped would be the destiny of her prospective son-in-law:

> My dear Fauré, I am asking you to take note of a charming pupil whom I had some years ago … I would be most grateful to you for anything you might be willing to do for this most interesting person. Thank you in advance, my dear, my dear Fauré, Please accept my best, rather elderly, wishes. Pauline Viardot[19]

1   This is how Viardot styles herself on the title-page of her edition of Schubert's *50 Mélodies*.

2   Carlo Caballero, *Fauré and French Musical Aesthetics* (Cambridge: Cambridge University Press, 2001), p. 74.

3   *Aubade*: Aspects of this song's interpretation are discussed in Chapter 16, p. 404.

4   *Tristesse*: Aspects of this song's interpretation are discussed in Chapter 16, p. 404.

5   *Barcarolle*: Aspects of this song's interpretation are discussed in Chapter 16, p. 404.

6   Jean-Michel Nectoux, *Gabriel Fauré: A Musical Life*, trans. Roger Nichols (Cambridge: Cambridge University Press, 1991), pp. 70–71.

7   *Puisqu'ici bas toute âme:* Aspects of this duet's interpretation are discussed in Chapter 16, p. 404.

8   Nectoux, *Gabriel Fauré: A Musical Life*, p. 70.

9   *Tarantelle*: Aspects of this duet's interpretation are discussed in Chapter 16, p. 405.

10 *Ici-bas!*: Aspects of this song's interpretation are discussed in Chapter 16, p. 405.

11 Francis Yvon Eccles, *A Century of French Poets* (London: Constable, 1909), 267.

12 Quoted in W.J. Robertson, *A Century of French Verse* (London: A.D. Innes & Co., 1895), p. 239.

13 *Au bord de l'eau*: Aspects of this song's interpretation are discussed in Chapter 16, p. 405.

14 A French proverb: 'everything passes, everything breaks'.

15 *Gabriel Fauré: A Life in Letters*, trans. and ed. Barrie Jones (London: B.T. Batsford, 1989), letter 31, p. 53.

16 *Après un rêve*: Aspects of this song's interpretation are discussed in Chapter 16, p. 405.

17 It seems that she sees her lover in a dream: and having awakened, is sad because she lost him; or that, after he was near her, and she fell asleep, she can no longer find him.

18 Marcel Proust, in a letter to Pierre Lavallée, Summer 1894. *Correspondance génerale de Marcel Proust*, Volume 4, Paris, 1933 p. 10. The original French describing *Après un rêve* is 'bien nul'.

19 Quoted in Nectoux, *Gabriel Fauré: A Musical Life*, p. 226.

Chapter Five

1878, a Transitional Year of Song

Paul de Choudens, Charles Grandmougin

Although one may say 'All's well that ends well' with regard to *l'affaire Viardot*, it would be a long time before Fauré could look back on the Marianne episode with any kind of equanimity. As an unintended compensation for this debacle, the publication by Choudens of *Lydia, Mai, Ici-bas!, Barcarolle* and *Au bord de l'eau* in December 1877 must have given his song-writing confidence a welcome boost (the first and second of these songs had been taken over from the original Hartmann edition of 1871). In the same month he travelled to Weimar in Germany to see the first performance of *Samson et Dalila* by Saint-Saëns. One senses that this was an essential recuperative break for the suffering young composer. He met Liszt on this occasion in Weimar; it is not certain whether the great pianist tried out Fauré's fiendishly difficult *Ballade* then (and found it too difficult to sight-read) or whether this celebrated incident occurred in 1882 when the two composers met again.

No creative artist lives in a vacuum, although Fauré sometimes gives the impression of having preferred to do so, particularly at times of emotional crisis. He was always so absorbed in his work, and the demands of making a living, that it might have been lost on him that his adopted city was more beautiful than it had ever been; the devastation of the Commune now appeared a distant nightmare and the correspondent of the *Musical Times* in London wrote a report in July 1878 which stated that Paris was the phoenix of cities: 'you may burn it, but a fairer Paris arises from the ashes'.[1]

With the exception of the two wars that inconvenienced and endangered opposite ends of his career (1870 and 1914–18), Fauré was spared, by twentieth-century standards at least, catastrophic upheaval. Having gone through the Franco-Prussian War and survived its aftermath he must have found the politics and current events of the following years rather dull. One wonders whether in 1878 the composer would have been disappointed on behalf of James McNeill Whistler, awarded deliberately risible damages of a farthing (the smallest coin of the realm) in a libel action against John Ruskin, who had disparaged the painter's *Nocturne in Black and Gold*. Whistler, already famous in Paris, had contributed memorably to the Paris Exhibition of 1878; his portrait of Robert de Montesquiou, Fauré's future patron, is among his finest works. The composer would have known next to nothing about musical life in England, and could hardly have guessed that he would become a regular visitor there in later years. Sir George Grove had just published a *Dictionary of Music and Musicians* in London that failed to mention Fauré; the composer eventually appeared in the appendix of the dictionary's fourth volume in 1899 (he had a short entry in the supplement to Fétis's

Biographie universelle des musiciens as early as 1881, where it is almost exclusively his early songs that are listed).

Dvořák, whose *Three Slavonic Dances* were composed in 1878, and Tchaikovsky, whose *Swan Lake* dates from the same year, were gradually becoming known to the French public at this time. Arthur Sullivan's *HMS Pinafore* was the smash hit of the London season, but of course it failed to register in Paris, and so did Thomas Hardy's novel *The Return of the Native*. Nevertheless this parallel productivity reminds us that the early days of the Third Republic coincided with an era of high Victorianism across the Channel, and France, before the loosening of stays in the late eighties and nineties of the century, had a quasi-Victorian side to its moral code, at least on the surface. The prevailing formality regarding courtship and marriage was at the heart of the series of bungled stand-offs that had led to the break with Marianne, not to mention the strangely uninvolved manner in which Fauré went about the selection of his wife in 1883 – almost as if he were playing a game of Russian roulette (see Chapter 6).

Release from the Viardots, even if it appeared like bitter exile at the time, had its compensations. The twelve months of 1878 were especially fecund for Fauréan song: if *Le Voyageur* and *Sérénade toscane* date from this year (which scholars agree is more than likely), there were eight *mélodies* written within a twelve-month period that also encompassed *O salutaris* for voice and organ and two works for violin – the *Berceuse*, Op. 16, and an unfinished concerto, Op. 14.

Eight songs hardly seem prolific in comparison with the numbers of vocal masterpieces composed by Franz Schubert in 1815, Robert Schumann in 1840 and Hugo Wolf in 1888. It so happens that Johannes Brahms also composed eight songs in 1878, but Wolf, ten years before the creative explosion of the *Mörike Lieder*, composed twenty-one songs in this year alone, many to texts by great writers such as Heine (an entire cycle by this poet), and some of them remarkably sophisticated for an eighteen-year-old. There was undoubtedly a difference between the song-composing cultures of the French and the Germans in the 1870s – the *mélodie* (as opposed to the outdated *romance*) was a stripling form in comparison with the lied. Apart from this the thirty-three-year-old Fauré was a late developer and far less driven than many of his contemporaries.

This composer refused to be hurried. He worked at his own pace, and in steadfast fashion, over many years (only Strauss among the German lieder composers can match Fauré for such productive and measured longevity). This was the beginning of a period when, more or less freed from the influence of the Viardot salon, the charming and elegant style of the *romances* and *mélodies* from the first *recueil* gradually gave way to the greater depth and intensity characteristic of the composer's second volume of songs. We shall later discuss the question of whether this is merely a perception encouraged by hindsight and the serendipity of publishing, or whether this really can be said to signify a new 'period' in the composer's career. It is a moot point however whether Fauré allowed his grief and disappointment in his failed engagement to influence his choice of song texts. That this is at least a possibility is reflected in the poems' world-weariness and unhappiness, depressive emotions that the composer had every reason to feel in his own right.

The early days of 1878 saw the composer appearing as a pianist at concerts of the Société Nationale de la Musique (SNM). On 5 January he took part in a performance of the Piano Quartet of Charles Lefebvre; the violinist on this occasion was Paul Viardot. The next day (6 January) *Après un rêve* was presented for approval to the committee of the SNM. The text of this song mentions an 'ardent mirage' and unfulfilled dreams of happiness, which must have seemed appropriate to Fauré's mood at the time. On 19 January at another SNM concert he accompanied a performance of the

Violin Sonata in A major, Op. 13 (the first performance had taken place in January 1877), as well as the first performance of the newly published *Au bord de l'eau*.

Apart from the composer's sometimes irksome duties as *maître de chapelle* at the Madeleine, such small-scale, yet significant, appearances as these were typical of the entire year's music-making. An exception was in June for a performance at the Universal Exhibition of Fauré's *Les Djinns* (to a poem of Victor Hugo) for four-part choir and orchestra, Op. 12. This involved 500 performers, a scale of event that he had not experienced before in his works, and one that no doubt awakened his interest in larger projects with massed forces. Following this première, the composer spent a quiet summer with his friends Camille and Marie Clerc in Villerville.

This was a period of emotional consolidation after the shock of the break-up with Marianne. On one hand he felt bruised by having loved and lost, but on the other he had gained his freedom. In terms of women the world was now his oyster. J.-M. Nectoux avers that the outcome of this crisis was to turn Fauré 'into something of a Don Juan'; it was necessary for him to find his own way as both musician and lover. He was in his early thirties and had stamped his own personality on works like the violin sonata, but the songs and duets of the Viardot years, with certain exceptions, seem uncharacteristically cosmopolitan. Now that he was no longer a prospective member of a multinational theatrical family he changed direction and realigned his gaze towards more local horizons. His inclination was now to stay within the literary borders of his own country. Nevertheless, Pauline Viardot's lingering influence (she continued to be his adviser in his search for a librettist) persuaded him to stray into quasi-Italian, and quasi-operatic, territory for one last time.

Viardot, the most famous Orfeo of the age (in Gluck's opera), would have thought nothing of singing the song of a gondolier *en travesti*, and we know she felt comfortable with the essentially male emotions of the Gautier setting dedicated to her, *Chanson du pêcheur*. It so happens that the performing of essentially male texts by female singers was very much part of the Fauré tradition: the soprano Emma Bardac sang the love poems written by Paul Verlaine for Mathilde Mauté in *La Bonne chanson*, and as late as 1908 the composer played *Sérénade toscane* with the American contralto Susan Metcalfe (later to marry the cellist Casals) at Buckingham Palace for Queen Alexandra and the Empress of Russia. The composer's lifelong preference for the female voice in almost all of his vocal music is discussed in Chapter 14 in relation to the single cycle for male voice, *L'Horizon chimérique*.

(24) *Sérénade toscane* (*Tuscan serenade*)[2]
1878?, Op. 3 No. 2, 'À Mme la Baronne de Montagnac, née de Rosalès', first Hamelle collection p. 22, B♭ minor, 9/8, *Andante con moto quasi Allegretto*

Ô toi que berce un rêve enchanteur,	*You whom a lovely dream lulls,*
Tu dors tranquille en ton lit solitaire,	*You sleep quietly in your lonely bed,*
Éveille-toi, regarde le chanteur,	*Awake, gaze at the singer,*
Esclave de tes yeux, dans la nuit claire!	*Enslaved by your eyes in the moonlit night!*
Éveille-toi mon âme, ma pensée,	*Awake, my soul, my thoughts,*
Entends ma voix par la brise emportée:	*Hear my voice borne on the breeze:*
Entends ma voix chanter!	*Hear my voice sing!*
Entends ma voix pleurer, dans la rosée!	*Hear my voice weep in the dew!*

Sous ta fenêtre en vain ma voix expire,	*Beneath your window my voice fades in vain,*
Et chaque nuit je redis mon martyre,	*And each night I tell my torment anew,*
Sans autre abri que la voûte étoilée,	*With no shelter but the starlit vault,*
Le vent brise ma voix et la nuit est glacée;	*The wind drowns my voice and the night is chill;*
Mon chant s'éteint en un accent suprême,	*My song dies on a final cadence,*
Ma lèvre tremble en murmurant je t'aime.	*My lips quiver as they murmur: I love you.*
Je ne peux plus chanter!	*I can no longer sing!*
Ah! daigne te montrer! daigne apparaitre!	*Ah! deign to show yourself! Deign to appear!*
Si j'étais sûr que tu ne veux paraître	*If I was sure you did not wish to appear,*
Je m'en irais, pour t'oublier, demander au sommeil	*I would go away to forget you, I would ask of sleep*
De me bercer jusqu'au matin vermeil,	*To cradle me until the rosy dawn,*
De me bercer jusqu'à ne plus t'aimer!	*To cradle me till I loved you no more!*

Romain Bussine (1830–1899), adapted from an anonymous Italian text

The French poem is a much closer rendition of the Tuscan original than *Après un rêve* composed in the previous year. Once again the source is the Tuscan section (*Canti toscani*) of Niccolò Tommaseo's *Canti popolari*. The underlay of the vocal line in *Sérénade toscane* fits both French and Italian texts (as is the case with *Après un rêve*). When she was living in Germany, Viardot may have discovered the Tommaseo collection by tracing it back as one of the sources of Paul Heyse's acclaimed German translations for his *Italienisches Liederbuch* (Berlin, 1860). Her own *Poèmes toscanes* songs were published in 1880. The immortal settings of these poems by Hugo Wolf were composed much later in Vienna (1891 and 1896).

Bussine cobbled together no fewer than three separate Italian *rispetti* from Tommaseo's collection in order to complete Fauré's serenade. For the song's first two verses the twelfth lyric (p. 124) in the *Altre serenate* section of *Canti toscani* begins:

O tu che dormi e riposata stai	*O lady, you who sleep and rest*
'N testo bel letto senza pensimento [pensamento],	*In this fine bed without a thought,*
Risvegliati un pochino, e sentirai	*Wake up just a little, and you shall hear*
Tuo servo che per te fa un gran lamento …	*Your servant who greatly grieves for you.*

The Italian sources for the remaining strophes of Bussine's poem-translation are to be found three pages further on in *Canti popolari*, a combination of two poems from the *Fine della serenata* section of *Canti toscani* – No. 2 on page 127 ('Non posso più cantar … Stanotte son dormito a ciel sereno'[3]) and No. 3 on the same page ('Non posso più cantar, che non ho voce / E m'entra in bocca, e non mi lassa dire …').[4] This last poem was Paul Heyse's source for the German translation 'Nicht länger kann ich singen', set to music by Hugo Wolf as No. 42 of his *Italienisches Liederbuch*. The Wolf song is richly comic but there is nothing amusing about Fauré's setting, even if such woebegone confessions of vocal limitations ('che non ho voce' or 'ma voix expire') are rare in Italian song.

The initial climb of the vocal line, followed by a fall in gradual stages, is yet another example of the 'Viardot motif' identified by Nectoux. The music is more refined and more individual than the earlier *Barcarolle*, with a similarly languid and luscious entwining of voice and piano. In *Barcarolle* the governing momentum is that of an oar plying through the Venetian lagoon; this song, like all serenades worthy of the name, is accompanied by one version or other of those gently strummed chords that are a pianistic stand-in for lute or guitar. The loping rhythm of this accompaniment, however, with chords placed on the first, third, sixth, seventh and ninth quavers of the bar, defies the commonplace and is typical of Fauré's ingenious ability to conjure something new from conventional means. The original key of B♭ minor is clearly associated with moonlight in the composer's mind, and is also the tonality of the greatest of all serenades in that key – the future *Clair de lune*.

The song's dedicatee Henriette de Montagnac (1851–1917) was married to the Baron Élisée de Montagnac. Both were close friends of Fauré's patrons and friends Marguerite ('Meg') and Eugène Baugnies. The two couples went on holiday to Egypt together in 1874. Meg Baugnies regarded Henriette de Montagnac as a lifelong confidante, and Henriette's link to Fauré via the Baugnies family is easy to fathom.[5]

CANTI

POPOLARI

TOSCANI CORSI ILLIRICI GRECI

RACCOLTI E ILLUSTRATI

DA N. TOMMASEO

MINISTRO DEL GOVERNO PROVVISORIO DELLA REPUBBLICA VENETA

Seconda edizione.

VOL. I.

VENEZIA

STABILIMENTO TASSO TIPOGRAFICO-ENCICLOPEDICO EDIT.

1848.

Title-page of Tommaseo's Canti popolari *(1848)*

(25) **Sylvie** (*Sylvie*)[6]
1878, Op. 6 No. 3, 'À Mme la vicomtesse de Gironde', first Hamelle collection p. 61, A♭ major, 3/4, *Allegro moderato*

Si tu veux savoir, ma belle,	*If you wish to know, my sweet,*
Où s'envole à tire d'aile	*Where the bird is hastening*
L'oiseau qui chantait sur l'ormeau,	*That was singing in the elm,*
Je te le dirai, ma belle,	*I shall tell you, my sweet,*
Il vole vers qui l'appelle,	*It flies to the one who calls it,*
Vers celui-là	*To the one*
Qui l'aimera!	*Who will love it!*
Si tu veux savoir, ma blonde,	*If you wish to know, my fair one,*
Pourquoi sur terre et sur l'onde	*Why on land and sea*
La nuit tout s'anime et s'unit,	*All things at night revive and merge,*
Je te le dirai, ma blonde,	*I shall tell you, my fair one:*
C'est qu'il est une heure au monde	*There is one hour in the world,*
Où, loin du jour,	*When far from day*
Veille l'amour!	*Love stands watch!*

Si tu veux savoir, Sylvie,	*If you wish to know, Sylvie,*
Pourquoi j'aime à la folie	*Why I love to distraction*
Tes yeux brillants et langoureux,	*Your bright and yearning eyes,*
Je te le dirai, Sylvie,	*I shall tell you, Sylvie,*
C'est que sans toi dans la vie	*That without you in my life,*
Tout pour mon cœur	*My heart feels*
N'est que douleur!	*Naught but pain!*

Paul de Choudens (1850–1925)

The would-be poet Paul de Choudens was a recently appointed partner in the publishing business of his father, Antoine de Choudens. The publisher's other son, Antony de Choudens, had published a volume of anodyne songs dedicated to Bizet – settings of Silvestre and Gautier among others. At this point Fauré had written nineteen *mélodies* (excluding three Hugo song settings – unpublished, and deemed by him unpublishable – and two duets) and a round figure of twenty was required. Paul de Choudens was a potential ally in Fauré's desire to see all his songs gathered together in a single *recueil*; the composer clearly decided to provide this twentieth song in the most charming possible way by keeping the poem in the publisher's family, as it were. He may also have been at a genuine loss at the time for something else suitable to set. In a letter to Marie Clerc of 3 October 1878 the composer writes:

> I have just performed a labour of Hercules, *viz* setting to music some lines by Choudens (Paul)! Yes, dear Madame, Lucette will be walking through life with an escort of four flats and twelve semiquavers into the bargain. See what you achieve when you tell me so kindly that the smallest piece of work from my hand gives you pleasure![7]

What is the reference here to 'Lucette'? If this had been the original title of the poem (as Nectoux suggests), the rhymes with 'Sylvie' in the third verse would have had to have been different. Perhaps Fauré accommodated the last-minute revisions of an inexperienced poet in this regard – but it is also very possible that he himself requested the alteration of the name, and this is entirely in line with the minute alterations he made to other poems in the interests of a smooth, unimpeded vocal line. The name 'Sylvie' is much more in keeping with the suave character of this music than 'Lucette', with an awkwardly explosive double 't' coming before the mute 'e' vowel. A mystery solved by Fauré's letter to Marie Clerc is to do with the song's original key (always a bone of contention in the case of early songs where the autographs have disappeared): when the composer writes to her about 'the escort of four flats' the tonality of A♭ major is clearly indicated. It is confusing however that in the long-awaited Choudens *recueil* of 1879 the song appears only in F major, the lower of the available tonalities in the first Hamelle collection.

The strain of the song's genesis does not show. As a paean of praise to female beauty, *Sylvie* succeeds where the earlier *Hymne* does not, precisely because Paul de Choudens was no Baudelaire. The text makes no demands beyond the conventions of a young man using flowery language to salute his paramour of the moment. If the text of the poem ever appeared in print, other than in Fauré's song, it could only have done so in a journal or newspaper. The shallowness of the verse gives Fauré musical room to manoeuvre in a way denied him by the greater poet. The result is a beautifully crafted song with deft piano writing that lies 'just so' under the hands. Any pianist, having first mastered the fingering of course, will acknowledge the pleasure of playing the gently rising figurations first encountered in bars 3 to 4. To reach the tonic chord with some delicacy after traversing a small thicket of sharps and flats in contrary motion is like executing a complicated embroidery stitch; it is as if the music, when it reaches the tonic, lands on its feet as delicately as a cat, to borrow Jankélévitch's simile.[8] This applies above all to the pianistic pleasure associated with playing this song in A♭ major, a physical sensation somehow lacking when negotiating the accompaniment in any other key. With its 'escort of four flats' the song is as neat and delicately perfumed as Sylvie herself. There is little room for error, and the pleasure of listener and performer is dependent on a perfectly clear and clean execution of the manoeuvre.

This is music for the salon, and it has the salon's light touch; the incessant semiquavers of the accompaniment suggest the fluttering of butterflies' wings. The composer modifies his *Allegro* with *moderato* in a song that should encompass both the industry and the laziness

Title-page of the first edition of Sylvie, published by Choudens

of a gently buzzing bee. 'Tes yeux brillants *et langoureux*', says the poet (my italics). The reconciliation of two such adjectives lies at the heart of achieving the 'golden mean' in Fauré performance; the music is on the move throughout, but it must never sound snatched or hurried. A fine singer can make much of the gentle undulations of the vocal line, and the ease with which the music unfolds belies the composer's skill in tonal manipulation. The piece is an example of Fauré's mastery in writing an eloquent, yet economical, bass (as in bars 34 to 39) that steers the progress of the music like a rudder. The style of Massenet (no friend of Fauré) comes to mind, not least because there is a *belle époque* languor in this music that co-exists quite easily with its ardour. On the other hand the tight and economical construction of the piece from a formal point of view is a marked contrast (and something of a reproof) to the flimsy *déshabillé* of rather too many of Massenet's *mélodies*.

The dedicatee of *Sylvie* was one of the powerful Parisian *beau monde* passionately interested in the music: the Vicomtesse de Gironde was often to be found on the guest lists of Marguerite Baugnies (later de Saint-Marceaux) and the Comtesse Greffulhe. Before her marriage she was Lucy Denière and was actually a cousin of Meg Baugnies. One is tempted to think that the composer had thought of the dedication to this elegant 'Lucy' when the song was still provisionally entitled *Lucette*. In any case, from the point of view of societal rank alone the publishing house of Choudens would have considered this an entirely suitable dedication.

❧   ❧   ❧   ❧

Paul de Choudens was born in Paris on 5 June 1850. He was made a partner in his father's firm in November 1874, together with his brother, the composer Antony de Choudens, who withdrew from 'Choudens, père et fils' some eleven years later. Antoine, the father, died in 1888. This left Paul in sole charge of one of France's most successful publishing businesses with a history that embraced collaborations with Bellini, Verdi, Gounod, Bizet, Berlioz (*Les Troyens*) and Offenbach. The publishing house moved from its address in the rue St Honoré to the boulevard des Capucines. Although by this time Fauré had long since departed from the ranks of Choudens composers, Paul de Choudens continued to work with Bruneau, Messager, Vidal and many others. Paul remained in charge of the firm until his death on 7 October 1925, thus outliving the composer who was to give him his sole claim to literary immortality.

∽   ∽   ∽   ∽

With *Poëme d'un jour* Fauré writes his first set of songs (with the opus number of 17 given mysteriously on the autograph). It has nothing of the architecture of the densely organised *La Bonne chanson*, whose network of cyclical borrowings and self-quotation were later developments of the composer's mature years. *Poëme d'un jour* is rather a cycle in the manner of Robert Schumann's *Frauenliebe und*

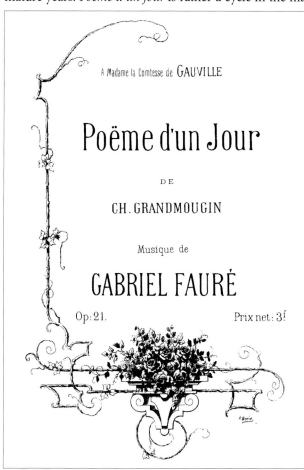

-*leben*, where each song is an individual entity in an implied narrative chronology. The Schumann cycle about a woman's life and love unfolds over at least a year, possibly much longer. Fauré sets tighter parameters: if *Poëme d'un jour* means what it says, this love affair, from meeting to parting, takes place in a single day. This fact alone limits the emotional range of the music; passion is illusory and impermanent, and the rueful farewell marks the end of a relationship so short that it cannot be taken any more seriously by the listener than it has been by the lovers themselves. A further factor in rendering the cycle lightweight is the versifying of Charles Grandmougin, which is typical of the sentimentality found in popular magazines of the time.

One wonders whether the notion of a work of this kind began in Fauré's mind as the temptation to compose a deliberate parody of Massenet's highly successful series of 'Poème' cycles (four of which had been published by 1878, the year of Massenet's enviable election to the Institut[9]). The texts of some of these works are unashamedly, even

Title-page of the first edition of Poëme d'un jour, *published by Durand*

114

embarrassingly, saccharine. At the same time as distrusting Massenet and disliking his music, Fauré would hardly have turned his nose up at the financial success of *mélodies* by the future composer of *Manon*. The desire to write a commercially viable cycle seems rather more important in the genesis of *Poëme d'un jour* than any need on the composer's part to give vent to his distress at the rupture of his engagement to Marianne Viardot. One can be certain that his emotions concerning this bruising episode in his life were far more complicated than those felt by the narrator of this cycle – a shadowy male persona invented by what is surely Fauré's juxtaposition of three unrelated Grandmougin poems.

The three songs of *Poëme d'un jour* were published in November 1880 in a single volume, as well as separately, by the firm of Durand. It would be thirty-three years before another of the composer's works was issued by this publisher.

Poëme d'un jour (*Poem of a day*)[10]
1878, Op. 21

(26) (i) *Rencontre* (*Meeting*)
1878, Op. 21 No. 1, 'À Madame la comtesse de Gauville', second Hamelle collection p. 16, D♭ major (original key), ♩, *Andante*

J'étais triste et pensif quand je t'ai rencontrée,	*I was sad and pensive when I met you,*
Je sens moins aujourd'hui mon obstiné tourment,	*Today I feel less my persistent pain;*
Ô dis-moi, serais-tu la femme inespérée	*O tell me, could you be the long hoped-for woman,*
Et le rêve idéal poursuivi vainement?	*And the ideal dream pursued in vain?*
Ô passante aux doux yeux, serais-tu donc l'amie	*O passer-by with gentle eyes, could you be the friend*
Qui rendrait le bonheur au poète isolé,	*To restore the lonely poet's happiness,*
Et vas-tu rayonner sur mon âme affermie	*And will you shine on my steadfast soul*
Comme le ciel natal sur un cœur d'exilé?	*Like native sky on an exiled heart?*
Ta tristesse sauvage, à la mienne pareille,	*Your timid sadness, like my own,*
Aime à voir le soleil décliner sur la mer!	*Loves to watch the sun set on the sea!*
Devant l'immensité ton extase s'éveille	*Such boundless space awakes your rapture,*
Et le charme des soirs à ta belle âme est cher.	*And your fair soul prizes the evenings' charm.*
Une mystérieuse et douce sympathie	*A mysterious and gentle sympathy*
Déjà m'enchaîne à toi comme un vivant lien,	*Already binds me to you like a living bond,*
Et mon âme frémit, par l'amour envahie,	*And my soul quivers, overcome by love,*
Et mon cœur te chérit sans te connaître bien.	*And my heart, without knowing you well, adores you.*

This is music of the greatest urbanity and elegance. It spins a line as surely as the male suitor spins his, a progression of murmured endearments with artfully placed climactic moments of ardour. How many men, with the greatest seriousness, have told a woman they have just met that they have experienced a 'coup de foudre' whereby a strange and mysterious chemistry inexplicably binds the two of them together? If the narrator claims to be 'triste et pensif', he is neither very sad, nor very thoughtful: we can be sure he has said these words, or words like them, many times before. The purling progress of the music seems to be on automatic pilot. The ceaseless flow of semiquavers, shared between the hands with seemingly effortless ease, adds to this impression. This is not to deny that Fauré's music is remarkable – indeed, only he could have written these harmonically sophisticated pages where the modulatory twists and turns are so discreetly managed that we are less aware than we should be of the music's considerable musical felicities.

There are some high notes for the singer, but for all its mellifluous progress the song lacks depth, one feels deliberately: it is as dapper as the elegantly attired young man who sings it. He is not exactly a Don Giovanni because, the ardour of *Toujours* notwithstanding, he clearly lacks the diabolical energy for heartless seduction. No, this lover has convinced himself of his sincerity, as far as it goes; but singers are well advised not to attempt to match the gushing hyperbole of the verse with meaningful (and unmarked) emphases inappropriate to the imperturbability of the music. Fauré is wise enough to avoid matching Grandmougin's grandiloquence in a phrase such as 'Devant l'immensité ton extase s'éveille', where the vocal line droops gently rather than rises. After all, this is not yet Verlaine in *La Bonne chanson*, hell-bent on marriage and contemplating connubial bliss. The inevitable parting is already foretold in the beginning of this liaison.

(27) (ii) *Toujours* (For ever)
1878, Op. 21 No. 2, 'À Madame la comtesse de Gauville', second Hamelle collection p. 20, F minor (original key of first edition; key of autograph F♯ minor), ♩, *Allegro con fuoco*

Vous me demandez de me taire,	*You ask me to be silent,*
De fuir loin de vous pour jamais	*To flee far from you for ever*
Et de m'en aller, solitaire,	*And to go my way alone,*
Sans me rappeler qui j'aimais!	*Forgetting whom I loved!*
Demandez plutôt aux étoiles	*Rather ask the stars*
De tomber dans l'immensité,	*To fall into infinity,*
À la nuit de perdre ses voiles,	*The night to lose its veils,*
Au jour de perdre sa clarté!	*The day to lose its light!*
Demandez à la mer immense	*Ask the boundless sea*
De dessécher ses vastes flots	*To drain its mighty waves,*
Et quand les vents sont en démence,	*And the raging winds*
D'apaiser ses sombres sanglots!	*To calm their dismal sobbing!*
Mais n'espérez pas que mon âme	*But do not expect my soul*
S'arrache à ses âpres douleurs	*To tear itself from bitter sorrow,*
Et se dépouille de sa flamme	*Nor to shed its passion*
Comme le printemps de ses fleurs!	*As springtime sheds its flowers!*

In this cycle there is a puzzling inconsistency in the singer's form of address: in the first song, having apparently just met his lady love, he nevertheless presumes to 'tutoyer' her; in the second and third songs, as intimacy is surely meant to increase, he addresses her as 'vous'. (Of course Grandmougin,

116

if he had anything to do with the construction of this cycle, may have made his protagonist revert to this stinging formality as a result of the girl's rejection – going back on the 'tu' form in this way signifies a relationship in considerable crisis.) It seems very much more likely however that Fauré took the three poems from disparate sources and constructed this narrative himself, inventing the Massenet-like title of the set and perhaps even adding titles to the poems to suit his scenario. On the other hand, it can't be ruled out that he asked for Grandmougin's help, and at least his permission.

Perhaps the defensive outburst of *Toujours* is occasioned by the otherwise silent woman's attempts to slow down the rapid onslaught of the man's affections. If so, the temporarily rebuffed lover plays the passion card; he invokes the stars and heavens in his anguish. These thundering triplets owe much to the excitement of Fauré's writing for chamber ensembles; the passion and power generated in the last movement of the Piano Quartet, Op. 15, for example, are formidable. Undulations between the hands are craftily deployed to generate a remarkable pianistic momentum. And crafty the song somehow remains. The effect, after the bluster has died down (which it does rather quickly, for this piece is short), is that of a storm in a teacup. The *piano* chords at the end admit as much; it is as if the young suitor is exhausted by his pose. Not for a moment do we share his pain – the imagery is too pat, and the vehement outpourings flow too smoothly, as if schooled by a shade too much experience. Of course he puts up a tremendous show as the wounded lover, and in a fine performance this song can be most exciting, but we never quite believe in this music, certainly not in the same way as we are drawn into the emotional world of such a potentially melodramatic song as *Spleen*, for example.

As far as the triptych of the story line is concerned the song is effective: we must assume that the protagonist gets his way with the woman as a result of these infatuated protestations. If we imagine a morning meeting (the first song), *Toujours* is sung over lunch, and there is the whole afternoon to be enjoyed – a lovers' siesta in a quiet hotel – before the inevitable evening parting. (Grandmougin's first published volume of poetry was *Les Siestes*, 1874, but these poems are not to be found in this collection, nor anywhere else in the poet's printed work.)

Officially of course this 'affair' is thwarted, it fizzles out in the third song without consummation. But the public, then as now, is invited to read between the lines. As Nectoux has written concerning Fauré's own extra-marital affairs:

> The moral code of the Third Republic was strict on the surface. Divorce was rare and socially unacceptable. But underneath this surface it is fair to say that morality was extremely flexible, as a result of both the rampant anti-clericalism of the times and of reaction to the restrictive codes of conduct established under the preceding regimes.[11]

It may be helpful to the prospective performers of these songs to realise that in the Paris of 1878 such a whirlwind romance including a sexual adventure in a single day would not have been possible between two unmarried people of a respectable class. A seduction involving an *ingénue* would have required the machinations of a Boccaccio or Casanova, including, for example, the drugging of chaperones. The scenario of the cycle suggests, surely, the involvement of a married woman (if not also a married man) whose commitments elsewhere made such a discreet encounter both possible and necessarily brief.

(28) (iii) *Adieu* (*Farewell*)

1878, Op. 21 No. 3, 'À Madame la comtesse de Gauville', second Hamelle collection p. 24, F major (original key of first edition), key of autograph G♭ major, ♩, *Moderato*

Comme tout meurt vite, la rose	*How swiftly all things die, the rose*
Déclose,	*In bloom,*
Et les frais manteaux diaprés	*And the cool dappled mantle*
Des prés;	*Of the meadows;*
Les longs soupirs, les bien-aimées,	*Long-drawn sighs, loved ones,*
Fumées.	*All smoke*
On voit dans ce monde léger	*In this fickle world we see*
Changer	*Our dreams*
Plus vite que les flots des grèves,	*Change more swiftly than waves*
Nos rêves,	*On the shore,*
Plus vite que le givre en fleurs,	*Our hearts change more swiftly than patterns*
Nos cœurs!	*Of frosted flowers!*
À vous l'on se croyait fidèle,	*To you I thought I would be faithful,*
Cruelle,	*Cruel one,*
Mais hélas! les plus longs amours	*But alas! the longest loves*
Sont courts!	*Are short!*
Et je dis en quittant vos charmes,	*And I say, taking leave of your charms,*
Sans larmes,	*Without tears,*
Presqu'au moment de mon aveu,	*Almost at the moment of my avowal,*
Adieu!	*Farewell!*

Adieu is surely the best song of the three. It is the first in a long line of *mélodies* in 4/4 with gently throbbing crotchet accompaniments, a kind of Fauré trademark when time is made to stand still by a quality of musical invention both self-effacing and revelatory. Over this seemingly neutral background, an inspired melodic line is cradled and nurtured – the same can be said, for example, of *Le Secret*, and of one of this composer's last songs, *Diane, Séléné*. The music for *Adieu* is ruefully relaxed; it denotes satiation rather than voluptuous languor. Fauré's relatively fleet metronome marking is important here, and it is clear that the singer is no longer motivated by passion. It is part of the amorous game to part from a lady with expressions of tender regret. We can only hope that his erstwhile partner is equally philosophical; we sense that *her* feelings are not even taken into account – but it is assumed that she will now return to the bosom of her unwitting, or forgiving, family – just as Emma Bardac was to return to her husband Sigismund once her affair with Fauré had run its course (see Chapter 9).

This cynical edge notwithstanding, Fauré's music is beautifully moulded; a *minore* middle section, a temporary touch of urgency, allows the music to regain the poise of the major key. The final 'Adieu!' is suspended on a high F, a tied pair of semibreves, as the two lovers float out of each other's lives and into each other's pasts. The song is an admirable exercise in restraint for those full-hearted singers who struggle to master the essential detachment inherent in Fauré's style; if *Adieu* sounds anything like Rodolfo's farewell to Mimi, the singer has entered the Parisian 'vie de bohème' through the wrong stage door (Fauré disliked Puccini's opera when he first heard it in 1900). Nevertheless a tenor able to sing *piano* in the higher register should perhaps consider reverting to the tonalities of Fauré's autograph for the second and third songs of the cycle (F♯ minor and G♭ major). Durand may have decided to avoid publishing the songs in these keys simply because they were considered unnecessarily complicated for amateur accompanists and too high for many singers.

The subjugation of emotion into form, which is a requirement everywhere in Fauré's music, is a necessity for these songs on interpretative, as well as stylistic, grounds. In this music a heart-on-sleeve emotiveness is singularly superfluous, both because Fauré's music itself does not require it – it never requires it – and because the rather self-centred gentleman who sings these songs pursues his amorous prey with an ardour that is, at heart and beneath the bluster, detached and cool. One may even choose to regard this cycle, *très belle époque*, as cynical and calculating, the complete opposite of the sugary sentimentality for which these songs are sometimes criticised.

This cycle is scarcely a lament for the unsuccessful engagement to Marianne Viardot, but one is tempted to see an autobiographical side to it that is perhaps nearer to Schumann's Heine triptych *Tragödie* than to *Frauenliebe und -leben*. The manner of conducting an affair as outlined in *Poème d'un jour* seems curiously prophetic of Fauré's many future liaisons. From 1883 he was caught in an unsatisfactory, and curiously co-dependent, marriage, but divorce was never contemplated, probably for the sake of his two sons. After the breakdown of the engagement with Marianne Viardot, and both before and after his largely arranged marriage (arranged by others, that is, in the belief that they were doing him a service), the soft-spoken composer exercised a magnetic attraction as far as women were concerned. The composer Casella noted 'the large languid and sensual eyes of an impenitent Casanova'.[12]

Fauré's affairs were legendary (there was even malicious gossip about illegitimate children); later on this inspector of the provincial conservatoires worked in conditions ideal for the unaccountable travelling Lothario, and visits to England also occasioned his infidelities. He was noted for his laconic charm, and he must have broken many hearts – particularly those of women who allowed themselves to imagine that he might eventually leave his difficult wife, having found 'true love'. There were mistresses of protracted influence (Emma Bardac, and above all Marguerite Hasselmans), but Fauré's affairs were, on the whole, 'poèmes d'un jour' (or 'de quelques semaines') with what must have been an inbuilt, deft exit strategy. He must have been adept at charm (the first song), showing just enough glints of genuine passion (the second), followed by something like the elegantly veiled retreat of the third. These extrications probably saved Fauré's marriage and reputation (compare Debussy's domestic linen washed disastrously in public), and increased his reputation for inscrutability, but they can have done little for his enduring happiness or emotional stability, not to mention that of his wife and children. It is notable however that the occasional pianistic glimpses of the flightiness of Fauré (the fond seducer) and the volubility of Fauré (the inveterate charmer of women) are more to be found in the earlier solo piano music than in the songs. The absence of real virtuosity in many of the song accompaniments gives little scope to display and celebrate the roaming fingers of the highly practiced lover and 'master of charms'; in a *mélodie* the presence of a poem by somebody else seems to have concentrated the composer's mind in a way that discouraged any temptation to gratuitous display.

To dedicate this cycle to any high-born lady, considering its subject-matter, might have been considered somewhat risky. The Comtesse de Gauville, née Paultre, had a salon in Paris and lived at the château of Le Theil at Bernay (in the Eure), where she was a neighbour and friend of the painter Charles Emmanuel Jadin, dedicatee of Fauré's *Le Voyageur* and *Clair de lune*. She was a long-time acquaintance of Meg Baugnies, who waspishly noted in her journal (1896) that Gauville was 'daughter of a notary' and 'capable of any and every villainy'.[13] At that time the Comtesse had become embroiled in a trial where she was accused of having stolen jewellery from a friend. One can only wonder whether as a younger woman she had enjoyed something of a reputation for amatory indiscretion; if so, Fauré might have regarded the dedication of this cycle as an amusingly skewed compliment or, who knows, he may himself have been the passing beneficiary of the wayward Comtesse's 'generosity'.

～　　　～　　　～　　　～

Charles-Jean Grandmougin was born in Vesoul on 17 January 1850. As a young man he was a passionate Wagnerian when the cause of that composer was still somewhat controversial. As a poet of *mélodie* texts his name is to be found in songs by Chaminade and Pierné, as well as these three famous Fauré settings. He was more famous as a librettist for operas and oratorios, and as a translator (in this respect he may be compared with Victor Wilder). He provided Massenet with the text for his *La Vierge* (1880) and Franck with *Hulda* (1894), after Bjørnson. He translated into French two operas of Weber (*Der Freischütz* and *Euryanthe*) and wrote *Etudes sur l'esthétique musicale*, a history of music from the time of the Greeks to the nineteenth century.

Grandmougin was more of a peripheral figure on the musical scene than a true poet; in this connection one thinks of such later writers as G. Jean-Aubry and René Chalupt, who later contributed to the song repertoire from the literary sidelines. Grandmougin died in Neuilly on 28 April 1930.

(29) *Nell* (*Nell*)[14]

1878, Op. 18 No. 1, 'À Mme Camille Saint-Saëns', second Hamelle collection p. 3, G♭ major, 3/4,
Andante, quasi allegretto

Ta rose de pourpre, à ton clair soleil,	*Your crimson rose in your bright sun*
Ô Juin, étincelle enivrée;	*Glitters, June, in rapture;*
Penche aussi vers moi ta coupe dorée:	*Incline to me also your golden cup:*
Mon cœur à ta rose est pareil.	*My heart is like your rose.*
Sous le mol abri de la feuille ombreuse	*From the soft shelter of shady leaves*
Monte un soupir de volupté;	*Rises a languorous sigh;*
Plus d'un ramier chante au bois écarté,	*More than one dove in the secluded wood*
Ô mon cœur, sa plainte amoureuse.	*Sings, O my heart, its love-lorn lament.*
Que ta perle est douce au ciel enflammé,	*How sweet is your pearl in the blazing sky,*
Étoile de la nuit pensive!	*Star of meditative night!*
Mais combien plus douce est la clarté vive	*But sweeter still is the vivid light*
Qui rayonne en mon cœur charmé!	*That glows in my enchanted heart!*
La chantante mer, le long du rivage,	*The singing sea along the shore*
Taira son murmure éternel,	*Shall cease its eternal murmur,*
Avant qu'en mon cœur, chère amour, ô Nell,	*Before in my heart, dear love, O Nell,*
Ne fleurisse plus ton image!	*Your image shall cease to bloom!*

Charles Marie René Leconte de Lisle (1818–1894)

The poem by Leconte de Lisle is from his first collection, *Poèmes antiques* (1852), where there is a quasi-Scottish subsection that includes the poems 'Jane' (set by the young Debussy), 'Nanny' (later a Chausson song) and 'La Fille aux cheveux de lin', set by Debussy in 1881 and also the inspiration for his famous piano prelude of 1910. 'La Fille aux cheveux de lin' is none other than Burns's 'Lassie with the Lint-White Locks' The poet adds the subtitles 'imités de Burns' – 'imitated from Burns'; in 'Nell' Leconte de Lisle combined the name of Nell Kirkpatrick, Burns's first love, with an opening image adopted from that immortal lyric beginning 'O my luve's like a red, red rose / That's newly sprung in June'. After this nod of homage to these first two lines the French poet goes his own way. The Scottish poet's third and fourth lines are 'O my luve's like the melodie / That's sweetly played in tune', and it is Fauré (certainly unversed in the Burns original) who happily provides us with just such a melody.

Everything in this song comes together to make a masterpiece, a milestone that represents a real step forward from *Sylvie*: melody, harmonic texture, depth of feeling, the matching of the literary means to the musical.

Title-page of Nell, *published by Hamelle*

There is a *pudeur* in this Parnassian-poetry-via-the-Highlands that perfectly suits this composer's personality. The music murmurs as gently as a cool mountain stream, but it is pungent as peat. When pianists first encounter these rippling semiquavers in G♭ major (the fingers of both hands are made to caress the black notes, making occasional sorties into the region of the whites) they discover a complex musical language – impossible to sight-read – that masquerades as insouciant simplicity. Each beat of the second and third bars is marked by a bass line that descends via the little finger of the left hand – a perfect mingling of harmony and concealed, or rather implied, counterpoint. Throughout the song every group of four semiquavers forms a new chord, sometimes two; this ever-changing progress, quietly subversive, makes us even more aware of the more restricted harmonic vocabulary of older French composers, Saint-Saëns for example. Fauré's range of colour (diatonic harmony enriched by the church modes) produces a kaleidoscope of sound ('rose de pourpre … clair soleil') that is both sumptuously muted and iridescent. One thinks of a canvas by a great impressionist or pointillist painter where hyperactive brushwork in close-up seems, at a distance, full of repose.

This extraordinary combination of peacefulness and harmonic restlessness is unique to this composer. But this is not simply the tonal conjuring for its own sake of which Fauré is occasionally guilty. In contrast to the *Poëme d'un jour*, we hear in *Nell* the core of the composer's being,

Title-page of Nell, *published in London by Metzler & Co.*

his better self; the whole song breathes an air of shy sweetness and an endless capacity for devotion – exactly the effect of the Burns lyric that inspired Leconte de Lisle in the first place ('And I will luve thee still, my dear, / Till a' the seas gang dry'). If the facts of the composer's own love life seem to contradict the sincerity of this music, one feels that Fauré himself would have been convinced of his capacity for being faithful to his paramours 'in his own fashion' (like Ernest Dowson to his 'Cynara'[15]). Robert Burns, the inspiration of *Nell*, was more than the composer's equal in terms of genuinely affectionate promiscuity.

The song has one of the most ill-fated of all Fauré's dedicatees, the wife of Saint-Saëns. This was of course merely an indirect way of offering the song, one of the finest so far, to Saint-Saëns himself. The older composer had married the nineteen-year-old Marie-Laure Truffot in 1875, although his redoubtable mother heartily disapproved of the match. The couple had two children, both of whom died in this very year of 1878, the younger boy (aged six months) from illness, the elder (aged two and a half) from a fall from a fourth-floor window. One cannot help wondering whether the dedication of *Nell* was also Fauré's way of expressing his sorrow and concern regarding this double tragedy, for which Saint-Saëns later blamed his wife. There are no extant letters between Fauré and his teacher from this period, although we must assume that Fauré was welcomed into the older composer's marital home, and that he met the young Madame Saint-Saëns; she was even young enough at twenty-two for the thirty-three-year-old Fauré to have found her attractive, a reaction that might well have come less naturally to Saint-Saëns. The marriage had lasted only another three years when Saint-Saëns suddenly walked out on Marie-Laure, never to see her again. She survived until 1950, by which time the song Fauré had dedicated to her had long been established as one of his canonical masterpieces.

Fauré signed a contract in 1896 with the English music publishing firm of Metzler & Co. (see Chapter 10). The new edition of *Nell*, issued with an English singing translation by Fauré's mistress of the time, Adela Maddison, is graced by the heading 'as sung by Madame Melba'. It is understandable that this Nellie, the most famous 'Nell' of the time, would have agreed to be associated with a piece that bore her name, indeed the firm of Metzler probably pushed this association in order to heighten sales. This celebrated diva made recordings of three of Debussy's melodies (including the tricky *Mandoline* and *En sourdine*), so it is likely that she did indeed have the Fauré song in her repertoire. This famous Australian with a legendarily sharp temper would have been completely unabashed at singing a song as if in praise of her considerable Antipodean self.

(30) *Le Voyageur* (*The wanderer*)[16]

1878?, Op. 18 No. 2, 'À M Emmanuel Jadin', second Hamelle collection p. 8, where it is printed in G minor (original key A minor), 3/4, *Allegro moderato*

Voyageur, où vas-tu, marchant
Dans l'or vibrant de la poussière?
— Je m'en vais au soleil couchant,
Pour m'endormir dans la lumière.

Wanderer, where are you bound,
Walking in the golden, quivering dust?
— I am going towards the sunset,
To fall asleep in the light.

Car j'ai vécu n'ayant qu'un Dieu,
L'astre qui luit et qui féconde.
Et c'est dans son linceul de feu
Que je veux m'en aller du monde!

For I have lived with only one God,
The sun which shines and makes fertile.
It is shrouded in his fire
That I wish to leave the world!

— Voyageur, presse donc le pas:
L'astre, vers l'horizon, décline …
— Que m'importe, j'irai plus bas
L'attendre au pied de la colline.

— Wanderer, you must hurry, then:
The sun slips towards the horizon …
— What do I care, I shall descend further
And wait at the foot of the hill.

Et lui montrant mon cœur ouvert,
Saignant de son amour fidèle,
Je lui dirai: J'ai trop souffert:
Soleil! emporte-moi loin d'elle!

And showing the sun my open heart,
Bleeding with faithful love,
I shall say: I have suffered too much:
Sun! Take me far away from her!

Armand Silvestre (1837–1901)

Although we cannot be sure about the date of this song, it would be reasonable to regard it as Fauré's first setting of one of his key poets, Armand Silvestre. It is also more than likely that the composer wrote it at about the same time as *Automne*, when he had not yet settled into the rather more per-fumed musical mood and manner that we broadly associate with Fauré's Silvestre period. *Le Voyageur* is untypical of the poet's settings, which are usually valued for their grace and easy charm, qualities that stem from what Jankélévitch calls the poet's 'sensibilité un peu facile'.[17] The poem appears in *Les Ailes d'or* (1880), in a subsection entitled *Vers pour être chantés*. The date of the collection shows that Fauré either found the poem in a newspaper or periodical, or was in contact with the poet himself. This is a vehement song, brusque and tinged with pessimism and the kind of social realism one expects more readily in a poet such as Jean Richepin (whose 'Au cimetière' was set by Fauré in 1888). *Le Voyageur* resembles the Richepin setting in some ways. The original key of A minor – later moder-ated to G minor by the publisher Hamelle (who must have judged the composer's key impractical for most amateur singers) is high enough to sound almost hysterically dramatic.

   An English equivalent of this music is Vaughan Williams's *The Vagabond* from his *Songs of Travel*; misanthropy and disdain for his fellow human beings hover not far beneath the surface of the trav-eller's replies to his interrogator. Fauré is only occasionally in as robustly pessimistic a mood as this (consider the song *Larmes*, or the much later opening movement of the First Cello Sonata, Op. 109). In the outer sections the accompaniment is in accented crotchets: a dotted rhythm on the first beat

Title-page of Le Voyageur, *published by Hamelle*

resounds through the entire bar like the tolling of a bell; the vocal line roams the stave with manly determination.

The imagery of verse 3, where a sun sets towards the horizon, inspires the song's great musical surprise. The vocal line is marked *dolce* and is suddenly muted and contained: the texture of the accompaniment is different from anything that has gone before. In fact, this extraordinary passage, brought to a close by a return of the louder music of the opening after eighteen bars, would not have seemed out of place in a late work such as *Mirages* – it is a prophetic glimpse of a much later style. As Jankélévitch points out, the song opens with a falling scale that recalls the first and third songs of *Poème d'un jour*, a contemporary work. This descent of the stave is none other than the Viardot motif. The bitter tone of the music is a possible indication of the composer's residual grief regarding the loss of Marianne. This is also the motif's final appearance, and it seems possible to interpret it as a musical line drawn firmly here under the whole sad affair. The next *mélodie* is dedicated to a beautiful woman, a mezzo-soprano replacement for Marianne Viardot – if only in Fauré's hopeful dreams.

(31) *Automne* (Autumn)[18]
1878, Op. 18 No. 3, 'À Mlle Alice Boissonet', second Hamelle collection p. 12, B minor, 12/8, *Andante moderato*

Automne au ciel brumeux, aux horizons navrants,	*Autumn of misty skies and heartbreaking horizons,*
Aux rapides couchants, aux aurores pâlies,	*Of swift sunsets and pale dawns,*
Je regarde couler, comme l'eau du torrent,	*I watch flow by, like torrential water,*
Tes jours faits de mélancolie.	*Your days imbued with melancholy.*
Sur l'aile des regrets mes esprits emportés,	*My thoughts, borne away on the wings of regret,*
— Comme s'il se pouvait que notre âge renaisse!	*— As though our time could come round again!*
Parcourent, en rêvant, les coteaux enchantés	*Roam in reverie the enchanted hills,*
Où jadis sourit ma jeunesse.	*Where long ago my youth once smiled.*
Je sens, au clair soleil du souvenir vainqueur	*In the bright sun of triumphant memory*
Refleurir en bouquet les roses déliées	*I feel untied roses reflower in bouquets,*
Et monter à mes yeux des larmes, qu'en mon cœur,	*And tears rise to my eyes, which in my heart*
Mes vingt ans avaient oubliées!	*At twenty had been forgotten!*

Armand Silvestre (1837–1901)

This is a justly famous song, one that would number in most people's top ten Fauré *mélodies*. The grandeur of these 'horizons navrants' has inspired a setting of genius, and some credit must be given to the poet for its success. This is the second of three Silvestre settings (out of ten) which opt for drama rather than charm; the others are *Le Voyageur* (already considered above) and *Fleur jetée*. The key is B minor, a tonality that seems exactly right for October storms; in fact, the song sounds curiously unconvincing in a higher transposition.

An opening bar of empty, restless triplets churns in the pianist's right hand; leaping on to the next available bar line, the left hand jumps a fifth in octaves – B to F♯ – before plunging a sixth down to A♮, and thence slipping down to the adjacent G♯. The rhetoric of this bass clef writing is intensified by the kick of syncopation, something bitter and querulous. This process is repeated, once again in left-hand octaves: up to F♯, and then down a seventh to a G♮, a note

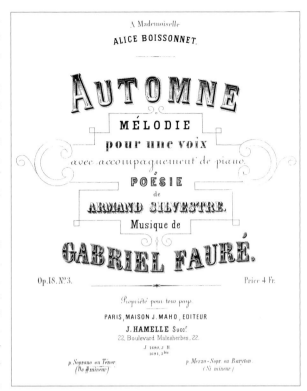

Title-page of Automne, *published by Hamelle*

which is repeated before settling on to the neighbouring F♯ in the depths of the instrument. There is something circular about this billowing piano writing, which punctuates the vocal outbursts with the movement of a mighty windmill. (Seasons come round again and again with this inevitable pull – the turning of the world.) This song is about memory, and the impossibility, even as one's mind moves in circles, of having one's time over again (as Verlaine also bemoans in the poem set to music by Fauré as *Prison*). At the time of its composition the composer was thirty-five, already old enough to look back on his youth with a measure of regret.

It is a miracle how, in the midst of this stormy music, a pianistic interlude of the purest sweetness and calm (bars 15–16) is allowed to flower as an introduction to the middle verse of this ABA structure. The right hand briefly abandons its restless oscillations for a simple yet heartfelt cantilena. This section leads to the ache of 'Où jadis sourit ma jeunesse', but it is capped by one of the most powerful vocal climaxes in the French *mélodie* – a high F♯ – at the end of the phrase 'Mes vingts ans avaient oubliées!' After this confession of anguished vulnerability, the postlude for piano seems divided into two parts: it first expresses the protagonist's feelings and then seems to comment on them from the viewpoint of a cynical observer, searing pain followed by a shudder of cold indifference. Once again the poem's publication in 1880 (as 'Chanson d'automne' in *Les Ailes d'or*) postdates the composition of the song.

Of Fauré's many settings this is one of the few in which a German-born lieder singer would feel at home – it is no salon *romance*, and the boundaries of the *mélodie* seem stretched to the limit. Nevertheless, a great performance of *Automne* requires an element of interiority, a communing with an inner world of memory and regret. This is music that suffers from over-loud and grandiloquent

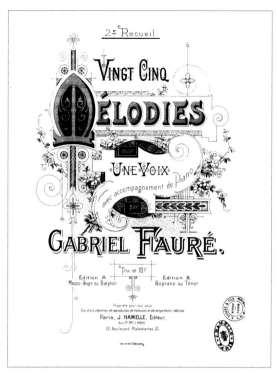

Title-page of the second recueil *of* Vingt-cinq mélodies
published by Hamelle in 1897

performances; in these less than subtle circumstances the use of diminished sevenths (amid many more subtle harmonies) can seem melodramatic and sentimental rather than haunting as the composer intended.

❧ ❧ ❧ ❧

It may have seemed arbitrary in this chapter to have concentrated on a single year in which Fauré composed a mere eight songs (and very little else). But 1878 was a watershed year, and the composer's release from the influence of the Viardot salon left him free to pursue his own developing and changing musical ideals. In general we find the composer somewhat betwixt and between; some of the songs remind us that Fauré had lost one guiding light and not yet found another. In *Sérénade toscane* we see the conclusion of Fauré's early Italian style; we must wait until his next visits to Italy, both imaginary and real (the *Shylock* songs of 1889, the *Mélodies 'de Venise'* of 1891) before his songs are irradiated with a Venetian atmosphere that is his own special creation. In the writing of *Sylvie* we see a straightforward piece of musical politics (the wooing of the publisher) turned to exceptionally elegant musical account; it is one of the most perfect songs of the first *recueil*, duly brought out under the title *Vingt mélodies* by the suitably flattered Choudens family at the end of 1879. The rest of the songs of 1878 are to be found in the second Hamelle *recueil* of songs. They were all published singly of course, but they were first gathered together in the *Vingt-cinq mélodies* of 1897. This volume of twenty-five songs was reissued and rearranged within two different instalments of *Vingt mélodies* (Hamelle volumes 2 and 3) in 1908.

There are a quiet sophistication and a discreet complexity in *Nell* that represent an advance on the achievements of *Au bord de l'eau*. For anyone who performs Fauré's songs this entry into the second Hamelle volume seems a significant step, a move into music that is both more mature and more demanding. It seems impossible to deny that there is a deepening of musical response here, but whether it represents a major change of direction is a moot point. *Le Voyageur* is the first setting of Armand Silvestre, the quintessential poet of the second *recueil*; with Silvestre's *Automne* as the volume's third item we have a dramatic song of a richness and depth that can only be compared to *L'Absent* in the earlier collection.

For this reason it has always been tempting to speak of the beginning of Fauré's 'second period' as coinciding with the first songs of this second *recueil* of songs. For those who work with Fauré's *mélodies* they do indeed seem roughly divided into *four* rather than three periods: each of the three Hamelle volumes seems conveniently to inhabit a period of its own, and the works not published by Hamelle (two separate songs, a vocalise and four further cycles) constitute a fourth and final period.

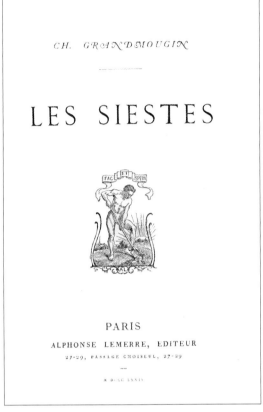

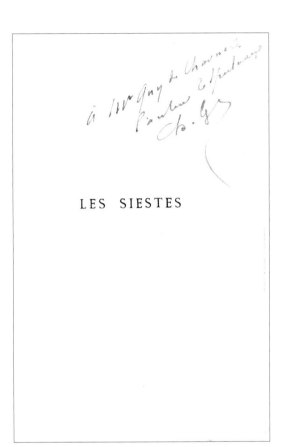

The title page of Les Siestes, *Charles Gandmougin's first published collection of poetry (1874) inscribed by the author*

This was the view of Fauré's first biographer, Louis Vuillemin, but it hardly suits the convention, established since Beethoven, that great composers' creative lives should be divided into three.

Of course one should not allow Beethoven's output to dictate the circumstances of Fauré's, but one must be wary of the arbitrary nature of these Hamelle volumes, which have governed the perceptions of the devoted performer and listener over the years – or at least since 1908. The musicologist has to be concerned with the composer's œuvre as a whole, not just the *mélodies*. Jankélévitch believed that the second period begins only with the *Cinq mélodies 'de Venise'* in 1891 (Nectoux has it beginning a few years earlier in 1888) and lasts until 1904. It would indeed be accurate to date Fauré's third and last period from 1905, with his change of publisher to Heugel. This charts Fauré's first period as lasting for nearly thirty years (1862–91), but so be it: he was a late and slow developer, and as exceptional as some of the songs are from the late 1870s and 1880s, these should surely be more accurately described as a later phase of a 'first period'. They clearly do not belong in the same 'second' stylistic category that begins in 1891 with the Verlaine settings 'de Venise' (with a foretaste by way of prologue in two Verlaine songs of 1887–88), and continues through *La Bonne chanson*.

The songs of the first and second *recueils* are different from each other, not least because the second marks a change of publisher from Choudens to Hamelle, and because *Le Papillon et la fleur* and *Nell*, which open each of the two *recueils* are notably different from each other in character. On the other hand, in the larger perspective of an exceptionally long career, they both fall under the larger umbrella of the composer's earlier work. If Fauré had already deepened considerably as a song composer by 1878, the listener who is following the composer's development and measuring his progress must be prepared for all sorts of further revelations, shocks and surprises. Such is the nature of this composer that just when we believe that we have got the measure of Fauré's music he perplexes us by moving forward relentlessly – usually by tiny increments – but with a slow determination that might be compared to that of a mighty tree – impressive even as a sapling, in its youth already capable of giving generous shade, but containing within itself the possibility of landmark height and grandeur that few would have suspected at first planting.

1   Quoted in Jessica Duchen, *Gabriel Fauré* (London: Phaidon, 2000), p. 53.

2   *Sérénade toscane*: Aspects of this song's interpretation are discussed in Chapter 16, p. 406.

3   'I can no longer sing … This night I slept beneath clear starlit skies.'

4   'I can no longer sing, for I have no voice / It remains within my mouth, and does not let me speak … .'

5   Marguerite de Saint-Marceaux, *Journal 1894–1927*, ed. M. Chimènes (Paris: Fayard, 2007), p. 34.

6   *Sylvie*: Aspects of this song's interpretation are discussed in Chapter 16, p. 406.

7   Gabriel Fauré, *Correspondance*, ed. Jean-Michel Nectoux (Paris: Flammarion, 1980), p. 83.

8   See Foreword, p. xvi.

9   The traditionally shortened form for 'Institut de France', a collective noun for the five French *académies* honouring the greatest living French artists and scientists, with a certain number of chairs (or *fauteuils*) reserved for musicians. A new member can be elected only on the death of someone in the same discipline, whose *fauteuil* is thus vacated.

10 *Poëme d'un jour*: Aspects of this cycle's interpretation are discussed in Chapter 16, p. 407.

11 Nectoux, *Gabriel Fauré: A Musical Life*, p. 34.

12 Quoted in Duchen, *Gabriel Fauré*, p. 63.

13 Saint-Marceaux, *Journal 1894–1927*, pp. 149–50.

14 *Nell*: Aspects of this song's interpretation are discussed in Chapter 16, p. 408.

15 Set to music by Delius with the refrain: 'I have been faithful to thee, O Cynara, in my fashion'.

16 *Le Voyageur*: Aspects of this song's interpretation are discussed in Chapter 16, p. 408.

17 Vladimir Jankélévitch, *Fauré et ses mélodies* (Paris: Librairie Plon, 1938), p. 68.

18 *Automne*: Aspects of this song's interpretation are discussed in Chapter 16, p. 408.

Chapter Six

Bachelor and Husband –
The Silvestre Years

Armand Silvestre, Victor Wilder

In 1878 eight songs had been composed; in this chapter we consider twelve *mélodies* written within a span of six years, 1879–85 – a period in the composer's life that is particularly poorly documented in terms of surviving letters and thus biographical information. These six years may not have been the most eventful in Fauré's career, but they saw the consolidation of his reputation and a deepening of his art. There were an increasing number of performances of his works, and his music began to appear regularly in print. Two Baudelaire settings as well as one of Hugo's *L'Absent*, and the more recently composed *Sérénade toscane*, were published by Choudens in January 1879; the first *recueil* of *Vingt mélodies* appeared under the Choudens imprint at the end of the same year, although by this time the composer was already considering a change of publisher and a move to Hamelle.

In April 1879 Fauré visited Cologne, where he saw productions of *Das Rheingold* and *Die Walküre* as well as paying his respects to the graves of Beethoven and Schumann. On returning to Paris he wrote one of his most famous songs, *Les Berceaux*; it is likely that he composed *Notre amour* at about the same time. In September he journeyed to Munich with Messager to see Wagner's *Ring*. By now Fauré was thoroughly acquainted with Wagner's works, but he seemed to have had the ability (unlike many other French composers) to keep his own harmonic and aesthetic agenda entirely separate from that of the master of Bayreuth. The most substantial work of 1879 was the *Ballade* for piano in F♯ major, Op. 19 (it is possible that Fauré showed it to Liszt as a work in progress in 1877). This is the piece that Debussy was many years later to characterise as a pretty woman adjusting her shoulder strap – the performer who inspired this withering comparison was Fauré's mistress, the pianist Marguerite Hasselemans, who apparently adjusted that item of her apparel between phrases.

Artistic bitchery apart, Debussy (hardly a paragon of virtue when it came to his relationships with women) had identified a crucial aspect of Fauré's creative personality. For J.-M. Nectoux, much of Fauré's music is redolent of the 'odor di femmina' (as Da Ponte's Don Giovanni put it).[1] If the composer were to have listed his lady friends (most of the names are not known to us) the result would have been a catalogue if not quite worthy of the 'mille e tre' vaunted by Leporello on Don Giovanni's behalf then at least far exceeding the twenty-one paramours of the female protagonist of Wolf's *Ich hab in Penna*. Throughout his life Fauré sought out women as lovers and mother-figures, sometimes united in the same person, although only the most important of these have a place in his biography. Marie Clerc continued to be Fauré's maternal substitute at this period, while the role of surrogate

129

elder sister was taken by the much more artistically ambitious Marguerite ('Meg') Baugnies, later Marguerite de Saint-Marceaux (1850–1930), whose musical salon was to become one of the most important in Paris.[2] Madame de Saint-Marceaux, amateur singer and pianist, was later to be the dedicatee of *Après un rêve* and Fauré's First Nocturne (as well as *La Flûte enchantée* from Ravel's *Shéhérazade*). Neither Marie nor Marguerite was the composer's lover as far as we know. Indeed, it was to Marie Clerc that Fauré confided his amorous feelings for the young singer who inspired the first song discussed in this chapter, an early masterpiece, composed in 1879.

(32) *Les Berceaux* (*The cradles*)[3]
1879, Op. 23 No. 1, 'À Mademoiselle Alice Boissonnet', second Hamelle collection p. 27, B♭ minor, 12/8, *Andante*

Le long du quai les grands vaisseaux,	*Along the quay the great ships,*
Que la houle incline en silence,	*Listing silently with the surge,*
Ne prennent pas garde aux berceaux	*Pay no heed to the cradles*
Que la main des femmes balance.	*Rocked by women's hands.*
Mais viendra le jour des adieux,	*But the day of parting will come,*
Car il faut que les femmes pleurent,	*For it is decreed that women shall weep,*
Et que les hommes curieux	*And that men with questing spirits*
Tentent les horizons qui leurrent.	*Shall seek enticing horizons.*
Et ce jour-là les grands vaisseaux,	*And on that day the great ships,*
Fuyant le port qui diminue,	*Leaving the dwindling harbour behind,*
Sentent leur masse retenue	*Shall feel their hulls held back*
Par l'âme des lointains berceaux.	*By the soul of the distant cradles.*

Sully Prudhomme (1839–1907)

This lyric appears in Sully Prudhomme's *Stances et poëmes* (1865), where it has the cumbersome heading 'Le Long du quai les grands vaisseaux'. In July 1879 Fauré, in a letter to Marie Clerc, mentioned that he had received 'a long and flattering letter from Sully Prudhomme'. This had addressed the composer's quandary regarding the work's title; 'I have the poet's authorization to call it *Les Berceaux*', Fauré wrote with some relief (there was another poem with the same title in the collection).[4]

This song was composed four years after *Au bord de l'eau*. Although both the Sully Prudhomme lyrics employ water imagery, *Les Berceaux* has a much closer musical affinity with one of the Armand Silvestre songs from 1878, *Automne*. These two songs, both conceived for the mezzo-soprano voice, are also linked by their dedicatee – one of Fauré's pupils in his harmony class, Alice Boissonnet. In one of his letters to Marie Clerc in May 1878 the composer refers to Alice as the 'spring rose of the month of May' (clearly he associated his feelings for her, give or take a month with the emotional rapture of the June-inspired *Nell*). This infatuation produced three wonderful songs before Alice married Henri de Lassus and bore him seven sons; after this she was no doubt busy rocking cradles of her own.

The theme of 'Les Berceaux' might be summed up in lines by Charles Kingsley: 'For men must work, and women must weep / And there's little to earn and many to keep / Though the harbour bar be moaning.'[5] Sully Prudhomme makes a play of words between the vessels ('vaisseaux') in which sailors go off to sea, and the smaller yet similarly shaped cradles ('berceaux') in which mothers nurse the children of sailors whose fathers are in danger of being lost at sea. Fauré has written an inspired combination of *berceuse* and barcarolle in the key of B♭ minor, a very special tonality in his songs. The introduction and the music of the opening section seem suitably intimate for the rocking of cradles; we are soon to hear how the same music will become imposingly majestic as it illustrates ships cradled on the ocean wave. The undulating accompaniment in triplets where the hands seem almost superimposed on each other is a masterful invention, one of many where Fauré dreams up a cunning new deployment of digital resource for the pianist; one has to be a pianist to *feel* under the fingers here the novelty and gentle inevitability of these syncopations between overlapping thumbs. It is also likely that Fauré had in mind the piano writing of Saint-Saëns's *Soirée en mer*, a song that had already influenced the much earlier Gautier setting *Les Matelots*.

Title-page of Les Berceaux, *published by Hamelle*

In the climactic central section ('Tentent les horizons qui leurrent') the music takes on a heightened dramatic tone with a rare dotted semibreve crowning the vocal line with anguish on '*leur*rent'. This kind of outburst is relatively rare in this composer's *mélodies*, but by no means unique; the intensity of this passage alone would be a sufficient riposte to Debussy's unfair assertion that Fauré is merely a 'master of charms'. With this climax we hear the heartbreak of the women left behind, who have come to regard the sea as their husbands' perpetually destructive mistress. This explosion of feeling subsides as suddenly as it arose, as if to emphasise the impotence of the women's jealousy in the face of the ocean's power. J-M Nectoux points out that it is also in this song that Fauré discovers, at the other end of the spectrum, the power of 'poignant sweetness' expressed within a pianissimo dynamic. [6]

The vocal range of the song encompasses an amazing thirteenth, from low A♭ to high F. It is a measure of Fauré's control of his musical material that he avoids any sense of helter-skelter contrast between the women at home and the men at sea. Everything is skilfully managed with poise, including a remarkably concise, and superbly effective, transition into the poem's third strophe. The *moto perpetuo* which is this haunting *mélodie* seems a perfect musical illustration for Whitman's contemporary words: 'Out of the cradle endlessly rocking … the musical shuttle … A reminiscence sing.' The distancing idea of a reminiscence is a useful one for performers because it discourages the singer from over-emoting in a way that has nothing to do with the Fauré style. Norman Suckling expressed this caveat perfectly when he wrote that 'The song as a whole conveys a desire to resolve feeling into form, rather than to be affected by feeling in itself.'[7]

Armand Silvestre by Kauffmann, frontispiece for Pour faire rire *(1883)*

Les Berceaux is a Sully Prudhomme setting with the musical breadth that we associate with the Silvestre songs. The close relationship between *Automne* and *Les Berceaux* is perhaps forged by the low and warm voice (and personality) of their common dedicatee, Alice Boissonnet, rather than by their different poets. Though Sully Prudhomme was taken rather more seriously as a poet than Armand Silvestre, it was to Silvestre's poetry that Fauré was to turn for inspiration for the next five years.

Paul-Armand Silvestre was born in Paris on 18 April 1837. Although much of his poetry is suffused with a veiled preoccupation with 'le corps féminin', a devotion to women and the 'odor di femmina', his prose style was altogether earthier, one may almost say Rabellaisian. Even if Fauré's Silvestre settings are not often in themselves overtly erotic, the poet's work seems perfectly suited at this stage of his career to Fauré the charming bachelor with a roving eye. Silvestre was a civil servant, an art critic (a specialist on the subject of the female nude) and a newspaper columnist. He worked in the archives and library of the Ministry of Finance, and then became *inspecteur des beaux-arts* in 1892. In 1866 he had published his first book of verse, *Rimes neuves et vieilles*, with a preface by someone no less distinguished than George Sand. His Parnassian poetry, a great deal of which he wrote over the years, was only one string to his bow; his fame with the general reader was based on his 'contes', amusing and sometimes *risqué* instalments that appeared first in that famous journal *Gil Blas* (from 1880) and were then republished in innumerable collections. The poet was fond of mildly scatological references in his humorous writings and, despite the rather prim disapproval of such older luminaries as the Goncourt brothers, his work amused the general public; his fame on the popular front ensured publication of an astoundingly prolific oeuvre that was very much part of the *esprit gaullois* of the *belle époque*. In Vicaire's bibliography Silvestre's publications occupy no fewer than thirty-two closely printed columns.[8] One can imagine these works, once so popular, thrown away in cartloads long before the First World War – judging by the comparative rarity of Silvestre's verse in the second-hand bookshops of today.

The poet was more than usually attracted to music; his first published collection of poems and five subsequent volumes each featured a section entitled 'Vers pour être chantés'. An alphabetical list of composers other than Fauré to have set his verse is impressive: Louis Aubert, André Caplet, Alexis Castillon (the influential and surprisingly early *Six poésies d'Armand Silvestre* of 1872), Emmanuel Chabrier (perhaps his least successful song, *Credo d'amour*, Sylvestrian eroticism comingled with religion), Ernest Chausson, Léo Delibes, Henri Duparc (*Testament* of 1884), Edouard Lalo, Jules

Massenet, André Messager, Gabriel Pierné. The poet's strongest musical connection was with Massenet, Fauré's *bête noir*, whose *faiblesse* for otherwise weak poets is a major reason for the neglect of his songs today. Though Silvestre was by far the most talented of Massenet's regular poets, Fauré's later song collaborators included writers of a much finer pedigree. Nevertheless, it is beyond contention that some of the Silvestre settings are among the most frequently sung and admired of Fauré's songs.

Perhaps the composer was drawn to Silvestre in the first place because the poet had contributed to Massenet's success as a *mélodie* composer (as early as 1866–68 with the *Poème d'avril*). Silvestre was also a successful librettist; he provided such composers as Godard (*Jocelyn*), Lalo, Litolff, Massenet (*Grisélidis*) and Saint-Saëns (*Henry VIII*) with libretti. Later on a personal friendship between Fauré and Silvestre was kindled during their work on an opera that never came to fruition, *Lizarda*, although a production at the Opéra-Comique had already been scheduled. The poet provided Fauré with decent musical verse; the composer set poetry that appealed to the music-buying public while still finding in Silvestre's imagery much that stimulated his own creative impulses. This was a useful collaboration, and at times, almost despite itself, it was a

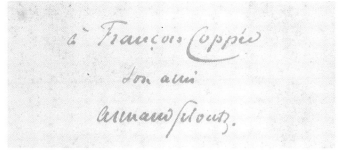

Armand Silvestre, frontispiece to Poésies *(1880) and the poet's dedication to F. Coppée*

partnership that touched greatness. Silvestre died on 19 February 1901 in Toulouse, where a statue was erected in his honour. Perhaps touched by news of his old colleague's death, Fauré was to return to the poetry of Silvestre twice in 1904 – *Le Plus doux chemin* and *Le Ramier*, both enchanting songs that look back nostalgically to a more complacent age of artistic expressivity. But it is significant that Fauré returned to the poet's earlier collections for these two settings; when one reads the books of poems indefatigably published by Silvestre after Fauré had discreetly abandoned him as he might an amiable mistress who was too busy with others to notice his absence (*Les Chemins des étoiles*, 1885; *Roses d'octobre*, 1890; *Les Tendresses*, 1898; *Les Fleurs d'hiver*, 1900) the style seems to become heavier and more marmoreal – these are lyrics that have lost their freshness, stuck in the 1880s, portentous and unwieldy when compared (an unkind comparison admittedly) with Verlaine's lyrics. Fauré seems to have moved on to different pastures at exactly the right time.

(33) *Notre amour* (*Our love*)[9]

*c.*1879, Op. 23 No. 2, 'À Mme C. Castillon', second Hamelle collection p. 30, E major, 6/8, *Allegretto*

Notre amour est chose légère	*Our love is light and gentle*
Comme les parfums que le vent	*Like fragrance fetched by the breeze*
Prend aux cimes de la fougère	*From the tips of ferns*
Pour qu'on les respire en rêvant.	*For us to breathe while dreaming.*
— Notre amour est chose légère.	*— Our love is light and gentle.*
Notre amour est chose charmante,	*Our love is enchanting,*
Comme les chansons du matin	*Like morning songs,*
Où nul regret ne se lamente,	*Where no regret is voiced,*
Où vibre un espoir incertain.	*Quivering with uncertain hopes.*
— Notre amour est chose charmante.	*— Our love is enchanting.*
Notre amour est chose sacrée	*Our love is sacred*
Comme le mystère des bois	*Like woodland mysteries,*
Où tressaille une âme ignorée,	*Where an unknown soul throbs*
Où les silences ont des voix.	*And silences can be heard.*
— Notre amour est chose sacrée.	*— Our love is sacred.*
Notre amour est chose infinie,	*Our love is infinite*
Comme les chemins des couchants	*Like sunset paths,*
Où la mer, aux cieux réunie,	*Where the sea, joined with the skies,*
S'endort sous les soleils penchants.	*Falls asleep beneath slanting suns.*
[— Notre amour est chose infinie]	*[— Our love is eternal]*,
Notre amour est chose éternelle	*Our love is eternal.*
Comme tout ce qu'un Dieu vainqueur	*Like all that a victorious God*
A touché du feu de son aile,	*Has brushed with his fiery wing,*
Comme tout ce qui vient du cœur,	*Like all that comes from the heart,*
— Notre amour est chose éternelle.	*— Our love is eternal.*

Armand Silvestre (1837–1901)

The poem comes from Silvestre's *Les Ailes d'or* (1880) although the song was composed before the poem's appearance in book form. There are five rather wordy strophes, and *Notre amour* is often heard as a breathless patter song where the whole performance is geared to the launching of the singer's final bars, which include an optional high B. If presented in this way the song impresses as a vocalise but fails as a *mélodie*. Suckling regards it as being 'still under the influence of the ballad form which required among other things a top-note just before the end'; one thinks of Roger Quilter's *Love's Philosophy* as an English equivalent.

With this number of words to put across (most of them proclaiming thoughtful sincerity rather than dizzy excitement) performers should observe the composer's *Allegretto*, a marking that allows for a certain *élan* while avoiding the demented gabble of an unbridled *Allegro*. The tonal architecture has a subtle asymmetry: the first and third strophes move from the E major tonic to G♯ minor and B major, the second from the tonic to F♯ minor and A major. For the fourth and fifth strophes the text suggests greater intimacy: the elegant sextuplets of the accompaniment are given deeper meaning by the affectionate counterpoint between the vocal line and an ascending five-finger scale in the pianist's left hand (at bars 21 to 23 and 26 to 27). Between these two verses, there is a beautiful interlude – an arched rainbow of sound suspended in the right hand over the lapping of the tide in the left – a perfect illustration of the poem's immediately preceding imagery.

This little interlude for piano at bar 25 replaces the poet's repetition of the line 'Notre amour est chose infinie' at the end of the strophe; in all the other verses Fauré follows Silvestre's repetition to the letter. The brief detour into G major for the penultimate 'chose éternelle' adds strength to the clinching vocal cadence. The postlude betokens the colloquy of mutual affection: undulating triplets alternate and mesh with five-finger scales, an

ARMAND SILVESTRE

————

LES AILES D'OR

POÉSIES NOUVELLES

1878 — 1880

————

PARIS

G. CHARPENTIER, ÉDITEUR

13, RUE DE GRENELLE-SAINT-GERMAIN, 13

—

1880

Title-page of Silvestre's Les Ailes d'or *(1880)*

exchange that symbolises the mingling of twinned souls, masculine and feminine. This is the kind of Silvestre-inspired eroticism in which Fauré excelled.

❧   ❧   ❧   ❧

In the summer of 1880 there was another visit to Munich for more Wagner performances. Fauré was much taken with *Die Meistersinger* and disappointed with *Tannhäuser*. This year was given over mainly to the performance of chamber and piano music: the *Berceuse*, the Violin Sonata, the Piano Quartet, the *Elégie* for cello (composed in 1880) and the *Trois romances sans paroles* for piano. Neither was the following year productive for Fauré in vocal terms; the *Messe des pêcheurs de Villerville* for three-part women's choir and soloists was composed in collaboration with André Messager (the two composers were guests of the Clercs in Normandy), but otherwise 1881 was remarkable chiefly for piano music – the Second Nocturne, the First Impromptu and probably the First Barcarolle. Partially concealed in this account is the shadow of the opera *Lizarda*, which Fauré worked on with Armand Silvestre; nothing at all remains of this work, but it is possible, if rather surprising, that the composer destroyed something that was already in an advanced state of preparation; indeed, a production at the Opéra-Comique had already been scheduled. A third visit to Munich to see Wagner operas was made, this time in the company of Marguerite Baugnies and her mother.

❧   ❧   ❧   ❧

135

There was only one song composed between 1880 and 1881, very possibly a by-product of *Lizarda*.

(34) *Le Secret* *(The secret)*[10]
1881, Op. 23 No. 3, 'À Mme Alice Boissonnet', second Hamelle collection p. 35, D♭ major, 2/4,
Adagio

Je veux que le matin l'ignore	*Would that the morn were unaware*
Le nom que j'ai dit à la nuit,	*Of the name I told to the night,*
Et qu'au vent de l'aube, sans bruit,	*And that in the dawn breeze, silently,*
Comme une larme il s'évapore.	*It would vanish like a tear.*
Je veux que le jour le proclame	*Would that the day might proclaim it,*
L'amour qu'au matin j'ai caché,	*The love I hid from the morn,*
Et, sur mon cœur ouvert penché,	*And poised above my open heart,*
Comme un grain d'encens il l'enflamme.	*Like a grain of incense kindle it.*
Je veux que le couchant l'oublie	*Would that the sunset might forget*
Le secret que j'ai dit au jour	*The secret I told to the day*
Et l'emporte, avec mon amour,	*And would carry it and my love away*
Aux plis de sa robe pâlie!	*In the folds of its faded robe!*

Armand Silvestre (1837–1901)

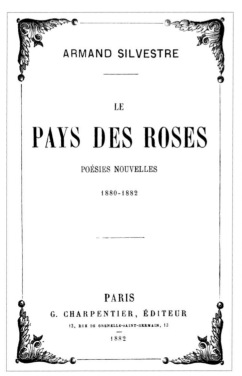

How pleased the alluring Alice Boissonnet must have been with this, the third Fauré song dedicated to her, and the third masterpiece. The poem was printed in Silvestre's collection entitled *Le Pays des roses* (1882), where its title is *Mystère*. Once again, the composer must have had the poem in his hands long before the appearance of the book. This is the Fauré–Silvestre collaboration at its best. If the gently flowing *Nell* personifies one kind of Fauré love song, *Le Secret* is the first and among the finest of another more contemplative genre. This is music that encompasses religious awe or devotion (the composer of the *Requiem* can be identified here, and the accompaniment often suggests the organ). Nectoux refers to a 'style psalmodié' and draws attention to the song's close relationship to the contemporary *Elégie* for violoncello and piano.[11]

In songs of this type the tempi of the beats (though not necessarily the smaller note values that make up those beats) can seem slow enough to approach a kind of

Title-page of Silvestre's Le Pays des roses *(1882)*

immobility. This achieves a transcendental effect with minimalist means – in short, a mystery worthy of the poem's printed title.

This is the first of several highly successful Fauré songs in five flats – D♭ major (a favourite Chopin tonality), or its relative minor B♭. The vocal line, wistful and heartfelt, is introduced by four crotchet chords; the second of these, on the third degree of the scale, introduces a Gregorian flavour to the music that Jankélévitch compares to the Franciscan fervour to be found in some of Liszt's piano and vocal music. The same writer finds that the delicacy of the two-bar interludes between Silvestre's strophes is like 'the breath of the beloved'. Like Schubert, Fauré has the ability to use the major key to write music that is tinged with melancholy – this silent worship expects, and receives, no reciprocation, a passivity that is typical of this composer's inability to impose himself, or his music, on the unreceptive ear.

A side of Fauré always doubted his own worth, and the worth of his work, but the following incident, recounted by the composer to Henri Malherbe, is revealing: 'I'd recently finished a song called *Le Secret*. I played it to Henri Duparc who began to tremble with emotion. The composer of *La Vie antérieure* began to punch me with his fists shouting "Savage! Brute!" I realised then that *Le Secret* was something good.'[12]

Title-page of Le Secret

During this period Fauré often acted as an accompanist for various recreational singing classes that were run for the benefit of well-to-do young ladies of a musical disposition. One of these choirs was organised by Pauline Roger (the mother of the soprano Thérèse Roger), and in 1881 Fauré obliged her by writing a piece for female chorus (mostly in unison) that includes passages for two soloists – also female voices. Like *Madrigal*, discussed later in this chapter, *Le Ruisseau* is vocal chamber music of exquisite craftsmanship, and it deserves to make an appearance from time to time in shared recital programmes when there a sufficient number of singers on stage. These two works, among the least-known of any of Fauré's piano-accompanied vocal music, can be performed by a number of good solo voices. While dispensing with the choral element may not be what the composer had in mind, such an approach might rescue music that is all but forgotten within the canon of his piano-accompanied vocal music.

(35) *Le Ruisseau* (*The stream*)

1881?, Op. 22, 'À Mme Pauline Roger', Hamelle, E♭ major, ♩, *Andante moderato*

Au bord du clair ruisseau,	*On the banks of a limpid stream*
Croît la fleur solitaire,	*Grows the solitary flower,*
Dont la corolla brille	*Whose corolla gleams*
Au milieu des roseaux;	*Amid the reeds;*
Pensive, elle s'incline	*Pensively she bows her head*
Et son ombre légère	*And her faint shadow*
Se berce mollement	*Rocks gently*
Sur la moiré des eaux.	*On the silky water.*
Ô fleur, ô doux parfum,	*O flower, O sweet perfume,*
Lui dit le flot qui passe,	*The passing billows say to her,*
À mes tendres accents	*To my tender words*
La tristesse répond!	*Sadness makes reply!*
À mon suave élan	*Come! unite your charm*
Viens marier ta grâce,	*To my dashing elegance*
Laisse moi t'entraîner	*Let me bear you away*
Vers l'Océan profond!	*Toward the deep ocean.*
Mais il entourne en vain	*But he surrounds her in vain*
De sa douce caresse	*With his sweet caress,*
Cette flottante image	*This floating vision*
Aux incertains contours,	*With its blurred outline*
Se dérobe au baiser	*Escapes the moist kiss*
Humide qui l'oppresse	*That oppresses her,*
Et le flot éploré	*And the weeping stream*
Tristement suit son cours!	*Goes sadly on her way!*

Unidentified poet

This poem of thwarted love between non-human participants reminds us of Fauré's first song, *Le Papillon et la fleur*, thus a text not to be taken very seriously. But it does give the composer a chance to luxuriate in water music and to make something of a quiet joke. This French stream is a miniature and obviously of very little consequence in comparison with the mighty Rhine – a river much on Fauré's mind in these years of travel to Germany to hear Wagner's operas. Fauré's quartet is also a miniature, and it follows that the figurations around the tonic chord of E♭ in the accompaniment that dominate the song's first page can only be interpreted as a smilingly deferential reference to Wagner's *Das Rheingold* with its famously extended prelude in the same key. In *Le Ruisseau* Fauré keeps up these unchanging E♭ major arpeggios for only four bars, but in a musical climate where every Wagnerian allusion was quickly spotted, this is long enough and he has made his point. The words 'suave élan' in the poem perfectly describe the mood of the music, with its windingly sensual melody and its succession of smooth modulations – the tempo never hurried, but never dragging either. The piece predictably moves into ever-flattening regions of recherché tonality, but we realise that the music was conceived for amateurs when the descent of some of the more demanding vocal lines is doubled by the accompaniment. The end of the second strophe ends climactically in G♭ major with mention of the deep ocean, and this sets up a return to E♭ and a musical recapitulation of the first verse.

The words 'Et le flot éploré / Tristement suit son cours' are repeated at the end to give the composer a chance to compose a musical envoi. In this closing passage, where, separate from the seraphic progress of the vocal line, the piano's semiquavers are led by a melody pricked out in the little finger of the pianist's right hand, we find an astonishing prophecy of the final page of *En sourdine* (1891) in the same key. In that masterpiece (with its words 'Voix de notre désespoir / Le rossignol chantera') the rustlings of E♭ major form a sad commentary on the loneliness of all beings, even when deeply in love. As the Romans observed, all animals are sad after coitus: 'Post coitum omnia animal triste'. After having temporarily submitted to the embrace of the stream, the flower must ruefully admit that their relationship is doomed. This renunciation inspires Fauré to music both plaintive and dignified, a combination of moods in the quartet's closing pages that would be recaptured in *En sourdine*, where the transience of the courtiers' late-afternoon dalliance is marked by the singing of the nightingale.

༃   ༃   ༃   ༃

Such was the composer's Wagnerian enthusiasm that he visited London for five days in May 1882 (the first of many visits to the British capital) in order to hear artists from Bayreuth sing the Ring. In July 1882 Fauré encountered Liszt for the second time; Fauré confessed that, according to Saint-Saëns, he turned green with shy embarrassment and pleasure when Liszt greeted him with open arms.[13] Perhaps it was on this occasion that Liszt sight-read the *Ballade* for piano and orchestra and then stopped as if defeated, saying he had 'run out of fingers'. Since then, almost every pianist or accompanist who has ever attempted (ill-advisedly) to play Fauré's music at sight has followed in Liszt's fingerprints and been forced to make more or less the same excuse. In return Fauré studied the music of Liszt and took it seriously; we have already quoted Jankélévitch on the harmonic world of *Le Secret*, and there are passages in Fauré's solo piano music that show a fleeting Lisztian influence, particularly when the composer moves into the higher reaches of the keyboard. At Villerville, as a guest of his friends Camille and Marie Clerc, Fauré completed a mythological scene for soloists, choirs and orchestra to words of Paul Collin, *La Naissance de Vénus*, Op. 29. Apart from this work, only two compositions date from 1882. These are both Armand Silvestre settings.

Title-page of Chanson d'amour

(36) *Chanson d'amour* (*Love song*)[14]

1882, Op. 27 No. 1, 'À Mlle Jane Huré', second Hamelle collection p. 37, F major, ♩, *Allegro moderato*

J'aime tes yeux, j'aime ton front,	*I love your eyes, I love your brow,*
Ô ma rebelle, ô ma farouche.	*O my rebel, O my wild one.*
J'aime tes yeux, j'aime ta bouche	*I love your eyes, I love your mouth*
Où mes baisers s'épuiseront.	*Where my kisses shall dissolve.*
J'aime ta voix, j'aime l'étrange	*I love your voice, I love the strange*
Grâce de tout ce que tu dis,	*Charm of all you say,*
Ô ma rebelle, ô mon cher ange,	*O my rebel, O my dear angel,*
Mon enfer et mon paradis!	*My inferno and my paradise.*
J'aime tout ce qui te fait belle,	*I love all that makes you beautiful*
De tes pieds jusqu'à tes cheveux,	*From your feet to your hair,*
Ô toi vers qui montent mes vœux,	*O you the object of all my vows,*
Ô ma farouche, ô ma rebelle!	*O my wild one, O my rebel!*

Armand Silvestre (1837–1901)

In his *Journal de mes mélodies* Francis Poulenc wrote that this was one of the songs he most hated when sung by female singers (Duparc's *Phidylé* was another) because of Silvestre's unambiguously masculine text with its typically veiled eroticism. Poulenc's distaste is reminiscent of Benjamin Britten's intense dislike of the *travesti* element in Strauss's *Der Rosenkavalier*. One suspects that Fauré, the ardent heterosexual, would have had nothing against the Sapphic undertone in Strauss's opera, and nothing against *Chanson d'amour* receiving a Cherubino-like performance, particularly if it was performed in the original mezzo key. He was more than happy for *La Bonne chanson*, with its ardently masculine poems, to be sung by Emma Bardac, its soprano dedicatee (admittedly this was in private, and he chose a tenor for the first public performance of that work).

Like *Le Secret*, the poem is from Silvestre's collection *Le Pays des roses*. Both the courtly words and the music bring to mind the Gounod setting *Ô ma belle rebelle*, a sixteenth-century evocation with a poem by Jean-Antoine de Baïf. The pattern of Gounod's accompaniment is a single left-hand note in the bass clef followed by three in the treble, an alternation between left and right hand that suggests the strumming of lute or guitar; in *Chanson d'amour* Fauré follows suit in perfect sympathy with the time-travelling tradition so beautifully demonstrated by the earlier master. Indeed, with the exception of the early *Puisque j'ai mis ma lèvre*, *Chanson d'amour* is Fauré's first exercise in his so-called madrigal style. (It is notable that Silvestre's volume of verse *La Chanson des heures* contains a twelve-poem sequence entitled 'Madrigaux dans le goût ancien', the source of Fauré's four-part *Madrigal*, Op. 35, discussed below.) Fauré transcends pastiche by taking the refined musical manners of an earlier age and incorporating them into the *pudeur* of his own creative spirit (Reynaldo Hahn, with a comparatively restricted musical language, was to do exactly the same thing more often and with greater *fin de siècle* self-consciousness).

In *Chanson d'amour* we also detect the origins of Fauré's 'Venetian' settings of Verlaine. As is often the case with Fauré, this is recherché music of the greatest subtlety that is only pretending to be simple. Countless inadequate performances have rendered this *fausse naïveté* merely banal. The performers must be sensitive to the song's harmonic nuances, the imitative flirtations between piano and voice (and between left hand and right), as well as the enharmonic puns that Fauré incorporates into the music as a chord pivots between two possible resolutions. The tiniest musical hesitation on the words 'Où mes baisers s'épuiseront' is indicated by the direction *senza rigore* (unique in Fauré's songs) in bars 9 and 28 (and interestingly different from the *poco rit.* on the same words in bar 49). One cannot help wondering whether this marking – not exactly in everyday use – was lifted by Proust from this song to appear, thirty-five years later, in *À l'ombre des jeunes filles en fleur*, where Odette (Mme Swann) is amused to describe the relative informality of her salons as being *senza rigore*, in contrast to those of the more formal Mme Verdurin.

The use of this direction in Fauré is paradoxical, for it is the rare exception that proves the rule of the composer's tight control over rhythmic nuance. (There are too many performers who employ a *senza rigore* attitude throughout this composer's output, and not only when permitted, as here, to do so.) There is something deliciously taunting about these tiny moments of relaxation that is specific to *Chanson d'amour*: the composer is playing with us as surely as the 'farouche rebelle' is toying with the affections of her serenader.

The creation of a musical refrain by re-using Silvestre's first verse twice more, (before verse 3 and again at the end, making five musical strophes in all), is a rare instance of Fauré expanding, rather than cutting, a poem. The enjambment, without a breath between 'rebelle' at the end of the fourth verse of music and the final repeat of the refrain is a charmingly ardent touch (again one thinks of the impatient Cherubino) in a song where every perfectly placed note betokens a smiling composer of the deepest seriousness.

(37) *La Fée aux chansons* (The fairy of songs)[15]
1882, Op. 27 No. 2, 'À Mme Edmond Fuchs', second Hamelle collection p. 41, F major, 2/4, *Allegretto vivo*

Il était une fée,	*There was a fairy,*
D'herbe folle coiffée,	*Crowned with rank weeds*
Qui courait les buissons,	*Who ran through the bushes*
Sans s'y laisser surprendre,	*Without being caught,*
En avril, pour apprendre	*In April, to teach*
Aux oiseaux leurs chansons.	*The birds their songs.*
Lorsque geais et linottes,	*When jays and linnets,*
Faisaient des fausses notes	*Sang wrong notes*
En récitant leurs chants.	*As they recited their songs.*
La fée, avec constance,	*The fairy, tirelessly,*
Gourmandait d'importance	*Sternly rebuked*
Ces élèves méchants.	*Those naughty pupils.*
Sa petite main nue,	*Her little bare hand,*
D'un brin d'herbe menue	*With a tiny blade of grass*
Cueilli dans les halliers,	*Plucked from the thickets,*
Pour stimuler leurs zèles,	*To stimulate their zeal*
Fouettait sur leurs ailes	*Would whip the wings*
Ces mauvais écoliers.	*Of those bad scholars.*

Par un matin d'automne,	*One autumn morning*
Elle vient et s'étonne	*She comes and is amazed*
De voir les bois déserts.	*To find the woods deserted.*
Avec les hirondelles,	*With the swallows,*
Ses amis infidèles	*Her unfaithful friends*
Avaient fui dans les airs.	*Had flown away on the wind.*
Et tout l'hiver la fée,	*And all winter long, the fairy,*
D'herbe morte coiffée,	*Crowned with dead grass*
Et comptant les instants,	*And counting time*
Sous les forêts immenses,	*In the vast forests,*
Compose des romances	*Composes songs*
Pour le prochain printemps.	*For the coming spring.*

Armand Silvestre (1837–1901)

Fauré wrote from Toulouse to the singer Henriette Fuchs (1836–1927) on 19 September 1882: 'I shall have the honour of bringing to you in Paris a little song I have composed for you and that I now ask permission to dedicate to you.'[16] This was *La Fée aux chansons*. Madame Fuchs was only an amateur, it is true, but she ran a respectable musical salon, and was the co-founder with Charles-Marie Widor of the Concordia choral society. Fauré seems to have been genuinely impressed by what he refers to in the same letter as her 'very great gifts'. In the distinguished roster of Fauré performers, Henriette Fuchs occupies a special place: she gave the first performances at Société Nationale de la Musique (SNM) concerts of a quartet of famous *mélodies* – *Après un rêve* and *Sylvie* (on 11 January 1879) and *Nell* and *Automne* (on 28 January 1881). Her daughter Noémi married into the Lalo family, and Fauré was moved by news of Noémi's death to write his Eleventh Nocturne in 1913. It would be interesting to know what Fauré saw in this lyric, which is unique in his output. Did he regard the women who nurtured and inspired him (and made him work harder, like Marie Clerc) as his personal good fairies – as if they themselves were supernatural composers at one remove?

If *Automne* is richly textured and low in tessitura, *La Fée aux chansons*, also a song of the seasons, is transparently light and high, its mirror-image and opposite. Gerald Moore selected this *mélodie* to be performed at his eightieth birthday concert in 1979. This shy and neglected song of aerial enchantment had long been one of his personal favourites, although the great accompanist admitted that it was tricky to play. It has a drawback common to the sweeter Silvestre settings, a kind of winsomeness that borders on (but does not fall into) the sugary trap of many of the Massenet songs. The harmonic structure of the Fauré piece is too strong and well planned for the music to collapse into the fey shapelessness that undermines many of his rival's *mélodies*. Of course the poem is nothing more than a cleverly crafted confection, but it is of a perfect shape (and length) for a fast song that sets to music one fleet syllable after the other. Silvestre was right to place it in his 'Vers pour être chantés' (in *Les Ailes d'or*).

Fauré is usually a composer wedded to the strength of his marvellously conceived bass lines, but occasionally, in the interests of sparkle and brightness, he transports us (as in some of his piano music) into the higher, relatively weightless regions of the treble clef. In *La Fée aux chansons*, the listener is sprinkled with glistening stardust by the lightest of fingers, and 'The Master of Charms'

142

(Debussy's phrase) does not seem an inaccurate soubriquet. But this song contains a special surprise that is reserved for the poem's fourth verse. We have been delighted by the lightness of the fairy's tread in spring and summer, but autumn brings different music. For fourteen bars (at 'Par un matin d'automne', marked *molto meno mosso*) we enter another harmonic sphere. Fauré allows himself to broach that world of mists and mysterious allusion which was soon to become Debussy's distinctive province and to be heard in an early song like *La Romance d'Ariel*. Here mellowness contrasts with the glitter of what has gone before – a ravishingly beautiful interlude; but Fauré does not allow himself to dally long. A swift rise of triplets transports us out of the autumnal reverie, and the flight of the swallows sweeps us up from the doldrums with precipitous grace. The postlude of this very superior piece of salon music is also feather-light and ineffably graceful. The charm of Cécile Chaminade's songs comes to mind, although she could not dream of possessing Fauré's dazzling, and almost perplexing, command of harmony; it is this that lifts what might have been commonplace into other-worldly realms of great subtlety.

∾   ∾   ∾   ∾

Fauré was now approaching the age of forty and he was still a bachelor, sharing an apartment in Paris with his younger *copain* André Messager. It was some six years since the severing of his engagement with Marianne Viardot, and it was clearly time for him to settle down and marry – at least his influential friend Marguerite Baugnies, a notorious match-maker, thought so. (She was later unsuccessfully to attempt, with the support of Chausson, to engineer the marriage of Debussy to the soprano Thérèse Roger.) The biographer is hampered by the lack of surviving letters to and from Fauré at this stage of his life. The story goes (according to the composer Georges Migot, a friend of the Baugnies) that three eligible young ladies' names were put into a hat by Marguerite – all with surnames beginning with F (Feuillet, Feydeau and Fremiet) – and that Fauré pulled out the piece of paper bearing the name of Marie Fremiet, daughter of a sculptor, Emmanuel Fremiet, who was quite well known at the time.[17] It seems that it was Marguerite Baugnies, and her mother, who visited the Fremiet family and who essentially negotiated the marriage. This shows just how unwilling Fauré was to embark for a second time on the kind of wooing, with proposal and counter-proposal, that he had painfully endured with Marianne Viardot. The absence of a romantic background for this large step in the composer's life seems peculiar to say the least; it is certainly inexplicable, by modern standards in the West, and suggests the arranged marriages of the Indian subcontinent – some of which are admittedly very successful. One can only imagine that the composer had come to believe in fate or magic and trusted that by the sheer power of chance Marie Fremiet would turn out to be his new 'feé aux chansons'.

The marriage took place on 27 March 1883, and the couple moved into a home at 93 avenue Niel in the seventeenth *arrondissement*, where they were to live for the following three years. On 29 December the composer's first son, Emmanuel, was born. Romain Bussine unkindly claimed that the new Madame Fauré was so plain that he thought the composer must have married his mother's chambermaid; Nectoux's verdict on Marie Fremiet is that she was 'without beauty, or wit, or a fortune'.[18] Sadly, but almost predictably, the alliance proved to be what might be termed a mis-match, although there were also certain long-term compensations; divorce, it seems, was never considered (the couple were both devoted to their two sons), but there was an emotional void in the composer's life, as well as in that of his highly strung wife, who cast herself as a domestic martyr and envied her husband his success (such as it was in the earlier years and later with increasing justification). She was

Marie Fauré (née Fremiet) (1856–1926) at the time of her marriage

the daughter of an artist, and now the wife of an artist, and she felt her own artistic potential was smothered by the demands of being a mother, a role she shouldered with relentless fortitude.

She stayed at home and made beautiful painted fans that were sold to supplement the family income; her over-protective fears for the safety of her two children (exacerbated no doubt by the accidental deaths of Saint-Saëns's two young sons) were an excuse to opt out of travelling with the composer on his many journeys for both business and pleasure. After the early days of the marriage, when the couple had attempted to make a go of it, one feels that Fauré was simply relieved to have his freedom. His many affairs were conducted with discretion, but they added to his wife's suffering. She was of a woman of her time, bound by convention, devoted to her children and the respectability of their joint family name, and she put up with her circumstances as best as she could. Although her struggle to be someone in her own right is completely understandable (there is something heartbreaking about her stoic fortitude), Marie's passive aggression while accepting her victimhood must have made for a tense and miserable atmosphere in the Fauré household.

Their relationship perhaps worked best at a distance, and there is evidence of this in the detailed letters that he wrote to her about his work, particularly after 1900. This correspondence is often our most accurate source of information concerning the composer's own opinions of his music, and they contain his own marvellously aware comments on the whole creative process. In this area, at least, he was able to achieve with Marie a frankness in regard to something absolutely central to his inner life, an openness that was denied to his friends and admirers. The composer's son Philippe published these *Lettres intimes*, and they do display closeness of a special kind, the intimacy born of loyalty separated from romance and sexual attraction. Marie was a major shareholder in the family firm, and almost despite herself she played a role in Fauré's life that was unique. In fact, it is difficult to imagine any other woman, given the composer's promiscuous nature, displaying so much self-abnegating control.

At first, judging from the amount of music composed in the early years of the marriage, one might have pronounced the relationship a success, but there were early signs that the composer missed his freedom, and that he sought to recapture it, almost immediately. At the beginning of December 1883 Fauré composed what is perhaps the least known of his Armand Silvestre settings. This piece is written for vocal quartet or choir, with piano or orchestral accompaniment, a companion piece to *Le Ruisseau* from a couple of years earlier.

(38) *Madrigal* (*Madrigal*)

1 December 1883, Op. 35, 'À M. André Messager', D minor, 3/4, *Andante quasi allegretto*

Les Jeunes Gens:
— Inhumaines qui, sans merci,
Vous raillez de notre souci,
Aimez! aimez quand on vous aime!

The Young Men:
— Inhuman women who, without mercy,
Make fun of our turmoil,
Love! Love when you are loved!

Les Jeunes Filles:
— Ingrats qui ne vous doutez pas
Des rêves éclos sur vos pas,
Aimez! aimez quand on vous aime!

The Young Women:
— Ungrateful men who do not suspect
The dreams you arouse in your wake,
Love! Love when you are loved!

Les Jeunes Gens:
— Sachez, ô cruelles Beautés,
Que les jours d'aimer sont comptés.
Aimez! aimez quand on vous aime!

The Young Men:
— Mark well, O cruel beauties,
That the days of loving are numbered.
Love! love when you are loved!

Les Jeunes Filles:
— Sachez, amoureux inconstants,
Que le bien d'aimer n'a qu'un temps.
Aimez! aimez quand on vous aime!

The Young Women:
— Mark well, inconstant lovers
That love has but a single season.
Love! Love when you are loved!

Ensemble:
Un même destin nous poursuit
Et notre folie est la même:
C'est celle d'aimer qui nous fuit,
C'est celle de fuir qui nous aime!

Together:
The same fate pursues us both
And our folly is the same:
That of loving those who flee us,
That of fleeing those who love us!

Armand Silvestre (1837–1901)

The work was dedicated to Messager, Fauré's former flatmate, who was himself about to get married. In this four-part song (the poet's title is 'Pour un chœur alterné') the men demand that the women (whom they regard as inhumanly cruel) reciprocate the love they receive; the women (who regard the opposite sex as ingrats) demand that the men should do the same. Once quavers in the accompaniment have begun to purl persuasively up and down the keyboard for the song's third verse, the music registers something of the silken fascination of the duet *Puisqu'ici-bas toute âme*. Both sexes ruefully admit to a fascination with the chase, and confess that love ceases to be interesting once one is the object of it. This is an elegant rationalisation of promiscuity, but Silvestre's worldly text suggests that temptations such as these are too strong to fight.

The poem from Silvestre's *Les Chansons des heures* (in the subsection *Vers pour être chantés*, where it is the second of the 'Madrigaux dans le goût ancien') is just a little bit too risqué and cynical to have appealed to a blissfully happy married man. The poet indicates that it is to be sung alternately by young men ('les Jeunes Gens') and women ('les Jeunes Filles'), and the composer obediently follows

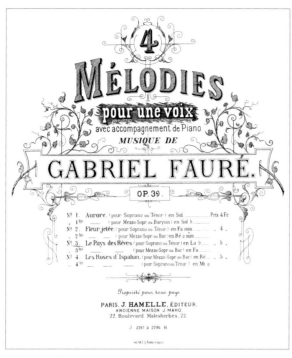

Title-page of Quatre mélodies, *Op. 39*

suit in the disposition of the writing for vocal quartet or choir.

Both the poem and the music subscribe to a kind of time-travel: the words, in the manner of a sixteenth-century rondel, are complemented by music that juxtaposes a suave modern sensuality (the fleet quavers at the end of piece – in D major at last – personifying those running away from the responsibilities of love are amusingly apt) with equally cheeky references to Johann Sebastian Bach. Charles Koechlin in his biography of Fauré was the first to unearth the source of these: the opening vocal line of *Madrigal* is derived from the beginning of Cantata No. 38 (*Aus tiefer Noth – From deepest need –* and perhaps this title said it all!), a fragment of melody that is also used as the theme of Fugue 8 of the first book of the *48 Preludes and Fugues*. Either of these works by Bach might have meant something special in the relationship between Fauré and Messager, who had been master and pupil since the exile of the École Niedermeyer in Switzerland in 1871. This was the only time that Fauré borrowed a musical idea from another composer in this way, and it seems to have been the nearest he came in his life to a public interchange of views on romantic or sexual matters with a male friend. The piece has the wittiness and suggestiveness of a speech by the best man at a wedding who has no real reason to assuage the worst fears of the bride, and it is significant that the composer found just what needed to be said in the poetry of Silvestre.

1884 was a busy and relatively productive year. In April the piano quartet was performed with its new finale, and in May three further Silvestre settings saw the light of day within less than a fortnight: *Aurore* (20 May); *Fleur jetée* (25 May) and *Le Pays des rêves* (30 May). Two of these were given their first performances in December – the songs of this year had an unusually quick turn-around. The summer was spent at Prunay with the composer's in-laws (Fauré had a particularly good relationship with his wife's father). Here he was able to work fruitfully on his D minor Symphony and on the second *Valse-caprice* for piano.

(39) **Aurore** (The dawn)[19]
20 May 1884, Op. 39 No. 1, 'À Mme Henriette Roger-Jourdain' G major, (, Andante

Des jardins de la nuit s'envolent les étoiles,	*Stars take wing from the gardens of night –*
Abeilles d'or qu'attire un invisible miel,	*Golden bees tempted by invisible honey,*
Et l'aube, au loin tendant la candeur de ses toiles,	*And the distant dawn, stretching its guileless veils,*
Trame de fils d'argent le manteau bleu du ciel.	*Weaves silver threads through the sky's blue cloak.*

Du jardin de mon cœur qu'un rêve lent enivre	*From the garden of my dream-enraptured heart,*
S'envolent mes désirs sur les pas du matin,	*My desires take wing as morning appears,*
Comme un essaim léger qu'à l'horizon de cuivre,	*Like a delicate swarm called to the copper horizon*
Appelle un chant plaintif, éternel et lointain.	*By a sad, never-ending and distant song.*
Ils volent à tes pieds, astres chassés des nues,	*They fly to your feet, stars banished from the sky,*
Exilés du ciel d'or où fleurit ta beauté	*Exiled from the golden heavens where your beauty thrives,*
Et, cherchant jusqu'à toi des routes inconnues,	*And, seeking to reach you by untried paths,*
Mêlent au jour naissant leur mourante clarté.	*They mingle their dying light with the dawning day.*

Armand Silvestre (1837–1901)

This is a morning song to follow a night of conjugal bliss, a kind of more respectable and less tortured 'C'est l'extase langoureuse', Verlaine's poem set by both Debussy and Fauré, where the love-making has taken place, by contrast, in the late afternoon.

The model for this kind of *mélodie* has already been established by *Le Secret* (1881), an earlier setting of Armand Silvestre. The accompaniment (as in so many later Fauré songs) begins in simple crotchets, slightly detached (an articulation suggestive of distant twinkling stars – see also *Diane, Séléné* from *L'Horizon chimérique*), seemingly uneventful, yet containing the seeds of huge harmonic promise. The flattened seventh of the scale plays an important part in both the vocal line and the accompaniment. With the gradual arrival of dawn the music builds and develops over four pages. After the rapt yet undemonstrative first strophe (Claude Rostand finds that the beginning of the song affects a deliberate coldness), the accompaniment (without a change of pulse or tempo) flowers into semiquavers for the second verse in the minor key. In the third strophe (the song has an ABA structure) the semiquavers are re-energised for a triumphant return to the major. With the warmth of a new dawn comes a new romantic confidence. The deployment of notes between the hands (a crotchet in the left, three semiquavers in the right) as well as the key of G major, prophesies the optimistic *N'est-ce pas?* from *La Bonne chanson*. The poem is the fourth in a dawn sequence of eight (entitled *Matutina*) from Silvestre's collection *Le Pays des roses*. The title *Aurore* is Fauré's own.

For a note on the song's dedicatee see the commentary on the Villiers de L'Isle-Adam setting *Nocturne* in Chapter 7.

(40) *Fleur jetée* (*Discarded flower*)[20]

25 May 1884, Op. 39 No. 2, 'À Mme Jules Gouïn', second Hamelle collection p. 51, F minor, 6/8, *Allegro energico*

Emporte ma folie	*Bear away my folly*
Au gré du vent,	*At the whim of the wind,*
Fleur en chantant cueillie	*Flower, plucked while singing*
Et jetée en rêvant.	*And discarded while dreaming.*
— Emporte ma folie	— *Bear away my folly*
Au gré du vent!	*At the whim of the wind!*

Comme la fleur fauchée	Like a scythed flower
Périt l'amour.	Love perishes.
La main qui t'a touchée	The hand that touched you
Fuit ma main sans retour.	Shuns my hand for ever.
— Comme la fleur fauchée,	— Like a scythed flower
Périt l'amour!	Love perishes!

Que le vent qui te sèche,	May the wind that withers you,
Ô pauvre fleur,	O poor flower,
Tout à l'heure si fraîche	So fresh just now
Et demain sans couleur!	But tomorrow faded,
— Que le vent qui te sèche,	— May the wind that withers you,
Sèche mon cœur!	Wither my heart!

Armand Silvestre (1837–1901)

The poem stands next to 'Notre amour' in Silvestre's collection entitled *Les Ailes d'or*. One of three stormy Silvestre settings by Fauré, it inspires a powerful song that is often compared to Schubert's *Erlkönig* because of the challenging octave repetitions of the piano writing. There is a melodramatic grandiloquence about this music that is not native to the composer, at least when he is composing *mélodies*. There are many more movements in his chamber works when the music builds into climactic moments of powerful abandon. When writing for solo voice and piano, Fauré seldom allows himself to become passionate in this manner. For this reason *Fleur jetée* is a useful foil for the more introverted *mélodies* when performers need contrast within a group of Fauré songs.

It is rare to find an instance where Fauré's teacher Camille Saint-Saëns has actually exerted an influence on his pupil, but the piano writing here, requiring both exact adherence to the tempo and clarity in its repetitive articulation, reminds us of the robust demands of certain passages in the Saint-Saëns piano concertos. One has only to speed up the accompaniment to Dalila's famous aria 'Mon cœur s'ouvre à ta voix' to find similarities with the semiquavers that hop up and down the staves of the whole central portion of *Fleur jetée*. The voice too, as in some of Saint-Saëns's songs, is unafraid to flirt with an operatic scale and manner; the problem is that within a Faurean context this easily becomes exaggerated.

There is plenty to admire in music that should not be judged by its most rowdy performances; the seamless harmonic progress of the music sweeps us along and blows us away, 'Au gré du vent', in one great *courbe*. As in *Notre amour*, the pulsating music for the right hand is interlaced with ascending and descending scale passages in the left hand. As always, one is astonished by the fecundity of Fauré's imagination in devising accompaniments that have an exploratory character in both pianistic and musical terms; in this respect Fauré's piano-writing for the voice has a great deal in common with Schubert's. Towards the end the time signature changes for three bars from 6/8 to 9/8 – an indication of how well Fauré understood the space that a voice needs to manoeuvre at the top of the stave when under this kind of expressive pressure. A polished performance of *Fleur jetée* can be thrilling, but the final high notes are often presented at the expense of the song as a whole. In his thundering postlude the poor pianist always risks humiliation by landing on a split final chord at the very last hurdle.

Lol!

148

The dedicatee of the song, Madame Jules Gouïn (née Marie-Thérèse Singer, 1856–1909), was an amateur singer and an early member of what became a distinguished musical family. Her end in 1909 was particularly tragic and a *cause célèbre*: she was robbed of her jewels in a railway carriage, murdered and thrown out of the window, her body mutilated by passing trains.[21] Her grandson Henry Gouïn and his wife Isabel (née Lang) were distinguished musical patrons of the 1930s, hosting concerts both in their home in Auteuil and at their other famous property, the Abbaye de Royaumant north of Paris, with its splendid (and continuing) history of musical performances.

(41) *Le Pays des Rêves* (*The land of dreams*)[22]
30 May 1884, Op. 39 No. 3, 'À Mlle Thérèse Guyon', A♭ major, 12/8, *Andante quasi allegretto*

Veux-tu qu'au beau pays des Rêves	*Shall we go to the land of Dreams,*
Nous allions la main dans la main?	*Holding each other's hand?*
Plus loin que l'odeur des jasmins,	*Further than the scent of jasmine,*
Plus haut que la plainte des grèves,	*Higher than the shore's lament,*
Veux-tu du beau pays des Rêves,	*Shall we together seek the road*
Tous les deux chercher le chemin?	*To the lovely land of Dreams?*
J'ai taillé dans l'azur les toiles	*I have fashionied from the blue sky the sails*
Du vaisseau qui nous portera,	*Of the ship that will bear us*
Et doucement nous conduira	*And gently lead us*
Jusqu'au verger d'or des étoiles.	*To the golden orchard of the stars.*
J'ai taillé dans l'azur les toiles	*I have cleaved the blue sky with the sails*
Du vaisseau qui nous conduira.	*Of the ship that will bear us.*
Mais combien la terre est lointaine	*But how distant the land is*
Que poursuivent ses blancs sillons!	*That these white furrows seek out!*
Au caprice des papillons	*Let us, with the impulse of butterflies,*
Demandons la route incertaine:	*Ask how to find the uncertain road:*
Ah! combien la terre est lointaine	*Ah! how distant the land is*
Où fleurissent nos visions!	*Where our visions can bear fruit!*
Vois-tu – le beau pays des Rêves	*You see: the lovely land of dreams*
Est trop haut pour les pas humains.	*Is too high for human steps.*
Respirons à deux les jasmins	*Let us both breathe in the jasmine*
Et chantons encor sur les grèves.	*And sing again on the shore.*
Vois-tu – du beau pays des rêves	*You see – Love alone knows the path*
L'amour seul en sait les chemins.	*To the lovely land of dreams.*

Armand Silvestre (1837–1901)

This song's beguiling invitations bring to mind Gounod's setting of 'Où voulez-vous aller?' (with its sailing-ship imagery) or Duparc's *L'Invitation au voyage*. In Silvestre's collection *Les Ailes d'or*, the second half of the poem (ignored by Fauré) is a Baudelaire-like sequel personifying the ominous dreams of the past. But there is nothing disturbing in the words set here, and the music rocks us gently, benignly, into the stratosphere. Suckling observes that this music is an upmarket version of the 'swing song', which towards the end of the nineteenth century 'shared a fashion with hammocks and croquet'. He must have been thinking of songs such as Liza Lehmann's *The Swing* (to R.L. Stevenson's poem, also set in English by Reynaldo Hahn), which was a favourite of Britten's when he was a child. There may be some similarity in the rocking rhythm of the accompaniment, but Fauré's other-worldly harmony, which spirits us away as we float high above the world's planted bowers with their fragrance of jasmine, is anything but common or garden. There are passages in this song where the musical discourse strays into the indeterminate ether in a manner of which no other French composer of the time was capable.

When Fauré decides to 'go walk-about' in this way he is uniquely able to avoid banality; at times it seems as if he delights in doing so by the skin of his teeth – sometimes it is only a single note in an chord that differentiates the ordinary from the sublime, and the insistence of this rocking rhythm requires (and delivers) any number of delicate harmonic surprises to mitigate its sameness. One is all too aware of how sickly and 'twee' this song could have become in other hands. Fauré's harmonic excursions are usually underpinned by strong bass lines, but here, as in another Silvestre setting, *La Fée aux chansons*, the composer abandons the F clef for much of the time in favour of higher, more etiolated regions of the keyboard. There are delicious ambiguities here, for example the pivotal role played by E♭ (D♯) in the keys of A♭ major (where it is the dominant) and E minor (where it is the leading note).

Jankélévitch hears similarities with Wolf's Mörike setting *An eine Äolsharfe*, composed in 1888. The two songs, light years apart in harmonic terms, share a *berceuse* rhythm and an other-worldly evanescence. Silvestre is clearly no Mörike, and it is Fauré's harmonic refinement that deflects attention from the sentimental streak of his poet and elevates the song to something more substantial than Silvestre could ever have imagined.

The song's dedicatee Thérèse Guyon was an amateur singer of some ability who came from a theatrical family. Her father, her sister Cécile, and her brother (Charles-Alexandre Guyon 1854–1923) were all well-known actors.

(42) *Les Roses d'Ispahan* (*The roses of Isfahan*)[23]
6 June 1884, Op. 39 No. 4, 'À Mlle. Louise Collinet', D major, 2/4, *Andantino*

Les roses d'Ispahan dans leur gaine de mousse,	*The roses of Isfahan in their mossy sheaths,*
Les jasmins de Mossoul, les fleurs de l'oranger	*The jasmines of Mosul, the orange blossom*
Ont un parfum moins frais, ont une odeur moins douce,	*Have a fragrance less fresh and a scent less sweet,*
Ô blanche Leïlah! que ton souffle léger.	*O pale Leilah, than your soft breath!*
Ta lèvre est de corail, et ton rire léger	*Your lips are of coral and your light laughter*
Sonne mieux que l'eau vive et d'une voix plus douce,	*Rings brighter and sweeter than running water,*
Mieux que le vent joyeux qui berce l'oranger,	*Than the blithe wind rocking the orange-tree bough,*
Mieux que l'oiseau qui chante au bord d'un nid de mousse …	*Than the singing bird by its mossy nest …*
Ô Leïlah! depuis que de leur vol léger	*O Leilah, ever since on light wings*
Tous les baisers ont fui de ta lèvre si douce,	*All kisses have flown from your sweet lips,*
Il n'est plus de parfum dans le pâle oranger,	*The pale orange-tree fragrance is spent,*
Ni de céleste arome aux roses dans leur mousse …	*And the heavenly scent of moss-clad roses …*

Oh! que ton jeune amour, ce papillon léger,	*Oh! may your young love, that airy butterfly,*
Revienne vers mon cœur d'une aile prompte et douce,	*Wing swiftly and gently to my heart once more,*
Et qu'il parfume encor la fleur de l'oranger,	*To scent again the orange blossom,*
Les roses d'Ispahan dans leur gaine de mousse!	*The roses of Isfahan in their mossy sheaths!*

Charles Marie René Leconte de Lisle (1818–1894)

This third appearance of Leconte de Lisle (*Lydia* had been the first many years earlier, followed by *Nell* in 1878) is among the most erotic, even decadent, of Fauré's *mélodies*. 'Decadent music for a decadent epoch!' is the verdict of Nectoux, who discerns the influence of Pierre Loti, a travel writer specialising in evocation of the East, whose *Fleurs d'ennui* is a work contemporary with this song. Instead of the Attic purity of *Lydia* and the Scottish *pudeur* of *Nell*, we have a kind of sensual oriental monotony. Jankélévitch, in an unusually prudish mood, judges its self-consciousness as unworthy of the real Fauré, but most of his admirers have always adored its highly perfumed sumptuousness. If this song suggests a *seraglio* draped in the opulent Parisian style of the 1880s, the spirit of the times is partly to blame: Huysmans's *A rebours* appeared alongside Leconte de Lisle's *Poèmes tragiques* in 1884, where the inner title-page of 'Les Roses d'Ispahan' is spelled 'Les Roses d'Hispahan', a sign that the ageing poet, always inclined to obfuscation in his spelling of foreign names, found it difficult to choose between variants. Although these two literary works are most unlikely bedfellows, it seems that even the austere master of Parnassus had been somewhat drawn into the *esprit décadent* (see Chapter 7). It is interesting that here Fauré first encounters Leconte de Lisle as a contemporary and sets a poem by him that is more or less hot off the press.

There is a unique undulation to this music that is partly created by a counter-melody, like a third voice, between the thumbs of the accompanist's hands. This gait, leisurely yet implacable, varied by occasional rhythmic displacements, suggests heavily laden camels swaying across the desert sands (as in Chausson's *La Caravane*, 1887). Every kind of rare perfume is for sale here, but nothing can match the fragrance of the absent Leïlah. The song's journey is suddenly interrupted by a personal aside: we had been expecting another appearance of the sinuous and hypnotic refrain (and indeed the song closes with this music), but with 'Ô Leïlah!' at the opening of the third strophe there is a sudden outburst; the lack of a preceding interlude makes it seem spontaneous, unplanned. This verse alone, one of Fauré's most heartfelt utterances, saves the song from relegation into the ranks of that overpopulated genre in French music, the oriental pastiche. The return to the song's fourth strophe with its familiar refrain is a miraculous piece of musical engineering. The soprano transposition (up into E major) is heard so often that one can easily forget the duskily erotic atmosphere created by the original lower key.

It is notable that Fauré takes the trouble to modify a tiny detail in the poet's text (the second-last line): 'les fleurs de l'oranger' has been modified to 'la fleur de l'oranger' in the interests of a less bulging vocal line – words like 'les' and 'tes' always entail a broadening of mouth position. The composer has left out two of the poet's strophes – the third and the fifth. Nectoux is surely correct in believing that Fauré found the following line in the third strophe offensive because he found that alliterations blocked the musical flow: 'Et l'eau vive qui flue avec sa plainte douce'. And when we search for the reasons why the fifth strophe has been found unsuitable, we need to go no further, surely, than the imagery of the 'duvet humide' of the first line with its unintentional bedroom banality.

The song's dedicatee, Louise Collinet, an amateur singer, was a close friend of Marguerite

Baugnies (de Saint-Marceaux). From 1894 she was better known in social circles as Madame Alfred Gentil de Vély. This marriage seems to have been arranged (as was the composer's) by the match-making hand of Madame de Saint-Marceaux.

∾   ∾   ∾   ∾

Fauré's musical energies in the year 1885 were given over to the performance and promotion of his D minor Symphony. This work was given its première at the Châtelet with Colonne conducting and was received without enthusiasm. The composer eventually destroyed the work following a final performance of the *Andante* in 1888. The composer's father died in July 1885 in Toulouse, and this event, together with the death of his mother in 1887, was to mark the definite end of an era. The Faurés – husband, wife and child – went to Néris-les-Bains in August so that Marie could take the waters. One senses that at this stage Fauré had not yet given up on his marriage and was still struggling to be a companionable and faithful spouse, albeit without much success. The single song of the period was considered too simple to be a *mélodie*, and because of its religious subject was classed as a *cantique*.

(43) *Noël* (*Christmas*)[24]
1885, Op. 43 No. 1, 'À mon ami A Talazac', first Hamelle collection p. 89, A♭ major, ♩, *Andante quasi allegretto*

La nuit descend du haut des cieux,	*Night falls from the sky,*
Le givre au toit suspend ses franges,	*Frost hangs its fringes along the roofs.*
Et, dans les airs, le vol des anges	*And the flight of angels in the sky*
Éveille un bruit mystérieux.	*Creates a mysterious sound.*
L'étoile qui guidait les mages,	*The star that led the Magi*
S'arrête enfin dans les nuages,	*Stops at last in the clouds,*
Et fait briller un nimbe d'or	*And casts a golden halo*
Sur la chaumière où Jésus dort.	*Above the cottage where Jesus sleeps.*
Alors, ouvrant ses yeux divins,	*Then, opening His divine eyes,*
L'enfant couché dans l'humble crèche,	*From His crib of fresh hay*
De son berceau de paille fraîche,	*The Child, lying in the humble manger,*
Sourit aux nobles pèlerins.	*Smiles at the noble pilgrims.*
Eux, s'inclinant, lui disent: Sire,	*They, bowing down, address Him: Sire,*
Reçois l'encens, l'or et la myrrhe,	*Receive the incense, gold and myrrh,*
Et laisse-nous, ô doux Jésus,	*And allow us, gentle Jesus,*
Baiser le bout de tes pieds nus.	*To kiss the tips of your naked feet.*
Comme eux, ô peuple, incline-toi,	*Bow down like them, O people,*
Imite leur pieux exemple,	*Follow their devout example,*
Car cette étable, c'est un temple,	*For this stable is a temple,*
Et cet enfant sera ton roi!	*And this Child shall be your king.*

Victor Wilder (1835–1892)

The position of *Noël* at the end of the first Hamelle collection does not reflect the work's real chronology. In a sweep of new publications issued in 1908 Hamelle was very keen (for the sake of symmetry) that sixty Fauré songs should be parcelled into three volumes of twenty each. One of the casualties of this arrangement was *Barcarolle*, an early song that found itself placed incomprehensibly at the end of the second volume. *Noël*, on the other hand, is a later work that was swept into the first *recueil* for convenience's sake. In a letter to Edgard Hamelle, the son of his former publisher (Fauré had transferred to the firm of Heugel in 1906), the composer attempted to argue against this decision: 'as regards *Noël*, I still think it should be left uncollected. Firstly because of its hybrid character, which is neither secular nor religious.'[25] Fauré also mentions the fact that the *ad libitum* harmonium accompaniment was 'really necessary' and that there was not room to insert this – the separate harmonium part in the original edition is indeed missing from

Title-page of Noël, *published by Hamelle*

the Hamelle volume. Worse still, it seems that Hamelle favoured the idea of grafting a new poem (by Charles Grandmougin) on to the existing music for *Noël*. Here Fauré really put his foot down:

> As for Grandmougin's poem (he sent it to me on his own initiative) it does not fit the music at all. Whether good or mediocre, this is *Christmas* music. Its innocent, expressionless character, its accompaniment conveying a *continuous* ringing of BELLS, goes with Wilder's somewhat lame lines, but does not go with Grandmougin's *tender, sentimental* little poem at all. So let's keep Wilder's lines because after all they inspired the character of the music, its *physiognomy*, its *looks*.[26]

Noël was clearly conceived as an occasional piece, a little Christmas song destined for a performance where a harmonium was available to add a festive carillon colour to the piano accompaniment. In the absence of this possibility pianists must do their best as solitary bell-ringers. Fauré sometimes seems to lack the practical touch: here he writes music 'for the people' (simplified to a degree, and seemingly designed for a popular market) and yet the vocal writing is far too demanding for any amateur, and the accompaniment would defeat most village organists. Great French composers seem permitted, almost as if by tradition, to write slightly awkward, and untypical, Christmas songs: thus Debussy's *Noël des enfants qui n'ont plus de maisons*, Ravel's *Noël des jouets* (both to the composers' own poems) and Poulenc's *Nous voulons une petite sœur*. The text embraces a traditional religiosity to which Fauré responds dutifully at the end of the piece, although a certain atypical unctuousness hovers uncomfortably over the music unless it is performed with open-hearted innocence. *Noël* belongs with the composer's smaller sacred works and *pièces d'occasion* rather than with his *mélodies*.

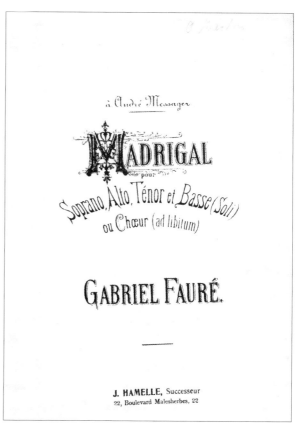

Title pages of the two choral pieces Le Ruisseau *and* Madrigal

It is included in this book simply because, whether the composer liked it or not, it has become part of the Fauré song repertoire thanks to the publishing history of the Hamelle edition.

Victor Wilder (Jerôme-Albert-Victor van Wilder) was born in Wettern in Belgium and moved to Paris in his twenties. He was more of a musicologist and literary critic than a poet, although composers such as Lalo and César Franck set his words to music, and Duparc used his translation of Goethe for his *Romance de Mignon*. He was best known in his time for biographies of Mozart and Beethoven, and for his championing of the German classics and early French performances of the oratorios of Handel. He was a devoted Wagnerian; ten years of his life translating the writings of his idol into French were rewarded by a lawsuit with the composer's publisher and widow. Wilder was a man of much greater originality, and of more importance to French music, than the 'lame lines' of *Noël* suggest.

Fauré's Silvestre period finds the composer in a Janus-like position. With each year he is clearly developing enormously as a musician and song writer; in this respect Fauré is looking to the future. But although the Silvestre collaboration represents real progress since the Viardot days, the composer is still pulled into a kind of backward-looking conventionality by his poet. It is as if the presence of Silvestre remains reassuring for Fauré in these years: a safety net, or an anchor to keep him cocooned within a narrow bourgeois world of emotions, perimeters within which he is comfortable and familiar even if this included the poet's tacit 'permission', as implied in *Madrigal*, for the composer to dally with other women at the same time as securing a home base with his wife and children. The slight suggestiveness in some of the Silvestre texts is no substitute for a genuinely daring outlook. It is for this reason, surely, that these songs, even those that are among the best-known, can hardly be considered to inaugurate a new period in Fauré's creative career.

It is anachronistic to dismiss Silvestre as a 'bad' poet; he is clearly nothing of the kind. Highly respected in his time, he was an extremely prolific and urbane writer, an astute critic, a complete professional who received, and deserved, the respect of his colleague Paul Verlaine, no less.[27] The success, indeed immortality, of the best Silvestre settings testifies to the poet's ability to inspire music of the highest quality. And yet in Fauré's case something is wrong when we judge the Silvestre texts by the most stringent standards: even if these lyrics are well made, they do not excite us in their own right, and we do not choose to recite them aloud; they lack charisma. In some ways this is no catastrophe: we can rely on Fauré to provide that very quality, and in the meantime

Fauré at the age of forty. © Bibliothèque nationale de France

the composer is not wasting time on unwieldy poems by Baudelaire; indeed, at times the words and music of the Silvestre songs of Fauré seem indivisible. But are they?

Fauré scarcely seems to need the *particularity* of Silvestre's words and images; he is always able to make a successful construction based on an assimilation of the poem's *generalities*. For this reason we get suave Silvestre songs, beautifully crafted and charming, rather than *mélodies* that owe their existence to the composer's engagement with the inner substance of the poems, perhaps because this substance is not interesting enough. They smack of the libretto where it is no great disaster if the orchestra drowns the detailed imagery of the words. If one were to be harsh, one might say that such an easy relationship with a poet makes for a rather lazy way of composing songs (Silvestre was the ideal poet for Massenet in this regard).

Silvestre's words sometimes do manage to come memorably across the footlights – Fauré's *Automne* is such a song, as are Duparc's *Testament* and both of Fauré's later Silvestre settings of 1904 (see Chapter 10). On the other hand, *Notre amour* and *Fleur jetée*, despite their vibrant tempi, lack a certain amount of internal electricity, and this has to be provided by the singers, who frequently over-compensate by singing too loud or too fast, perhaps because insufficient excitement is generated from within the words-to-music axis. Both *Le Secret* and *Chanson d'amour* are much more personal, but *Le Pays des rêves* and *La Fée aux chansons*, admittedly both charming songs, might just as easily have been written as pieces for violin and piano. The composer has expertly, indeed, exquisitely, captured the moods of both these poems, but once he has done so in musical terms, the actual words themselves can all too easily seem almost redundant in performance.

In this context, the inner glow of a song such as *Les Roses d'Ispahan*, with its poem by Leconte de Lisle, comes as something of a shock and revelation. This lyric is not merely a frame on which to hang an oriental water-colour; it demands our attention (and the composer's) bar by bar – the woman in question is not merely sketched, she is painted in oils; she is the beautiful and unique Leïlah, and not simply a stand-in for any woman of curvaceous build in Silvestre's capacious gallery of nudes.

Silvestre's affinity with the 'odor di femmina' has a weakness: the women praised are too general and are neither specific nor individual enough. It is the same graceful anonymity that we find in *Sylvie* or the *Poëme d'un jour* triptych. In many of the Silvestre settings, the listener longs in vain for the specificity, the clear-cut imagery that would bring the union of word and tone into the sharpest focus. By the time Fauré sought once more this kind of non-specific literature in the symbolist poetry of Charles Van Lerberghe (from 1906) it was a deliberate choice; his musical language had evolved to such an extent that the marriage between word and tone was of a completely different order.

1   Jean-Michel Nectoux, *Gabriel Fauré: A Musical Life*, trans. Roger Nichols (Cambridge: Cambridge University Press, 1991), p. 34.

2   For a full discussion of Marguerite de Saint-Marceaux see Myriam Chimènes, *Mécènes et musiciens* (Paris: Fayard, 2004) as well as her *Journal 1894–1927* ed. Myriam Chimènes (Paris: Fayard, 2007).

3   *Les Berceaux*: Aspects of this song's interpretation are discussed in Chapter 16, p. 409.

4   *Gabriel Fauré: His Life through his Letters*, ed. Jean-Michel Nectoux, trans. John Underwood (London and New York: Marion Boyars, 1984), letter 35.

5   Charles Kingsley, 'The Three Fishers' (1851).

6   J-M Nectoux, Gabriel Fauré, *La Voix du clair obscur*, 2nd edition, Paris, 2008, p. 128.

7   Suckling, *Fauré*, p. 68.

8   Georges Vicaire, *Manual de l'amateur de livres du XIXe siècle*, vol. 7 (Paris: Librairie A. Rouquette, 1894), pp. 509–43.

9   *Notre amour*: Aspects of this song's interpretation are discussed in Chapter 16, p. 409.

10   *Le Secret*: Aspects of this song's interpretation are discussed in Chapter 16, p. 410.

11   Nectoux, *Gabriel Fauré: A Musical Life*, p. 176.

12   Quoted in ibid., p. 492.

13   Letter to Marie Clerc, 9 July 1882, in *Gabriel Fauré: His Life through his Letters*, letter 45, pp. 104–5.

14   *Chanson d'amour*: Aspects of this song's interpretation are discussed in Chapter 16, p. 410.

15   *La Fée aux chansons*: Aspects of this song's interpretation are discussed in Chapter 16, p. 410.

16   *Gabriel Fauré: His Life through his Letters*, letter 48, pp. 109–10.

17   Nectoux, *Gabriel Fauré: A Musical Life*, p. 36.

18   Ibid., p. 37.

19   *Aurore*: Aspects of this song's interpretation are discussed in Chapter 16, p. 410.

20   *Fleur jetée*: Aspects of this song's interpretation are discussed in Chapter 16, p. 411.

21   Marguerite de Saint-Marceaux, *Journal 1894–1927*, ed. Myriam Chimènes (Paris: Fayard), 2007, p. 568.

22   *Le Pays des Rêves*: Aspects of this song's interpretation are discussed in Chapter 16, p. 411.

23   *Les Roses d'Ispahan*: Aspects of this song's interpretation are discussed in Chapter 16, p. 411.

24   *Noël*: Aspects of this song's interpretation are discussed in Chapter 16, p. 411.

25   *Gabriel Fauré: His Life through his Letters*, letter 150, pp. 274–5.

26   Ibid.

27   See the sonnet addressed to Silvestre in Verlaine's *Dédicaces* (Paris: Vanier, 1894).

Chapter Seven

Crisis and Decadence

Auguste Villiers de L'Isle-Adam, Jean Richepin, Edmond Haraucourt, Stéphan Bordèse

In different branches of the arts there is often little synchronicity between the waxing and waning of certain broad artistic ideas and influences. Thus the term 'romanticism' means something rather different in literature from what it does in music, and in each case it encompasses a somewhat different period. It seems that music almost always takes a certain amount of time to catch up with literature and painting (nothing could illustrate this better than the time-gap between visual and musical impressionism). Music is more influenced by literature than the other way around: in the world of song there is usually a gap, sometimes quite a long one, between the publication of a poem and its musical settings. Whether a song can ever be said to embody the characteristics of the school to which its poet belongs, rather than its composer, is a moot point. In this matter of classification the music surely takes precedence.

French historians had proposed the idea of *décadence* at various times since the Revolution. Long before the defeat of France by the Germans in the war of 1870, some philosophers likened Napoleon III's empire to the physical and moral degradation of its Roman equivalent. Pessimists diagnosed the gradual but inevitable putrefaction of the French state, but optimists among the artistic community noticed only a new air of freedom and, in the second decade of the Third Republic, a revival of the *dandyisme* of the 1860s. By the 1880s the once-forbidden imagery of the 'decadent' Baudelaire was recognised, by other artists at least, as integral to the greatness of his art: if Rome was burning it was the artist's role to strike the lyre extolling the conflagration and to stoke the fire. For a time it was as if Nero was a hero. Rather than fighting to reverse the decadence of French life, why not accept decline and sink insolently into the satin cushions of the imperial couch? Why not feast and make love until the Barbarians knocked on the gates, and why not be too drugged and drunk to notice their arrival? This was *Après nous le déluge* all over again. The feeling that civilisation was coming to a colourful, if rather languorous, end was well conveyed by the phrase *fin de siècle*.

Verlaine's poem 'Langueur' of 1883 – 'Je suis l'Empire à la fin de la décadence' – and his enthusiasm for 'toutes les splendeurs violentes' of a corrupt civilisation seemed a battle cry for various sybaritic groups of the Latin quarter: the Hydropathes, the Hirsutes (with their revue entitled *Lutèce*), the Zutistes, the Jemenfoutistes and so on. Periodicals rather more serious than these were to remain of supreme importance as far as Fauré's literary self-education was concerned: the *Revue wagnérienne* first appeared in 1885, and the influential *Revue blanche* (a periodical regularly read by Fauré) dated from the end of the decade.

Flaubert's *Hérodias* (1877) is already characteristic of the *décadence*, as are the paintings of Gustave Moreau and Félicien Rops. The stage performances of *monstres sacrés* such as Sarah Bernhardt (later to be a colleague of Fauré at the Conservatoire, and an enemy of his reforms) and Edouard de Max (who was to take the speaking role of Prométhée in Fauré's *tragédie lyrique* at Béziers in 1900), and the sumptuous theatricality of their off-stage life-styles, appear to the modern reader to have been more camp than challengingly decadent. (De Max when older delighted in appearing at parties as that most effeminate of emperors, Heliogabalus, with a retinue of slave boys.) Much of the thrust behind the *esprit décadent* came from proselytisers for the love that had not dared speak its name, but now was doing so with increasing confidence, not to say insouciance.

The rise of Oscar Wilde across the Channel and the Aesthetic Movement (parodied in Gilbert and Sullivan's *Patience*) seem to have been propelled by the same modernising audacity that empowered the French *décadence*. It did not end well. With Wilde's trial and imprisonment (in the year of Verlaine's death in 1896) an increasingly brazen delight in forbidden sensation was snuffed out in London, albeit temporarily, as if by a cold blast of wind ('fresh air' some would have insisted) blown by the *Zeitgeist* in a frostier mood. In Paris fashion had simply moved on and the decadents had become passé, as is the eventual fate of everything in that most modish of cities. From the ashes of those once-flagrant fires the more enduring symbolist movement rose phoenix-like; the *Manifeste de symbolisme* ('Manifesto of symbolism') by Jean Moréas had first appeared in 1886, and it was Moréas who proposed replacing the term *décadent* with *symboliste* and *décadence* with *symbolisme*. The way was now prepared for the poet Mallarmé to lead French literature in a new direction, but that is to jump forward into Fauré's song-composing future in another century – as we have already noted, music takes some time to catch up with the latest literary trends.

ᘓ   ᘓ   ᘓ   ᘓ

We return to the middle 1880s, at about the time when Joris-Karl Huysmans wrote *A rebours* (translated as *Against Nature*), the story of the neurasthenic hyper-aesthete Des Esseintes, a character based (neither accurately nor particularly fairly) on the young Comte Robert de Montesquiou-Fezensac, cousin of the Comtesse Greffulhe. The novel was a wild success, and it brought renown to such living artists mentioned in its text as the poet Mallarmé, and the painters Moreau and Redon, who were vaunted as the favourite artists of the fictional Des Esseintes. Oscar Wilde's response to this novel in 1890 was his own *A Picture of Dorian Gray*. If we have elsewhere praised the Attic purity of Fauré's *Lydia*, this novel, where Wilde's eponymous anti-hero hides his deteriorating portrait at the top of the house, might well be described as a work of attic impurity – a facetious observation certainly, but the kind of word-play that might have been indulged in by the followers and admirers of Wilde who were busy making themselves implacable enemies in the strait-laced Anglo-Saxon world.

Marie Joseph Robert Anatole, Comte de Montesquiou-Fenzensac (1855–1921), was fortunate to live in Paris and in a rather less censorious society. One story about him encapsulates his sensibilites: when challenged one autumn day as to why he was dressed entirely, and exquisitely, in black, he replied that he was in mourning for the dead leaves. Montesquiou's sensitivity regarding nuances of colour and texture was legendary. Sir William Rothenstein once met him at a concert wearing a mauve suit with a shirt to match and a bunch of pale violets at his throat in place of a necktie 'because', he explained, 'one should always listen to von Weber in mauve'.[1] W.S. Gilbert with scarcely disguised homophobia (not that he would have understood the term) would certainly have thought Montesquiou was

A most intense young man
A soulful-eyed young man
An ultra-poetical, super-aesthetical
Out-of-the-way young man.[2]

Many years later, Marcel Proust in his series of great novels *A la recherche du temps perdu* was to model the predatory Baron Charlus on the ageing Montesquiou (among other older homosexual acquaintances, including Saint-Saëns).

In 1886, many years before he had turned into anything resembling this saturnine voluptuary character, Robert de Montesquiou met Gabriel Fauré and offered to become his 'literary adviser'. For the time being, the composer was happy to accept. The immediate effect was that the composer dropped such seemingly outdated poets as Leconte de Lisle and Armand Silvestre, although he was to return to both of these in his own good time.

Fauré was not homosexual himself, but he seems to have been perfectly comfortable with those who were. Female friends such as Winnaretta Singer and both his female poets (Dominique and Brimont) were lesbian. According to Georges Servières, Fauré was 'a feminine type without being in the least effeminate'. He was not the kind of man to relish competitive battle with other men for a woman's favours, and it is likely that he found the company of gay men unthreatening in this regard. Someone who had been an inmate of a cloistered boarding school from the age of nine to twenty is unlikely to have been shocked by the subject. In any case Fauré was considered attractive by certain men on account of his dreamy unavailability and his sultry good looks. His teacher and devoted friend Camille Saint-Saëns was the first of several infatuated male admirers; the playful, familiar tone in the eighteen-year-old Fauré's letters to his teacher had made it clear that he was aware that the older man was attracted to him; and Saint-Saëns was capable of being self-revealing enough to end a letter (on 1 January 1867) with the words 'Meanwhile a thousand kisses! But kisses on paper are not the same thing at all.'[3] One cannot help feeling that Tchaikovsky, with his almost tender regard for Fauré's music (the two composers first met in 1886), was not insensible to the physical attraction of his colleague five years younger. He wrote to Taneyev in that year that he much approved of Fauré 'both as a man and as a musician'. It also seems that a spell was cast for personal as well as musical reasons on Frank Schuster, a wealthy Englishman of German extraction who lived in London and who played host to Fauré in his luxurious home in Westminster at 22 Old Queen Street, a genuine address that surpasses malicious invention.

It made no difference to Fauré that among his younger colleagues, the singer Maurice Bagès and the composer Pierre de Bréville (who were lovers), the pianist Léon Delafosse, Reynaldo Hahn, Marcel Proust of course, and so on, were all homosexual. There is even a passage in Proust's novel (in *Sodome et Gomorrhe* to be precise), concerning the liaison between Baron Charlus and the violinist Morel, where someone we may take to be Fauré makes an anonymous appearance as 'an eminent musician … a member of the *Institut* … exclusively and passionately a lover of women' who aids and abets the relationship of the two men by arranging for the Baron to attend rehearsals at which the young violinist was playing.[4] Proust puts this down to a kind of moral indifference on the part of the eminent musician, who is a man of the world; he is tolerant and kind, and he is able to read the requirements of his highly born patrons. He is not shocked at all by the fact that the two men are having an affair. Indeed, in the novel he asks of a fellow guest the startlingly modern and tolerant question – less remarkable by the standards of our own time – 'Have they been together long?', as if he were enquiring of a liaison between a man and his mistress. As Richard Davenport-Hines writes: 'This morally disinterested dignitary is an honourable figure in the Proustian universe.'[5] The writer clearly admires the real-life model of such a heterosexual character, to whom he ascribes this kind of humanity in fictional terms. It is likely that this figure, seemingly modelled on Fauré, was created as the result of an actual incident observed by Proust with his *omnium gatherum* eyes and ears.

One feels that the younger Montesquiou's interest in his new and still handsome composer (he was thirty-one when he met Fauré, who was forty-one) might not have been entirely altruistic, although there is no doubt that his reactions to Fauré's music were genuinely enthusiastic and knowledgeable – as were those of Proust (himself a Montesquiou protégé) many years later. In terms of other important social connections we have already mentioned Fauré's friendship with Marguerite Baugnies (later Madame de Saint-Marceaux), dedicatee of *Après un rêve*, who was something of an inspiration to Proust when it came to his creation of Madame Verdurin. This is a troubling parallel for those who would like to see the composer's relationship with this formidable and influential woman as wholly constructive. Proust's Sidonie Verdurin – middle-class society hostess ruthlessly on the make, and eventually to marry into the Guermantes family – is one of the most calculatingly ambitious characters in French literature, and there was also undoubtedly an unpleasant side to 'Meg' Baugnies – one has only to think of the bizarre and somewhat meddling role she had played in 'arranging' Fauré's marriage. The fact remains, however, that the salon of the legendary Madame de Saint-Marceaux (she held court at 100 boulevard Malesherbes) was an absolutely indispensable part of Parisian musical life; she was a highly competent singer and pianist (if not sublimely talented herself, she recognised the talents of others in a meticulously graded hierarchy), and in terms of running a successful salon attended by every significant musician of the day she was something of an organisational genius.[6] Her full stature has only very recently come to light with the publication of her massive *Journal* (1894–1927), which encompasses almost every important name in French music of the time and is marked by the rapier-like thrust of her perspicacious and often acerbic musical assessments.[7] Fauré's long-standing and continuing friendship for her is proved by some hundred exchanged letters; he was fond enough of her to ask her to be the godmother of his second son, Philippe. She was officially a woman of rigid moral principles (she disapproved of the composer's extra-marital adventures) but she ended up by bowing to genius and, in later years, received two of Fauré's mistresses (Adela Maddison and Marguerite Hasselmans) in her home. One can only wonder if she ever felt guilty about the part she herself had played in Fauré's unsuccessful marriage.

ॐ　　　ॐ　　　ॐ　　　ॐ

There now came a period in the composer's life (this is the period of the Fourth Barcarolle and Second Piano Quartet) when he began to move regularly in aristocratic circles, that very *gratin* of high society frequented by Proust and later mercilessly analysed by him. Fauré's dalliance with the luxurious world of Montesquiou was a retreat from the grinding drudgery of his everyday existence where he had to travel three hours a day by train in order to visit pupils in their homes in outlying areas of Paris. His music was always wonderfully balanced between fantasy and practical reality, but Montesquiou's world was a fairytale one where phrases like 'art for art's sake' and 'hot-house exquisiteness' scarcely encompassed the extravagance and self-indulgence of a Parisian prince who, apart from the penning of his verses, had never done a day's work in his life.

This luxurious credo that was in the air during the 1880s and 1890s was as far as can be imagined from Fauré's everyday existence. He was continually short of money; lacking even the amount of capital behind him of the moderately comfortable Chabrier, he considered his job at the Madeleine to be seldom more than a chore, and his teaching could be a torture. The situation at home with a wife who was dissatisfied with her lot in life was such that the domestic hearth failed to lure him home – this despite the fact that in October 1886 the Faurés had moved into a large and comfortable apartment on the top floor of 154 boulevard Malesherbes in the seventeenth *arrondissement* (in the same street as the Baugnies), and were to remain there for the following twenty-five years. The composer clearly preferred to spend his evenings away, and he could always (and with some justification) describe this social activity, the networking of modern parlance, as essential to his career. The opportunity to be fêted in elegant surroundings was also something of a comfort to a man who was insecure about himself, and surprised, as ever, that anyone should like his work.

Robert de Montesquiou (1855–1921) by Félix Vallotton from Le Livre des Masques *(1896) by Rémy de Gourmont*

Jean-Michel Nectoux gives us a list of the society hostesses at whose homes the composer was received,[8] and it is indeed a Proustian roll-call of princesses and countesses, quite apart from the painters, sculptors and writers who were also part of the composer's circle. Many years later Debussy, writing in connection with the rival versions of *Pélleas et Mélisande*, was to describe Fauré as 'the musical servant of a group of snobs and imbeciles'.[9] This was scarcely fair, particularly coming from a man who had could be extremely ruthless and focused when using other people to serve his musical and personal ends. Fauré knew that 'playing the game' was a necessary part of survival for an artist in Paris, but he had no illusions about the emptiness of the charade. For a man of the composer's background, imbued with the calm good sense of the Ariège, Montesquiou's aesthetic, and the often mindless pursuit of pleasure associated with the aristocracy, were essentially at odds with his honesty and *clarté*, in short the sincerity, of Fauré's true nature.

Despite all the elegance and wealth of his new-found admirers the composer felt himself to be getting nowhere in his career, and he suffered from a series of deep depressions that reactivated the neuralgic head-pains and dizziness he had suffered as a younger man. This was an exceptionally unhappy time in his life. Nevertheless, when confronted with the high society that he considered to be the only outlet for his music at the time, he had the capacity to be charm itself. Camille Bellaigue describes this aspect to his character, which stood him in such good stead with those who had the power to support his music and provide the arenas for its performance:

No one possessed to the same degree as Fauré the mysterious gift that no other can replace or surpass: charm. In and around him, all was seductive. Very tanned of face, with dark eyes and hair, illuminated now and then by the youthful twinkle of a street-urchin. The sound of his voice was soft and deep.[10]

Winnaretta Singer, c. 1896 (Collection Jean-Michel Nectoux)

In 1891 Fauré was to find both an artistic and a personal way out of this impasse in his career, and it was thanks to someone rich and powerful, a woman rather than a man, for, apart from Saint-Saëns, it was usually women who exerted the greatest influence on his behaviour. His saviour was the young Winnaretta Singer, Princesse de Scey-Montbéliard, later Princesse de Polignac. Her salutary role in Fauré's career will be more fully discussed in the next chapter, but her description of the composer at this stage of his life may usefully be quoted here, particularly because it throws some light on his home situation, and gives us grounds to spare a thought for the loneliness of Marie Fauré:

> Although he was sensitive and sentimental, he was easily carried away by new affections, and was not always a faithful and perfect friend, being too much interested in new ties to trouble much about his old ones. No one could resist his charm of manner, his gaiety, his tenderness, above all his utter sincerity when a new fancy took his heart and mind, as it too often did.[11]

In later years the pianist Marguerite Long, envious of the composer's attachment to another gifted young woman pianist (Marguerite Hasselmans), would write of Fauré's 'somewhat volatile affections'.[12] As if to prove the veracity of this observation in his professional as well as amatory life, the influence on Fauré of Montesquiou was to wane once Winnie Singer had entered the composer's life, but the super-aesthete remained a devoted, and surprisingly humble, admirer of the composer and a generous promoter of Fauré's works in his salon. As late as 1919 he paid a visit to Fauré, who remarked dryly that it was not at all a tiring occasion because the Comte had done all the talking. In fact the composer in later life confessed to his son that he had always thought Montesquiou to be a 'crackpot'. In this remark made within the safety of the family home we detect the slipping of a mask of affability worn by the composer for many years in the gilded salons of the nineteenth century, and mainly for reasons of professional survival.

162

(44) *Nocturne* (Nocturne)[13]
1886, Op. 43 No. 2, 'À Mme Henriette Roger-Jourdain', E♭ major, 3/4, *Andante*

La Nuit, sur le grand mystère,	*Onto a landscape of great mystery,*
Entr'ouvre ses écrins bleus;	*Night half-opens its blue caskets;*
Autant de fleurs sur la terre	*As many flowers on earth*
Que d'étoiles dans les cieux!	*As stars in the sky!*
On voit ses ombres dormantes	*Its sleeping shadows are seen*
S'éclairer à tous moments,	*Brightening every moment,*
Autant par les fleurs charmantes	*As much by charming flowers*
Que par les astres charmants.	*As by charming stars.*
Moi, ma nuit au sombre voile	*My own darkly veiled night*
N'a, pour charme et pour clarté,	*Has for charm and light*
Qu'une fleur et qu'une étoile:	*But one flower and one star:*
Mon amour et ta beauté!	*My love and your beauty!*

Auguste Villiers de L'Isle-Adam (1838–1889)

The poem is from the *Contes cruels* by Villiers de L'Isle-Adam, horror stories influenced by the work of Edgar Allan Poe and one of the cult books of the decadents, published in 1883; it was almost certainly on the reading list for Fauré prepared (at least metaphorically) by Montesquiou. (Some of the aesthete's recommended poets, such as Lucie Delarue Mardrus, whom he had re-discovered, clearly made no impression on Fauré at all.) The overwhelmingly larger part of Villiers de L'Isle Adam's collection is prose; in a section beginning on page 302, under the heading *Conte d'amour*, there are seven poems. Léon Boëllmann (a gifted organist and composer and the arranger of Fauré's *Shylock* music for piano duet) set all seven as a cycle. Fauré composed the first of these (*Éblouissement*) with the title *Nocturne*; Chausson set the second, retaining the poet's heading *L'Aveu*; *Les Présents* is the third. We know that Fauré would have liked to turn all three of these poems into *mélodies*, but he regarded Chausson's setting as definitive.

Nocturne is a beautiful song that can boast neither an exceptional melody nor a chance for a singer to make a dramatic impression. But it does conjure a mood of infinite peace and calm, the composer's own version of the Baudelaire–Duparc 'Luxe, calme et volupté'. That reference to Baudelaire is appropriate enough: Villiers de L'Isle-Adam's lines are clearly modelled on that poet's lines 'Un soir fait de rose et de bleu mystique' from the poem *La Mort des Amants*.

The title 'Éblouissement' implies a dazzling sight; exclamation marks at the end of the first and third strophes (omitted in the musical setting) betoken a heady enthusiasm typical of the poet (see below). Fauré is far more *en sourdine*; his own title of *Nocturne* (he had already written his first five nocturnes for piano) prepares us better for the languid unfolding of this music in a muted tessitura. (Nectoux finds that the 'incantatory' aspect of this song reminds him of Erik Satie's *Gymnopédies*.)[14] At the moments when the 3/4 rhythm gives way to a rocking 6/8 one might even think of a swing-song or *berceuse*. The form is essentially AAB. In the first two strophes the home key of E♭ is reached relatively easily after momentary excursions into E♭ minor and G♭ major. The third strophe is more

163

exploratory and takes us on a restless tonal journey; we reach E♭ major at the end, but only after an unexpected detour into G minor for the word 'beauté!' If the poet rejoices in the possession of his beloved, the composer mourns her unavailability with only a momentary loss of composure.

Norman Suckling comments on the song's use of a scale where the second and third degrees waver between a flat and a natural, as well as the flattened leading note of the vocal line – 'the whole resembling the oriental songs produced by the Russian composers'. Music of this kind was clearly popular with the public at the time: Mimi Daitz informs us that *Nocturne* was available to the music-buying public in an astonishing range of tonalities: E♭ major, G♭ major, G major, A♭ major, B♭ major and C (the last of these is the high key printed in the second Hamelle *recueil*). This latter option is an astonishing sixth higher than the original, and the accompaniment for this version had to be printed a third *lower* than the original to

Auguste Villiers de L'Isle Adam. Photograph by Nadar

stop it falling off the top of the keyboard. Such information should be a reminder to modern singers and pianists that for all the Fauré songs printed by Hamelle, the single printed transposition (for either a higher or lower voice, depending on the original) is not the only possibility. Fauré, like all composers, preferred to hear his songs in the original keys, but once transposing becomes necessary there is nothing sacrosanct or irreversible about the printed alternatives beyond the extra trouble necessary for the performers to come up with a more comfortable, or better-sounding, option.

The dedicatee of *Nocturne* was Henriette, the daughter of the painter Léopold de Moulignon and the wife of the painter Roger Jourdain (1845–1918), who was half-brother of Marguerite de Saint-Marceaux and a friend and colleague of Fauré's painter friend Emmanuel Jadin (dedicatee of *Clair de lune*). Henriette Roger-Jourdain (as she was styled by Fauré) must have been a beautiful woman: she was also the dedicatee of the Silvestre setting *Aurore* and of the composer's Third Barcarolle (1885).[15] Henriette and Roger Jourdain were among Fauré's fellow guests in Venice during the magical and productive holiday in 1891 organised for him and a hand-picked group of friends by Winnaretta Singer (the Princesse de Scey-Montbéliard as she was at the time).

The poet Philippe Auguste, Comte de Villiers de L'Isle-Adam might have been, in some respects at least, yet another model for Huysman's Des Esseintes in *À rebours*. He was born on 7 November 1838 and came from a noble and eccentric family steeped in tradition and religion. But he lacked the money to explore his neuroses as luxuriously as Des Esseintes, and lived in Paris in abject poverty;

Villiers de L'Isle Adam as an older man

his somewhat alarming appearance as a tramp, the greatest contrast to the aristocracy of his background, was noted by his contemporaries. The fastidious Montesquiou, who had been introduced to Villiers de L'Isle Adam by Mallarmé, nevertheless recommended these texts to Fauré. Villiers did not write much poetry, and he specialised in the occult and horror stories of a gothic kind; he was also an avid Wagnerian, being skilled as both a singer and a pianist. If Fauré had not grasped the full range of the poet's output, he seems to have understood its neurasthenic sensitivity and sense of masochistic isolation; perhaps he had indeed read the whole of the *Contes cruels*, as these poems are more or less hidden two-thirds of the way through a volume dominated by prose. When the young Maurice Maeterlinck came to Paris in 1885 he was deeply influenced by his meetings with Villiers de L'Isle Adam and other symbolists. Villiers died on 19 August 1889. It does not seem to have occurred to Fauré to seek out any personal contact with him, although he may have attended one of Victor Wilder's salons between 1880 and 1890, where the poet was a regular visitor alongside such composers as Messager, D'Indy and Chabrier.[16] Perhaps the reputation of Villiers de L'Isle-Adam for eccentricity was to blame. According to Jules Lemaître he was a 'grandiose mystifier', but this seems unjust to a very real talent.

Madame Chabrier was said to have been been terrified of him; the description of the poet by Verlaine's friend Edmond Lepelletier reveals a more disturbing side of the poet's personality than we can even begin to suspect on hearing Fauré's settings:

He was gifted with a genius that bordered on madness … He had in him something of the magician, something of the mountebank. He seemed intoxicated with air; some said he smoked opium. We listened with astonishment, admiration, even fear. We almost dreaded when he narrated some strange tale, emphasised by fantastic gesture, some crisis that would cause him to fall down in a fit of epilepsy or hurl himself bodily on his auditors. He affected a strange pronunciation, punctuating his phrases, emphasising his verbs, and sounding his adjectives … ringing out like a clarion.[17]

This clarion-like emphasis is entirely lacking in the two settings by Fauré of this poet. As we have already seen, the composer adopted a mood of infinite refinement, almost as if Robert de Montesquiou had penned the texts himself.

(45) *Les Présents* (*The gifts*)[18]
1887, Op. 46 No. 1, 'À M. le comte Robert de Montesquiou', second Hamelle collection p. 74,
F major, 2/4, *Andante*

Si tu demandes quelque soir	*If you should ask one evening*
Le secret de mon cœur malade,	*The secret of my sick heart,*
Je te dirai, pour t'émouvoir,	*I shall tell you, to move you,*
Une très ancienne ballade.	*A very ancient ballad.*
Si tu me parles de tourments,	*If you talk to me of torments,*
D'espérance désabusée,	*Of shattered hopes,*
J'irai te cueillir, seulement,	*I shall simply pick for you,*
Des roses pleines de rosée.	*Roses full of dew.*
Si, pareille à la fleur des morts,	*If, like the flower of the dead,*
Qui fleurit dans l'exil des tombes,	*Which blossoms only in the exile of the grave,*
Tu veux partager mes remords . . .	*You should wish to share my remorse . . .*
Je t'apporterai des colombes.	*I shall bring you doves.*

Auguste de Villiers de L'Isle-Adam (1838–1889)

Fauré's *Les Présents* is dedicated to Comte Robert de Montesquiou (the author remembers rejoicing in noticing, as he bowed from the concert platform, that his portrait by Whistler graced the back wall of the recital room of the Frick Museum in New York). Jankélévitch remarks on the song's 'charmante morbidezza' with its alternation between F major and A♭ major in its opening bars.[19] In some ways this *berceuse* is a variant of *Le Secret*, but the music is rarefied, less heartfelt and more world-weary; there is something of the occult about it plus the languor of *décadence*. Something obsessive is at work in musical terms – this is reflected in the way in which after every chromatic excursion, no matter how exotic, the music returns in circular fashion to F major. These modulations, employing all the cleverness of the composer's enharmonic resources, are particularly ingenious at 'Je t'apporterai des colombes.' – an image that recalls the English composer Lord Berners, an English Montesquiou of a later age, who dyed his pigeons in the park of Faringdon House in various pastel shades.

The poet envisaged his text as a litany where both the first and second verses begin with 'Si tu me parles'. Fauré's alteration of the opening strophes to 'Si tu demandes' seems rather insensitive to this fact, but it is clear that the music itself creates this repetitive effect without making the text undertake the same task.

At the end of the song, the intrusion of an F♯ in the fifth and third bars from the end attempts to pull the music into G major, but to no avail. The setting is the musical equivalent of a futile attempt to escape the controlling influence and addiction of a 'cœur malade' – flights of imaginative fancy are reined in as the music is drawn back again and again to the doleful, velvet-lined reaches of the home key. In an exquisite and somewhat self-conscious song like this the art of Fauré and that of Debussy (in *Beau soir* for example) seem closer than they had ever been, or were ever to be in the future – at least until the song cycle *Mirages* of 1919, composed after Debussy's death (see Chapter 14).

In early 1887 Fauré performed his Second Piano Quartet at the Société Nationale de la Musique

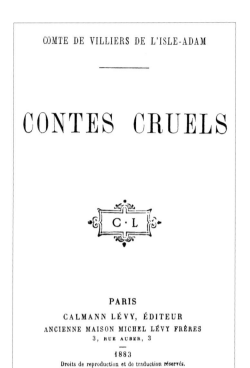

Title-page of Contes cruels *(1883) by Villiers de L'Isle Adam*

Elisabeth de Caraman Chimay, Comtesse Greffulhe

(SNM). In April Comte Robert de Montesquiou hosted a starry gathering at his home in Paris, an 'Audition de mélodies de Fauré', devoted to the composer's songs. The programme was exquisitely printed on pink Japanese vellum. In the summer of this year Fauré was the guest of Montesquiou's cousin, the beautiful Elisabeth de Caraman Chimay, Comtesse Greffulhe, at her sumptuous villa, 'La Case', built on the cliff top at Dieppe. She was the queen of French society, and another crucial character-template for Proust's novel. To her is dedicated Fauré's celebrated *Pavane*, Op. 50, with words (in the style of 'Mandoline' from Verlaine's *Fêtes galantes*) by Montesquiou himself; this is the only piece of music by Fauré with a poem by his literary adviser. In fact it is not even a setting as such because Montesquiou had to undertake 'the difficult and thankless task of setting to this music which is already complete, words that will make our *Pavane* fit to be both danced and sung'.[20] This post-facto task was indeed rather demeaning for someone like Montesquiou who so highly prized his own artistry, but we note here something that has radically changed about Fauré since the Viardot years: the composer is now unable to dissemble regarding his estimation of a poet's worth, however influential Montesquiou was as a *mécène*. The Comte had clearly hoped for a greater reciprocation of admiration from his favourite composer.

Fauré's rise in social status in Parisian artistic life was indicated by the fact that Montesquiou's friend Jacques-Emile Blanche painted the composer's portrait. The masterpiece *Clair de lune*, Fauré's first Verlaine setting, dates from this time (1887). Montesquiou's greatest contribution to Fauré's life and career was that he introduced the composer to Verlaine's poetry. We need no more evidence than a letter that Fauré wrote to Montesquiou at the end of February 1888 thanking him for the loan of 'the Verlaine books' (the precious first editions of the poet's work from the Comte's library) and

167

arranging to pass his house and return them.[21] This is a significant statement as we shall see, because it shows that once Fauré had selected a poem to set to music in 1887 (*Clair de lune*) the potential source of further poetic inspiration from Verlaine went out of his hands until he was able to obtain his own copies of the poetry. Fortunately the publisher Léon Vanier had issued second editions of *Fêtes galantes* and *Romances sans paroles* in 1886 and 1887 respectively, but it is impossible to say when Fauré searched them out for himself. The second edition of *Sagesse*, source of *Prison*, was first published in 1881 and reappeared only in 1889.

On 9 November 1887 Fauré wrote to Montesquiou concerning the poem for the *Pavane*; but he also had news that was rather more important for the history of the *mélodie*:

> How I should like to acquaint you with the last song: 'Your soul is a charming landscape' [here Fauré misquotes Verlaine with 'charmant' instead of 'choisi']. My publisher [Julien Hamelle] is very worried about the *masques* and *bergamasques*. Having successively consulted his wife, his children, and all his clerks he announced triumphantly 'You see, no-one knows what it means!'

It is clear that Fauré enjoys sharing a joke with Montesquiou at the expense of the philistine Hamelle, who was bewildered by Verlaine's use of a word going back to the sixteenth century describing a dance from Bergamo in Italy that resembled a tarantella. He clearly had never heard of the 'bergomask' danced by the mechanicals at the end of Shakespeare's *A Midsummer Night's Dream*.

It is typical of Fauré to use an amusing story to play down the significance of such a work as *Clair de lune*. He must have realised in his heart of hearts that he was making light of a piece of music that was soon to be recognized as an immortal masterpiece. In November 1888, in the same spirit of ironic obfuscation he wrote a letter to the Countess Greffulhe in which he described three recent songs– *Au cimetière*, *Larmes* and *Spleen*, as being 'all very cheerful!' In fact they are amongst his most angst-ridden works.

In chronological terms, the two early Verlaine settings *Clair de lune* (1887) and *Spleen* (1888) should be considered at this point in the narrative, when the composer was still influenced by *l'esprit décadent*, although they represent the upbeat to a new phase rather than the coda to an old one. It is clear that Montesquiou had lent the composer at least two exquisite (and already rare) volumes: Verlaine's *Fêtes galantes* of 1869 (from which Fauré took *Clair de lune*) and the possibly even more rare *Romances sans paroles* of 1874. As we have seen the composer then returned the Verlaine collections with care; the bibliophile Montesquiou would have expected no less. *Romances sans paroles* was reprinted in 1887 and *Spleen* ('Il pleure dans mon coeur') was probably set in 1888 from the pages of this new edition. Three years later, in 1891, the poetry of Verlaine was to provide the clue to Fauré's exit from the creative impasse in which he found himself at about the time he went to Venice as the guest of Winnaretta, Princesse de Scey-Montbéliard. Fortunately the publisher Léon Vanier reissued both the *Fêtes galantes* and the *Romances sans paroles* in that very year of 1891 in third editions, and it is probable that Fauré took at least the first of these newly available books, his own copy of *Fêtes galantes*, with him to Venice. Although the composer's early encounter with Verlaine (1887–88) is strictly speaking separate from the later (1891), the importance of the entry of Verlaine into Fauré's life is such that it deserves to be considered separately. For this reason these two earlier settings will be discussed in the next chapter, where all the Verlaine songs before *La Bonne chanson* are grouped together.

ɷ   ɷ   ɷ   ɷ

The year 1888 also saw the first performances of Fauré's *Requiem* – that is if we mean the first, austere version of the piece, the one in five movements (without tutti violins and excluding the *Dies irae*) written during the time following his mother's death. In later years the composer was to deny any connection between the two events, personal and musical. The *Requiem* was later expanded into seven movements; it is an irreplaceable masterpiece of course, but it is not the most highly prized of works for all admirers of Fauré in modern times, particularly those who are smitten by the master's later music. In his older age, with a fine opera to his credit that was virtually ignored, the composer might have resented being known chiefly as the Fauré of the *Requiem*, rather than of *Pénélope*, but the enduring fame of this religious work has continued to be a mixed blessing: a justifiable affection for the *Requiem* sometimes blinds members of the public to the composer's secular achievements.

In May 1888 the composer took part in a performance of Chabrier's opera *Gwendoline* at the imposing salon of the American heiress Winnaretta Singer; she had first met Fauré a decade or so earlier, during one of those summers he spent with the Clercs on the Normandy coast in the late 1870s. This was at a time when the mother of the adolescent Winnaretta had propelled herself (and her daughter) into the ranks of the French aristocracy thanks to her second marriage to a Luxembourgeois duke. Winnaretta herself had later married the Prince de Scey-Montbéliard and became a close friend of Marguerite Baugnies, whose weekly salons were to be the inspiration for her own. The formidable Princesse quickly became one of the most important, and serious, music patrons in Paris; we shall hear much more of her in the following chapter.

In July 1888, in the company of Messager, Fauré travelled to Bayreuth for the first time and was cordially received by Wagner's family. Performances there of *Die Meistersinger* and *Parsifal* moved him greatly. Back in Paris in November, less exalted subject-matter awaited his attentions: Paul Porel of the Odéon had commissioned him to write the incidental music for *Caligula* by Alexandre Dumas *père*. This is a portrait of imperial Rome where the composer's choral depictions of life at Caligula's court aim openly at pleasure-giving voluptuousness; Nectoux avers that 'the sensuality of Fauré's harmonies here reaches its apogee and it is not far from the borders of bad taste'.[22] At times we fancy we might be hearing film music written for a heavily costumed Cecil B. de Mille Roman epic, with tinges of exotic harmony that seem suitably pagan; it was surely only at this time in his career that he would have cared to embrace this 'dedcadent' subject-matter, and in such a way. Nevertheless, the closing chorus of the work, 'César a fermé la paupière', is as magical a piece for chorus as Fauré ever wrote. *Caligula* was given its first performance in April 1889; Tchaikovsky was in the audience and noted in his diary that Fauré was 'delightful', adding an exclamation mark for good measure.[23]

The three *mélodies* of 1888 could not be more different – it is strange to think of Fauré labouring over the poetry of the gruff and hirsute giant Jean Richepin (whose collection *La Mer* had appeared in 1886) at the same time as Hugo Wolf was creating his glorious *Mörike Lieder*. At first glance it seems likely that Fauré's self-appointed 'literary adviser' Montesquiou would have disapproved of Richepin, a Parisian Diogenes who gloried in a kind of social realism. The waves of Richepin's *La Mer* would seem to have threatened to overturn the delicate barque that wafted the Comte and his disciples to their exquisite imaginary Cytherea. Richepin belonged however to a more rugged side of the same left-bank bohemian culture that had spawned the decadents in the first place. He sang of the forgotten poor and the dregs of society, but works such as the erotic *Les Caresses* (1877) and the violently atheistic *Les Blasphèmes* (1884) had put him on the wrong side of the law in a way that appealed to the minorities that delighted in shocking respectable bourgeois society. Richepin's collaboration with

Chabrier for *La Sulamite* (1885) and as a ghost writer for the libretto of that composer's opera *Le Roi malgré lui* (1887) would have been known to Fauré and may have served to draw his attention to the poet. The controversial side of his writing had quietened down by the time he wrote *La Mer*, but he was still considered something of an anti-establishment troublemaker with an ability to scandalise middle-class opinion (the once-grisly poet eventually became a paid-up member of the establishment). Fauré's temporary espousal of poems by Richepin represented an experiment that was as temporary as his affiliation with Montesquiou and his circle.

It is worth noting that the composer considered his setting of Verlaine's *Spleen* as a suitable companion to publish with the two Richepin settings of his Op. 51; one should remember that at this time Verlaine, a one-time convict and well-known alcoholic, was anything but a 'respectable' choice as a collaborator in the eyes of those of a conservative or religious disposition. On the other hand, the poet was increasingly admired, already revered, by liberal opinion for his literary achievements.

The rise of *décadence* coincided with the loosening of the stays of the Third Republic and a sign of an increasing divergence from the Victorian values to be found rigidly, if hypocritically applied, across the Channel. Within a decade there would be official separation between Church

Caricature of Jean Richepin

and State in France. Entrenched right-wing prejudice was still to be found in the country, as was to be evident in the Dreyfus case, but obsession with a citizen's private sexual life (as in the case of Oscar Wilde) was viewed by the French as a peculiarly Anglo-Saxon obsession. As the nineties began, the stage was set for Fauré to embark on a new period in his compositional life at the same time as he began a series of relationships and would-be relationships with women that no longer required the clandestine discretion of an earlier, more censorious, epoch.

(46) *Au cimetière* (At the cemetery)[24]
1888, Op. 51 No. 2, 'À Madame Maurice Sulzbach', third Hamelle collection p. 8, E minor (transposed down into D minor for the Hamelle edition), 3/4, *Andante*

Heureux qui meurt ici	*Happy he who dies here*
Ainsi	*Even*
Que les oiseaux des champs!	*As the birds of the fields!*
Son corps près des amis	*His body near his friends*
Est mis	*Is laid*
Dans l'herbe et dans les chants.	*Amid the grass, amid the songs.*

Il dort d'un bon sommeil	*He sleeps a good sleep,*
Vermeil	*Crimson*
Sous le ciel radieux.	*Beneath the radiant sky.*
Tous ceux qu'il a connus,	*All those he has known*
Venus,	*Are come*
Lui font de longs adieux.	*To bid him a long farewell.*
À sa croix les parents	*By the cross his weeping*
Pleurants	*Parents*
Restent agenouillés;	*Remain kneeling,*
Et ses os, sous les fleurs,	*And his bones beneath the flowers*
De pleurs	*With tears*
Sont doucement mouillés.	*Are gently watered.*
Chacun sur le bois noir	*On the black wood all*
Peut voir	*Can see*
S'il était jeune ou non,	*If he was young or not,*
Et peut avec de vrais	*And can with true*
Regrets	*Regret*
L'appeler par son nom.	*Call him by his name.*
Combien plus malchanceux	*How much more unfortunate*
Sont ceux	*Are they*
Qui meurent à la mé,	*Who die at sea,*
Et sous le flot profond	*And beneath deep waters*
S'en vont	*Drift*
Loin du pays aimé!	*Far from their beloved land!*
Ah! pauvres, qui pour seuls	*Ah! poor souls! whose only*
Linceuls	*Shroud*
Ont les goëmons verts	*Is the green seaweed,*
Où l'on roule inconnu,	*Where they roll unknown,*
Tout nu,	*Unclothed,*
Et les yeux grands ouverts.	*And with wide-open eyes.*
Heureux qui meurt ici	*Happy he who dies here*
Ainsi	*Even*
Que les oiseaux des champs!	*As the birds of the fields!*
Son corps près des amis	*His body near his friends*
Est mis	*Is laid*
Dans l'herbe et dans les chants.	*Amid the grass, amid the songs.*

Jean Richepin (1849–1926)

Title-page of Au cimetière, published by Hamelle

Like 'Les Berceaux' this is a poem that compares life at sea with life on dry land, and in this case death at sea with a decent burial. The atheist Richepin fails to mention any Christian consolation in being buried in a churchyard – the dead man's parents may be kneeling in religious observation, but the corpse's implied preference for burial among family and friends, rather than alone at sea, is based on a pantheistic desire to be laid to rest among the trees and birds, the gentler manifestations of nature, rather than in the inhospitable reaches of uncharted waters. The outer strophes are set in a cemetery, and the initial peacefulness of this evocation precedes the savage contrast of music for victims of wave and storm. In the music a mood of rarefied simplicity (the *Requiem* is, after all, a contemporary work) reminds us that we are on hallowed ground. In this way the composer adds a whiff of religiosity to the picture that is not strictly to be found in Richepin's poem. The haunting opening cantilena is required to be *dolce e sereno*, a marking unique in Fauré's song output. The modal purity of these chordal progressions shines out with rare conviction. In the Fauré *mélodies* such chords often embark on complicated harmonic journeys; their rhythm is plain and undemonstrative, yet the effect, as here, is poignant and noble in its understatement.

At the end of the poem's fourth strophe a huge crescendo in the original tonic key (E minor, despite the printing of the song a tone lower in Hamelle) plunges the mood into bitterness with amazing speed. All hell now breaks loose with a merciless chromatic tightening, a tidal wave of anguish in a dangerously high tessitura. Left-hand triplets smash like breakers on to the second beats of the bar, the buffeting of a gigantic storm at sea. At the frightening image of 'Et les yeux grands ouverts' the accompaniment drifts like a body sinking to the depths. This is Fauré truly let off the leash, and unless both singer and pianist are masterful the result, unfamiliar in music by this composer, can be bombastic – it was almost certainly this part of the song that caused Proust to brand *Au cimetière* as 'truly awful'.[25] (In any case Richepin was not exactly a Proustian role-model.) Then, in a typically Fauréan ellipsis, as neat and almost as sudden as a cinematic change of shot (and reminiscent of *Les Berceaux*), we return to the safety of the churchyard and a recapitulation of the first verse. It is printed thus in Richepin's poem, but Fauré, wishing to round out the musical shape in binary form, repeats the poet's second strophe also.

Brahms's great setting of Detlev von Liliencron, *Auf dem Kirchhofe* Op. 105 No. 4 (1886), is an almost contemporary work; the poet and composer, both atheists, achieve something similar to

Richepin's sleight of hand abetted by Fauré. The casual listener may imagine that a song set in a churchyard and ending in the peace and tranquillity of the major key (as is the case with both the Fauré and the Brahms settings) might point to a depiction of the peace of a Christian afterlife. Closer reading of both texts reveals a simple longing for rest from earthly toil and troubles rather than any hopeful belief in a heavenly apotheosis. Liliencron deciphers the word 'Genesen' on the tombstones, showing that the dead, luckier than he, have been 'cured' of life – as if it were a sickness; this has not prevented the inappropriately unctuous performance of this song at many a funeral or remembrance service.

The dedicatee of *Au cimetière*, Madame Maurice Sulzbach (née Frincsel), was an amateur singer who, thanks to the largesse of her husband, a banker and collector, ran a thriving salon at 52bis avenue d'Iéna as well as at her château outside Paris. Her vocal ability was severely criticised by Marguerite de Saint-Marceaux (although the latter was not above singing duets with her); she was a friend of Chausson and Massenet, both of whom dedicated songs to her. Even Debussy frequented her gatherings for a time in the 1890s. She delighted Proust by telling him that she would give all of Beethoven's music for one work by Fauré.[26]

(47) *Larmes* (Tears)[27]

1888, Op. 51 No. 1, in the first edition 'À Madame la Princesse de Scey-Montbéliard', in later editions 'À Madame la Princess Edmond de Polignac', third Hamelle collection p. 3, C minor, 3/4, *Molto moderato*

Pleurons nos chagrins, chacun le nôtre.	*Let us mourn our sorrows, each his own.*
Une larme tombe, puis une autre.	*One tear falls, another follows.*
Toi, qui pleures-tu? Ton doux pays,	*You, who do you mourn? Your sweet native land,*
Tes parents lointains, ta fiancée.	*Your distant family, your betrothed.*
Moi, mon existence dépensée	*And I – my existence, wasted*
En vœux trahis.	*On vows betrayed.*
Pleurons nos chagrins, chacun le nôtre.	*Let us mourn our sorrows, each his own.*
Une larme tombe, puis une autre.	*One tear falls, another follows.*
Semons dans la mer ces pâles fleurs.	*Let us bestrew the sea with these pale flowers.*
À notre sanglot qui se lamente	*To our sobbing lament*
Elle répondra par la tourmente	*It will reply with the storm*
Des flots hurleurs.	*Of howling waves.*
Pleurons nos chagrins, chacun le nôtre.	*Let us mourn our sorrows, each his own.*
Une larme tombe, puis une autre.	*One tear falls, another follows.*
Peut-être toi-même, ô triste mer,	*Perhaps you yourself, O dismal sea,*
Mer au goût de larme âcre et salée,	*That tastes of acrid and salty tears,*
Es-tu de la terre inconsolée	*Are the inconsolable earth's*
Le pleur amer.	*Bitter weeping.*

Jean Richepin (1849–1926)

Title-page of Larmes, *published by Hamelle*

The frankness and vehemence of the song betoken a mid-life crisis. Dangerous though it often is to equate musical creation with biography, *Larmes* strikes so unusual a note in Fauré's song oeuvre that one feels that either he deliberately sought out the text to reflect his feelings, or his response to Richepin's melodramatic text unexpectedly dredged up a host of suppressed emotions. At the age of forty-three the composer seems to have been tormented about the direction of his career, the state of his finances and a marriage in which he was unfulfilled. It is clear that becoming a socially acceptable member of high society, an artist-in-waiting to the aristocracy, had brought him neither lasting pleasure nor security. The convulsive accompaniment is jagged and peremptory, and the pianist brings forth heavy teardrops in accented crotchets that are sustained under the hands while quaver rests punctuate other layers of the accompaniment. This ingenious deployment of fingers provides an unusual texture where the piano sound is both snatched away and insistent, like a stifled sob. (Wilhelm Müller's *Wasserflut* from Schubert's *Winterreise* uses similar imagery for tears that turn into a river.) At 'Moi, mon existence dépensée / En vœux trahis' we are reminded of the interaction between voice and piano in *Chanson du pêcheur*. The pathos of 'Une larme tombe' followed two beats later by 'puis une autre' is that of a great French *tragédien* pausing between phrases for effect. Yet the vocal line is a thing of shreds and patches; it never settles into a satisfying *cantilena* (appropriately enough for music where anything but satisfaction is described), although it achieves a bitter heroism at the close. A bewildering sequence of enharmonic progressions makes a slew of flats and sharps compete for the same harmonic space; the song's complex orthography mirrors the emotional confusion and distress of its subject.

Sylvia Kahan in her biography of Winnaretta Singer makes the fascinating suggestion that the anguish of *Larmes* might be connected with the composer's empathy with the mental state of its dedicatee who had recently suffered a family bereavement and who was imprisoned, like Fauré, in an unhappy marriage. Fauré, moreover, was probably enamoured of the Princesse at the time.

Like the poem for 'Au cimetière', *Larmes* is taken from Richepin's bulky collection of often melodramatic verse entitled *La Mer*; Richepin, elected a member of the Académie Française in 1908, became one of the most patriotic of poets during the First World War. His death in 1926, on the day before the publication of the *Manifeste surréaliste*, represents the unlikely juxtaposition of two irreconcilable poetic worlds. Richepin's life was rich in such paradoxes. He was someone from a middle-class background (his father was an army surgeon) who relished the world of outcasts and left-wing insurgents; he was a seaman, a dock labourer and a travelling salesman who understood ancient Greek.

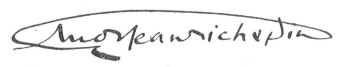

He remarked of his own poetry that it was 'bitter wine – not for the cream-licking palates of our children but for strong stomachs and powerful brains'. Although he is not as great a poet as Walt Whitman there is something Whitmanesque about Richepin's breadth of utterance, and Fauré's two settings of this poet were instinctively invested with a corresponding musical grandeur that borders on eccentricity.

∾   ∾   ∾   ∾

Shylock is a 'comédie en trois actes et sept tableaux' by Edmond Haraucourt (1856–1941), whose poetry has been described as belonging to the Parnassian aftermath. Haraucourt was ignored by most song composers, but there are at least six *mélodie* settings by Charles Koechlin. This 'drame adapté de Shakespeare' (from *The Merchant of Venice*) was given its first performance in Paris at the Théâtre National de l'Odéon on 17 December 1889. In October 1893 Fauré wrote to Saint-Saëns: 'Incidental music for the stage is the only kind that is suited to my limited means.' The later successes, however mixed, of *Prométhée* and *Pénélope* were eventually to prove him unduly pessimistic.

Fauré wrote this music during the busy summer and autumn of 1889 when he had also sat for his portrait by John Singer Sargent, composed an *Offertorium* for baritone solo to add to the first version of the *Requiem* and played host to the visiting Russian composer Glazunov in Paris. His second son Philippe was born in July 1889. Between writing the *Shylock* music and conducting it at the Odéon he had slipped away to holiday at the home of the Comtesse Greffulhe at Bois-Boudran (Seine-et-Marne). The music was dedicated to Paul Porel, director of the Théâtre de l'Odéon, who had invited Fauré to provide incidental music to Dumas's *Caligula* in 1888. Two of the *Shylock* numbers are songs that appeared separately in the third Hamelle *recueil*.

Many years ago the author of this book acquired a bound volume of music that had belonged to Leo Francis ('Frank') Schuster, the friend and patron of Fauré (and of Elgar), who lived in London. In this collection was a copy of the complete *Shylock* suite in a rare version where the two songs are accompanied by a single pianist, and the instrumental numbers are arranged for piano duet (with Fauré's approval) by the much younger composer Léon Boëllmann (1862–1897). Boëllmann was married to the daughter of Niedermeyer, and was one of Fauré's trusted collaborators. The composer had already asked him to make a four-hand version of the *Allegro symphonique*, the first section of the ill-fated Symphony in F; Boëllmann would have been first choice to make the piano version of the *Requiem*, but his early death intervened.

On the third disc of the complete Fauré songs issued by Hyperion records (CDA 67735) the two *mélodies* from *Shylock* were performed in the context of Op. 57 as a whole, although this suite for piano duet essentially differs in several respects from the version heard in the theatre. There is no music associated with any scene involving the money-lender of Haraucourt's play. Commentaries for the complete incidental music are given here the better to place the two *mélodies* in context. These two songs have four slightly different (and somewhat confusing) existences: as part of the original incidental music for the play (this music for reduced orchestra remains unpublished): as Nos 1 and 3 of the version (sometimes referred to as a 'suite' in the concert hall) for full orchestra and, in two of the numbers, tenor voice (*Shylock, Musique de scène* Op. 57; as part of the piano-duet accompanied version arranged by Louis Boëllmann as explained above; and as separate piano-accompanied songs (Op. 57 Nos 1 and 3), published in the third Hamelle collection.

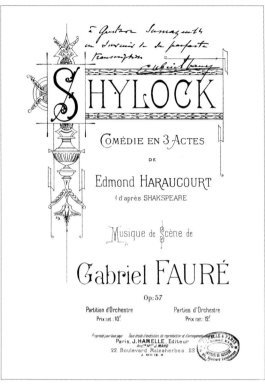

Title-page of Shylock by Haraucourt (1889)

Title-page of the orchestral score of Shylock, inscribed by Fauré
to the critic Gustave Samazeuilh

Shylock (*Haraucourt*)
1889, Op. 57

(48) *Chanson* (*Song*)[28]
1889, Op. 57 No. 1, third Hamelle collection p. 22, B♭ major, 12/8, *Allegretto*

Oh, les filles! Venez, les filles aux voix douces!
C'est l'heure d'oublier l'orgueil et les vertus,
Et nous regarderons éclore dans les mousses,
    La fleur des baisers défendus.

Oh, girls! Come, girls with the sweet voices!
It is time to forget your pride and virtue,
And we shall watch forbidden kisses
    Flower among the mosses.

Les baisers défendus, c'est Dieu qui les ordonne.
Oh, les filles! Il fait le printemps pour les nids,
Il fait votre beauté pour qu'elle nous soit bonne,
    Nos désirs pour qu'ils soient unis.

Forbidden kisses – it's God that orders them.
Oh, girls! He creates springtime for nesting,
He creates your beauty so that it seems good to us,
    And our desires that they might be joined.

Oh, filles! Hors l'amour, rien n'est bon sur la terre,
Et depuis les soirs d'or jusqu'aux matin rosés
Les morts ne sont jaloux, dans leur paix solitaire,
    Que du murmure des baisers.

Oh, girls! Except for love, there is nothing good on earth,
And from the gold of evening to the pink of dawn,
The dead, in their solitary peace, are jealous only
    Of murmured kisses.

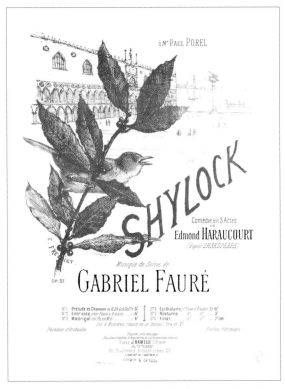

Title-page of an arrangement of the Shylock *suite for piano duet.*
Illustration by Fauré's father-in-law, Emmanuel Fremiet

This music opens Act I, Tableau II, scene 2 (thirty-two pages into the play). The stage directions read: 'La nuit, sur le canal; clair de lune. Au fond, la façade de la maison de Shylock. À gauche un pont. Les gondoles traversent la scène.' ('Night on the canal, moonlight. In the background the front of Shylock's house. To the left a bridge. Gondolas cross the stage.') In the orchestrally accompanied *Musique de scène*, the song is marked Allegretto moderato and is prefaced by twenty introductory bars (Boëlmann's version for piano duet is called a Prélude) for muted cellos and harp arpeggios; towards the end of the passage the violas and violins amplify the texture before the singer launches the *Chanson* in bar 21. In the Hamelle edition, as almost certainly in the original stage music, there are only two introductory bars. It is a curiosity of the orchestral score that the time signature for the whole opening number is in common time, while the vocal line is clearly written in 12/8 without a separate time signature of its own. During the *Chanson* (a voice singing in the distance), Jessica stands enveloped in a large, dark cloak and leans against a column on the terrace as she awaits her fiancé Lorenzo. The music for this distant voice is suitably plaintive and Italianate. On closer hearing, it is infinitely subtle – as elusive as the female qualities described in the poem. As Jankélévitch remarks, harmonies seem to dissolve as soon as they appear to have been established. The beautifully transparent orchestration is for strings, harp, flute, horn and clarinet. Considering that this music was conceived for an off-stage singer to a rather wooden text that owes nothing to Shakespeare, Fauré did his best to ensure that this insouciant barcarolle-*berceuse* somehow suggested the Rialto. In the stage version the two strophes were separated by spoken text, and there was a third strophe tacked on for the spiriting away in a gondola of a willing Jessica.

Entr'acte
Op. 57 No. 2 (title on autograph: 'Scene of the Caskets'), A major, 2/4, *Andante moderato – Allegretto*

On 27 September 1889 Fauré wrote from Bougival to Haraucourt asking urgently for the 'act with the caskets' – the part of *Shylock* for which this entr'acte was written. He also invited the playwright to lunch the following week in order to hear the two songs, the *Chanson* and *Madrigal* from the play, sung by a 'young friend', possibly Maurice Bagès (who was to give the first performance of *La Bonne chanson* five years later). It is interesting that the composer seems to have been scrupulously concerned to fulfil the wishes of Haraucourt in musical terms.

Fauré lavishes his musical talents on this movement as lovingly as Schubert provided *Rosamunde* with its three entr'actes in 1823. By the 1880s the musical entr'acte was a tradition that was dying in the theatre. In the case of *Shylock* we might have imagined that it would be played during the changing of scenery between Acts I and II, just as we are about to meet the important characters of Portia and her maid Nérissa for the first time. In fact, Nectoux has established that in the stage version the fanfares were played separately for the entrances of the Bey of Morocco and of the Prince of Aragon (Act II scene 3), and that most of the remaining music was played extremely quietly *during* the rest of the scene.[29] This is the point in the plot where the suitors are required to choose one of three caskets in gold, silver or lead. At the heart of Fauré's music there is a ravishing melody for violin solo (marked *espressivo*), which is then taken up by solo clarinet. This theme would surely have been linked with Bassanio, with whom Portia is enamoured.

(49) *Madrigal* (Madrigal)[30]
Op. 57 No. 3, third Hamelle collection p. 25, F major, 3/4, *Allegretto*

Celle que j'aime a de beauté	*She whom I love has more beauty*
Plus que Flore et plus que Pomone,	*Than Flora and Pomona,*
Et je sais, pour l'avoir chanté,	*And I know, for having sung it,*
Que sa bouche est le soir d'automne,	*That her mouth is an autumn evening*
Et son regard la nuit d'été.	*And her gaze a summer night.*
Pour marraine elle eut Astarté,	*Astarte was her godmother,*
Pour patronne elle a la Madone,	*The Madonna her patroness,*
Car elle est belle autant que bonne	*For she whom I love*
Celle que j'aime!	*Is as lovely as she is good.*
Elle écoute, rit et pardonne,	*She listens, laughs and forgives,*
N'écoutant que par charité:	*Listening only from charity:*
Elle écoute, mais sa fierté	*She listens, but her pride*
N'écoute, ni moi ni personne,	*Listens neither to me nor anyone,*
Et rien encore n'a tenté	*And nothing yet has tempted*
Celle que j'aime!	*She whom I love.*

Edmond Haraucourt (1856–1941)

This is heard in Act II scene 1, before the 'Scene of the Caskets'. Fauré clearly decided that for his *Shylock* suite he did not wish to have the two numbers for tenor appearing consecutively; in the original incidental music to Haraucourt's play there was an *Interlude*, discarded from the suite, which separated them. Portia and Nérissa discuss the demerits of her various suitors: she calls the Neapolitan 'Un pot de pomade, / Un fleuve de parfums' ('a jar of pomade, a river of perfumes'); the Palatine count is dismissed as a German ogre; the French prince is 'Plus noble que la reine et plus vieux que Bourbon'; the Englishman Fauconbridge is dismissed for his 'jargon anglais'; the Scottish lord is scotched for his meanness; and the Duke of Saxony's nephew is damned as a drunk. Suddenly there is the sound of a guitar from outside. This is the Prince of Aragon. Mention of his up-coming 'aubade' (morning serenade) is rhymed with 'malade' (sick) – Portia fears that all this wooing will indeed make her sick. Once again Fauré has the task of providing music for an off-stage tenor (in all likelihood Maurice Bagès). When the *Madrigal* ends, Portia is witheringly funny at the expense of the poem sung by the hapless Aragon, who, she says, 'sings like a blind man and burns like a candle'. Nectoux is damning of both the music ('The melodic lines droop, and the accompaniment, with its predictable harp entries, is banal') and the piano-writing of the two songs, which he finds uncharacteristically thin in comparison with Fauré's usual accompaniments.[31]

This music is indeed banal, but might it have been a deliberate attempt at humour on the composer's part? Perhaps Fauré has turned this futile serenade into something of a character piece. He is incapable of writing music that is not polished and elegant (Jankélévitch praises its harmonic subtleties to the skies), but it is hard to believe that the woebegone mood created by this music is inadvertent – one has only to hear the cello introduction, which seems to poke gentle fun at the love-sick prince – a French equivalent of Hugo Wolf's delight in poking fun at lovelorn Italian serenaders. The hyperboles in praising Portia are deliberately ridiculous in Haraucourt's lyric, and the composer must have felt free to allow the melodic lines to droop to match the mood of the lovesick Aragon.

Epithalame
Op. 57 No. 4, C major (original printed key; key of autograph B♭ major), 2/4, *Adagio non troppo*

By the terms of her father's will, Portia must marry the suitor who chooses the correct casket, and Bassanio has successfully selected the casket of lead. At the end of Act II scene 3 Portia and Bassanio are wed. In *Shylock* the marriage takes place in full view of the unsuccessful suitors, the Bey of Morocco and the Prince of Aragon. At the same time Nérissa, Portia's maid, marries Gratiano; both the couples kneel before the priest. This piece looks forward to Fauré's most successful incidental music, that for Maeterlinck's *Pelléas et Mélisande*. In Fauré the influence of Wagner is rarely to be heard, but here we can discern something of *Parsifal* in the noble unfolding of music that also incorporates the love theme from the so-called *Entr'acte*, as well as echoes of the fanfares for the foreign dignitaries. Fauré's final orchestration for the published suite is far more sumptuous than that of the stage version; the composer predicted that after the first three performances of the play he would have to work with an 'inferior bunch of hacks', and that it was no fun conducting such musicians in the Odéon orchestra. It was also presumably not much fun for the composer that this beautiful score was mere background music, not only for movement on stage, but for speech as well. Few of the original audience would have noticed the felicities of this composition, and the critics made little comment on it at the time.

Nocturne
Op. 57 No. 5, D major (original key), 3/4, *Andante molto moderato*

Not all the love music in *Shylock* is related to Portia and Bassanio. We have already encountered Jessica, Shylock's daughter, in the first act. After the taxing trial scene involving Shylock and his pound of flesh there is clearly need for a change of mood. The stage directions for Act III scene 2 of *Shylock* are 'La nuit. Clair de lune. Le jardin de Portia'. Jessica and Lorenzo celebrate their love in a scene which is one of the most beautiful in all Shakespeare (see *The Merchant of Venice*, Act V). Some of Haraucourt's imagery takes its cue from the Bard, but there is nothing to rival the rapturous words of Lorenzo that Vaughan Williams set in his *Serenade to Music* ('How sweet the moonlight sleeps upon this bank!').

Nevertheless, Fauré's music proves worthy of the original Shakespearean mood; this, his only bard-inspired music, is one of his loveliest creations, and is scored entirely for *divisi* strings. He had found the inspiration for this music in the beautiful park of Bois-Boudran that belonged to the Comtesse Greffulhe. In the third bar we hear a melody, a drop of a fifth followed by a seven-note ascent of the stave; this theme occurs in varied forms in the *Romance* for cello and piano, and in the opening of the song *Soir*. The composer referred to it as 'a musical phrase with a certain penetration, like Venetian moonlight'. Fortunately there is a break in the text ('on entend les accents lointains d'une musique', 'one hears the distant sounds of music' the playwright observes) where at least some of Fauré's score might have been allowed to make its point. It seems certain, however, that after a short while the play's dialogue continued to obscure some of the most moving 'background music' ever written. Nectoux points out that at rehearsal letter B in the orchestral score there is a modulation which seems to have been inspired wholly by the prelude to Wagner's *Parsifal*.[32] Koechlin,

Edmond Haraucourt

taken with the sumptuousness of this music's colouring compared it to the work of Vittore Carpaccio – an allusion worthy of Marcel Proust's reverence for this Venetian painter, and for Fauré.

Final
Op. 57 No. 6 (original title *Aubade*), F major, 3/4, *Allegretto vivo*

One might have imagined that this marvellously deft and light-hearted movement was meant to be played right at the end of *Shylock*, rather like the bergamasks that were traditionally danced after the Shakespeare plays in Elizabethan times. Instead, Fauré was charged with writing background music for the last scene (Act III scene 2), where all the lovers come together and everything is resolved. Because the dialogue had to be audible above the music, Fauré relied less on melody here and provided a remarkable assortment of rhythms and articulations (pizzicato, staccato, spiccato), all giving the impression of light-hearted banter without interfering too much with the actors – a thankless task. This movement of the suite was thus more sumptuously orchestrated than the incidental music was allowed to be. It could be extremely unrewarding for a composer to undertake this kind of work. In 1901, after having written incidental music for Georges Clemenceau's play *Le Voile du bonheur*, Fauré asked the playwright if the music was all right. 'Perfect, perfect,' was the response, 'one couldn't hear a thing'.[33] The scherzo was one of which Fauré could be proud.

The fragments of fanfare and melody show a not very thorough attempt to incorporate some of the earlier musical ideas in a final portmanteau piece. He was to achieve just such an effect, triumphantly, at the end of *La Bonne chanson*.

(50) *La Rose* (*Ode anacréontique*) (*The rose (ode in the style of Anacreon)*)[34]
August 1890, Op. 51 No. 4, 'À M. Maurice Bagès', F major, 3/4, *Andante*

Je dirai la rose aux plis gracieux.	*I shall speak of the rose with its graceful petals.*
La rose est le souffle embaumé des dieux,	*The rose is the scented breath of the gods,*
Le plus cher souci des Muses divines.	*The most cherished care of the divine Muses.*
Je dirai ta gloire, ô charme des yeux,	*I shall speak of your glory, O delight of the eyes,*
Ô fleur de Kypris, reine des collines!	*O flower of Cypris, queen of the hills!*
Tu t'épanouis entre les beaux doigts	*You bloom between the beautiful fingers*
De l'Aube écartant les ombres moroses;	*Of Dawn, brushing gloomy shadows aside;*
L'air bleu devient rose, et roses les bois;	*The blue air turns rose, and rose the woods;*
La bouche et le sein des vierges sont roses!	*The lips and breasts of virgins are roses!*
Heureuse la vierge aux bras arrondis	*Happy the virgin with rounded arms*
Qui dans les halliers humides te cueille!	*Who gathers you in moist thickets!*
Heureux le front jeune où tu resplendis!	*Happy the young brow that you adorn!*
Heureuse la coupe où nage ta feuille!	*Happy the cup where your leaves float!*
Ruisselante encor du flot paternel,	*Streaming still from the paternal waters,*
Quand de la mer bleue Aphrodite éclose	*When from the blue sea Aphrodite emerged*
Etincela nue aux clartés du ciel,	*Glistening naked in the brilliant sky,*
La Terre jalouse enfanta la rose;	*Jealous Earth gave birth to the rose:*
Et l'Olympe entier, d'amour transporté,	*And all Olympus, transported by love,*
Salua la fleur avec la Beauté!	*Greeted the flower with Beauty!*

Charles Marie René Leconte de Lisle (1818–1894)

This song, with its Botticellian references to the birth of Venus, returns to territory covered ten years earlier in the cantata *La Naissance de Vénus*. It has its problematic aspects in that the date of the finished manuscript (August 1890) is a full two years after its companion songs in Op. 51 (the two settings of Richepin and Verlaine's *Spleen*) had been composed. Finishing *La Rose*, like completing *Soir* in 1894, seems to have caused Fauré some difficulty, and it is probable that the song was set aside to be reconsidered at a later date. Even then (as we discuss below) Fauré remained in two minds about the work's ending.

Leconte de Lisle's ode (*Poèmes et poésies*) was already thirty-five years old, but the composer valiantly defies the time-warp. He clearly admired the gardener in this Parnassian poet whose roses from Isfahan had bloomed in his musical past, and whose roses from Lahore (*Le Parfum impérissable*) lay in his musical future. This prize-winning specimen of a rose is from Delos, and it inspires the composer to a very personal response; he manages to relax the poet's majestic and statuesque pose with music that remains warm and sensual despite the statuesque mythological references. Flowers are a metaphor for women of course, and all Fauré's experience in apostrophising the female form in his Silvestre songs here comes to his aid in silken progressions that paint elusive erotic visions.

Title-page of La Rose, *published by Hamelle*

There are no separate strophes in this single sweep of a text, and the composer allows himself only a brief piano interlude before the fourteenth line of the poem. Apart from this respite, voice and piano flower together in a texture that, if not exactly overgrown, signifies profusion: this is no single rose but an overgrown hillside where the passer-by is overwhelmed by the flowers' scent, a veritable 'odor di femmina'.

The ingenuity and impetus of the music either hold the listener's attention or are a source of confusion. Constantly changing harmonies (on a row of descending basses with Mixolydian colourings) are meant to delight, but, as in the future *La Bonne chanson*, the ear is in danger of being unsettled by too much diversity. The final page successfully incorporates a touch of the grandeur of Zeus (and Leconte de Lisle's apotheosis as high priest of Parnassus), but it risks obliterating the slender grace of the flower. It is only here that one feels a slight artificiality in the music, as if the composer were playing a sacerdotal role that did not come as naturally to him as to the poet. One may even say that the composer has captured the spirit of Leconte de Lisle too successfully for the music's good. The postlude, like that for Schubert's *Ganymed*, restores classical poise within a *piano* dynamic in the wake of a more boisterous heavenly rejoicing. Suckling notes that this music is marked *Andante* 'but displays quite a Mozartian reluctance towards any sagging into an adagio'. Although Mozart is scarcely the composer to cite with regard to a texture as effulgent as this, Suckling correctly points out that *La Rose* is an example of 'the *unimpeded* character of Fauré's songs'. (It would be even more appropriate to mention Bach and what Nadia Boulanger refers to as both composers' 'incomparable sense of self-unfolding melody'.)[35] Once begun, the music flows to its destination, the final chord, with the inevitability of a mighty river.

It is fascinating to see that Fauré had second thoughts about the concluding vocal phrase of this song to the words 'avec la Beauté'. In the version sung universally today (and printed in volume 3 of *Vingt mélodies*, published by Hamelle) the singer's final note is a sober F. In fact, the composer had originally ended the song with a high A, as shown in Example 7.1 (from *Vingt-cinq mélodies*, 1897). He had asked, moreover, that this high A should be sung in a challengingly difficult *piano* dynamic.

This high-flown ending, almost without parallel in the composer's mature songs (unless we compare the discarded climax of *Soir* discussed in Chapter 10), might seem at first glance to break free from the restrictions implied by classical restraint, but this is no climactic celebration; in fact it works only when the singer has a *piano* high A at his or her easy disposal (very few do, particularly on this vowel). Fauré changed this song either because such control was simply impractical for most artists, or because he wished to 'rein in' a song in danger of becoming too dramatic (involuntarily,

Example 7.1 Original ending of La Rose

for those not able to end the song quietly). The pianist will find that the approach to the *forte* F major chord under 'Beauté' falls a good deal more easily under the fingers in this earlier version. In the more familiar printed peroration the pianistic jump between 'Beau-' and '-té' seems slightly unnatural – as if a cut has been made, as is indeed the case.

The song is dedicated to Maurice Bagès (1862–1908), whose full name was Maurice Bagès Jacobe de Trigny, a gifted amateur tenor straight out of Proust. He must have been a formidable musician, and a good singer too, for the composer to have dedicated to him a song of this complexity and difficulty. If it was relatively rare for Fauré to dedicate a song to anyone other than a woman, Bagès had no wife via whom the dedication could be made, as was often the custom of the time. *La Rose* is almost always sung by a soprano, sometimes a mezzo, and one is reminded that the heroism of the final pages, like the closing section of Duparc's *Phidylé*, may sound more convincing sung by the male voice and an octave down from the printed pitch. Bagès was associated above all with the great Verlaine settings: he sang the first public performance of *La Bonne chanson* at the home of the painter Madeleine Lemaire, the first performance of *Clair de lune* at a concert of the SNM and the first performance of the *Cinq mélodies 'de Venise'*.

Left-to-right: the composers Henri Duparc and Pierre de Bréville with the tenor Maurice Bagès (banjo) at the 'Fêtes de Marnes-la-Coquette', 1895 (Collection Jean-Michel Nectoux)

(51) *En prière* (In prayer)[36]

1890, first published in *Contes mystiques* (Durand, 1890), 'À Mme Leroux-Ribeyre', second Hamelle collection p. 66, E♭ major, ♩, *Moderato*

Si la voix d'un enfant peut monter jusqu'à Vous,
    Ô mon Père,
Écoutez de Jésus, devant Vous à genoux,
    La prière!
	If a child's voice may rise up to You,
	    O Father,
	Hear the prayer of Jesus who kneels
	    In prayer!

Si Vous m'avez choisi pour enseigner Vos lois
    Sur la terre,
Je saurai Vous servir, auguste Roi des rois,
    Ô Lumière!
	If You have chosen me to teach Your laws
	    On earth,
	I shall serve You, august King of kings,
	    O light!

Sur mes lèvres, Seigneur, mettez la vérité
    Salutaire,
Pour que celui qui doute, avec humilité
    Vous révère!
	On my lips, O Lord, place truth that is
	    Beneficient,
	So that he who doubts may with humility
	    Revere You.

Ne m'abandonnez pas, donnez-moi la douceur
    Nécessaire,
Pour apaiser les maux, soulager la douleur,
    La misère!
	Do not abandon me, give me the kindness
	    Required,
	To ease pain, console sorrow
	    And misery!

Révélez-Vous à moi, Seigneur en qui je crois
    Et j'espère:
Pour Vous je veux souffrir et mourir sur la croix,
    Au calvaire!
	Reveal Yourself to me, Lord, in whom I believe
	    And hope:
	For you I would suffer and die on the Cross,
	    On Calvary!

Stéphan Bordèse (1847–?)

This is not a *mélodie* but rather a *cantique*, like *Noël*. *En prière* was included in the *Vingt-cinq mélodies* of 1897, and it remained in the second Hamelle *recueil*. Countless singers and pianists have performed this attractive prayer-like song as if it were a bona fide *mélodie*, and if it is going to be performed at all in the concert hall, there is no other choice. Its seraphic mood may be problematic to those who do not whole-heartedly admire Fauré's *Requiem*, more or less a contemporary work. On the other hand, like the religious songs of Schubert, this music never cloys; Gounod or Franck identify with their texts in a more personal way, which makes a different impression. Fauré has learned much from Gounod, particularly in a setting like this, but as in *Clair de lune* he keeps his distance as if avoiding avowals made in the first person. This is a portrait of devotion, a picture of someone at prayer, rather than the composer imagining *himself* at prayer. The creation of an atmosphere of heartfelt piety seems effortless, the progression of harmonies a miracle of fluidity. Only Fauré could have written this music. At 'Révélez-Vous à moi' the triplet accompaniment cedes to a motif of crotchets that wafts across the stave as if the Holy Spirit is revealed – wonderfully mysterious, yet somehow casual and without undue fuss. On the song's last page this alternates in an almost liturgical manner with triplets, and is repeated no fewer than five times, as if in benediction. It is paradoxical that the shadow of Wagner's mighty *Parsifal* should fall on one of Fauré's slightest songs. Nadia Boulanger told Nectoux that the composer delighted in accompanying this song for her sister Lili, who sang it exquisitely.[37]

Stéphan Bordèse, born in 1847, was the son of Louis Bordèse (1815–1886), an Italian-born composer who emigrated to Paris in 1834 and worked there as a famous singing teacher. The collection of twelve religious poems by Bordèse entitled *Contes mystiques* (published by Durand), set to music by various composers, dates from 1890. Alongside Fauré this includes works by Augusta Holmès, Théodore Dubois, Charles Lecocq, Jules Massenet, Emile Paladilhe, Camille Saint-Saëns, Pauline Viardot and Charles Widor. It may be unfair to come to the conclusion that the son of the affectionately regarded Louis Bordèse traded on the friendship from his father's circle to elicit this response to his rather indifferent religious verse. It sounds like the sort of project that comes off only with a certain amount of legerdemain: Widor, for example, is possibly informed by the wily *animateur* of the project that Saint-Saëns has already contributed to the collection, and vice versa,

STÉPHAN BORDÈSE

CONTES MYSTIQUES

Musique
de

Ed. Diet. — Th. Dubois
G. Fauré. — Augusta Holmès. — Ch. Lecocq
Ch. Lenepveu. — H. Maréchal. — J. Massenet
E. Paladilhe. — C. Saint-Saëns
Pauline Viardot. — C.-M. Widor

* * * *

Dessin de G. Rochegrosse

Paris

A. DURAND & FILS
4, Place de la Madeleine, 4

Déposé selon les traités internationaux. — Propriété pour tous pays.
Tous droits d'Exécution publique, de Reproduction, de Traduction et d'Arrangements réservés pour tous pays
y compris la Suède, la Norvège et le Danemark.

1890

Title-page of Contes mystiques *published by Durand (1890)*

and no one wishes to be left out in such company. Widor and Lecocq also took part in another such poet-oriented collection, the idea clearly stolen by Hamelle from Durand and Bordèse: in 1891 Paul Gravollet of the Comédie-Française wrote a set of undistinguished poems under the title *Les Frissons* and asked a new generation of composers to set a poem each. Amazingly he persuaded Debussy, Ravel, Caplet, D'Indy, Chaminade and fifteen others (though not Fauré) to take part in the published collection. Alphonse Duvernoy, Marianne Viardot's husband, contributed a song that is seemingly dutifully influenced by the Viardot taste for Italian *verismo*. Stéphan Bordèse also furnished Massenet with song texts; he provided two libretti for operettas by Charles Lecoq, and collaborated with Saint-Saëns on *Lola* (1900) – a *scène dramatique*.

If the songs of Chapter 5 had represented the transition between the first and second *recueils* – in itself a significant deepening of stylistic expressivity – the songs of this chapter are the gateway into the second period. Where one period ends and another begins is something of a grey area. *Nocturne* and *Les Présents* (the two Villiers de L'Isle-Adam settings) represent a change (Montesquiou-approved) from the texts of Armand Silvestre, but they are merely an upbeat to the rebirth of Fauré's muse that occurred as the poetry of Paul Verlaine entered into his life. It is *Clair*

Whistler's Arrangement in Black and Gold *(1891-1892): Comte Robert de Montesquiou-Fezensac. © The Frick Collection, New York*

de lune (1887) and *Spleen* (1888), composed and published at a deceptive distance from the *Cinq mélodies 'de Venise'* (1891), which give notice of a second period in Fauré's *mélodies*. For some commentators they mark the beginning of the second period itself. The miracle was that this poet came to Fauré's aid (although in no personal sense) at exactly the right time.

The Jean Richepin settings (*Au cimetière* and *Larmes*) are also clearly songs of a different kind, but their overwrought stylistic character is something of a blind alley in terms of the composer's search for a way out of the creative impasse that had tormented him (alongside his migraine-like headaches and bouts of depression) in these, his busiest salon years. His flirtation with the prevailing decadent *Zeitgeist* is an indication of a creative soul temporarily lost, and searching for new, meaningful collaboration. As we shall see, a Venice sojourn, the friendship of a young woman of power and wealth and two small volumes of Verlaine's verse were to conjure a solution to this problem. If the *Cinq mélodies 'de Venise'* represent the true beginning of the second period, the music for Haraucourt's *Shylock*, and his setting of *La Rose* are transitional; these songs clearly benefited from the new artistic vistas that had been revealed by the composer's first encounters with Verlaine in 1887 and 1888. And that epiphany went back to his fateful meeting with Montesquiou. It is no wonder that after completing a concert at the Frick I felt honoured to bow, from the stage to the imposing portrait of the exquisitely attired Comte – Whistler's title for the painting is *Arrangement in Black and Gold*. And who could be surprised by his icy indifference? It is as if Montesquiou remains permanently and magnificently impervious – as he had been in life – to a passing parade of less important artists and poorly dressed admirers.

---

1   Recounted in *Cornelia Otis Skinner, 'Robert de Montesquiou: The Magnificent Dandy', in Elegant Wits and Grand Horizontals: Paris la belle époque* (London: Michael Joseph, 1962), p. 45.

2   From the Savoy opera *Patience* by Gilbert and Sullivan.

3   *Gabriel Fauré: A Life in Letters*, trans. and ed. Barrie Jones (London: B.T. Batsford, 1989), letter 6, p. 21.

4   Marcel Proust, *Remembrance of Things Past* (originally *A la recherche du temps perdu*), trans. C.K. Scott Moncrieff, vol. 4: *Cities of the Plain* (originally *Sodome et Gomorrhe*), part 2, pp. 265–7. The passage begins in the original 'Un grand musicien, membre de l'Institut, haut dignitaire officiel …'.

5   Richard Davenport-Hines, *A Night at the Majestic* (London: Faber and Faber, 2006), p. 166.

6   See J-M Nectoux, *Musique et beaux arts: Le Salon de Marguerite de Saint-Marceaux*, in *Les Saint-Marceaux, Une famille d'artistes en 1900*, Les Dossiers du Musée d'Orsay (Paris: Réunion des Musées Nationaux, 1992), pp. 62–90.

7   Marguerite de Saint-Marceaux, *Journal*, ed. M. Chimènes (Paris: Fayard, 2007).

8   Jean-Michel Nectoux, *Gabriel Fauré: A Musical Life*, trans. Roger Nichols (Cambridge: Cambridge University Press, 1991), p. 225.

9   In the original French, 'porte-musique d'un groupe de snobs et d'imbéciles'. Debussy in a letter to Georges Hartmann, 9 August 1898, in *Debussy Letters*, ed. François Lesure and Roger Nichols, trans. Roger Nichols (London: Faber, 1987), p. 99.

10   Quoted in Orledge, *Gabriel Fauré* (London: Eulenburg, 1979), p. 11.

11   Quoted in Sylvia Kahan, *Music's Modern Music: A Life of Winnaretta Singer, Princesse de Polignac* (Rochester, NY: University of Rochester Press, 2003), p. 88.

12   Marguerite Long, *Au piano avec Gabriel Fauré* (Paris : Gérard Billandot, 1963), p. 15, where the original phrase is 'un coeur peu volage de Gabriel Fauré'.

13   *Nocturne*: Aspects of this song's interpretation are discussed in Chapter 16, p. 411.

14   Nectoux, *Gabriel Fauré: A Musical Life*, p. 174.

15   Myriam Chimènes, *Mécènes et musiciens* (Paris: Fayard, 2004), p. 357.

16   Ibid., p. 445.

17   Edmond Lepelletier, *Paul Verlaine: His Life, his Work*, trans. E.M. Lang (London: T. Werner Laurie, 1909), pp. 109–11.

18   *Les Présents*: Aspects of this song's interpretation are discussed in Chapter 16, p. 412.

19   Vladimir Jankélévitch, *Fauré et ses mélodies* (Paris: Librairie Plon, 1938), p. 89.

20   Letter from the composer to Elisabeth Greffulhe, 1887, in *Gabriel Fauré: His Life through his Letters*, ed. Jean-Michel Nectoux, trans. John Underwood (London and New York: Marion Boyars, 1984), pp. 130–31.

21   Gabriel Fauré, *Correspondance*, ed. J.-M. Nectoux (Paris: Flammarion, 1980), letter 104, p. 198.

22   Nectoux, *Gabriel Fauré: A Musical Life*, p. 140.

23   Ibid., p. 279.

24   *Au cimetière*: Aspects of this song's interpretation are discussed in Chapter 16, p. 412.

25   Marcel Proust in a letter to Pierre Lavallée, Summer 1894. *Correspondance génerale de Marcel Proust*, Volume 4 (Paris, 1933), p. 10. The original French describing *Au cimetière* is 'vraiment affreux'.

26   Chimènes, *Mécènes et musiciens*, pp. 191–2.

27   *Larmes*: Aspects of this song's interpretation are discussed in Chapter 16, p. 412.

28   *Chanson*: Aspects of this song's interpretation are discussed in Chapter 16, p. 412.

29   Nectoux, *Gabriel Fauré: A Musical Life*, p. 144.

30   *Madrigal*: Aspects of this song's interpretation are discussed in Chapter 16, p. 412.

31   Nectoux, *Gabriel Fauré: A Musical Life*, p. 144.

32   Ibid., p. 145.

33   Quoted in Claude Rostand, *L'Œuvre de Gabriel Fauré* (Paris: J.B. Janin, 'La Flûte de Pan', 1945), p. 134.

34   *La Rose*: Aspects of this song's interpretation are discussed in Chapter 16, p. 413.

35   Quoted in a lecture given at the Rice Institute in 1925 by Nadia Boulanger, transcribed in Don G. Campbell, *Master Teacher – Nadia Boulanger* (Washington DC: The Pastoral Press, 1984), p. 108.

36   *En prière*: Aspects of this song's interpretation are discussed in Chapter 16, p. 413.

37   The composer Lili Boulanger was born in 1893; she was eight years younger than her sister Nadia, Fauré's composition pupil.

Chapter Eight

Fauré and Paul Verlaine (I)

With the arrival of the poet Verlaine into the world of Fauré's *mélodies*, something new and special comes into focus: it must have been with something of the same sense of destiny that (Schubert came across Goethe's poetry in 1814.) Fauré is truly Verlaine's composer, although he was not the first to set the poet to music. Some fourteen months older than Fauré, Verlaine was the youngest poet apart from Grandmougin with whom Fauré had so far collaborated (when he eventually did so in 1887). Because their association came towards the end of the poet's life and career it seems appropriate to begin this chapter with an outline of Verlaine's extraordinarily turbulent biography.

❧   ❧   ❧   ❧

Paul Verlaine was born into a military family in Metz on 30 March 1844. Like Fauré, Verlaine moved from the provinces to Paris as a boy. In 1853 he was registered as a pupil at the Institution Landry in the rue Chaptal (in 1854 Fauré began at the nearby École Niedermeyer). In 1862, at about the time when Fauré was composing his first Hugo settings, Verlaine left school (the Lycée Bonaparte, later renamed Condorcet) and began to study law.

After falling in with the younger Parnassian poets he abandoned his legal studies and became an insurance salesman. He then decided to be a 'poète-fonctionnaire'; he realised that a boring but regularly paid civil service job would enable him to concentrate on his writing. At this time the poet was in love with his cousin, Elisa Moncoble, who lived near Douai, and with whom he spent his holidays. It was in this period at the salon of Nina de Callias in rue Chaptal, not far from his first school, that Verlaine met Emmanuel Chabrier; and he was later to dedicate a sonnet of retrospective admiration to the composer. The pair had worked on two operettas in 1864 – *Fisch-Ton-Kan* and *Vaucochard et fils Ier*; fragments from the latter survive in piano score.

Verlaine's father died in 1865 and the poet became even closer to his mother, who was both indulgent and controlling – and often not quite controlling enough. He had already published a number of poems in magazines and reviews, but 1866 marks the appearance of seven of Verlaine's poems in *Le Parnasse contemporain* (see Chapter 3) and also in his first published collection, *Poèmes saturniens*. These were issued at the author's expense (or that of his mother) by the dynamic new publisher Alphonse Lemerre. In August 1867 Verlaine went to visit Victor Hugo in Brussels; in September he was present at Baudelaire's funeral.

Paul Verlaine sitting in a bar, much as Fauré must have encountered him. Photograph by Dornac, c.1896

In 1869 Lemerre published the small volume of poems Verlaine entitled *Fêtes galantes*. This has as much claim as any collection of French poetry to have altered the history of the *mélodie*. Many of its twenty-two poems have been set to music. Below are listed only the poems that Fauré set (in the order they are to be found in Verlaine's little volume), together with the dates of those Fauré songs, and a selective list in brackets of the composers who have set the same poems.

No. I 'Clair de lune', 1887 [Claude Debussy, Joseph Szulc]
No. XV 'Mandoline', 1891 [Claude Debussy, Reynaldo Hahn with the title *Fêtes galantes*, Gabriel Dupont, Joseph Szulc]
No. XVI 'À Clymène', 1891
No. XXI 'En sourdine', 1891 [Claude Debussy, Reynaldo Hahn, Poldowski (Lady Dean Paul), Joseph Szulc]
Composers who set further poems from *Fêtes galantes* include Claude Debussy, Charles Koechlin, Charles Cuvillier, Gustave Charpentier, Poldowski, Catherine Urner, Maurice Ravel.

Edmond Lepelletier, Verlaine's lifelong friend and colleague, speculated on the genesis of the collection:

I suppose two contemporary events directed the poet's mind towards the marquis and the marquises, the pierrots and columbines, and all the merry throng in the sylvan glades of Lancret and Fragonard; where the sound of the fountain is heard in the moonlight among the marble statues. For one thing, Edmond and Jules de Goncourt had just published several very beautiful studies of the eighteenth century and the charming artists of this fascinating period, the Saint-Aubins and Moreaus; and they had narrated the life and adventures of the great actresses, La Guimard and La St-Huberti, and written the only true and non-defamatory history of Madame Dubarry, queen of the *Fêtes galantes*, whose end was so tragic and undeserved. It is possible that from these works Verlaine acquired a taste for poetical dalliance in the world evoked by the Goncourts. Then again, the Galerie Lacaze in the Louvre had just been opened to the public, and we never tired of going to admire the Gilles, the embarkation for Cythera, Fragonard's swings, Nattier's interiors, the Lancrets and the Chardins; all the art at once intimate and idyllic, realistic and poetical in which Greuze, Watteau and Boucher are past masters. Perhaps too we owe the *Fêtes galantes* to the very strong impression produced by 'La Fête chez Thérèse' in Hugo's *Les Contemplations*, a poem for which Verlaine felt an admiration so great that it is the only one by a well-known author which I ever heard him repeat by heart.[1]

PAUL VERLAINE

FÊTES GALANTES

PARIS
ALPHONSE LEMERRE, ÉDITEUR
PASSAGE CHOISEUL, 47

M.D.CCC.LXIX

Title-page of first edition of Fêtes galantes *(1869) published by Lemerre*

Turning to Hugo's 'La Fête chez Thérèse' (published in 1856), we can indeed see Verlaine's *Fêtes galantes* prophesied in the closing lines, describing an outdoor party in the heady days of the *ancien régime*. It is a moving indication of the strength and enduring influence of Hugo, on all his successors:

Ils sentaient par degrés se mêler à leur âme,
À leurs discours secrets, à leurs regards de flamme,
À leur cœur, à leurs sens, à leur molle raison,
Le clair de lune bleu qui baignait l'horizon.

As it mingles gradually with their soul,
Their secret talk, their fiery gaze,
Their heart, their senses, their languid mind,
They feel the blue moonlight suffusing the horizon.

Verlaine was no Hugolien hero and had none of that poet's single-mindedness. His exquisitely controlled verses (though sometimes less controlled than some of his Parnassian colleagues would have wished) were created amid the alarming counterpoint of increasing signs of his emotional instability: in 1869 he shocked his friends and family with his drunkenness – an ongoing problem, this – and he attempted to kill his mother. His entire life was typified by violent contrasts redolent of Dr Jekyll and Mr Hyde: religious observation alternated with blasphemy, periods of purity with dissolute sexual behaviour, gentleness with uncontrollable anger. He saw marriage as a heaven-sent solution to his woes and insecurities (rather like the similarly homosexual Tchaikovsky seven years later), and he impulsively proposed to Mathilde Mauté, the half-sister of one of his friends, the composer of popular music Charles de Sivry (1848–1900).

Paul and Mathilde were married in August 1870; it turned out to be an unfortunate year for France as well as the newly-weds. At first there was a glow of feverish activity: Verlaine published *La Bonne chanson*, a sequence of poems for Mathilde that constitutes a hymn to the marvels of imagined marital love; nine of these lyrics were set to music by Fauré over twenty years later, and this period in both artists' lives is discussed more fully in Chapter 9. The political debacles of 1870 initiated by the Franco-Prussian War soon cast a shadow over Verlaine's existence. He joined the national guard and remained in Paris during the Commune, serving the rebels as a press officer. His Communard sympathies were stronger when he was in one of his reckless and aggressive moods – once again a part of his equivocal Jekyll-and-Hyde nature. The fall of the Commune and the establishment of the Third Republic left the poet in permanent fear of retribution for this phase of his life.

At this unsettled time the couple lodged with Mathilde's parents in a small flat in the rue Nicolet. It was there in September 1871 that the seventeen-year-old Arthur Rimbaud turned up on the doorstep, invited by an impulsive Verlaine, who had enclosed a postal order to help with his younger colleague's travelling expenses. Rimbaud had read Verlaine's poems, particularly the *Fêtes galantes*, and regarded the older man if not as his literary master, then at least as the only poet worth bothering with among the effete Parnassians. It was not the boy-wonder's first trip to Paris from his native Charleville – he had already visited Paris four times in the previous six months, and had fought together with the Communards. When he came to stay with Verlaine, Rimbaud brought with him the manuscript of a work that early announced his precocious genius, *Le Bateau ivre*. He was taken in at the Mauté flat out of the kindness of its female inhabitants, but when Monsieur Mauté returned he had to be lodged temporarily with Théodore de Banville until Verlaine found (and paid for) a room elsewhere.

Verlaine and Rimbaud: detail from Coin de table, *painted by Henri Fantin-Latour, 1872, Paris, Musée d'Orsay*

192

Verlaine took his young protégé to see all the celebrities, including the kindly Hugo, who pronounced Rimbaud a 'Child Shakespeare'. It was at this time that Fantin-Latour painted the two poets together in his *Coin de table*. Soon after this Rimbaud misbehaved disgracefully in the company of Verlaine's colleagues and was excluded from their meetings. (It is said that he interjected 'Merde' ["shit"] after each line of a poetry reading.) Verlaine took Rimbaud's side and lost the support of many of his fellow writers; it was clear he was obsessed with the brilliant, charismatic teenager. He became increasingly short-tempered, and even violent, with his wife. On 30 October his son Georges was born.

The relationship that was developing between the two poets was passionately tormented on Verlaine's side, flagrantly manipulative and seemingly without compunction on Rimbaud's. The contrast between the personalities of the two men was enormous, but they experienced a powerful creative complicity temporarily inflamed, though scarcely cemented, by a sexual relationship – seemingly deeply emotional on Verlaine's side and audaciously experimental on the part of Rimbaud – a young man determined to experience everything while shocking society in every way possible. It is hardly surprising that Mathilde left her husband in January 1872. She made it a condition that if she returned he should break off any contact with his new paramour. Instead the two men departed together on the open road for Belgium on 7 July. Many years later (in 1887, on learning – erroneously – that Rimbaud had died) Verlaine attempted to tell the story of their friendship in verse:

Nous avions laissé sans émoi	*We had left behind without emotion*
Tous impédiments dans Paris,	*Everything that held us back in Paris*
Lui quelques sots bernés, et moi	*He, a bunch of bigots, and me*
Certaine princesse Souris,	*A certain Princess Mouse,*
Une sotte qui tourna pire …	*A stupid girl who turned out worse …*

Verlaine, 'Laeti et errabundi' from Parallèlement *(1889)*

After trudging through the Belgian countryside (Charleroi, Walcourt, Malines, Brussels) they went on to England, where they took cheap lodgings at 34 Howland Street,[2] off Tottenham Court Road. At the time London was full of exiled Communards – officially tolerated in the land of free speech but actually closely monitored by the English authorities. The tumultuous story of the two poets during this period of *vagabondage* is dramatised in Christopher Hampton's play *Total Eclipse*. If this were a fictional tale involving two of the most important men in French literary history, it would have seemed impossibly far-fetched. One wonders if Verlaine was aware at the time that he was part of a scabrous succession of wandering minstrels of questionable morality, a tradition in French literature that had begun with the medieval troubadour Rutebeuf and continued with François Villon and such figures as Mathurin Régnier and Alexis Piron. Verlaine wrote his *Ariettes oubliées* and the *Paysages belges* during this time; both groups of lyrics (important for both Fauré and Debussy) were to be included in the collection published in 1874 as *Romances sans paroles* when Verlaine was in prison.

Arthur Rimbaud also wrote poems that would contribute to his own extraordinary literary fame. He mercilessly captured Verlaine's impulsive and weak character in *Une saison en enfer* (1873). In this overpowering work, contemporary with his *Illuminations* (some of which were memorably, if controversially, set to music by Benjamin Britten some sixty-five years later), the younger poet cast Verlaine as 'la vierge folle' who, in a sobbing monotone, describes his submission to Rimbaud, and the humiliation he suffered at the hands of the younger man, the self-appointed 'Epoux infernal' – the infernal husband. The 'vierge folle' (representing Verlaine) is made to say 'À côté de son cher corps endormi, que d'heures de nuit j'ai veillé, cherchant pourquoi il voulait tant s'évader de la réalité' ('beside his dear sleeping body, how many hours of the night have I stayed awake searching for the reason why he so wanted to distance himself from reality'). In these lines that paint a picture of a dependent and lachrymose Verlaine, we can easily recognise as the same person the poet of *Green* ('Et que je dorme un peu / Puisque vous reposez') and *C'est l'extase* ('Cette âme qui se lamente / En cette plainte dormante').

In April 1873 the two exiles returned briefly to France, but Verlaine was terrified of being arrested as an erstwhile Communard – this had been the fate of his brother-in-law Charles Sivry (as well as Debussy's father). The semi-fugitive holed up, first at Namur and then Jéhonville in the Ardennes. By the end of May both Verlaine and Rimbaud returned to London and stayed at the more celebrated of their two London addresses, 8 Great College Street, Camden Town[3] – they rented a garret in a house that is still extant as the middle building in a broken-down terrace of four. Here they loved, worked and squabbled incessantly.

In July the often stormy relationship between the two poets came to a tragic climax. In a fit of pique Verlaine abandoned Rimbaud in London and returned across the Channel to Brussels, where the younger man, first conciliatory, then bitter, joined him. The presence of Verlaine's mother inflamed an already incendiary situation. On 10 July Rimbaud arrived in Brussels and said that he wanted to leave Verlaine permanently; but he demanded money before he left. The distraught Verlaine fired two revolver shots at Rimbaud. One of the bullets entered his left wrist (it was removed three days

8 Royal College Street, Camden Town (formerly Great College Street). Photos © Malcolm Crowthers

later); Verlaine had not of course intended to hurt the eighteen-year-old. With Rimbaud's wound bandaged by Madame Verlaine the two poets walked to the station and fell into another argument on the way. It looked as if Verlaine was reaching once again for his gun. Rimbaud appealed to the police on the street, and this resulted in the arrest of the older man, who was wildly brandishing a revolver.

Verlaine was eventually sentenced to two years' solitary confinement and was transferred from the Prison de Carmes in Brussels to Mons to serve his time. The severity of this punishment was probably due to the fact that the Belgian authorities, in deference to their French colleagues, lost no chance to punish Verlaine for having been a suspected Communard. The poet found himself in prison between the summer of 1873 and January 1875.

PAUL VERLAINE

ROMANCES SANS PAROLES

ARIETTES OUBLIÉES
PAYSAGES BELGES. — BIRDS IN THE NIGHT
AQUARELLES

PARIS
CHEZ TOUS LES LIBRAIRES
—
1874

Title-page of the first edition of Romances sans paroles *(1874)*

It was Verlaine's great friend Edmond Lepelletier who saw *Romances sans paroles* through the press in 1874 as the poet was incarcerated at the time. It seems that the previously supportive Lemerre would not touch it, such had Verlaine's personal reputation plummeted, and the work had to be published privately. The edition of forty-eight pages, now a bibliophilic treasure of the greatest rarity, was limited to 300 copies. *Romances sans paroles* was reprinted in 1887 by the publisher Léon Vanier, but it was almost certainly the volume printed privately in the Burgundian town of Sens and available in Paris 'Chez tous les libraires' that was placed into Fauré's hands (together with the *Fêtes galantes* in very small format from 1869) by the Comte Robert de Montesquiou. Below are listed the poems from *Romances sans paroles* that Fauré eventually set, the dates of those settings and the names of some of the other composers who set the same poems.

Ariettes oubliées (subsection):

No. I 'C'est l'extase langoureuse', 1891 [Claude Debussy]

No. III 'Il pleure dans mon cœur' as *Spleen*, 1888 [Claude Debussy, Dinu Lipatti]

Aquarelles (subsection):

No. I 'Green', 1891 [Claude Debussy, Reynaldo Hahn with the title *Offrande*, Paolo Tosti with the title *Rêve*, André Messager, Dinu Lipatti]

Composers who set further poems from this collection include Claude Debussy, Charles Bordes, Reynaldo Hahn, Poldowski (Lady Dean Paul), Charles Loeffler, Jean Cras, Florent Schmitt.

∾ ∾ ∾ ∾

During 1874 the poet and his wife were legally separated, and as a result of the regime of prison life Verlaine, always a creature of extremes, immersed himself in a life of contemplation and religion. When he emerged from incarceration, with time off for good behaviour, he tried unsuccessfully to heal the breach with Rimbaud, and even travelled to Stuttgart in an attempt to do so. His efforts to convert Rimbaud to his re-discovered Catholicism irritated the younger man no end, and Verlaine was left bleeding on the banks of the Neckar for his trouble.

There now followed what was to become a typical back-tracking in the poet's life after any period of excess, a kind of self-chastening of the spirit. To effect this penance Verlaine deliberately sought out the emotional and sensual deprivation of exile in provincial Victorian England (he was already a knowledgeable reader of Shakespeare and Dickens and was now to add Swinburne and Tennyson to his enthusiasms). For more than a year he taught in a village school in what must have seemed the middle of nowhere, first in Stickney, a long way from any temptation of the flesh or bottle, and then in Boston (both in Lincolnshire). In October 1876, as if returning to the normality of city life in stages,

PAUL VERLAINE

———

SAGESSE

PARIS

SOCIÉTÉ GÉNÉRALE DE LIBRAIRIE CATHOLIQUE

PARIS | BRUXELLES
Ancienne Maison VICTOR PALMÉ | Ancienne Maison HENRI GOEMAERE
76, rue des Saints-Pères, 76 | 29, rue des Paroissiens, 29

M DCCC LXXXI

Title-page of first edition of Sagesse *(1881). Société Générale de Librairie Catholique*

he took up another job at St Aloysius College in Bournemouth; the poem 'La Mer est plus belle' (later set to music by Debussy) dates from this time. He then travelled back to the Ardennes, a favourite haunt with Rimbaud, and taught at the school at Notre Dame de Rethel.

There in 1878 he met the replacement for Rimbaud that his spirit craved, part lover and part son (the Mauté family scarcely allowed him to see his own son Georges). The new liaison was with Lucien Létinois, a school student from local farming stock, seventeen and a half years old, the same age as Rimbaud when the two men had first met. At this time Gabriel Fauré was recovering from the emotional shock of the break-up of his engagement to Marianne Viardot, but in comparison with Verlaine's lurid story he appears to have led a completely uneventful life.

In 1879 Verlaine travelled again to England, this time with Létinois in tow, and taught in Leamington Spa. They moved back to the Ardennes in 1880. In the following year, 1881, the poet published one of his most important collections of verse, *Sagesse*. This volume, printed by a private Catholic press (and once again at the poet's expense), gathered together the poetry of the prison years and beyond, much of it with an openly religious slant. *Sagesse* was greeted at first with scant enthusiasm; there were many who regarded the poet as a spent force, and few musicians were drawn to the more religious of the poems.

Fauré set only one poem from this collection – and this was his last Verlaine setting:

'Le ciel est pardessus le toit' (the sixth poem of Part III of the collection with the composer's own title of *Prison* 1894 [Reynaldo Hahn as *D'une prison*, Déodat de Séverac, Ralph Vaughan Williams as *The Sky above the Roof*]

Composers who set other poems from *Sagesse* include Claude Debussy, Ernest Chausson, Charles Bordes, Reynaldo Hahn, Poldowski (Lady Dean Paul), Charles Loeffler, Jean Cras, Florent Schmitt, Maurice Ravel, Arthur Honegger, Edgar Varèse (whose entry certificate into the Paris Conservatoire was signed by Fauré as its ageing principal – a coming together of two entirely different musical worlds) and Igor Stravinsky. Fauré probably worked from the second edition of the poems (Léon Vanier, 1899), as almost certainly did the other composers on this list, including Debussy. The religious and well-to-do Chausson was the kind of reader who would have taken the trouble to acquire a first edition from the Société Génerale de Librairie Catholique.

❧   ❧   ❧   ❧

At about the time when *Sagesse* was first published Verlaine embarked on one of the more unlikely, not to say bizarre, experiments of his life – running a farm in the Ardennes with Létinois. This part idyll, part folly ended in 1882 when the poet returned to live in Paris after more than a decade away from the capital. The Rimbaud incident and its aftermath had engendered such a scandal that his reputation with all but the most broad-minded colleagues was ruined; his Communard past made it impossible to reclaim his old job in the civil service at the Hôtel de Ville. In 1883 Létinois died of typhoid. Verlaine moved back to the Ardennes, this time living with his mother. The year 1884 was completely unproductive, and Verlaine was invisible as far as his literary colleagues were concerned, apart from the appearance in print of *Les Poètes maudits* and the collection *Jadis et Naguère*, which included the famous sonnet 'Langueur'. From this time Verlaine's works were published by Léon Vanier, who was to reprint the earlier volumes of verse that gradually established themselves as national classics.

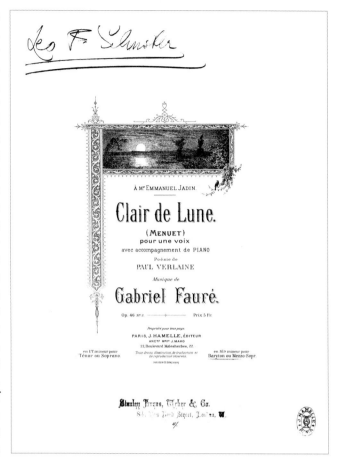

Title-page of Clair de lune, *with the signature of Fauré's London patron Frank Schuster*

In 1885, after attacking his mother violently, the poet was sentenced once again to prison, this time in Vouziers. When he emerged after two months behind bars he returned to Paris, where he and Madame Verlaine were forced to lodge in a cheap and sordid hotel in the rue Moreau. Mother and son had once enjoyed rather substantial means but the whole of the family fortune, such as it was, had been whittled away. At the age of forty-one Verlaine's life was in free fall. The death of his mother in 1886 was a catastrophic loss; in this year he spent two periods in hospital – in the final decade of his life he was to find himself in one pauper's ward after another. Life was indeed bleak: prematurely aged, he was tormented by the consequences of syphilis, his knee was diseased, and he suffered from cirrhosis of the liver. He was by now already 'pauvre Lélian', that ingenious anagram of 'Paul Verlaine' that was his own self-pitying invention.

Much of 1887 was spent in hospital. It was at this point that Verlaine entered stealthily into the creative life of Gabriel Fauré thanks to 'Clair de lune', a poem that had been published eighteen years earlier. As we have seen, this was the result of the match-making skills of the Comte Robert de Montesquiou, Fauré's 'literary adviser'.

(52) *Clair de lune* (Menuet) (Moonlight)[4]

1887, Op. 46 No. 2, 'À M. Emmanuel Jadin', second Hamelle collection p. 76, B♭ minor, 3/4, *Andante quasi allegretto*

Votre âme est un paysage choisi	*Your soul is a chosen landscape*
Que vont charmant masques et bergamasques	*Bewitched by masquers and bergamaskers,*
Jouant du luth et dansant et quasi	*Playing the lute and dancing and almost*
Tristes sous leurs déguisements fantasques.	*Sad beneath their fanciful disguises.*
Tout en chantant sur le mode mineur	*Singing as they go in a minor key*
L'amour vainqueur et la vie opportune,	*Of conquering love and life's favours,*
Ils n'ont pas l'air de croire à leur bonheur	*They do not seem to believe in their fortune*
Et leur chanson se mêle au clair de lune,	*And their song mingles with the light of the moon,*
Au calme clair de lune triste et beau,	*The calm light of the moon, sad and fair,*
Qui fait rêver les oiseaux dans les arbres	*That sets the birds dreaming in the trees*
Et sangloter d'extase les jets d'eau,	*And the fountains sobbing in their rapture,*
Les grands jets d'eau sveltes parmi les marbres.	*Tall and svelte amid marble statues.*

Paul Verlaine (1844–1896)

As he stood on the threshold of a new phase in his creative life, Fauré composed what is for many people the quintessential French *mélodie*. The poem (the opening of Verlaine's *Fêtes galantes*, 1869) is a flawless jewel, and the music follows suit. The young Debussy had already set this text for his mistress, the soprano Marie-Blanche Vasnier, in 1882 – a *menuet* of stately intent overlaid with the winsome charm of Massenet. That the teenage composer was in early possession of these lyrics, as well as those from the equally rare *Romances sans paroles* (1874), can only be attributable to his link with Madame Mauté, who must have shown the young composer (her erstwhile piano pupil) the publications of her increasingly famous, not to say notorious, son-in-law, with a mixture of pride and foreboding. Debussy's second version, from the first set of his *Fêtes galantes*, the mature master at the top of his form, was composed in 1891.

Between these, in terms of chronology, is Fauré's song – sublimely indifferent to his rival's earlier setting, and unthreatened by the success of the later. The two are worlds apart: Debussy uses five sharps, Fauré five flats, the irreplaceable colour of B♭ minor. (Vladimir Jankélevitch avers that with Fauré there is 'an entire poetics of flat-key sonorities, which acts to filter light, giving expression to the penumbra, the half-tint, half-day').[5] This *Clair de lune* stands in the hearts and ears of many listeners as a kind of definition of French vocal music with piano – similar to the status of Schubert's *Gretchen am Spinnrade* in the German lied. It also has some similarity to *Das ist ein Flöten und Geigen* from Schumann's *Dichterliebe*, where singer and pianist take independent paths – in both Schumann's and Fauré's songs the so-called accompaniment is in fact a piano piece in its own right, and the voice embroiders this as a kind of obbligato. Fauré's sketch book containing this song (one of very few surviving pieces of evidence that shows the composer's manner of working) indicates that the piano piece came to him much more easily than the vocal line.

The paintings of courtly revels in the gardens of Versailles by Watteau and his contemporaries set the tone; the autograph of the poem pictured below shows us that the line 'Au calme clair de lune

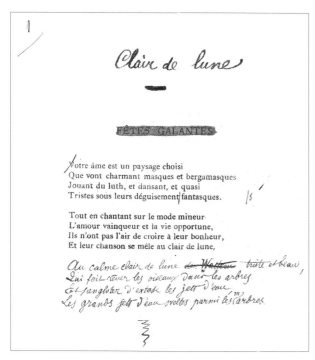

Verlaine's correction of the proof for his 'Clair de lune', with the autograph addition of the poem's third verse

triste et beau' had originally been conceived as the rhyming 'Au calme clair de lune de Watteau'. Fauré responds to these wonderful words with that air of tenderness, boredom and distance which is the nineteenth century's view of how the eighteenth felt about itself. Time-travel of this kind is familiar enough, but not one of the many *menuets*, *sarabandes* and *bourdons* that abound in French song can match this *Clair de lune*. Under the unruffled surface of this music, passion and spontaneity are tightly corseted by etiquette and intrigue; Jankélévitch sees in Fauré's simulated nonchalance an iron fist in a velvet glove.[6] He writes that these courtiers 'feign indifference in moments of their passion and passion in those of their indifference', a paradox that lies at the heart of the *Fêtes galantes*. It was Ravel who noted that the phrase 'mode mineur' strays into the major key; perhaps this is a musical metaphor for the fact that the suave words of a courtier never mean exactly what they say. After the celebrated twelve-bar introduction, voice and piano perform an insouciant *pas de deux*, sometimes coalescing (as at 'Au calme clair de lune triste et beau' – Fauré struggled with the shape of this melody just as Verlaine had struggled with his rhyme) yet always seeming to lead independent existences. Claude Rostand saw this work to be a surrealist creation before surrealism, with the voice lost as if in one of those dark avenues in the gardens of Versailles with their disturbingly ambiguous statues, a landscape evoked by the implacable accompaniment.[7] Verlaine's poem reflects the chasm between public utterance and private life; he who writes poems of courtly love is not necessarily a courtly lover. The solitary melancholy in this song seems apt for an unhappily married composer for whom the scandal of divorce was unthinkable. Whatever pleasure is arranged *au clair de lune* it will be felt at one remove; the thrill of pursuit is already marred by the certainty of the final parting.

It may well be that the dedication of the song to Fauré's friend the painter Emmanuel Jadin (1845–1922) implies a gallant reference to the dedicatee's possible forebears, a large and well-known family of court musicians at Versailles during the reign of Louis XVI. Louis-Emmanuel Jadin (1768–1853), the most famous of the family, probably gave piano lessons to Marie-Antoinette. Who could be better to receive the dedication of this particular song than someone who might have descended from a long line of the original 'donneurs de sérénades', as the poem 'Mandoline' has it?[8] *Clair de lune* reappears as an orchestrated work in Fauré's work list as No. VI of the *divertissement Masques et bergamasques*, Op. 122, a work made up of some old material freshly orchestrated, some new, and prepared as a *divertissement* for the Prince of Monaco in 1919. As for the completely forgotten dedicatee of the song, he made his debut as a painter at the salon in 1868 having studied with his father,

Louis Godefroy Jadin, and Napoleon III's favourite historical painter Alexandre Cabanel. He was a great friend and Parisian neighbour of Marguerite de Saint-Marceaux and went fishing with René, her husband. The painter Roger Jourdain, whose wife Henriette was the dedicatee of *Aurore*, had been a pupil of Jadin *père*. This couple visited Venice as Fauré's fellow house-guests and heard him accompany the first performance of *Mandoline* on the waters of the Grand Canal.

(53) *Spleen* (*Spleen*)[9]

1888, Op. 51 No. 3, 'À Mme Henri Cochin', third Hamelle collection p. 13, D minor, 3/4, *Andante quasi allegretto*

Il pleure dans mon cœur	*Tears fall in my heart*
Comme il pleut sur la ville ;	*As rain falls on the town;*
Quelle est cette langueur	*What is this torpor*
Qui pénètre mon cœur?	*Pervading my heart?*
Ô bruit doux de la pluie,	*Ah, the soft sound of rain*
Par terre et sur les toits!	*On the ground and roofs!*
Pour un cœur qui s'ennuie	*For a listless heart,*
Ô le chant de la pluie!	*Ah, the song of the rain!*
Il pleure sans raison	*Tears fall without reason*
Dans mon cœur qui s'écœure.	*In this disheartened heart.*
Quoi! nulle trahison? …	*What! Was there no treason? …*
Mon deuil est sans raison.	*This grief's without reason.*
C'est bien la pire peine	*And the worst pain of all*
De ne savoir pourquoi	*Must be not to know why*
Sans amour et sans haine	*Without love and without hate*
Mon cœur a tant de peine!	*My heart has so much pain!*

Paul Verlaine (1844–1896)

Fauré may well have been attracted by this poem when he borrowed the first edition (1874) of *Romances sans paroles* (together with *Fêtes galantes*, 1869) from Robert de Montesquiou in 1887. We know that the composition of *Clair de lune* was a direct result of that loan, but the composer returned these precious volumes to Montesquiou in February 1888. It was probably the re-publication of *Romances sans paroles* by Vanier in 1887 (enabling Fauré to obtain his own copy of these lyrics) that facilitated the setting in 1888 of the song he entitled *Spleen*.

Here we must compare Fauré's setting with Debussy's. *Il pleure dans mon cœur*, the second of that composer's *Ariettes oubliées*. Rather confusingly the song that Debussy names *Spleen* is another Verlaine setting altogether, 'Les roses étaient toutes rouges', which closes that composer's cycle on a haunting note of desperation. In fact Debussy's *Spleen* accurately uses Verlaine's title, and it was Fauré who decided to re-name *Il pleure dans mon cœur* as *Spleen* – a word that he himself used to describe his own bouts of depression.

PAUL VERLAINE

———

Romances

SANS PAROLES

ARIETTES OUBLIÉES

PAYSAGES BELGES — BIRDS IN THE NIGHT

AQUARELLES

Édition nouvelle

PARIS

LÉON VANIER, LIBRAIRE-ÉDITEUR

19, QUAI SAINT-MICHEL, 19

———

1887

Portrait and title-page of the second edition of Verlaine's Romances sans paroles. *Published by Vanier (1887)*

There is no sign of Fauré being influenced by the younger composer's *Ariettes oubliées* (already published in 1888, and issued in a revised version dedicated to Mary Garden, the first Mélisande, in 1903). This is music of genius that invites, and always receives, instant admiration. In terms of style there are prophecies of *Pelléas* (as well as echoes, considering the revised version and its dedicatee), yet some of the songs still seem to be under Massenet's spell, with vocal lines and sumptuous, swooning harmonies designed more to ravish than to disturb the listener's senses. It is the vocal climax on an anguished high note in the last song of the cycle (*Spleen* in fact) that provides the cycle's greatest moment of surprise and drama. Debussy's *Il pleure dans mon cœur*, the second song, is more muted – it suggests the languorous enervation of listless depression and *décadence*. Fauré on the other hand goes for a darker and altogether more intense mood, as anguished as he ever allowed himself to be – which is not to say boisterous or loud. All the Fauré songs of 1888 (the others in the same opus number are *Au cimetière* and *Larmes*) are *cris de cœur*, and anything but pastels.

Both composers effectively, yet quite differently, evoke the falling of rain on the miserable London lodgings that Verlaine shared with Rimbaud in the autumn of 1872. Debussy's oscillations in monotone thirds masterfully evoke the grey drizzle of this kind of English weather. Fauré's staccato semiquavers, coloured with the pedal, alternate closely between the hands, and they do indeed suggest more substance to the downfall than Debussy's almost imperceptible rain. Perhaps this is why the younger composer was later to adopt the pianistic figuration found between the hands in Fauré's *Spleen* to depict falling snow in *La neige danse* from the *Children's Corner* (1908). In any case, as

201

Fauré himself wrote 'the sound of the drops of water is only a secondary factor. The important thing is the malaise in the lover's lament.'[10] Accordingly, this pattering motif is overtaken by churning triplets and the emotional turbulence they represent. Fauré's whole construction is undeniably tighter, more of a piece, than Debussy's: the latter's 'Quoi! nulle trahison?' is set as a recitative indicative of enervation; with Fauré this desperate exclamation is kept within the song's ongoing momentum, and sounds more frightened than lethargic as if the singer had discovered in himself a frightening propensity for mental disintegration.

Exhaustion and hopelessness set in later. The diminuendo, as well as the freezing of the harmonic movement in the piano writing after 'Sans amour et sans haine', speaks volumes. 'Mon cœur a tant de peine' is set to a downward scale, drained of its confidence; we can imagine the poet turning his face to the wall. The seven-bar postlude is undemonstrative, almost offhand, in the manner of the depressed person who after having been roused to a vehement outburst sinks back into silence.

The dedicatee of this song, Mme Henri Cochin, had married into the musical family for whom the honour was surely intended: Henri Cochin and his brother Denys were well-known patrons and amateur musicians – Henri was a good violinist and, as a lifelong friend of Vincent D'Indy, played an active role in the creation of the Schola Cantorum; Denys was a renowned art collector (Goya, Delacroix, Corot, Manet) and had a salon in the rue de Babylone. The Cochin brothers attended many of the social events frequented by Fauré.

~ ~ ~ ~

When in May 1888 Chabrier's opera *Gwendoline* was performed at the home of Winnaretta Singer (at that stage unhappily married to Prince Louis de Scey-Montbéliard), Fauré played the harmonium. But Chabrier's opera was not the only work on a programme that inaugurated the Princesse's salon (Winnaretta's musical 'Tuesdays' were to become complementary to her friend Marguerite Baugnies's 'Fridays'). Fauré orchestrated his song *Clair de lune* for a soirée that marked the deepening of a remarkable relationship between the Princesse and himself – something that might almost be termed an artistic partnership, a friendship that survived vicissitudes and deserves the epithet 'lifelong'. In 1889 Winnaretta parted from her husband (on grounds of sexual incompatability) and initiated the process of seeking a papal annulment. It was at this time that she sat for her portrait by her friend, and Fauré's admirer, John Singer Sargent. It was not unknown for this great painter to make his subjects appear more beautiful or imposing than they really were – more a question of selectivity and perspective than misrepresentation. In this case we feel that Sargent has been enjoined to tell the whole truth. He avoids depicting the Princesse in profile, however; her aquiline features bore an uncanny resemblance – noticed by Stravinsky among many others – to those of the poet Dante. 'La mère Dante' was Jean Cocteau's irreverent label for her in later years – 'Tante Winnie' was the more usual nickname.

By January 1891 we find Fauré writing to Winnaretta, who was visiting Paignton in Devon, England, for the marriage of a relative: 'I can't tell you how greatly you are missed here, how painful a process it is to get out of the habit of seeing you at frequent intervals. Talking about you amongst ourselves is but poor consolation! … Fridays are not the same without you.'[11]

It is clear that at this point, and for some time afterwards, the composer harboured affectionate thoughts for the formidable Winnaretta that extended to feelings both romantic and sexual.[12] Fauré must have been aware that her own preference was lesbian (something that her husband, the Prince de Scey-Montbéliard, had apparently not realised), but this aspect of her unattainability perhaps intensified the erotic aspect of his regard for her. She was, after all, twenty years younger, highly intelligent,

The Princesse Louis de Scey-Montbéliard (Winnareta Singer), by John Singer Sargent

motivated, determined and extremely cultured ('d'une vaste culture générale' as Stravinsky affirmed many years later, also remarking on her genuine talent as a painter).[13] She was a powerful woman, and Fauré seems to have found that side of her very attractive; there was always a side of him that longed for a woman to look after him. And 'Winnie' certainly had the means to change the lives of those with whom she came into contact.

The subtle electricity between the composer and his new patroness was something that went both ways for entirely different reasons. Winnaretta had the good sense and taste to realise that Fauré was a genius; her perspicacity in matters such as this was extraordinary, all the more so when we realise that her perception of the composer's importance was far from universally shared. She wrote back from Paignton and offered him the sum of 25,000 francs for a musical work, a one-act opera perhaps, with a libretto by someone who would be selected between them. On her return to Paris the Princesse and Fauré settled on Paul Verlaine as the appropriate poet to write a libretto. Fauré had already composed two of his most significant songs to Verlaine texts; she had read copies of *Le Décadent*, the review founded by Verlaine in 1886, and was fascinated by this entire school (to which, however, it could never be said that the always elusive Verlaine truly belonged).

Since 1888 the poet had been in and out of hospital (in 1892 he was to publish his rather audacious autobiographical monograph *Mes hôpitaux*, and in 1893 the sequel, *Mes prisons*). Who in French literature, apart from François Villon perhaps, could have provided similar catalogues of vagabond woe in such an inspired, even endearing, manner? He continued to write poetry, although the late Verlaine of such collections as *Amour* (1888) and *Parallèlement* (1889) has never appealed to composers. The first edition of the collection *Dédicaces* (1890) includes a frontispiece portrait of the poet in hospital attire as if it were a uniform to wear with a kind of defiant pride. This collection is a largely genial array of sonnets, each dedicated to one of Verlaine's (mostly literary) friends and contemporaries (the poem recollecting his early friendship with the composer Chabrier is No. XXXIII of these *Dédicaces*). No. VIII is posthumously dedicated to Villiers de L'Isle Adam, one of Verlaine's 'poètes maudits' – a celebrated anthology of essays published in 1888, the other 'cursed poets' being Corbière, Rimbaud, Mallarmé, Desbordes-Valmore (the only woman), and Verlaine himself in the anagrammatic guise of 'Le Pauvre Lélian'. In *Dédicaces* Verlaine imagines Villiers, a fellow down-and-out, ensconced in heaven and fêted by God, thus revealing both his own devout nature and that of the recently departed vagabond poet. Verlaine is impatient to grant to this admired writer 'la gloire d'un élu' – the glory of one of the elect. Sonnet No. XVII is enthusiastically addressed to Armand Silvestre and serves as a reminder to us that Silvestre, now almost forgotten, was once a famed and valued personality in Parisian literary life. After saluting George Sand's early belief in the young Armand, Verlaine compares the poet to Orpheus – able to charm men and women as well as the animals. Silvestre's books, readable and re-readable, are a gift from nature, even if they view life from a male angle – something that Verlaine does not mind in the least. (By this time his own quasi-pornographic collection *Femmes* had already appeared in a limited edition, for sale under the counter). He admires Jean Richepin (sonnet No. LXI) in a rather more down-to-earth way – as a 'bon bougre et gentil copain'; the paupers and beggars to be found lovingly described in Richepin's poems (as well as the rough sailors encountered in *La Mer*) do not go down well with the bourgeois and those who attend the Opéra-Comique, but Verlaine is firmly on the side of the rough-hewn defender of the proletariat. The poem following this (No. LXII) is more famous because it is addressed to Arthur Rimbaud, an ex-lover soon to die: 'Mortel, ange ET démon, autant dire Rimbaud / Tu mérites la prime place en ce mien livre' (Mortal, angel AND demon as much as being called Rimbaud / You deserve first place in this, mine book). Sonnet No. CI is dedicated to the Comte Robert de Montesquiou-Fézensac. This brilliant pen-portrait captures the vain and neurotic aspects of the would-be poet ('Le poète infini qui doublant et triplant / Les nuances') while remaining more or less kindly to the 'Cavalier exquis'. If this book had been prepared even a year later we might have had a poem addressed to Gabriel Fauré. As it is, we have in *Dédicaces* a remarkable survey of the literary scene, circa 1890; other writers accorded a dedicatory sonnet include Mallarmé, Huysmans and Bouchor.

∾   ∾   ∾   ∾

The last two amatory arrangements of Verlaine's life were with women of ill-repute – Philomène Boudin and Eugénie Krantz – although he failed to renounce his homosexual activities, his parlous state of health notwithstanding. By 1891, when the Princesse approached him for a libretto on Fauré's behalf, Verlaine was all but 'down and out'. He didn't want any money, he told the Princesse, but would be grateful if she could open an account for him at his tailor's or boot-maker's.

Fauré, always the consummate professional, attempted to initiate a correspondence with the poet in order to set the parameters of their proposed collaboration, but to no avail – Verlaine disappeared. When he surfaced it was once again in hospital, officially for rheumatism, but really for an addiction to absinthe. Fauré went to see him twice in the Hôpital St-Antoine, braving the stale smell of sicknesses and medicines; he was horrified by Verlaine's dirty clothes and bed linen, and appalled by the rules that allowed the poet visits only twice a week, and no lamp or candle after nightfall.

After this visit he wrote a letter to the Princesse (on 30 January 1891) including his own drawing of Verlaine's head:

Well, I have seen him, this Verlaine! … What a singular, strange, incomprehensible character! How can any human being who is so marvellously gifted revel in this endless toing-and-froing between hostelry and hospital! … In physical terms he is ugliness itself, however there is a great deal of gentleness and liveliness in his deep-set, Chinese-like slanting eyes; the face of a child on an old body.[14]

It must have seemed terrible that the poet of 'Clair de lune' was afflicted in this way; the composer had reason to be profoundly grateful to Verlaine but he became increasingly wary of him. The prospects of writing an opera were not altogether hopeful – 'his mind has now fallen back to the delusions of unspeakable shame [la folie de l'invouable] and his most recent productions would bring a blush to the cheeks of a hussar.'[15] The composer here refers to Verlaine's collection of explicitly homoerotic poems *Hombres*, which was only published posthumously in 1904, and he was only pretending to be shocked; indeed, he knew that Winnie would enjoy gossip of this kind.

The Princesse was determined to have her libretto. She offered to pay Verlaine's hospital fees, and gave him *carte blanche* in terms of a choice of subject. Fauré was told to extract the text from the poet who, once he had left the hospital, played a game of hide and seek with the composer in cafés and other pre-arranged ren-

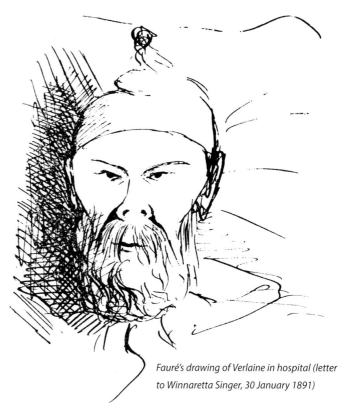

Fauré's drawing of Verlaine in hospital (letter to Winnaretta Singer, 30 January 1891)

dezvous. After months of wooing Verlaine's reluctant muse, and always being the recipient of tearful and seemingly sincere excuses, the composer became utterly exasperated. He was not prepared to make an opera out of Verlaine's extant play *Les Uns et les autres*. He wrote to Winnaretta that he had come to the conclusion that Verlaine was simply incapable of the concentration and application such work would require – 'nothing matters to him as long as he has something to drink'.[16]

It was in the middle of all this, in April 1891, that Winnaretta decided to go to Venice for an extended holiday. She rented a small palace on the Grand Canal for herself and her brother and his wife and their guests. The Palazzo Volkoff, belonged to a Russian count, a one-time friend of Wagner; later owners include the great Italian actress Eleanore Duse and Woody Allen, the American film director. Fauré was invited there for a holiday, as were two painters, Roger Jourdain and Ernest Dueze, both with their wives, who, as it happened, were fairly well-known amateur singers. There seems to have been no question of an invitation for Marie Fauré. In grave need of a rest, the composer arrived in Venice on 18 May and stayed five weeks, among the happiest of his life; he wrote back to Marguerite Baugnies that 'Divine' would be an inadequate word to describe the life they were leading. The composer clearly had Verlaine much on his mind. Denied a collaboration in the present, he went back into the poet's past to find the greatness that his musical imagination needed for its inspiration. A poem such as 'À Clymène', with the 'mystique barcarolles' of its opening, must have seemed singularly appropriate for his Venetian surroundings. In her memoirs Winnaretta recalled:

I carefully prepared a quiet room for piano as a study for Fauré to work in, but I had forgotten how fond he was of cafés; and I am obliged to say that he wrote his *Cinq mélodies de Venise* at a little marble table on the Piazza, in the midst of the noise and turmoil of a busy Venetian crowd, rather than in the peaceful room I had arranged for him.[17]

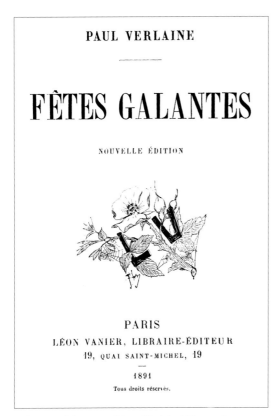

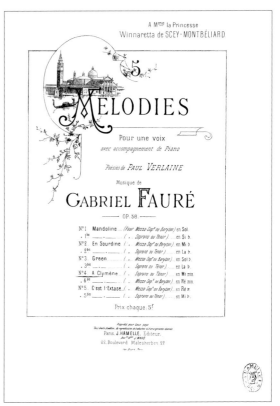

Title-page of the 1891 edition of Verlaine's Fêtes galantes

Title-page of Cinq melodies 'de Venise', *with a dedication to Winaretta Singer, still officially Mme la Princesse de Scey Montbéliard*

Fauré clearly took either the 1886 edition of the *Fêtes galantes* with him to Venice or the newly issued third edition. It is always tempting to imagine with song composers that the recent appearance of a volume in a bookshop had been the spur to new activity – this is certainly often the case with Schubert and his sudden acquaintance with old eighteenth-century poets reissued in new local Viennese editions. Fauré composed *Mandoline* and *En sourdine*, the first and second song of the set, his third and fourth settings of Verlaine, in Venice itself. Apart from the veiled references in *À Clymène*, the poems are not about 'Serenissima', but the composer regarded these *mélodies* as being 'of Venice', the fruit of a much-needed rest where he was able to relax in beautiful surroundings thanks to the generosity of his patroness. This association is celebrated by the songs' first editions, which feature a charming illustration of a gondola on a lagoon with the Campanile and the San Marco basilica in the background. This edition features the title the Princesse still used, but was shortly to change, 'Mme la Princesse Winaretta de Scey-Montbéliard'. In a letter to the cycle's dedicatee Fauré refers to the songs as being 'a sort of Suite, a story'.[18] Nectoux agrees with this – he sees the songs in terms of a chamber music work with an opening prelude (*Mandoline*), first slow movement (*En sourdine*), scherzo (*Green*), second slow movement (*À Clymène*) and finale (*C'est l'extase*). But such a description on Fauré's part also suggests someone who had been offered a 25,000-franc commission to write an opera, and who very much hoped that these songs, with a dramatic content of their own, might be accepted to stand in for that purpose.

206

There is no connecting narrative to Verlaine's texts, of course, but, as we shall see, Fauré effected a wonderful weave of musical inter-connections between the songs that are a new feature of his so-called second, or middle, period. The composer wrote to the Princesse: 'You will see that I have attempted a form that I take to be new, or at least I know nothing like it; indeed to try to create something new is really the least I can do when I work for you, the person who is the least like anyone else in the world.'[19] In fact this is something of a cycle within a cycle: the songs *En sourdine*, *Green*, *À Clymène* and *C'est l'extase* are indeed connected by shared musical tissue, whereas *Mandoline* plays little or no part in the overall structure (it is for this reason, no doubt, that Nectoux designates it a *Prélude*). For the moment the Princesse was prepared to play hostess as Fauré wrote his new cycle, but she was still determined to have her operatic work at a later date.

Cinq mélodies 'de Venise' *(Five 'Venetian' Songs)* [20]
1891, Op. 58

(54) (i) *Mandoline* (*Mandolin*)
1891, Op. 58 No. 1, À Mme la Princesse Winnaretta de Scey –Montbéliard, third Hamelle collection p. 29, G major, ♩, *Allegretto moderato*

Les donneurs de sérénades	*The gallant serenaders*
Et les belles écouteuses	*And their fair listeners*
Échangent des propos fades	*Exchange sweet nothings*
Sous les ramures chanteuses.	*Beneath singing boughs.*
C'est Tircis et c'est Aminte,	*Tirsis is there, Aminte is there,*
Et c'est l'éternel Clitandre,	*And tedious Clitandre too,*
Et c'est Damis qui pour mainte	*And Damis who for many a cruel maid*
Cruelle fait maint vers tendre.	*Writes many a tender song.*
Leurs courtes vestes de soie,	*Their short silken doublets,*
Leurs longues robes à queues,	*Their long trailing gowns,*
Leur élégance, leur joie	*Their elegance, their joy,*
Et leurs molles ombres bleues	*And their soft blue shadows*
Tourbillonnent dans l'extase	*Whirl madly in the rapture*
D'une lune rose et grise,	*Of a grey and roseate moon,*
Et la mandoline jase	*And the mandolin jangles on*
Parmi les frissons de brise.	*In the shivering breeze.*

In a letter to Marguerite Baugnies written from Venice on 12 June 1891 Fauré wrote:

The fact of the matter is that I am having an excellent holiday, feeling better than I have ever felt before, and filling my eyes with marvellous things and my mind with delightful memories! I certainly lack the peace and quiet I need for work and the little something I have sketched out to some lines by Verlaine may possibly turn out well once I am back at my desk in Paris amid the peace of my home and with my children whom I should love to have in my arms now.[21]

This 'little something' is *Mandoline*, and once again we feel that Fauré would not be above down-playing its import with his own particular brand of mischievous self-deprecation.

As we have already discussed, Verlaine's second collection of poems, *Fêtes galantes* (first published in 1869), evokes the subtle spirit of Watteau, who had painted courtly life at Versailles in an epoch governed by the trivia of extreme formality. Twenty years after the collection of poems appeared, the centenary (1889) of the French Revolution sparked a collective nostalgia for the *ancien régime*. The citizens of the Third Republic were now amused to take part in costume balls in the style of Watteau; the painter Adolphe Monticelli (1824–1886) – possibly also admired by Verlaine – had returned to this period for inspiration, making something new from a period in French history that seemed to have been completely detached from reality. The time was ripe for music to follow suit: in *Clair de lune* there is a deepening of Fauré's madrigal style, time-travelling in music that preserved (and even enhanced) the Fauréan essence. This composer was superbly suited to evoke an era that combined outrageous self-indulgence with the rigours of an exaggerated *politesse*. *Mandoline* has a sprightly charm, certainly, but it is also powered by a *pudeur* that is appropriate to Fauré at the height of his technical powers. The courtiers go by the nicknames of Tircis (perhaps a deliberate reference to the pet-name of the male lover of the disgraced seventeenth-century poet Théophile le Viau), Clitandre and Aminte. These nymphs and shepherds of eighteenth-century pastorals were freed by the Enlightenment, and extremely libidinous – we only have to look at the Haydn songs and part-songs (full of similar pastoral names) as evidence of this. At Versailles, however, the court was ruled by rigid rules of etiquette, as was Fauré's musical world; in this clash between licentiousness and restraint the energy of the music was born.

This microcosmic world is divided between those who serenade (accompanied by a plucked lute rendered in pianistic staccato) and their beautiful listeners, a game that is both meaningless and full of hidden meaning for the initiates. The veneer of heartless elegance cracks sufficiently to reveal deep feeling and real humour (that boring Clitandre!); Fauré's courtiers are not made of stone – we sense that they too long for true love in that milieu of slightly apathetic melancholy engendered by too much luxury and too little responsibility.

It is this subliminal ache that is beneath the surface in Fauré's song; it is lacking in Debussy's whirlwind setting, which creates a madcap feeling, as does Hahn's (entitled *Fêtes galantes*). In Fauré's infinitely more subtle song the very *justesse* of the correct tempo and the

Illustration by Léon Lebègue for 'Mandoline' in Verlaine's Fêtes galantes, *published by Ferroud (1913)*

elegant exactitude of the staccatos betoken a world where everything is a matter of guarded calcula-tion, where passion is played out partly as a power game, where nothing can be out of place, nothing left to chance. At Versailles, luxury and licence were always accompanied by the constraints of courtly life. The musical equivalent of this etiquette is the rigorous self-control of the conscientious professional musician responsible for the accuracy of each note and the measuring of each beat, the singer determined not to allow her coloratura to be smudged carelessly. Only Verlaine purists may object to Fauré choosing – in popular song manner – to repeat the poet's first strophe to bring the song to its satisfyingly inevitable musical conclusion. What an inscrutable courtier Fauré might have made in the eighteenth century! The semi-sincere and ultimately melancholic world of *Mandoline* is a metaphor for Fauré's dealings with the whole race of high-flying Parisian aristocrats, where his affection and regard for some of them was inevitably complicated by considerations of finance and class; the courtiers of junior rank and their distant descendants, the composers of Paris, were skilled above all in the art of survival. 'Fauré, as always, hides his greatest audacities under a cover of regularity.'[22] Never was Jean-Nectoux's axiom more true than in these songs *de Venise*, where the composer pays lip-service to the *ancien régime* of Versailles while plotting a revolution of his own devising.

(55) (ii) *En sourdine* (*Muted*)
1891, Op. 58 No. 2, third Hamelle collection p. 34, E♭ major, ♩, *Andante moderato*

Calmes dans le demi-jour	*Calm in the twilight*
Que les branches hautes font,	*Cast by lofty boughs,*
Pénétrons bien notre amour	*Let us steep our love*
De ce silence profond.	*In this deep quiet.*
Mêlons nos âmes, nos cœurs	*Let us mingle our souls, our hearts*
Et nos sens extasiés,	*And our enraptured senses*
Parmi les vagues langueurs	*With the hazy languor*
Des pins et des arbousiers.	*Of arbutus and pine.*
Ferme tes yeux à demi,	*Half-close your eyes,*
Croise tes bras sur ton sein,	*Fold your arms across your breast,*
Et de ton cœur endormi	*And from your heart now lulled to rest*
Chasse à jamais tout dessein.	*Banish forever all intent.*
Laissons-nous persuader	*Let us both succumb*
Au souffle berceur et doux	*To the gentle and lulling breeze*
Qui vient à tes pieds rider	*That comes to ruffle at your feet*
Les ondes des gazons roux.	*The waves of russet grass.*
Et quand, solennel, le soir	*And when, solemnly, evening*
Des chênes noirs tombera,	*Falls from the black oaks,*
Voix de notre désespoir,	*That voice of our despair,*
Le rossignol chantera.	*The nightingale shall sing.*

This song ranks high as a favourite among the composer's *mélodies*; it is indeed a classic example of his song-writing art at its most organic, although he wrote that he found the work 'difficile à conduire' in Venice and it cost him considerable trouble to compose. The progression of Fauré's music here seems to trace a perfect arc in the late-afternoon sky of the lovers' assignation – the first phrase moving ineluctably to the last in an inevitable, if languid, trajectory. The accompaniment in fronds of semiquavers makes a shady bower for this reverie in the half-light; the rippling between the pianist's hands is as graceful and measured as it is imperturbable. The vocal line is a model of seemingly laconic poise despite the considerable chromatic undulation beneath the surface. *Mandoline* is now only a distant echo, although the lovers' assignation may well have been confirmed with a discreet exchange of glances during that sprightly *moment musical*.

In contrast, *En sourdine* breathes the peaceful melancholy of satiation to be found in the earlier nocturnes for piano; it is clear that temporary fulfilment has been achieved, but at a price. The intrusion of the word 'désespoir' at the end of the song suggests subterfuge; the warning song of the nightingale unmasks this idyll as a stolen joy. (One of Verlaine's favourite poems, Victor Hugo's 'La Fête chez Thérèse', also contains this motif: 'Le rossignol, caché dans son nid ténébreux, / Chanta comme un poëte et comme un amoureux' – 'The nightingale concealed in his dark nest, sang like a poet and like a lover'). Nevertheless for the few moments left in each other's arms there is a touch of defiance, a sublime determination to enjoy together the remains of the day. Seventy years later W.H. Auden would enjoin his lover of the moment to 'Lay your sleeping head, my love, / Human on my faithless arm …' despite the impermanence of his ever-roving desire. In Verlaine's collection this is the penultimate poem; *Fêtes galantes* closes with the chill of 'Colloque sentimental' – the contrasted nostalgic regret and cold indifference of the two lovers' ghosts – a poem that was set masterfully by Debussy in his second set of *Fêtes galantes* (1904).

Mandoline and *En sourdine* were given their first performance in Venice sung by Amélie Duez, the wife of the painter. The guests of the Princesse were often taken out on a fishing boat in the evening; there was an instrument on board, a 'yacht piano' with the range of a harpsichord. We must imagine the composer accompanying his first two *mélodies* 'de Venise' on board the boat, adapting the range of his accompaniments as best he could to the restrictions of the instrument. But the abiding memory of those lucky enough to be there must have been the sound of *En sourdine*, a masterpiece only recently given to the world, sung sweetly and wafted into the warm evening air, Fauré's inimitable harmonies mingling with the plashing water of the lagoon. Debussy's exquisite setting of the same text dates from the same year, but it could not be more different. Fauré allows the sound of the nightingale to permeate the music in such a way that there seems no need for illustrative birdsong; the latter is precisely what Debussy gives us in repeated notes that throb allusively in the keyboard's treble. Fauré digests and captures the mood of the whole (from the very first laconic, yet evenly spaced, semiquavers of the accompaniment); Debussy, with the legerdemain of a superb musical journalist, and a man of the theatre to boot, peoples the song with changing pictures, and the nightingale sings on cue. As Jankélévitch puts it: 'the melody of [Fauré's] *En sourdine* is coextensive with Verlaine's poem and nevertheless does not tangle itself up in the details of the text, preferring to drown them in the unvarying pianissimo of the arpeggios, in the penumbra, in the end taking no account of the nightingale's singing.'[23]

Drawing parallels with English music, lovers of Fauré's art might prefer the Hardy cycle of Gerald Finzi, and those who prefer Debussy's Verlaine songs might admire Benjamin Britten's *Winter Words*, his more theatrically aware Hardy cycle. It must be said of this analogy that although Britten is a greater composer than Finzi by far, Finzi enjoys an almost preternatural affinity with his chosen poet and, much to do with this fact, has a loyal following among performers and listeners. Likewise, even when the Verlaine settings of Fauré face stiff competition from other great musicians, one can never underestimate the uncanny link between this poet and this particular (in every sense) composer, a match of inborn affinities that is as important as any in the history of song.

Returning to Paris, the composer was still looking for a librettist. He flirted with the idea of working with Maurice Bouchor (Chausson's poet for *Poème de l'amour et de la mer*) but disliked the theme of the life of Buddha proposed by the Princesse. Verlaine suddenly re-surfaced with an unexpected and rather autobiographical suggestion: he wanted to write something associated with the *commedia dell'arte* to be entitled *L'Hôpital Watteau* (although he constantly misspelled the painter's name as 'Wateau'). The Princesse liked this idea, but Fauré was unconvinced; neither did her idea of a Buddha project with Bouchor seem feasible. He tried to divert his patron by drawing her attention to the fact that he had written a piano quintet that should be performed in her home. And of course there was the 'Venice' cycle, which needed to be completed.

Illustration by Léon Lebègue for En sourdine *in Verlaine's* Fêtes galantes, *published by Ferroud (1913)*

(56) (iii) *Green* (*Green*)

1891, Op. 58 No. 3, third Hamelle collection p. 39, G♭ major (higher key), 3/4, *Andante con moto*

Voici des fruits, des fleurs, des feuilles et des branches	*Here are flowers, branches, fruit and fronds,*
Et puis voici mon cœur qui ne bat que pour vous.	*And here too is my heart that beats just for you.*
Ne le déchirez pas avec vos deux mains blanches	*Do not tear it with your two white hands*
Et qu'à vos yeux si beaux l'humble présent soit doux.	*And may the humble gift please your lovely eyes.*
J'arrive tout couvert encore de rosée	*I come all covered still with the dew*
Que le vent du matin vient glacer à mon front.	*Frozen to my brow by the morning breeze.*
Souffrez que ma fatigue à vos pieds reposée	*Let my fatigue, finding rest at your feet,*
Rêve des chers instants qui la délasseront.	*Dream of dear moments that will soothe it.*
Sur votre jeune sein laissez rouler ma tête	*On your young breast let me cradle my head*
Toute sonore encor de vos derniers baisers;	*Still ringing with your recent kisses;*
Laissez-la s'apaiser de la bonne tempête,	*After love's sweet tumult grant it peace,*
Et que je dorme un peu puisque vous reposez.	*And let me sleep a while, since you rest.*

With a change of residence from Venice back to Paris in the summer of 1891 comes a change of poetry. For *Green* the composer abandons Verlaine's *Fêtes galantes* and turns to the *Aquarelles* section of the same poet's *Romances sans paroles*. This collection had been issued first in 1874 (Montesquiou's copy), but the publisher Vanier had issued second and third editions of the work in 1887 and 1891 (together with, in the latter year, a third edition of *Fêtes galantes* and the first printing of *La Bonne chanson* since 1870). By this time, and probably since the composition of *Spleen*, Fauré was surely the proud owner of a *Romance sans paroles* of his own. The *Aquarelles* subsection boasts a number of poems with English titles. *Green* is a breathless confession of devotion (the composer required it to be both 'slow moving' and 'halétant', or 'breathless'), the latter indication of speed and mood unique for a poem that celebrates the aftermath of lovemaking, were it not for Debussy's setting, which is arguably even more enthusiastic and passionate. If there is an adorer and an adored in every relationship, this is music for the former, and those who equate adoring with suffering may prefer the languidly masochistic overtones of *Offrande*, Reynaldo Hahn's version in his *Chansons grises*. This interpretation touched Verlaine, judging by his tears on hearing Hahn's songs. Nevertheless, Fauré's *Green* is enchanting. In a letter to the Princesse de Polignac in late July 1891 he described the song as a 'vivid, melancholy, country scene … the harmony must try and underline the deeper meaning which the words do no more than hint at'.

Just before 'J'arrive tout couvert encor de rosée' the mezzo-staccato quaver accompaniment blossoms into a graceful little figure that links a falling third with a rising second, two semiquavers followed by a quaver, light as a caress, but contained within a legato, a gesture both soothing and conciliatory. This unassuming yet emollient motif binds the song together, and is heard again in the next two songs, a cyclic feature that makes a bow of acknowledgement in the direction of César Franck, and also prophesies *La Bonne chanson*. The composer himself summed up the song's paradoxes in acknowledging its interpretative difficulties in the same letter to the Princesse: 'If on first hearing it doesn't please you, will you promise not to lose heart and read it again? It is a difficult one to interpret: Slow-moving but agitated in feeling, happy and miserable, eager and discouraged! So many things in thirty bars!'[24] In another letter, this time to Marguerite Baugnies, his advice is subtly different: 'I can't insist too strongly that it musn't be sung *slowly*: it has to be *lively*, passionate, almost *out of breath*!'[25]

In sending the score to Winnaretta at her palatial residence on the avenue Henri-Martin (since renamed as avenue Georges-Mandel) he quotes the poem and begs that she should not 'tear it up with your two white hands'. The implication that the composer feels, or has felt, amorously for the song's dedicatee is indisputable. It also lets us know that Fauré was attempting to assuage Winnaretta's mounting irritation with the fact that her commission for an opera by Fauré and Verlaine (or even Fauré and another poet) was unlikely to materialise (and it was never to do so).

(57) (iv) *À Clymène* (*To Clymène*)
1891, Op. 58 No. 4, third Hamelle collection p. 43, E minor, 9/8, *Andantino*

Mystiques barcarolles,	*Mystical barcarolles,*
Romances sans paroles,	*Songs without words,*
Chère, puisque tes yeux,	*Sweet, since your eyes,*
Couleur des cieux,	*The colour of skies,*

212

Puisque ta voix, étrange	*Since your voice,*
Vision qui dérange	*Strange vision that unsettles*
Et trouble l'horizon	*And troubles the horizon*
De ma raison,	*Of my reason,*
Puisque l'arome insigne	*Since the rare scent*
De ta pâleur de cygne,	*Of your swan-like pallor,*
Et puisque la candeur	*And since the candour*
De ton odeur,	*Of your fragrance,*
Ah! puisque tout ton être,	*Ah! since your whole being –*
Musique qui pénètre,	*Pervading music,*
Nimbes d'anges défunts,	*Haloes of departed angels,*
Tons et parfums,	*Sounds and scents –*
A, sur d'almes cadences,	*Has in sweet cadences*
En ses correspondances	*And correspondences*
Induit mon cœur subtil,	*Led on my receptive heart –*
Ainsi soit-il!	*So be it!*

We now return to Verlaine's *Fêtes galantes*. It is rather curious that the Mendelssohnian second line of 'À Clymène' – 'Romance sans paroles' ('Songs without words') – is also the title of the later poetry collection that contains 'Green'. The combination of music, colour and perfume 'sur d'almes cadences' is Verlaine's bow in the direction of the synaesthesia of Baudelaire, and thus his conscious use of one of the most famous of that poet's words – 'correspondances'. (Rimbaud was also absorbed by the idea of synaesthesia in his 'Voyelles'.) This spell-binding Clymène is an eighteenth-century court beauty whom one imagines reclining in an imitation gondola on the Bassin d'Apollon at Versailles (see the description at the end of this chapter of a Venetian-styled soirée at Versailles in 1908).

Of the 'Venise' songs this is perhaps the least often heard on the concert platform; as a rather nebulous hymn of praise in a single uninterrupted progression of over-abundant imagery it challenges its interpreters, and no other composer of significance has set these words. The first three poems of this opus have been cast in ABAB quatrains; here the rhyme scheme is AABB. It is doubtless a deliberate technical ploy on Verlaine's part that these paired lines, light as helium, lack the ballast of a further clinching rhyme: they never weigh anchor. The third to fifth strophes comprise a single, rambling phrase; we wait, in a flurry of subordinate clauses, for the verb 'Induit' in the penultimate line. As a piano piece with a vocal line weaving in and out of the swaying barcarolle (sequences of seductive triplets, a rarefied and other-worldly mood), *À Clymène* has undeniable beauties, though it is hard to say whether the song is adrift or merely drifting. As the performer struggles with it, Fauré's own description of the piece (according to Claude Rostand) as 'lunaire et lunatique' seems apt.[26]

The crucial little motto in semiquavers that had been the leitmotif of *Green* is here expanded into more leisurely quaver triplets. The modal tinge in the music, a sign of the composer's exceptionally rich harmonic vocabulary, recalls Reynaldo Hahn's label for Fauré – 'a gregorianizing voluptuary'. This song has more in common with the music of César Franck than any of Fauré's other *mélodies*

– just as the entire 'Venise' cycle seems indebted to Franck's cyclical procedures. The composer's younger colleague Camille Benoit pronounced the music 'incoherent and obscure', advising Fauré to abandon Verlaine, who was clearly leading him up the garden path.[27] Fauré on the other hand was concerned that he was too classical in approach for this challenging poem. The change of metre for the second strophe (9/8 giving way to 4/4 *un poco più mosso*) is a cunning depiction of quickening pulses leading to momentary blurred vision, like a sudden squall of wind that might rock the equilibrium of a gondola on the Grand Canal. From rhythmic juxtapositions such as these we can tell that *La Bonne chanson* is just around the corner. Also typical of that future cycle is a coda with the breadth of a benediction: here the words 'Ainsi soit-il!' give rise to a beautifully poised nine-bar envoi.

(58) (v) *C'est l'extase* (*It is rapture*)
1891, Op. 58 No. 5, third Hamelle collection p. 48, D♭ major, 3/4, *Adagio non troppo*

C'est l'extase langoureuse,	*It is languorous rapture,*
C'est la fatigue amoureuse,	*It is amorous fatigue,*
C'est tous les frissons des bois	*It is all the tremors of the forest*
Parmi l'étreinte des brises,	*In the breezes' embrace,*
C'est, vers les ramures grises,	*It is, around the grey branches,*
Le chœur des petites voix.	*The choir of tiny voices.*
Ô le frêle et frais murmure!	*O the delicate, fresh murmuring!*
Cela gazouille et susurre,	*The warbling and whispering,*
Cela ressemble au bruit doux	*It is like the sweet sound*
Que l'herbe agitée expire …	*The ruffled grass gives out …*
Tu dirais, sous l'eau qui vire,	*You might take it for the muffled sound*
Le roulis sourd des cailloux.	*Of pebbles in the swirling stream.*
Cette âme qui se lamente	*This soul which grieves*
En cette plainte dormante	*In this subdued lament,*
C'est la nôtre, n'est-ce pas?	*It is ours, is it not?*
La mienne, dis, et la tienne,	*Mine, and yours too,*
Dont s'exhale l'humble antienne	*Breathing out our humble hymn*
Par ce tiède soir, tout bas?	*On this warm evening, soft and low?*

Paul Verlaine (1844–1896)

The poem is from the 'Ariettes oubliées' section of *Romances sans paroles* – indeed it opens the entire volume. The more famous Debussy setting, the first of his cycle, emphasises the 'langoureuse' aspect of this 'fatigue amoureuse'. Fauré, on the other hand, finds just the right 'shiver' for the mezzostaccato accompaniment to illustrate 'les frissons des bois'. The whole *mélodie* is alive with nervous syncopation and hovering harmony, ever changing yet always seeming to stay more or less in the same place (a Fauré speciality, this) – like light dancing before the eyes of an impressionist painter. Integrated into a song that unfolds seamlessly we hear motival echoes of *Green* and *En sourdine* (this last, in Fauré's words, writing to his patron Princesse, 'a cry of frustration, ever deeper and more intense right up to the end'[28]). For Fauré, love was perhaps too complicated an issue for this cycle to end in a mood of 'happiness ever after'. That was to be the future theme of *La Bonne chanson*. In contrast with those optimistic poems addressed by Verlaine in 1870 to his ill-starred fiancée, the poet was in a more vulnerable mood in the wake of his disastrous affair with Arthur Rimbaud and in his various phases of believing that a reconciliation with this wife was somehow possible. Debussy understood this: the panicked 'dis' ('say!') in his setting of 'C'est la nôtre, n'est-ce pas? La mienne, dis, et la tienne' begs in vain for a confirmation of reciprocal feeling. This passage, responsive to every verbal inflection, might have come from *Pelléas et Mélisande*.

Fauré prefers a musical, rather than a dramatic, solution: the listener is carried along by the composer's determination to unite the cycle's strands in a magnificent whole, a hymn to love echoed by, and reflected in, every aspect of nature. Beneath the surface, seemingly complacent to inattentive ears, we can detect the 'cry of frustration, ever deeper and more intense'.[29] Woven into this garland in love's honour there is an unmistakable strand of renunciation. Such subtle ambivalence is the trademark of a great composer.

                ❧   ❧   ❧   ❧

It seems that at this time Fauré came very near to making a fool of himself regarding the Princesse, whom he now plied by letter with such untypically extravagant phrases as 'your every word becomes a note of music'. There is no doubt that he was smitten; it is likely that Winnaretta had to suppress her irritation with him in ignoring this emotional onslaught. Besides, there was still business to attend to: if neither Verlaine nor Bouchor were to write a libretto, what about a Buddha project with the poet Albert Samain? In the meantime she, still formally known as the Princesse de Scey-Montbéliard, was the dedicatee of the completed *Cinq mélodies 'de Venise'*. The work was given its first performance by the tenor Maurice Bagès with Fauré at the piano on 2 April 1892.

The occasion was the opening of the Princesse's new music *atelier*. At vast expense the original hôtel on the avenue Henri-Martin (where Chabrier's *Gwendoline* had been performed), in the sixteenth *arrondissement*, was now linked, via a connecting garden, with another house on the adjacent rue Cortambert that housed a gigantic music room complete with a Cavaillé-Coll organ. (The whole property was to be completely redesigned and rebuilt in 1905.) We remember that the Princesse's original 25,000-franc commission was for a large work to open her new *atelier*; instead her *Mélodies 'de Venise'* were performed for the first time in public.

In February 1892 Winnaretta received the news that her supplications to the Vatican had been rewarded with success: her unhappy marriage to Scey-Montbéliard had finally been granted an annulment. A downgrading from the rank of Princesse must have seemed as inevitable as it was unthinkable. Most fortunately there was at hand another Prince, a potential second husband of unimpeachably aristocratic birth who would expect nothing from her sexually, whom she could like and respect, and even admire, and whose work she could, and would, promote. Edmond de Polignac was in his late fifties (Winnaretta was still only twenty-eight) and was contentedly homosexual; he was a member of one of the oldest aristocratic families in France, though virtually penniless (one can see the advantage of the match from his point of view); he was a serious and interesting, if only moderately gifted, composer whom Fauré already knew. Comte Robert de Montesquiou brought Edmond and Winnaretta together and cruelly exulted in having promoted a marriage of heartless convenience. But the couple quickly became genuinely devoted to each other and during the short course of their marriage confounded all of high society's negative prognostications. The knot was tied in December 1893; Winnaretta could at last use the almost legendary name by which she would always be known by musicians everywhere: the Princesse Edmond de Polignac.

She grew into her legend with increasing authority. Cocteau's quip about her loving music as a sewing machine loves sheets was blatantly unfair. Enthroned in her high-backed tapestried chair (placed in front of the first row of her guests in a central position), this imposing woman was set regally to preside for the next forty years over some of the finest music-making imaginable, much of it music she herself had commissioned.

Frontispiece by Léon Lebègue for Verlaine's Fêtes galantes, published by Ferroud (1913)

With the *Cinq mélodies 'de Venise'* Fauré triumphantly embarks on his second period. 'A composer had arisen', writes Norman Suckling, 'in whose name French song could hold its head high against any in the world.' The two earlier Verlaine settings from 1887 and 1888 are touched with a similar magic, proving that it was the voice of the poet, not just the passage of time, that was responsible for releasing in Fauré such a vital response. Not only was each of the 'Venetian' songs a triumph in its own right, but the composer had produced, for the first time in his career, a *set* of songs that were ingeniously inter-related in terms of musical motifs There had been nothing quite like it in the history of the *mélodie*, and he knew it – and this, in turn, energised him for the years to come. The various periods of aimlessness that had characterised some of his song composing were now over. Looking back on his first period, Fauré himself may have identified a streak in his own nature that attempted to please other people, to provide what they wanted. This too was a thing of the past. It would be fair to say that from now until the end of his life, the composer's songs were written to please himself (or sometimes his lovers) and in a totally focused manner.

Of course the 'Venetian songs', apart from the barcarolle of *À Clymène*, had little to do with Venice itself, except that it was a holiday in Venice that made this creative mood possible. Whereas the Venetians themselves probably regarded their carnival as an excuse for a riotous saturnalia, Suckling points out that the French had long imagined that Venice at carnival time was a 'perfect frame for a life of moonlight confidences and subtle evasions'. This is a useful image for those performers who might wish to conflate the *masques* and *bergamasques* of Versailles with the magical mood of the city on the water that Fauré absorbed with such unalloyed delight in 1891. Both the Versailles of the *Fêtes galantes* and the Venice of the *mélodies 'de Venise'* are enchanted landscapes of dreams and deception, playgrounds of the rich whose tyrannical power is disguised by elaborate games and

*The Palazzo Volkoff on the Grand Canal with the Princesse's
Venetian guests (including Fauré) assembled on the balcony, 1891.*
© *Bibliothèque nationale de France*

softened by make-believe scenarios decorated with lavish costume and adorned with glittering *courtoisie*. And Fauré, the visitor to Venice who could not afford to stay there on his own account, and who was born too late to observe Versailles at its apogee, is the ideal observer of all this at one remove, the detached chronicler of these 'donneurs de sérénades', whether painted by Watteau or accompanied with his own fingers on an undulating barge on the Grand Canal.

∾   ∾   ∾   ∾

This was not the last time Fauré accompanied his songs afloat. On a magical evening in June 1908 (described by Marguerite Saint-Marceaux as 'cette soirée inoubliable') the twinned themes of Venice and Versailles were united in honour of the celebrity that the composer became following his appointment as director of the Conservatoire in 1905. This magnificently extravagant outdoor concert in the gardens of Versailles, evidence of a gilded prosperity that would have been unimaginable after the First World War, was the brainchild of Vicomte Robert d'Humières, a friend of Robert de Montesquiou. After an orchestral performance of the *Pavane*, poetry readings about the château and its park and an exquisite dinner, the hand-picked guests descended the 'tapis vert' (accompanied by the sounds of a hidden orchestra conducted by Inghelbrecht) and having reached the Bassin d'Apollon embarked on a fleet of gondolas adorned with Venetian lanterns as if on the Grand Canal. In the first of these gondolas were placed a Pleyel piano, the singer and composer Reynaldo Hahn and Fauré himself as accompanist. The Venetian barques floated gently (as if) downstream while the deliciously warm evening resounded with orchestral music from *Shylock* (now performed from the steps of the Petit Trianon); this was followed by the unmistakable timbre of Reynaldo Hahn's slender but charming singing voice floating across the water. The final song in Reynaldo's recital of about eight or nine Fauré masterpieces was *Clair de lune*:

And finally, when I sang the words 'Au calme claire de lune, triste et beau' the moon suddenly appeared above the trees and its reflection on the lake seemed to prolong like a luminous echo the last notes of the exquisite and melancholy refrain. Then Fauré gently shut the piano and for some moments we remained silent.[30]

1   Edmond Lepelletier, *Paul Verlaine: His Life, his Work*, trans. E.M. Lang (London: T. Werner Laurie, 1909), pp. 130–31.

2   London W1, west of Tottenham Court Road, two blocks north of Goodge Street which is parallel to Howland Street. The dwelling shared by the poets was demolished in the 1930s and is the site of the Post Office, or Telecom, Tower, a monument to a more modern kind of communication.

3   This is now Royal College Street, London NW1 not far from the new Eurotunnel terminus at St. Pancras. In recent years there has been an ongoing battle regarding the future of this building between London property developers and Verlaine and Rimbaud enthusiasts who wish to establish a museum there with poetry workshops. At one time the French government was interested in funding this project.

4   *Claire de lune*: Aspects of this song's interpretation are discussed in Chapter 16, p. 413.

5   Valdimir Jankélévitch, *Music and the Ineffable* (1961, rev. 1981), trans. Caroline Abbate (Princeton, NJ: Princeton University Press, 2003), p. 115.

6   Vladimir Jankélévitch, *De la musique au silence: Fauré et l'inexprimable* (Paris: Plon, 1974), p. 98.

7   Claude Rostand, *L'Œuvre de Gabriel Fauré* (Paris: J.B. Janin, 'La Flûte de Pan'), p. 87.

8   This connection is doubted by Nectoux, who points out that Jadin is not an unusual French name; it seems to me that the shared 'Emmanuel' may point to family usage that is something more than coincidence.

9   *Spleen*: Aspects of this song's interpretation are discussed in Chapter 16, p. 414.

10 Jean-Michel Nectoux, *Gabriel Fauré: A Musical Life*, trans. Roger Nichols (Cambridge: Cambridge University Press, 1991), p. 175.

11 Quoted in Sylvia Kahan, *Music's Modern Muse: A Life of Winnaretta Singer, Princesse de Polignac* (Rochester, NY: University of Rochester Press, 2003), p. 51.

12 Ibid.

13 Igor Stravinsky, *Chroniques de ma vie* (Paris: Denoel, 1962), p. 118.

14 *Gabriel Fauré: His Life through his Letters*, ed. Jean-Michel Nectoux, trans. John Underwood (London and New York: Marion Boyars, 1984), letter 83.

15 Ibid.

16 Quoted in Sylvia Kahan, *Music's Modern Muse*, p. 52.

17 Quoted in ibid., p. 52.

18 Nectoux, *Gabriel Fauré: A Musical Life*, p. 178.

19 Ibid., p. 179.

20 *Cinq melodies 'de Venise'*: Aspects of this cycle's interpretation are discussed in Chapter 16, pp. 414–16.

21 *Gabriel Fauré: His Life through his Letters*, p. 178.

22 Nectoux, *Gabriel Fauré: A Musical Life*, p. 190.

23 Jankélévitch, *Music and the Ineffable*, p. 53.

24 Nectoux, *Gabriel Fauré: A Musical Life*, p. 178.

25 Ibid., p. 178.

26 Quoted in Rostand, *L'Œuvre de Gabriel Fauré*, p. 102. This phrase attributed to Fauré himself was perhaps recounted to Rostand by Marguerite Hasselmans, whom he interviewed for his book.

27 Quoted in Nectoux, *Gabriel Fauré: A Musical Life*, p. 179.

28 Ibid., p. 179.

29 Ibid., p. 179.

30 Reynaldo Hahn, *Thèmes variés* (Paris: J.B. Janin, 1946), p. 138. The evening is also discussed and described in Myriam Chimènes, *Mécènes et musiciens* (Paris: Fayard, 2004), pp. 372–4.

Chapter Nine

Fauré and Paul Verlaine (II)

La Bonne chanson

As we have seen, Fauré had faced insuperable difficulties in 1891 in attempting to coax a libretto out of the wily and uncooperative Verlaine at the behest of the implacable Princesse de Polignac. On the other hand, the *Cinq mélodies 'de Venise'* (to poems written twenty years or so earlier) had been hugely important in re-establishing the composer's creative self-confidence. Here was poetry, at last, to which he could genuinely respond without compromising anything of his artistic integrity. These texts fitted him like a glove: they were more naturally *musical* than anything he had set in the past ('De la musique avant toute chose … De la musique encore et toujours!', as Verlaine famously wrote[1]: 'Music above everything … music again and forever!').

As the most sheerly musical of song composers, Fauré was able to be completely himself, almost *more* than himself, in setting these poems. As J.-M. Nectoux has written, 'Verlaine's aesthetic can be defined in terms of its musicality, its feeling for line, its mingling of discretion and audacity, and its gently probing "spleen".[2] These words might also be used to describe Fauré's own aesthetic of course. When compared with this partnership, his other favourite poets all had their drawbacks – Silvestre's weaknesses were a tendency to generalisation and over-ripe sweetness; Richepin, on the other hand, was self-consciously masculine and gruff; Leconte de Lisle, master of Olympian control, could also be stiff and portentous. Certainly Fauré had negotiated all these hurdles for years as part of the job of being a song composer, but what a pleasure it must have been to collaborate, even at a distance, with a kindred spirit – in matters of art at least. Verlaine was a man of the composer's own age and epoch who always struck the right note (and who enabled the composer to strike the right note in return) provided there was no attempt to work with him in person. The unveiling of the *Cinq mélodies 'de Venise'* at the Princesse's *atelier* was a kind of dress-rehearsal for the first performance at the Société Nationale de la Musique (SNM) on 2 April 1892. Fauré was delighted that for this, his first real song cycle, he had hit upon a format for the songs with interlinking musical cross-references that he felt was genuinely new. If only he had known Verlaine many years earlier in his career (when they were both in their twenties or thirties) they might have been able to astonish the world with an opera for the demanding 'Winnie'. Or perhaps not – she had been only a schoolgirl then, and the earlier period of Verlaine's life had been even more disturbed and unreliable than the perpetual shuttle between hostelry and hospital of his later years.

There are many who believe that success in the opera house represents a higher level of achievement than the writing of mere songs; at heart the Princesse de Polignac, for all her cultivation, seems to have been tempted into this opinion. An opera would surely have provided her with the maximum amount of glory in her role as *mécène*. Despite the dedication of the glorious *Venise* cycle she continued to insist, like the straightforward, no-nonsense woman she was, on the work for which she had paid; this was to lead to a distinct, if temporary, cooling in the relations between her and Fauré. The beginning of 1892 saw a continuing struggle to find a suitable text. The poet Albert Samain (who was later to make a significant contribution to Fauré's *mélodies*) went ahead and wrote 750 lines on the subject of *La Tentation de Bouddha* that were never used, a most embarrassing situation. The Princesse was still disappointed about the composer's rejection of Verlaine's idea for *L'Hôpital de Watteau*, and the failure of this project to get off the ground (for which she blamed Fauré) haunted her as one of the great 'might-have-beens' in her long life in support of music. The resolution to this awkward situation was effected only belatedly with the composer's dedication to the Princesse de Polignac of his incidental music to Maeterlinck's *Pelléas et Mélisande* in 1898.

In any case, the Princesse had moved on to a new marital alliance, and Prince Edmond de Polignac, a composer in his own right, now occupied a great deal of her time and attention. Fauré's tentative romantic advances in Winnie's direction, if such they were, had been made very much in the light of each of them being aware of the other's unhappy marriage. Who knows if he had ever fantasised about leaving his wife for a life of luxury with Winnaretta? She had been brought up to make alliances on a more exalted level altogether and would certainly have scoffed at such a notion; even the aristocracy of Fauré's genius would not have been sufficient. In any case, the composer had other patrons, less Amazonian but equally influential, such as the beautiful Elisabeth de Caraman Chimay, Comtesse Greffulhe (1860–1952), reigning queen of Parisian society and a member of an extremely musical family; she played the piano well, was capable of judging a work from the orchestral score (she was an early patron of Gustav Mahler) and had very good literary taste. She was, moreover, kindness itself to Fauré's wife and children, sending them thoughtful gifts. The artistically possessive Winnaretta did not approve of such rivals, indeed she was jealous of them, but Fauré's emotional life was now moving away from her direct influence although his professional life would remain entwined with her assiduously cultivated musical pursuits.[3]

On 1 June 1892 he was appointed inspector of musical instruction, a post he would hold for thirteen years and which would take him on journeys throughout the country visiting the provincial conservatoires and making sure that they were up to the mark. Of course, being a government functionary meant greater financial security, but the drudgery of this job with its incessant train journeys and bad hotels in uninteresting towns (and the writing of reports when he would have preferred to write music) took Fauré even more systematically away from hearth and home. Later in the summer it must have been a bitter disappointment that the dyspeptic Ambroise Thomas blocked his candidature as professor of composition at the Conservatoire.

❧   ❧   ❧   ❧

It was during this same summer spent with his parents-in-law at Prunay near Bougival (a delightful quarter beloved of artists, outside Paris, on the Seine and near the island of Chatou) that the composer fell in love with one of his holiday neighbours, Emma Bardac, née Moÿse. (It is little wonder, therefore, that we suddenly hear a good deal less of the Princesse de Polignac in Fauré's life.) Emma, who was just thirty at the time, was spending the summer near Prunay with her husband,

Emma Bardac

the banker Sigismund Bardac, and her two young children, Raoul and Hélène, the latter still a baby.

Emma was a gifted soprano, a good sight-reader who adored performing in the salon. Although she was not exactly beautiful (she was cosy in build rather than statuesque) she had the ability to charm intelligent men with the wit of her conversation, and an inborn elegance. The friendship between her and Fauré seems to have become ardently romantic during the summer of 1892. Fauré had earlier said that he had set all the Verlaine poems he could, but perhaps he had not quite read everything when he made that remark; indeed, it is highly likely that the very rare first edition of *La Bonne chanson* (Lemerre, 1870), printed during the Franco-Prussian War, was not among the volumes of Verlaine's poetry loaned to Fauré in 1887 by Comte Robert de Montesquiou. The work had long been unobtainable and was reissued by Vanier in its second edition only in 1891; it is very possible that these poems, supremely appropriate to Fauré's new role of ecstatic lover, were new discoveries for him at the time.

The lyrics were paeans of love written by Verlaine in a mood of high exaltation, and they mirrored the joy that Fauré felt in his new collaboration with Emma, both personal and artistic. We can assume that someone of her culture and musical sophistication admired innovation and daring, and was enchanted by Fauré's compositional mastery. The exuberant harmonic profligacy of this cycle stemmed in part from an understandable desire on Fauré's part to impress Emma with music written for her delectation; she was someone who valued the avant-garde all her life.

By 9 August 1892 the first song, *Donc, ce sera par un clair jour d'été* was already composed. *Une Sainte en son auréole* followed in September. *La Bonne chanson* as a whole was to be Fauré's most complex vocal work, and so it has remained for each generation of challenged listeners and hardworking singers and pianists. Nectoux writes,

Fauré's passion for Emma Bardac not only disrupted the even, bourgeois tenor of his life but, unusually for him, had the effect of completely reorientating his compositional activity … he cast off from the moorings of what was reasonable, what was respectable, what 'sounded well' and at a stroke achieved the sovereign liberty that marks the great creative artist.[4]

Fauré himself said that he had never written anything so spontaneously, although he gave full credit to Emma; in later years he was to speak lovingly about the cycle, and 'the singer [Emma of course] who was to remain its most moving interpreter … the pleasure of seeing those little sheets of paper come alive as soon as I brought them to her was one I have never experienced since.'[5] According to Roger-Ducasse, Fauré was not above taking Emma's musical advice and rewrote the postlude to *La Lune blanche* at her behest. The composer was also to say to Albert Samain in May 1896 (of the song *Soir*), 'You will never hear it sung better'[6]. To profoundly admire those whom one loves is not given to everyone; but when this is the case, intellectual and physical passion powered by both head and heart, become indivisible and mutually enthralling. As it happens this very phrase 'You will never hear it sung better' was addressed to me (out of the singer's hearing), by Benjamin Britten after conducting Peter Pears in a performance of Bach's *St John Passion* in 1971. Bearing in mind the considerable talents of Marguerite Hasselmanns, and even Adela Maddison, the composer's future mistresses, it was clearly an important bonus for Fauré that he should be able to admire the artistic achievements of the women in his life, and not only their feminine charms. This adds yet more pathos to the plight of poor Marie Fauré and her unremitting attempts to become an artist of significance in her own right.

Work continued on the cycle between May and December of 1893 (all the songs are individually dated and with care, and as we shall see the order of their composition bears no resemblance to the order of the published cycle). Nos 2, 3, 8 and 5 date from 1893; by February 1894 the composer had finished the last three songs (Nos 4, 6 and 9), and the work was issued by Hamelle in April 1894 with a dedication to Emma, officially Madame Sigismund Bardac. The first public performance took place with Maurice Bagès accompanied by the composer on 25 April at the salon of that important *mécène* the Comte de Saussine (it was at the home of Henri-de-Gault-de-Saussine that Fauré had first met Marcel Proust in 1893). One could say that the poems required a masculine interpreter, but it is also clear that for the mistress of the composer to sing in public such overwhelmingly passionate songs (also dedicated to her) was a step too far in terms of what was acceptable in society. The Bardacs seem to have enjoyed a kind of *fin de siècle* open relationship where they were both allowed their sexual freedom, but Emma was not entirely insensible to the danger of exposing her husband to gossip and mockery. The freedom of this kind of modern marriage was in marked contrast to the moral climate of France a quarter of a century earlier when Verlaine had married Mathilde Mauté, or indeed when Fauré's hopes of marriage to Marianne Viardot had been extinguished.

We must now retrace the story of how these poems came to be written. Having last seen Verlaine in this narrative in irreversible decline (he was to die on 8 January 1896), we have to imagine him at a time in his life a quarter of a century earlier when he felt that he had a genuine chance to overcome, with the help of a wife, what he considered to be the flaws in his nature – his homosexual proclivities, his alcoholism, his tendency to irrational violence.

As a young man Verlaine believed himself to be physically ugly, even repulsive (as he got older he seemed to care far less, and it was said that he seemed to grow into his looks). This verdict on his own lack of attractiveness, particularly when he was a younger man, and before he had acquired his fame, is confirmed by the poet's friend Edmond Lepelletier.[7] It seems that although Verlaine had been infatuated with his cousin Elsa, his only sexual contacts with women were of a professional nature – their profession, not his, to invoke the old joke. Against the flood of evidence to the contrary, and all the publicity surrounding the Rimbaud scandal, Lepelletier foolishly attempted to deny his friend's homosexual inclinations in his biography *Paul Verlaine: His Life, his Work.*[8] From the point of view of an affectionate heterosexual friend the poet seemed to be merely shy, awkward, lonely, ill at ease in female company and uninterested in the social outings that brought his male friends into normal, lively contact with girls. Verlaine, according to Lepelletier, only ever visited brothels when he was drunk.

One day in 1869 the poet visited his friend Charles de Sivry, who lived in Montmartre in the home of his stepfather Monsieur Mauté de Fleurville, a retired notary and a man of irreproachable respectability. Sivry was a musician who longed to write operettas in the mould of Offenbach's *La Belle Hélène*; he was to become the conductor of the orchestra for the cabaret at the famous 'Chat noir', and he imagined that the young poet of the recently published *Poèmes saturniens* and *Fêtes galantes* would make a good librettist for one of his works. Verlaine's feelings for Sivry were less clear; there may have been an initial element of sexual attraction, almost certainly one-sided, on the poet's part. Verlaine was talking earnestly with

Mathilde Mauté

Sivry in his room when there was a knock. A young girl, no doubt curious about the guest, put her head around the door. She apologised for disturbing the two men's discussion but was encouraged to stay and meet Verlaine.

The poet was never to forget that moment as Mathilde Mauté, a brunette wearing a frilled dress of grey and green ('En robe grise et verte, avec des ruches' as we discover in one of the poems in *La Bonne chanson* not set to music), entered the room. It seems that Sivry had already discussed the poet with his family (including Mathilde, his half-sister) and that he had shown them Verlaine's work. Mathilde was not (and was never to be) interested in literature, but she made some charmingly complimentary remarks. This meeting was a *coup de foudre* for Verlaine. This young girl of sixteen seemed to look at him with a preternatural understanding and sympathy; he did not feel judged by her, she was too inexperienced, and too protected by her parents, to have absorbed the cynicism that he would have encountered in more worldly women. She seemed unperturbed by his unusual looks, and able to see into the depths of his soul.

She too was greatly affected by the hour she spent with Verlaine. She was a cosseted, rather uneducated girl, but she was clearly no fool. Her half-brother too must have vaunted Verlaine's prospects before his arrival in the house. Her mother was a fine musician, a piano teacher (an erstwhile pupil of Chopin, who numbered the young Debussy among her pupils) and a woman who, when her own daughter's marriage deteriorated, was intelligent enough to understand Verlaine's crises beyond any reasonable expectation (thus earning the poet's enduring gratitude). Madame Mauté enjoyed proximity to men who were talented and creative.

Her mother's admiration for artists in general might have influenced Mathilde in Verlaine's favour. She was of an age at which she was looking for a husband, but there was no need to hurry. In her indulgent parents' house she wanted for nothing, and she felt no pressure to leave the rue Nicolet. She was in a position to hope for the hand of a comfortably middle-class husband with a good income. Verlaine was by no means rich, but this fact does not seem to have concerned her. The tragedy for this couple who never should have married was that Verlaine's fantasy, and his belief that this meeting was somehow pre-ordained, was unaccountably matched by similar feelings on the part of Mathilde. Although she was never to lose her head (in the manner of a good middle-class girl she resisted Verlaine's pre-marital impatience), it seems that she too had fallen in love at first sight.

Verlaine, *bouleversé* and needing to think about this unexpected turn of events, left Paris and went into the country. For a brief period he was also unable to touch his customary absinthe; he even made himself believe that the power of love had vanquished his need for drink. He wrote a long letter to Charles de Sivry almost demanding the hand of his half-sister, and completely forgot the role of Mathilde's parents in such a negotiation. This course of action makes us suspect, perhaps more than we should, a unconscious displacement of the poet's attraction to Sivry, and its transferral to his half-sister; certainly this is what happened when Saint-Saëns, only five years later, proposed marriage with a similar impulsiveness, and with unhappy results, to the sister of a good-looking young man of his acquaintance. In any case such a letter ignoring parental consent was a completely unconventional approach to the etiquette of courtship, but even this failed to ring alarm-bells with the Mauté family. Family approval was forthcoming for a number of reasons: the poet was employed in a good civil-service job and had some prospects; he was an only son and thus had a small family fortune of his own; the Mautés had two daughters, and the poet's willingness to take the hand of Mathilde 'sans dot' – without dowry – was a distinct advantage. Mother and daughter said a provisional 'yes', the whole question to be settled finally after their return from two months' holiday in Normandy.

The favourable reply from Sivry put Verlaine in a transport of happiness. At moments like this, it seems, he was more excited by the *idea* of Mathilde than by her physical presence. Rather than immediately rushing back to Paris to spend time in her company he mused on his wonderful good fortune and wrote poetry in her praise. He had never believed that someone so irreproachably pure, so *good*, could love him for himself. When he did go back to Paris, even his mother was not openly averse to the marriage, aware that her son badly needed stability in his life. In any case she had noticed a distinct improvement in his daily habits; he was obsessively careful not to make a drunken impression at the crucial interview that would confirm his suit. He corresponded with Mathilde in Normandy (his letters were ardent and humorous and included some of his latest lyrics) and he even discussed by letter various details concerning the future with Madame Mauté, such as the situation and furnishing of the marital apartment.

When the Mautés returned to Paris the poet, dressed up in his smartest attire, was formally received by the family. On this occasion he had to broach Monsieur Mauté himself, who is brilliantly, if unsympathetically, described by Lepelletier: 'an ex-notary with the ruddy face and shrewd air of a countryman grown rich, kind-hearted in reality, but with a keen eye to his own interests, and the unintellectuality and the suspicion of a business man'.[9] The preparations for the marriage were set in motion. Verlaine dutifully absented himself from his friends and drinking companions, and was to be found every evening paying court at the rue Nicolet.

During this time the ardent verses of *La Bonne chanson* were written, and many more of them than the twenty-one that eventually appeared in the published collection.[10] There had originally been a number of much racier and more passionate poems that were suppressed by the poet. This is a pity, and he himself later came to regret the puritan aspect of this decision. If Verlaine's infatuation had occasionally seemed to his readers more red-blooded and physical, less head-in-the-clouds and idealistic, it might have changed posterity's one-sided perspective on the unrealistic nature of the poet's relationship with Mathilde. The emotions he felt for her certainly did include physical desire; awareness of Verlaine's homosexuality, that other side of his bisexual nature, has often roused readers to cynical disbelief with regard to the sincerity of these verses. But what Lepelletier says is true: 'La Bonne chanson is a transition from objective, descriptive, plastic verse [as in Fêtes galantes, for example] to personal expression, the soul's confession.'[11]

The courtship in real life was protracted and dogged with difficulties caused by outside circumstances. The marriage date was postponed on several occasions, once because Mathilde had chickenpox, and again when Madame Mauté was ill. In July 1870 the poet dedicated La Bonne chanson to his fiancée, whom he was later to describe (in Romances sans paroles) less than charitably as a 'child wife'. By then he had forgotten that in La Bonne chanson he had briefly seen himself reborn as a new man. The poems glow with Verlaine's optimism and high-flown belief that his darker side could be obliterated by the healing power of transcendental love.

By a stroke of bad luck the marriage was set for August 1870, just when the German forces, as it turned out, were advancing on Paris. Verlaine, twenty-six years old, was called up to military service with other bachelors of his year; one of his closest friends committed suicide rather than report for duty. The poet was persuaded by his future in-laws to ignore the call-up. Nevertheless, the nuptial ceremony at the town hall of Montmartre and Notre-Dame-de-Clignancourt took place against a background of bloodshed and cannon-fire, a sinister omen. It is an extraordinary thought that had Fauré stayed in Paris that summer (instead of fleeing the Commune and taking refuge in Switzerland) he might have found himself the organist at Verlaine's wedding.

La Bonne chanson was printed in a very small edition by Lemerre in December 1870. Victor Hugo, no less, recently returned from exile, greeted the cycle as 'a bouquet in a cannon shell'. This no doubt referred to the appearance of the poems during the German bombardment of Paris, but the great old poet may well have had some inkling of the highly-strung, even explosive nature of the creator, and of an idyll where the expression of happiness sometimes strikes a jarringly desperate note. Mathilde is scarcely seen as a real woman; she is a magical force, the idealised Madonna, an answer to the prayers of a man hitherto plagued by his demons.

Both Lepelletier and Mathilde Verlaine, in a book she wrote in 1907 (Mémoires de ma vie), made a case for the depth and veracity of the poet's romantic feelings for his fiancée. Posterity has judged differently: the writing of the poems has been largely seen as part of a wish-fulfilment fantasy. Whether or not Robert Orledge is correct to observe that 'the predominantly homosexual Verlaine put more genuine passion into La Bonne chanson than he ever found for Mathilde', there is no doubt that this is how it has seemed to later generations.[12] By the time Fauré came to set these texts, the tragic outcome was already an outdated scandal and literary history. We know that Verlaine failed to suppress his drunkenness and his inclination to violent rages; less than two years after the publication of the poems he left his wife and baby and went off, as we have seen, with the teenage poet, Arthur Rimbaud, with whom he was besotted. This was his farewell to a life of respectability, and the beginning of a long downhill spiral into vagabondage and destitution.

ॐ   ॐ   ॐ   ॐ

225

Below are listed the poems from *La Bonne chanson* that Fauré set, together with the names of some of the other composers who have tackled the same poems.

No. IV [2 in Fauré's cycle] 'Puisque l'aube grandit'

No. V [6 in Fauré's cycle] 'Avant que tu ne t'en ailles. There are some fifteen settings of this lyric, including one by Frederick Delius.

No. VI [3 in Fauré's cycle] 'La lune blanche' [Massenet (as *Rêvons, c'est l'heure*), Ernest Chausson, Ange Flégier (both as *Apaisement*), Reynaldo Hahn, Poldowski (both as *L'Heure exquise*)]. There are some 130 settings of this poem.

No. VIII [1 in Fauré's cycle] 'Une Sainte en son auréole'. Fauré seems to have been the only composer to set this to music.

No. XV [5 in Fauré's cycle] 'J'ai presque peur, en vérité'

No. XVII [8 in Fauré's cycle] 'N'est-ce-pas?' [also set by Charles Koechlin]

No. XIX [7 in Fauré's cycle] 'Donc, ce sera par un clair jour d'été [also set by Reynaldo Hahn as *Tous deux* in his *Chansons grises*]

No. XX [4 in Fauré's cycle] 'J'allais par des chemins perfides' [Charles Bordes as *La Bonne chanson*]

No. XXI [9 in Fauré's cycle] 'L'hiver a cessé'

Charles Koechlin also set of this cycle No. I 'Le Soleil de matin', No. III 'Une robe grise et verte' (as *Un jour de juin*) and No. XII 'Va, chanson'. Charles Bordes set No. I 'Le Soleil de matin' (as *Promenade matinale*), and Reynaldo Hahn set No. XI 'La dure épreuve va finir' (as *La Bonne chanson*).

Fauré set nine of the twenty-one poems; with the exception of the beginning of *J'allais par des chemins perfides* he avoided lyrics that expressed doubt or anguish. He paid no attention whatever to the poet's ordering, apart from choosing to end his cycle with Verlaine's final poem. As we can see above, Fauré selected Nos IV, V, VI, VIII, XV, XVII, XIX, XX and XXI from Verlaine's cycle. These were reshuffled into a new order as far as the song cycle Op. 61 was concerned: VIII, IV, VI, XX, XV, V, XIX, XVII, XXI. As we have already seen, the first eight songs were composed in 1892 and 1893; the last was not ready until February 1894.

The complexity of *La Bonne chanson* won Fauré few friends in the short term; his old teacher Saint-Saëns was no less than horrified by its wilful complexity. The main criticism concerned

PAUL VERLAINE

LA

BONNE CHANSON

PARIS

LÉON VANIER, LIBRAIRE-ÉDITEUR

19, QUAI SAINT-MICHEL, 19

1891

Tous droits réservés.

Title-page of the 1891 edition of Verlaine's La Bonne chanson what other people termed the incessant modulations, which Fauré regarded merely as adventurous harmonic colourings. Fauré had always tended to revel in his mastery of harmony but, as Nectoux observes: 'Harmonic instability in *La Bonne chanson* reaches a pitch rarely equalled in Fauré's output. Tonality is undermined by tortuous chromaticism so that at times … a sense of key is almost obliterated.'[13] Camille Bellaigue, in a review of October 1897, complained that 'all the sonorous elements appear in contradiction: the voice with the accompaniment … the chords with each other, and the notes of the vocal part amongst themselves.'[14] Proust, noting that he was in disagreement with Debussy's own low estimate of Fauré's new cycle, wrote: 'The young musicians are almost unanimous in disliking *La Bonne chanson*. It appears that it is needlessly complex … but I don't care, I adore it.'[15] It appears possible, if we are to believe Emma, that even Debussy softened in his attitude to the work much later, towards the end of his life, when working on it with his wife – the cycle's dedicatee.

Proust's remarkably astute view was to prevail with Fauré enthusiasts, but as Orledge remarks of critics like Bellaigue, and for many members of the public, Fauré's 'good' *chansons* were his old *chansons*, not this new cycle.[16] Indeed, the work remains inaccessible to many an admirer of the earlier Fauré; it is often the performers, rather than the audiences, who emerge from the concert hall singing the cycle's praises: it seems that the enthusiasm which lights up the singer and pianist in mastering this work generates more heat 'à deux', between the performers themselves, than can often be found in the auditorium. Fauré is usually considered to be rather self-effacing; when he flexes his musical muscles, as in this cycle, many a listener is disconcerted by the resulting creative exuberance. At the instigation of a wealthy patron of the arts, Frank Schuster (see Chapter 11), the cycle was arranged with a string quintet and piano accompaniment for a performance in London in 1898, a version that Fauré disliked and came to regard as pointless. As with the orchestrated songs of Duparc and Wolf, in *La Bonne chanson* the listener finds the silken effect of string accompaniment (admittedly effective in some of the songs, the first for example) no match for the more percussive energy of piano sonorities.

There are five main themes in the cycle, noted by both Jankélévitch and Orledge: the 'Carlovingien' theme A, first heard in No. 1, bars 15 to 16 and 79 to 80 (Example 9.1):

Example 9.1

the 'Lydia' theme B, named after the melody of the song *Lydia*, heard most plainly in No. 3, bars 9 to 12 (Example 9.2):

Example 9.2

the 'Que je vous aime' theme C, first heard attached to those very words in No. 5, bars 65 to 69 (Example 9.3):

Example 9.3

D, the pair of jauntily dotted figurations at the *Allegro moderato* of No. 6 (bars 8 to 9) that introduce the singing quails (Example 9.4):

Example 9.4

and E, the 'Sunrise' theme (first heard in No. 6, bars 72 to 73), denoting the power of nature (Example 9.5):

Example 9.5

The deployment of these motifs in different songs is the musical glue that gives this work its astonishing cohesion, as well as an obsessive, almost disturbing, single-mindedness. However, when Fauré was interviewed in 1903 by Louis Aguettant regarding these various motifs the composer would at first only acknowledge the presence of the 'Lydia' theme in the work. Aguettant took Fauré over to the piano and showed him the other motifs in the score. Of course the composer could not deny their presence, but his nonplussed reaction tells us that unless he was extremely forgetful these links of compositional unity had been employed unconsciously, and forged in the heat of creative inspiration. Benjamin Britten once remarked that until he had read an analytical article by Hans Keller he had no idea of how 'clever' he had been in composing the opera *Billy Budd* – an exceptionally integrated work bound together by motival cross-references.

La Bonne chanson[17]
1892–94, Op. 61, 'À Mme Sigismond Bardac', Hamelle, 1894

(59) (i) *Une Sainte en son auréole* (*A saint in her halo*)
17 September 1892, Op. 61 No. 1, A♭ major, 3/4, *Allegretto con moto*

Une Sainte en son auréole,	*A Saint in her halo,*
Une Châtelaine en sa tour,	*A Chatelaine in her tower,*
Tout ce que contient la parole	*All that human words contain*
Humaine de grâce et d'amour;	*Of grace and love;*
La note d'or que fait entendre	*The golden note of a horn*
Un cor dans le lointain des bois,	*In forests far away,*
Mariée à la fierté tendre	*Blended with the tender pride*
Des nobles Dames d'autrefois;	*Of noble Ladies of long ago;*

Avec cela le charme insigne	*And then – the rare charm*
D'un frais sourire triomphant	*Of a fresh, triumphant smile,*
Eclos dans des candeurs de cygne	*Flowering in swan-like innocence*
Et des rougeurs de femme-enfant;	*And the blushes of a child-bride;*
Des aspects nacrés, blancs et roses,	*A nacreous sheen of white and pink,*
Un doux accord patricien:	*A sweet patrician harmony –*
Je vois, j'entends toutes ces choses	*All these things I see and hear*
Dans son nom Carlovingien.	*In her Carolingian name.*

We begin with a portrait of the beloved, a 'Châtelaine en sa tour', the poet's fiancée Mathilde presented here as a saint with a halo (and on a pedestal), an image suggested by her 'Carlovingien' name, which evokes the age of Charlemagne. Fauré's usual time-travelling music often suggests the seventeenth-century madrigal, or the eighteenth-century *fêtes galantes* of Versailles, but here his part-writing and counterpoint imitate the rigorous devotion of a medieval motet – somewhat 'archaïsant', as Suckling puts it – without sacrificing a jot of his own style or sound-world. One remembers the contemporary passion for 'Art nouveau', but this 'demoiselle élue' could also be a pre-Raphaelite beauty were it not for a certain rigour and spareness in the texture that eschews pre-Raphaelite voluptuousness. The music has a firmness that discourages sentimentality; Fauré understands that the function of this chatelaine is to improve her husband, as well as to motivate and inspire him – a kind of purity by example. The entire song breathes an air of seraphic calm despite a tempo that moves forward with implacable assurance – as if to say 'this is ordained'. There is some word-painting: a D♭ concealed in the accompaniment (with the following F♭

Title-page of La Bonne chanson, *published by Hamelle*

a minor third above) mournfully suggests the 'golden note' of the horn in the distant forest. This unexpected touch from a composer who usually refrains from such illustrative details reminds us of works by Debussy as yet uncomposed – the Verlaine setting *Le Son du cor*, and Golaud's horn-call in the prelude to *Pelléas et Mélisande*.

The curvaceous characteristics of theme A are to be heard traced in the introduction to the song, and in many a bar of the piano writing, but the actual theme appears for the first time only at bar 15 (just before 'de grâce et d'amour'; Example 5.1); Jankélévitch refers to this six-crotchet motif as being 'as pure and lily-like as the neck of a woman'. This 'Carlovingien' theme reappears three times in the song's last two lines; we will hear it again in Nos 3, 4, 5, 6 and 9 of the cycle.

Parenthetical mention should be made here of a much later work for solo harp, *Une châtelaine en sa tour*, Op. 110 (1918), which takes its name from the poem set to music here by Fauré, and which has what might be termed a 'Verlainian' atmosphere. The music, in triple time with an element of canonic repetition, is like a distant reminiscence of the opening number of *La Bonne chanson*. It was composed for the young harpist Micheline Kahn, who had been a member of Alphonse Hasselman's class at the Conservatoire (we shall hear a great deal more of this surname in later chapters). From the faintly flirtatious tone of his correspondence with Micheline Kahn there is no doubt that the composer found his dedicatee both personally charming and musically dedicated. She transcribed several other pieces for harp with Fauré's blessing.

(60) (ii) *Puisque l'aube grandit* (*Since day is breaking*)
1893, Op. 61 No. 2, G major, **c**, *Allegro*

Puisque l'aube grandit, puisque voici l'aurore,	*Since day is breaking, since dawn is here,*
Puisque, après m'avoir fui longtemps, l'espoir veut bien	*Since hope, having long eluded me, would now*
Revoler devers moi qui l'appelle et l'implore,	*Return to me and my imploring,*
Puisque tout ce bonheur veut bien être le mien,	*Since all this happiness will truly be mine,*
Je veux, guidé par vous, beaux yeux aux flammes douces,	*I shall, guided by your fair eyes' gentle glow,*
Par toi conduit, ô main où tremblera ma main,	*Led by your hand in which I place my trembling hand,*
Marcher droit, que ce soit par des sentiers de mousses	*Walk straight ahead, on mossy paths*
Ou que rocs et cailloux encombrent le chemin;	*Or boulder-strewn and stony tracks;*
Et comme, pour bercer les lenteurs de la route,	*And while, to ease the journey's languid pace,*
Je chanterai des airs ingénus, je me dis	*I shall sing some simple airs, I tell myself*
Qu'elle m'écoutera sans déplaisir sans doute;	*That she will surely hear me without displeasure;*
Et vraiment je ne veux pas d'autre Paradis.	*And truly I crave no other paradise.*

A song about the birth of love, this music is the first of several explosions of joy in this cycle. Fauré is better known as a famous master of the nocturne, a painter of the *demi-jour* and of emotions *en sourdine*, but here he greets the dawn with undisguised happiness – and not for the first time in his songs. The melisma on the word 'l'aurore' (bar 4) is one of the most open-hearted phrases in all his *mélodies*, and its energy seems to light up an entire landscape. (Incorporated in this vigorous phrase for the voice is a hidden appearance of motif B – the 'Lydia' theme.) This exuberance, to be found also in three further songs of the cycle, is a rare aspect of Fauré's song writing. The accompaniment consists of incessantly changing semiquaver sextuplets, rolling between the hands and exploring every nook and cranny of harmonic well-being with implacable curiosity. There is even an opportunity in bars 24–5 for a subtle musical quotation inspired by the word 'mousse', placed there, one feels, to make Emma Bardac smile in acknowledging that she was now the composer's beloved 'Leïlah': the seven notes of the phrase 'par des sentiers de mousse' are an exact quotation from *Les Roses d'Ispahan* (bars 9–10), where Leconte de Lisle's words are 'dans leur gaine de mousse'.

230

Fauré ruthlessly cuts Verlaine's references to 'funestes pensées' or 'rancune abominable' in this long poem and sets only strophes 1, 5 and 7 of the original text. The third of these (the final musical verse) initiates a change of note-values rather than tempo – sextuplets are replaced by triplets, and the vocal line becomes more expansive without any sense of rallentando. All this leads towards the radiant fervour of the crowning and concluding phrase 'je ne veux pas d'autre Paradis'. The whole of this strophe is in fact a coda, the first of several in the cycle where, instead of allowing the piano to sign off in the manner of a Schumann cycle, Fauré invents a new concept – that of the vocal postlude where both voice and piano participate together in the envoi, as if they were one united instrument.

(61) (iii) *La Lune blanche* (*The white moon*)
20 July 1893, Op. 61 No. 3, F♯ major, 9/8, *Andantino*

La lune blanche	*The white moon*
Luit dans les bois;	*Gleams in the woods;*
De chaque branche	*From every branch*
Part une voix	*There comes a voice*
Sous la ramée …	*Beneath the boughs …*
Ô bien-aimée.	*O my beloved.*
L'étang reflète,	*The pool reflects,*
Profond miroir,	*Deep mirror,*
La silhouette	*The silhouette*
Du saule noir	*Of the black willow*
Où le vent pleure …	*Where the wind is weeping …*
Rêvons, c'est l'heure.	*Let us dream, it is the hour.*
Un vaste et tendre	*A vast and tender*
Apaisement	*Consolation*
Semble descendre	*Seems to fall*
Du firmament	*From the sky*
Que l'astre irise …	*The moon illumines …*
C'est l'heure exquise.	*Exquisite hour.*

This lyric was the first of Verlaine's to be set by any composer of note – by Massenet in his duet *Rêvons, c'est l'heure* (1872). Many years later Massenet's pupil Reynaldo Hahn composed another setting as part of his *Chansons grises* – the celebrated *L'Heure exquise*. That languid little miniature could not be more different from the purposeful unfolding of Fauré's evocation densely packed with flowing triplets and ceaseless harmonic activity. As befits a nocturne following the joyful *aubade* of the cycle's second song, the mood is gentle, but this music is far from somnolent or retiring. The climax at 'Ô bien-aimée' reaches an unashamed *forte*. Just before this, under the phrase 'Sous la ramée …', we hear the unwinding coil of motif B (the 'Lydia' theme; see Example 9.2) in the piano. In the Leconte de Lisle song *Lydia* this music had depicted a shy Greek beauty; here the music, by the composer's own admission, is associated with the cycle's dedicatee, Emma Bardac – someone like Lydia from whom 'delights without number' flow – as Leconte de Lisle's poem has it.

The deep mirror of the pool glints with the colours of many different changing harmonies, and the passage beginning 'Rêvons, c'est l'heure' is accompanied by a kaleidoscope of sound. The pianist must convey a sense of restful ease throughout: he or she should never allow the crotchet–quaver groupings of the right-hand triplets to bounce rather than float; no matter how wide the stretch, or awkward the fingering, this accompaniment must remain smooth and relaxed – which is no excuse to slacken the tempo. The setting of the poem's third strophe is another vocal postlude (with another appearance of the 'Lydia' theme). This sets up the final phrase, 'C'est l'heure exquise', initiated by the jump of an octave in the vocal line. This ravishing benediction is marked *dolcissimo* and is one of Fauré's most exquisite moments (an effect that will be recapitulated on the cycle's closing page). The song's valedictory bars are enriched by a succession of ascending scales (derived from the same 'Lydia' motif) in the accompaniment, a musical metaphor for reflection and thus a mirror-image of the 'Apaisement' that seems to fall gently from the sky. These limpid quavers rise delicately through both staves of the piano-writing, like incense wafting upwards into the still night air. Listeners attuned to the perfection of this music are lost in these fragrant, spiralling shifts of harmony, and yield, like the lovers who people Verlaine's poems, to the preternatural calm of a cherished exquisite hour. This is Fauré's only song in F♯ major, a tonality we associate with the seductive *Ballade* for piano and orchestra.

(62) (iv) *J'allais par des chemins perfides* (*I walked along treacherous ways*)
1892, Op. 61 No. 4, F♯ minor, 3/4, *Allegretto quasi andante*

J'allais par des chemins perfides,	*I walked along treacherous ways,*
Douloureusement incertain.	*Painfully uncertain.*
Vos chères mains furent mes guides.	*Your dear hands guided me.*
Si pâle à l'horizon lointain	*So pale on the far horizon*
Luisait un faible espoir d'aurore;	*A faint hope of dawn was gleaming;*
Votre regard fut le matin.	*Your gaze was the morning.*
Nul bruit, sinon son pas sonore,	*No sound, save his own footfall,*
N'encourageait le voyageur.	*Encouraged the traveller.*
Votre voix me dit: 'Marche encore!'	*Your voice said: 'Walk on!'*
Mon cœur craintif, mon sombre cœur	*My fearful heart, my sombre heart*
Pleurait, seul, sur la triste voie;	*Wept, lonely along the sad road;*
L'amour, délicieux vainqueur,	*Love, that charming conqueror,*
Nous a réunis dans la joie.	*Has united us in joy.*

The sudden change between the F♯ minor of this song and the F♯ major of *La Lune blanche* is dramatic and intentional. Just for once Fauré allows himself to set a poem that describes something of Verlaine's previous sorrows and predicaments; this permits the composer to depict how these doubts are triumphantly solved and removed in the second half of the song. These 'chemins perfides' are perfectly illustrated by the anguished harmonic tussle of the opening, where we are scarcely aware of the song's tonality. This is reminiscent of the tortured, self-castigating chromaticism of the religious songs from the more or less contemporary *Spanisches Liederbuch* by Hugo Wolf, and for a moment we are unexpectedly reminded of both composers' debt to the anguish of Amfortas in Wagner's *Parsifal*.

Redemption is close at hand. The upbeat to bar 13 introduces the upwardly spiralling quavers, derived from motif B, that have brought the previous song to a close. Above these we hear the words 'Vos chères mains furent mes guides'. This consolatory music does battle with the poet's darker thoughts and his 'cœur craintif'; the accompaniment achieves its musical contrast by switching between tortured crotchet chords turning in on themselves (as if the poet were pacing in a prison cell) and the flow of a quaver accompaniment that betokens freedom from such introspection. A double bar announces a change of key into the major tonality, and a change of tempo (*un poco più mosso*). The music is suddenly suffused with motif A, as if the 'Carlovingien' girl stands before the poet as the personification of love. It is a magical moment. This melody is traced by the pianist's right hand while the left hand ascends seraphically in various permutations derived from motif B. The unification of the two lovers (and the unification of these two themes) is crowned by the sudden appearance of triplets, like a pulse quickening in ardour, under the melisma on the final word, 'joie'.

(63) (v) *J'ai presque peur, en vérité* (In truth, I am almost afraid)
4 December 1893, Op. 61 No. 5, E minor, c, Allegro molto

J'ai presque peur, en vérité,	*In truth, I am almost afraid,*
Tant je sens ma vie enlacée	*So much do I feel my life bound up*
À la radieuse pensée	*With the radiant thoughts*
Qui m'a pris l'âme l'autre été,	*That captured my soul last summer,*
Tant votre image, à jamais chère,	*So deeply does your ever-dear image*
Habite en ce cœur tout à vous,	*Inhabit this heart that is wholly yours,*
Ce cœur uniquement jaloux	*This heart, whose sole desire*
De vous aimer et de vous plaire;	*Is to love you and please you;*
Et je tremble, pardonnez-moi	*And I tremble, forgive me*
D'aussi franchement vous le dire,	*For telling you so frankly,*
À penser qu'un mot, qu'un sourire	*To think that one word, one smile*
De vous est désormais ma loi,	*From you is henceforth law to me,*
Et qu'il vous suffirait d'un geste,	*And that one gesture would suffice,*
D'une parole ou d'un clin d'œil,	*One word, one single glance,*
Pour mettre tout mon être en deuil	*To plunge my whole being in mourning*
De son illusion céleste.	*From its heavenly illusion.*

Mais plutôt je ne veux vous voir,	*But I would sooner not see you –*
L'avenir dût-il m'être sombre	*However dark the future might be*
Et fécond en peines sans nombre,	*And full of untold grief –*
Qu'à travers un immense espoir,	*Could I not, through an immense hope,*
Plongé dans ce bonheur suprême	*Immersed in this supreme happiness,*
De me dire encore et toujours,	*Repeat to myself again and again,*
En dépit des mornes retours,	*Despite bleak reversals,*
Que je vous aime, que je t'aime!	*That I love you, I love thee!*

This is the fastest song of the cycle and it admirably conveys the panic of the lover who both fears and longs for commitment; the song ends with the reassurance he finds in his fiancée. As in the previous number, a negative state of mind is set up in order to be knocked down by the composer's mastery of musical contrast. The conversational and confessional tone of the poem ('pardonnez-moi / D'aussi franchement vous le dire'), something that Fauré usually avoids, is remarkably captured, especially considering the speed of the music and the rapid progress of the text across the singer's lips. The breathless accompaniment is anchored by two left-hand minims per bar with palpitating quavers marked mezzo-staccato off the beat. The falling figure in the piano writing in bars 10 to 12 (after the words 'l'autre été') is derived from motif A. Underneath the lines 'Ce cœur uniquement jaloux / De vous aimer et de vous plaire' the piano's left hand introduces a clear quotation of motif B for three bars. The effect is to allow a ray of Lydian sunlight into a darkened room.

The poet worries that his well-being is so dependent on every glance and gesture of his beloved. In response to the words 'son illusion céleste' the music moves from the minor key to the major and provides just that celestial illusion in musical terms. The key words in this remarkable passage are 'Plongé dans ce bonheur suprême': the effect of this music is for the listener to feel bathed in light and suspended in a state of happiness. The poem may talk about 'a dark future' or 'untold grief' at this point, but these images are subsumed in music that cradles the singer as if he or she were float-ing and contained within the safety of the womb. At this point the song treads water in a daze of joy; the listener is content simply to enjoy the singer's state of grace.

Breaking free from this stasis after some twenty bars, the poet initiates a new phase in his relation-ship – the change from the formal 'vous' to 'tu' in addressing his beloved. The manly virility of 'Que je vous aime' is a gallant marvel; this upward arpeggio is motif C (Example 9.3), which we will hear again in the cycle's three last songs. Even more breathtaking is the follow-up 'que je t'aime'. The music for this, at first intimate and vulnerable (marked *senza rall.* in the score), seems to gather courage as the phrase develops. Reaching the home key is like a ship coming safely home to port against all expectations. In these contrasting phrases we have heard the progress of a relationship into a new sphere of intimacy.

It is a curious footnote concerning musical taste that Francis Poulenc, a composer who admitted to finding much of Fauré's music physically intolerable, found that the modulation on 'Que je vous aime' was one that particularly pained him. This transition is admittedly somewhat convoluted. But what seems merely rich and ingenious to some is indigestible to others, and it reminds us that this cycle in particular among Fauré's *mélodies* has always had its detractors.

(64) (vi) *Avant que tu ne t'en ailles* (*Before you fade*)
1892, Op. 61 No. 6, D♭ major, 3/4, *Quasi adagio* – 2/4, *Allegro moderato*

Avant que tu ne t'en ailles,	*Before you fade,*
Pâle étoile du matin,	*Pale morning star,*
– Mille cailles	* – A thousand quail*
Chantent, chantent dans le thym. –	*Are singing, singing in the thyme. –*
Tourne devers le poète,	*Turn to the poet*
Dont les yeux sont pleins d'amour,	*Whose eyes are full of love,*
– L'alouette	* – The lark*
Monte au ciel avec le jour. –	*Soars heavenward with the day. –*
Tourne ton regard que noie	*Turn your gaze drowned*
L'aurore dans son azur;	*In the blue of dawn;*
– Quelle joie	* – What delight*
Parmi les champs de blé mûr! –	*Among the fields of ripened corn! –*
Puis fais luire ma pensée	*And make my thoughts gleam*
Là-bas, – bien loin, oh! bien loin!	*Yonder, far, ah far away!*
– La rosée	* – The dew*
Gaîment brille sur le foin. –	*Glints brightly on the hay. –*
Dans le doux rêve où s'agite	*Into the sweet dream where still asleep*
Ma mie endormie encor …	*My love is stirring …*
– Vite, vite,	* – Make haste, make haste,*
Car voici le soleil d'or. –	*For here's the golden sun. –*

The poet has created a new form here, and, in switching back and forth between two contrasting tempi, the composer follows suit. Two poems are superimposed on each other and dove-tailed into one: if the reader chooses one of the two sets of couplets (and ignores the other) both poems make perfect, and separate, sense. The sudden musical changes instigated by Fauré acknowledge and highlight a poetic duality that is later encountered in some of Poulenc's Apollinaire settings.

This is another *aubade*, but the energy is more contained than in the cycle's second number, at least at the outset. The song begins as music of the half-light, the point when night yields to day; the stillness that precedes the birds' dawn chorus is admirably conveyed in the song's first seven *Adagio* bars. There is as yet no warmth in the dawn, and there are no sounds of life. Not for the first time in this cycle one thinks of Hugo Wolf: a contemporary lied from the *Italienisches Liederbuch* comes to mind – 'Schon streckt' ich aus im Bett die müden Glieder', which also describes the repose (and dreams of the beloved) that precede a burst of energetic activity.

Suddenly everything changes: the key signature, the time signature and the tempo marking (a contrasting *Allegro moderato*). The effect is of two songs cohabiting within one musical structure where the pianist is like a computer operator, switching between two programmes on a single screen simply by touching the keyboard (although simply to touch the keyboard is clearly not enough for the pianist in a fiendishly difficult song such as this). Tight dotted rhythms high in the treble, and the whirring wings of left-hand triplets, denote the singing of the quail, or rather thousands of these small birds. It is the twittering of their song that prophesies the victory of the light, and this pair of dotted figurations is motif D of the cycle (Example 9.4), set to return even more triumphantly in the cycle's last song. It is too early in the day, however, for the dark to have renounced its hold entirely on the poet's spirit; the accompaniment plunges from the heights of the keyboard and returns to the regions of the opening *Quasi adagio*.

After six bars of introspective music there is once again a change of key and metre, and once again this leads to avian exultation: the lark soars high in the heavens until it swoops downwards, following the path of the pianist's hands across the keyboard. This music, superbly descriptive of both the sound of a singing bird and the trajectory of its flight, takes wing in an elemental way that is unique in Fauré's *mélodies*; but we have not yet reached the apogee of excitement that we will experience in this music. There is a third *Adagio* passage, and another switch to *Allegro moderato*, this time a paean to the beauty of the sunlight on the cornfields. After mention of 'les champs de blé mûr' the return to the coolness of the morning star that we have come to expect does not materialise. Instead the music begins to broaden towards a sumptuous sunrise, although the composer makes us wait for the climactic moment. For the first time in the song we feel the resonance of the bass clef, in triplets, adding a new warmth to music that mirrors a wonder of nature. For the glistening of the dew the piano's left hand quickens into a semiquaver accompaniment; in the right hand there are glinting off-beat accents. There is another key change, and now it is as if all nature is singing. The sudden *pianissimo* intimacy of 'Dans le doux rêve' is a case of 'reculer pour mieux sauter'. Thoughts of the beloved prompt a trace of the 'Carlovingien' motif A (Example 9.1). In the song's remaining twelve bars, Fauré masterfully builds the tension so that we feel the dazzling impact of the sun's golden rays at their most potent on the word 'd'or', the climax (and last note) of the vocal line. The triumphant piano phrase that accompanies this image of sunrise is the last of the cycle's five motifs, E (Example 9.5). This is surely one of the grandest, and most diverse, of all French *mélodies*.

(65) (vii) *Donc, ce sera par un clair jour d'été* (So, on a bright summer day it shall be)
9 August 1892, Op. 61 No. 7, B♭ major, **c**, *Allegro non troppo* – 9/8, *Molto più lento*

Donc, ce sera par un clair jour d'été:	*So, on a bright summer day it shall be:*
Le grand soleil, complice de ma joie,	*The glorious sun, my partner in joy,*
Fera, parmi le satin et la soie,	*Shall make, amid the satin and the silk,*
Plus belle encor votre chère beauté;	*Your dear beauty lovelier still;*
Le ciel tout bleu, comme une haute tente,	*The sky, all blue, like a tall canopy,*
Frissonnera somptueux à longs plis	*Shall quiver sumptuously in long folds*
Sur nos deux fronts qu'auront pâlis	*Above our two brows, grown pale*
L'émotion du bonheur et l'attente;	*With pleasure and expectancy;*
Et quand le soir viendra, l'air sera doux	*And when evening comes, the breeze shall be soft*
Qui se jouera, caressant, dans vos voiles,	*And play caressingly about your veils,*
Et les regards paisibles des étoiles	*And the peaceful stars looking down*
Bienveillamment souriront aux époux.	*Shall smile benevolently on man and wife.*

This song, with words that look forward to the poet's wedding day, was the first setting from *La Bonne chanson* that Fauré composed. It thus contains the musical seeds of much that is to be found reappearing elsewhere in the composer's masterly cycle. The tempo and impetus of the opening section are those of *Puisque l'aube grandit*. The 'grand soleil' mentioned in the song's first verse seems to be a natural sequel to the triumphant sunrise that has concluded the previous song. Accordingly it is no surprise that the motif that governs much of the music is E, the figuration that closes *Avant que tu ne t'en ailles*. The radiance, the iridescence, of this music was the key to the entire cycle – it was as if Fauré had suddenly unlocked a new reservoir of immense joy within himself and his creative personality; the music bristles with energy, sexual excitement, and a heightened sensual awareness of nature. The rushing sextuplets of the accompaniment die down gradually (via a 3/2 bar where semiquavers are grouped in fours rather than sixes), and the music becomes calm and nocturnal: a mood that harks back to *La Lune blanche* in terms of the cycle's order, but which actually looks *forward* to that song in terms of the sequence in which the music was composed.

The rising arpeggio motif on which the last two pages of this song's accompaniment is based comes from motif C (Example 9.3), last heard at the end of *J'ai presque peur, en vérité* to the words 'Que je vous aime'. The song ends in quiet rapture. Verlaine envisages the calm of the night following his marriage, but, true to the poet's suppression of the more risqué aspects of his creativity in 1870, the music suggests sacred exaltation rather than sexual bliss. The music gives us the impression that an idealised relationship has been solemnised and written in the stars. From Fauré's point of view it seems inconceivable that when he composed this music he thought of himself as being merely erotically attached to Emma Bardac; this is music of utter commitment, and in receiving it as her own, she could hardly have been blamed for believing that art would one day be reflected by life. As Claude Rostand says, these were the most burning words of love that the composer had ever proferred.[18] That this shining promise was never to be kept seems a poignant and unintentional link between the composer, living in a cocoon of happiness, and his haplessly idealistic poet.

(66) (viii) *N'est-ce pas?* (*Is it not so?*)
25 May 1893, Op. 61 No. 8, G major, 3/4, *Allegretto moderato*

N'est-ce pas? nous irons, gais et lents, dans la voie
Modeste que nous montre en souriant l'Espoir,
Peu soucieux qu'on nous ignore ou qu'on nous voie.

Is it not so? Happy and unhurried we'll follow
The modest path where Hope directs us with a smile,
Little caring if we are neither known nor seen.

Isolés dans l'amour ainsi qu'en un bois noir,
Nos deux cœurs, exhalant leur tendresse paisible,
Seront deux rossignols qui chantent dans le soir.

Isolated in love as in a dark wood,
Our two hearts, breathing gentle peace,
Shall be two nightingales singing at evening.

Sans nous préoccuper de ce que nous destine
Le Sort, nous marcherons pourtant du même pas,
Et la main dans la main, avec l'âme enfantine

With no thought of what Destiny
Has in store, we shall walk along together,
Hand in hand, our souls like those of children

De ceux qui s'aiment sans mélange, n'est-ce pas?

Whose love is unalloyed, is that not so?

This music is the building of castles in the air. In asking 'N'est-ce pas?' the poet seeks reassurance from the invisible fiancée that he is not deluding himself. He is of course doing precisely this, and Mathilde remains silent in the face of rhetorical questions. If there is any self-doubt expressed anywhere in this cycle, it is in this song (there is another insecure 'N'est-ce-pas?' phrase in the Verlaine poem that begins 'C'est l'extase …', towards the end, and set to music rather differently by Fauré and Debussy, the latter more desperately). The music has a simplicity and an intimacy that are very different from the grandeur of the cycle's joyful outbursts. The composer leaves out Verlaine's first strophe, which rails against the 'sots et méchants' who are the couple's enemies. Verlaine's fourth and fifth strophes are also omitted on account of imagery Fauré thought unsuitable for music.

The song's opening is accompanied by a simple little figure – a left-hand crotchet followed by three right-hand semiquavers. This is new to the cycle, yet unexceptional in comparison with some of Fauré's other pianistic ideas. In the interlude following this strophe, motif theme C ('Que je vous aime') makes the first of four increasingly passionate appearances in the accompaniment. After the second line of the second strophe (ending with the words 'tendresse paisible'), the 'Lydia' motif (B) is to be heard for four bars decorating the idea of the song of the two nightingales (a wonderful melisma on the word 'chantent' here). The third verse is accompanied by the same figuration as the opening, but motif C returns in the last eight bars of music; it entwines with the final 'n'est-ce pas?' Verlaine certainly imagines a reply in the affirmative from his equally deluded beloved – 'Yes, we *shall* be happy!' – and so does Fauré. After all, the composer had no obligation to make of this cycle an accurate depiction of Verlaine's biographical circumstances; instead he needed to reflect his happiness in his new relationship with Emma Bardac. In doing so he seems to have been living his life one day at a time, enjoying the passion while it lasted, and not scanning the more distant future with any interest.

Fauré's optimism was to prove just as misplaced as the poet's. As a father of two sons and wary of damage to his reputation, he would not contemplate divorce; for this reason alone his long-term relationship with Emma was just as doomed as Verlaine's with Mathilde.

(67) (ix) *L'Hiver a cessé* (*Winter is over*)
February 1894, Op. 61 No. 9, B♭ major, **c**, *Allegro*

L'hiver a cessé: la lumière est tiède	*Winter is over, the light is soft*
Et danse, du sol au firmament clair.	*And dances up from the earth to the clear sky.*
Il faut que le cœur le plus triste cède	*The saddest heart must surrender*
À l'immense joie éparse dans l'air.	*To the great joy that fills the air.*
J'ai depuis un an le printemps dans l'âme	*For a year I have had spring in my soul,*
Et le vert retour du doux floréal,	*And the green return of sweet May,*
Ainsi qu'une flamme entoure une flamme,	*Like flame encircling flame,*
Met de l'idéal sur mon idéal.	*Adds an ideal to my ideal.*
Le ciel bleu prolonge, exhausse et couronne	*The blue sky prolongs, heightens, and crowns*
L'immuable azur où rit mon amour.	*The steadfast azure where my love smiles.*
La saison est belle et ma part est bonne	*The season is fair and my lot is happy*
Et tous mes espoirs ont enfin leur tour.	*And all my hopes are at last fulfilled.*

Que vienne l'été! que viennent encore
L'automne et l'hiver! Et chaque saison
Me sera charmante, ô Toi que décore
Cette fantaisie et cette raison!

Let summer come! Let autumn
And winter come too! Each season
Will delight me, O you graced with
Imagination and good sense!

Paul Verlaine (1844–1896)

This remarkable song draws together all the threads of the cycle into a quasi-symphonic conclusion. This is a miniature 'rite of spring' that celebrates a cosmic pantheism prefiguring the profundities of *La Chanson d'Ève*. Jankélévitch refers to the build-up of this music as representing 'the great dizziness of spring'.[19] The introduction of seven and a half bars is one of Fauré's longest in a *mélodie*, and it is uniquely exciting. The first thing we hear is motif D, last heard in *Avant que tu ne t'en ailles*. Like a growing chorus of voices, or melting tributaries conjoining in a mighty river, what has begun as the call of the quail in the pianist's right hand (the 'thousand quail' described in the cycle's sixth song) gathers strength over four stirring bars into a grand reprise of motif E, the sunrise music first heard at the end of the same song. Both Beethoven and Schubert in their settings of Sauter's poem 'Der Wachtelschlag' ('The quail call') depicted this bird-song in a similar way, in punctiliously dotted rhythm.[20] Their pious quails sing in three notes repeated on the same pitch – as if they were saying 'Lobe Gott', or 'Praise to God'. Fauré's quails may be less religious, but they sing in exactly the same rhythm in a marvellously energised motif that incorporates a rising fourth.

After this extraordinary build-up, the way the voice part enters with the words 'L'hiver a cessé' is thrilling – rather like a surfer catching a wave to be carried triumphantly over the crest. In this strophe the ascending arpeggio to which the words 'du sol au firmament clair' are set is a variant of motif C. Fauré omits Verlaine's second strophe, which damns Paris as a 'sick' city. The song's second verse ('J'ai depuis un an') is set to new musical material, but very much in the manner of *Puisque l'aube grandit*; the swirling colours of this section are truly 'floréal'. This music elides into the third strophe; the ceaseless energy of the accompaniment has launched a heady vocal eloquence that builds into something more imposing than almost anything else in French song. With the words 'ma part est bonne' ('my lot is happy') we wonder whether the secret of the cycle's title has been revealed: Verlaine's 'good' love song for Mathilde is also the song of his fate. The end of this strophe signals a reappearance of the 'quail' theme (motif D) in the piano, underneath 'Que vienne l'été!' At 'Me sera charmante' the vocal line is fashioned from motif B, culminating in a glorious eight-note melisma on 'charmante' that conjoins with the piano into an explosive interrupted cadence.

After a moment of silence, what follows by way of epilogue (with a change to a slower tempo and triple metre) is a masterstroke: the words 'ô Toi' are set to the octave jump of 'C'est l'heure exquise' (in *La Lune blanche*). After 'décore', the piano quotes motif A in gently undulating 9/8 triplets, and we have come full circle to the music for Mathilde, the 'Châtelaine en sa tour'. This passage, beginning 'Cette fantaisie et cette raison!' (with yet another time change – to a benignly flowing 3/4, and semiquaver scales to accompany the caress of the last two words), is heartfelt while avoiding the bathos of self-conscious peroration. The head of steam worked up during this long song has now been gently diffused. The cycle ends with a postlude containing the same murmuring music (once again in triplets) that concluded *Donc, ce sera*.

ω   ω   ω   ω

With *La Bonne chanson* Fauré's song writing reached the apogee of its complexity. According to Claude Rostand, Ravel referred to the work as an 'incomparable symphonie … un vaste poème lyrique émouvant et parfait'.[21] The next stages of the composer's development represented a movement sideways rather than continuing in the same direction. There was a retreat from the bristling difficulties of the cycle. Never again would the composer's *mélodies* challenge the listener's ear in quite this way, and only in *La Chanson d'Ève* is there a return to cyclical cross-referencing, although on nothing like the same scale of complexity.

There is one more Verlaine setting, *Prison*, which was composed more or less as Fauré's farewell to a poet who had opened up new expressive vistas to him, and thus new avenues in his career. It is a brief but devastatingly moving pendant to *La Bonne chanson*, composed eight months after that cycle had been published. Perhaps the circumstances surrounding the poem's creation need to be briefly recapitulated.

∾   ∾   ∾   ∾

In the summer of 1873 the tension between those run-away lovers Rimbaud and Verlaine had reached breaking point. The pair had travelled backwards and forwards between London and Brussels. It was in the latter town on 10 July that the overwrought Verlaine wounded Rimbaud twice with a revolver, though not severely, and then, on the way to the station, seemed to threaten further violence. Rimbaud alerted a policeman who arrested Verlaine. The discovery on his person of a letter from Victor Hugo (offering to intercede with Verlaine's wife and help effect a reconciliation) impressed the police to treat the poet as something better than the vagabond he otherwise seemed to be. Verlaine was transferred to the Prison de Carmes, where he was given a cell to himself; he was allowed to exercise in a courtyard from where he could see a poplar tree and hear the murmuring sound of life on the outside. While awaiting trial Verlaine wrote the poem below, perhaps his most famous lyric.

He was tried in October, and sentenced to two years in prison. This was a harsh sentence, but in England, where the incident could just as easily have taken place, Verlaine might have been treated even more severely, not only because he was already thought by the police to be politically subversive, but because a quarrel of this kind between lovers of this ilk would probably have provided further excuse for punitive censure. The poet spent the whole of 1874 in custody in Mons prison; during that time he reconverted to Catholicism and received communion. He was released in January 1875, and a few months later he took up a position as a teacher in the remote village of Stickney, Lincolnshire – a prison of another kind.

(68) *Prison* (Prison)[22]
4 December 1894, Op. 83 No. 1, third Hamelle collection p. 61, E♭ minor, 3/4, *Quasi adagio*

Le ciel est, par-dessus le toit,
    Si bleu, si calme!
Un arbre, par-dessus le toit,
    Berce sa palme.

The sky above the roof –
    So blue, so calm!
A tree, above the roof,
    Waves its crown.

79

VI

Le ciel est, par dessus le toît,
Si bleu, si calme!
Un arbre, par dessus le toît,
Berce sa palme.

La cloche dans le ciel qu'on voit
Doucement tinte.
Un oiseau sur l'arbre qu'on voit
Chante sa plainte.

Mon Dieu, mon Dieu, la vie est là
Simple et tranquille.
Cette paisible rumeur là
Vient de la ville.

— Qu'as tu fait, ô toi que voilà
Pleurant sans cesse,
Dis, qu'as-tu fait, toi que voilà,
De ta jeunesse?

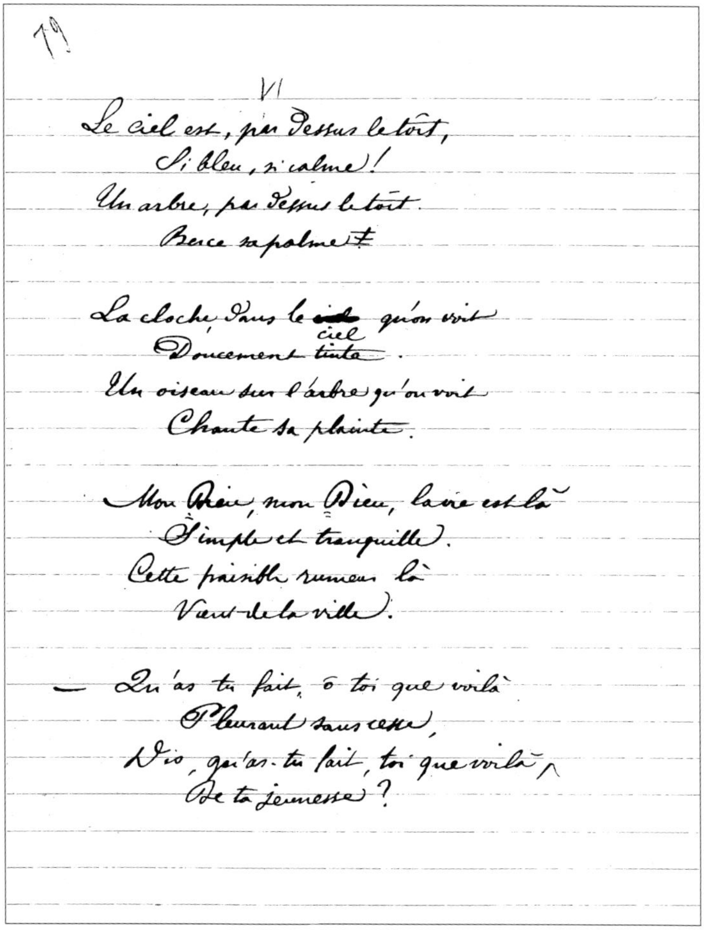

Verlaine's autograph for 'Prison'

La cloche, dans le ciel qu'on voit,
Doucement tinte.
Un oiseau sur l'arbre qu'on voit
Chante sa plainte.

Mon Dieu, mon Dieu, la vie est là,
Simple et tranquille.
Cette paisible rumeur-là
Vient de la ville.

— Qu'as-tu fait, ô toi que voilà
Pleurant sans cesse,
Dis, qu'as-tu fait, toi que voilà,
De ta jeunesse?

The bell, in the sky that you see,
Gently rings.
A bird, on the tree that you see,
Plaintively sings.

My God, my God, life is there,
Simple and serene.
That peaceful murmur out there
Comes from the town.

O you, what have you done,
Weeping without end,
Say, what have you done
With your young life?

Paul Verlaine (1844–1896)

The text for *Prison* – Fauré's pithy title allows the uninformed listener to place these words in context – appeared without heading in *Sagesse*, a collection of poetry published in 1881 under a Catholic imprint, evidence of Verlaine's chastened state of mind, albeit only temporary. (For a fuller discussion of *Sagesse* see Chapter 8.) The song is among Fauré's most powerful, and it is certainly his most concise. In that most melancholy of keys, E♭ minor, the clarity of the light, the muted poignancy of the chiming clock (in octaves on the third beats of bars 4, 7, 10 and 13), the enviable simplicity of life on the outside, the birdsong ruefully appreciated in the distance – all these things are depicted with rigorous economy. Writing eighteen years after the composition of *Prison*, the composer claimed that he was very proud of the two successive sevenths on 'La cloche' and 'doucement tinte'. At the time he wrote this song he regarded these as something new and daring.[23] In Fauré's setting the anguished middle section, beginning 'Mon Dieu, mon Dieu, la vie est là, / Simple et tranquille', is no appeal to a higher power, but the self-castigating outburst of a battle-scarred ne'er-do-well poet desperate to salvage something from what he now considered a wasted life.

The composer was a master of the religious miniature when he wished to be, but he chooses to ignore Verlaine the ecstatically devout, repentant sinner, who emerges, by way of contrast, in Déodat de Séverac's setting of this poem. The final lines of Fauré's song are accompanied by inexorably rising harmonic progressions on an E♭ pedal. This heartbreaking music signifies an evaporation of youthful hopes, the draining away of life's vital substance, the disappearance of good fortune over the distant horizon, but hardly religious penitence. Debussy had the good sense not to attempt a rival setting. Reynaldo Hahn's *D'une prison* has languid charm, but it suggests an idyllic sojourn on a desert island, or the luxurious incarceration available only to the wealthy in a South American banana republic.

In the ineluctable rhythmical impulse of Fauré's music, quiet and gentle though the opening is, we can somehow *hear* the bars of the prison cell inherent in the held rhythm, and we realise that the iron has entered the poet's soul. This is the music that Fauré composed as he contemplated his fiftieth birthday, his 'jeunesse' a thing of the past. What a different, chastened world this poem encompasses in comparison with the optimism of *La Bonne chanson*.

༄   ༄   ༄   ༄

The relationship between Fauré and Emma Bardac developed under the very nose of Marie Fauré and of Emma's husband Sigismund Bardac, a man with beetling eyebrows in his thirties whom the poet Albert Samain later described as 'charming, absolutely charming'. He would need to be it seems. As a boy on holiday with his parents and grandparents at Bougival, Emmanuel Fauré recalled performances of songs from *La Bonne chanson* by his father and Emma on warm summer evenings. Was the lad aware of any tension in the house? If Marie Fauré suffered paroxysms of jealousy, Fauré did not allow his wife's feelings to deter him. A psychiatrist may come to the conclusion that in conducting his affair with Emma at such close quarters the composer was punishing his mother for her neglect in the person of his wife; very occasionally one is permitted to glimpse in Fauré, that famous lover of women, the cruelty that is the inevitable counterpoint to Casanova's charming manner. Emma was outgoing, amusing, articulate, all the things that Marie was not. She also had great warmth and a mothering side to her personality that the composer would have found irresistible. Emma was ideally suited to be a creative man's muse and companion; she was an enthusiast for new music (unkind observers might have used the expression 'groupie' if it had been at their disposal); talented composers were her romantic weakness to such an extent that her indulgent husband even teased her about it. The Bardacs' son Raoul (1881–1950) later became a respected composer and

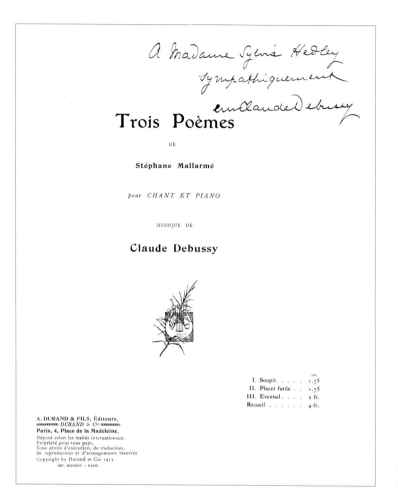

À Madame Sylvia Hedley
sympathiquement
emClaudeDebussy

Trois Poèmes

DE

Stéphane Mallarmé

pour CHANT ET PIANO

MUSIQUE DE

Claude Debussy

	net
I. Soupir	1.75
II. Placet futile . .	1.75
III. Eventail	2 fr.
Recueil	4 fr.

A. DURAND & FILS, Éditeurs,
DURAND & Cie
Paris, 4, Place de la Madeleine.
Déposé selon les traités internationaux.
Propriété pour tous pays.
Tous droits d'exécution, de traduction,
de reproduction et d'arrangements réservés
Copyright by Durand et Cie 1913.
IMP. MOUNOT - PARIS

Title-page of Debussy's cycle Trois poèmes de Stéphane Mallarmé, *signed by 'Em-Claude Debussy'*

studied with both Fauré and Debussy. When Fauré first encountered Emma she had recently given birth to a daughter, Hélène, who bore the nickname Dolly. It has long been something of a legend that Dolly Bardac was Fauré's daughter (he did after all write the *Dolly Suite* for piano duet in her honour), and Madame de Tinan, the grown-up Dolly, who visited England frequently in later years, did little to discourage this inference – sometimes referring only to her father's great charm, a quality that belonged to Bardac as much as to Fauré. In any case the facts spoil a good story: the dates simply do not accommodate this theory that Fauré was the father of 'Dolly' Bardac.

In many ways Emma was the love of Fauré's life, but the affair seems to have faded away after four years or so. We can only speculate as to why it ended – was there already another woman in Fauré's roving sights, or was it because Emma realised that the affair had no future and that Fauré would never make a complete break from his long-suffering wife? The volatility of Emma's affections should also not be underestimated: sheerly on a physical level she might have simply tired of a man who was seventeen years her senior. It is one of the quirky facts of musical history that she was the muse and lover of two great French composers, Fauré as well as Debussy (who was almost exactly her own age), and she had tried for a third! Debussy first met Emma in 1903 as a result of his giving lessons to her son Raoul. Shortly before this it is said that she attempted, without success, to seduce

243

Maurice Ravel, who was one of Fauré's pupils introduced to the Bardac salon in the rue de Berri; it is significant that Ravel dedicated his *L'Indifférent* from his *Schéhérézade* song cycle to Emma – this is a setting of a Tristan Klingsor text that describes a beautiful and androgynous young man who ignores the advances of a smitten female admirer.

Sigismund welcomed Emma back home once her relationship with Fauré was over, and he no doubt fully expected her to return to the marital fold once the liaison with Debussy had run its course. After all, as Bardac is said to have remarked with a smile (according to Pierre Louÿs in a gossipy letter to his brother Georges[24]), he was the man with the money: 'She'll be back.' However, in 1904 Emma was to leave her husband in order to live with Debussy, a move that caused Lilly, the composer's wife, to attempt to kill herself with a revolver, a great scandal at the time – made worse by the fact that Gaby Dupont, Debussy's previous paramour, had also attempted suicide in 1897. In 1905, shortly after the first performance of *La Mer*, Emma bore the composer a daughter, Claude-Emma, known as Chouchou; after her divorce from Bardac in 1908 she became the second Mrs Claude Debussy, styling herself Emma-Claude.

There is a strange postlude to *La Bonne chanson* and the story of Fauré's relationship to Emma Bardac. There is no doubt that the prevailing awkwardness between him and Debussy (they very rarely spoke about each other, though their correspondence was cautiously polite) was exacerbated in later years by the fact that Fauré had once been the lover of the second Madame Debussy. When Fauré looked back to the time of *La Bonne chanson* he must have recalled, with a considerable twinge of regret, the termination of a golden time of love united with a mutual joy in music-making that had been unique in his life.

After Debussy died in March 1918 Fauré wrote a letter of condolence to Emma, and he received the following reply. It seems, in some ways, to be an all-purpose letter, something that could be copied out in the stupor of her grief and sent to everyone. It is the more personalised words after the signature that bear the greatest resonance: Emma could not resist mentioning the great song cycle that came into being because Fauré had once loved her, and she could not resist defensively chiding Fauré as if he was guilty, in her view, of underestimating Debussy as a human being:

I thank you profoundly, my dear friend, for your affectionate feelings of respect over this terrible bereavement that has struck me.

I feel totally incapable of putting into words the cruel anguish which has taken hold of me since his decease and which will continue to grow.

I am trying to be brave by thinking of Chouchou (how lovely she looks!) and also of all the beauty which he leaves behind and which in war-time one often forgets (at our house!). But to think I shall see him no more is a piercing stab wound which tortures me …

I have not replied to the telegrams which you have sent me … it will be necessary to forgive my unintentional forgetfulness – I can perhaps be excused.

…

Emma Claude Debussy

He was so happy last summer to study *La Bonne chanson* …
People were unaware of his kindness, his sincerity, and his loyal affection for 'the music'.[25]

∾   ∾   ∾   ∾

La Bonne chanson is a climactic work; there is nothing like this cycle before or since in Fauré's catalogue of *mélodies*. There are certainly many other great songs from Fauré's pen, from both before and after this date, but there is nothing to match this eruption of energy, optimism and dizzying creativity. And yet, even today, these songs have not found the understanding and popularity that one might have imagined to be their automatic due. From the point of view of singer and pianist this is an exhilarating and eventually deeply moving work to study, to sing, to play, but many listeners, particularly those who have come to the cycle with an 'innocent ear' and without any preparation, are bewildered and, in the short term at least, unenthusiastic.

La Bonne chanson bears little relation to the immediately appealing songs of the first period, and even the cycle's blood-relations, the *Cinq mélodies 'de Venise'* and *Prison*, seem immediately accessible by comparison. Saint-Saëns, Hahn, Debussy and Poulenc were all 'doubters' regarding this cycle, and it is surely significant that Debussy's change of heart (if we are to take his widow at her word) came about only when he had the time, as he lay grievously ill, to study the work, as opposed merely listening to it. Poulenc recorded the work with the baritone Pierre Bernac for EMI, but these 78 rpm discs were never issued because of Poulenc's dissatisfaction with his own piano playing, a different matter entirely from that of whether he had become converted to the work as he practised it.

If one seeks for a reason for the controversial nature of *La Bonne chanson*, it is that the listener can all too easily give up in exasperation, as if he or she were being force-fed a rich meal without being given time to digest the preceding courses. For some listeners too much seems to happen within the space allotted to the music, which appears to be too 'busy', the harmonic changes too unrelenting, the texture never allowing the ear or the fingers a moment's respite. There is no time for the kind of spacious charm that is so valued by most admirers of the *mélodie*, and at which a composer such as Reynaldo Hahn so excelled. *La Bonne chanson* seems to have so much crammed into it in terms of musical activity, such a wealth of highly wrought detail, that one needs to dissolve it, as if it were a stock cube, in order to allow all this musical flavour to fill a larger space (Chabrier used just this analogy concerning one of his own works, the opera *Gwendoline*). This is exactly what seems to happen when one practises the work, plays it through slowly, and gets to know it gradually. At first it seems impossibly dense, even impenetrable, but with time it opens out and becomes filled with joy, light and air.

The reason why so much has been packed into this work so tightly seems to me to have to do with Fauré's own struggle with his feelings at that most vulnerable time for a man, his approaching middle age, when any new romance seems to signal a final opportunity for happiness. This is usually referred to as a mid-life crisis. The affair with Emma Bardac seems to have brought out a side of the composer's nature that was normally easily subdued and kept under wraps; it is he who seems always to have controlled the ebb and flow of his love affairs, and yet, probably for the first time in his life, he was in the thrall of someone who was his intellectual equal, a woman who was as strong as he was. His reaction might have been to abandon his restraint altogether, to write music where all the stays were loosened, where emotion was subjectively expressed in the way that had hitherto been foreign to his nature. And yet the thought of a Fauré transformed into a composer in the manner of a neo-romantic or naturalist like Gustav Charpentier or Alfred Bruneau can scarcely be imagined.

Instead, the composer made a superhuman effort to *contain* his emotions, more active than perhaps they had ever been, within the rigorous form of a work remarkable for its lack of sentimentality. It was fortunate for him that the work's talented dedicatee would have completely understood this kind of sacrifice. It is entirely possible that Emma Bardac's musical personality, and her manner of singing (something that is lost to us in the absence of recordings), had an enormous influence on the style of the music, not only in this cycle but also in a later song such as *Soir* that is also associated with her.

For Norman Suckling *La Bonne chanson* is 'the supreme example in musical history of a work, written to an amorous programme, which loses nothing and gains a great deal by its tone of exqui-

Emma Bardac with her two children, Raoul (aged 16) and Hélène (Dolly) in Italy c.18

site urbanity and by the sense of design, rather than of passionate outpouring, that pervades it'.[26]

Suckling may be going too far in describing the cycle as 'urbane', and averring that the work's design is more important than the passionate outpourings that are part and parcel of its effect in performance. And yet it is surely the tension between the realities of life and the exigencies of art that makes *La Bonne chanson* the extraordinary work that it is, a triumph of form over naked emotion. The mighty struggle is beneath the surface of the work, like taut muscles covered by a smooth skin. We may not wish to be reminded of this struggle on the concert platform, but singers and pianists are aware of it because of the huge effort to master the nuts and bolts of the work on a technical level. They have to work very hard to resolve the work's fearsome challenges in favour of a performance that is characterised by extended passages of exquisite calm and control rather than the helter-skelter of *verismo* effects that these words might easily have unleashed in another composer. But if the listener is unaware of what this reconciliation between content and form is costing the composer and his performers, *La Bonne chanson* can easily appear to be simultaneously overwritten and underpowered, hardly a winning combination for the innocent ear. A piece of music such as this that bristles with technical difficulties and gleams with the ebullience of idealistic love can seem far less demonstrative in the concert hall than expected. The review by Léon Delafosse in *Le Figaro* of the first performance (given by Maurice Bagès with the composer at the salon of the Comte de Saussine) makes a point of mentioning the lukewarm public reaction ('une réception restreinte')[27] as well as the presence of the Princesse de Polignac. Was she similarly unimpressed? The gossip about Fauré's affair with Emma would certainly have reached her omniscient ears, and she might have been jealous of the composer's dedication of a second Verlaine cycle, even more significant than her own, to an adulterous Jewess.

Fauré had reason to be grateful for the perception and understanding of his Jewish friends and their sympathy for the marginalised. Proust was one of the rare contemporary listeners who immediately, and instinctively, understood the process whereby the hardest and most concentrated technical challenges lead, via a kind of glorious renunciation, to a perfect work of art, *more* powerful because subdued by the form that contains it. This is surely the first of Fauré's works that, for better or worse, is best understood by 'the initiates', the successors to Proust, that ardent Fauréan, in all succeeding generations. But the fact remains that there are few important works of art in the whole song repertoire that have provoked such dissension among listeners; the jury of recital enthusiasts seems to have returned an open verdict as to whether or not the work is Fauré at his best when for every sheerly musical reason this cycle is clearly Fauré at the height of his powers. Doubts nevertheless persist. *La Bonne chanson* has never been short of respectful admirers, but the spark that turns respect into love, the sort of adoration that Proust felt for the work, is ignited in the heart of the listener rather less often than its composer deserves. It is perhaps its performers who love this work best, those who have been lucky enough to experience (or re-experience) at first hand something of the excitement and energy, the life-enhancing joy, that first went into the making of this masterpiece –and there is no other word for this cycle, no matter what anyone says.

1   Paul Verlaine, *Jadis et Naguère*, in *L'Œuvres poétiques complètes*, Edition de la Pléiade (Paris, Gallimard, pp. 326-7).

2   Jean-Michel Nectoux, *Gabriel Fauré: A Musical Life*, trans. Roger Nichols (Cambridge: Cambridge University Press, 1991), p. 174.

3   Fauré was far too great a composer to be dropped by someone who was all too aware of his stature. The Princesse continued to include works by Fauré in her concerts and from time to time even planned whole programmes in his honour.

4   Nectoux, *Gabriel Fauré: A Musical Life*, pp. 185–6.

5   Ibid., p. 181.

6   Quoted in Nectoux, *Gabriel Fauré: A Musical Life*, p. 172

7   "His skull was too large, his face pushed in, his eyes oblique, his pug nose too small and tipped up. He'd lost most of his hair at an early age and compensated for it by growing sparse, wispy whiskers". Edmund White: *Rimbaud, The double life of a rebel*, London 2008, p.59.

8   Edmond Lepelletier, *Paul Verlaine: His Life, his Work*, trans. E.M. Lang (London: T. Werner Laurie, 1909).

9   Lepelletier, *Paul Verlaine*, p. 195.

10 Only three of these extra poems appear in the Pléaide Edition of Verlaine's poems. Others must have been destroyed at the time.

11 Ibid.

12 Orledge, *Gabriel Fauré*, p. 81.

13 Nectoux, *Gabriel Fauré: A Musical Life*, p. 185.

14 Quoted in Robert Orledge, *Gabriel Fauré* (London: Eulenburg, 1979), p. 84.

15 Letter to Pierre Lavallée, September 1894, in *Correspondance de Marcel Proust*, ed. Philippe Kolb (Paris: Plon, 1970), p. 338.

16 Ibid., p. 84.

17 *La Bonne chanson*: Aspects of the cycle's interpretation are discussed in Chapter 16, pp. 416–18.

18 Claude Rostand, *L'Œuvre de Gabriel Fauré* (Paris: J.B. Janin, 'La Flûte de Pan', 1945), p. 107.

19 Vladimir Jankélévitch, *De la musique au silence: Fauré et l'inexprimable* (Paris: Plon, 1974), p. 149.

20 Schubert's song is D742, Beethoven's WoO (Work without Opus Number) 129.

21 Quoted in Rostand, *L'Oeuvre de Gabriel Fauré*, p. 105.

22 *Prison*: Aspects of this song's interpretation are discussed in Chapter 16, pp. 418.

23 Fauré, letter to the music theorist René Lenormand, 1912.

24 Quoted in Nectoux, *Gabriel Fauré: A Musical Life*, p. 181.

25 *Gabriel Fauré: A Life in Letters*, ed. Jean-Michel Nectoux, trans. John Underwood (London and New York: Marion Boyards, 1984), p. 171.

26 Norman Suckling, *Fauré* (London: Dent, 1946), pp. 72–3.

27 Myriam Chimènes, *Mécènes et musiciens* (Paris: Fayard, 2004), p. 229.

Fauré, in later life, emerging from a walk 'Dans la forêt de septembre', Chamonix, 1918. © Biblioteque nationale de France

Chapter Ten

Crossing the Divide –
Towards the Late Style

Molière, Albert Samain,

Maurice Maeterlinck, Catulle Mendès

This extended chapter encompasses eleven years of Fauré's life (1893–1904), and the same number of songs. It finds the composer betwixt and between, in a state of change and evolution. The 'divide' of the chapter title refers to the journey from the end of one century to the beginning of the next, as well as the progress from the composer's late forties to the threshold of his sixties. The later music of the second period leads us to the very portals of the last cycles and thus to perhaps the greatest, and certainly the most individual, music of Fauré's long career. A new generation of performers was now discovering Fauré's music with enthusiasm and the composer's fame was widening to include other countries, particularly England, where he was gradually to become a familiar and admired figure. Although far from financially secure, he was beginning to reap the rewards, slow to come to fruition, of years of unobtrusive creative work.

Fauré was no longer the youthful creator, but he was not yet the inscrutable sage of the late works. In terms of his songs the vernal explosion of *La Bonne chanson*, completed in 1894, can be seen as the late fruit of his middle years, its energy and complexity a defiant riposte to the crisis that often overtakes those of his age who are ill at ease with their lives. But the affair with Emma Bardac was a temporary respite rather than a permanent solution. The relationship with her was over by 1896; the fact that no songs were composed in 1895 might seem indicative of a cooling of affection, although the *Salve regina* Op. 67 was written for Emma in March of that year, and in March 1896, exactly a year later, Fauré and Emma invited the poet Samain for an evening together in order to perform *Soir* for him. The pianist Marguerite Hasselmans became the composer's companion from 1900. Between these two younger women there was someone else of charm and talent to fulfil the role of Fauré's mistress, the English composer Adela Maddison. But as we shall see, it was the loving support that Fauré found with Hasselmans for the rest of his life, combined with an affectionate letter-writing accommodation with his wife, that enabled him to embark on the last great phase of his career as a composer.

The composition of *La Bonne chanson* – begun in 1892 and finished in 1894 – had taken some seventeen months from first song to last. In the meantime Fauré, denied a teaching post in the Paris Conservatoire by the intransigence of Ambroise Thomas, had no choice but to continue with his job as inspector of the provincial conservatoires. This involved a great deal of train travel and restricted his composing timetable. In 1893, between May and September, essentially during the summer holidays, there were four songs composed from the Verlaine cycle. In February 1893 he began the com-

249

position of incidental music for Molière's *Le Bourgeois gentilhomme*. This was at the request of Saint-Saëns, who found that he did not have time to undertake the commission. After working on Dumas's *Caligula* and Haraucourt's *Shylock*, Fauré perhaps thought he could reckon on a career of writing music of this kind as an alternative to the operatic project that had, as yet, consistently eluded him.

(69) *Sérénade du Bourgeois gentilhomme* (Serenade from 'The bourgeois gentleman')[1]
Monday 27 February 1893, Heugel, 1957, F minor, 9/8 (no tempo marking)

Je languis nuit et jour, et ma peine est extrême	*I languish night and day, and my pain is extreme,*
Depuis qu'à vos rigueurs vos beaux yeux m'ont soumis;	*Since your lovely eyes have subjected me to your severity:*
Si vous traitez ainsi, belle Iris, qui vous aime,	*If, lovely Iris, you treat him who loves you thus,*
Hélas! que pourriez-vous faire à vos ennemis?	*How, alas, would you treat your enemies?*

Molière (Jean-Baptiste Poquelin) (1622–1673)

There were five performances at the Odéon of Molière's play in 1893, but it seems that Fauré's music was not used. It would certainly be a rare actor who was capable of performing this song, and perhaps the production costs did not run to hiring a professional singer. It had become established practice to revamp the original incidental music of Lully from 1670, and even Gounod had only attempted to modify this rather than replace it. The *Sérénade* is heard in Act I scene 2 of the play; it is part of the music lesson of the philistine Monsieur Jourdain, the 'bourgeois gentilhomme' himself. He is attended by both the Mâitre à Danser and the Mâitre de Musique. The music master says that he wishes Monsieur Jourdain to hear the serenade that he has required to be set to music – one of his pupils has fulfilled the commission. Effortlessly offensive, Monsieur Jourdain (who believes he merits only the very best) asks why a mere pupil, rather than the master himself, has done the job. He then asks one of his footmen (or 'Laquais') for his robe in order, he says, to hear the music better.

Fauré reverts to his famous madrigal style for this little-known song. Semiquavers sweep gently up the keyboard, and the vocal line has a courtly grace that might suggest the seventeenth century, even if the harmony does not do so. In the final bars a rising twelve-note unaccompanied vocalise leads up to an elegantly turned trill before the final cadence. This quasi-cadenza is the only moment that even vaguely suggests time-travel. Under the fingers the pianist cannot help noticing the *Sérénade*'s similarity to another 9/8 song with similar dotted rhythms, and in a similarly wistful mood: the Samain setting *Arpège*, which was composed four years later. After the performance Monsieur Jourdain judges the song to be 'lugubre' (Fauré makes sure it is anything but in order to emphasise Jourdain's pretentiousness and inability to appraise music); the music master is commanded to brighten it up, a little bit here, a little bit there. The Mâitre de Musique replies with a phrase that goes completely over Monsieur Jourdain's head: 'Il faut, Monsieur, que l'air soit accommodé aux paroles' ('Sir, the music must suit the words').

A haunting *Sicilienne*, touched with the cadences of *le grand siècle*, was originally sketched as part of the incidental music for the same production. This music eventually found its way into the suite for *Pelléas et Mélisande*, but it is better known of course in its incarnation as a delightful piece for cello and piano.

Portrait of Molière by Mignard

Molière was the pseudonym of Jean-Baptiste Poquelin (1622–1673). He was a famous actor and playwright active from the middle 1650s, and he frequently performed before Louis XIV at Versailles. His plays specialised in ridiculing the various types of folly, pedantry and human weakness that were to be observed in society. He used humour to make his point, and concentrated on creating types (rather than individuals in the manner of Shakespeare), as can be seen by the generic titles of many of his works. Perhaps his greatest play, the controversial *Tartuffe*, was first performed in 1664; this was followed by *Le Misanthrope* in 1666 and *L'Avare* in 1668. *Le Bourgeois gentilhomme*, a telling and hilarious exposé of the ignorance and pompous self-regard of the newly rich, dates from 1670. Molière's last play was *Le Malade imaginaire* (1673), in which he took the part of Argan. He fell ill during a performance and died soon after. As a celebrated lampoonist of cant and hypocrisy he, hardly surprisingly, had powerful enemies, particularly those connected with the Church. As a result Molière was buried secretly at night, and without the pomp that was his due as one of France's greatest writers. He was much copied by the English Restoration playwrights, who borrowed freely from his plays, but there is a whimsy and fantasy about Molière that is entirely his own, and inimitable.

ॐ　　　　ॐ　　　　ॐ　　　　ॐ

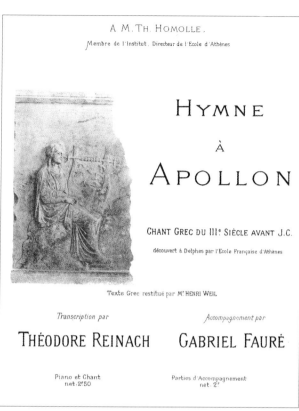

Marie and Gabriel Fauré at Prunay in 1889. © Bibliothèque nationale de France. The composer is holding an instrument that might at first glance appear to be like a reconstruction of a Greek lyre. In fact it is a lute-like instrument ('ombi') from Guinea. On the right is the title-page of the vocal score of Hymne à Apollon

In April 1893 Fauré began to work with Catulle Mendès on a new opera entitled *Lavallière*. This libretto about one of the mistresses of Louis XIV retains a connective thread with the composer's work on Molière's play. Just as the Princesse de Polignac had supported the abortive Verlaine operatic project, this venture was underwritten by the Comtesse Greffulhe; it too came to nothing. The summer of 1893 was spent at Prunay at the home of Fauré's in-laws. Apart from continuing the work on *La Bonne chanson*, he completed the third *Valse-Caprice*, and began the fourth. The death of Gounod found Fauré officiating at the organ of the Madeleine for the funeral, and improvising on a theme from the late composer's *La Rédemption*.

In late 1893 or early 1894 Fauré provided an accompaniment (for harp, flute and two clarinets) for a curious musicological project entitled *Hymne à Apollon*. The title-page informs us that this 'Hymn to Apollo' is an ancient Greek song from the third century BC discovered in Delphi in 1893 by the archaeological excavations of the French School in Athens under the direction of Théodore Homolle (the arrangement's dedicatee). The 'song' was engraved on two pieces of marble; the notes were represented by figures of the Greek alphabet inscribed above the corresponding words. The vocal line was deciphered by Théodore Reinbach and presented as seven pages of chant in the printed score. Fauré harmonises this strange work (mainly in the Phrygian mode) more successfully in the hymn's first three pages, when the accompaniment is in simple chords. This dubious musical result is hardly helped by the extraordinarily long sentences in the French translation of Eugène d'Eichtal. Everything attempts to be so faithful to what was then perceived as authentic Greek performing practice that this work, impossible to shorten, is unsustainable on the concert platform – outside the kind of specialist seminar in which it was first performed on 12 April 1894. On that occasion Fauré accompanied Jeanne Remacle on the harmonium with the addition of harp. In the same year the *Hymne à Apollon* appeared as a supplement to the *Musical Times* in London. Working on this hymn no doubt reinforced the composer's sense of affinity with ancient Greek subjects– both *Prométhée* and *Pénélope* lay in his future. As Jankélévitch points out,[2] the text glorifies the waters of Castalia, pure and clear and chaste, the waters by which strolled Phaedrus and Socrates, and surely a tributary stream to the colourless and innocent waters of C major that biblical Eve would later apostrophise in the song *Eau vivante*.

The *mélodies* of 1894 are almost entirely settings of Verlaine – the completion of *La Bonne chanson* in February and its first performance in April, and then the final Verlaine song *Prison*, which was written at the beginning of December. At this time Fauré had the energy of a man still young enough to be enlivened, emboldened, by the love of an intelligent and attractive woman: the artistic fruits of Fauré's liaison with Emma Bardac were still in full flower.

The other works of this extraordinarily busy and inspired year are the First Piano Quintet, the most famous nocturne of all, the Sixth (composed between July and August), the sacred choral work *Tantum ergo* (also August), and the Fifth Barcarolle (September, composed at Prunay). The Sixth Nocturne is a noble and unforgettably haunting masterpiece, but it is the dizzying yet suave harmonic complexity of the Fifth Barcarolle – veering between F♯ minor and F♯ major via multi-tudinous other tonalities – that seems the most appropriate pianistic companion to the composer's great song cycle. In it we can also hear the doubt and unease that are missing from Verlaine's texts in *La Bonne chanson*, the awareness that the composer's happiness with Emma was finite. There were Fauré festivals in Geneva and a concert devoted to the composer in the St James's Hall in London.

Another operatic libretto was proposed, this time on the German writer Friedrich de la Motte Fouqué's *Undine* (a subject that would later ensnare Fauré's pupil Ravel with his *Ondine* for solo piano). Yet again these plans failed to lead to the hoped-for opera. Almost as soon as Fauré had fin-ished composing his last Verlaine song he began work on his first setting of the poet Albert Samain. Although Samain was far less celebrated than Verlaine, he was a far from negligible figure. Emma Bardac was already a Samain enthusiast; when she and Fauré invited the poet to dinner in order to perform *Soir* for him in 1896, she proudly showed him his volume of verse, *Au Jardin de l'Infante*, 'bound in kind of mauve silk with her monogram embroidered on it'.[3] She told Samain that the book was a present from a woman friend who knew she liked the work. This gift would almost certainly have gone back to 1893, the year in which the collection of poems appeared.

Samain was already known to the composer as an aspiring librettist. As we have seen, in 1892 the Princesse de Polignac had already attempted, and failed, to bring Samain and the composer together to write an opera entitled *La Tentation de Bouddha*. Although Fauré had also first encountered Verlaine as a poet some years before he was proposed as a potential operatic collaborator, all but two of the Verlaine settings post-dated the failure of their operatic collaboration. Similarly, it was only after he had decided against writing a theatre piece with Samain that the composer turned to his poetry and went on to fashion four significant songs from these lyrics.

(70) *Soir* (Evening)[4]
17 December 1894, Op. 83 No. 2, D♭ major, 3/4, *Andante molto moderato*

Voici que les jardins de la Nuit vont fleurir.	*Now the gardens of Night begin to flower.*
Les lignes, les couleurs, les sons deviennent vagues.	*Lines, colours, and sounds begin to blur.*
Vois, le dernier rayon agonise à tes bagues.	*See the last rays expire on your rings.*
Ma sœur, entends-tu pas quelque chose mourir! …	*Sister, can you not hear something die? …*
Mets sur mon front tes mains fraîches comme une eau pure,	*Place your hands, cool as pure water, on my brow*
Mets sur mes yeux tes mains douces comme des fleurs;	*Place on my eyes your hands as sweet as flowers;*
Et que mon âme, où vit le goût secret des pleurs,	*And let my soul, with its secret taste of tears,*
Soit comme un lys fidèle et pâle à ta ceinture.	*Be like a lily at your waist, faithful and pale.*
C'est la Pitié qui pose ainsi son doigt sur nous;	*It is Pity that lays thus its finger on us;*
Et tout ce que la terre a de soupirs qui montent,	*And all the sighs that rise from the earth*
Il semble qu'à mon cœur enivré le racontent	*Seem uttered to my enraptured heart*
Tes yeux levés au ciel si tristes et si doux.	*By your sad sweet eyes raised to the skies.*

Albert Samain (1858–1900)

Unless one was lucky enough, like Emma Bardac, to receive the book as a gift with a fine silk binding, Albert Samain's first collection of poetry, *Au Jardin de l'Infante* (1893), was issued in a dark olive green paper cover with red lettering. In a unique gesture of confidence in his lover's literary taste and perspicacity, the composer obtained for Emma another copy of the book (now in the Bibliothèque Nationale in Paris) and gave it to her with the following inscription, dated May 1894: 'I beg you to accept this book and choose the poems you would like to sing.'

In Samain's collection the poem 'Elégie' follows on from the poem 'Larmes' (which Fauré later set as the duet *Pleurs d'or*). 'Elégie' has nine strophes, of which the composer selected only the last three. In the book of poems that Fauré gave to Emma Bardac, her pencil markings show that she had indeed selected this poem for music. There are also pencil marks against the poem 'Dilection' (which Fauré began to compose but never finished), against 'Arpège' (which he did set, of course)

First edition of Soir, *printed as a supplement for* L'Illustration, *18 April, 1896*

254

and against 'Promenade à l'étang', for which the composer sketched a sophisticated tonal plan without composing any actual music.

The great soprano Claire Croiza used to read the first six strophes of the poem 'Elégie', and under the closing lines of these ('soothe our hearts alone at evening on the road') the pianist would enter with the beginning of the accompaniment to *Soir*, which Croiza would then go on to sing. Most singers, even native French speakers, will not have the ability both to read and sing convincingly, but these initial verses of the poem are beautiful enough to be quoted in full:

Quand la nuit verse sa tristesse au firmament,	*When night pours down its sorrow from the sky*
Et que, pâle au balcon, de ton calme visage	*And, pale on the balcony, your calm face*
Le signe essentiel hors du temps se dégage,	*Releases that essential, timeless sign,*
Ce qui t'adore en moi s'émeut profondément.	*My adoration for you is deeply stirred.*
C'est l'heure de pensée où s'allument les lampes,	*It is the hour of thought, when the lamps are lit,*
La ville, où peu à peu toute rumeur s'éteint,	*The town, where gradually all sounds are stifled,*
Déserte, se recule en un vague lointain	*Draws back, deserted, into the hazy distance*
Et prend cette douceur des anciennes estampes.	*And takes on this mellowness of ancient prints.*
Graves, nous nous taisons. Un mot tombe parfois,	*We stand in solemn silence. Occasionally a word is spoken,*
Fragile pont où l'âme à l'âme communique.	*A fragile bridge through which souls communicate,*
Le ciel se décolore; et c'est un charme unique	*The sky fades; time seems to flit by –*
Cette fuite de temps, il semble, entre nos doigts.	*Unrivalled delight – between our fingers.*
Je resterais ainsi des heures, des années,	*I could remain like this for hours, for years,*
Sans épuiser jamais la douceur de sentir	*Without ever diminishing the sweetness of feeling*
Ta tête aux lourds cheveux sur moi s'appesantir,	*The weight of your tresses fall on me,*
Comme morte parmi les lumières fanées.	*As though lifeless amid the faded lights.*
C'est le lac endormi de l'heure à l'unisson,	*A lake asleep in harmony with time,*
La halte au bord de puits, le repos dans les roses;	*A pause beside a well, a rest among the roses;*
Et par de longs fils d'or nos cœurs liés aux choses	*And our hearts, linked by long golden threads*
Sous l'invisible archet vibrent d'un long frisson.	*Beneath an invisible bow, quiver with sustained delight.*
Oh! garder à jamais l'heure élue entre toutes,	*Ah! to preserve forever this most choice hour,*
Pour que son souvenir, comme un parfum séché,	*So that its memory, like faded perfume,*
Quand nous serons plus tard las d'avoir trop marché,	*When later we are tired from so much walking,*
Console notre cœur, seul, le soir, sur les routes.	*Will soothe our hearts, alone, at evening, on the road;*

[Accompaniment begins.]

Voici que les jardins de la nuit … [etc.]	*Now the gardens of Night … [etc.]*

The form of this *mélodie* is ABA, broadly speaking, but as in the great modified strophic songs from the later years of Schubert's life nothing is taken for granted – the music is continually rethought and newly invented. The accompaniment for this nocturne begins modestly in simple arpeggiated semiquavers (like the Verlaine setting *En sourdine*, to which it is distantly related) and flowers in the second strophe into a dizzying complexity of chromaticism that somehow remains tranquil and unruffled. In both texture and appearance the piano writing in the middle section of the song recalls that of *C'est l'extase* (1891) and is prophetic of the ninth variation from Fauré's masterful *Thème et variations* (1895). *Soir* is a work that combines a relaxed melodic attractiveness with the harmonic richness of *La Bonne chanson* – the latter attribute hardly surprising when we are reminded that this song was also inspired by Emma Bardac.

The accompaniment deftly returns to a single stave at the beginning of the third verse, and the ardent harmonic subtleties leading to this last transition are simply miraculous. In the Verlaine setting *C'est l'extase* (1891), we have heard 'le frêle et frais murmure' of nature. This kind of music, an attempt to describe almost inaudible sound, returns in *Soir*, triggered by the words 'entends-tu pas quelque chose mourir?' In both cases a delicate descant to the vocal line is traced in the little finger of the right hand; this is supported by off-beat mezzo-staccato harmonies that change constantly, glinting and palpitating. This musical pointillism is prickly in close-up, but it blurs into a marvellously glowing picture from a distance. The final bars ('si tristes et si doux' followed by the postlude) encapsulate both the depth and economy of Fauréan expressiveness. As Robert Orledge has shown,[5] the composer had some trouble in finding this ending, which may explain why a work that was all but complete in December 1894 was only published in 1896. (It was performed for the poet by Emma and Fauré at a dinner party in March of that year.) Orledge's article examines the last ten bars of the song and the composer's many adjustments, sometimes only tiny, of harmony and orthography. The climactic A♭ on 'Tes *yeux*' clearly jumps outside the dream-like frame of the song and does not survive the first version. The closing words of the song, 'Et si doux', exist in no fewer than three versions: in the first of these the words are set to a repeated A♭ in the D♭ tonic chord; in the second F♭ ('Et') falls to E♭ ('si') before rising a fourth to A♭ ('doux'). In the printed version there is the definitive and haunting rise of a third from F♭ ('Et') to a repeated A♭ ('si doux'). Fauré's work on these revisions shows his capacity at this stage of his career to take infinite pains over his songs; in a letter to his wife he was later to liken this kind of fine-tuning to a bear licking its cubs all over to make them clean and presentable.[6]

Soir was given its first public performance at the Société Nationale de la Musique (SNM) on 3 April 1897 by Thérèse Roger, whose name had earlier been linked with that of Claude Debussy and whose fiancée she had briefly been some four year earlier. (*Prison* was on the same programme, sung by the same singer). By this time Fauré and Emma Bardac had definitely parted; how would she have felt about 'her' *Soir* being performed by another woman, not one of Fauré's girlfriends (as far as we know) but an attractive and talented female singer nevertheless? The fact that Roger had also once been Debussy's fiancée and that Emma was later to marry Debussy is a tiny illustration of a certain incestuous tendency in the world of Parisian music-making. There is evidence that Fauré's relations with the Bardacs remained amicable – that is in the period after Emma broke up with Fauré and before she definitively left her husband for Debussy. The couple were invited to a Fauré concert in March 1902 *chez* the Girette family at the composer's behest.[7]

For a thematic link between this song and the *Nocturne* from the *Shylock* suite, see the commentary on this work in Chapter 7.

Albert Samain was born in Lille on 4 April 1858 and was thus the youngest of Fauré's poets so far. Samain was part Parnassian, part decadent, part symbolist and wholly a master of poetic technique. He came from humble beginnings and, very shy by nature, he worked his way up in a firm of sugar brokers. Like Verlaine when a young man, he combined an initially small-scale literary career with employment in the civil service, in this case at the Préfecture de la Seine. Advised by Richepin (a poet of completely different temperament), he joined a group of young poets called 'Nous autres' and declaimed his verses at the newly opened cabaret, *Le Chat noir*. His existence until his early thirties was monotonous and unfulfilled save for occasional holidays in London and on the Rhine. In 1889 he helped to found the publishing house of Société du Mercure de France, and most of his writing was published by this firm that later issued the first editions of such important works as *Les Chansons de Bilitis* by Pierre Louÿs and the poetry of Henri de Régnier. When Samain's *Au Jardin de l'Infante* appeared in 1893 it was enormously successful – these poems, evocations of the soft and mysterious landscapes viewed by a Spanish princess who has withdrawn into a remote and exotic palace, seemed perfectly attuned to the *fin de siècle* mood of the times. An indication of this is Ravel's celebrated *Pavane pour une Infante défunte*, a piece for piano (also orchestrated) that unashamedly derived its title from the poet's collection. It was this music, indirectly inspired by Samain, that Marcel Proust was to choose for his own funeral.

Albert Samain

François Coppée hailed Samain as 'un poète d'automne et de crépuscule, un poète de douce et morbide langueur, de noble tristesse' ('a poet of autumn and of twilight, of a soft and morbid langour, of noble sadness'). The reception of this first book was so enthusiastic that the backlash that swept Samain back into obscurity some years later was perhaps inevitable, a reversal of fortune that he did not live to experience. *Au Jardin de l'Infante* was published when he was thirty-five, and he was slow to follow up with his next collection, *Aux Flancs de vase* (1898). He died of consumption aged forty-two, on 18 August 1900, still a celebrated figure, but not for very long. The posthumous *Le Chariot d'or* was issued in 1901, and his tragedy *Polyphème* was produced on the Parisian stage in 1908. While acknowledging that Emma Bardac was 'pretty, elegant, a woman of the world' and that she had ' a real feeling for nuance and an unusual purity of style', the poet was sadly no true admirer of the music that keeps his fame, such as it is, alive today. It is obvious that his impoverished background had allowed him little chance of a musical education. He wrote to his sister after a soirée *chez* Emma Bardac: 'Why was the music so modern? Ah those gentlemen of the SNM (D'Indy, Chausson, Fauré) punish me severely.'[8] Samain clearly preferred the past to the present: yearning for far-off imagined lands is the supreme emotion of his poetry combined with memories of lost delight and faded glory. The poet's simplicity and noble perfection have been regarded as a continuation of Verlaine, and it is exactly this role that his poems played in the canon of Fauré's songs.

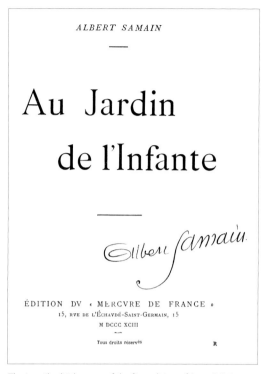

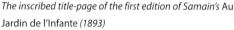

The inscribed title-page of the first edition of Samain's Au Jardin de l'Infante *(1893)*

Albert Samain by Félix Valloton from Le Livre des Masques *(1896) by Rémy de Gourmont*

By now Fauré was influential enough for his approval of a poet to influence the literary choices of his younger contemporaries. It was just as well that Samain was spared, on the occasion mentioned above, the complex settings of his verse by Charles Koechlin (twelve Samain *mélodies*); he might have preferred the two settings of Poldowski (Lady Dean Paul); Pierné and Casella wrote one song each. George Hüe, Nadia Boulanger and Charles Tournemire all composed Samain songs, as did the Belgian Joseph Jongen and the German-American Charles Loeffler; Florent Schmitt wrote a song with orchestra, and Jean Cras created an opera from Samain's *Polyphème*. The latter piece was performed in 1922; after that the poet's name all but ceases to be heard in connection with music.

∾   ∾   ∾   ∾

Soir was composed at the end of 1894; it would be another sixteen months before Fauré composed another song – in fact a duet – and when the time came, it would be another Samain setting.

1895 was one of the composer's songless years. The greatest creative event of these twelve months was the *Thème et variations* for solo piano. There were high-profile performances of *Shylock* and *La Naissance de Vénus*. At the end of November, Fauré travelled to London to discuss a publishing deal with the London firm of Metzler, which came into force in January 1896. For a few years, until the arrangement collapsed, many of the *mélodies* were published more or less simultaneously in France and England (see p. 122 with regard to the song *Nell*) – the composer's popularity in Britain had grown slowly but surely, bolstered by a handful of devoted enthusiasts in London.

In January 1896 Fauré played the organ at the funeral of Paul Verlaine, who had died at fifty-one.

(71) *Pleurs d'or* (*Tears of gold*)[9]

21 April 1896, Op. 72, 'À Mlle Camille Landi et M. David Bispham', E♭ minor, 12/8, *Andante quasi allegretto*[9]

Larmes aux fleurs suspendues,	*Tears clinging to flowers,*
Larmes aux sources perdues	*Tears from springs lost*
Aux mousses des rochers creux;	*In the moss of hollowed rocks;*
Larmes d'automne épandues,	*Tears shed by autumn,*
Larmes de cors entendues	*Tears from horns sounding*
Dans les grands bois douloureux;	*In great doleful forests;*
Larmes des cloches latines,	*Tears of church bells,*
Carmélites, Feuillantines …	*Of Carmel and Feuillants convents …*
Voix des beffrois en ferveur;	*Devout belfry voices;*
Larmes des nuits étoilées,	*Tears of starlit nights,*
Larmes des flûtes voilées	*Tears of muffled flutes*
Au bleu du parc endormi;	*In the blue of the sleeping park;*
Larmes aux grands cils perlées,	*Pearly tears on long lashes,*
Larmes d'amantes coulées	*A beloved's tears flowing*
Jusqu'à l'âme de l'ami;	*To her friend's soul;*
Larmes d'extase, éplorement délicieux,	*Tears of rapture, delicious weeping,*
Tombez des nuits! Tombez des fleurs! Tombez des yeux!	*Fall at night! Fall from the flowers! Fall from these eyes!*

Albert Samain (1858–1900)

The title of Samain's poem is *Larmes*, but Fauré had already given this title to the Richepin setting of 1888. He omits the poet's fourth stanza and the poem's last three lines, which are even more highly perfumed than the rest of the lyric:

Et toi, mon cœur, sous le doux fleuve harmonieux,
Qui, riche du trésor, tari des urnes vides,
Roule un grand rêve triste aux mers des soirs languides.

> *And you, my heart, beneath the sweet, harmonious river flow*
> *Which, rich with the parched treasure of empty urns,*
> *Rolls great and sorrowful dreams towards the seas of languid evenings.*

We are familiar enough with Fauré's taste to know that whereas he might have set the last of these three lines, he was utterly defeated by the idea of finding music for 'urnes vides', 'empty urns'. The singer Emilie Girette tells us that the word 'Schumann' – the composer's name – when it appeared in another Samain poem was enough to put Fauré off. The composer once remarked that the phrase

'Hélène aux pieds blancs' ('Helen with white feet') made a charming literary impression, but with music added the effect of those feet would be clumsily gigantic.

In *Pleurs d'or* the flowing triplets of this 12/8 *Andante quasi allegretto* suggest the flow of water music, but this is water, almost holy water, in a state of suspension. The imagery of convent bells adds an aura of piety. (It was in the Feuillants convent near the Tuileries that Marie Antoinette took refuge during the mob insurrection of August 1792.) Off-the-beat crotchets in the accompaniment are distilled drop by drop – mezzo-staccato dew on the rose-petalled surface of the music. These golden tears are turned into something audible in the sounds of different bell sonorities and of veiled flutes; they are transfigured as pinpricks of stars in the heavens. There is a voluptuous sensuality in this music that is not often encountered in Fauré; indeed, one might regard it as a late example of his *décadent* style if the music were less inspired, less radiant. It is very likely that, when writing it, the composer was already once more in love, and no longer with Emma Bardac. The entwined vocal lines swoon as if responding to a caress, a touch of Massenet perhaps; there is in this music a sybaritic voluptuousness of manner that we almost never hear in Fauré's mature work.

The sentiment of the duet is still that of the second period; the harmonic progressions are recherché without having embraced the *pudeur* of the third – this is scarcely the music of renunciation, and Fauré exploits to the full the luxurious casting of two voices. The duet is written for soprano and tenor and begins with a succession of answering phrases, each of the voices presenting their vocal lines as a solo. The convergence of the two is such that they cross into each other's tessituras with a wonderful sense of mingled sonority. With two well-matched sopranos the voices can seem totally entwined; this is a magical effect even if the composer had intended a colloquy between lovers, male and female; for this reason he had altered Samain's singular 'amante' in the poem to 'amantes'.

〜　　　〜　　　〜　　　〜

The duet was first published by the British firm of Metzler. The composer clearly took the manuscript with him when he journeyed to London a few days after he had finished it on 21 April 1896. He had a date for a sitting with John Singer Sargent at the end of the month; this had been arranged to tie in with a London recital on 1 May in which *Pleurs d'or* was given its first performance by the soprano Camille Landi and the famous tenor and icon of late Victorian music-making, David Bispham (to whom Fauré dedicated the duet). At the same concert he collaborated with strings in playing his First Piano Quartet.

In June 1896 Fauré was promoted within the hierarchy of the Madeleine from the position of choirmaster to organist, replacing Théodore Dubois, a worthy but rather mediocre composer whose work had received all the public recognition that had unaccountably been denied to Fauré. In August he travelled for the second time to Bayreuth, this time as a member of the Princesse de Polignac's party, to hear Wagner's *Ring*. On 1 October Fauré, at long last, got his foot through the door of the Conservatoire. Massenet, who had gambled and lost in a bid to become director of the institution, resigned in pique as professor of composition, and Fauré unexpectedly succeeded him. In Marie Clerc's words in a letter from much earlier in the composer's career, this was a victory over the politically cunning and 'adroit' Massenet by the 'droit', or upright, Fauré. How much difference in the addition of a single letter of the alphabet, Marie had bemoaned. Fauré's continuing dislike for Massenet and his music is shown in a phrase he wrote in a letter to his wife (1 October 1909), where he refers to the 'vulgar and passionate writhings of Massenet'.[10]

Until this time there had been a great amount of official resistance to appointing someone to the post who was an outsider, someone who had not himself been trained at the Conservatoire. Despite his tendency to say very little at his composition lessons, Fauré proved to be an enduringly popular professor. Through his hands passed some of the greatest talents of the time: Maurice Ravel, Florent Schmitt, Charles Koechlin, Georges Enesco, Nadia Boulanger and many others. He was often the subject of his pupils' veneration. Of course, his personal authority stemmed from the esteem in which his music, by now increasingly published and well known, was held by other musicians, but he had an inclusive way of dealing with different talents and styles that nurtured his students' progress. He was never overbearing or dictatorial; his disapproval was more eloquently expressed by silence than by anger. Fauré was now able to give up his peripatetic music teaching, and he was spared incessant train travel to give lessons. But he was still inspector of conservatoires, and the down-side of this prestigious new Conservatoire appointment was that it gave him even less time for composition.

A disappointing aspect of 1896 was the composer's failure, for the second time, to be elected to the Institut. A by-product of Fauré's campaign for this position was that a list of his opus numbers was printed for the first time – he felt he required such a catalogue at the time to consolidate his reputation with his prospective supporters and potential electors. It was thus that the opus numbers between 2 and 8 first appeared; they had not as yet been allocated to any music, and Hamelle now endeavoured to backdate the earlier songs by matching them, often quite arbitrarily, with opus numbers and subdivisions of numbers, many of them inaccurate in terms of any realistic chronology. The unravelling of the correct sequence of Fauré's earlier songs is an ongoing task; even someone so finely attuned to Fauré's style as Jean-Michel Nectoux has not yet published a definitive sequence – that is if one can ever be decided upon.

In September 1896 Fauré visited English friends who had a holiday home at Saint-Lunaire near his old stamping ground of Rennes in Brittany. These were Frederick Maddison and his wife, Adela (née Katherine Mary Adela Tindal, a beautiful brunette of Irish descent), a couple whom he had met in London in 1894. Maddison was a lawyer with connections to music publishing and with the firm of Metzler and Co. (later J.B. Cramer) in particular. It was no surprise therefore that earlier in the year Fauré had concluded an agreement with Metzler and Co. to publish his works. As we have seen above, *Pleurs d'or* was the first vocal work to come out in an English edition. Between 1896 and 1899 Metzler published over twenty of Fauré's best pieces, some of them even before Hamelle had issued them. In 1896 Metzler also published Liza Lehman's cycle for vocal quartet, *In a Persian Garden*. Fauré's songs had been rather awkwardly rendered into English by Adela Maddison; we can only assume that she was more gifted as a composer than a translator – Fauré even wrote to Samain praising Adela's settings of the poet's 'Hiver' and 'Silence', and some of her songs had been performed at the same concert in which *Pleurs d'or* received its first performance. Metzler brought out a volume of Adela's songs, and Choudens followed suit two years later, probably on Fauré's recommendation.

It was the Maddisons who proposed yearly concerts in London to be entirely devoted to Fauré's music. This idea showed admirable enthusiasm – the couple were swept away by the composer's achievements – but they were guilty, perhaps, of an over-optimistic attitude when it came to calculating how best to popularise Fauré's music with the English public. At some point Adela Maddison became another in the select line of Fauré's significant musical mistresses, the only one who was not French and the only one who was a fellow composer (of the composer's other amatory adventures when abroad– and there were almost certainly a number of these – there is no surviving information). The end of 1896 saw a Fauré Festival in London (at St James's Hall, Piccadilly, a large concert hall no longer extant), at which the Second Piano Quartet was performed as well as a broad selection of piano pieces. He was still pianist enough at this time (Saint-Saëns had commented that Fauré was a remarkable pianist and organist 'when he wanted to be') to play the exacting piano part of his A major violin sonata in London. In fact he went on playing this piece in public for years. Sadly the London concerts were not to be a regular, yearly event as originally planned.

1897 was relatively rich in performances, particularly of piano music, but there were only two new compositions, both songs, in August and September of the year.

(72) *Le Parfum impérissable* (*The imperishable perfume*)[11]
22 August 1897, Op. 76 No. 1, 'À Paolo Tosti', E major, 3/4, *Andante molto moderato*

Quand la fleur du soleil, la rose de Lahor,	*When the flower of the sun, the rose of Lahore,*
De son âme odorante a rempli goutte à goutte	*Has drop by drop from her scented soul*
La fiole d'argile ou de cristal ou d'or,	*Filled the phial of clay or crystal or gold,*
Sur le sable qui brûle on peut l'épandre toute.	*It can all be scattered on the burning sands.*
Les fleuves et la mer inonderaient en vain	*Rivers and oceans would flood in vain*
Ce sanctuaire étroit qui la tint enfermée:	*This narrow sanctuary where it was confined:*
Il garde en se brisant son arome divin,	*On shattering it keeps its heavenly scent,*
Et sa poussière heureuse en reste parfumée.	*Which still perfumes its happy dust.*
Puisque par la blessure ouverte de mon cœur	*Since through the gaping wound of my heart*
Tu t'écoules de même, ô céleste liqueur,	*You likewise flow, O heavenly nectar,*
Inexprimable amour, qui m'enflammais pour elle!	*Ineffable love which inflamed me for her!*
Qu'il lui soit pardonné, que mon mal soit béni!	*May she be pardoned and my pain be blessed!*
Par delà l'heure humaine et le temps infini	*Beyond this world and infinity*
Mon cœur est embaumé d'une odeur immortelle!	*My heart is embalmed with immortal fragrance!*

Charles Marie René Leconte de Lisle (1818–1894)

In a remarkable fan letter written by Marcel Proust to Fauré in 1897, this song is the only one mentioned by name: 'The other evening I took my first intoxicating draught of *Le Parfum impérissable*, and it is a dangerous intoxication for I have been back every day since. At least it is a clear-sighted intoxication for I told Reynaldo Hahn things about that fragrance that he found fitting even from the musical standpoint, and God knows how harshly he judges the musical views of men of letters.'[12]

This is Fauré's farewell to Leconte de Lisle;[13] the song was taken from the late collection *Poèmes tragiques* (1884). We know that this poem was set at the suggestion of the famous and devastatingly beautiful actress Julia Bartet, nicknamed 'la divine'; since the days of Pauline Viardot and Montesquiou the composer had not been too proud to be guided in his searches for suitable song texts, and in fact we know that when he felt stuck in this regard he appointed friends as scouts to help find him new poems. The first performance of the song was given on 4 November 1897 by the Belgian baritone Émile Engel, who was the teacher, and later the husband, of Jane Bathori, a soprano who was to figure in the performance of Fauré's songs in later years.

This setting is an intimation of things to come and a precursor of the style of the late song cycles.

LECONTE DE LISLE

POÈMES
TRAGIQUES

PARIS

ALPHONSE LEMERRE, ÉDITEUR

27-31, PASSAGE CHOISEUL, 27-31

M DCCC LXXXIV

Le Parfum impérissable

Quand la fleur du soleil, la rose de Lahor,
De son âme odorante a rempli goutte à goutte
La fiole d'argile ou de cristal ou d'or,
Sur le sable qui brûle on peut l'épandre toute.

Title-page of Leconte de Lisle's Poèmes tragiques *(1884) and the opening lines of 'Le Parfum impérissable'*

The dedication of this other-worldly masterpiece to the urbane Paolo Tosti, professor of singing at the Royal Academy of Music, London, and master of the *canzone*, would seem almost ironic if he had not been a highly cultivated man more than capable of appreciating this song's beauties. The opening bar is the mezzo-staccato chord of a tenth shared between left hand and right, thrice repeated – nothing more. The articulation is a preparation for the way in which rare and precious harmonies will be measured out 'goutte à goutte' by the composer–alchemist. As soon as the voice enters in the second bar we begin a musical journey that scarcely pauses for breath – the progress is unhurried but ineluctable, as if the singer were 'high' on an exquisite substance, almost drug-like in its effect. This morbidity, also known as unrequited love, is at the heart of the song's mournful ecstasy. The constant returning to the home key at important cadences acknowledges the presence of the perfume's bass note, all the peripheral harmonies a variation on this obsessive, predominant aroma. Referring to the manner in which bar 5 of the song begins in the home key of G♭ and returns to this key in bar 9 (the music for the third and fourth lines of the poem), Nadia Boulanger writes, 'one knows not what to admire most in such harmony: the richness and accuracy of its allusions to foreign keys or the deftness with which it returns to the point from which it started'.[14]

The piano's only ostensible function here is to support the voice; any pianist who encounters this song for the first time is astonished at just how many side-steps, back-steps and half-steps are available to the fingers as they ceaselessly pivot from one astonishing harmony to the next. In fact this song, so unlike anything Debussy wrote, is perhaps Fauré's most distinguished experiment with the harmonic ladder of the whole-tone scale; it is this that gives the gently restless music its space and mysterious

263

grandeur. In 1912 Fauré, conscious of certain innovations of which he could be proud, wrote of 'the harmonic progressions (or non-progressions) in *Le Parfum impérissable*'.[15] The large stretches in the left hand suggest the strumming of a guitar or perhaps an oriental harp. Is the exotic sweep of these chords part of the composer's response to a poem that evokes the roses of Lahore? This is music about subtle persistence – of an aroma that survives all attempts at its destruction, and an aroma that has the Proustian power to restore the past through deep inhalation. But the theme of subtle persistence also seems a metaphor for Fauré's great art, each drop of perfume an incremental measurement of its indestructible progress from note to note and from harmony to astonishing harmony, each new idea the result of steady accretive growth from month to month, and from year to year. Thus the composer's contribution to the treasury of song grows like some infinitely precious pearl in the oyster.

(73) *Arpège* (Arpeggio)[16]
6 September 1897, Op. 76 No. 2, 'À Mme Charles Detellbach', E minor, 9/8, *Andante quasi allegretto*

L'âme d'une flûte soupire	*The soul of a flute is sighing*
Au fond du parc mélodieux;	*Deep in the melodious park;*
Limpide est l'ombre où l'on respire	*The shade is limpid where one breathes*
Ton poème silencieux,	*Your silent poem,*
Nuit de langueur, nuit de mensonge,	*Night of languor, night of delusion,*
Qui poses d'un geste ondoyant	*That with a flowing gesture*
Dans ta chevelure de songe	*Sets in your dreamy hair*
La lune, bijou d'Orient.	*The moon, that Orient jewel.*
Sylva, Sylvie et Sylvanire,	*Sylva, Sylvie and Sylvanire,*
Belles au regard bleu changeant,	*Beauties with eyes of shimmering blue,*
L'étoile aux fontaines se mire,	*Fountains reflect the morning star –*
Allez par les sentiers d'argent,	*Go along the silvery paths,*
Allez vite – l'heure est si brève!	*Go quickly – time is so short!*
Cueillir au jardin des aveux	*To gather in the garden of vows*
Les cœurs qui se meurent du rêve	*The hearts which are dying of the dream*
De mourir parmi vos cheveux …	*Of dying enveloped in your hair …*

Albert Samain (1858–1900)

This is another poem from Albert Samain's *Au Jardin de l'Infante* and another poem selected for setting by Emma Bardac's pencil, although it seems to have been composed some time after the relationship between her and Fauré had ended. The song is the composer's final farewell to the courtly world of Verlaine's *Fêtes galantes* in a new manifestation – the park that is mentioned here with its 'nymphs' suggests a moonlit eighteenth-century landscape. Samain's poem itself is part of a fantasy sequence (an extended 'Embarquement pour Cythère') which begins with 'L'Île fortunée', a parody of Gautier's 'Où voulez-vous aller?' – known best in Berlioz's setting *L'Île inconnue*. Next, 'Nocturne', the poem before 'Arpège', describes a 'fête à Bergame', where 'Lulli' conducts a *bergamasque* orchestra of strings and flutes. We have already noted that Jean-Baptise Lully, Louis XIV's *surintendant de musique*, wrote the original music for *Le Bourgeois gentilhomme* in 1670. *Arpège* has a strong similarity to the *Sérénade* from Fauré's music for the same Molière play (1893; see p. 250) – a 9/8 metre with skipping dotted rhythms, and similar trills and ornaments. Were these musical allusions meant to amuse Emma Bardac, fan of Samain's poetry and knowledgeable about Fauré's recent music (which she would, with some justification also regard as *her* music)? Or by this time was there someone new in the composer's life, Adela Maddison, perhaps, who, being a song composer herself, might have recognised this allusion, and smiled at a cross-reference meant only for the ears of initiates?

The music for the first strophe in the minor key is elegant and deft, somewhat malign (as is appropriate for a 'nuit de mensonge'); the second strophe recalls the barcarolle of the Venetian *À Clymène* (see p. 212) (gondolas are indeed a feature of this Samain fantasy sequence); the final verse in the major key is perhaps the most original, with its sighing descents of triplets in octaves – music for a swoon, if not a *Liebestod* – and compressed sequences of harmony in continual metamorphosis. The postlude, now in the major key, traverses the keyboard light-heartedly, bottom to top, as if to admit that the whole of this song has been nothing more than a *jeu d'esprit* at a fancy-dress ball.

Lanvin's famous perfume 'Arpège' was created in 1927. It seems even more of an inspired brand name if one knows this song. Jeanne Lanvin's pride and joy, her daughter, the soprano Marie-Blanche de Polignac, certainly did so and she probably sang *Arpège* in that same silvery voice that is to be heard in Nadia Boulanger's classic recordings of the Monteverdi madrigals. Even if Fauré's and Samain's influence had entered the realm of haute couture (for Lanvin was famous chiefly as a dress-designer) their *Arpège* is no classic *Parfum impérissable*; it remains one of the composer's least-performed *melodies*, its rarity ensures it still sounds and feels elusive to listeners' ears and pianists' fingers.

The song's dedicatee, Doris Dettelbach, was an amateur singer of some repute who was a friend of Proust, Massenet and Reynaldo Hahn (who frequently accompanied her in his own songs). Her salon at 13 rue Christophe Colomb (where performances could be heard by such artists as Artur Rubinstein, André Caplet and Claire Croiza) continued until the 1930s.

(74) *Mélisande's Song*[17]
31 May 1898, part of Op. 80, D minor, 3/2, *Lento*, first published in 1937

The King's three blind daughters	*Les trois sœurs aveugles,*
Sit locked in a hold.	*(Espérons encore).*
In the darkness their lamps	*Les trois sœurs aveugles,*
Make a glimmer of gold.	*Ont leurs lampes d'or.*
Up the stairs of the turret	*Montent à la tour,*
The sisters are gone,	*(Elles, vous et nous).*
Seven days they wait there	*Montent à la tour,*
And the lamps they burn on.	*Attendent sept jours.*
What hope? says the first	*Ah! dit la première,*
And leans o'er the flame.	*Espérons encore,*
I hear our lamps burning,	*Ah! dit la première,*
O yet if he came!	*J'entends nos lumières.*

O hope! says the second
    Was that the lamp's flare
Or a sound of low footsteps?
    The Prince on the stair!
	Ah! dit la seconde,
	    (Elles, vous et nous).
	Ah! dit la seconde,
	    C'est le roi qui monte.

But the holiest sister,
    She turns her about.
Oh no hope now for ever,
    Our lamps are gone out.
	Non, dit la plus sainte
	    (Espérons encore).
	Non, dit la plus sainte,
	    Elles se sont éteintes …

translated Jack W. Mackail (1859–1945) from Maurice Maeterlinck (1862–1949)

There is one lyric in Maeterlinck's play *Pelléas et Mélisande* that must be sung by Mélisande as she sits in the window of her tower in Act III scene 2, just before Pelléas interrupts her musings. In the original 1892 edition of the play this lyric begins 'Mes longs cheveux descendent jusqu'au seuil de la tour'. Maeterlinck later provided a leading lady with alternative words that no longer emphasised the length of the heroine's hair – sometimes awkward to stage. The only Paris performances of the play took place at the Théâtre des Bouffes Parisiens in May 1893 (Debussy was in the audience). The music on that occasion was by Gabriel Fabre (1858–1921), and Mélisande sang an alternative song about a king's three blind daughters – *Les trois sœurs aveugles*. By this time this replacement lyric had found its way into later printings of the play. In his opera Debussy chose to set the original lyric (the opening of Act III of *Pelléas et Mélisande*, vocal score p. 116), which accounts for the fact that the later words set by Fauré, as printed above, are nowhere to be found in Debussy's opera.

In 1898, when Debussy was still occupied with bringing his masterpiece to the stage, he was invited, rather cheekily, to provide a preview of a certain amount of its material as incidental music for a London production, in English, of the original play. He refused, rather understandably, and Fauré was asked in his stead. It seems that Debussy was not informed about this turn of events. In a letter to Georges Hartmann (9 August 1898) he rails against both Maeterlinck and Fauré on this account. Debussy reminds Hartmann that Maeterlinck is 'a Belgian! which is to say, a trifle vulgar and badly brought up' and that Fauré 'hasn't had the good manners to keep me informed'. At the same time the younger composer assures his correspondent, not altogether convincingly, that he is not at all rattled by the reported success of Fauré's music.[18] The play's translation and the incidental music were commissioned by the English Mélisande, Mrs Patrick Campbell. In her autobiography she recounts how she met Fauré at Frank Schuster's house in London in late March or early April 1898, and read him in French those parts of the play that she believed needed music: 'Dear Mr Fauré, how sympathetically he listened, and how humbly he said he would do his best!'[19] She is pictured with Fauré in a beautiful full-face depiction of the composer in charcoal by John Singer Sargent. The drawing is dated June 1898 (thus during the subsequent run of *Pelléas et Mélisande* in London) and was made during a party at 'The Hut', the sumptuous house of Frank Schuster at Bray-on-Thames.

'Mrs Pat' was delighted with the composer's work. She wrote that Fauré 'had grasped with most tender inspiration the poetic purity that pervades and envelops M. Maeterlinck's lovely play'.[20] The orchestral suite taken from the play is indeed Fauré's orchestral masterpiece, and its dedication to the Princesse de Polignac (it was given its first performance at a Lamoureux concert in 1901) helped to defuse the tension between Fauré and Winnie regarding his non-fulfilment of her opera commission.

On the private front, the presence of Adela Maddison (perhaps she became the composer's mistress during this trip, perhaps earlier) was another perfect reason for Fauré to find himself living and working in London. His London host Frank Schuster at 22 Old Queen Street (today the offices of the *Spectator* magazine) would have done anything necessary to facilitate clandestine meetings between the lovers, all in the tradition of the Edwardian house-party that already held sway in late Victorian times.

The translator of Maeterlinck's French was John ('Jack') William Mackail, the brother-in-law of the play's designer Burne-Jones; he published an important life of William Morris in 1899. We catch sight of him again in Fauré's life when he was present at the first performance of *Prométhée* in Béziers with Adela Maddison and the Princesse de Polignac. It seems that Mackail was a somewhat fastidious translator: while being happy to translate 'Les trois sœurs aveugles' to be sung, he was unhappy about the loss of a lyric, rich in symbolism, that crucially mentioned Mélisande's hair – 'Mes longs cheveux descendent'. Accordingly it

Fauré, with Mrs Patrick Campbell in the background. Drawing by John Singer Sargent

seems that this passage was reinstated in the English version, but it was spoken, rather than sung, from Mélisande's tower by Mrs Patrick Campbell. The song (*Les trois sœurs aveugles*) was confusingly shifted to the preceding scene, where Mélisande is at her spinning wheel.

The music was completed in a great hurry to be ready for the first performance on 21 June 1898, in the production by Sir Johnston Forbes-Robertson (who also played Golaud to Martin Harvey's Pelléas). In a revival of this production Sarah Bernhardt, who delighted in *travesti* roles, took over the role of Pelléas (with Mrs Patrick Campbell, and in French). Mary Garden, Debussy's first Mélisande, compared Bernhardt's performance to that of Robin Hood in a pantomime. [21]. Fauré had to ask his pupil Charles Koechlin for help in orchestrating the music. This mysterious lyric is Fauré's only song in English; it is accompanied by sparse but haunting harmonies and scored for flute, clarinet and strings. There is some disagreement about whether it was heard at all in the London performances: Charles Koechlin thought not; Reynaldo Hahn (Koechlin's diary informs us that Hahn was at the London performance) averred that it would have been beyond the abilities of Mrs Patrick Campbell as it required the considerable breath control of a professional singer; but Nectoux, in examining the parts and cue sheets used in the theatre production, could find no evidence that *Mélisande's Song* had been cut.[22]

Hahn was correct about the limited singing capabilities of most actresses, but 'Mrs Pat' could have sung the song, even if not very well. She had decided where all the music was to appear in the production, and why else would she have commissioned a song from Fauré if not for herself? The source of Koechlin's confusion (as well as Hahn's) was that the actress had obviously spoken, rather than sung, the reinstated 'Mes longs cheveux'. They had clearly both forgotten that she had in fact sung 'The king's three blind daughters' at an earlier point in the production. This mistaken memory, many years after the event, is surely the result of their knowing Debussy's more famous setting of Maeterlinck's play rather better than Fauré's incidental music.

The rising motif that opens this song is also the basis of the *Molto adagio* movement that closes Fauré's *Pelléas et Mélisande* orchestral suite, first performed in 1901. This poignant music describes and accompanies the death of Mélisande, and was chosen to accompany the procession of the catafalque at the state funeral granted the composer by the French government in 1924.

This was the last of Fauré's songs to be composed in the nineteenth century; it was first performed in Paris on the concert platform in December 1936.

∾   ∾   ∾   ∾

Arguably the two greatest French composers, Fauré and Debussy owe some of their finest and most refined work to Belgian writers – this song is Fauré's only connection with Maeterlinck, but it was followed by eighteen settings of his compatriot and colleague Charles Van Lerberghe who, by curious coincidence, was in the audience for the première of the London production of *Pelléas et Melisande* in June 1898, but made no comment on the music (he did write of the 'golds and liquid greens' of the costumes by Edward Burne-Jones). It is also very possible that the composer and the poet met at a party given by Frank Schuster on 21 June 1898, following the first performance of the Maeterlinck play, but they probably merely shook hands and had no idea of the important role they were later to play in each other's lives.

The link between the two Belgian poets, Maeterlinck and Van Lerberghe, is reinforced by the fact that the musical material of *Mélisande's Song* reappears eight years later in two songs from Fauré's great song cycle *La Chanson d'Ève*, first in *Crépuscule* (June 1906) and then in *Paradis*, composed in the autumn of the same year. This musical idea clearly signifies something special in the composer's mind. The king's three blind daughters experience a living death: they are lost in primeval darkness, as if before the dawn of creation, and they are denied that radiant outcome. This music of 'nothingness' must have seemed to Fauré an ideal starting point for the 'isle of oblivion' and the 'cry in the night' of *Crépuscule* or a landscape that awaits the intervention of divine grace such as in *Paradis*, just as Haydn's *Creation* depicts Chaos before a blaze of redemptive light.

There is another moment in *Mélisande's Song* that finds an echo in a later work, the opera *Pénélope*: the orchestral phrase following Ulysse's great outburst at the end of Act I (after the second of his 'Épouse chérie!') quotes the melody for the words 'The Prince on the stair'.[23] At this point in *Mélisande's Song* the sisters hope in vain for the redemptive return of the king; Pénélope awaits the same thing in her longing for the return of Ulysse.

∾   ∾   ∾   ∾

Maurice Maeterlinck was born in Ghent, Belgium, on 29 August 1862. As a student he became friends with his slightly older but less worldly compatriot Charles Van Lerberghe, a name that will dominate Chapters 12 and 13 of this book. Maeterlinck was an exact contemporary of the composer Claude Debussy, whose opera would confer immortality on the poet in the eyes of music lovers everywhere. This is despite the fact that the poet Mallarmé, when reviewing *Pelléas et Mélisande* in 1893 (the play, of course, not the opera), dismissed the idea that these words would ever need a musical accompaniment. In Maeterlinck's art, said Mallarmé, everything becomes music anyway.

Maeterlinck's first published collection of verse appeared in 1889 – a limited edition of *Serres chaudes* ('Hothouses'), a group of poems that took the literary world by storm and enchanted Ernest Chausson, who set a number of them to music. Works for the theatre followed soon after – *L'Intruse* and *Les Aveugles* (both 1890), *Les Sept princesses* (1891) and *Pelléas et Mélisande* in 1892. Within a few years the name of this poet-playwright had become very famous and synonymous with the term 'symbolism'. His plays were translated into many languages: as we have seen, the English version of *Pelléas*, for which Fauré wrote the music, was seen on the London stage in June 1898. The poet's relationship with the actress and singer Georgette Leblanc lasted more than twenty years – she was his muse and managerial interpreter; Debussy went to a great deal of trouble to avoid having her sing the title role in his opera. Maeterlinck was also an author of essays – usually meditations on philoso-phy and nature. He was deeply interested in

Maurice Maeterlinck

animal and insect life, and his *La Vie des abeilles* (1901) remains a classic.

Although he claimed to be the least musical of poets in terms of his knowledge of music itself, Maeterlinck's long and fruitful career was rich in music and musicians. Paul Dukas's opera *Ariane et Barbe-bleue* (1907), a work that impressed Fauré greatly, is to a Maeterlinck text. The playwright's *Sœur Béatrice* was considered, then rejected, as a libretto by Fauré after he had worked on the project for two years (1900–1902; no sketches have survived). Among the other composers who set Maeterlinck to music were Lili Boulanger, Jean Absil and Arthur Honegger. And if it were not a sufficient compli-ment to the musical power of *Pelléas et Mélisande* that both Debussy and Fauré wrote music for this play, the symphonic poem of Arnold Schoenberg (1903) and the incidental music of Jean Sibelius (1905) on the same subject are testaments to the power of the story to fascinate musicians.

On 8 May 1912, Fauré, at the time deeply involved in the composition of his opera *Pénélope*, found time to conduct in Brussels a performance of his music for *Pelléas et Mélisande* as part of a homage to Maeterlinck in his fiftieth birthday year. Maeterlinck died on 6 May 1949 in Nice.

∾   ∾   ∾   ∾

We might describe 1898 as Fauré's British year: there were three visits in all – March–April, June–July and October. By now he was able to write letters in English after a fashion; after signing one of these 'Yours very sincerely, Gabriel Fauré' he added as a footnote 'Jeune élève d'anglais'.[24] After the success of *Pelléas et Mélisande* in London, he stayed at Llandough Castle in Wales as guest of the striking Mrs George Swinton (handsomely painted by Sargent), who was also a singer of his songs;

she went on to perform some of these with the composer in Manchester in 1908. In Wales Fauré completed his Seventh Nocturne and dedicated it to Adela Maddison, who by now was deeply in love with him – a devotion that as far as we know he reciprocated, at least for a while. In October he was back in London, where *Pelléas et Mélisande* was revived at the Lyceum. At some time along the way, and probably much earlier than this, Emma Bardac, so crucial to the composer's emotional happiness at the time of *La Bonne chanson*, had quietly slipped out of Fauré's life; it is by no means certain whether Adela Maddison's new position as Fauré's mistress was the cause, or the result, of the break-up of this historically productive relationship.

In 1898 Adela abandoned her husband and two children and moved to Paris to be nearer Fauré. For her bravery in following the man she loved she was admired by Marguerite Baugnies (now Madame de Saint-Marceaux), who set aside her scruples and played hostess to the couple at her country home in 1899 when Fauré brought with him the manuscript of the Seventh Nocturne as a gift for his English paramour. The publishing arrangement with Metzler and Co. was not renewed after 1901 – it was an inefficient firm, certainly, but the cuckolded Frederick Maddison, connected with Metzler, might not have regarded Fauré in the kindest of lights. These were the dramas, internal, private, above all discreet, of the composer's life. Of the dramatic *dénouement* of the Dreyfus case in 1899, a political crisis that had polarised the whole of French society, there is little sign in Fauré's biography, although this may be because of a lack of surviving documentation. The older Fauré was far from impervious to the events of the outside world, although there are periods of his life when this impression is created by a dearth of surviving correspondence.

In August 1899, at the behest of Fernand Castelbon de Beauxhostes, a rich patron of the arts, Fauré visited the town of Béziers in the Languedoc. There, in a large modern amphitheatre, he conducted a revival of the opera *Déjanire* by Saint-Saëns, a work commissioned for the town. Fauré was asked to write something of a similarly epic nature for the following year. For a composer such as Fauré this was an unusual, not to say daunting, task; his career had been built on intimate music-making, but the unexpected success of his lyric drama *Prométhée*, given its first performance in Béziers in August 1900, showed that he was more than capable of working on a very large scale. *Prométhée*, a *tragédie-lyrique*, had a libretto by Jean Lorrain and André-Ferdinand Hérold. The orchestration reminds us of Britten's original conception for his *War Requiem*, where a symphony orchestra and a chamber ensemble were controlled by different conductors; in *Prométhée* the wind band was conducted by Charles Eustace, and a string orchestra by Fauré himself. When performed in this vast space the work must have seemed a cross between an opera and a blockbuster pageant. This was the era directly preceding the advent of the cinema as a popular art form; the cast of 800 performers, encompassing hundreds of actors, 200 singers and 400 instrumentalists (including twenty harpists), was seen by an enthusiastic audience of 15,000 spectators. The classical subject of *Prométhée* was very much to the taste of the composer of *Lydia* despite the vast disparity in the sheer scale of the two works.

This was an important turning point for Fauré; it seems to have helped remove his writer's block in composing an opera, and it is significant that when this constraint was finally lifted with the creation of *Pénélope*, it too was on a classical subject. Above all it is the bareness of the late style, as well as its accompanying grandeur of utterance, that stems from the breakthrough of *Prométhée*.

This gateway year into the new century finds Fauré truly 'crossing the divide': the third and final period is now distinctly visible on the horizon. One of the members of the audience at the première of *Prométhée* was Adela Maddison, whom he had been seeing less and less in Paris, but who remained devoted to him. By this time she had branched out, and had made friends on her own

account with the Princesse de Polignac and with other expatriate British artists in Paris, including Delius. She continued to compose; indeed her opera *The Talisman* was performed in Leipzig in 1910. She was able to play her own piano and chamber music, which, according to Madame de Saint-Marceaux (Marguerite Baugnies), was a pleasant enough mixture of Debussy and Fauré. To judge from her *Trois mélodies de Goethe* published by A. Quinzard of Paris in 1902, Adela, soon after parting from Fauré, seems to have graduated to the style of the Baudelaire settings of Debussy, or the *Prose lyriques*: the third song, the effusive *Maifest*, is clearly influenced by Debussy's *Le Balcon*.

Adela's presence in Béziers had been an embarrassment to the composer, who had moved on in his affections, as was his lifelong wont. He had very recently met the twenty-four-year-old pianist Marguerite Hasselmans, daughter of Alphonse Hasselmans, harp professor at the Conservatoire, whose help was enlisted by Fauré in providing all the harpists needed for the Béziers performances. Marguerite's brother was Louis Hasselmans, a cellist (dedicatee of the First Cello Sonata) and a fine conductor.

Marguerite was a good-looking young woman who dressed strikingly; she was formidably intelligent and very much a 'modern', as well as possessing rare discretion and a disinclination for self-advertisement. She was clearly a young lady with an eye for the older man, a father-figure perhaps; at the age of fifty-five the composer was clearly lucky to have found her, although there is nothing to suggest that a roving eye ceased to be the adjunct of his perpetually restless sexual spirit. Marguerite was a pianist of great sensibility; Albéniz was to dedicate to her the third book of *Iberia*, and she was Fauré's own favourite interpreter of his piano works (whatever was claimed and written to the contrary by that 'other' Marguerite, the hugely talented but self-serving Madame Long). Mademoiselle Hasselmans spoke Russian, read philosophy and smoked in public; on the other hand she was an extremely private person who avoided publicity of any kind. Fauré was completely *bouleversé* by her, and the couple began a relationship (even though the composer was the same age as her father) that would last for the rest of the composer's life.

Draining though it was to his finances, Fauré installed Marguerite, in the time-honoured fashion for a mistress, in an apartment in the avenue Wagram, Plaine Monceau, from where she gave piano lessons. It was known to everyone that 'Mme H', as the composer called her, played a special role in Fauré's life, and from now on she accompanied him on all his long working holidays in the summers. This was a kind of second marriage in an era when divorce was socially unacceptable. The humiliation of this development – a permanent mistress, young, beautiful talented – must have been indescribably bitter to Marie Fauré, who became more and more of a recluse over the years.

Perhaps this is the reason why the advent of this relationship coincided with a profound change in the composer's epistolary habits. Heart-searching letters to such diverse female muses or mother figures as Marie Clerc, Marguerite Baugnies, the Princesse de Polignac and Elisabeth Greffulhe were now a thing of the past. Unfortunately there are no surviving letters to Marguerite Hasselmans (she was in any case at the composer's side as often as was possible). Instead, the correspondence with Fauré's wife Marie really comes to the fore as our most valuable source of sometimes daily information concerning work in progress and his thoughts about music. It is as if he felt he owed her, as the recipient of important letters relating to his oeuvre, this small sliver of the immortality that she so longed for on her own account (in trying to follow in her father's footsteps, she had even turned her hand to sculpting).

In June 1901 Robert de Montesquiou arranged a Fauré recital at his home at 96 boulevard Maillot in Neuilly, a dwelling built in Louis XVI's reign which he christened the 'Pavillon des muses'. Maurice Bagès as an accustomed interpreter of Fauré songs was joined by the famous baritone Victor Maurel (allocated *Au cimetière*, *Clair de lune* and *Spleen*) and the equally celebrated soprano Félia Litvinne (she performed *Automne* and *Les Berceaux*). The programme was divided into two parts by Litvinne's performance of Wagner's *Liebestod*.[25] In the autumn of this year Fauré worked on the Chinese-influenced incidental music to Georges Clemenceau's play *Le Voile de bonheur*. Although given the opus number 88, this music has never been published. In November of that year Maurice Ravel dedicated his famous piano piece *Jeux d'eau* to his teacher.

It was some time since Emma Bardac had been the composer's muse, and this perhaps explains the absence of songs (apart from *Mélisande's Song*) in the composer's catalogue for over four years. The relationships with Adela Maddison and, more importantly, Marguerite Hasselmans had turned the composer's mind towards the piano at the expense of the *mélodie*. Female intervention was needed to reverse this trend. This came in the form of a beautiful young contralto named Émilie Girette. 'Mimi', as Émilie was known, was the daughter of a famous architect, Jean Girette (her parents, both amateur musicians, had a distinguished musical salon at 11 avenue de Villiers),[26] and in 1903 she married the ebullient Edouard Risler, a young and good-looking Alsatian pianist on his way to the top. (Émilie fell in love with him as he accompanied her in Fauré songs unknown to him – 'her' *Accompagnement* among others – but which he sight-read perfectly.) She was in a very privileged position as the daughter of an important patron of the arts: her other accompanists, apart from Fauré himself, were Alfred Cortot and Reynaldo Hahn. It was thanks to the Girettes, undaunted by the scale of the works that they presented in their home, that Fauré's *Prométhée* was revived in Paris in 1902 under the baton of Alfred Cortot; Émilie sang the role of Gaïa, which she studied with the composer himself. He accompanied her in a group of songs at the Salle Erard at the beginning of March 1902: *Les Roses d'Ispahan*, *Aurore*, *Automne*, *Les Berceaux* and even Schubert's *Gretchen am Spinnrade*. On one Sunday in April 1902 Fauré persuaded Émilie to join him in the organ loft at the Madeleine and hear him improvise; she noted this down in her diary with all the innocence of an ingénue, and without any sense of having been invited to 'view the composer's etchings'. On another occasion Fauré shared a box at the Opéra with her for a performance of *Siegfried*; her diary describes her joy at sharing Fauré's impressions in the music, as well as his 'amusantes et fines remarques'.[27] With women one senses that Fauré was always a gentleman, but he was never remiss in giving the chosen ones every opportunity, should they so wish, to get to know him better.

Despite his attachment to Marguerite Hasselmans it would not have been lost on Fauré, incapable of being faithful for very long, that Émilie was a beautiful young lady. He was inspired to turn his hand to a group of *mélodies* to be sung by her, and in a sense written in her honour. Surprisingly, as if there had been no time-gap between *Arpège* and this newly reinvigorated creative impulse, he reached for the poetry of Albert Samain, taking up where he had left off in the book which was first his gift to Emma Bardac and was then returned to him with her annotations regarding which poems he should set. The Girettes had hosted a great Fauré concert at their home on 25 March 1902, when Fauré played piano duets with Alfred Cortot and *La Bonne chanson* was performed, as well as the *Requiem* with organ accompaniment. A few days later Fauré completed *Accompagnement*. Émilie's diary ingenuously recounts what Fauré had told her in advance: 'From the musical point of view it will be like *Soir* … in writing it he is thinking of me and my voice … He's afraid I shan't like it … He told me he thought there was a little of me in it and that he'd worked on it heart and soul.'[28]

(75) *Accompagnement* (*Accompaniment*)[29]
28 March 1902, Op. 85 No. 3, 'À Madame Edouard Risler', third Hamelle collection p. 82, G♭ major, 3/2, *Adagio*

Tremble argenté, tilleul, bouleau …	*Silver aspen, lime, birch …*
La lune s'effeuille sur l'eau …	*The moon sheds itself on the water …*

Comme de longs cheveux peignés au vent du soir,   *Like long hair combed by the evening breeze,*
L'odeur des nuits d'été parfume le lac noir.   *The scent of summer nights perfumes the black lake.*
Le grand lac parfumé brille comme un miroir.   *The great perfumed lake gleams like a mirror.*

Ma rame tombe et se relève,	*My oar dips and rises,*
Ma barque glisse dans le rêve.	*My boat glides in the dream.*
Ma barque glisse dans le ciel	*My boat glides in the sky*
Sur le lac immatériel …	*On the insubstantial lake …*
En cadence, les yeux fermés,	*In cadence, with closed eyes,*
Rame, ô mon cœur, ton indolence	*Row, O my heart, your indolence*
À larges coups lents et pâmés.	*In broad slow swooning strokes.*

Là-bas la lune écoute, accoudée au coteau,   *Over there the moon, against the hillside, listens*
Le silence qu'exhale en glissant le bateau …   *To the silence of the gliding boat …*
Trois grands lis frais-coupés meurent sur mon manteau.   *Three large fresh-cut lilies die on my cape.*

Vers tes lèvres, ô Nuit voluptueuse et pâle,   *Is it their soul or mine that reaches out*
Est-ce leur âme, est-ce mon âme qui s'exhale?   *To your lips, O pale and voluptuous night?*
Cheveux des nuits d'argent peignés aux longs roseaux …   *Hair of silver nights combed by tall reeds …*

Comme la lune sur les eaux,	*Like the moon on the waters,*
Comme la rame sur les flots,	*Like the oar on the waves,*
Mon âme s'effeuille en sanglots!	*My soul sheds itself in sobs!*

Albert Samain (1858–1900)

This is the composer's third, and last, dalliance with Samain, and among the least-performed of all his *mélodies*. Less obviously voluptuous than *Pleurs d'or*, it shows the composer on the verge of his third period. The music has some of the harmonic characteristics of Fauré's late style, but it has yet to achieve the transparency and lucidity of the four final cycles.

Émilie Girette in her diary (for the spring of 1902) describes the process of composition as recounted to her by the composer – this in itself is a sign of an intimate friendship, although almost certainly not as intimate as Fauré might have wished:

> He told me he was composing in his head first of all, starting with the words; it's the poetry that inspires him – the melodic line grows gradually within him, maturing even without his conscious application, and then comes the labour of putting everything in order which is far from being the easiest part.[30]

This extended *mélodie* is best understood as a series of pictures, each reflecting, Monet-like, the composer's lifelong fascination with water imagery in music. The first of these (the poem's opening five lines) is accompanied by pulsating mezzo-staccato quavers. At first glance these seem as restless as the off-beat throbbings of the accompaniment to *J'ai presque peur, en vérité* from *La Bonne chanson*. The difference is that this restless rhythm, ever changing yet somehow immobile, manages to suggest shimmering moonlight on the flat and mirror-like surface of 'Le grand lac parfumé'.

In the next seven lines the singer plies an oar in 'broad slow swooning strokes'. Each plunge in *forte* quavers and triplets sets off a series of subsidiary ripples in *piano* semiquavers. (This is a study for the marvellous, and rather different, depiction of ripples of water in *Mirages* many years later.) The next two strophes (from 'Là-bas la lune écoute') inspire yet another pattern: limpid sextuplets spiral between the pianist's hands, and from the lower stave to the higher, a miracle of teeming uneventfulness (see also *Eau vivante* in *La Chanson d'Ève*), the gliding of the boat in unearthly silence.

This is water music, simultaneously nocturne and barcarolle, whose upward drift is also redolent of the wafting fragrance of the lilies mentioned in the text. The final strophe of the poem is set to the music of the opening as both moon and poet's oar touch the surface of the water. The vocal line is neither melody nor recitative, but a continually evolving combination of both – pure music that simplifies an over-aesthetic text not best-suited to music. It is interesting that *Accompagnement* was not one of the poems selected by Emma Bardac for setting eight years earlier. Nevertheless if the song taken as a whole proves not to be one of Fauré most perfect successes, it contains ample evidence of his own ineffable mastery of tone and atmosphere. It is significant that Charles Koechlin, one of the composer's fervent admirers, composed his own setting of *Accompagnement*. In his short biography of Fauré he remarks that in this song Fauré had missed some of the poem's meaning by 'a too scrupulous fidelity to the poem'. Koechlin's own sprawling setting is rich in a chordal polytonal atmosphere, but his three-stave 'accompagnement' is almost impossible to play.

The manuscript of the song (in the Bibliothèque Nationale) is inscribed to 'ma délicieuse interprète et amie Mlle. Mimi Girette'. It is hardly surprising that *Le Plus doux chemin*, a song of indomitable courtly devotion and Don Ottavio-like self-control, is dedicated to the same singer.

(76) *La Fleur qui va sur l'eau* (*The flower on the water*)[31]
13 September 1902, Op. 85 No. 2, 'À Mademoiselle Pauline Segond', second Hamelle collection p. 77, B minor, 3/2, *Allegretto molto moderato*

Sur la mer voilée	*On the sea*
D'un brouillard amer	*A bitter fog has veiled,*
La Belle est allée,	*The Fair Lady set out,*
La nuit, sur la mer!	*At night, on the sea!*
Elle avait aux lèvres	*Between her lips,*
D'un air irrité,	*Indignantly, she held*
La Rose des Fièvres,	*The Rose of Fevers,*
La Rose Beauté!	*The Rose of Beauty!*
D'un souffle farouche	*With its savage breath,*
L'ouragan hurleur	*The shrieking storm*
Lui baisa la bouche	*Kissed her mouth*
Et lui prit la fleur!	*And took the flower!*
Dans l'océan sombre,	*In the sombre ocean,*
Moins sombre déjà,	*Less sombre now*
Où le trois-mâts sombre,	*The three-master sinks,*
La fleur surnagea.	*The flower floated.*
L'eau s'en est jouée,	*The waves toyed with it*
Dans ses noirs sillons;	*In their black furrows –*
C'est une bouée	*Like a buoy*
Pour les papillons.	*Attracting butterflies.*
Et l'embrun, la Houle	*And since that night,*
Depuis cette nuit,	*The spray, the swell,*
Les brisants où croule	*The breakers crashing*
Un sauvage bruit,	*With a savage roar,*
L'alcyon, la voile,	*The halcyon, the sails,*
L'hirondelle autour;	*The circling swallows,*
Et l'ombre et l'étoile	*The shadows and the stars –*
Se meurent d'amour,	*All have been dying with love,*
Et l'aurore éclose	*And the dawn breaking*
Sur le gouffre clair	*Over the clear depths –*
Pour la seule rose	*With love for the only rose*
De toute la mer!	*In all the sea!*

Catulle Mendès (1841–1909)

We may surmise that after completing *Accompagnement*, Fauré was not altogether convinced that Samain's poetry was as congenial to him as it had been in the closing years of the nineteenth century – he looked elsewhere for his next texts, and clearly he was after something less rarefied, more overtly dramatic. We must not forget that the experience of having composed *Prométhée*, a successful work on a grand scale with its share of bombastic passages, was bound to have had some effect on his taste – the epic nature of the Greek drama had brought him out of his shell, at least to a certain and temporary extent. *La Fleur qui va sur l'eau* is a modern *Fleur jetée* written eighteen years after that famously tricky song from 1884, with its *Erlkönig*-like repeated octaves. In the earlier *mélodie* a flower is thrown to the winds, here it is tossed by stormy waves. Although it may not seem to be the case, the accompaniment for *La Fleur qui va sur l'eau* trumps *Fleur jetée* in terms of difficulty: this must be one of the most ingenious, as well as the most maddeningly tricky, accompanying patterns ever devised by a song composer. The amount of tension generated by

Title-page of Trois mélodies, *Op. 85*

these restless, but surprisingly delicate, semiquavers oscillating between the hands is tremendous, but as in *Accompagnement*, Fauré understands better than anyone the secret of uniting hectic movement with an inner stillness. Despite the fingery detail that sets this cauldron rhythmically a-bubble, the composer also manages to suggest something fragile bobbing on the waves, a rose on the surface cradled by water that seems to simmer from beneath.

The singer receives no help at all from the pianist in maintaining his or her own rhythm in longer note values; in the midst of a maelstrom of notes he or she must count or die (the terms 'at sea' or 'cut adrift' come to mind). This separateness is an indication perhaps of the two different worlds to be found adjacent in the song – the tumultuous seascape represented by the piano writing, and the human anguish of the voice part. The accompaniment becomes gradually calmer as the song progresses; by the last page broad groups of quavers and an elegiac vocal line suggest a bitter requiem for lost struggles. Perhaps Mendès has in mind a floral metaphor for a beautiful woman drowned and afloat, a symbolist Ophelia. The imagery of the rose's union with the sea, an aquatic deflowering, could also be descriptive of some violation or disgrace that has led to suicide. There is certainly a rage to this music ('un air irrité', at the very least) that suggests a dramatic (and even melodramatic) subtext of this kind. The song has been compared to *La Vague et la cloche*; it deserves at least as many performances as Duparc's quasi-operatic blockbuster, but its difficulties (which do not sound as formidable as they prove to be under the fingers and in the voice) have discouraged generations of singers and pianists.

(77) *Dans la forêt de septembre* (*In the September forest*)[32]
29 September 1902, Op. 85 No. 1, 'À Mlle Lydia Eustis', third Hamelle collection p. 72, G♭ major,
3/4, *Adagio*

Ramure aux rumeurs amollies,	*Foliage of deadened sound,*
Troncs sonores que l'âge creuse,	*Resonant trunks hollowed by age,*
L'antique forêt douloureuse	*The ancient, mournful forest*
S'accorde à nos mélancolies.	*Blends with our melancholy.*
Ô sapins agriffés au gouffre,	*O fir-trees, clinging to chasms,*
Nids déserts aux branches brisées,	*Abandoned nests in broken branches,*
Halliers brûlés, fleurs sans rosées,	*Burnt-out thickets, flowers without dew,*
Vous savez bien comme l'on souffre!	*You well know our suffering!*
Et lorsque l'homme, passant blême,	*And when man, that pale wanderer,*
Pleure dans le bois solitaire,	*Weeps in the lonely wood,*
Des plaintes d'ombre et de mystère	*Shadowy, mysterious laments*
L'accueillent en pleurant, de même.	*Greet him, likewise weeping.*
Bonne forêt! promesse ouverte	*Good forest! Open promise*
De l'exil que la vie implore,	*Of exile that life implores,*
Je viens d'un pas alerte encore	*I come with a step still brisk*
Dans ta profondeur encor verte.	*Into your still green depths.*
Mais d'un fin bouleau de la sente	*But from a slender birch by the path,*
Une feuille, un peu rousse, frôle	*A reddish leaf brushes*
Ma tête et tremble à mon épaule;	*My head and quivers on my shoulder –*
C'est que la forêt vieillissante,	*For the ageing forest,*
Sachant l'hiver où tout avorte,	*Knowing that winter, when all withers,*
Déjà proche en moi comme en elle,	*Is already close for me as for her,*
Me fait l'aumône fraternelle	*Bestows on me the fraternal gift*
De sa première feuille morte!	*Of its first dead leaf!*

Catulle Mendès (1841–1909)

The composer found this poem in the issue of *Le Figaro* dated 21 September 1902; along with the preceding poem in this chapter, it seems not to have been published in a collection of poetry. The slowly dying forest (Mendès treats it almost as a human presence) looks with benign fellow-feeling on the ageing poet's peregrinations. One is somehow reminded of a famous quatrain from *Les Fleurs du mal*,[33] words that we can be certain that Mendès, the avid Wagnerian, knew well because they also appear as a quotation in Baudelaire's *Richard Wagner et Tannhäuser*:

La Nature est un temple où de vivants piliers	*Nature is a temple whose living pillars*
Laissent parfois sortir de confuses paroles;	*Sometimes let fall confused words;*
L'homme y passe à travers des forêts de symboles	*There man passes through forests of symbols*
Qui l'observent avec des regards familiers.	*Which observe him with familiar glances.*

Jankélévitch, master commentator on late Fauré in particular, notes that the sad grandeur of this song draws attention to the ambiguous poem's simultaneous charting of old age (the autumn of life) and autumn (the ageing of the year).[34] More than a touch of modal harmony (the cadence at 'L'accueillent en pleurant, de même', for instance) also ages the music, a distancing whereby certain passages suggest a sixteenth-century madrigal. Earlier autumnal songs such as *Chant d'automne* and *Automne* had been composed by a younger man struggling to turn back the clocks, but this song strikes a different note, that of an older man's philosophical acceptance of his mortality, despite the fact that the composer was only fifty-seven at the time. He is still young enough to walk briskly into the forest, but in the leaf-shedding autumn of their own life the trees are not fooled – the gradually dying forest recognises that one of its own is in its midst. Is there any significance in the fact that in 1920 Fauré chose to make a gift of the manuscript of this song to the American composer Charles Martin Loeffler, who was one of a number of Americans who contributed a generous sum of money (a 'fraternal gift' perhaps) to help the composer with the expenses of his vulnerable old age?

The key is G♭ major, and the song is a rather more static companion piece to the equally enigmatic *Soir*, also rich in flats. The music glides resourcefully forward, always defying our tendency to second-guess the master's infinitely subtle harmonic twists and turns. This is an accompaniment for the soft footfall among the yellowing leaves, and the contemplation that comes from a future with a limited horizon, all expressed in haunting music of noble reticence. The melodic line is an extraordinary hybrid, tuneful in its way, but also near to a kind of recitative where the accentuations of the spoken word animate the music from within. If Fauré avoided the direct influence of Debussy's opera *Pelléas et Mélisande*, this music definitely inhabits a post-*Pelléas* world. In fact it was composed a few months after Fauré had heard several performances of this work at the Opéra-Comique.

There are some songs of Fauré's late style that perplex the listener, but this one, on the very borders of the forest that forbids entry to all but the brave and determined, is one of the most immediately accessible. I have never encountered a singer who has worked on this song and not fallen in love with it. As Nectoux points out, there is a cadence in a passage from this song (bars 36–40, between 'Mais d'un fin bouleau' and 'tremble à mon épaule') that reappears in Antinoüs's recitative from *Pénélope*.[35]

The dedicatee of the song, Lydia Eustis, was an amateur mezzo-soprano of some distinction. Like her equally well-known soprano sister, Anita Kinen (Madame Georges Kinen), she sang frequently in the important Parisian salons, including that of Marguerite de Saint-Marceaux.

❧   ❧   ❧   ❧

Earlier in the autumn of 1902 Fauré had sketched a song to a poem ('Dans le ciel clair') by a poet whom he had some justification in regarding as an old faithful, Leconte de Lisle. This did not turn out satisfactorily (it would have been the composer's sixth setting by that poet), so he searched for a new collaborator and found one in another poet of the old guard. Catulle Mendès was more or less a contemporary of Fauré's. Of Jewish background, he had been singularly good-looking and powerfully charming in his youth and had been associated with all the great literary figures of Paris since the 1860s. By the time the composer came across a few examples of the late flowering of his poetry in 1902, the seventy-year-old writer was more or less resting on old laurels – he had been, after all, editor of *Le Parnasse contemporain* and was the famous historian of the Parnassians (see Chapter 3). He had also been Gautier's son-in-law (married to Judith Gautier, who had been famous as Wagner's mistress), Chabrier's librettist (for *Gwendoline*) and the lover of the formidable woman composer Augusta Holmès. Perhaps Fauré was reminded of Mendès at this time as a result of an interview he gave to Louis Aguettant in 1902. When discussing the *mélodies* of Saint-Saëns (Aguettant was unimpressed), Fauré, in defending his old friend's work, came up with a title of an 'exquisite' Saint-Saëns *mélodie* from 1866 entitled *Clair de lune*, with a text by … Catulle Mendès.

Mendès had always been a relentlessly ambitious member of the literary establishment; his early success links him with the extravagances of the Second Empire although he was not much older than Fauré – born on 21 May 1841. Together with his wife Judith and the poet Villiers de L'Isle Adam (see Chapter 7), he visited Wagner in Tribschen as early as 1869.

Catulle Mendès

Despite his wife's celebrated liaison with the composer, and the inevitable tension between French and German artists as a result of the Franco-Prussian War, Mendès remained a faithful Wagnerian, and wrote a number of books on the composer. Apart from his connection with Chabrier (which included providing the disastrous libretto for *Gwendoline* as well as the poems for the ravishing song *Chanson pour Jeanne*, and the delightful *Lied*, both *c*.1886) Mendès wrote opera libretti for Pessard, Messager, Pierné (there are also *mélodie* settings of Mendès by Pierné), Lecocq, Hahn and Massenet. He provided Debussy with the text for *Rodrigue et Chimène*, an opera project that was subsequently abandoned. He translated Humperdinck's *Hänsel und Gretel* into French. Mendès is the author of a very useful survey of poetry of the period, *Le Mouvement poétique français de 1867 à 1908*, in which he allots himself a princely amount of space.

Mendès died on 8 February 1909 as a result of a bizarre accident: it is assumed that when his train stopped he mistakenly thought he had arrived at the station and dismounted; his body was found in the tunnel the next morning. The story is told in *Portraits-souvenirs* by Jean Cocteau,[36] who had come to know Mendès as a teenager – a strange collision of two different worlds where the future progenitor of 'Les Six' was entertained in the plush ambience of the poet's dining room, a makeshift aviary for rare birds that flew around squawking and pecked food from the table. Such theatrical eccentricity marks Mendès out as an untypical Fauré collaborator; it is significant that the two failed to get going on a proposed operatic collaboration, *Lavallière*, in the 1890s.

∾   ∾   ∾   ∾

1903 was not a year of musical creativity in Fauré's life, but it brought news both gratifying and alarming. The composer's music was achieving more frequent public performance with each passing year, and a new generation of performers (such as the cellist Casals) was taking it up with proselytis-

279

ing enthusiasm. Ravel dedicated his String Quartet in F to his teacher Fauré. In March the composer was appointed music critic of *Le Figaro*, a post he had long coveted; this brought him extra money, and his appointment as an *officier* of the Légion d'Honneur betokened serious recognition. He was nevertheless still on the treadmill as inspector of conservatoires. With his composition class at the Conservatoire, as well as his duties as a critic (work for which he scrupulously prepared in advance), the years between 1903 and 1905 were perhaps the most stressful on a day-to-day basis.

The strain of this hectic life began to tell in a most unpleasant way: in the summer of this year there were the first disturbing signs that the fifty-eight-year-old composer was having trouble with his hearing. He spent his holidays in Lausanne, where he returned to work on a piano quintet, first sketched in January 1891, temporarily abandoned, and then worked on again in the summer of 1894. From there he wrote to his wife:

> I am stunned by this curse which has struck me down in the very place where I most need protection. It is disrespectful, or at the very least inconsiderate, to think of Beethoven! Nevertheless the latter half of his life was *nothing but a long period of despair.* Now there are areas of music, sonorities, where I can hear *nothing, nothing*! Of my own, as well as others. This morning I put some manuscript paper on my table; I wanted to try to work. Now I feel only a mantle of misery and discouragement on my shoulders …[37]

Work on the piano quintet was continued into the late summer and early autumn of 1904 when the composer stayed in Zürich. Otherwise his hardly arduous creative work included a Conservatoire sight-reading piece for harp as well as an impromptu for the same instrument. The composer was now inclined to look back into his past to rediscover the felicities of his former poetic collaborators. He returned to Armand Silvestre for two songs in 1904.

(78) *Le Plus doux chemin* (Madrigal) (*The sweetest path*)[38]
1904, Op. 87 No. 1, 'À Mme Edouard Risler', F minor, 2/2, *Moderato*

À mes pas le plus doux chemin	*The sweetest path for me*
Mène à la porte de ma belle,	*Leads to my fairest's door,*
– Et, bien qu'elle me soit rebelle,	*– And though she resists me,*
J'y veux encor passer demain.	*I shall tomorrow pass by once more.*
Il est tout fleuri de jasmin	*It is all a-bloom with jasmine*
Au temps de la saison nouvelle,	*When the new season arrives,*
– Et, bien qu'elle me soit cruelle,	*– And though she resists me,*
J'y passe des fleurs à la main.	*I go there bearing flowers.*
Pour toucher son cœur inhumain,	*To touch her inhuman heart*
Je chante ma peine cruelle,	*I sing of my cruel pain,*
– Et, bien qu'elle me soit rebelle,	*– And though she resists me,*
C'est pour moi le plus doux chemin!	*It is for me the sweetest path!*

Armand Silvestre (1837–1901)

280

This enchantingly mournful serenade of a gently persistent, if unsuccessful, lover, is Fauré distilled to the essentials – indeed, it is a latter-day, rather more resigned, *Chanson d'amour*. It is remarkable how spare this accompaniment is in comparison with the fulsome deployment of the pianist's fingers in *Accompagnement* and *La fleur qui va sur l'eau* from only two years earlier. In this 'madrigal' the gentle plucking of a lute contrasts with the strength of a bass line, almost a counter-melody in itself, that depends on the legato tone of a piano to make its effect. The harmonic plan suggests time-travel; G♭ and D♮ in the key of F minor add a Gregorian flavour to the cadences. The song's mood defies easy description: Jankélévitch fancifully likens its effect to 'the smell of the rain on the pathways on a warm autumn evening'.[39] Elsewhere he refers to the song's 'bergamasque charm' (a trait he sees as being shared with the *Agnus Dei* from the *Requiem*) and 'the indefinable and irreducible strange flavour that impregnates the Andantino entitled *Le plus doux chemin*'.[40] Despite Sylvestre's reference to 'la saison nouvelle', autumn does indeed predominate in musical terms; Fauré was now facing his sixtiethth birthday with a mixture of graceful acceptance and regret. The composer's choice of Silvestre shows a nostalgia for the past; the poem goes back to the poet's early published collection, *La Chanson des heures* (1878), but we do not know what impulse encouraged Fauré to return to a poet whom he had dropped as soon as he came under the influence of the ultra-fastidious Robert de Montesquiou.

We feel that the gallant Don Ottavio, who treads this pathway, will always pay court to feminine beauty while dreaming of more youthful days. The overall tone of the serenade rules out the ardent protestation of a younger man, confident of his suit. Perhaps there is some significance in the fact that Fauré dedicates his song to Madame Édouard Risler, the beautiful, though clearly unobtainable, contralto Émilie Girette. It is more than likely that the composer had a terrible crush on her. The poem's last syllable is dovetailed with a six-bar postlude, a fragmented version of the opening melody that is repeated like a lover's despondent sigh in a lower register of the keyboard. Aaron Copland once remarked of this song that 'all of Fauré is contained in its three short pages'.[41]

This song reappears in an orchestrated version as No. 4 of the amalgam of songs and dances, some new and some old, that appeared under the title of *Masques et bergamasques* in 1919. In this work, with a libretto by René Fauchois, it is sung by Clitandre, that long-winded participant ('l'éternel Clitandre') in Verlaine's *Fêtes galantes* who sits alone on a bench with a guitar slung from his shoulders, singing to his own accompaniment. Silvestre's words are retained for this music of course.

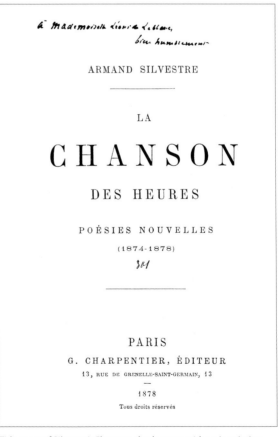

Title-page of Silvestre's Chanson des heures, *with an inscription from the poet*

(79) *Le Ramier* (*Madrigal*) (*The ring-dove*)[42]

1904, Op. 87 No. 2, 'À Mlle Claudie Segond', third Hamelle collection p. 70, E minor, 3/4, *Andantino*

Avec son chant doux et plaintif,	*With its gentle plaintive song,*
Ce ramier blanc te fait envie:	*This white ring-dove makes you envious:*
S'il te plaît l'avoir pour captif,	*If you want it as a captive,*
J'irai te le chercher, Sylvie.	*I'll go and seek it for you, Sylvie.*
Mais là, près de toi, dans mon sein,	*But there, near you, in my breast,*
Comme ce ramier mon cœur chante:	*Like this ring-dove, my heart sings:*
S'il t'en plaît faire le larcin,	*If you would like to steal it,*
Il sera mieux à toi, méchante!	*It will be better for you, wicked girl!*
Pour qu'il soit tel qu'un ramier blanc,	*For it to be like a white ring-dove,*
Le prisonnier que tu recèles,	*The prisoner that you conceal,*
Sur mon cœur, oiselet tremblant,	*Place your hands like two wings*
Pose tes mains comme deux ailes.	*On my heart, a trembling little bird.*

Armand Silvestre (1837–1901)

In 1904 the company Il Gramofono of Milan commissioned a series of short pieces from a number of contemporary composers with the idea that each composer should accompany his new work on a single-sided gramophone record. Giordano and Leoncavallo recorded their contributions, but Fauré did not; the failure of the project seems indicative of the composer being at odds with the technology of the new century. (Other composers commissioned but not recorded included Puccini and D'Indy.) *Le Ramier* marks the composer's farewell to Silvestre after an intermittent working relationship of twenty-six years. The lyric comes from the poet's first collection, *La Chanson des heures* (1878), where its title, like that of *Le Plus doux chemin*, is 'Pour une voix'. Despite its age, the lyric fulfils remarkably well the literary requirements of a composer who, more than a quarter of century later, finds himself working on the borders of poetic symbolism.

   This bird music could not be more different from the ecstatic tremblings for quail and lark in *La Bonne chanson*. This billing and cooing is much more low-key but adorable nevertheless; the dropping fifth and the mezzo-staccato quavers of the accompaniment are surprisingly evocative of this bird-like sound. If Schubert's *Die Taubenpost* is too exalted a comparison, *The Doves* by that gifted American composer Theodore Chanler – who owes much to Fauré via Nadia Boulanger – is perhaps more apt. This is one of Fauré's least appreciated, least sung, little gems, and is music that is the gateway into Fauré's late style. As Jankélévitch puts it, 'Fauré is on the threshold of a long and admirable old age'.[43] Each note and each progression has been carefully planned, yet seems casual and relaxed. The syncopations and off-beat accents, as well as a suggestion of counterpoint, all prefigure the late style with a suave quirkiness. Fauré might have been tempted to write a song in popular style for the Gramophone company; instead he wrote a song that is far from popular, but near perfection, right up to the ravishing final cadence.

   The music has the rueful charm of a man nearing sixty who realises that his days as a Lothario, if not quite over, are at least numbered. This does not necessarily imply a diminution of sexual energy;

we have to remind ourselves that Fauré was 'unofficially' attached to Marguerite Hasselmans, who accompanied him on all his journeys, whenever possible. Nevertheless, bidding farewell to his days of roving was a mournful matter, even for a man with a beautiful and talented young mistress. The name 'Sylvie' (evocative because of Fauré's setting of that name in 1878) no longer prompts an 'escort' of passionate semiquavers. If he can no longer promise his lady friends the passion of *La Bonne chanson*, he can at least offer civilised companionship and this *compliment galant*. In every respect this is a wonderful example of the 'madrigal' style from an ageing but ever-gallant troubadour.

∾ ∾ ∾ ∾

Eleven years and six poets, two of them (Leconte de Lisle and Silvestre) recapitulations from former times … This period finds Fauré, for the second time in his song-composing career, searching for a new direction. Until he finds it he feels free to compose in subtly different genres – from light-hearted pastiche to music of the deepest seriousness.

Each song here is remarkable in a different way. *Sérénade, Accompagnement, La Fleur qui va sur l'eau* and *Le Ramier* are the least performed among them, but any of these would grace a recital if properly programmed. *Sérénade* has been handicapped by the relative unavailability of its music; *Accompagnement* requires (and rewards) a patient deciphering from both singer and pianist it seldom receives; the complexities of *La Fleur qui va sur l'eau* will not be taken on lightly by any accompanist, particularly if his or her singer is not infallibly rhythmic. It is a mystery to me why more singers do not include *Le Ramier* in their programmes; *Mélisande's Song* with its English text seems to appear far more often on English recital programmes than French; it is something of a companion piece to that single Shakespeare song in English by Francis Poulenc, the enchanting *Fancy*.

This leaves us with six masterpieces, of which the fugitive and exquisite *Arpège* is the least known. *Pleurs d'or* requires two excellent singers with perfect intonation, but it is to be heard with delight at many of the best duet recitals, one of the most immediately attractive of all Fauré songs, and one that admirers of Massenet (and those songs of Debussy influenced by Massenet) would take to like ducks to water. Best-known from this period are *Soir* and *Le Plus doux chemin*, entirely unlike each other but representing two kinds of time-honoured Fauré *mélodie*, the first genre made famous by another vocal nocturne, *En sourdine* with its similar evenly spaced semiquaver accompaniment, and the second an even lovelier variation on the imitation sixteenth-century madrigal style of *Chanson d'amour*. These songs look to their earlier models, and arguably excel them, certainly in the case of *Le Plus doux chemin*, which, in turn, shows the way to the etiolated but fascinating *Chanson* (Henri de Régnier) of the next chapter.

There are two songs, *Le Parfum impérissable* and *Dans la forêt de septembre*, that look out towards the future, even though their use of modal harmony also evokes the past. This music knocks gently and solemnly on the door of the third period. Both songs have accompaniments of deceptive simplicity from the point of view of digital dexterity, but they are sprinkled with the many accidentals that unlock their harmonic subtlety and complexity. The first is *Andante molto moderato* in E major, and the second *Adagio* in G♭ major. Both these tonalities, the sharp and the flat, are favourite keys that will play an important role in the third period. It is in these two songs that time seems to stand still; Fauré's music is timeless, although its rhythmic impetus is implacable, and there is no trace of sentimentality. We have our first intimation here of how Fauré can create a new style, shorn of superficially exciting musical events, that is nevertheless mesmerising. Even those who remain unconvinced by the music of the last period are struck by the haunting beauty of these two songs.

Designs by A. Giraldon for Samain's Au Jardin de l'Infante *(1920)*

Arpège with its fleet arabesques will very soon be a bagatelle of the past as far as the composer is concerned, as will the busy virtuosity of *La Fleur qui va sur l'eau*. Coming into focus we now see the future image of an old man sitting at the keyboard playing slow crotchets; he is scarcely able to hear the singers by his side, but he trusts them to keep in time; as chord succeeds chord he metronomically traverses the score from one end to the other; his short fingers on the keyboard scarcely seem to move as he accompanies voices that negotiate the stave in small and exquisitely calculated intervals. Everything seems effortless under those compact hands but the subtly woven web of sound that supports and enfolds those lucky singers is painstakingly measured and unfurled – the work of a lifetime, subtle and sublime harmony: nothing less than the music of the spheres.

1   *Sérénade*: Aspects of this song's interpretation are discussed in Chapter 16, p. 418.

2   Vladimir Jankélévitch, *Music and the Ineffable* (1961, rev. 1981), trans. Caroline Abbate (Princeton, NJ: Princeton University Press, 2003), p. 104.

3   Albert Samain, letter to his sister, 8 March 1896.

4   *Soir*: Aspects of the cycle's interpretation are discussed in Chapter 16, pp. 418.

5   Robert Orledge, 'The Two Endings of Fauré's *Soir*', *Music and Letters*, 60/3 (1979), 316–22.

6   Gabriel Fauré, *Lettres intimes*, ed. Philippe Fauré-Fremiet (Paris: La Colombe, 1951), 16 September 1915, pp. 226–8.

7   Myriam Chimènes, *Mécènes et musiciens* (Paris: Fayard, 2004), p. 142.

8   Robert Orledge, *Gabriel Fauré* (London: Eulenburg, 1979), p. 87.

9   *Pleurs d'or*: Aspects of the cycle's interpretation are discussed in Chapter 16, pp. 419.

10 *Gabriel Fauré: A Life in Letters*, trans. and ed. Barrie Jones (London: B.T. Batsford, 1989), p. 136.

11 *Le Parfum impérissable*: Aspects of the cycle's interpretation are discussed in Chapter 16, pp. 419.

12 *Gabriel Fauré: A Life in Letters*, letter 75, p. 86.

13 There was to be one further attempt to set a poem by Leconte de Lisle in 1902. *Dans le ciel clair* was sketched but never finished. The fragment is discussed at length in Orledge, *Gabriel Fauré*.

14 Quoted in a lecture given at the Rice Institute in 1925 by Nadia Boulanger, transcribed in Don G. Campbell, *Master Teacher – Nadia Boulanger* (Washington DC: The Pastoral Press, 1984), p. 107.

15 Fauré, letter to René Lenormand, 1912.

16 *Arpège*: Aspects of the cycle's interpretation are discussed in Chapter 16, p. 420.

17 *Mélisande's Song*: Aspects of the cycle's interpretation are discussed in Chapter 16, p. 420.

18 Debussy in a letter to Georges Hartmann, 9 August 1898, in *Debussy Letters*, ed. François Lesure and Roger Nichols, trans. Roger Nichols (London: Faber, 1987), p. 99.

19 Orledge, *Gabriel Fauré*, p. 124.

20 Ibid., p. 124.

21 Quoted in Jean-Michel Nectoux, *Gabriel Fauré: A Musical Life*, trans. Roger Nichols (Cambridge; Cambridge University Press, 1991), p. 161.

22 Ibid., p. 157.

23 Gabriel Fauré, *Pénélope*, vocal score (Paris: Heugel, 1930), p. 115.

24 Orledge, *Gabriel Fauré*, plate VIII.

25 Chimènes: *Mécènes et musiciens*, pp. 369–70.

26 Ibid., p. 138.

27 Quoted in ibid., p. 141.

28 Quoted in Nectoux, *Gabriel Fauré: A Musical Life*, pp. 299–300.

29 *Accompagnement*: Aspects of the cycle's interpretation are discussed in Chapter 16, p. 420.

30 Quoted in Nectoux, *Gabriel Fauré: A Musical Life*, p. 357.

31 *La Fleur qui va sur l'eau*: Aspects of the cycle's interpretation are discussed in Chapter 16, p. 420.

32 *Dans la forêt de septembre*: Aspects of the cycle's interpretation are discussed in Chapter 16, p. 420.

33 Charles Baudelaire: *Les Fleurs du mal* (1861), No. IV, 'Correspondances'.

34 Vladimir Jankélévitch, *De la musique au silence: Fauré et l'inexprimable* (Paris: Plon, 1974), p. 164.

35 Nectoux, *Gabriel Fauré: A Musical Life*, p. 300.

36 Jean Cocteau, *Œuvres complètes*, vol. 9 (Paris: Marguerot, 1923).

37 *Gabriel Fauré: A Life in Letters*, p. 111.

38 *Le Plus doux chemin*: Aspects of the cycle's interpretation are discussed in Chapter 16, p. 421.

39 Jankélévitch, *De la musique au silence: Fauré et l'inexprimable*, p. 165.

40 Jankélévitch, *Music and the Ineffable*, pp. 111–12 and 107.

41 Aaron Copland, 'Gabriel Fauré: A Neglected Master', *Musical Quarterly*, 10/4 (1924), 573–86.

42 *Le Ramier*: Aspects of the cycle's interpretation are discussed in Chapter 16, p. 421.

43 Jankélévitch, *De la musique au silence: Fauré et l'inexprimable*, p. 167.

Chapter Eleven

Interlude: The Silent Gift

Jean Dominique, Henri de Régnier

Faure's sixtieth birthday year, 1905, was a real turning point in his life. His fifties had been a period of running simply to keep still: there was less music written, and in return for greater financial security (brought about by the job as music critic of *Le Figaro*) there had been huge demands made on his physical energy, which was, in any case, in gradual decline. He was drained of most of his *joie de vivre*, and frequently depressed about his health, in particular his increasingly poor hearing; this would gradually develop into an epic struggle with tinnitus that would cruelly distort what musical sounds he could hear – according to his son, these made the higher notes of the stave sound a third lower, and the lower notes a third higher. Only the musical range represented by the middle register of the piano, though faint, was spared this cacophonous refraction of sound. It is extraordinary, and extremely unlucky, that Fauré's hearing was affected mainly in musical terms at first; it seems that his hearing as far as speech was concerned was slower to deteriorate, although a certain amount of lip-reading, obviously impossible with music, may have helped.

On the other hand, success and public recognition were steadily consolidated, but this was mainly with the music he had composed long ago. After the gratifying success of *Prométhée* in 1900 there was very little new music, something that possibly indicated a composer in gradual retreat towards retirement: a handful of songs, the *Huit pièces brèves* for piano (some of which are re-workings of pieces that go back to as early as 1869), the revised *Tantum ergo* for soprano solo and mixed four-part chorus (1902), and some instrumental pieces for conservatoire consumption. It is true that since 1903 he had been working afresh on the piano quintet that he had begun in 1891, but even this needed a new impetus to encourage its completion. At the beginning of 1905 he made a visit to Germany, where he played his Violin Sonata in A major and First Piano Quartet and in Frankfurt paid a visit to Elise Sommerhoff, one of the surviving daughters of Robert and Clara Schumann. Fauré was also in touch with the great violinist Joseph Joachim at this time. There was a wave of interest in Fauré's *mélodies* in Germany – as he noted, 'Everyone here sings my "chansons", as they call them!' This misnomer stems from a too-literal translation of 'song'. In the 1840s, inspired by the new appearance of Berlioz's *Irlande* (settings of Thomas Moore's *Irish Melodies*), the French had uniquely adopted this foreign word *mélodie* as a term for an art song with piano. This was specifically to differentiate it from

Opposite: Gabriel Fauré at his desk as Director of the Paris Conservatoire. © Bibliothèque nationale de France

chanson, which meant something lighter and more popular altogether. The generic 'French *chanson*' (when what is meant is 'French *mélodie*') is an incorrect usage that persists in Germany, England and America to this day.

﹏﹏﹏﹏﹏﹏﹏﹏

One of the most momentous changes in the composer's life took place in the summer of 1905. On 15 June, to everyone's astonishment, Fauré the outsider, Fauré, who had never won the Prix de Rome, and was not yet a member of the Institut, Fauré the alumnus of the École Niedermeyer who had once been blocked by Ambroise Thomas for a post as composition professor, was appointed director of the Paris Conservatoire (he had more than proved himself as a popular teacher of composition there since 1896). He was to take up his new job in October with a salary of 12,000 francs.

A contributory factor to the change of regime was the upheaval caused by *l'affaire Ravel*. The composer of *Jeux d'eau*, Fauré's most famous pupil, had persisted in his attempts to win the Prix de Rome long after less tenacious composers would have thrown in the towel. When Ravel tried again in 1905 he failed to reach the final. The six candidates to do so were all Conservatoire pupils of Charles Lenepveu, who was also on the jury. This blatant favouritism, allied to discrimination against a composer who was already well known with the public, but still eligible as a candidate, caused such a furore that Théodore Dubois was forced to resign, leaving the directorship of the Conservatoire vacant. We may surmise that a French government averse to controversy needed to place an important, and potentially volatile, educational institution into a safe and moderate pair of hands. At this time Fauré's apolitical nature seems to have served him well; he was someone whose reputation had been acquired by steady, hard work over many years. If he was conservative in some ways, he was also completely open to the younger composers and their right to create music in their chosen way. He was a discreet but firm opponent of the Schola Cantorum (despite his personal respect for Vincent D'Indy), the musical institution that most favoured closeness to Rome. The Third Republic was endeavouring to distance itself from the Vatican, and the separation of Church and State was a controversial issue of the period. The times called for exactly the kind of non-partisan and tactful moderation that had always characterised this composer's professional life.

Thanks mainly to the wisdom of François Dujardin-Beaumetz, the under-secretary for fine arts, Fauré, the complete antithesis of the prevailing *arrivisme*, was the chosen man. Ysaÿe's letter of congratulation offered a hug 'for the whole of France', so pleased was he by the appointment. In a letter to the American composer Loeffler of July 1905, Fauré noted with wonder and satisfaction that 'the conservatives of the musical world have applauded it as much as the more progressive elements'. He was especially pleased that he was to be spared most of the administrative duties and that his job would be purely artistic. Of course, things did not quite work out in the way the composer intended.

Fauré became famous overnight with people who would otherwise have been unaware of his existence; this appointment raised his profile to the extent that it affected the sales of his music and the number of performances he enjoyed. Those who imagined, however, that the incumbent's reign as a figurehead would preserve the status quo were in for a rude surprise. A seven-point plan for the rejuvenation of the Conservatoire was published in November 1905. This included sweeping reforms that required the reorganisation of the whole institution. First-year singing students, for example, would now be allowed to study only exercises and vocalises (there is many a wise and old-fashioned singing teacher of today who would welcome such a rule, but there would also be many opponents). The removal of restrictions placed on repertoire for singers (who had been forced to choose music only from the current theatrical repertoire at the Opéra) were hugely welcome; for the first time the German lied was an acceptable subject for study. There was to be much more ensemble music-making and fewer examinations, and composition students were expected to receive a grounding in musical history. Howls of protest greeted Fauré's reorganisation of the corrupt auditioning process whereby professors smuggled their private pupils into the conservatoire system or made entry into the institution conditional on private lessons in advance. Fauré invited both Debussy and D'Indy on to the *conseil supérieur* of the Conservatoire (they both accepted), and Ravel, who had been treated as an unsuccessful student in 1905, found himself on the counterpoint jury in 1906 – this possibly designed to cock a snook at Théodore Dubois, who resigned from the *conseil supérieur* of the Conservatoire claiming that Fauré was turning the institution into 'a temple for the music of the future'.

Fauré was indeed one of the most innovative of all the Paris Conservatoire's directors – one might even say that he dragged the institution kicking and screaming into the twentieth century; because these reforms required radical changes, resulting in numerous resignations, he acquired the nickname of 'Robespierre'. In the process he became a household word. As Claude Rostand put it: 'C'est la guerre, mais la célébrité.'[1]

The new job left Fauré with little time to compose during the academic year, but his heightened status was a remarkable boost to his creative powers and self-confidence. He was able to resign from the Madeleine (he played the organ for the last time there on 1 October 1905, gleefully and irreverently improvising on a French folksong), and this release from an obligation that he had never really enjoyed gave him the time he needed to pursue many dormant compositional ideas. We soon notice the difference in the catalogue of his compositions: in August the Seventh Barcarolle was completed on holiday in Zürich, followed by the Fourth Impromptu. The long-awaited piano quintet was finished by January 1906, with a first performance in March led by Ysaÿe, the work's dedicatee.

Among the composer's first acts following the new appointment had been the termination of his dealings with the publisher Julien Hamelle (1836–1917), whose dilatory and patronising attitude to Fauré's music had been a thorn in the composer's flesh for a number of years. With a decisiveness that signalled a new lease of life, he now signed a contract with the house of Heugel, publisher of Charpentier's opera *Louise*, with effect from the beginning of 1906. Henri Heugel himself (1844–1916) was a somewhat younger and more innovative man than his predecessor. For the student of Fauré's songs who has grown up with the three *recueils* of *mélodies*, peremptorily arranged by Hamelle in 1908 into twenty songs each, this distribution may seem convenient and orderly. In reality, the arrangement lacked any scholarly respect for the chronology of the composer's work; it was simply a rearguard action on the part of the publisher to tidy up loose ends while finding an effective commercial means of packaging the work of a composer who had left their stable and in whose future good opinion Hamelle had little interest. Nevertheless, these volumes have long been an indispensable fact of life (in recent years, American editions with a larger type-face and added commentary have made inroads into the firm's monopoly), and the three *recueils* in their distinctive yellow or buff covers have long seemed conveniently to enshrine (with the exception of four forward-looking songs at the end of the third volume) the vocal parameters of the nineteenth-century Fauré.

As the new century advanced the compact size of those Hamelle volumes (slightly smaller in height and width than a Peters lieder volume) now gave way to the broader and more spacious editions of Heugel, a far more glamorous if somewhat impractical luxuriance of wide-margined paper forever associated with French music by anyone aged over fifty (most of the printed music in present-day France has become smaller in format and disappointingly standardised in appearance). We are now prepared for the late cycles, the first of which was published by Heugel before Fauré made yet another move to Durand, Debussy's publisher. There is only one sticking point, or rather a pair of them: two songs were written in 1906 neither of which were part of a big cycle, and they were also excluded from the sixty-song pseudo-symmetry of the Hamelle volumes. As a result these two beautiful pieces of music, printed in a much larger format than Hamelle's, have always had something of an orphan status, and are not nearly as well known as they might otherwise be. In this period Fauré also composed a beautiful *Vocalise-Étude* for voice and piano (Leduc) that has always lingered in the same kind of library limbo as *Le Don silencieux* and *Chanson*.

(80) *Le Don silencieux* (*The silent gift*)[2]

20 August 1906, Op. 92, 'À Mme Octave Maus', Heugel, published separately, 1906, E major, **c**, *Andante molto moderato*

Je mettrai mes deux mains sur ma bouche, pour taire	*I shall place my two hands over my mouth, to silence*
Ce que je voudrais tant vous dire, âme bien chère!	*What I so wish to tell you, dear heart!*
Je mettrai mes deux mains sur mes yeux, pour cacher	*I shall place my two hands over my eyes, to hide*
Ce que je voudrais tant que pourtant vous cherchiez.	*What I still so wish you to seek.*
Je mettrai mes deux mains sur mon cœur, chère vie,	*I shall place my two hands over my heart, dear life,*
Pour que vous ignoriez de quel cœur je vous prie!	*That you may not know with how much heart I entreat!*
Et puis je les mettrai doucement dans vos mains,	*And then I shall place them gently in your hands,*
Ces deux mains-ci qui meurent d'un fatigant chagrin! …	*These two hands that die of a wearying sorrow! …*
Elles iront à vous pleines de leur faiblesse,	*They will come to you, full of their weakness,*
Toutes silencieuses et même sans caresse,	*All silent and even without a caress,*
Lasses d'avoir porté tout le poids d'un secret	*Weary of having borne all the weight of a secret*
Dont ma bouche et mes yeux et mon front parleraient.	*That my lips and eyes and brow would reveal.*
Elles iront à vous, légères d'être vides,	*They will come to you, light at being empty,*
Et lourdes d'être tristes, tristes d'être timides;	*Heavy at being sad, sad at being shy;*
Malheureuses et douces et si découragées	*Unhappy and gentle and so downcast*
Que peut-être, mon Dieu, vous les recueillerez! …	*That maybe, my God, you will gather them up! …*

'Jean Dominique' (1875–1952)

The poem is the last (No. XXVIII) in the collection entitled *L'Anémone des mers* (1906) by Jean Dominique, the pseudonym of the Belgian poet Marie Closset. There is no heading to the lyric, and thus the evocative title may have been the composer's own, or it may have been the idea of Jean Dominique herself. Fauré had originally thought of *Offrande* as a suitable title (a name that even then must have seemed to belong, as of right, to Reynaldo Hahn's setting of Verlaine's 'Green'). The work's

290

Belgian dedicatee, Madeleine Maus, was clearly the poet's friend, and the composer wrote to her husband, his friend Octave Maus, having no idea at this point that Jean Dominique was a woman:

> I'm counting on Mme Maus to get the poet to pardon me for giving the title *Offrande* to this poem which doesn't have one of its own … If Jean Dominique doesn't like this title, which I've had to think up because of my publisher's insistence, then tell him the *thirteen-foot lines* with which he has decorated his poetry, nice though they are, have given me more than enough to get my teeth into! Still, I hope my music has allowed them to retain their suppleness. I've done my best at least.

Title-page of Le Don silencieux

As we have seen, *Le Don silencieux* is a rarity simply because it was published separately, and was never part of one of the *recueils*. When it was out of print, copies of the music circulated among singers and pianists, who guarded the pages with devotion (I first acquired it in the 1970s in a battered photocopy from my senior colleague Dalton Baldwin).

    Fauré was not often inclined to discuss his songs at length, but here he wrote the following words to his wife:

> It does not in the least resemble any of my previous works, nor anything that I am aware of; I am very pleased about this. There is not even a main theme; the song is of a free nature which would strongly upset Théodore Dubois. It translates the words gradually as they unfold themselves; it begins, opens out, and finishes, nothing more, nevertheless it is unified.[3]

With these words, and with this song, five days' work, Fauré embarks on his third period. Of course there are similarities here to earlier works: the dreamy, introverted nature of *Le Secret* and *Les Présents*, the guitar-like madrigal accompaniment of *Chanson d'amour* and *Le Plus doux chemin*, the economy of *Le Ramier* and also of *Chanson*, the immediate contemporary of *Le Don silencieux*. This music represents evolution rather than revolution, but there is also something new that is beyond technical analysis – a reserve, a melancholy, a *renunciation* that breaks the heart in its lack of self-pity and its honesty. The song seems peeled right down to the deepest level of self-revelation. It is thus difficult not to equate this 'don silencieux' with the gift of Fauré's music to the world, and his noble disinclination to push himself, and his art, under our noses. No music, and no song, better illustrates the composer's 'indifference to success'.

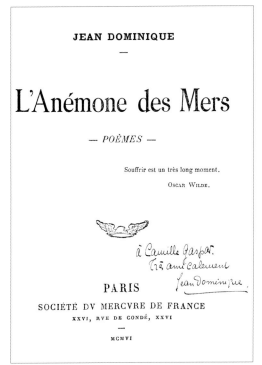

JEAN DOMINIQUE

—

L'Anémone des Mers

— *POÈMES* —

Souffrir est un très long moment.

Oscar Wilde.

*à Camille Gaspar.
Très amicalement
Jean Dominique*

PARIS

SOCIÉTÉ DV MERCVRE DE FRANCE

XXVI, RVE DE CONDÉ, XXVI

—

MCMVI

Title-page of Jean Dominique's L'Anémone des mers
(1906), with the poet's dedication

Like the silent lover who keeps his distance, the gift of this composer's music is easy both to ignore and refuse; indeed, it must first be gathered up, and taken to heart, before it can be understood and cherished. It is little wonder that this strange little song, with the lop-sided and almost halting gait of its accompaniment, and almost no melody to speak of, has always been an article of faith among enthusiasts. A mere mention of *Le Don silencieux* can make admirers of Fauré go misty-eyed; it used to be that an awareness of its very existence was taken as a measure of true devotion to his *mélodies*.

The song was given its informal first performance by Pauline Segond accompanied by the composer in January 1907; this was in a concert of Fauré's works organised by Albert Blondel, director of the firm of Erard pianos (on this occasion Risler played the piano music, and the Capet Quartet collaborated in the First Piano Quintet). Pauline Segond had earlier been the dedicatee of the very different *La Fleur qui va sur l'eau*; Pauline's daughter Claudie Segond was the dedicatee of Fauré's last Silvestre setting, *Le Ramier*.

The composition of *Le Don silencieux* has everything to do with Fauré's ongoing connection with Belgium. The official first performance of this work was reserved for the benefit of Fauré's many friends and allies in that country: Jane Bathori sang *Le Don silencieux* in Brussels on 12 March 1907. Fauré had been an enthusiastic guest there since 1888 when he first met Octave Maus, founder of 'Les Vingt', a group of twenty artists (painters, writers, musicians) who went out of their way to remain in contact with similarly anti-estabishment artists in other countries, and to arrange annual exhibitions and concerts. It was through this brotherhood of symbolists that Fauré first encountered the great violinist Eugène Ysaÿe. The composer was in Brussels for four days in March 1906; the main event was the Belgian première of his Piano Quintet in D minor Op. 89 on the 23rd, but there was a gathering at the home of Octave Maus on the 20th, when piano music, songs and the *Dolly* duets were performed. *Le Don silencieux* was later dedicated to his hostess, Madame Octave Maus. We imagine that Jean Dominique's latest book of poems may have been pressed into Fauré's hand by her, or one of the many Belgians who were justly proud of their native literature. It was also during this visit that Albert Mockel (1866–1945), founder of the revue devoted to Belgian writing, *La Wallonie*, and a considerable poet in his own right (Edmond Gosse referred to him as the Belgian Ariosto[4]), introduced Fauré to *La Chanson d'Ève* and the poetry of Mockel's protégé Charles Van Lerberghe.

In France the years leading up to the First World War were awash with books of poetry by female poets of wildly differing abilities: names, now largely forgotten, such as Nicolette Hennique, Anne Osmont and Elsa Koeberlé join that of Marie Closset (Jean Dominique) as followers and emulators of Mallarmé's symbolism. Dominique was published (as were Henri de Régnier and Charles

Title-page of Chanson

Jean Dominique (Marie Closset) on her deathbed

Van Lerberghe) by the influential Société de Mercure de France; *L'Anémone des mers* was her fifth volume of poetry, and she issued five more collections between 1909 and 1945. She chose as her Muse the figure of Watteau's Gilles, the sad clown clothed all in white (*L'Anémone des mers* opens with a cycle of poems entitled *L'Amour du Gilles*). She numbered the painters Henri-Edmond Cross and Théo van Rysselberghe among her admirers. Van Rysselberghe painted a wonderful portrait of Octav Maus in 1885, and through Maus and his wife we find the thread that linked Dominque to Fauré.

Jean Dominique, known to her friends as Jean-Do, was something of a Belgian literary Nadia Boulanger, venerated in particular by a succession of female disciples. One of the last of these was the American feminist May Sarton (1912–1995), a novelist and poet whose debt to Dominique is acknowledged in many of her writings. Jean-Do was an exceedingly charismatic individual, thin and bird-like with haunting grey eyes, famous in Brussels as an educator. She was in charge of a school, the Institut Belge de Culture Française, where the children who passed through her hands never forgot her (one of these was the young Sarton, who spent a year of her school life in Belgium). Dominique's life as an educationalist and as a *feuilletoniste* (for the Brussels newspaper *Soir*) out-lasted her career as a poet, but she remained a woman of exquisite verbal sensibility. She lived in a female *ménage à trois* in a rosy brick house on the avenue de L'Échevinage in Uccle near Brussels, an address that became a place of pilgrimage for many writers. She had a painful old age because she was blind and exceedingly frail, but she remained indomitable in spirit.

When Fauré encountered the work of this writer she had only just turned thirty. From everything written about her and her capacity for love and friendship, it is clear that the honour that Fauré did her by setting her touching poem was richly deserved. The composer conferred on Jean Dominique a certain slender musical immortality denied her elsewhere. She was far from an inconsiderable poet, and she seems to have been a truly extraordinary and much-loved human being.

(81) *Chanson* (Song)[5]
1906, Op. 94, Heugel, published separately, 1907, 3/4, E minor, *Andante quasi allegretto*

Que me fait toute la terre	*What use to me is all the earth*
Inutile où tu n'as pas	*Where you have not left*
En marchant marqué ton pas	*The imprint of your steps*
Dans le sable ou la poussière!	*In the sand or the dust!*
Il n'est de fleuve attendu	*I await no river*
Par ma soif qui s'y étanche	*To quench my thirst*
Que l'eau qui sourd et s'épanche	*But the waters that well and flow*
De la source où tu as bu;	*From the spring where you have drunk;*
La seule fleur qui m'attire	*The only flower which attracts me*
Est celle où je trouverai	*Is that on which I'll find*
Le souvenir empourpré	*The crimson memory*
De ta bouche et de ton rire;	*Of your lips and your laughter;*
Et, sous la courbe des cieux,	*And beneath the sweep of the sky,*
La mer pour moi n'est immense	*The sea for me is only immense*
Que parce qu'elle commence	*Because it begins*
À la couleur de tes yeux.	*With the colour of your eyes.*

Henri de Régnier (1864–1936)

This is Fauré's last song in madrigal style, and one of the most piquant. It would surely be better known if an accident of publishing had not consigned it to be issued as a single song by Fauré's new publisher, Heugel (as we have seen, the other 'orphan' song which shares this fate is *Le Don silencieux*). The text comes from Henri de Régnier's collection *La Sandale ailée*, hot off the press. (It is curious how the poetry of Jean Dominique, this book and the *Chanson d'Ève* were all published by the Société de Mercure de France, a firm that went back with Fauré to his settings of Albert Samain.) It is possible that Fauré was drawn to Régnier by the example of Albert Roussel, four of whose settings of this poet were performed by Jane Bathori in Paris in April 1906; the same singer was to perform *La Bonne chanson* the following month at an all-Fauré festival. The title is the poet's own, a kind of *compliment galant* in the manner of the first of Ravel's *Don Quichotte* songs. Paradoxically, the extravagant tone of the words gives them a courtly formality. Régnier's pastiche of a madrigal (it is a twentieth-century equivalent of Verlaine's 'Mandoline') is matched by Fauré with similar time-travel; his song is accompanied by a piano standing in for a lute, and that instrument is depicted with more accuracy than in any of the *fêtes galantes* settings.

We should note here that Henri de Régnier was the third of a trio (after Verlaine and Samain)

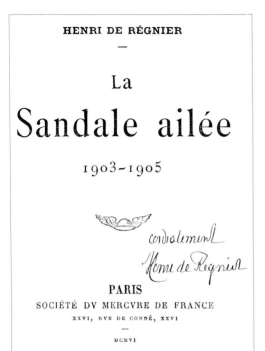

Title page of Régnier's La Sandale ailée, *with the poet's*
inscription

Henri de Régnier, by Jacques Émile Blanche

of Fauré's Watteau-inspired poets fascinated with the contrast between Versailles at its height, and its melancholy role as a museum in republican France in the aftermath of the revolution. Jean Dominique's fascination with Watteau has also been noted in the previous commentary (see p. 293), although this does not emerge in the single Fauré setting of her poetry.

Chanson is rightly prized by those who admire musical economy – this is a fine example of *multum in parvo*, a piece of musical conjuring where the most slender means achieve eloquence. Indeed, this song is typical of many a creation from Fauré's third period in that it is a highly wrought piece of work that masquerades as a trifle. Notes used with sparing discernment, a strong bass line and an implacable rhythm create a harmonic world of subtlety and disguised richness. The change from E minor into the four sharps of E major is a masterclass in modulation. Nadia Boulanger, that great teacher of composition and Fauré's pupil at one time, doubtless adored *Chanson*. It is no coincidence that the music of many of her pupils, including the young Lennox Berkeley, aspired to this lean texture with never a note too many. This music has the characteristics of Stravinsky's neo-classicism before Stravinsky himself had shown any such leanings; by the time the Russian composer pared down his music to this extent, *Le Jardin clos* had already beckoned Fauré into pastures more rarefied still.

❧   ❧   ❧   ❧

Henri François Joseph de Régnier was born at Honfleur on 28 December 1864. He is not to be confused with Mathurin Régnier (1573–1613), the more famous satirist. Like the work of Albert Samain, Régnier's poetry, world-weary and full of regret for the past, seems far less significant now, at the beginning of the twenty-first century, than it seemed at the start of the twentieth. These poems

295

(and there were at least eight volumes of verse published before the one chosen by Fauré) occupy the middle ground between the Parnassians and the symbolists; their indeterminate, gentle melancholy might easily have appealed to Fauré on a more productive scale had he discovered the poetry earlier – he set this poem some twenty years after Régnier had published his first lyrics.

Born into an aristocratic family, Régnier was fascinated by historical associations; some of his most eloquent poems, as well as ornate and allusive novels, are evocations of a deserted Versailles, haunted by its past. 'His luxurious temperament, afflicted with the *lacrimae rerum*, loves to evoke the external objects with which it finds durable associations: naiads and fauns, swift horses, marble busts, laurels and moss-grown fountains, with gates of brass and golden sunsets – emblems of regret and glory and ancient peace.'[6] As a young man Régnier had attended the receptions of Leconte de Lisle and had been in touch with Chausson and Debussy since the early 1890s, but in terms of a composer setting his verse Albert Roussel's name is the most notable – nine settings including that little masterpiece, *Le Jardin mouillé* (1903), a song that recalls Ravel's *Jeux d'eau* for piano (1901), itself a work dedicated to Fauré and prefaced by a quotation from Régnier; neither should one forget that hauntingly spare Ravel song from 1907, *Les Grands vents venus d'outre-mer*, the sole setting of this poet by a composer who had long admired Régnier and was one of his firm friends. Perhaps the appearance of Fauré's song reminded Ravel that he owed the poet some kind of musical homage.[7] Fauré had known Régnier's name for quite some time of course: that group of poets known as *Le Cénacle* had as its founder members both Régnier and Ferdinand Hérold, who had collaborated with Jean Lorrain in the libretto for Fauré's *Prométhée* in 1900. Fauré might also have been amused that Régnier had used that famous decadent archetype, Comte Robert de Montesquiou, as a model for one of the characters of his *Le Mariage de minuit* (1903). The poet's wife was Marie de Heredia, daughter of the poet José-María; like Jean Dominique she wrote under a male pseudonym – Gérard d'Houville. Henri de Régnier died on 23 May 1936.

(82) *Vocalise-étude*[8]

1906, published by Leduc without opus number, E minor, **c**, *Adagio molto tranquillo*

The other 'stray' vocal work of 1906 was the *Vocalise-étude*, published by Leduc without an opus number. The key is E minor, and the marking of *Adagio molto tranquillo* allows a stately unfolding of the melody in common time. This is one of ten *vocalises-études* (in the first volume of a series) that were published under the direction of A.L. Hettich, singing professor at the Paris Conservatoire. Naturally the *Vocalise* of Fauré, as the newly appointed director of the conservatoire, is placed at the beginning of the volume, which also contains similar exercises by Koechlin, Ropartz, Schmitt and Vierne among others. Fauré's music is a solemn march with his characteristic mezzo-staccato crotchet accompaniment. It is carefully crafted to contain a number of vocal challenges, including the singing of intervals as wide as a tenth, and the pitching of unusual harmonies. This piece tests not only the voice, but also the exactitude of rhythm without which no singer should approach a Fauré *mélodie*. As in *Chanson*, it is the skill in which the music moves from E minor to E major that is particularly memorable. It is a haunting and beautiful piece of music in its own right, which deserves to be better known, but Ravel's *Vocalise en forme de Habañera* of the following year (published in Hettich's second collection) seems to have obliterated all competition in the genre. Under the different title of *Pièce* this oddly haunting music by Fauré can be heard in arrangements for different orchestral instruments.

The aptly titled *Le Don silencieux* marks the beginning of Fauré's third period, the celebrated late style, although it is difficult to work out exactly when and how these demarcation lines really begin. Two shadowy presences hover in the background to the songs of 1906: the figures of Prometheus and Penelope, both classical legends, the former already a stage work, the other as yet a phantom. The *tragédie-lyrique* written about Prometheus in 1900 and the opera to be written around Penelope between 1907 and 1913 were of crucial importance. *Prométhée* had shown Fauré the way to the spacious grandeur inherent in simplicity; it is a key work in the formation of the late style. *Pénélope* had been a long time coming, a dream child of whom the composer had despaired many times in the previous thirty years. This work, in turn, could come into being only because Fauré felt newly empowered and vindicated by his new position at the Conservatoire. With three such enchanting but slight pieces as the vocal works considered in this chapter, it is tempting to forget that from now on nothing in

Cover of Répertoire moderne de vocalises-études

Fauré's output was independent of his mission to write something for the stage at last – the outdoor spectacle *Prométhée* was a significant move in that direction, but not the real deal. As for the songs he was yet to write, anyone planning to sing or play the two Van Lerberghe cycles should not fail to study Fauré's only opera, a work he regarded with justification as his masterpiece.

1   Claude Rostand, *L'Œuvre de Gabriel Fauré* (Paris: J.B. Janin, 'La Flûte de Pan', 1945), p. 144.

2   *Le Don silencieux*: Aspects of the cycle's interpretation are discussed in Chapter 16, p. 421.

3   Jean-Michel Nectoux, *Gabriel Fauré: A Musical Life*, trans. Roger Nichols (Cambridge: Cambridge University Press, 1991), p. 304. This is a translation of Fauré's letter to his wife of 17 August 1906, published in Gabriel Fauré, *Lettres intimes*, ed. Philippe Fauré-Fremiet (Paris: La Colombe, 1951), p. 121.

4   Edmund Gosse, *Aspects and Impressions* (London: Cassell, 1922), p. 269.

5   *Chanson*: Aspects of the cycle's interpretation are discussed in Chapter 16, p. 421.

6   Francis Yvon Eccles, *A Century of French Poets* (London: Constable, 1909), p. 307.

7   The British novelist Allan Hollinghurst prefaces *The Folding Star* (1994) with Régnier's 'Les grands vents d'outre-mer'.

8   *Vocalise*: Aspects of the cycle's interpretation are discussed in Chapter 16, p. 421.

Chapter Twelve

Fauré and Charles Van Lerberghe (I)

La Chanson d'Ève

The years leading up to the Great War were given over to two large vocal projects: in 1906 Fauré began the song cycle *La Chanson d'Ève* (completed in 1910), and in 1907 the opera *Pénélope* (performed for the first time in 1913). The confident grandeur of the *La Chanson d'Ève* would almost certainly have been inconceivable if the composer had not been engaged simultaneously in writing a work on a larger, operatic scale, and on so broadly human and generous a theme as the steadfast faithfulness of Penelope awaiting the return of Ulysses.

Fauré's opera was performed twelve years before D'Indy conducted his version of Monteverdi's *Il ritorno d'Ulisse in patria* in Paris in 1925, almost certainly the first performance of this work in modern times, and a year after Fauré's death. Fauré was no stranger to the music of Monteverdi (Nadia Boulanger's studies of this composer began in Fauré's composition class), but we shall never know what Fauré might have learned from Monteverdi as a dramatist had he had the chance to hear this opera before pondering his own work. Perhaps his natural modesty would have prompted him to search for another operatic subject altogether.

Eve and Pénélope (uncompromising women of imposing stature) are Fauré's quietly defiant replies to a musical world stirred up to fever pitch by Salome and Elektra, not to mention Mimi and Tosca. A few years earlier, Fauré might have imagined that any opera of his would be compared with Debussy's single contribution to the genre, but there were composers further afield whose recent success, and appeal to the popular taste, would render the reception of his own music even more problematic. In October 1900, soon after the success of *Prométhée* in Béziers, Fauré visited Brussels, where he was forced to be present, as he confided to his wife, at the Belgian première of 'a dreadful Italian work called *La Bohème*'.[1] In 1903 he wrote to her from Switzerland bemoaning the imminent première at the Opéra-Comique of *Tosca* and 'the bizarre school of music to which the composer of the music belongs, Puccini'.[2] In Fauré's eyes this 'neo-Italian art' was 'a kind of soup where every style from every country gets all mixed up. And everywhere, alas! they are welcomed with open arms.'[3] When he actually heard *Tosca*, Fauré was very impressed by the scene in Scarpia's chamber in Act II; and by the time he heard *Madama Butterfly* in 1906 he had become, almost despite himself, an admirer of Puccini's genius. He only regretted that the best and most popular works of Messager, to take one example, were not given equal recognition.

The composer continued to use the summer months (when he was accompanied as always by

Marguerite Hasselmans) for composition; certainly the directorship of the Paris Conservatoire had eased the financial worries of the Fauré household, but his determination to reform the institution from within cost him much time and energy. New artists who enthused for his music were constantly entering his life. In May 1906 we see for the first time the name of the pianist Marguerite Long (1874–1966) at a recital at the Société Nationale de la Musique (SNM), as well as that of Jane Bathori (1877–1970) on the same programme, a mezzo-soprano who would do more to further the cause of contemporary French vocal music than anyone else of her generation. On this occasion Fauré accompanied her in *La Bonne chanson*. On 4 June he completed *Crépuscule*, the first of his Van Lerberghe settings; he sent it off to the publisher without perhaps realising that it was to be the kernel of a mighty new cycle. *Le Don silencieux* (see Chapter 11) was the next song to be composed (at Vitznau in Switzerland); it was given its first performance by Jane Bathori and the composer the next year in Brussels. By Lake Maggiore Fauré met Umberto Giordano, the composer of *Andrea Chénier*, one of the few of the *verismo* school of composers whose music he could tolerate, and whom he was able to help enormously with a favourable mention in *Le Figaro*. After that he was in Italy for nearly a month, staying at the Hôtel des Borromées in Stresa at the edge of the same lake. Fauré described the garden which surrounded the hotel: 'With an extraordinary variety of shrubs and bushes and superb flowers and trees of every kind this garden is a paradise cared for at night, certainly, by gardeners who are incontestably angels.'[4] Fauré was overwhelmed by these beauties and also delighted by the guitars and mandolins of the hotel's Neapolitan serenaders. By this time he had received the proofs of *Crépuscule*, a song that was published as an independent entity. It was in Stresa that the composer returned to Van Lerberghe's *La Chanson d'Ève* and conceived the idea of a constructing a new cycle that would somehow encompass *Crépuscule* and would be a pendant to *La Bonne chanson*. There was as yet no overall plan to this – the cycle was something that evolved song by song with the titles being shuffled and reordered as time went along.

He now began work on *Paradis*, his longest song and the one that was destined to open the cycle. As we shall see, the poet Van Lerberghe had also been enchanted by an Italian garden when the idea of his cycle on the life of Eve first came into his mind.

Fauré wrote to his wife about the challenge facing him: 'My text is difficult … and then I have to make God the Father speak, and Eve, his daughter. Ah! It's not very convenient when one has to deal with such important personages.'[5] Two days later he wrote: 'I have worked for seven hours and I have resolved the problem of how to make God sing. You will see what constitutes his eloquence, and you will all be surprised that it has taken me so much time to find the solution. But alas! bare simplicity is what is most difficult to conceive.'[6]

Fauré completed *Paradis* on 8 September, but no sooner had he provided the finishing touches than he fell ill, no doubt exhausted by the intensity of his work. Many years later his son Philippe Fauré-Fremiet mused as to whether his father had been punished for tasting the fruits of Eden.[7] He also reminds us that it was at exactly this time that Van Lerberghe was stricken with the illness, a sudden stroke, that would lead to his death the following year. It was back in Lausanne on a strict diet and prescribed rest by the doctor that Fauré composed the second song in the work, *Prima verba*. By now three numbers had been completed; two more were composed in 1908, and three in 1909 in Lugano, but the cycle was not completed until early 1910 with the addition of two further songs, making ten in all. The birth-pangs of this extraordinary work were unlike anything else in the composer's output.

In the summer of 1907 the problems affecting Fauré's ears, and now also his eyes, were diagnosed as arterio-sclerosis, an affliction that would increasingly torment him right up to his death, his discomfort increasing slightly with each passing year. There is a strong possibility that this was a hereditary condition. In February of that year Lucienne Bréval had asked the composer to write her an opera on the subject of Penelope from Homer's *Odyssey*.

In a composer's life there are many such seemingly importunate demands made by performers; these are usually politely put to one side with a rueful smile. But every so often, what had seemed to be entirely impossible becomes the key to a new chapter in a musical career, because it was requested at exactly the right time. Thanks to Bréval's astonishingly ambitious suggestion a key was turned in a locked door that scores of others in the preceding decades, including Pauline Viardot, Winnaretta Singer and numerous poet–librettists, had failed to open. Another factor was the success of *Ariane et Barbe-bleue*, the Maeterlinck opera by Fauré's friend Paul Dukas that received its première at the Opéra-Comique in May 1907; as far as the admiring Fauré was concerned it proved that there was such a thing in the French operatic world as life after *Pelléas*.

He was able to commence work on *Pénélope* at the end of August with René Fauchois as his librettist; this was the beginning of five years' hard labour. When not immersed in his opera, or adding songs to the Van Lerberghe cycle, the composer turned his attentions to piano music. The Ninth and Tenth Nocturnes (Op. 97 and Op. 99) were composed in 1908; the Ninth Barcarolle (Op. 101) and the Fifth Impromptu (Op. 102) between 1908 and 1909; the Nine Preludes (Op. 103) between 1909 and 1910. With this wealth of piano music, it is not hard to see that the primary emotional relationship in his life was with the devoted virtuoso Marguerite Hasselmans, who now accompanied him (to accompany Fauré remains a delicate task for any solo pianist!) on all his summer working holidays.

In both the spring and late autumn of 1908 the composer visited London, where he had his biggest success so far. He may have missed being in touch with the Maddisons, who had made his earlier London visits so enjoyable, but his relationship with Adela was a thing of the past; instead he was now invited into aristocratic circles more exalted than ever before. He performed for Queen Alexandra (who, like the composer, had problems with her hearing) and the Prince and Princess of Wales. What the future King George V and Queen Mary made of Fauré's art is not certain; his music was always more likely to be patronised and underestimated by the great and good to cause any offence.

The composer was once again the house guest at 22 Old Queen Street, Westminster, of his old friend the flamboyant Frank Schuster, a descendant of a wealthy Jewish banking family that had followed Albert, the Prince Consort, to London in the 1840s. The poet Stephen Spender descended from this line.[8] Frank (his official first names were Leo Francis) supported the arts with inherited money, and was particularly devoted to the music of Elgar; he features in the Siegfried Sassoon diaries, and was Lady Ottoline Morrell's guest at Garsington Manor. He was genuinely musical, and a lavish host, both in London and at his beautiful house, 'The Hut', at Bray-on-Thames. It was very convenient for Fauré that Schuster, something of an Anglo-German Montesquiou, though less precious and fastidious, had conceived a passion for his music; 'ma nourrice' ('my nurse'), as Fauré openly referred to Frank, seemed to have liked nothing better than arranging concerts, bringing famous names together and ensuring that his favourite artists enjoyed the luxurious treats that he felt were their due.

A female guest at one of Schuster's musical gatherings compared Fauré's economy of form to Mozart's; the composer savoured 'this not-so-banal eulogy' and shared it delightedly with his son Emmanuel in a letter (17 March 1908). On the same visit Fauré lunched at the home of an admirer,

In the foreground, Frank Schuster photographed by Lady Ottoline Morrell some years after the composer was in regular contact with him, but still sporting a rather Fauréan moustache. © National Portrait Gallery, London

the painter John Singer Sargent, amid a number of unfinished portraits. Sargent's portrait of Fauré in subtle tones of grey already hung in the composer's studio in Paris.

The two singers with whom he appeared in London were the redoubtable mezzo Jeanne Raunay, *créatrice* of *La Chanson d'Ève*, and the American contralto of Swiss parentage Susan Metcalfe, who would later marry Pau Casals. His second English visit of the year was at the end of November 1908, when he performed for the French Concert Society in Manchester and accompanied his violin sonata and his *Fantaisie* for flute; on this occasion his songs were sung by Mrs George Swinton (see p. 48), a staunch ally and a patroness of the arts. The concert also included the music of Ethel Smyth.

Schuster (the dedicatee of Elgar's overture *In the South*) ensured that Fauré was present at the first performance of that composer's First Symphony, conducted by Hans Richter in Manchester on 3 December 1908. There is no record of Fauré's reaction to this music, so very different from his own, but he compared the 'black, smoky, foggy, dreadful city' of Manchester with the capital city – 'Today London seems like an Eden!' – a comparison that has a richer meaning in the light of his continuing work on his song cycle. It may be that Schuster had been offended by what we might take to be Fauré's logical lack of enthusiasm for the grandeur of Elgar's style, or that he was no longer enthused by the infinitely more sparse music that Fauré was composing; from now on Schuster's name and money seem to fade from the chronicles of the composer's intimate life.

If London was an Eden, it made perfect sense that one of the very first performances of *La Chanson d'Ève* was to take place there in the Bechstein Hall. Many years later Elgar was to communicate in a letter that he had admired Fauré, and that he felt him to be have been unjustly underrated. This remark places in perspective any impression we may have had that Fauré was wildly popular in London at this time; outside a relatively small circle of initiates this was sadly not the case. To fill Bechstein Hall (now Wigmore Hall, but still with about 500 seats) from a population the size of London is pleasing, a *succès d'estime*, but hardly indicative of a popular runaway success.

By now Fauré was something of a globetrotter on a modest scale. The English visit had been preceded by a successful concert of chamber music and songs in Berlin. In March 1909 he visited Barcelona. While there he was at long last elected to the Institut, that elite body of the leading lights of the arts in France where only the death of a member opens up a highly contested vacancy. He narrowly beat the composer and organist Widor (by eighteen votes to sixteen) for the chair that had once been occupied by Berlioz; the voting had to go to five ballots before the result was declared. On this occasion, as he waited tensely for news of the outcome, Fauré displayed much less *sang-froid* than usual. Serious lobbying was always required of the various factions, and Saint-Saëns had returned from Algeria to throw his considerable weight behind his former student's campaign.

Fauré's famous indifference to success was suspended during that breathless evening of waiting in Barcelona – he was clearly on tenterhooks, and relieved and delighted with the result. Belonging to the Institut was no empty honour: the members exerted real influence on the artistic life of France, and this was a time in his life when Fauré needed to exert that influence.

His new position as director of the Paris Conservatoire had already made him an important figure in the French world of music. There was no equivalent to this position in London; the principals of the English music colleges, despite the fact that they were usually knighted, never enjoyed quite the power and prestige that came with the appointments of their single all-powerful French counterpart. Fauré knew full well that his acceptance of the presidency of a break-away group, the Société Musicale Indépendante (SMI), would be regarded as a significant departure from tradition. This new body was born of a general dissatisfaction that the concerts of the SNM (Fauré had been a founder-member of this organisation in 1871) had simply become an exclusive shop front for the music of the Schola Cantorum. In a letter to Fauré of the utmost civility (14 February 1909), Claude Debussy agreed to become a member of the governing body of the Paris Conservatoire.

Honours were now being showered on Fauré at a time when they were almost too late to make a great deal of difference. He told his wife, who was sadly, but predictably, jealous of his success, that he regarded the establishment of his reputation as a necessity for the good of his family's monetary well-being, little more. As it turned out, even the directorship of the Conservatoire did him little good when it came to his long-term financial security.

1910 began with the composition of *Ô mort, poussière d'étoiles*, eventually to be the last song of *La Chanson d'Ève*, but otherwise it was a bad year. There was further deterioration in the composer's health (he went to Bad Ems during the summer in a futile attempt to find a cure for his affliction) and in September Emmanuel Frémiet, his beloved father-in-law, died. By way of compensation there was a two-week journey further east than he had ever travelled – to Helsinki, St Petersburg and Moscow. In

Bust of Gabriel Fauré by his father-in-law, Emmanuel Fremiet

Russia Fauré was handsomely hosted by the Ukrainian pianist and conductor Aleksandr Ziloti, and lauded at a reception at the Moscow Conservatoire by another Aleksandr, Glazunov, whom he had earlier entertained in Paris. He was also friendly with César Cui, that least famous member of 'The Five', who admired him deeply. At the St Petersburg Conservatoire Fauré was cheered to the rafters. 'What a pity that Dubois and Widor were not able to see it from the outside!' the composer joked somewhat maliciously with his wife by letter.[9] Despite his poor hearing he was still able to play his violin sonata with Ysaÿe (composed thirty-five years earlier), and the Second Piano Quartet with members of the Capet Quartet. A Russian critic on the Moscow review *Apollo* found both Fauré's conducting and piano playing disappointing and dull. In 1922 the composer confessed to Marie Fauré that he had not really heard what he had been playing at the piano for many years:

> Can you imagine that with my poor ears there are times when I have been unable to tell where I was in the music. I have *never played, neither for myself nor anyone else*, a single note of *Pénélope* since its inception, which was in Lausanne in 1907, if I am not mistaken. All this because even at that time my hearing was faulty, and when my fingers were hitting certain notes, it was *other notes* which I *heard*.[10]

Fauré continued to take part in concerts as pianist and accompanist deep into old age. He was almost always paid a fee for these public appearances, and we can guess that he must have needed the money. When he accompanied singers in salon performance, it was not unusual, if the singer dragged, for the composer to finish the accompaniment several bars ahead. Did the same thing happen in the very many chamber music performances? Perhaps string players were better able to accommodate themselves to the composer's playing, which was, by all accounts, metronomic. There must have been accidents, however, and these would probably have been acutely embarrassing to Fauré. That he refused to renounce performing as a result of his affliction is admirable but also sad, especially if his motive was largely financial. It seems that performers (and audiences) were willing to tolerate any defects: this was after all the composer himself, the authoritative voice (he now seldom played other composers' music). His affliction must have been something like an open secret among musicians, and they were prepared to put up with it, and work their way around it, out of respect and love.

In April 1910 *La Chanson d'Ève* appeared in print for the first time as a *recueil*; on 10 April, as part of the first concert of the newly formed SMI, Jeanne Raunay gave the first performance of the entire ten-song cycle. There was an awkward confrontation between Fauré and Sarah Bernhardt (who believed that 'Le Conservatoire national de Musique et de Déclamation', with its courses for actors, should be led by someone with theatrical credentials) as well as other rebellious members of his staff. This was neatly resolved in the composer's favour when his tenure as director was extended by the ministry for a further five years. The end of the year saw Fauré appointed a *commandeur* of the Légion d'Honneur.

❧   ❧   ❧   ❧

The substantial book of poems by Charles Van Lerberghe with the title *La Chanson d'Ève* appeared in 1904 (published by Mercure de France and dedicated to Emile Verhaeren, whom Van Lerberghe venerated as the greater Belgian poet). In a letter to Albert Mockel (published as a postscript to the 1926 Brussels edition of *La Chanson d'Ève*), Van Lerberghe said that he had no choice but to dislike Milton's *Paradise Lost*, even if it was a venerated masterpiece. He deplored that work's 'methodist Adam who has contributed nothing to the birth of mine, because my poem has no Adam … Milton's Eve is nothing more than a *cuisinière* … stupidly submissive to her God and her master.'[11] In *La Chanson d'Ève*, on the other hand, there is a cast of one person, a figure of Botticelli-like beauty, who is both the poem's subject and its narrator. Van Lerberghe speaks of his desire to create

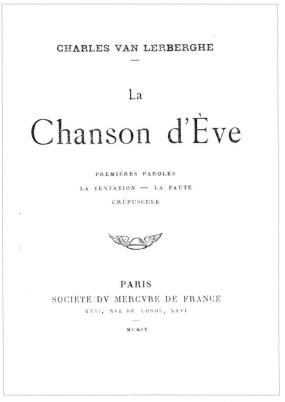

a feminine soul, very sweet and pure, very tender, very dreamy, very wise and at the same time very voluptuous, very capricious, very fantastic … the soul that I should have had in another existence, when men did not yet exist, and when everyone still had a little of the soul of the young Eve … It is a speaking soul … almost everywhere I could replace this word 'Eve' with 'my soul' … I do not excuse myself for being 'jeune fille' in this regard – naturally, like them I am envious of, and prefer good-looking men … Verhaeren, for example, to whom I wanted to pay homage in dedicating my book to him.[12]

The title-page of the first edition of Van Lerberghe's La Chanson d'Ève.

There is no attempt to follow the Bible story, and Milton's blazing religious conviction is certainly not to be found in *La Chanson d'Ève*. It is rare for a symbolist poet to have launched an entire book in this manner around a single subject; Van Lerberghe thought of his *recueil* in quasi-Wagnerian terms, and planned its architectural proportions; he even claimed that the work was unified by the use of verbal equivalents of the Wagnerian leitmotif.

Alfred Mockel, a name at the heart of Belgian symbolism as its major theoretician and a mutual friend of Fauré and Van Lerberghe, introduced the composer to this poetry in 1906; it was only a matter of months before Fauré began work on the first song of what would eventually turn into a cycle. By this time, the autumn of 1906, he had already spent a year as director of the Conservatoire, and had turned his back on his work at the Madeleine. This renunciation of the world of religious music, at the time of embarking on these settings, is also indicative of changed attitudes in the Third Republic. The year 1905 saw the official separation of Church and State in France; since 1903 Pope Pius X had been fighting a vehement rearguard action against the forces of religious modernism in France, but when the separation became a matter of official government policy Fauré shed no tears; indeed he was irritated by the religious Right's threats of eternal condemnation for a country out of step with the Holy See. Those musicians who supported the aesthetic of the Schola Cantorum were more likely to be of this mind, and Fauré was certainly not of their number; his appointment to head the Conservatoire had fortified that position. It was clearly a time when he could write a piece of music with an ostensibly biblical theme that was (for want of a better defining word) pantheistic, as opposed to conventionally religious. By this time the composer would certainly have had no fear that a musical re-writing of Genesis might affect his career adversely.

True to his enigmatic nature, Fauré never admitted to being an atheist. As part of his address to the Cercle Royal Gaullois in Brussels in 1954, Philippe Fauré-Fremiet assured his audience that his father had an absolute confidence (according to the evidence of Fauré's *Requiem*) in a 'supreme leniency that could only be divine' whereby 'the human soul dreams of being cradled like a child' – a statement that hardly answers any serious questions about Fauré's religious affiliations.

He would never have been so foolish as to deny the existence of God earlier in his career – dependent as he was on a living from the church authorities at the Madeleine. From the very beginning of his time as a church musician in Rennes in the late 1860s, when he had left the organ loft to smoke cigarettes during the sermon, and had played the organ in tails following a night on the tiles, he had shown an indifference to organised religion and its proprieties. The unconventional nature of the *Requiem*, which refuses to contemplate a vengeful or even judgmental God, places him side by side with Schubert, a composer eminently capable of writing religious music that could stir its listeners to the most devout feelings without being in the least dogmatically religious himself.

Van Lerberghe's readers found the poet similarly difficult to pin down. The cycle of poems takes no clear position on the question of whether Eve is human or divine, an ambiguity deliberately fostered by the poet for artistic reasons. In fact, his own feelings were absolutely clear. In the year of writing *La Chanson d'Ève*, the anti-clerical Van Lerberghe moved towards an unequivocal atheism; he regarded Christian myth as a poetic source but he came to believe that Darwin's theory of evolution was the only acceptable theology.

Van Lerberghe's work contains ninety-six poems, and we notice a combination of biblical imagery with a pantheism that is subtly different from that of the pagans. The first readers of the book saluted a beguiling new purity and naivety in the character of Eve, who seems to be in direct communication with the 'Universal substance' as Jacques Rivière put it; she sees herself not as a human worshipper of the gods (as an ancient Roman might have done), but as part of the pantheistic substance itself, together with the trees, flowers and birds. All this adds to her cosmic stature.

The book is divided into five sections: Fauré passes over the *Prélude* and begins his cycle with the first poem of *Premières paroles* (No. III), followed by Nos VIII, VII, XII, XVI and XXII from the same book. This is the most joyous and optimistic section of the poet's work. It is clear that the wonder of the Creation, and the beauties of the garden of Eden, interested Fauré far more than any other phase of Eve's life. Eve is never promised immortality, and her progress to death via self-knowledge and gradually growing human awareness is a natural development; it has little to do with the conventional biblical version of the expulsion from Eden as divine punishment. As Van Lerberghe put it, 'Eve is born, she walks in the garden, she talks there a little to the angels and other creatures, she dreams there a great deal, she allows herself to be tempted there, she succumbs there, and dies there.'[13] Throughout the cycle God speaks to Eve in words of advice and admonishment; she has a mentor who monitors her progress, but this murmuring presence is unable, and unwilling, either to raise her up to the heavens or to cast her into hell. Apart from a sentence in the opening song, *Paradis*, God as a character is written out of Fauré's music. In much the same way the Prince de Cynthie in Van Lerberghe's short story *Sélection surnaturelle* (1900) throws the word 'God' out of his vessel, gradually lightening his ship of every heavy aspect of the dictionary until only the phrase 'I aspire' remains to speak truly to his soul.

In Van Lerberghe's poem, part of *La Tentation*, Eve eats the golden fruit that glistens in the shadows. This terrible deed extinguishes the Holy Spirit and God dies. In part of 'La Faute' (the fourth subsection of the poem) that Van Lerberghe chose to modify and somewhat soften before publication, Eve is made to exult:

Il n'existe pas, il n'existe plus!	*He does not exist, he no longer exists!*
Ô mon ennemi mort, repose!	*O rest my dead enemy!*
Mon âme chante, mes yeux s'ouvrent,	*My soul sings, my eyes are opened*
Je suis égale à Dieu!	*I am the equal of God!*
Pour la première fois, je vois et je comprends,	*For the first time, I see and I understand,*
Comme Dieu même.	*Like God himself.*

Van Lerberghe plays with Christian and mythological aspects a great deal more than we are allowed to hear in Fauré's cycle: there are fairies, spirits and a serpent in the poet's original that depict temptation in a way that has conventionally religious undertones. After she dies we sense that Eve's soul is travelling somewhere in a kind of apotheosis that is not unrelated to the soul's journey in Christian terms.

The composer will have none of this; he dramatically cuts the poet's entire scenario – for reasons of length he had no other choice, but there is also a controlling hand here that suggests a rigorous suppression of even the ghost of fanciful sentimentality. As Carlo Caballero writes in *Fauré and French Musical Aesthetics* (2001): 'while the poet casts more than one backward glance on the ancient Roman Catholic edifice, Fauré turns away, and keeps going'. Caballero, more succinctly than any other writer, also sums up the composer's aim in writing the cycle:

Fauré abolishes original sin from the garden of Eden and forces us to imagine Eve's relation to the world anew. Unredeemed because never guilty, Eve does not transcend the world through personal immortality but rather returns to the world, is absorbed by it, becomes it. Fauré specifically suggests the inseparability of life and death through Eve's immersion and reflection in nature, in which joy and suffering are part of the same mortal mystery.[14]

Fauré introduces a single poem from *La Tentation* (No. XXXIX into the work, before a return to *Premières paroles* (No. XXIX). The eighteen poems of 'La Faute' are ignored entirely. If the composer has no interest in promoting the presence of God in the cycle, he has equally no interest in setting to music Eve's notification of the death of as God quoted above. The cycle ends with poems Nos LXXXVI and XCIV (the third-to-last poem) from the subsection *Crépuscule*, which the composer also adopts as the title of the penultimate song; thus Fauré's cycle follows Van Lerberghe's chronology only to a generalised extent; it skims the surface of the poet's portrait of Eve while deepening it with matchless music. The opening lines of the poems are their only headings, thus *Paradis*, *Prima verba* and *Eau vivante* are Fauré's own titles.

Another aspect of this mighty work is the time-scale envisaged by poet and composer. In a sense this is a 'Poëme d'un jour' – as if Eve is born and dies at opposite ends of the same cosmic day – a day perhaps encompassing millennia. Evening arrives in *Crépuscule*, the ninth song of the cycle, and in the last song death comes together with nightfall. Twilight is also depicted in the first song of the work – but in the broadest terms the poems trace the trajectory of a vast cosmic sun across

The soprano Jeanne Raunay, also known professionally as Jeanne Raunay-Demeny.

the heavens. The middle of the cycle is filled with sunlight and the fullness of day, the 'soleil radieux' of *Roses ardentes*. Carlos Cabellero points out that 'the sensory events of the sixth song, *Veilles-tu, ma senteur de soleil* seem to take place at night, but the exhilaration Eve expresses in this nocturnal fantasy comes from her intensified sensation of all the smells of daytime persisting in the night air'.[15] The effect of this time-scale in Van Lerberghe's complete poem is even more remarkable with many different stages of the days marked and differentiated, but the progress of this 'solar drama' from dawn to dusk is something that Fauré also takes care to preserve in his much pared-down sequence of chosen poems. Van Lerberghe had not envisaged this kind of timetable when he first wrote the poem, and a footnote from Mockel tells us that the poems were reordered in a way to give the sequence a more convincing dawn-to-dusk shape.

In motivic terms *La Chanson d'Ève* is a less complex musical composition than *La Bonne chanson*, which had five recurring themes. In other ways, despite the fact that the music seems far less dense on the page, the later cycle is rather more ambitious. Fauré, not yet as old as Haydn when he wrote *Die Schöpfung*, undertakes nothing less than a 'Creation' of his own. The music is imposing without appearing to be, certainly without trying to awe us: in the first song we hear the voice of God Himself, a rare if not quite a unique event in the song repertoire (Wolf's *Herr, was trägt der Boden hier* and Britten's *Canticle II* come to mind), superbly managed by a composer who brilliantly downplays the portentousness of the Almighty's pronouncements. The murmur of God's words is something that he imagines playing in Eve's own mind, like the development of her conscience and the ripening of her judgement – each of His phrases marked by a subtly heightened modulation. Towards the beginning of Van Lerberghe's work she asks, 'Who can tell me where I end / where I start?' This question is unanswerable, of course, but her discovery of the world around her deepens her and prepares her for her own eventual demise.

So absorbing is this burgeoning picture of Eve's outer, and inner, world that the complete absence of Adam seems hardly worthy of comment. In the sixty-first year of his life, Fauré is ready to take his listeners fearlessly by the hand and show them a garden of Eden lacking both a punishing God and a God of salvation. Instead he gives voice to a remarkable being who personifies the entirety of creation. That the heroine of his great cycle is a woman and not a man makes entire sense to those who have followed the emotional life of a composer who had always been dependent on the company and support of the fairer sex. But how far we have travelled from Leporello's 'Odor di femmina', and how distant is Eve from the women who inspired, say, the poetry of Armand Silvestre!

The first public performance of *La Chanson d'Ève* (although only three songs were sung) took place at an all-Fauré concert at the Bechstein Hall (now the Wigmore Hall), London, on 17 March 1908. The composer wrote to his wife two days later:

> The concert took place at half-past three in a pretty music room of Bechstein pianos (of Berlin). The second half of the room was filled with critics or professional musicians and singers. On the other hand, the first half was very much like a salon where everyone knew each other. First Mme Raunay sang songs, old and new [the Van Lerberghe settings came into the latter category] then an excellent London pianist played my *Ballade* which I accompanied on a second piano; finally Mme Raunay ended with *La Bonne chanson*. A charming and very warm reception for all these different things, very well interpreted too.[16]

The critic of the London *Times* remarked that 'the composer accompanied throughout the concert in a most artistic style'. A more complete performance of the cycle (seven out of the ten songs) was given at the Salle Érard in Paris on 26 May 1909, also by Jeanne Raunay with Fauré accompanying. As we have noted above, the first complete performance of the work as we know it today was in April 1910.

La Chanson d'Ève (*The song of Eve*)
1906–10, Op. 95[17]

(83) (i) *Paradis* (*Paradise*)
3–8 September 1906, sent to the engraver 3 October 1906, published January 1907
The second song in the cycle to be composed, E minor – E major, 3/2, *Andante molto moderato*

C'est le premier matin du monde.	*It is the first morning of creation.*
Comme une fleur confuse exhalée de la nuit,	*Like an abashed flower breathed on the night air,*
Au souffle nouveau qui se lève des ondes,	*With the pristine whisperings that rise from the waves,*
Un jardin bleu s'épanouit.	*A blue garden blooms.*
Tout s'y confond encore et tout s'y mêle,	*Everything is still blurred and indistinct,*
Frissons de feuilles, chants d'oiseaux,	*Trembling leaves, singing birds,*
Glissements d'ailes,	*Gliding wings,*
Sources qui sourdent, voix des airs, voix des eaux,	*Springs that rise, voices of air and water,*
Murmure immense;	*An immense murmuring;*
Et qui pourtant est du silence.	*Which yet is silence.*
Ouvrant à la clarté ses doux et vagues yeux,	*Opening to the light her soft and vacant eyes,*
La jeune et divine Ève	*Young, heaven-born Eve*
S'est éveillée de Dieu.	*Is awakened by God.*
Et le monde à ses pieds s'étend comme un beau rêve.	*And the world lies at her feet like a lovely dream.*

Or Dieu lui dit: Va, fille humaine,	*Now God says to her: Go, daughter of man,*
Et donne à tous les êtres	*And bestow on all beings*
Que j'ai crées, une parole de tes lèvres,	*That I have created a word from your lips,*
Un son pour les connaître.	*A sound that we might know them by.*
Et Ève s'en alla, docile à son seigneur,	*And Eve went, obedient to her Lord,*
En son bosquet de roses,	*Into her rose grove,*
Donnant à toutes choses	*Bestowing on all things*
Une parole, un son de ses lèvres de fleur:	*A word, a sound from her flower-like lips:*
Chose qui fuit, chose qui souffle, chose qui vole …	*On all that runs, that breathes, that flies …*
Cependant le jour passe, et vague, comme à l'aube,	*Day meanwhile passes, and hazy, as at dawn,*
Au crépuscule, peu à peu,	*Eden falls slowly asleep*
L'Éden s'endort et se dérobe	*In the twilight and steals away*
Dans le silence d'un songe bleu.	*In the silence of a blue dream.*
La voix s'est tue, mais tout l'écoute encore,	*The voice is hushed, but everything still hearkens,*
Tout demeure en attente;	*Waiting in expectation;*
Lorsque avec le lever de l'étoile du soir	*When with the rising of the evening star,*
Ève chante.	*Eve sings.*

'Nothing equals the purity, the grandeur, the chastity of *La Chanson d'Ève*, this *Bonne chanson* of the golden age.'[18] So wrote Vladimir Jankélévitch, and it is the first song of the cycle that most reflects those three qualities of purity, grandeur and chastity.

At ten pages, this is by far the longest song of the cycle, and the longest of Fauré's *mélodies*. It opens with a succession of bare semibreves that demurely flower into etiolated chords (see Example 12.1):

Example 12.1

These six bars of accompaniment might be labelled the 'Eden' motif, A; even by their appearance on the page (as in Wolf's *Grenzen der Menschheit*) these notes made up of open circles seem to depict expanses of space over which hovers the hand of the Creator.

This music for the dawning of life itself had first been heard in *Mélisande's Song* (see Chapter 10) and later reappears in *Crépuscule* (actually the first song in the cycle to be composed). At the end of the poem's first verse, following 'Un jardin bleu s'épanouit', another theme, B, is first heard (in bars 21 to 23) in a piano interlude that coincides with a change of key signature into E major (see Example 12.2):

Example 12.2

This pattern of intervals descends the stave while doubling back on itself – a simple succession of minims (in the song's accompaniment concealed, as if in a garden, within a foliage of surrounding crotchets): D♯ falls to C♯, and then there is a semitone rise to D♮, a drop of a minor third to B♮ and then a rise back up to C♯. This is the motif of Eve herself – 'la damoiselle élue'. From this seed the composer brings paradise to life: crotchet triplets enrich the 3/2 texture as if with a profusion of tropical vegetation and flowing rivers. There is nothing like this 'murmure immense' in all song: a magical, deliberately blurred hum that is nevertheless as silent as a spinning top (the diminuendo and thinning of texture at the end of the second strophe remind us of this). This is followed by a return to theme A for the awakening of Eve, and then the heightened reappearance of music derived from B where the increasingly ecstatic grandeur of the picture threatens to break the boundaries of the musical possibilities of voice and piano.

This magnificent passage in triplets gives way to the voice of God, hushed in his understated reasonableness (*Andante* with a change of time signature to **c** and a luminously simple musical landscape where the accompaniment is dominated by minims and semibreves). The world is now ready for the naming of flowers, birds and animals. There are no more overgrown triplets, only music that shows Eve as newly appointed mistress of her domain; the momentary quickening into life at 'Chose qui fuit … souffle … vole' (*Più mosso*) is the very act of creation magically turned into music. The world's first day passes – a mere moment in the 'cosmic day' of the cycle as a whole – and theme A paints the twilight (verse 6) in the same terms as dawn, now in a lower, darker tessitura (*Meno mosso*). The final strophe (*Andante*, with a return at last to the 3/2 of the opening) is a drawing together of musical threads: theme A climbs in the pianist's left hand, quietly flowing quavers ripple in the right hand; with the words 'Ève chante' ('Eve sings') theme B returns for a song without words, a postlude of seraphic calm – Eden has been created and ordered, and is now in the care of its Earth Mother. The relatively strict polyphony of this song (something not exactly new for Fauré, but not by any means to be found in all his songs) is a characteristic, to a lesser or greater extent, of every number in the cycle. The composer omits the poet's last strophe and the effect is to forge a stronger link with the following text beginning 'Comme elle chante'.

(84) (ii) *Prima verba* (*The first words*)
28 September 1906, sent to the engraver 3 October 1906, published January 1907
The third song in the cycle to be composed, G♭ major, **c**, *Adagio molto*

Comme elle chante	*How it sings*
Dans ma voix,	*In my voice,*
L'âme longtemps murmurante	*The constantly murmuring soul*
Des fontaines et des bois!	*Of the springs and woods!*
Air limpide du paradis,	*Clear air of paradise*
Avec tes grappes de rubis,	*With your ruby grape-clusters,*
Avec tes gerbes de lumière,	*With your sheafs of light,*
Avec tes roses et tes fruits;	*With your roses and your fruits;*
Quelle merveille en nous à cette heure!	*How we marvel at such a moment!*
Des paroles depuis des âges endormies	*Words that had slumbered for aeons*
En des sons, en des fleurs,	*Finally come to life on my lips*
Sur mes lèvres enfin prennent vie.	*As sounds, as flowers.*

Depuis que mon souffle a dit leur chanson,	*Since my breath uttered their song,*
Depuis que ma voix les a créées,	*Since my voice created them,*
Quel silence heureux et profond	*What deep and blissful silence*
Naît de leurs âmes allégées!	*Is born from their unburdened souls!*

In this G♭ major meditation Eve expresses herself in direct speech for the first time. The images of ruby-coloured grapes, roses and fruits, and Fauré's response to them in music that recalls *Le Parfum impérissable*, seem to locate Eden in the hot-house luxuriance of the biblical Middle East in the composer's mind, although we know that Italy was the real inspiration. This earlier song has prepared us for the simple crotchet chord accompaniment of *Prima verba* as it shadows the vocal line with anything but simple harmonies.

Once again the first bar of the piano part presents an empty vista on which will soon be imposed every manner of subtle and recherché twist and turn, a dense forest of accidentals created with the greatest deliberation. In the piano's left hand, after 'Depuis que ma voix les a créées' there is a veiled reference to theme B – the G♭ pedal through this section signifying stability – the 'silence heureux et profond' of ordered creation. The sudden presence of a C♮ in the penultimate bar (an echo of 'allégées') is like balm to the burdened soul, a reminder of primal innocence.

Nectoux informs us that the music for 'Depuis que mon souffle a dit leur chanson' is a quotation from the *Agnus Dei* of the *Messe de Villerville* of 1881, an unpublished work that Fauré was revising at this time for Heugel so that it could appear in 1907 (as if a new work) as the *Messe basse*.[19]

(85) (iii) *Roses ardentes* (*Fiery roses*)
June 1908, sent to the engraver 22 July 1908, published November 1908
The fourth song in the cycle to be composed, E major, 3/4, *Andante*

Roses ardentes	*Fiery roses*
Dans l'immobile nuit,	*In the motionless night,*
C'est en vous que je chante,	*It is in you that I sing*
Et que je suis.	*And have my being.*
En vous, étincelles,	*It is in you, gleaming stars*
À la cime des bois,	*High in the forests,*
Que je suis éternelle,	*That I am eternal*
Et que je vois.	*And given sight.*
Ô mer profonde,	*O deep sea,*
C'est en toi que mon sang	*It is in you that my blood*
Renaît vague blonde,	*Is reborn, white wave*
Et flot dansant.	*And dancing tide.*
Et c'est en toi, force suprême,	*And it is in you, supreme force,*
Soleil radieux,	*Radiant sun,*
Que mon âme elle-même	*That my very soul*
Atteint son dieu!	*Reaches its god!*

312

Roses are everywhere in this cycle: in this song, where they are red, in the eighth song, where they are white, and in the 'roses chaudes' of the seventh song. In the first strophe Eve identifies herself with this flower, the initial impetus behind her gently palpitating hymn of rapture, passionate but always 'pudique'. As Carlo Caballero writes, 'She suffuses herself and her senses in the roses, the stars and the sea, and she in turn is suffused by them.'[20] When the stars are included in Eve's litany, mezzo-staccato quavers seem admirably suitable for pinpricks of light. The deepest bass note, and a *forte* dynamic, are reserved for sea imagery (in this music for 'flot dansant' we can hear the beginnings of *Je me suis embarqué* from the last Fauré cycle, *L'Horizon chimérique*). The song's climactic final strophe aspires to the sun, the climbing vocal line widening in distance from the falling bass to encompass the majesty of this solar 'force suprême'.

In a letter to Isaac Albéniz written on Conservatoire-headed notepaper in June 1908, Fauré excuses himself for not having written earlier: 'I am absolutely over-burdened with work, because I am trying, in the middle of everything else (from contractual necessity), to compose, and my poor brain, such as it is, is in a complete whirl!'[21] This song and *L'Aube blanche* were the songs that the composer was working on at the time; needless to say they give no hint of the pressed circumstances in which they were written. The two motifs of the cycle make no appearance here.

(86) (iv) *Comme Dieu rayonne* (How radiant is God)
Before 26 May 1909, sent to the engraver 5 June 1909, published October 1909
The sixth song in the cycle to be composed, C minor – C major, **c**, *Quasi adagio*

Comme Dieu rayonne aujourd'hui,	*How radiant is God today,*
Comme il exulte, comme il fleurit.	*How he exults and blossoms*
Parmi ces roses et ces fruits!	*Among these roses and fruits!*
Comme il murmure en cette fontaine!	*How he murmurs in this fountain!*
Ah! comme il chante en ces oiseaux …	*Ah! how he sings in these birds …*
Qu'elle est suave son haleine	*How sweet is his breath*
Dans l'odorant printemps nouveau!	*In the new fragrant spring!*
Comme il se baigne dans la lumière	*How he bathes in light*
Avec amour, mon jeune dieu!	*With love, my young god!*
Toutes les choses de la terre	*All earthly things*
Sont ses vêtements radieux.	*Are his dazzling raiments.*

Since a young virile Adam has been ruled out of this cycle by Van Lerberghe himself, the first-time reader of these lines will imagine that the poet is describing a traditional view of the Creator. But there is a subtle sign here of a transformation whereby that God of religion, the 'Dieu' with a capital letter of the first strophe, is subsumed into the world of his own creation; he is at one with the fountains, the singing of birds and the springtime flowers, and he turns into a symbol, the 'dieu' in the lower case of the final strophe. The phrase 'mon jeune dieu' removes the concept of an Old Testament God and replaces it with a joyous personification of a young creative force, the divinity of nature, and Eve's equal, not her superior.

For a poem that expresses the pantheistic concept of God as all-in-all, the composer's genius for reductive concision seems heaven-sent. For the first two strophes the pared-down piano writing, suggestive of an almost Bach-like rigour, could easily be transcribed for string quartet. The poem ascribes nature's flowering to one divine source; to mirror this, the accompaniment for the first strophe germinates solely from theme A, restated in each of the opening four bars. In the second verse theme B is concealed (in diminution) in the undulating quavers of the tenor (or viola) line as part of the piano's four-part texture. The third verse weaves a glorious light-filled tapestry of sound: the accompaniment, now grandiose, quickens with semiquavers while theme B resounds like a bell in octaves as the right-hand accompaniment. This peroration leads to the remarkable change of colour from C minor to the C major of the closing bars, where Eden seems bathed in heavenly light.

(87) (v) *L'Aube blanche* (*The white dawn*)

June 1908, sent to the engraver 22 July 1908, published November 1908
The fifth song in the cycle to be composed, D♭ major, 3/4, *Andante*

L'aube blanche dit à mon rêve:	*The white dawn says to my dream:*
Éveille-toi, le soleil luit.	*Awake, the sun is shining.*
Mon âme écoute, et je soulève	*My soul listens, and I raise*
Un peu mes paupières vers lui.	*My eyes a little towards it.*
Un rayon de lumière touche	*A ray of light touches*
La pâle fleur de mes yeux bleus;	*The pale flower of my blue eyes;*
Une flamme éveille ma bouche,	*A flame awakens my mouth,*
Un souffle éveille mes cheveux.	*A breeze awakens my hair.*
Et mon âme, comme une rose	*And my soul, like a rose*
Tremblante, lente, tout le jour,	*That is trembling and listless all day,*
S'éveille à la beauté des choses,	*Awakens to the beauty of things,*
Comme mon cœur à leur amour.	*As my heart awakens to their love.*

On the page this piece can be overlooked as unexceptional – there is no sign of either of the motifs that mostly govern this cycle. Instead, there is an unchanging accompanying pattern, a left-hand crotchet followed by three right-hand semiquavers, and a rather undemonstrative vocal line that moves in small steps. But this would be to reckon without Fauré's harmonic (and enharmonic) genius, which is demonstrated here in rich measure. This is the music of awakening, in the sun's warmth, not only of the new world, but of Eve's awareness. In the first verse, at 'le soleil luit', we hear a sybaritic gear-change of harmony that, if heard in isolation, one might ascribe to Debussy; nevertheless, for the most part, in this music for the listening soul, Fauré moves from chord to chord in a way that is his alone. Without making us aware of it, he traverses huge distances in incremental steps that defy ordinary analysis (Jankélévitch refers to a 'thousand different nuances'[22]). Having radiantly returned us to the home key on the word 'amour', the composer omits the poem's last verse.

Manuscript of the first page of Eau vivante

(88) (vi) *Eau vivante* (*Spring water*)

Before 26 May 1909, sent to the engraver 5 June 1909, published October 1909
The seventh song in the cycle to be composed, C major, 3/4, *Allegretto moderato*

Que tu es simple et claire,	*How simple and clear you are,*
Eau vivante,	*Spring water,*
Qui, du sein de la terre,	*Who, from the heart of the earth,*
Jaillis en ces bassins et chantes!	*Surges into these pools and sings!*
Ô fontaine divine et pure,	*O divine, pure fountain,*
Les plantes aspirent	*The plants breathe in*
Ta liquide clarté;	*Your liquid limpidity;*
La biche et la colombe en toi se désaltèrent.	*The doe and the dove quench in you their thirst.*
Et tu descends par des pentes douces	*And you descend by the gentle banks*
De fleurs et de mousses,	*Of flowers and moss*
Vers l'océan originel,	*Towards the primeval ocean,*
Toi qui passes et vas, sans cesse, et jamais lasse,	*You who come and go, without cease or fatigue,*
De la terre à la mer et de la mer au ciel.	*From the land to the sea and from the sea to the sky.*

Fauré's water music has so far been associated with gently flowing rivers, or the rocking of the ocean waves in various moods. In *Eau vivante* the water is a natural spring, self-replenishing, from deep within the earth; there are no glittering cascades in the treble clef. A *moto perpetuo* of winding and ascending semiquavers in the middle of the accompaniment's texture – like a dovetailing between viola and second violin – flows with the quiet persistence of a water-main that has burst underground, and is just as difficult for the pianist's hands to find and contain. The ancients said that one could not step into the same river twice: restless harmonic metamorphoses reflect a ceaseless, ever-changing flow. This effect is rendered even more hypnotic by the fact that this in this song Fauré makes one of his very occasional whole-hearted sorties into the whole-tone scale, an ideal colorant for this glistening current and rhapsodic overflow.

Van Lerberghe's line concerning the watery journey from land to sea, and from sea to sky, echoes Goethe's 'Gesang der Geister über den Wassern'. In the song's final page (particularly in the two-bar interlude after 'sans cesse, et jamais lasse') the music seems to be aspiring ever upwards as chromatic manoeuvrings rise in ascending sequences. As in *L'Aube blanche*, resolution is to be found only in the closing bars: the water has journeyed from the subterranean depths and finds its way to the ocean and thence to the broad expanses of the sky – a rediscovery of C major that sounds like the birth of a new tonality. It is interesting and arresting that the singer's climax occurs ahead of that of the pianist, who has to play two further bars of music to catch up with the voice. Having arrived at such a remarkable cadence, Fauré ignores the last verse of Van Lerberghe's poem.

Jankékélevitch uses the poem's first verse, as printed above, as his motto for his book on Fauré *mélodies*. He clearly believed that these words summed up the nature of the composer's] creative gift – the clarity of the water a metaphor for the fluidity and subterranean source of Fauré's inspiration, the purest life-giving refreshment derived 'from the heart of the earth'. Neither of the cycle's two motifs appears here.

(89) (vii) *Veilles-tu, ma senteur de soleil?* (*Are you awake, my fragrant sun?*)
January 1910, sent to the engraver 15 January 1910, published February 1910
The ninth song in the cycle to be composed, D major (original key), 2/4, *Allegretto con moto*

Veilles-tu, ma senteur de soleil,	*Are you awake, my fragrant sun,*
Mon arôme d'abeilles blondes,	*My scent of bright-coloured bees,*
Flottes-tu sur le monde,	*Do you drift across the world,*
Mon doux parfum de miel?	*My sweet aroma of honey?*
La nuit, lorsque mes pas	*At night, while my steps*
Dans le silence rôdent,	*Prowl in the silence,*
M'annonces-tu, senteur de mes lilas,	*Do you, who scent my lilacs*
Et de mes roses chaudes?	*And vivid roses, proclaim me?*
Suis-je comme une grappe de fruits	*Am I like a bunch of fruit*
Cachés dans les feuilles,	*Hidden in the foliage,*
Et que rien ne décèle,	*That nothing reveals*
Mais qu'on odore dans la nuit?	*But whose fragrance is felt at night?*
Sait-il, à cette heure,	*Does he know at this hour*
Que j'entr'ouvre ma chevelure,	*That I am loosening my tresses*
Et qu'elle respire;	*And that they are breathing;*
Le sent-il sur la terre?	*Does he sense it on earth?*

Sent-il que j'étends les bras,	*Does he sense that I reach out my arms,*
Et que des lys de mes vallées	*And that my voice – which he cannot hear –*
Ma voix qu'il n'entend pas	*Is fragrant*
Est embaumée?	*With lilies from my valleys?*

Among the many animal and insect poems in the French song repertoire (by Chabrier, Poulenc, etc.) this song is overlooked as one of the most perfect bee songs ever written, alongside Mahler's *Blicke mir nicht in die Lieder*. In the piano's unceasing sextuplet tremolos, implacable in their rhythmical exactitude, an apian hum (inspired admittedly by only a passing image in the poem) whirrs with the concentrated energy one associates with insects going about their work on a hot summer's day. It is interesting that a 'ruche' of this kind whereby heat is combined with a sound resembling a bee-hive is described by Philippe Fauré-Fremiet as being part of his father's earliest aural memories at the convent at Montgauzy (see Chapter 1).[23] Of course this glinting dynamo of an accompaniment serves more than one illustrative purpose – in this shimmering buzz we are aware of the radiation of the sun, a primal force in nature. Writers commenting on these songs in the past have mistakenly taken the 'he' referred to here as Adam, but a reading of the two poems on either side in the collection ('Tandis que tu reposes sur mon cœur' and 'Toutes blanches et toutes d'or') clarifies the situation: the male presence referred to here by Eve is less palpable than a husband and more symbolic – in this case 'Amour', god of Love. The song depicts the burgeoning of her sexuality; it is the only text that comes from the section of the book entitled *La Tentation*, and Eve manages to generate sensual excitement from the natural stimuli around her without requiring the presence of an Adam, or even an Adam's apple, in her life.

The music is prophetic of the first song in the *L'Horizon chimérique* cycle, *La Mer est infinie* (in the same key of D major), which defines the movement of the ocean in a similar, though rather less bracing, *moto perpetuo*. In this song sunlight, like water, is uncontainable: with Fauré's help it searches out and pervades every nook and cranny of harmonic possibility.

(90) (viii) *Dans un parfum de roses blanches* (*Amid the scent of white roses*)
Before 5 June 1909, sent to the engraver 5 June 1909, published October 1909
The eighth song in the cycle to be composed, G major, 3/4, *Andantino*

Dans un parfum de roses blanches	*Amid the scent of white roses*
Elle est assise et songe;	*She sits and dreams;*
Et l'ombre est belle comme s'il s'y mirait un ange.	*And the shade is fair, as if an angel were mirrored there.*
L'ombre descend, le bosquet dort;	*Darkness falls, the grove sleeps;*
Entre ses feuilles et les branches,	*Among the leaves and branches,*
Sur le paradis bleu s'ouvre un paradis d'or.	*A golden paradise opens out over the blue.*
Une voix qui chantait, tout à l'heure, murmure.	*A voice which sang but now, now murmurs.*
Un murmure s'exhale en haleine, et s'éteint.	*A murmur is breathed, and dies away.*
Dans le silence il tombe des pétales	*In the silence petals fall .....*

The harmonic complexities of this song are manifold with scarcely a nod towards the home key until the coda. This is because the chromatic theme B, not heard since *Comme Dieu rayonne*, returns as a bass line, a kind of passacaglia in gently sonorous crotchets. A concealed melody in the thumb of the pianist's right hand also traces the same theme with gentle insistence as the treble stave answers the bass. After the poem's first strophe even the vocal line (at 'L'ombre descend' and 'le bosquet dort') is fashioned from theme B. The superimposition of these three strands creates another 'murmure immense' indicative of a blurred dream, where a 'paradis d'or' will open out of the blue. With this search for an image of golden light in the second and third strophes the striving of the restless bass line recalls 'Vite, vite, / Car voici le soleil d'or' (*Avant que tu ne t'en ailles* from *La Bonne chanson*).

The relative calm of the song's final page is the kind of envoi we have come to expect in the songs from this cycle – the *berceuse* of the last three bars reveals Eve in a gentle shower of rose petals, a meeting of Eastern and Western religious imagery as if a Madonna-like figure were meditating within an Indian temple. The closing chord of G major, with a D at the top, already contains the opening note of *Crépuscule*, but nothing can prepare us for the coming of nightfall that follows. The first eight songs of this cycle have pulsated with life and joy, and now everything is set to change.

Fauré cuts the first line of Van Lerberghe's third verse. Other adaptions attempt to free the vocal line from a succession of sibilants, his least favourite cornucopia. Thus Van Lerberghe writes in his second strophe 'Le soir descend, le bosquet dort / Entre ses feuilles et ses branches'. Fauré unobtrusively amends this to 'L'ombre descend, le bosquet dort / Entre ses feuilles et les branches'. This poem is italicized by Van Lerberghe, the only one in 'Premières paroles' to be printed thus.

(91) (ix) *Crépuscule* (*Twilight*)
4 June 1906, sent to the engraver 13 June 1906, published August 1906
The first song in the cycle to be composed, D minor – D major, 3/2, *Adagio non troppo*

Ce soir, à travers le bonheur,	*This evening, amid the happiness,*
Qui donc soupire, qu'est-ce qui pleure?	*Who is it that sighs and what is it that weeps?*
Qu'est-ce qui vient palpiter sur mon cœur,	*What comes to flutter in my heart,*
Comme un oiseau blessé?	*Like a wounded bird?*
Est-ce une voix future,	*Is it a premonition,*
Une voix du passé?	*A voice from the past?*
J'écoute, jusqu'à la souffrance,	*I listen, till it hurts,*
Ce son dans le silence.	*To that sound in the silence.*
L'Île d'oubli, ô Paradis!	*Isle of oblivion, O paradise!*
Quel cri déchire, dans la nuit,	*What cry in the night cracks*
Ta voix qui me berce?	*Your voice that cradles me?*
Quel cri traverse	*What cry pierces*
Ta ceinture de fleurs,	*Your girdle of flowers,*
Et ton beau voile d'allégresse?	*And your lovely veil of happiness?*

Fauré first began work on his cycle with this song (in the office of the director of the Conservatoire), with a recapitulation of the music for *Mélisande's Song* from *Pelléas et Mélisande* and in the same key. Perhaps the imagery of the 'oiseau blessé' reminded the composer of the eponymous princess of Maeterlinck's play, or perhaps it is that both songs predict the deaths of their respective heroines. Fauré was under contractual pressure from his new publisher Heugel to produce a certain number of new works per year; this sent him looking for pieces from the past that could be adapted and recycled. Thus *La Chanson d'Ève* began by of taking the unpublished *Mélisande's Song* in English and grafting new words to it while making such accomodations as cutting the first line of Van Lerberghe's second strophe. If the original had not resurfaced in 1937 we would never have been any the wiser about the origins of *Crépuscule*.

This is the first time in this mighty work when we have heard of Eve's suffering and pain, and because Fauré has telescoped Van Lerberghe's lengthy cycle into a shape fit for music, the change of mood from joy to unhappiness is sudden rather than gradual, as in the extended poem-sequence. By now Eve has tasted the golden fruit of the forbidden tree and rejoiced in the death of God; because she has seen the fading of flowers, and the dying of the day, she understands that she is mortal (it is never claimed in the poem that she is anything else). She must die as everything in nature dies. The musical material is theme A, of course, although one fancies that one already hears theme B in the pianist's left hand in bar 29 as the sparse accompaniment gradually fills out with thirds, sixths and ninths and becomes a thing of power and grandeur.

Eve's final question as asked in the poem remains unanswered in the void of the infinite, but Fauré's music, particularly in the last-minute change into the major key, momentarily suggests a kind of transfiguration. This glimmer of hope is soon to be extinguished in the next song. Some months later the composer went on to write what would become the cycle's opening song, *Paradis*, another song of the half-light – the dawn of the world rather than Eden's twilight – where theme A is lifted into E minor, rather than reappearing in the more sombre light of its original key.

(92) (x) *Ô mort, poussière d'étoiles* (*O death, starry dust*)
January 1910, sent to the engraver on 15 January 1910, published February 1910
The last song in the cycle to be composed, D♭ major, **c**, *Andante molto moderato*

O mort, poussière d'étoiles,	*O death, starry dust,*
Lève-toi sous mes pas!	*Rise up where I tread!*
Viens, ô douce vague qui brille	*Come, gentle wave that shines*
Dans les ténèbres;	*In the darkness:*
Emporte-moi dans ton néant!	*Bear me off into your void!*
Viens, souffle sombre où je vacille,	*Come, dark sigh in which I tremble,*
Comme une flamme ivre de vent!	*Like a wind-intoxicated flame!*
C'est en toi que je veux m'étendre,	*It is in you that I wish to be absorbed,*
M'éteindre et me dissoudre,	*To be extinguished and dissolved,*
Mort, où mon âme aspire!	*Death, to which my soul aspires!*
Viens, brise-moi comme une fleur d'écume.	*Come, break me like a flower of foam,*
Une fleur de soleil à la cime	*A speck of sun in the crest*
Des eaux,	*Of the waves,*

319

Et comme d'une amphore d'or	*And like a golden amphora's*
Un vin de flamme et d'arome divin,	*Flaming wine of heavenly fragrance,*
Épanche mon âme	*Pour my soul*
En ton abîme, pour qu'elle embaume	*Into your abyss, that it might perfume*
La terre sombre et le souffle des morts.	*The dark earth and the breath of the dead.*

Charles Van Lerberghe (1861–1907)

Philippe Fauré-Fremiet, the composer's younger son, described this exceptionally dark song as 'a sort of funeral march, towards an open-armed Nirvana'.[24] Carlo Caballero points out that this observation is appropriate in that, particularly in the Hindu adaptation of a principal tenet of Buddhism, Nirvana 'is likened to a blowing out of the flame of life and an overthrow of all continuing personal passions and identity'.[25] In a letter to his wife of 6 April 1922 the composer writes, 'the clearest sign of the misery in which man finds himself is this promise, the very best he can be offered: the obliteration of *everything*, the Hindu nirvana, or the Catholic *Requiem aeternam*'.[26]

This type of slow and static crotchet-accompanied vocal line, going nowhere (and yet going everywhere in terms of harmonic exploration), is a familiar trademark of the late Fauré. The song's final strophe reintroduces theme B with a gradual, stately descent in both piano staves, a mingling of harmonies and rhythms that makes a haunting effect entirely consonant with that of fading away, a kind of musical vaporisation (see also *Inscription sur le sable*, which closes *Le Jardin clos*). The reader of Van Lerberghe's entire *Chanson d'Ève* will have followed a longer and more complex chronicle of Eve's life and her long progress to self-knowledge and death. But any religious aspect that has been retained as a residue of Van Lerberghe's erstwhile Catholicism (such as the consolatory angel Azreäl) fails to engage the composer. Fauré is very much in control here: he transposes the order of strophes 2 and 3 of the poem, and omits two lines each in strophes 4 and 5. The final shape is certainly no accident. In this last song Fauré omits the lines that refer to God.

In the final poem of Van Lerberghe's book (not set to music) the poet gently extinguishes Eve's breath as she sleeps, and her soul fades into the dawn, 'returning to the universe she sang'. Fauré's Eve does not even receive this amount of consolation; she is beyond religion, a symbol of pantheism and womanhood; her death, as natural as that of flowers and trees, is described without the slightest suggestion of salvation. Like everything else in this cycle the manner of her dissolution into the ether is implacable. In this music we can glimpse both Fauré's sense of wonder and his unsentimental grasp of reality – especially in relation to his own old age. The composer's son felt that his father's confidence had been shaken when contemplating the abyss represented by this song, but Jankélévitch the great musician–philosopher, saw it differently – as a song of ecstasy, 'a cosmic ecstasy which is in complete communion with nothingness, or better, a fusion into *total presence*'.[27] Almost certainly, Fauré had no belief in a personal resurrection; but there is no reason to suppose that he was unable to contemplate his own end with detachment. Like Eve herself, he understood the necessity of dying, yet this bleak song in the major key suggests the calm of acceptance rather than fear and revulsion.

ೲ   ೲ   ೲ   ೲ

In a letter to Fauré dated April 1910, Maurce Ravel wrote:

> My dear Master, How I should have liked to express my happiness to you as strongly as I experienced it yesterday, after *La Chanson d'Ève!* I was much too moved, and in any case, how could I, in the middle of that crowd? … One experiences a sense of closeness, at wonderful moments like these.'[28]

With this letter from a younger contemporary of this distinction Fauré's *mélodies* are gravely welcomed by a much younger man into his (Ravel's) own realm – that of twentieth-century music.

    ∽   ∽   ∽   ∽

Charles Van Lerbergh

Charles Van Lerberghe was born in Ghent in Belgium in 1861, at about the time when Fauré was composing his first Victor Hugo settings. Ghent is a Flemish-speaking city now, but in those days French was Belgium's sole literary language; in addition, Van Lerberghe's mother was Walloon, and thus French-speaking. The poet lost his parents early, but his mother was to remain for him a source of mystical memory and piety. An uncle of Maurice Maeterlinck became his guardian, and he studied literature at the University of Brussels. His Ibsen-inspired play, *Les Flaireurs* (*The trackers*), was produced in Paris in 1892. Far from being influenced by Maeterlinck (as was claimed at the time), this little play, written before Maeterlinck's *L'Intruse*, was a pioneering work in the history of the symbolist theatre. Indeed it may be said that Maeterlinck's *Pelléas et Mélisande* (and thus Debussy's opera) might not have been written without its pioneering establishment of an atmosphere of anguish and terror while using the simplest of literary means. Van Lerberghe spent time in Germany, Italy and England (where he admired the poems of Yeats as well the paintings of Burne-Jones and other pre-Raphaelites). His first volume of poetry, *Entrevisions* (*Glimpses*), appeared in 1898, poetry of the half-light and haunting, and haunted, visions that veiled more than they revealed. It was from this volume, as we shall see in the next chapter, that Fauré took the poems for his next cycle entitled *Le Jardin clos*.

La Chanson d'Ève, considered Van Lerberghe's masterpiece, was published in 1904, but, like Fauré's song cycle, it had a long period of gestation. In 1901 the poet had joined his friend Alfred Mockel in Torre del Gallo, near Florence. Mockel sets the scene:

> The windows of the villa opened out onto a garden planted with green oaks and pink laurel. The panorama rivalled that which one sees in Fiesole … as soon as he was in the garden, Charles Van Lerberghe recognised it as Eve's paradise. On certain evenings this enchanted garden was invaded by swarms of fireflies that we would see whirling like soaring sparks of light.

Added to this, the poet believed that he had met Eve herself, his Eve for whom he had searched so long; … But he decided that the attraction he felt was not to be expressed. He lived his feelings rather than defining them. His soul regaled itself with fugitive images and sensations, with many memories to which he did not yet dream of giving a definitive form.[29]

The poem was written not in Italy, but in Bouillon in the Ardennes (we are reminded of Fauré's words describing the garden of the Hôtel Borromée in Stresa as he began to work on *Paradis*). For both poet and composer the inspiration of the light and vegetation of the south is everywhere to be found in *La Chanson d'Ève*. For an idea of how Van Lerberghe imagined the appearance of the figure of Eve herself we must think of the female creations of painters, such as the poet's favourite Botticelli and the Englishman Burne-Jones. Reading between Mockel's lines we imagine that it was possible that Van Lerberghe, rather too young to be compared to Thomas Mann's ageing Aschenbach in Venice, had fallen in love with some angelic female Tadzio, out of reach, perhaps, because too young.

Some twenty years earlier the student Debussy had discovered the beauties of Dante Gabriel Rossetti's *The Blessed Damozel*, the inspiration for *La Démoiselle élue*, while reading in the gardens of the Villa Medici in Rome a book of English poetry translated into French. There were also contemporary writers, apart from Van Lerberghe's fellow Belgian symbolists, who played their part in the formation of the poem, and figures such as Yeats; the whole of Eve's narrative (taking place in a single day of creation from dawn to dusk, a vast arc of primordial experience) is a kind of extended variation on Mallarmé's 'L'Après-midi d'un faune', with its references to the shores of Sicily.

In this connection, the play *Pan* (published in 1906, but written before *La Chanson d'Ève*) was another of Van Lerberghe's attempts to mingle religion with symbolism, and written from the point of view of an atheist – a modern parody of the life of Christ. The poet died on 26 October 1907 following a stroke that had incapacitated him for a year; it was at a time when Fauré had set aside his work on *La Chanson d'Ève* in favour of *Pénélope*, and Van Lerberghe was never to know of the song cycles that would make his name known to musicians everywhere. Perhaps Fauré and his poet had shaken hands after the performance of *Pelléas et Mélisande* in London in 1898 (see Chapter 10), but the two men never corresponded; no doubt the situation would have changed if Van Lerberghe had lived for a few more years. Despite his very small output, he is still admired among connoisseurs of literature in French as being one of the most consistent and idealistic of the symbolist poets, capable of creating an atmosphere of serenity and mystery – the art of transcending reality in the creation of dreamy insubstantiality.

Charles Van Lerberghe. Frontispiece woodcut by Albert Delstanche from edition of La Chanson d'Ève *published by Crès in 1926.*

La Chanson d'Ève remains perhaps the greatest challenge of all for the Fauré interpreter. The sheer scope and length of the cycle are demanding enough (the range is that of a high mezzo) without the 'casting' that is necessary to make the work believable in performance – the work requires a singer with a measure of moral authority, and a sovereign sense of rhythm.

The formidable Jeanne Raunay, daughter of the painter Jules Richomme and the first singer and dedicatee of this work, was a very serious artist; as far as we know she was not one of the pretty singers for whom the composer felt a *frisson* of attraction. In 1898 she had refused Debussy's invitation to sing the first performance of his *Chansons de Bilitis* because she felt the texts to be immoral[30]. Although capable of the grand manner in her operatic singing (Gluck's *Iphigénie en Tauride* and Wagner), she was modest and highly intelligent, as was her well-known husband, the *littérateur* and novelist André Beaunier. Fauré counted the couple as personal friends.

The presence of an extremely attractive woman on the platform has seldom harmed a song recital, all other things (such as vocal and interpretative talent) being equal. But an Eve with a self-consciously sexy allure would undermine a performance of this work. Eve must be unaware of her beauty – if indeed she is conventionally beautiful – she is a cosmic figure, unawakened to temptation, but somehow still an earth-mother. She is not a wafting fairy, although she can be slight and unsubstantial; equally, she can be large and curvaceous and fundamental. Appearance is less important by far in a work that requires a kind of charismatic selflessness where the normal 'ego' issues of the singing voice become irrelevant. Eve is a mouthpiece for poems that belong to a primordial Eden and are not of this world, and Fauré sets these utterances to music in a way that matches them – there can be no higher compliment to the composer's ability to enter the world of his poet.

In my generation there have been few singers who are suited to the role. I shall never forget the performance of *Paradis* by Jennifer Smith, pupil of Winifred Radford and Pierre Bernac, who took part in a Songmakers' Almanac celebration of Fauré in 1980. We had worked very hard on all the tempi and gear-changes for this hugely difficult song, and when it came to the performance the music simply poured from the singer as if she was the mouthpiece for something beyond the confines of her own body. This was a valuable early lesson for me in Fauré's style. There was no way any producer could have told a singer how to 'act' this role; the luxury of expressing her own emotions had been sacrificed by the singer to the rigours of the music's form of which she was acutely aware.

Needless to say this does not happen very often. The euphoria that accompanies self-surrender is something extraordinary to hear and behold, but simply 'letting go' is not exactly the answer either: the songs are musically difficult, and the composer's directions have to be followed to the letter. The challenge, somewhat the same as singing oratorio at the

The title-page of the collected edition of Fauré's cycle La Chanson d'Ève *published by Heugel.*

most spiritual level, is to depersonalise the music without turning it into something heartless and robotic. In singing *La Chanson d'Ève*, the 'gloss' the music all too easily acquires, a patina of self-consciousness when it is being 'performed' by a 'successful' singer, must be avoided. On the other hand, if complete control over the musical material in terms of rhythm and diction is retained, the artist capable of this is more than likely to be eminent in her field, in other words 'successful'.

If a singer is able to master the difficulties of *Paradis* (and the cycle's other songs) it is something to be proud of, but Eve in her primal innocence is unaware that such a thing as pride exists. In this music even efficiency and determination can be mistaken for an arrogance that is utterly foreign to Eve in her wide-eyed humility. The paradoxes and challenges facing the performers of the late songs of Fauré will always be as ineffable as the music itself.

1   Letter of 27 October 1900, in Gabriel Fauré, *Lettres intimes*, ed. Philippe Fauré-Fremiet (Paris: La Colombe, 1951), p. 55.

2   *Gabriel Fauré: A Life in Letters*, trans. and ed. Barrie Jones (London: B.T. Batsford, 1989), letter 106, p. 103.

3   Ibid., letter 117, p. 111.

4   Fauré, *Lettres intimes*, p. 126.

5   Ibid., p. 129.

6   Ibid.

7   In an address to the Cercle Royal Gaulois Artistique et Littéraire on 14 October 1954, reprinted in *Synthèses* (September–October 1962).

8   Information from Lady Natasha Spender.

9   *Gabriel Fauré: A Life in Letters*, letter 175, p. 141.

10 Ibid., letter 290, p. 198.

11 C. Van Lerberghe, *Lettres à Albert Mockel, 1887–1906*, ed. Robert Debever and Jacques Detemmerman (Brussels: Editions Labor, 1986), p. 300.

12 Ibid., p. 301.

13 Ibid.

14 Carlo Caballero, *Fauré and French Musical Aesthetics* (Cambridge: Cambridge University Press, 2001), p. 205.

15 Ibid., p. 300, n. 132.

16 *Gabriel Fauré: A Life in Letters*, letter 152, p. 130.

17 *La Chanson d'Ève*: Aspects of this cycle's interpretation are discussed in Chapter 16, pp. 421–3.

18 Vladimir Jankélévitch, *De la musique au silence: Fauré et l'inexprimable* (Paris: Plon, 1974), p. 178.

19 Jean-Michel Nectoux, *Gabriel Fauré: A Musical Life*, trans. Roger Nichols (Cambridge: Cambridge University Press, 1991), p. 369.

20 Caballero, *Fauré and French Musical Aesthetics*, p. 200.

21 Gabriel Fauré, *Correspondance*, ed. Jean-Michel Nectoux (Paris: Flammarion, 1980), letter 152.

22 Jankélévitch, *De la musique au silence: Fauré et l'inexprimable*, p. 196.

23 Philippe Fauré-Fremiet, *Gabriel Fauré* (Paris: Les Éditions Rieder, 1929), p. 19.

24 Fauré-Fremiet, *Gabriel Fauré,* p. 272.

25 Caballero, *Fauré and French Musical Aesthetics*, p. 216.

26 Fauré, *Lettres intimes*, p. 99.

27 Jankélévitch, *De la musique au silence: Fauré et l'inexprimable*, p. 202.

28 *Gabriel Fauré: A Life in Letters*, letter 166, p. 136.

29 Van Lerberghe, *Lettres à Albert Mockel*, quoted in Philippe Fauré-Fremiet, 'La Chanson d'Eve', *Synthèses* (September–October 1962).

30 François Lesure, *Claude Debussy* (Paris: Fayard, 2003), p. 228.

Chapter Thirteen

Fauré and Charles Van Lerberghe (II)

Le Jardin clos

The years between 1911 and 1914 (for we must traverse this period in the composer's life before we encounter him once again as a creator of *mélodies*) were hugely busy. The sheer excitement of creating a large work in which he passionately believed, the opera *Pénélope*, carried him forward in terms of body and spirit. Fauré's health was not improving but no medical complaint, no difficulty with his hearing, could impede the progress of his great task. As he wrote to his son, 'In truth, one really ought to have nothing else to do apart from that which one is destined for – when one is destined for something.' The central misfortune of Fauré's life – as well as the good fortune of Schubert's, who managed precisely this, despite having even less money than the French composer – is encapsulated in this wistful sentence. Throughout his life Fauré had to snatch time to compose amid the hurly-burly of making a living. Not very much changed for him in this regard during the first decade of the twentieth century: his day-to-day work at the Conservatoire was demanding although less time-consuming and stressful than crossing from one end of Paris to the other to give lessons, or from one end of France to the other to inspect conservatoires. When circumstances permitted him to do so, he spent extended periods working on *Pénélope*, and these seemed positively idyllic.

By the summer of 1911 the remarkable first act of *Pénélope* was complete, and the second act was recast. After a quarter of a century at 154 boulevard Malesherbes in the seventeenth *arrondissement*, the Fauré family moved in April to 32 rue des Vignes in the rather grander sixteenth. This was where Fauré died in 1924, and the same apartment, full of family treasures, where the young Jean-Michel Nectoux visited the composer's daughter-in-law some forty-five years later.

The year 1912 was more or less given over to the evolving opera: there were three weeks in Hyères in April composing the third act, and the work was finally completed in short score in Lugano on 31 August. To celebrate this achievement Fauré wrote to his wife, quoting the words that are sung at the end of the opera: 'Gloire à Zeus', 'Praise be to Zeus' – an ironic acknowledgement of the religious gratitude of composers like Bach or Haydn in having completed a work. The orchestration was begun almost immediately. Soon afterwards Lucienne Bréval, who was to create the title role, read through her part accompanied by Alfred Cortot (who had joined the staff of the Paris Conservatoire thanks to Fauré, and much to the fury of Marguerite Long, who had wanted the position for herself). An encouraging letter from D'Indy on 12 August 1912 contains this observation about Fauré's forthcoming opera: 'the man who has written *Lieder* as dramatic as yours ever since the early *Berceaux*, up to *Spleen*

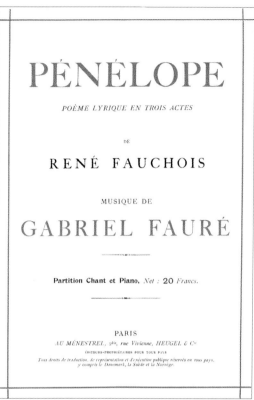

Cover (left) and title-page (right) of Pénélope

and *La Bonne chanson*, this man must write a real drama, and a good one.'[1] The two men, despite their opposing musical sympathies, had remained friends, and D'Indy reminded Fauré that they had been chums for so long that they could remember meeting each other at the homes of Duparc and Chabrier.

By mid-November the whole opera was ready for a read-through, which took place at the apartment of Marguerite Hasselmans. The orchestration was finished by 12 January 1913; the composer did about four-fifths of this himself, but ran out of time and called on the services of Fernand Pécoud to assist him.

Fauré felt it necessary to spend the Christmas of 1912 in Monte Carlo preparing for the work's première there at the beginning of March 1913, a sign that at this tense time he needed the company and support of the vivacious Marguerite Hasselmans rather than that of his pessimistic wife. Back in Paris there was another read-through of the work in the Director's office at the Conservatoire and, once again, Cortot presided at the piano. After a reasonable rehearsal period in Monte Carlo, *Pénélope*, conducted by Léon Jehin, was given its first performance on 4 March 1913. The work was dedicated to Saint-Saëns, who wryly admitted to shedding a tear on learning of this honour, but who nevertheless wrote somewhat acerbic letters to Fauré regarding various production, rather than musical, details; these were typical of the kind of proprietorial bossiness that one might expect from a rather crotchety old man with an eagle's eye for pitfalls. We also sense that, in criticising the librettist René Fauchois for misinterpreting Homer (Saint-Saëns was horrified that the suitors are

326

made to flirt with the servants in front of Penelope), the older composer was doing his best to avoid discussing the music, with which he was completely out of sympathy.[2]

The *succès d'estime* of the Monte Carlo performances was followed, on 10 May, by a triumphant first night in Paris at the Théâtre des Champs-Élysées. There were eleven further performances. It is curious to think that at this very theatre on 19 May, before the run of *Pénélope* was over, Stravinsky's *Le Sacre de printemps* had been given its historic, and riot-provoking, first performance. According to Stravinsky himself Fauré was present at one of the ballet's performances. On 26 June, on the day his opera came to the end of its run, Fauré signed a contract with Jacques Durand, the publisher of Saint-Saëns (since 1877) as well as of Debussy (since 1884). It is not at all clear why he effected this change. The relationship between composer and publisher is always severely tested during the preparation of a huge project like an opera, but Fauré seems to have been satisfied with Heugel in regard to *Pénélope*.

Durand was the last of the firms to be charged with printing Fauré's *mélodies*. The historical line-up of the composer's song publishers is as follows: Choudens, Hartmann, Choudens again, Durand (for the three songs of *Poëme d'un jour* issued in 1880 and the first appearance of *En prière* in 1890), Hamelle (the longest association by far), Fromont (very briefly), Metzler in London (for three years only), Heugel, and again Durand. The strange *Hymne à Apollon* was published by Bornemann. The Gramophone Company published the first edition of *Le Ramier* in Milan, and Leduc the *Vocalise*. Some of Fauré's songs and piano music were published posthumously by various publishers: Costallat undertook the *Souvenirs de Bayreuth* for piano duet. When we consider the oeuvre as a whole, we must add Schoen, who published the *Cantique de Jean Racine*, and Breitkopf & Härtel and Schirmer, who published, at opposite ends of the composer's life, the First Violin Sonata in A, Op. 13, and the First Piano Quintet, Op. 89, respectively.

The summer of 1913 was spent in Lugano; the composer was still fretting about *Pénélope*, but it was at this time that he began to think of writing songs again. On 6 August he wrote to Marie Fauré: 'I have just received a volume of poetry by Van Lerberghe, which one of his Belgian friends is lending me (for the work is out of print). Perhaps I will find something to do in the said volume.'[3] Fauré went on to say that the piano piece he was just beginning to compose (the Tenth Barcarolle) was 'the fiftieth, or more of my piano pieces: with rare exceptions, pianists just let them pile up without playing them. After 20 years their turn will come!'[4] At this time the composer's twenty-nine-year-old elder son Emmanuel, already a distinguished biologist, married into the Henneguy family; the father-in-law of Fauré *fils* was a professor of embryology at the Collège de France, where Emmanuel, in turn, also became a professor.

As Fauré feared, the Paris revival of *Pénélope* in October 1913 was insufficiently rehearsed. The bad luck that has dogged this work ever since set in at this point; the performances deteriorated in quality as the run progressed. The opera was withdrawn after six performances, and the promoter, Gabriel Astruc, went bankrupt. *Pénélope* was not revived until January 1919; after attending a performance at that time, the composer Gabriel Pierné wrote to Fauré in words that might also be used to describe the reaction of all those enthusiasts who are in love with the music of the composer's final period:

I was ready to cry my eyes out at certain passages, you know which ones I mean – it's so beautiful, so restrained, there is so much discretion in the work, it is full of subtleties so unpretentious that the experienced musician thinks he is the only one who can appreciate some of the finer points and selfishly rejoices over a beauty others fail to see!

In the autumn Fauré made five piano-roll recordings for the firm of Welte Mignon, including the First Barcarolle and a piano arrangement of the *Pavane*. These show his fingers to have been in good working order; playing on his own he had none of the difficulties in listening and ensemble that he experienced as an accompanist. At the beginning of December *Pénélope* had its Brussels première with the incomparable Claire Croiza in the title role.

In February 1914 the first biography of Fauré, by Louis Vuillemin, also a composer of songs, was published. Fauré was pleased, and the beautiful *Je me poserai sur ton cœur* from *Le Jardin clos* was later to be dedicated to Vuillemin's wife as a sign of the composer's gratitude. Fauré was still able to travel, and he was still determined to play the challenging piano parts in his chamber music works. He was a guest performer in a series of London concerts in which Robert Lortat (the dedicatee of the Twelfth Nocturne of 1915) played Fauré's complete music for solo piano; the series took place in the Aeolian Hall, New Bond Street, London in June 1914. This was a gratifying turn of events considering the composer's pessimistic letter of the previous year concerning his neglected piano works: the

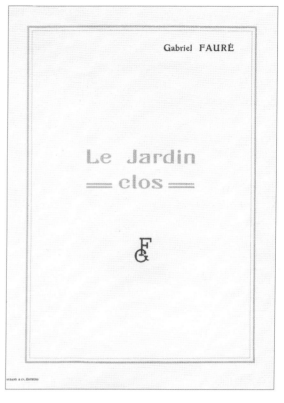

Title-page of Le Jardin clos, *published by Durand. The 'GF' monogram was invented by Durand to match the famous and long-established monogram for the published works of Debussy*

young Lortat had approached him in Paris, and to Fauré's stupefied surprise, was able to play by heart everything for piano that the composer had ever written. It is heartening that there was at least something of a public for such a project in London, although the press questioned the wisdom of devoting entire concerts to a single composer. Fauré has never been a mainstream 'box-office' composer, and he was certainly not regarded as such by the English critics of the time.

At the end of July he decided to return to Bad Ems near Wiesbaden in Germany to take the waters: this had been the scene of a productive holiday in 1910. He stayed there between 21 and 30 July 1914 and worked on the opening songs of *Le Jardin clos*. From Ems he wrote to Marie (21 July 1914) that he was working on the new Van Lerberghe settings. He added: 'I can find nothing, alas! in today's French poets, nothing, which calls for music.'[5] It is interesting that at more or less the same time Debussy was drawn in his song-writing to poets of the distant past such as François Villon, Charles d'Orléans and Tristan L'Hermite, rather than to his literary contemporaries. In 1913 both Debussy and Ravel had set poems by Stéphane Mallarmé, works inspired by the first *édition complète* of Mallarmé's *Poésies* in that year. We have to remind ourselves that Mallarmé was born three years before Fauré, and had died in 1898. He was hardly a new discovery in historical terms, although his work was 'modern' well before its time, and sounded particularly avant-garde in the context of these remarkable Debussy and Ravel settings.

328

As it turned out, Ems was a spectacularly unfortunate choice of holiday destination. The outbreak of the First World War at the end of July descended on Europe (and on Fauré) with scarcely any warning. His younger son, Philippe, joined up and was to see action at Verdun and Salonica. Fauré had to leave Germany and return to France via Switzerland – the journey via Basel was difficult and took three days. He made his way to Geneva, and from there to Pau in the Pyrenees, where he visited his brother Fernand and his family, and then eventually returned to Paris. This time, however, Fauré was not going to take four years to write a new set of songs, even considering the uncertainties of war. With an admirable sense of concentration, and clearly very taken with Van Lerberghe's *Entrevisions*, his new poetic discovery, he completed the cycle in the autumn of 1914. This was a complete contrast to the extended and convoluted genesis of *La Chanson d'Ève*, where the final shape of the cycle evolved over a long period.

Le Jardin clos was given its first performance on 28 January 1915, the composer accompanying Claire Croiza as part of the 'Concerts Casella' series. At the same concert Ravel's mesmerising Piano Trio in A minor also received its first performance. With due dispatch the songs were published in May 1915 by the firm of Durand, no doubt anxious to issue the first vocal work since *Poème d'un jour* by its new composer (it had already published the Eleventh Nocturne and the Tenth Barcarolle in 1913, and the Eleventh Barcarolle in 1914).

∾   ∾   ∾   ∾

Gardens have served as spiritual centres from the earliest times. From their protected spaces we may direct our gaze inward, toward our thoughts and feelings, or outward, toward a beautiful detail: light shining through the calyx of a flower, a lover's hand, the sky between the leaves, the crossing of clouds and stars, whatever is serene and desirable … . Fauré's music so often seeks to find this place of contemplation, to create a landscape unto itself, which cannot be precisely fixed in time and space.[6]
Carlos Caballero

Between 1906 and 1910, as we have seen in Chapter 12, Fauré had set ten poems from Van Lerberghe's *La Chanson d'Ève*. This great cycle had seemed to be Fauré's quiet, but mighty, riposte to the prevailing challenge of Debussy's music and aesthetic. These two great composers had Verlaine in common, but between them there had always been a wide divergence of literary, and other, tastes. It is curious, therefore, that they looked to different members of the same group of Belgian writers for the symbolism that was to define the great works of their maturity – Debussy to Maeterlinck for *Pelléas et Mélisande*, and Fauré to Van Lerberghe for two song cycles, *La Chanson d'Ève* and *Le Jardin clos*. The two Belgian poets were closely linked in terms of their lives and work, but Maeterlinck led Debussy to his opera, a story full of atmosphere and drama, and Van Lerberghe gave Fauré a kind of pre-Raphaelite language of idealised feminine beauty and grace where the mysterious imagery discourages a story line. (There is a very loose narrative in *La Chanson d'Ève*, none at all in *Le Jardin clos*.) This poetry seems to achieve, in Fauré's hands, a remarkable depth of utterance. Without his music and in the harsh light of a less perfumed epoch, these lyrics can seem dated and mannered; but they were the catalyst that released in the ageing composer a new and powerful vein of lyricism.

The texts for the cycle are taken from Van Lerberghe's first collection of verse, *Entrevisions* (*Glimpses*), published by the Brussels firm of Paul Lacomblez in 1898. The manuscript had originally consisted of some three thousand lines of poetry. Van Lerberghe had drawn on the philosopher Henri Bergson's theory of duration (whereby nothing is static, everything is in a state of change and evolution) to help him create verbal imagery of transient beauty.[7] A jury of the poet's friends, including Albert Mockel, Fernand Séverin and Maurice Maeterlinck, was brought together to find a title for the work, and to choose which of the poems to publish. Maeterlinck in particular was very critical of Van Lerberghe's language and his overuse of naive and insipid imagery, including what he termed an 'abus d'eau de rose'. It is certainly true that roses and the perfume of roses pervades the poet's work in general (*La Chanson d'Ève* in particular) and that *Le Jardin clos* contains many repetitions of such words as 'rêve', 'doux', 'radieux' and so on. Fauré seems to have found these almost-Wagnerian leitmotifs entirely acceptable; the potentially dangerous monotony and vagueness of the vocabulary seems somehow to have set him free.

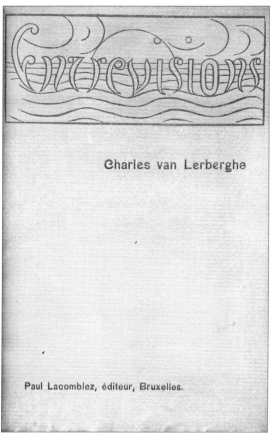

The first edition of Charles Van Lerberghe's Entrevisions *(1898)*

Entrevisions is divided into three parts, of which *Le Jardin clos* is the second. In fact only Nos 7, 4 and 2 of the song cycle are to be found in this part of the work; each of these three poems is preceded by a Latin epithet, translated in the commentaries below, that is adapted from the biblical *Canticum canticorum*, the Song of Songs. Fauré allowed himself to choose freely from the remainder of *Entrevisions*, where the other poems are contained under Van Lerberghe's subheadings *Jeux et songes* and *Sous le portique*. The title-page of *Jeux et songes* is prefaced by that marvellous quotation from one of Goethe's *Römische Elegien* – 'sehe mit fühlendem Aug, fühle mit sehender Hand' – which describes the poet's sensual awakening in Italy, where he learned, like a sculptor, to divine the inner shape of Roman marble turned to the reality of human flesh, how to 'see with a feeling eye, feel with a seeing hand'. Needless to say, the thematic links between the texts that one might expect in this cycle, representing an actual walled garden for instance, are very nebulous. For that reason Fauré referred to the work as a 'suite' rather than a cycle.

There is no doubt that the composer's memories of the vegetation and fragrances of the garden at Montgauzy (see Chapter 2), the enclosed space that had entranced his earliest years, had become more powerful with the passing of the decades, and that these childhood recollections played a crucial part in the selection of texts for both the Lerberghe cycles, and for *Jardin nocturne*, the third song of the *Mirages* set.

The poetry of Van Lerberghe's first collection has much in common with *La Chanson d'Ève* in drawing its inspiration from a kind of subverted religiosity: what might first appear to be Christian imagery is soon revealed as pagan. The Virgin can take on the name of Psyche or Venus; the nymph in the grotto ('Dans la nymphée'), sleeping with open eyes, is an antecedent of Eve in Van Lerberghe's verse. The use of the Song of Songs for headings in Latin gives a misleading impression of a biblical slant, but it is a signpost to the poet's veiled erotic agenda. After all, a seraglio can also be housed within a walled garden, each bloom therein a metaphor for pliant female pulchritude, although Van Lerberghe was undoubtedly more high-minded than a sultan. Albert Mockel (who introduced Fauré to this poetry) wrote of *Entrevisions*:

> The verses of Van Lerberghe make one think of angels that would follow the cortège of Venus: half veiled by their wings, they hide their astonished blue eyes and their lips, as if the delights of the senses have just been revealed to them. They are pagan angels, or if one wishes, they are simply young girls.[8]

Once again Fauré was attracted to verse that retreated from reality, but not so far as to lose all connection with real feminine beauty, in this case a distant echo of that amorous drive that had governed so much of his life as an ardent, yet necessarily discreet, lover of women. Van Lerberghe, deeply attracted to the feminine imagery of the pre-Raphaelites and Botticelli, had simply wanted to compose poetry which had a beauty that was both intense and mysterious. As such, these poems, and the music to which they are set, exert a fascination that exists without any confessed philosophical intention on the part of their creator. J.-M. Nectoux points out that this poetry is related to the paintings of the great Belgian symbolist Ferdinand Khnopff and to the writing of Georges Rodenbach, particularly *Bruges-la-morte* of 1892.[9]

Since 1903 the composer had been suffering, as we have seen, from tinnitus and hearing problems: when he played the piano, both low and high registers were distorted, only the middle remaining clear. This is often given as a reason for the restricted range of both the vocal line and the accompaniments in the late cycles. It is clear that practical considerations played their part in the evolution of the works, but the phlegmatic style of vocal writing, sparing in its intervals but melodically memorable and capable of intense emotion, seems an entirely natural and organic evolution from the later songs of the second period. The composer's hearing problems did not dictate the boundaries of the late style so much as fortify them.

Fauré himself hesitated to compare himself with Beethoven in this regard, but we may do so without embarrassment: the composer's terrible struggle with this illness at this time of his life seems to have given his music a kind of almost indefinable nobility and strength born of quiet suffering and heroic stoicism. With this music, *pace* those who sadly find they can only love the 'melodic' Fauré of earlier years, we are never short-changed. We are never led to regret the deafness and tinnitus, save for the pain and distress it caused an admired and loved master. In a similar way, how many lovers of Beethoven's music, however grateful they may be to the man, would now be willing to wish away that Titan's deafness, and its consequences?

In Fauré's development, as in his songs themselves, one thing always leads to another. Whether *La Chanson d'Ève* opened the way to the use of a new expressive vocabulary in *Pénélope* or vice versa is hardly important. *Le Jardin clos* is the beneficiary of the refining fire through which the composer passed in the process of working on his opera. Both cycles were written for a woman's voice; both cycles encompassed a tribute to the mystery of the eternal feminine. The distanced eroticism of *Le Jardin clos* seems a leave-taking – still passionate, ever discreet, but a valediction nevertheless. It is completely free of self-pity, but there is a sadness here that had not been evident in the vast unpopulated innocence of *La Chanson d'Ève*. In the best performances of *Le Jardin clos* there is an unforced sense of renunciation that can break the heart.

Le Jardin clos [10]
Op. 106

(93) (i) Exaucement (*Fulfilment*)
July–November 1914, Op. 106 No. 1, 'À Mme Albert Mockel', C major, 4/4, *Allegretto*

Alors qu'en tes mains de lumière	*When in your hands of light*
Tu poses ton front défaillant,	*You rest your swooning head,*
Que mon amour en ta prière	*May my love enter your prayer*
Vienne comme un exaucement.	*Like a fulfilment.*
Alors que la parole expire	*When words expire*
Sur ta lèvre qui tremble encor,	*On your still trembling lips,*
Et s'adoucit en un sourire	*And mellow into a smile*
De roses en des rayons d'or;	*Of roses and golden rays;*
Que ton âme calme et muette,	*May your calm and silent soul –*
Fée endormie au jardin clos,	*Asleep like a fairy in a walled garden –*
En sa douce volonté faite	*With its sweet desire now attained,*
Trouve la joie et le repos.	*Find delight and peace of mind.*

In the sleep of the beloved there is a kind of balm to the spirit. This music is almost too transparent to exist in reality. The rippling chords beginning and ending in C major take us on a journey both uneventful and packed with incident. The vocal line is undemonstrative, yet almost painfully eloquent. This simplicity could not be more different from the recherché textural and harmonic explorations of Ravel in his contemporary Mallarmé settings (1913). Unlike the music of Satie, whose minimalism sometimes seems childlike, *Exaucement* has the simplicity of a great sage. When pianists sympathetic to this music attempt this accompaniment the harmonies seem so magically in place, so inevitable, that they seem to dissolve under the fingers as soon as they are translated from page to keyboard.

Faure's achievement here is to distil the essence of French song – one might be tempted to say of music itself. In this handful of gentle oscillations one can sense the huge numbers of notes that have been eliminated by their composer over many years of self-pruning to achieve this almost unworldly limpidity. For those with the ears to discern discipline and self-sacrifice turned into music, something almost unbearably beautiful is created from thin air. Here we first experience something that runs throughout this marvellous cycle – a state of musical grace that is all the more touching for trying so little to engage the attention of the listener.

The song's dedicatee, the wife of the poet, Albert Mockel, was an amateur singer. The name of Mockel at the head of Faure's cycle is an indication of his gratitude for the role that the Belgian literati had played in his life as a song composer.

(94) (ii) *Quand tu plonges tes yeux dans mes yeux*

(*When you immerse your eyes in mine*)

July–November 1914, Op. 106 No. 2, 'À Mlle Germaine Sanderson', F major, 3/4, *Andante moderato*

Quand tu plonges tes yeux dans mes yeux,	*When you immerse your eyes in mine,*
Je suis toute dans mes yeux.	*I am wholly in my eyes.*
Quand ta bouche dénoue ma bouche,	*When your lips part mine,*
Mon amour n'est que ma bouche.	*My love is my lips alone.*
Si tu frôles mes cheveux,	*When you stroke my hair,*
Je n'existe plus qu'en eux.	*I no longer exist but there.*
Si ta main effleure mes seins,	*If your hand but brushes my breasts,*
J'y monte comme un feu soudain.	*I quicken there like a sudden fire.*
Est-ce moi que tu as choisie?	*Is it I that you have chosen?*
Là est mon âme, là est ma vie.	*There is my soul, there is my life.*

The motto from the Song of Songs printed at the head of the poem is 'Ego dilecto meo et dilectus meus mihi'. This is one of the most famous quotations from this book of the Bible: 'I am my beloved's, he is mine'. The meditation based on this text by Francis Quarles (1633) was set by Benjamin Britten as *Canticle 1*. It is more than likely that Van Lerberghe took the title *Le Jardin clos* itself from the 'hortus conclusus' in the Song of Songs.

Quiet and understated though it is, this is a voluptuous song. In Debussy's *Chansons de Bilitis* the seeming innocence of the eponymous narrator enhances the erotic effect of the music. Something similar happens here, although it is far removed from the heady pseudo-ancient-Greek world of the poetry of Pierre Louÿs. In terms of rhythm and pace the song inhabits the same world as *J'ai presque peur* from *La Bonne chanson*. Fear is the key word, or perhaps trepidation. There is a pulsation here that also recalls another Verlaine song, *Green*, with its palpitating accompaniment, a song that similarly describes sexual devotion within a halo of self-doubt and diffidence – as if to say 'Am I beautiful enough, desirable enough, good enough to be the chosen one?' The possibility of rejection and abandonment is implicit in such whole-hearted commitment to another, and sets the heart, and music, a-quiver. Needless to say, downcast eyes of modesty, a touch of submissiveness (at the return to the home tonality of F major at 'Je suis toute dans mes yeux', for example), adds to the erotic impulse. The composer has created a song that is breathless with innocence and sexual experience at the same time.

The song's dedicatee Germaine Sanderson, a soprano, had recently performed extracts from Bréville's *Éros vainqueur* under Messager's baton. She was active in the salon of Marguerite de Saint-Marceaux (who wrote witheringly of her 'talent d'amateur', but considered her 'aimable and bonne'). Sanderson, like the more famous Jane Bathori, often accompanied herself at the piano, although Saint-Marceaux notes in her journal a recital on 10 May 1911 where Fauré himself accompanied Sanderson.[11]

(95) (iii) *La Messagère* (*The messenger*)

July–November 1914, Op. 106 No. 3, 'À Mlle Gabrielle Gills', G major, 3/4, *Allegro*

Avril, et c'est le point du jour.	*April, and day has broken.*
Tes blondes sœurs qui te ressemblent,	*Your fair sisters who resemble you,*
En ce moment, toutes ensemble	*At this moment, all together*
S'avancent vers toi, cher Amour.	*Advance towards you, dear Love.*
Tu te tiens dans un clos ombreux	*In your shady enclosure*
De myrte et d'aubépine blanche:	*Of myrtle and white hawthorn:*
La porte s'ouvre sous les branches;	*The door opens beneath the branches;*
Le chemin est mystérieux.	*The path is full of mystery.*
Elles, lentes, en longues robes,	*Slowly, in long gowns,*
Une à une, main dans la main,	*One by one, hand in hand,*
Franchissent le seuil indistinct	*They cross the blurred threshold*
Où de la nuit devient de l'aube.	*Where night becomes dawn.*
Celle qui s'avance d'abord,	*She who first draws near,*
Regarde l'ombre, te découvre,	*Looks at the shade, discovers you,*
Crie, et la fleur de ses yeux s'ouvre	*Cries out, and her flower-eyes open,*
Splendide dans un rire d'or.	*Resplendent in golden laughter.*
Et, jusqu'à la dernière sœur,	*And the sisters without exception*
Toutes tremblent, tes lèvres touchent	*All tremble, your lips touch*
Leurs lèvres, l'éclair de ta bouche	*Their lips, the brilliance of your mouth*
Éclate jusque dans leur cœur.	*Erupts into their very hearts.*

This is a big song, and bristling with extraordinary élan, at least in the opening section, which suggests a fanfare for the arrival of the deputation of sisters, the kind of poetic symbol that is also beloved of Van Lerberghe's compatriot Maeterlinck. The onset of spring is associated with the awakening of love, and there is a priapic note in the energy of this music, an upbeat tempo that is not heard again until the seventh song in the cycle. Right-hand semiquavers ripple in Fauré's implacably fast metronome marking, while the left hand, at first engaged in canonic imitation with the vocal line, drives the music forward. In this register of the piano we might imagine a horn combining with glistening harp sonorities.

For the poem's third verse ('Elles, lentes, en longues robes') Fauré provides music that is extraordinarily apt for the image of spirits crossing the 'blurred threshold' of night and dawn. This accompaniment of gently oscillating quavers glides forward like an army of willowy female ghosts – one can almost hear the rustling of invisible silk gowns (perhaps the Burne-Jones costumes admired by Van Lerberghe in the London production of *Pelléas et Mélisande*) as one harmony melts imperceptibly into the next. Playing this passage for the first time is a revelation for any pianist – a nightmare of accidentals certainly, but also an induction into the Fauréan mysteries. A word of warning to singers and pianists: despite this song's energy it describes the half-light of a misty morning before the eruption of dawn. Performers must control their ebullience and preserve the interiority of this music, which must never jump outside the frame that contains the cycle as a whole.

The dedicatee of this song, Gabrielle Gills, earlier Madame Mannheim, was an amateur soprano who was an intimate childhood friend of a famous patroness of music, Jeanne Salomon, later Madame Léonard Rosenthal. The Rosenthals, who supported a number of young promising musicians, were the hosts of a highly successful salon, in the avenue Ruisdaël, that reached its height in the twenties. Gills was part of a circle that included the young Nathan Milstein and Vladimir Horowitz, as well as singers like Claire Croiza. Jacques Durand in his memoirs recalls accompanying Gills in Fauré songs (she apparently sang them delectably) at the salon of Madame Petit de Villeneuve. It is notable therefore that Gill's name features on the pages of the first of the composer's cycles to be published by the firm of Durand.[12] Marguerite de Saint-Marceaux compared her unfavourably to Croiza and wrote of 'a pretty voice without a shade of feeling'.[13]

(96) (iv) *Je me poserai sur ton cœur* (*I shall alight on your heart*)
July–November 1914, Op. 106 No. 4, 'À Mme Louise Vuillemin', E♭ major, 3/4, *Allegretto moderato*

Je me poserai sur ton cœur	*I shall alight on your heart*
Comme le printemps sur la mer,	*Like springtime on the sea,*
Sur les plaines de la mer stérile	*On the plains of the barren sea,*
Où nulle fleur ne peut croître,	*Where no flower can grow*
À ses souffles agiles,	*In its lithe breezes,*
Que des fleurs de lumière.	*Save flowers of light.*
Je me poserai sur ton cœur	*I shall alight on your heart*
Comme l'oiseau sur la mer,	*Like a bird on the sea,*
Dans le repos de ses ailes lasses,	*Resting its weary wings*
Et que berce le rythme éternel	*And rocked by the eternal rhythm*
Des flots et de l'espace.	*Of waves and space.*

The motto from the Song of Songs printed at the head of the poem is 'Ut signaculum' – 'set me as seal [upon thine heart]'.

The is one of Fauré's most touching creations; Nectoux finds its 'utterly human tenderness' unique in the composer's songs.[14] The poet's metaphor here becomes the musical *raison d'être*. The image of a bird, a tiny and vulnerable creature, pinpointed as a dot on a seascape, is at the heart of Fauré's musical illustration of 'le rythme éternel / Des flots et de l'espace'. Thus in the middle of a cycle purportedly about a walled garden we have music that suggests the gentle rocking of the sea seen at a distance, and the breadth of a marine landscape. This drifting and bobbing is caught to perfection by the seemingly simple device of a syncopated bass, the displacement of a quaver across the bar line which also makes the imploring lover seem to tug gently at the sleeve of the person to whom this hymn of devotion is addressed. In the half-barcarolle, half-*berceuse* of this wonderful music, the harmonies are as ever-changing as the sea glimpsed in different glinting lights.

There is a sublime visit to the key of G♭ major (in second inversion) for the setting of the poem's second strophe, a moment of calm on the water, a halcyon day. Even more wonderful, and ever more protected from the storms, is the way the music briefly slips into C major at Fauré's repeat of the first two lines of the poem before making its gliding return into the home key of E♭.

The song's dedicatee, also known as Lucy Vuillemin, was the wife of Fauré's first biographer, the composer Louis Vuillemin (1879–1929). She and her husband performed songs by Albert Roussel at a concert of the Société Nationale de la Musique (SNM) in August 1919, when Madeleine Grey created Fauré's cycle *Mirages* with the composer at the piano.

(97) (v) *Dans la nymphée* (*In the grotto*)

July–November 1914, Op. 106 No. 5, 'À Mme Claire Croiza', D♭ major, 4/4, *Andante molto moderato*

Quoique tes yeux ne la voient pas,	*Though your eyes do not see her,*
Pense, en ton âme, qu'elle est là,	*Think, in your soul, that she is there,*
Comme autrefois divine et blanche.	*Divine and pristine, as of old.*
Sur ce bord reposent ses mains.	*Her hands rest on this bank,*
Sa tête est entre ces jasmins;	*Her head is among the jasmine,*
Là, ses pieds effleurent les branches.	*There her feet brush the boughs.*
Elle sommeille en ces rameaux.	*She sleeps amid these branches.*
Ses lèvres et ses yeux sont clos,	*Her lips and eyes are closed,*
Et sa bouche à peine respire.	*And her mouth is scarcely breathing.*
Parfois, la nuit, dans un éclair	*Sometimes, at night, like lightning*
Elle apparaît les yeux ouverts,	*She appears with open eyes,*
Et l'éclair dans ses yeux se mire.	*The lightning mirrored in her eyes.*
Un bref éblouissement bleu	*A brief blue glare*
La découvre en ses longs cheveux;	*Reveals her with her long tresses;*
Elle s'éveille, elle se lève.	*She awakes, she rises.*
Et tout un jardin ébloui	*And the whole dazzled garden*
S'illumine au fond de la nuit,	*Is lit up in the depths of night,*
Dans le rapide éclair d'un rêve.	*In the swift flash of a dream.*

Drawing of Claire Croiza with the composer 'chez Madame de Saint-Marceaux' (1922), by William Ablett

336

This great and powerful nocturne lies at the heart of this cycle, just as the enchanted grotto is the most secret of places within the walled garden. It is impossible to say who this spirit is, which nymph, who lies asleep here, a metaphor perhaps for the loved one who is yet to be discovered like some sleeping princess, and whose awakening will signal a burst of radiance.

We are reminded of an earlier masterpiece, *Le Parfum impérissable*. This is one of the last in a great line of Fauré's song accompaniments that grow out of a slow succession of chords mainly in stately crotchets, and this one turns into a processional that is perhaps the most magnificent of its type in the composer's œuvre. Only Fauré, like a musical high-priest of Olympus, writes hymns of this kind where a deceptively simple opening leads to a display of harmonic virtuosity that is entrancingly, and perplexingly, sophisticated. It is amazing how static and mild this music seems on paper and how, in performance one glowing harmony changes to the next, like the opening, leaf by leaf, of a gorgeously coloured exotic flower. It was another sage, Goethe, who had described the organic metamorphosis of plant life in mesmerising poetry, and in his old age Fauré seems as wise, inscrutable, and self-contained as the German magus.

The dedicatee of *Dans la nymphée*, Claire Croiza, had recently sung the role of Pénélope in Fauré's opera in its Brussels première; that this great *mélodie* singer was rewarded thus is an indication of Fauré's estimation of her worth as well as the song's.

(98) (vi) *Dans la pénombre* (*In the half-light*)
July–November 1914, Op. 106 No. 6, 'À Mme Houben-Kufferath', E major, 3/4, *Allegretto moderato*

À quoi, dans ce matin d'avril,	*With what, this April morning,*
Si douce et d'ombre enveloppée,	*So sweet and swathed in shadow,*
La chère enfant au cœur subtil	*Is the dear and tender-hearted girl*
Est-elle ainsi toute occupée?	*So preoccupied?*
Pensivement, d'un geste lent,	*Pensively and slowly,*
En longue robe, en robe à queue,	*In a long flowing robe,*
Sur le soleil au rouet blanc	*Spinning blue wool*
À filer de la laine bleue.	*On the sun's white wheel.*
À sourire à son rêve encor,	*Still smiling at her dream*
Avec ses yeux de fiancée,	*With the eyes of one betrothed,*
À travers les feuillages d'or	*Across the golden foliage*
Parmi les lys de sa pensée.	*Among the lilies of her thought.*

In the genre of the spinning song (Schubert's *Gretchen*, Schumann's *Spinnelied* duet, Wagner's chorus in *Der fliegende Holländer*, Ravel's *Chanson du rouet*) this is the slowest and most unusual. Yet it is extraordinary how believably the accompaniment evokes spinning at the wheel in a more realistic way than the whirring centrifuge of other more obvious evocations. The threads of the accompaniment bring together warp and woof in right hand and left, and the composer proves himself as masterful in this skill as Ulysses' Penelope – in his opera he had proved himself remarkably successful in writing music to describe the weaving and unravelling of the shroud. It may be that Fauré was thinking more of the use of the spinning wheel's foot-pedal in each of these paired phrases of right-hand quavers than of the actual depiction of a rotating wheel. In the half-light, in the shade on a beautiful April day, the task is accomplished slowly and carefully, *en sourdine*.

This is another portrait of the imagined lover, the 'chère enfant'; she is earnest rather than voluptuous, 'toute occupée' and concentrating deeply. Sexual allure is still part of the picture: the sensuous cut of her flowing 'robe à queue' is part of the strange, gestural music in wafting crotchets that is the song's middle section. We can almost hear the material of her dress gently dragging across the floor. As always in such music the harmonic progressions defy anything but the most complex analysis; a synthesis of complexity and transparent simplicity is particularly apparent in this shy but moving song.

Fauré omits the second strophe in Van Lerberghe's poem. Nectoux writes that the reason for this was the large number of sibilants in this passage (nine 's's making too explosive a vocal effect), which offended the ever-practical composer.[15] But it is also likely that the intrusion of the personal narrative 'Je', and a male 'I' to boot, was not to his taste; and the repetition of 'Je ne sais pas' when set to music *twice* would also have been a problem. After all, the composer had told Louis Aguettant that the conversationally casual 'on veut croire' in the Verlaine poem 'Le son du cor s'afflige' was enough to stop him setting the poem.[16] Here are Van Lerberghe's excised words, too precious to lose entirely for those studying the song in depth:

La trace blonde de ses pas	*The golden trace of her steps*
Se perd parmi les grilles closes;	*Is lost among the closed railings;*
Je ne sais pas, je ne sais pas,	*I do not know, I do not know,*
Ce sont d'impénétrables choses.	*These are impenetrable things.*

(99) (vii) *Il m'est cher, Amour, le bandeau* (*Love, the blindfold is dear to me*)
July–November 1914, Op. 106 No. 7, 'À Mme Faliero-Dalcroze', F major, 3/4, *Allegro*

Il m'est cher, Amour, le bandeau	*Love, the blindfold is dear to me*
Qui me tient les paupières closes;	*That screens my eyes;*
Il pèse comme un doux fardeau	*It weighs like a sweet burden*
De soleil sur de faibles roses.	*Of sun on languid roses.*
Si j'avance, l'étrange chose!	*If I move forward – how strange!*
Je parais marcher sur des eaux;	*I seem to walk on water;*
Mes pieds plus lourds où je les pose,	*Wherever I place my too heavy feet,*
S'enfoncent comme en des anneaux.	*They sink as if into rings.*
Qui donc a délié dans l'ombre	*Who, then, has loosened in the shade*
Le faix d'or de mes longs cheveux?	*The golden weight of my long tresses?*
Toute ceinte d'étreintes sombres,	*All enclosed by dark embraces,*
Je plonge en des vagues de feu.	*I plunge into waves of fire.*
Mes lèvres où mon âme chante,	*My lips, where my soul sings*
Toute d'extase et de baiser,	*Of naught but rapture and kisses,*
S'ouvrent comme une fleur ardente	*Open like an ardent flower*
Au-dessus d'un fleuve embrasé.	*Above a blazing river.*

338

The somewhat intoxicated motto from the Song of Songs printed at the head of the poem is 'Fulcite me floribus' – 'Stay me with flagons [confer me with apples]'.

There are only two fast songs in this cycle, and this is the second of them. The blindfolded lover describes the strange sensations of walking into unknown territory – on water, into waves of fire. It is no surprise then that in this music (where the key of F major in root position is reached only in the song's final five bars) one feels the ground disappearing beneath one's feet. The Latin subtitle suggests that the disorientation described by the poet may have had its origin in alcohol. There is pleasure and excitement in this surrendering of control (surely also a sexual metaphor), but danger too in this song of precarious impetuosity. This is music that is vertiginous to play; the pianist's right hand must move between these oscillating chords (each one a glinting beam of harmonic light) with exquisite precision.

As in *Je me poserai sur ton cœur* the music is constructed, broadly speaking, on a dominant pedal; as a result the music stands on tiptoe, always hoping to be allowed to go home. Jankélévitch talks of the 'azure' of F major, and it is true that this resembles music of the great outdoors, very different from the perfumed enclosures of *Dans la nymphée* for example.[17]

(100) (viii) *Inscription sur le sable* (*Inscription on the sand*)
July–November 1914, Op. 106 No. 8, 'À Mme Durand-Texte', E minor, 4/4, *Andante quasi Adagio*

Toute, avec sa robe et ses fleurs,	*Entire, with her gown and flowers,*
Elle, ici, redevint poussière,	*She here became dust once more,*
Et son âme emportée ailleurs	*And her soul, borne off elsewhere,*
Renaquit en chant de lumière.	*Was reborn in a song of light.*
Mais un léger lien fragile	*But a light and fragile link,*
Dans la mort brisé doucement,	*Gently broken in death,*
Encerclait ses tempes débiles	*Encircled her sickly temples*
D'impérissables diamants.	*With imperishable diamonds.*
En signe d'elle, à cette place,	*As a token of her, in this place,*
Seules, parmi le sable blond,	*Alone among the pale sand,*
Les pierres éternelles tracent	*The eternal stones still trace*
Encor l'image de son front.	*The image of her brow.*

Charles Van Lerberghe (1861–1907)

La Chanson d'Ève ends with a hymn to death, *Ô mort, poussière d'étoiles* – a majestic, even frightening song of great darkness and power. The death described in *Inscription sur le sable* is of an entirely different order. Mention of jewellery and pale sand prompts thoughts that these words may describe an Egyptian queen or princess from thousands of years ago, her body mummified and turned to dust. Reading these words always reminds me of 'Fleurs', the poem by Louise de Vilmorin about the burning of love letters that Poulenc set in his cycle *Fiançailles pour rire*. Phrases by Vilmorin such as 'sable de tes baisers' and 'les beaux yeux sont de cendre' seem faint footprints on those shifting sands where surrealism was once symbolism. It is extraordinary that in two composers so unlike each other the musical solutions share a similar mournful gravity, the music drained of melodrama and undue emphasis – and both songs happen to be in E minor.

There is ceremony and hierarchy in this music, but all sense of personal tragedy has been erased by the passing of time; it is true that the closing bars, a particularly arid passage in the bass clef, have a finality that allows no court of appeal. It is also the only song in the entire cycle written in the minor key. It appears that at some point Fauré decided this ending was too harsh. The manuscript copy belonging to the firm of Durand has an ending on an E major chord. This does not appear in the printed copy; in the end the composer went for silence on the other side of the grave, rather than imply any hope of redemption.

༄ ༄ ༄ ༄

In a letter of 16 October 1915, Saint-Saëns wrote to Fauré:

> I have just read through *Le Jardin clos*. For all its apparent simplicity it is not particularly easy to read; but how engaging and how engrossing. I shall need time to take full possession of it. So far it is No. 1 that I like the best, but we shall see. Meanwhile I congratulate you on writing accompaniments that are genuinely written for the piano and not lavish orchestrations arranged for that instrument and unplayable, and on writing for the voice in a vocal and literary manner. As regards the literature itself, these are certainly fine lines showing a craftsman's hand, but often quite obscure; there are things I found impossible to understand. As Christ said, it's not the poor light, it's your bad eyes. I assume in my humility that it's the same thing here.[18]

Nearly twenty years earlier Saint-Saëns, loyal friend though he was, had also reacted to *La Bonne chanson* with incomprehension. With that work there was perhaps something to rail against – above all, the over-frequent changes of harmony. Here, with the best will in the world, he seems just as mystified by his famous pupil's work, but with fewer grounds for actual objection. He must nevertheless search for compliments in order to be polite. There could be no better illustration of the large and unbridgeable gap between the brilliant professional composer that Saint-Saëns always was and the visionary genius that Fauré had become, someone who had long since soared beyond the artistic reach of all but his most exalted contemporaries.

It is rather touching to see Saint-Saëns struggling to take seriously a work he might have belittled had it come from another source; and perhaps he truly sensed that there was *something* marvellous about this amalgam of word and tone that was beyond his grasp. Some years later in the music that Saint-Saëns wrote right at the end of his life there is occasionally a sign that he is seeking to assimilate Fauré's late style – his only Verlaine setting, *Le Vent sur la plaine*, is a case in point. Nevertheless, in 1915 he was far from convinced. On 27 December he could not resist a sequel that incorporated his penchant for the writing of verse as he expressed his nostalgia for the music of Fauré's second period:

> Do not curse me if I confess to you that *Le Jardin clos* is not taking me into its confidence and that the poetry is as unhospitable to me as the music:

Combien ce jardin fermé par des épines	*To this garden closed by thorns*
Impitoyablement	*In a pitiless way*
Je préfère celui que perfument divines,	*I do prefer that which imparts its divine fragrance,*
Les roses d'Ispahan	*The Roses of Ispahan*[19]

༄ ༄ ༄ ༄

The war years were not easy for any French family; the sword of Damocles hung over those who had children fighting at the front. Fauré spent a great deal of time performing in charity concerts in aid of the war effort, and he lost a number of friends and acquaintances in the hostilities – for example the highly cultured critic and musicologist Joseph de Marliave, husband of Marguerite Long, who was killed in August 1914. Fears for the well-being of Philippe Fauré tormented the Fauré household, and with some justification: he took part in the notorious Dardanelles expedition of 1915. Marie Fauré was particularly susceptible to fearful, pessimistic thoughts regarding her son's chances of survival; with the bombardment of Paris in 1918 she was forced to leave the family home in the rue des Vignes (Fauré was already in the south of France).

It was at this time that fate added insult to injury with a Spanish flu epdemic; the beautiful contralto Émilie Girette was one of its many fatalities.

On 25 March 1918 Debussy died from cancer; his musical response to the war had included a bitter little song with words of his own, *Noël des enfants qui n'ont plus de maisons*. Saint-Saëns busied himself with a great deal of anti-German bluster, both verbal and musical, and made rather a fool of himself – especially in the light of the fact that he had been among the first, and most enlightened, among French composers, fifty years earlier, to welcome the influence of German music into France.

These were indeed dark days, and Fauré's riposte was characteristically wordless, and in the field of chamber music: between August 1916 and May 1917 he composed his Second Violin Sonata in E minor, Op. 108, and a cello sonata in D minor, Op. 109. These works were published by Durand in 1917 and 1918 respectively. The cello sonata in particular has a grandeur, even a violence (always within the parameters of containment that we have come to expect from this master), that is the composer's response to the tragedy of the times. This music – much of it, though not all, removed from the translucent detachment of *Le Jardin clos* – contains, nevertheless, all the characteristics of the late style that we have learned to recognise through the songs. In the jagged opening of the cello work we hear the same economy of means, the same pared-down textures that we have encountered in the Van Lerberghe cycles, but the music itself seems to be twisted in fanfares of pain and reproach. It is fascinating that Debussy's Cello Sonata, also in D minor and also completed in 1917, was similarly coloured by his response to the war.

The pianist at the first performances of the two Fauré sonatas was Alfred Cortot, and it was for Cortot that Fauré composed a piece for piano and orchestra, the *Fantaisie* in G major, Op. 111 (1918), among the least known of his works. The pianist's failure, following its première, to programme the *Fantaisie* dedicated to him, and Fauré's disappointment on this account, occasioned one of the most bitter letters that a composer has ever addressed to one of his interpreters, all the more potent for its politeness. Fauré seems to have been less irritated by the fact that the work was ignored than by Cortot's insincere protestations of undying reverence and devotion.

During the war years Fauré refused to leave the country for the summer holidays in Switzerland that had long been his custom. Instead he stayed within France and rediscovered the glories of the Midi, and Nice in particular. In 1918 he even made a pilgrimage to his home town of Pamiers. With the approach of the Armistice in November, a complete change of musical atmosphere occurred in September 1918, when Albert I of Monaco commissioned a stage work for Monte Carlo. This was *Masques et bergamasques*, a mixture of music old and new, including orchestral versions of the songs *Clair de lune* and *Le Plus doux chemin*. The librettist for this entertainment was the same René Fauchois who had collaborated with Fauré on *Pénélope*. On hearing this music Reynaldo Hahn remarked that it was as if Mozart had imitated Fauré.

At the end of the year the new director of the Opéra-Comique visited Fauré and asked his permission for a revival of *Pénélope*; this opened in January 1919. Claire Croiza was indisposed, so Germaine Lubin took over a role that was perhaps better suited to her amplitude of voice than to Croiza's. Lubin was an enthusiastic Wagnerian, and tragically destined to be tainted by the accusations of collaboration with the Germans during the Second World War, as was Alfred Cortot.

∾   ∾   ∾   ∾

It is hard to think of a work such as *Le Jardin clos*, with its unworldly calm, belonging to the terrible vicissitudes of the war years. With its exquisite delicacy of thought and musical nuance, it is a rebuttal of barbarity in that it refuses to countenance the very existence of a philistine world outside the boundaries of a garden enclosing and protecting civilisation itself. We cannot help but think of Monet working behind the garden walls of Giverny at the same time. Fauré, increasingly immured in his own world, an ivory tower of sound built painstakingly and gradually, brick by exquisite brick over fifty years, could scarcely have meant to write a confrontational work. Nevertheless, *Le Jardin clos* remains a testament to the values that were under threat during the 1914–18 war, and have been under threat ever since. If this cycle does not achieve, or aim for, the cosmic grandeur of *La Chanson d'Ève*, it is arguably a more perfect work precisely because it is less ambitious; it is certainly one of the great masterpieces in all French music for voice and piano, although far too seldom recognised as such.

Perhaps the tunefulness of Fauré's earlier songs has led the public to expect something different; one feels that in some quarters the composer has been punished for his change of style as a kind of betrayal of his early willingness to please. It seems that Webern's songs, contemporary with this cycle, have met less resistance in the concert hall, perhaps because audiences have no expectation of hearing anything more accessible from him. Maybe it would be easier if we simply admitted that Gabriel Fauré, the inaccurately dubbed 'Master of Charms', had gradually turned into an avant-garde composer in his own inscrutable way.

There is a good deal more likelihood of getting a fine performance of this cycle than of fielding a perfect, or even near-perfect *La Chanson d'Ève*, where the finding of a suitable singer is a much harder task. *Le Jardin clos* is still underestimated, a mystery to many, and it remains necessary for the cycle's enthusiasts to convince the sceptical. The problems with performances of this work always stem from the unwillingness of singers and pianists to trust the composer and simply to do what he asks of them. Singers and accompanists, sometimes quite famous ones, imagine that they must help the poor old composer by 'shaping' the music he has written in some well-meaning attempt to make it more palatable to present-day audiences. The result is always a musical catastrophe that infuriates enthusiasts while winning no new friends at all for Fauré.

If converts are to be made to his cause, there is no advocacy or persuasion that can turn them into believers, for this is a composer who resists all proselytising. Listeners must be ready to allow the music to speak to them. When it does so, it will not be the result of any special 'communication' on the part of the performers. They have only to allow themselves to be lost and contained in Fauré's creation while the listener responds to this art that conceals art.

I have spent an entire career playing the Fauré songs, many of them more obviously 'beautiful' and 'accessible' than this music of the last period. But I confess that it is when listening in the audience to a rare performance of *Le Jardin clos* that tears of admiration and gratitude are never far away. Part of that reaction is a tribute to the inscrutable nature of the work itself (as Van Lerberghe says, 'Ce sont d'impénétrables choses'), but if one senses in the performers a selfless devotion to the music, their sacrifice of ego becomes absorbed into the work itself and becomes part of its astonishing and revelatory power.

1 *Gabriel Fauré: A Life in Letters*, trans. and ed. Barrie Jones (London: B.T. Batsford, 1989), letter 183, p. 145.

2 See Saint-Saëns letter to the composer Charles Lecoq in which he accuses Fauré of violating harmonic rules and setting a bad example to his pupils, the younger generation. Quoted in Saint-Saëns- Fauré *Correspondance*, Paris, 1994, p. 26n.

3 Ibid., letter 202, p. 133.

4 Ibid.

5 *Gabriel Fauré: A Life in Letters*, letter 205, p. 159.

6 Carlo Caballero, *Fauré and French Musical Aesthetics* (Cambridge: Cambridge University Press 2001), p. 247.

7 See Vladimir Jankélévitch, *Henri Bergson* (Paris: Presses Universitaires de France, 1959).

8 C. Van Lerberghe, *Lettres à Albert Mockel, 1887–1906*, ed. Robert Debever and Jacques Detemmerman (Brussels: Editions Labor, 1986).

9 Jean-Michel Nectoux, *Gabriel Fauré: A Musical Life*, trans. Roger Nichols (Cambridge: Cambridge University Press, 1991), p. 373.

10 *Le Jardin clos*: Aspects of this cycle's interpretation are discussed in Chapter 16, pp. 423–4.

11 Marguerite de Saint-Marceaux, *Journal 1894–1927*, ed. Myriam Chimènes (Paris: Fayard, 2007), p. 648.

12 Myriam Chimènes, *Mécènes et musiciens* (Paris: Fayard, 2004), pp. 197 and 252.

13 Saint-Marceaux, *Journal*, ed. Chimènes, p. 850.

14 Nectoux, *Gabriel Fauré: A Musical Life*, p. 274.

15 Ibid., p. 353.

16 Caballero, *Fauré and French Musical Aesthetics*, p. 246.

17 Vladimir Jankélévitch, *De la musique au silence: Fauré et l'inexprimable* (Paris: Plon, 1974), p. 213.

18 *Gabriel Fauré: A Life in Letters*, letter 218, pp. 165–6.

19 Ibid., letter 219, p. 166.

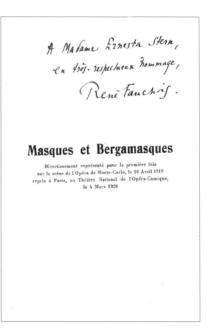

Title page, with author's inscription, of the libretto by René Fauchois for the 'divertissement' Masques et Bergamasques *(1919)*

Chapter Fourteen

Mirages and Horizons

Renée de Brimont, Georgette Debladis,

Jean de La Ville de Mirmont

But Time, to make me grieve,
Part steals, lets part abide;
And shakes this fragile frame at eve
With throbbings of noontide.
Thomas Hardy[1]

After the performance of *Masques et bergamasques* in Paris on 4 March 1919 and in Monte Carlo in April 1919, and the first performance in Paris in May of the *Fantaisie* for piano and orchestra with Cortot, Fauré decided to spend the summer in Annecy-le-Vieux in the Haute-Savoie, perched high above the lakeside town of Annecy. This was to be the first of several occasions on which he stayed in a location associated in later years with the composition of the Piano Trio and String Quartet. These tranquil surroundings with luscious vistas of water and vegetation no doubt played an inspirational role in the music composed there. Thanks to his friends, the banker Fernand Maillot and his wife Louise (dedicatee of the astonishing Thirteenth Nocturne), Fauré was to derive enormous pleasure from the calm of Annecy-le Vieux during the last summers of his life.

A letter written to Marie Fauré on 23 July 1919 included the lines 'I have sketched – very slowly, without straining myself – a song to a poem which M. Hanotaux has brought to my attention: just the thing to get me going'.[2] Albert-August-Gabriel Hanotaux (1853–1944) had been minister of foreign

Gabriel Fauré (second from right) with Marguerite Hasselmans on his right, Savoie, c.1919. On Hasselmans's right are the pianist Robert Lortat and his wife

345

affairs until 1898– it is possible that Fauré first met him at the salon of their mutual friend the Comtesse Greffulhe. He abandoned politics in favour of a life as a full-time historian, making special studies of Cardinal Richelieu, Joan of Arc and the First World War. The dedication of the cycle to Hanotaux's wife is an indication of the composer's admiration for her distinguished husband.

A little over a week later, by 2 August, the composer reports that he has finished one song, is in the process of finishing a second, and has sketched a third. This is the beginning of the cycle *Mirages*.

༄   ༄   ༄   ༄

The poems by the relatively unknown Renée Baronne de Brimont had not long been published when Gabriel Hanotaux presented them to the seventy-four-year-old Fauré. The composer selected four of the sixty Brimont texts. Four was now the magic number for a composer who, working on his Second Piano Quintet, Op. 115, seemed to be thinking in terms of chamber music movements where the slow movement was placed in second position. (The second song in *Mirages* is also the slowest, if only by a very small margin in terms of its metronome markings.)

Cover of Mirages *by Renée de Brimont*

The poems were published in a beautiful, if frail, paperback edition with woodcuts by Georges Barbier and issued under the imprint of 'Émile-Paul Frères, sur la Place Beauveau, à Paris MCMXIX' – this poetess, despite (and perhaps because of) her title, had failed to interest the important Parisian publishers in her verse, at least on this occasion – a time of post-war austerity. The book's cover has a small vignette in black and gold where a *putto* holds a circular mirror which reflects the mouth, neck and hair of a beautiful woman. Inside, the book's title is writ large; above this bold 'MIRAGES' is Barbier's drawing of a swan (a white one, despite the black swan of the cycle's first song) on a rippled pond beside which a voluptuous nude sits in profile, sweeping back her hair with both hands; underneath a full moon, an androgynous figure stands over the seated nude with a leg pressed close up against the nymph's naked buttocks.

A reading of these verses makes it fairly clear that whatever her married status, Brimont was almost certainly discreetly bi-sexual – thus the 'caresses de sœur' in the cycle's second song, and the naked eroticism of *Danseuse*. The poems are preceded by a motto, dated June 1918, that reminds us that the First World War had only just ended: 'Music [*Musiques*] singing to the ear of the poet, visions from before the torment; dreams and nostalgia, reflections or mirages of that which persists despite everything, and which brings us calm in Nature's eternity.' These introductory words might have been written specifically for Fauré, so exactly do they mirror the aesthetic of his third period; perhaps they served to lure him into the book's inner pages.

Fauré might well have noticed that the very first line of poetry in the book is 'Dans la pénombre', the title of one of his songs from *Le Jardin clos*. Having composed his two great cycles to poems by Van Lerberghe, Fauré obviously felt at ease with this kind of symbolism, which is more accessible than, say, that of Mallarmé. Brimont's poetry, neither great in itself nor so negligible as to be easily dis-

MIRAGES

Title-page of Mirages

missed, permitted the composer the things he needed for his music – a framework of uneventful passion and event-filled calm. In any case, he felt no compunction in making cuts to serve his purposes. One of these was to provide the young singer Madeleine Grey, one of his recent protégées, with a new work to perform – a reward for her fine advocacy of *La Chanson d'Ève* in May 1919. In a letter to Grey of 10 August of that year (which ends with the words 'fond kisses from your old friend'), Fauré tells her that 'I'm enjoying the pure, revivifying air and working. I am even working at something which you, in fact, will sing particularly well. Unfortunately it is not with orchestra.'[3]

The composer wrote again to Grey on 31 December 1919, soon after the first performance of *Mirages*:

Dear triumphant one! … very modestly you speak to me about the success of the composer and ignore the success of the interpreter … you have revealed to people who are particularly difficult to satisfy, a voice, a talent and a musical feeling *remarkable beyond all bounds* and quite unsuspected! Well done! I cannot tell you how happy I am to have been, for many of my friends, the occasion of so *dazzling* a revelation [4]

The composer was clearly smitten with his new performer in a way that had not been evident with those other interpreters of his later songs, Jeanne Raunay and Claire Croiza … or perhaps the letters that might tell us otherwise about Fauré's more personal reactions to the charms of these singers have simply been lost or destroyed. This composer was, as always, elusive, and one never knows.

Mirages[5]
1919, Op. 113, 'À Mme Gabriel Hanotaut'

(101) (i) *Cygne sur l'eau* (*Swan on the water*)
1919, Op. 113 No. 1, F major, 3/4, *Andantino*

Ma pensée est un cygne harmonieux et sage
qui glisse lentement aux rivages d'ennui
sur les ondes sans fond du rêve, du mirage,
de l'écho, du brouillard, de l'ombre, de la nuit.

Il glisse, roi hautain fendant un libre espace,
poursuit un reflet vain, précieux et changeant,
et les roseaux nombreux s'inclinent quand il passe,
sombre et muet, au seuil d'une lune d'argent;

My mind is a gentle, harmonious swan
Gliding slowly along the shores of ennui
On the fathomless waters of dreams and delusion,
Of echo, of mist, of shadow, of night.

He glides, a haughty monarch cleaving a path,
Pursuing a vain reflection, precious and fleeting,
And the countless reeds bow as he passes,
Dark and silent before a silver moon;

et des blancs nénuphars chaque corolle ronde	*And each round corolla of the white water-lilies*
tour à tour a fleuri de désir ou d'espoir …	*Has blossomed by turn with desire or hope …*
Mais plus avant toujours, sur la brume et sur l'onde,	*But ever forward on the mists and the waves,*
vers l'inconnu fuyant glisse le cygne noir.	*The black swan glides toward the receding unknown.*
Or j'ai dit: «Renoncez, beau cygne chimérique,	*And I said: 'Renounce, beautiful chimera of a swan,*
à ce voyage lent vers de troubles destins;	*This slow voyage to troubled destinies;*
nul miracle chinois, nulle étrange Amérique	*No Chinese miracle, no exotic America*
ne vous accueilleront en des havres certains;	*Will welcome you in safe havens;*
les golfes embaumés, les îles immortelles	*The scented gulfs, the immortal isles*
ont pour vous, cygne noir, des récifs périlleux;	*Await you, black swan, with their perilous reefs;*
demeurez sur les lacs où se mirent, fidèles,	*Remain on the lakes which faithfully reflect*
ces nuages, ces fleurs, ces astres, et ces yeux.»	*These clouds, these flowers, these stars, and these eyes.'*

This is the opening poem in the section entitled *De l'eau et des paysages* – the frontispiece is decorated with a woodcut of a stylised fountain that spouts equally stylised ribbons of water surrounded by birds, white on a black background. Fauré realises that the poet's reference (in her second strophe) to the swan's neck being like an unfurling snake would strike a false note in music of such ineffable calm. He accordingly cuts the following quatrain:

Il glisse … Et lentement se déroule, s'allonge	*He glides … And slowly his neck stretches out,*
Son col, tel un serpent vaguement balance,	*Extends like a gently swaying serpent,*
Et son aile luisante est la conque où le songe	*And his gleaming wing is the conch where dreams*
Repose avec l'oubli, la paix et le passé.	*Dwell with oblivion, peace and the past.*

Fauré also leaves out the final three strophes of the poem, which add little new to the overall picture; besides, the last verse of Brimont's construction is merely a re-working of the first verse with the lines rearranged in a different order.

There are nevertheless rather strange images that the composer *does* allow – 'No Chinese miracle, no exotic America / Will welcome you in safe havens'. This swan, who can only exist in his own lake, and for whom foreign travel is now pointless, is surely Fauré himself – a haughty monarch on the 'shores of ennui' who must now realise that he will never visit China, never visit America in the few years that are left to him – neither does he wish to. In the closing phase of his life he exists in 'fathomless waters of dreams and delusion, / Of echo, of mist, of shadow, of night'. Thus the uncrowned king of French music pursues his noble, lonely path in a miasma of hearing difficulties and corporeal disintegration; he sails serenely 'on the mists and the waves … toward the receding unknown'.

The music is a marvel. The simple and static opening chords of the accompaniment in F major are identical to those that precede the song *Lydia* in the same key and from so long ago; even the rising shape of the vocal line (a motif of a tetrachord that runs through all the songs in this cycle) recalls the melodic range of the same song written nearly half a century earlier. The transformation from one age to the other has been gradual and organic, something that seems part of nature itself: one is tempted, not for the first time, to compare Fauré's third period to the lofty sagacity of the elderly

Goethe who, in a poem from 1818, 'Um Mitternacht', describes the unfolding of his life in three strophes, the last making a circular reference, *Lydia*-like, to the first.

At the beginning of the second verse of *Cygne sur l'eau* the accompaniment quickens into oscillating semiquavers based on broken chords. J.-M. Nectoux has pointed out that this figuration is something that has been heard already in the Eleventh Nocturne, and it will reappear in the second movement of the Second Cello Sonata, as well as in the opening of *L'Horizon chimérique*, the coda of the Thirteenth Nocturne and the beginning of the Piano Trio. This kind of forward-moving oscillation seems ideally suited to the movement of a swan in water; when the accompaniment changes back into more static quavers at 'Renoncez, beau cygne chimérique' it is as if, with the stilling of these waters, the Fauréan swan has decided to rein in his horizons and his dreams. No one is better at the music of renunciation than this composer. The seemingly self-effacing accompaniment steers the music through harmonic straits of a seemingly shallow range, yet this lake is as deep as any sea, and this music as profound as any in the French *mélodie* repertoire.

Le Cygne of Saint-Saëns, from *Le Carnaval des animaux*, enjoys an immortality with music lovers of all ages; *Le Cygne*, that wonderfully greedy creature from Ravel's celebrated *Histoires naturelles* song cycle (Jules Renard, 1906), is a remarkably beautiful, and more sophisticated, creation. But here we have a third, chronologically the last and the least known: a regal black swan conjured equally miraculously from thin air by Saint-Saëns's ageing pupil, who is also Ravel's ageing teacher.

(102) (ii) *Reflets dans l'eau* (*Reflections in the water*)
1919, Op. 113 No. 2, B♭ major, 4/4, *Quasi adagio*

Étendue au seuil du bassin,	*Lying at the pool's edge,*
dans l'eau plus froide que le sein	*In water more cold than the breasts*
des vierges sages,	*Of wise virgins,*
j'ai reflété mon vague ennui,	*I saw reflected my vague ennui,*
mes yeux profonds couleur de nuit	*My deep and night-dark eyes*
et mon visage.	*And my face.*
Et dans ce miroir incertain	*And in this uncertain mirror*
j'ai vu de merveilleux matins …	*I have seen wondrous mornings …*
J'ai vu des choses	*I have seen things*
pâles comme des souvenirs,	*As pale as memories*
Sur l'eau que ne saurait ternir	*On the water that no morose wind*
nul vent morose.	*Could mist.*
Alors – au fond du Passé bleu –	*Then on the bed of the blue Past*
Mon corps mince n'était qu'un peu	*My slight body was but a shred*
d'ombre mouvante;	*Of moving shadow;*
sous les lauriers et les cyprès	*Beneath the laurel and cypress*
j'aimais la brise au souffle frais	*I loved the cool breath of wind*
qui nous évente …	*That fanned us …*

J'aimais vos caresses de sœur,	*I loved your sisterly caresses,*
vos nuances, votre douceur,	*Your light and shade, your softness,*
aube opportune;	*Timely dawn;*
et votre pas souple et rythmé,	*And your supple rhythmic step,*
nymphes au rire parfumé,	*You nymphs pale as the moon*
au teint de lune;	*With scented laughter;*
et le galop des aegypans,	*And the gallop of the Aegypans,*
et la fontaine qui s'épand	*And the fountain cascading*
en larmes fades …	*In saltless tears …*
Par les bois secrets et divins	*In the secret and sacred woods*
j'écoutais frissonner sans fin	*I heard the hamadryad's*
l'hamadryade.	*Endless quivering.*
Ô cher Passé mystérieux	*Cherished, mysterious Past,*
qui vous reflétez dans mes yeux	*Reflected in my eyes*
comme un nuage,	*Like a cloud,*
il me serait plaisant et doux,	*It would be pleasant and sweet for me*
Passé, d'essayer avec vous	*To embark with you, O Past,*
le long voyage! …	*On the long voyage! …*
Si je glisse, les eaux feront	*If I slip, the waters will ripple*
un rond fluide … un autre rond …	*In rings … in rings …*
un autre à peine …	*In rin …*
Et puis le miroir enchanté	*And then the enchanted mirror*
reprendra sa limpidité	*Will grow limpid once more,*
froide et sereine.	*Cold and serene.*

The titles of all the Brimont poems in this section of her book are 'on' or 'in' water: thus 'Dialogues sur l'eau', 'Rires sur l'eau', 'De l'orage et de l'eau', 'Solitude au bord de l'eau' (another title with an earlier Fauréan echo!), 'Soleil sur l'eau', 'Pétales sur l'eau' and so on. In Fauré's hands *Reflets dans l'eau*, the reflections of a female Narcissus, is another momentous journey; it begins with the apparent musical cliché of seemingly aimless oscillating quavers underpinning even less of a melody, as such, than we have encountered at the beginning of the cycle. From these tiny, unassuming cells grows a song of considerable, yet quiet, power – a match for the muted self-obsession of Brimont's words.

In the song's fourth verse the bass line of the piano unexpectedly takes on a new stride for the 'supple rhythmic step' of the nymphs, a loping gait also appropriate to the strange 'Aegypans', faun-chasing satyrs, and the 'hamadryade', a wood-nymph encased in the tree she inhabits. These are as exotic a pair of images as the composer ever allowed himself in a song text. The 'cher Passé mystérieux' of the sixth verse seems connected with the almost drugged introspection of Duparc's *La Vie antérieure* with its 'naked slaves all drenched in perfume'. In the long sweep of the history of the *mélodie* from 1884 to 1919 the burnished sensuality of Duparc's Baudelairean vision, already a memory of a former life, has given way to mere whispers in the watery corridors of post-war memory.

The final strophe of *Reflets dans l'eau* contains an effect which is unique (although Fauré has already tested these waters in *Accompagnement*). At 'Si je glisse, les eaux feront / Un rond fluide … un autre rond …' the poet, who has been staring deeply into the pool, imagines what would happen were she to slip beneath the mesmerising surface: the ripples formed on the lake would be first strong, then gradually weaker. This dispersal of energy is reflected on the surface of the music by three phases of musical reaction whereby the accompaniment's triplets dissolve into duplets, which then melt into silence. Nectoux compares the effect of this to the scene in Debussy's *Pelléas* when Mélisande drops her ring into the well (Act II scene 1);[6] at that moment in the orchestral writing we hear an eerie parallel to the haunted watery silences that punctuate the last verse of *Reflets dans l'eau*.

In this cycle, perhaps more than in any other work, the vocal line fails to register a tune as such. As usual, Fauré's undertone disdains any attempt to grab attention from an uncooperative pair of ears. The intervals are always small – seconds, thirds and fourths – and numbers of words are often set to the same note. This suggests the flexibility of speech, the so-called 'chant parlé'; one is also reminded of ecclesiastical chant, and it is tempting to think of the composer reverting to his early induction into the mysteries of church music at the École Niedermeyer. And yet, because Fauré was a composer who had thought all his life in terms of the most refined harmony, this is also melody distilled to its essence of a kind that recalls the vocal lines of Debussy's *Pelléas et Mélisande* (as already noted above), an opera in which there is also a great deal of water imagery.

Is it too fanciful to imagine that Fauré might be making a late, if very gentle, bow in the direction of Debussy? In the case of someone who could scarcely hear his own music without troubling about other people's, who confessed to his wife that he had never heard a note of his own *Pénélope* except in his head, the answer might be yes, this is indeed too far-fetched a theory. But Fauré's ability to assimilate what was going on around him without trying was legendary, and having heard Debussy's opera several times he probably retained an astonishingly complete aural picture of it. The composition of *Pelléas* lay many years in the past, of course, but its composer had died little over a year earlier. Fauré had been informed by his former mistress, Emma Debussy (see the letter quoted in Chapter 9, p. 244), that her late husband had been 'so happy' to study *La Bonne chanson*. Was Fauré moved by this short postlude to her letter where she had made an attempt somehow to bind the two great musical strands of her life into a more friendly congruity?

In these circumstances something points to at least the possibility of a posthumous reconciliation between the two composers, with *Mirages* cast, even if subconsciously, as a *tombeau* for the younger composer. In a similar way, perhaps, Fauré composed his *Fantaisie* for piano and orchestra after an idea that had come from Debussy, via the publisher Jacques Durand, to write a *concertante* work for piano and orchestra. Once Debussy died Fauré took this idea over, more homage than robbery surely, just as the title *Masques et bergamasques* was Debussy's title for a ballet that he had intended to write for Diaghilev in 1910. It was in Fauré's conciliatory nature to mend fences; for instance, after the quarrel with Marguerite Long and her husband that had estranged them for many years, he attempted without success to arrange a rapprochement from his deathbed.

The circumstances that governed the strange relationship of these two composers were such that a gesture of this kind from Fauré during Debussy's lifetime would have been out of the question. But the fact that *Reflets dans l'eau* is also the title of one of Debussy's most famous piano pieces, and that Brimont's allusive poem contains echoes of both Mallarmé's *L'Après-midi d'un faune* and Louÿs's *Chansons de Bilitis*, may have counted for something. Did they encourage Fauré, in this one song at least, to acknowledge the permanent changes wrought in French music by the younger composer whom he had unexpectedly survived? If so, this is the same generous-hearted Fauré who years earlier had tried in vain to persuade his publisher Hamelle to take up Debussy's *Cinq poèmes de Baudelaire*, a work that was in search of a publisher at the time. Fauré, who knew from first-hand experience how hard it was to set Baudelaire's poems to music, had generously declared Debussy's cycle to be a 'work of genius'.[7]

History does not relate whether Fauré sent a copy of *Mirages* to Emma – or Emma-Claude, as she called herself by this time. But even if there was no conscious link, the achievements of this cycle, to my mind at least, tie the two composers' names together with an exquisite ribbon of watered silk. The ingenuity, in *Reflets dans l'eau*, of the gradually receding ripples of water (mentioned above), and the almost avant-garde nature of the effect and its realisation, give rise to one of the most arresting moments in all French song. At this point (and this is not to deny that there were many other instances) Fauré's response to verbal imagery was more than a match for Debussy's at the apex of French creative sensibility. Absolute serenity is restored at the end of the song; the piano's harmonies are ever-changing, yet the surface of the water is unruffled. Fauré is a practised expert in simultaneously depicting movement and stasis.

The composer cuts three strophes of Brimont's poem (the second, seventh and eighth), including a reference to herds of goats with the smell of their curdled milk. His instinct for avoiding images that could not be incorporated in his increasingly rarefied stylistic world is infallible. We are only puzzled, and somewhat delighted, that he has allowed those perplexing Aegypans and that hamadryade through his guarded portals. As already noted, there is an echo here of the hybrid mythological world of *Le Tombeau des Naïades* from Debussy's *Bilitis* songs.

(103) (iii) *Jardin nocturne* (*Nocturnal garden*)
1919, Op. 113 No. 3, E♭ major, 3/4, *Andantino*

Nocturne jardin tout empli de silence,	*Nocturnal garden brimming with silence,*
voici que la lune ouverte se balance	*Now the full moon is swaying*
en des voiles d'or fluides et légers;	*In light and liquid veils of gold;*
elle semble proche et cependant lointaine …	*Close she seems, yet far away …*
Son visage rit au cœur de la fontaine	*Her face is laughing at the heart of the fountain*
et l'ombre pâlit sous les noirs orangers.	*And shadows pale beneath dark orange-trees.*
Nul bruit, si ce n'est le faible bruit de l'onde	*No sound, save perhaps the whispering wave*
fuyant goutte à goutte au bord des vasques rondes,	*Trickling drop by drop from round basins,*
ou le bleu frisson d'une brise d'été,	*Or the blue quiver of a summer breeze,*
furtive parmi des palmes invisibles …	*Furtive among invisible palms …*
Je sais, ô jardin, vos caresses sensibles	*I know, O garden, your keen caresses*
et votre languide et chaude volupté!	*And your languid, torrid voluptuousness!*
Je sais votre paix délectable et morose,	*I know your delicious and sullen peace,*
vos parfums d'iris, de jasmins et de roses,	*Your scents of iris, of jasmine, of rose,*
vos charmes troublés de désir et d'ennui …	*Your beauty ruffled by desire and ennui …*
ô jardin muet! – L'eau des vasques s'égoutte	*O silent garden! The waters in the basin drip*
avec un bruit faible et magique … J'écoute	*With a faint and magical sound … I listen*
ce baiser qui chante aux lèvres de la Nuit.	*To this kiss singing on the lips of Night.*

No one who has listened to the astonishingly beautiful 78 rpm recording of this song performed by Pierre Bernac, accompanied by Francis Poulenc,[8] could doubt the haunting quality of the music: a *moto perpetuo* that is somehow suspended in time – a real achievement this, and one that reflects the inscrutable workings of nature. Bernac and Poulenc recorded only one song from *Mirages*, a cycle conceived for female voice by the composer, but one that can easily survive sympathetic masculine performance. Nectoux believes that its position as the third in a set, where all the songs are of a similar *andante* tempo, has militated against its effectiveness.[9] On the other hand the near unity of tempi in the cycle is something that may well have been deliberate on Fauré's part. The listener can certainly put up with this hypnotic unanimity more readily, particularly in music of this quality, than if the cycle had consisted of eight or ten songs.

The composer happily embraces all three of the poet's strophes. The water music is that of a distantly lapping fountain – comparisons with Debussy's Baudelaire setting *Le Jet d'eau* (1889) come to mind, though one thinks more of that song's limpid opening pages ('Tes beaux yeux sont las, pauvre amante') than of the cascading semiquaver figurations that depict the plashing of water later in Debussy's song. For Fauré of the third period decorative aqueous arpeggio patterns such as these are far too obvious. In *Jardin nocturne* the articulation of the left hand, now flowing and now interrupted by rests, dispenses water, as if it were falling drop by drop into the fountain's basin. The right hand of the pianist, gently doubling the vocal line from time to time, eerily limns this distant sound. Apart from this hypnotic background the enchanted garden is indeed 'tout rempli de silence'. This is why Claude Rostand finds in this music 'an attenuated and distant reflection of some garden of the dead',[10] although the composer describes something far more pleasurable and sensual than a cemetery. Just as he can write music that moves while stationary, Fauré knows better than anyone the secret of writing music that resounds with its own silence: the heavenly calm evoked by 'Nul bruit' alone, a phrase that for a moment stands on its own in the music as if the composer were wanting us to hear the silence, accomplishes this seemingly impossible task.

Key words flow past illuminated by the glinting moonlight of the music: 'lointaine', 'invisibles', 'volupté', 'morose', the erotic 'délectable' and the almost heartbreaking 'faible et magique' – the second word plunging a sixth, by far the biggest interval in the song: a descent into the depth of dreams.

In this great song we hear the wisdom of an old man who has learned to put the passions of yesterday behind him. The 'caresses sensibles' of a lifetime of adult ardour are now confined to memory and are at one with the mystical connections that the composer felt for the monastery garden at Montgauzy that had thrilled him in his early childhood, the isolated place where he first learned to interpret the sounds, smells and sights of the natural world. This revelation of nature in all her mysterious glory is only a step away from the site of the central epiphany of his childhood – the deserted chapel where he had first made music on the old harmonium.

The aged Fauré still had five more years to live, but this is surely the song where the fascinations of his childhood meet the artistic concerns of his old age in full circle. 'En ma fin gît mon commencement', as Mary Stuart's motto had it or, in T.S. Eliot's inversion, 'In my beginning is my end'.

(104) (iv) *Danseuse* (*Dancer*)

1919, Op. 113 No. 4, D minor, 2/2, *Andantino*

Sœur des Sœurs tisseuses de violettes,	*Sister of violet-weaving sisters,*
une ardente veille blémit tes joues …	*A scorching vigil pales your cheeks …*
Danse! Et que les rythmes aigus dénouent	*Dance! And let the shrill rhythms unfurl*
tes bandelettes.	*Your sashes.*
Vase svelte, fresque mouvante et souple,	*Svelte vase, supple and moving fresco,*
danse, danse, paumes vers nous tendues,	*Dance with palms outstretched before us,*
pieds étroits fuyant, tels des ailes nues	*Slender feet flying like the naked wings*
qu'Éros découple …	*Which Eros unbinds …*
Sois la fleur multiple un peu balancée,	*Be the multiple flower swaying a little,*
sois l'écharpe offerte au désir qui change,	*Be the scarf proffered to fickle desire,*
sois la lampe chaste, la flamme étrange,	*Be the chaste lamp, the strange flame,*
sois la pensée!	*Be thought!*
Danse, danse au chant de ma flûte creuse,	*Dance, dance to the song of my hollow flute,*
sœur des Sœurs divines. – La moiteur glisse.	*Sister of sacred sisters. Moisture trickles,*
baiser vain, le long de ta hanche lisse …	*A vain kiss, along your lithe hip …*
Vaine danseuse!	*Vain dancer!*

Renée de Bonnières, Baronne Antoine de Brimont (1880–1943)

The poem is prefaced by a quotation in Greek from the sixth century BC, describing the psycho-spiritual condition of the anonymous poet quoted by the later writer Plutarch. The transliteration runs 'egô fâmi ioplokôn Moisân eu lakhemen' – 'I declare I have been truly possessed of the dark-tressed Muses'. It seems to be, in this context, a confession of the poet's own source of erotic inspiration, concealed by a diaphanous veil of ancient language. The dancer is both energetic and intangible. Fauré has written a song that seems to cloak its sexual allure in the ethereal shroud of time.

The poem itself strikes something of a Rimbaud-like note without Rimbaud's startling originality; *Antique* ('Gracieux fils de Pan') set by Britten in *Les Illuminations* comes to mind at the opposite pole of same-sex attraction. Fauré cuts two strophes of the six, one of which contains lascivious references to the dancer as a 'doux reptile', her breasts anointed with oil for lovemaking in the 'nuits stériles' of her sisterhood. Seven years after the first appearance of the *travesti* embraces of Strauss's *Der Rosenkavalier*, Fauré chose not to flirt as openly as Brimont with the new sexual freedom and openness that pervaded the post-war world. Far from encouraging a Straussian *Dance of the Seven Veils*, Fauré allowed this dancer even less freedom than those who appear in *Pénélope*. Yet this music belongs to the twentieth century in a different way from the other songs of the cycle.

Norman Suckling salutes *Danseuse* as 'one of the most vertiginous things ever written – and that without the aid of dynamics or acrobatics'.[11] If we have already been made to think of *Pelléas et Mélisande* in this cycle, it is the later, war-chastened, Debussy that we can hear in *Danseuse*, the Debussy of the late sonatas who was already measuring himself by the yardstick of the neo-classical

Stravinsky, who, in turn, had already abandoned the extravagances of his Russian ballets. One might imagine the last movement of Debussy's Cello Sonata (in the same key as this song) danced as a whirling finale by a young member of the erotic sisterhood created by Brimont.

Fauré undoubtedly knew Debussy's *Pelléas et Mélisande*, but it is unlikely that he would have had the time or inclination in 1919 to peruse that composer's instrumental sonatas; any similarities must be put down to the *Zeitgeist* whereby all things, including the expensive art of music, took on a more economical and slimmed-down shape during and after the war.

We have already seen how Fauré almost unconsciously entered into the new musical spirit of the age with *Masques et bergamasques*. There was a new thirst for simplicity, a new distaste for bombast – in short an artistic climate of imaginative economy that would have much favoured Fauré's easy-going personality as a young man. He was

Greek dancer from second edition of Les Chansons de Bilitis *(1900) by Pierre Louÿs*

perfectly aware of some of the work of 'Les Six'; did he ever wonder what it would have been like to have been young again if he had been born among their refreshingly insouciant number? Certainly the lightly entertaining *Masques and bergamasques* is not that far away from the aesthetic of these younger composers, all the more astonishing for coming so soon after such uncompromising works as the Second Violin Sonata and the First Cello Sonata.

If we discount any likelihood of outside influence, it is clear that in *Danseuse* Fauré is continuing to evoke the modal aspects of the ancient world, something that began with his *Lydia* about 1870, and which was taken up by Ernest Chausson in *Hébé* (1882) and by Reynaldo Hahn in his *Études latines* (1900). Fauré's own opera *Pénélope* embraced a restrained, though not unpassionate, Hellenism. In *Danseuse* we have no bargain-basement pastiche, rather the purest evocation of Attic economy and precision. Even if the music of the ancient Greeks did not sound like this (and the composer had already created an unconvincing accompaniment for a *Hymne à Apollon*) – in any case an impossible task, we feel that Fauré has captured something of its essential spirit. Jankélévitch calls this the music of 'perfect nudity', and it is true that the song is stripped to its essentials.[12] If its tireless balletic rhythms also contain the energy of the Dionysiac (an obsessive concentration on a dominant pedal on A pervades much of the song), this seems filtered by time and distance into a dance both chaste and remote, a merging of the sacred and the profane.

On 28 November 1919 Madeleine Grey came to Fauré's office at the Paris Conservatoire to sing through the new cycle in the presence of his publisher Jacques Durand, the Baronne de Brimont (an attractive woman in her early thirties at the time) and a few other friends. The first performance at a concert of the Société Nationale de la Musique followed on 27 December and was a great success, as Fauré himself confirmed in a letter to the singer. It was also the last time Fauré was to play at a concert of this musical organisation that had been so important a part of his life.

Portrait of Renée de Brimont, from the frontispiece of
Les Fileuses *(1937)*

Robert Orledge confirms that Renée de Brimont was well aware that Fauré had conferred unexpected immortality on her verses; these manage to be simultaneously slender and padded, but it would be wrong to say that she was merely an amateur poet. She was clearly a woman of means, able to have her verses published exquisitely (and probably at her own expense), but some of her writings clearly sold well enough. A separate page at the front of *Mirages* lists two works by the same author: *L'Essor*, published by Plon et Nourrit, and *Tablettes de cire*, published by the famous firm of Calmann-Lévy. Born Renée de Bonnières de Beaumont in 1886, she married the Baron Antoine de Brimont, and died in 1943. One wonders if she was somehow related to Robert de Bonnières (1850–1905), patron of the arts, amateur musician, critic and incidentally poet of his next-door neighbour Duparc's *Le Manoir de Rosemonde*. The main part of her literary career was in the 1920s and 1930s and post-dated the composition of *Mirages*. She was the great-niece of Lamartine, with access to his papers, and wrote two charming monographs about her distinguished relative, which included unpublished verse contemporary with the poet–politician's celebrated *Graziella*. Other works by Brimont are *Psyché* (1924), *L'Arche* (1927), *Belle Rose* (1931), *Les Oiseaux* (1932), *Ariane* (1936) and *Les Fileuses* (another volume of poems, 1937). Her salon at 14 avenue Bosquet welcomed such figures as Natalie Clifford Barney, Rémy de Gourmont (a favourite poet of the composer André Caplet), Paul Valéry, Marie Laurencin and the Princesse de Polignac (who, like Barney and Laurencin, may have been drawn to Renée by her striking good looks). She interested herself in the career of Jean Wiéner, a song composer of somewhat popular bent whose settings of Robert Desnos are extremely charming.[13] According to Orledge, Brimont was a literary acolyte of the French-Lithuanian poet, and translator of Goethe, Oskar Vladislas de Lubicz Milosz (1877–1939), who regarded her as 'the living torch'[14] – presumably a beacon to the young poets of the time. Sadly this was empty hyperbole: although the posthumous reputation of Milosz as a poet has never been higher than at the present time in France, Brimont now seems to be a completely forgotten figure, except among grateful Fauréans.

❧   ❧   ❧   ❧

Shortly after the first public performance of *Mirages*, Fauré travelled to Monte Carlo, where he had to grapple with an unenviable task. As music critic of *Le Figaro*, he was occasionally required by his editor to take part in projects that were calculated to connect the everyday public with higher culture. The composer had already avoided a commission for a work celebrating the allied victory, but he was unable to wriggle out of agreeing to set to music the newspaper's prize-winning poem about the peace. He had no doubt hoped for an evocation of still and calm sent in from the provinces, something akin to the poetry on which he had been working for the last thirteen years. In the event he was exasperated with the winning entry that praised peace only by invoking war-like overtones. Fauré regarded this text by someone otherwise unknown in the world of literature as a 'horrible little poem'.

(105) *C'est la paix* (*Peace has come*)

8 December 1919, Op. 114, published in *Le Figaro* on 10 October 1920, A major, 3/4, *Allegretto giocoso*

Pendant qu'ils étaient partis pour la guerre,	As long as they were at the wars,
On ne dansait plus, on ne parlait guère,	We danced no more, we hardly spoke,
On ne chantait pas.	We did not sing.
Mes sœurs, c'est la paix! La guerre est finie,	My sisters, peace has come! The war is over.
Dans la paix bénie,	In this blessed peace,
Courons au devant de nos chers soldats.	Let us run to meet our dear soldiers.
Et joyeusement, toutes, en cadence,	And joyfully, keeping time,
Nous irons vers eux en dansant la danse	We shall all move towards them, dancing
Qu'on danse chez nous.	The dance we dance at home.
Nous les aimerons! La guerre est finie.	We shall love them! The war is over.
Ils seront aimés, dans la paix bénie,	They shall be loved in this blessed peace,
Sitôt leur retour.	As soon as they return.
Pour avoir chassé la horde germaine	For having routed the German hordes,
Ils auront nos cœurs, – au lieu de la haine	They shall have our hearts – instead of hate,
Ils auront l'amour.	They shall have love.

Georgette Debladis[15]

In composing music for this project, the composer, as Nectoux puts it, somehow salvaged his self-respect.[16] In the end he was even rather proud of the result, calling it 'a small tour de force'. Dotted rhythms pervade the song, which recalls the music for Ulysse's triumphant return in *Pénélope*, but this is music that has clearly also come from the same pen that wrote *Danseuses* from the *Mirages*. It is as if the composer has taken his cue from Debladis's words 'Mes sœurs' – as if he has imagined the celebration of peace taking on something of a Dionysian ritual among a group of women. For this listener, and performer, the dotted rhythms, so beguiling for the young Grecian 'danseuse', seem strangely stiff and inappropriate to the dancing in the street that one would have expected at the Armistice. Instead, one is reminded of newsreel footage of the Great War where great generals and their confident troops are depicted in quick, jerky movements, the faded black and white of their images casting an eerie pall over the cinematic shuffling of bodies that were soon to be blasted into dust.

It is clear that Fauré, unlike his rabidly anti-German mentor Saint-Saëns, was no triumphalist. It takes some time for the rejoicing tonality of A major to be established, and even then Fauré manages to overcome any jingoistic bluster in favour of gratitude and relief. Built into this somewhat muted music there is a veil of sadness, the same veil employed by the 'danseuse', in this case designed to camouflage the pointlessness and waste of war. The prize-winning poetess, Georgette Debladis, had entered the competition under a curiously unattractive anagram of her own name – and not even a proper anagram at that: Gilette Besgador. She was not in the least impressed by the unusual honour accorded to her meagre verses by Fauré. She objected in razor-sharp manner to the composer cutting her poem in half (only what Fauré used is printed here) and replacing the patriotic slang 'poilus' ('hairies') with the simple word 'soldats'. Fauré pointed out that a word like 'poilus' sounded effective in speech, but horribly out of place in a song.

A very different use of slang from the Great War is to be found in Poulenc's *Bleuet* (1938), a song of such unearthly calm that it appears to be about peace although it is set in the trenches just before the soldiers are due to go over the top and face the enemy. The poem by Apollinaire had been written before 1918, its author a victim of head wounds that gradually got the better of him. 'Bleuet' (cornflower) was a colloquial term for a young soldier, and one that is rather more poetic than 'poilu'.

∾   ∾   ∾   ∾

Fauré was now ready to retire from his exacting job at the Conservatoire. He should have gone in 1919, but stayed one year longer. As he was now seventy-five, the authorities, grateful though they were for his contribution to the well-being of the institution, were insistent that the ailing composer should leave his post. But there was a seemingly insurmountable problem: Fauré had started working for the government as an inspector of conservatoires in 1892, at the age of forty-seven, and by 1920 he would have been twenty-eight years in employment. This was two years short of the thirty that would have entitled the composer to a pension. Much of 1919 and 1920 was spent in attempting to negotiate with the relevant ministry on financial matters.

Fauré retired officially in October 1920, but in the meantime he was given an extended leave of absence so that he could stay in the more hospitable southern climes. This effective end of all his administrative duties freed the composer to work with redoubled energy on his Second Piano Quintet, first in Monte Carlo, and later in the summer at Annecy with his friends the Maillots at their home 'Les Charmilles'. He had been appointed a *grand officier* of the Légion d'Honneur in April 1920, a promotion within the ranks of the order – this was partially the government's compensation for the pension fiasco, but it was of no practical help in terms of his financial position. Fauré's successor as director of the Conservatoire was Henri Rabaud (1873–1949), who held the position until 1941.

In the end the composer received a pension, but it was significantly less than he had hoped for. Although his sons by this time were making their own living, he was concerned with the future upkeep of Marguerite Hasselmans, as well as that of his wife. In the face of these inadequate financial arrangements, a group of English and American admirers sent the composer a large sum of money in 1921 – among the contributors was John Singer Sargent. In return Fauré sent the great painter the manuscript of the Second Piano Quintet, Op. 115.

This work had been completed in the beginning of 1921 and was performed with great success at an SNM concert. According to Philippe Fauré-Frémiet the performers were 'incandescent, white hot' with their enthusiasm and belief in this new quintet.[17] It was dedicated to the composer Paul Dukas, a friend of Fauré's later years whose powerful intellectuality and perceptive critical reviews attracted the older composer rather more than Dukas's music. The composer's son tells how his father, now aged seventy-six, felt that the challenges of his career were never-ending: 'When he was back home, at the moment he was ready to retire, he said to us as he sat on his bed, "Of course, an evening like this is a joy, but what is really almost *maddening* about it is that afterwards you must settle down again; you must try to do even better".'[18] Shortly, we will see how he took this advice to himself to heart.

Fauré was commissioned by the State to compose a *Chant funéraire* for Napoleon. Much more significant was his work on a Second Cello Sonata. Illness during the summer delayed its completion, but it was given its first private performance in December. Two weeks after that, on the last day of 1921, Fauré completed his Thirteenth (and final) Nocturne. This was some two weeks after the news that his beloved teacher, mentor and friend Camille Saint-Saëns, had died in Algiers, aged eighty-six. Their destinies had been so different yet so entwined that it is difficult to imagine Fauré greeting this news without a sense of foreboding regarding his own future. In the meantime, there were good tidings for *mélodie* enthusiasts: in the autumn of 1921 Fauré had written a new set of songs.

∾   ∾   ∾   ∾

Fauré's fulfilment of his awkward obligation to set *C'est la paix*, the clumsy poem of Georgette Debladis, could not lay to rest his feelings about the war, quite the opposite. His soldier son had returned home safely, but there could so easily have been another outcome. The war had caused both him and his wife countless days of worry, and much energy that he could scarcely afford. He was acutely aware that far too many did not return from the fray. One of these, a cross-Channel comrade-in-art to Rupert Brooke and Wilfred Owen (though far less famous), was Jean de La Ville de Mirmont (1886–1914). Dead at the age of twenty-eight, the poet was not the youngest writer to be killed in the war, but he was one of the most promising. There was the added fascination that he was a poet of the sea, and Fauré seems to have found his posthumously published work irresistible.

As a preface to the second edition of Jean de la Ville's poems (1929) François Mauriac drew a touching pen-portrait of the poet: a talented fellow student from Bordeaux – a good-looking young man, tall and thin and of the greatest sensibility. Born in a busy port, he wrote poetry full of dreams and travel fantasies: journeys never undertaken, visits to continents as yet undiscovered and from which no vessel has ever returned. Literary commentators of the time claimed that *L'Horizon chimérique* had been influenced by the wanderlust of the eponymous hero of *The Narrative of Arthur Gordon Pym of Nantucket* (1838) by Edgar Allen Poe, a novella that the poet of *L'Horizon chimérique* would have known in Baudelaire's translation. It is in fact Baudelaire with his 'L'Invitation au voyage'

JEAN DE LA VILLE DE MIRMONT

L'HORIZON CHIMÉRIQUE

POÈMES ORNÉS DE BOIS

*GRAVÉS PAR LÉON DUSOUCHET
et publiés par la Société
littéraire de France
10, rue de l'Odéon
A PARIS*

M. CM. XX.

Title-page of the first edition (1920) of L'Horizon chimérique *by Jean de La Ville de Mirmont*

Jean de La Ville de Mirmont

359

that is the background influence on these poems, although the imagery of unknown lands also owes something to Leconte de Lisle. With this kind of pedigree it is no surprise that Fauré was attracted by these poems.

The only book by Jean de La Ville de Mirmont that was published in his lifetime appeared in an edition of only 300 copies at the beginning of 1914. This little masterpiece is the *conte philosophique* entitled *Les Dimanches de Jean Dézert*, a work that should be much better known than it is. The anti-hero of this tale, written in an elegantly humorous – even sarcastic – style, is a civil servant who 'considers life to be like a waiting room for third-class passengers'. Jean Dézert is a failure; even his attempt at suicide is unsuccessful. His humdrum existence raises questions as to whether he has the right to say that he is alive at all. Another of the *contes*, *Le Piano droit*, published posthumously in 1923, is on a musical theme: the sad story of an old lady who is a piano teacher unable to install her upright piano in her new apartment, thus losing her friends and ending up in an old people's home. It is impossible to read this without imagining in this story an augury of the eventual fate of Marguerite Hasslemans. The prose writing is very distinguished; it is for this that Jean de La Ville de Mirmont would have been remembered, if remembered at all, had Fauré not intervened.

Cover of *L'Horizon chimérique, published by Durand*

Jean de La Ville de Mirmont died bravely in action in the first year of the war, on 28 November 1914, leaving only a few unfinished works – *Lettres de guerre*, sent to his parents from the front, and a slim *recueil* of poems in reflective and melancholy mood, something entirely different in character from his sharply focused prose. This collection was published in 1920 by the Société Littéraire de France, with engravings by Léon Dusouchet. The title of the first group of fourteen poems (from a total of forty-one) gave its name to the entire collection – *L'Horizon chimérique* – and to Fauré's cycle. The other sections are entitled *Jeux*, *Attitudes* and *Chansons sentimentales*. The poems the composer chose for setting are numbered XIII, XIV, XI and V in the poet's sequence. Fauré might have refused to write a work celebrating the Allied victory, but one feels that he wished to honour a talent from the ranks of the fallen. Very untypically, he did not alter a word of the poet's texts (although he did excise one strophe). The work was given its first performance by its dedicatee, the talented young baritone Charles Panzéra (destined to become one of the most famous of *mélodie* singers), on 13 May 1922, accompanied by his wife, Madeleine Panzéra-Baillot.

L'Horizon chimérique (*The illusory horizon*)[19]
1921, Op. 118

(106) (i) *La Mer est infinie* (*The sea is boundless*)
1921, Op. 118 No. 1, D major, 3/4, *Andante quasi allegretto*

La mer est infinie et mes rêves sont fous.	*The sea is boundless and my dreams are wild.*
La mer chante au soleil en battant les falaises	*The sea sings in the sun, as it beats the cliffs,*
Et mes rêves légers ne se sentent plus d'aise	*And my light dreams are overjoyed*
De danser sur la mer comme des oiseaux soûls.	*To dance on the sea like drunken birds.*
Le vaste mouvement des vagues les emporte,	*The waves' vast motion bears them away,*
La brise les agite et les roule en ses plis;	*The breeze ruffles and rolls them in its folds;*
Jouant dans le sillage, ils feront une escorte	*Playing in their wake, they will escort the ships,*
Aux vaisseaux que mon cœur dans leur fuite a suivis.	*Whose flight my heart has followed.*
Ivres d'air et de sel et brûlés par l'écume	*Drunk with air and salt, and stung by the spume*
De la mer qui console et qui lave des pleurs,	*Of the consoling sea that washes away tears,*
Ils connaîtront le large et sa bonne amertume;	*They will know the high seas and the bracing brine;*
Les goélands perdus les prendront pour des leurs.	*Lost gulls will take them for their own.*

In his very last creative phase Fauré rediscovers a new energy which animates his music in a remarkable manner. He emerges here from the veiled mysticism of *Mirages* and places his hand firmly on the tiller of life. This return to the positive, even joyful, aspects of music-making is partly encouraged by these fine poems of the sea, Fauré's beloved medium of water: transparent and opaque, restless and peaceful, never the same from one moment to the other. (In the same way the composer's music changes harmony in a seemingly imperceptible manner from one chord to the next.) The *moto perpetuo* semiquaver accompaniment of the song brings to mind *Veilles-tu, ma senteur de soleil?* from *La Chanson d'Ève*. It is a good example of this music of subtle 'sea-change' – undramatic yet teemingly eventful, and demanding enough to sink even the best sight-reader at the keyboard.

The infinite vistas of the horizon are mirrored by the implacable rise of the vocal line through an entire octave. In *Accompagnement* and *Mirages* we have encountered the eerie stillness of lakes; here we rediscover for the first time since *La Fleur qui va sur l'eau* a composer not shy of suggesting the buffeting of real waves at climactic points (as at 'Ivres d'air et de sel'); the composer, at home in this amalgam of reverie-fantasy and vigorous determination, revels in his starring role in 'The Old Man and the Sea', *avant* Hemingway, and much more benign. This is someone whose only foe and potential combatant was his own body, racked with illness. In this music the composer allows his fragile mortal form to be energised by the joyful buoyancy of buffeting waves. The inspiration of Panzéra's voice (broader and richer than that of any typical salon singer) must have played its part in encouraging the composer to paint with a broader brush dipped in testosterone. The result remains utterly Fauréan, but the music itself seems more easily accessible to the general listener than many of the earlier third-period songs.

(107) (ii) *Je me suis embarqué* (*I have embarked*)
1921, Op. 118 No. 2, D♭ major, 3/4, *Andante moderato*

Je me suis embarqué sur un vaisseau qui danse	*I have embarked on a ship that reels*
Et roule bord sur bord et tangue et se balance.	*And rolls and pitches and rocks.*
Mes pieds ont oublié la terre et ses chemins;	*My feet have forgotten the land and its ways;*
Les vagues souples m'ont appris d'autres cadences	*The lithe waves have taught me other rhythms,*
Plus belles que le rythme las des chants humains.	*Lovelier than the tired ones of human song.*
À vivre parmi vous, hélas! avais-je une âme?	*Ah! did I have the heart to live among you?*
Mes frères, j'ai souffert sur tous vos continents.	*Brothers, on all your continents I've suffered.*
Je ne veux que la mer, je ne veux que le vent	*I want only the sea, I want only the wind*
Pour me bercer, comme un enfant, au creux des lames.	*To cradle me like a child in the trough of the waves.*
Hors du port qui n'est plus qu'une image effacée,	*Far from the port, now but a faded image,*
Les larmes du départ ne brûlent plus mes yeux.	*Tears of parting no longer sting my eyes.*
Je ne me souviens pas de mes derniers adieux …	*I can no longer recall my final farewells …*
Ô ma peine, ma peine, où vous ai-je laissée?	*O my sorrow, my sorrow, where have I left you?*

In this vocal farewell to his beloved key of D♭ major, Fauré matches and illumines the obsessive wanderlust of the poet. Although the poet must have had a larger sailing ship in mind, the composer harks back to his *Chanson du pêcheur*, *Barcarolle* and *Accompagnement* by creating a bass-clef motif that suggests an oar plying its way through water. Thus the oar of the imagination cleaves through the constraints that keep the poet grounded on dry land, giving the song terrific thrust and momentum. The insistent dotted quaver-plus-semiquaver figuration launches the music and propels it forward.

The remarkable cradling music at the end of the second verse temporarily abandons this rhythm: a welcome respite, and one of the composer's most inspired use of *hemiola* – the ear is led to hear six bars of 2/4 instead of the four bars of 3/4 that appear on the page. Fauré chooses to end on a most untypical (for him) note of pathos ('Ô ma peine, ma peine'), something that a larger-than-life singer like Panzéra could carry off with conviction, perhaps because of that 'extra physical dimension that organises, surpasses and overturns the whole cultural part of music' (this is Roland Barthes, writing of Panzéra's powers, a point that is further discussed and somewhat disputed in Chapter 16).[20]

Jean de La Ville de Mirmont provides a last strophe, omitted by the composer, which announces the poet's departure for a destination beyond the Antilles. He asks whether his heart (which is the only cargo he will take with him) will appeal to the savages as a cheap trinket. These lines show the poet in ironic mood and Fauré does not set them to music. Such black humour might not have been out of place in the composer's private life, but it would seem strange in his song writing, and especially in a visionary incantation of this kind.

(108) (iii) Diane, Séléné (*Diana, Selene*)
1921, Op. 118 No. 3, E♭ major, 4/4, *Lento ma non troppo*

Diane, Séléné, lune de beau métal,
Qui reflètes vers nous, par ta face déserte,
Dans l'immortel ennui du calme sidéral,
Le regret d'un soleil dont nous pleurons la perte.

Ô lune, je t'en veux de ta limpidité
Injurieuse au trouble vain des pauvres âmes,
Et mon cœur, toujours las et toujours agité,
Aspire vers la paix de ta nocturne flamme.

Diana, Selene, moon of beautiful metal,
Reflecting on us, from your deserted face,
In the eternal tedium of sidereal calm,
The regret of a sun whose loss we lament.

O moon, I begrudge you your limpidity,
Mocking the fruitless commotion of wretched souls
And my heart, ever weary and ever uneasy,
Longs for the peace of your nocturnal flame.

This hymn to the goddess Diana is the last in a line of evocations of antiquity threading its way from *Lydia* to *Pénélope* and beyond; in the chords of the infinite calm of the song's opening we can also detect an echo of the noble beginning of Duparc's *Phidylé*, in itself a tribute to the static, seemingly inexpressive chordal repetitions that had opened certain songs by Fauré since those magical evocations *Lydia* and *Le Secret*. This is also the composer's last vocal nocturne, simpler and more direct than many of the others. The accompaniment consists of crotchet chords which glide without haste, seemingly laconic but implacably determined nevertheless. This circular progress from the opening to the closing E♭ chords seems a journey charted in the stars (one thinks of another sailor's hymn to sidereal beauty, Schubert's Mayrhofer setting *Lied eines Schiffers an die Dioskuren*).

For his vocal line Fauré has somehow conjured a memorable tune out of the unremarkable inflections of speech. In the vast calm of this picture the tiniest details seem significant, such as the clash, the glint of 'beau métal', between B♭ and A♮ in the pianist's hands. This is one of several such touches: the drop of a fourth on 'perte' (of no account in most songs, but here signifying something utterly bereft); an address to the moon ('Ô lune, je t'en veux de ta limpidité'), where the baritone voices his plea in a higher and lighter tessitura. Seven bars from the end, as the accompaniment's single pair of enlivening quavers stirs in a becalmed sea of crotchets, the word 'agité' is contrasted with 'paix', the harmonisation of which unfurls like a white flag and prepares the way for the truce of the closing cadence. Those wonderful words 'mon cœur, toujours las et toujours agité' incidentally express a central paradox in the composer's life and music.

It is notable that *Diane, Séléné*, the third song of *L'Horizon chimérique*, is cast here as the slow movement of a four-movement cycle; in the same way, the slow movement of the Second Cello Sonata Op. 117 is also the work's third, preceding its finale. Another contemporary work that seems intimately related to *L'Horizon chimérique* is the Thirteenth Nocturne for piano.

(109) (iv) *Vaisseaux, nous vous aurons aimés en pure perte*

(*Ships, we shall have loved you to no avail*)
1921, Op. 118 No. 4, D major, 12/8, *Andante quasi allegretto*

Vaisseaux, nous vous aurons aimés en pure perte;	*Ships, we shall have loved you to no avail,*
Le dernier de vous tous est parti sur la mer.	*The last of you all has set sail on the sea.*
Le couchant emporta tant de voiles ouvertes	*The sunset bore away so many spread sails,*
Que ce port et mon cœur sont à jamais déserts.	*That this port and my heart are forever forsaken.*
La mer vous a rendus à votre destinée,	*The sea has returned you to your destiny,*
Au delà du rivage où s'arrêtent nos pas.	*Beyond the shores where our steps must halt.*
Nous ne pouvions garder vos âmes enchaînées;	*We could not keep your souls enchained,*
Il vous faut des lointains que je ne connais pas.	*You require distant reaches unknown to me.*
Je suis de ceux dont les désirs sont sur la terre.	*I belong to those with earthbound desires.*
Le souffle qui vous grise emplit mon cœur d'effroi,	*The wind that elates you fills me with fright,*
Mais votre appel, au fond des soirs, me désespère,	*But your summons at nightfall makes me despair,*
Car j'ai de grands départs inassouvis en moi.	*For within me are vast, unappeased departures.*

Jean de La Ville de Mirmont (1886–1914)

Long gone are the days when the composer would attempt a complicated ending for a cycle in the manner of the last of the Venetian songs or the conclusion of *La Bonne chanson* – both of these had cleverly incorporated themes from earlier songs of their respective sets. For the closing of *L'Horizon chimérique* we merely return to the D major of the opening song, and the second number of the set is recalled in a modified recapitulation of its rhythmical emphases. This is more of a *berceuse* than the other numbers in the set, but it is a lullaby on a grand scale, though much less suave than *Les Berceaux*; indeed the repeated accompanying pattern gives the music enormous strength. The waves sweeping upwards in triplets have an open-air quality and are allowed to roll easily between the hands in a way that looks back to the early *Chanson du pêcheur*. Here a man of seventy-seven seems able to summon as much youthful ardour as he needs. At first hearing this may seem to be a song of action, but its poignancy lies in its unfulfilled longing.

The poet, who never fulfilled his desire to travel the world, remains land-locked alongside the ageing composer whose life is drawing to a close. Already very frail, Fauré assures us that he too has many great new departures left in him. Even if these songs were not the first that the composer had ever written specifically for the male voice, it had been very many years since he had imagined any of his songs in terms of a tenor or a baritone timbre. It is perhaps a pity that Fauré did not explore this vein of masculine *camaraderie* more in his career. In the open, outdoor music of this cycle one can sense his desire to write something gratifying for an agreeable male friend, the young Panzéra. For most of his life his songs, apart from their matchless musical value for their own sake, had always been superbly adaptable instruments of a kind of refined seduction, the calling cards of a subtle suitor, a means of staying close to a singer in order to admire her musicality and to revel in the unique female sound and aura of the soprano or mezzo voice.

Cradled in this environment where musical and visceral admiration could be combined in a civilised manner, the composer felt safe and inspired, as well as gratified. Performing songs with women meant rehearsing songs with women, and rehearsing songs meant goodness knows how many other opportunities for intimate colloquy and private discussion. Of course men had often performed his songs, singers like Maurice Bagès and Reynaldo Hahn (who were both homosexual and completely different as singers from the leonine Panzéra), but *La Bonne chanson*, which Bagès sang in public, had been written for Emma Bardac in private, and there are many enthusiasts who maintain that the work is much better suited to the female voice than to the male.

The list of female singers is a long one – Caroline Miolan-Carvalho, Pauline Viardot, the duetting Viardot daughters (of whom one, Marianne, had been Fauré's fiancée), Thérèse Roger, Henriette Fuchs, Alice Boissenet, Émilie Girette, Mrs George Swinton, Jeanne Raunay, Jeanne Remacle, Claire Croiza, Madeleine Grey, Suzanne Balguerie and many more. His affection for amateur singers led him to write songs for the pupils of his friend Marie Trélat, who was both a powerful socialite and a singing teacher, and whose pupils included such names as Pauline and Claudie Segond and Anna and Lydia Eustis. The dedicatees of most of the seven songs of *Le Jardin clos* were also female singers. Perhaps in this instance, 'odor di femmina' and 'voce di femmina' meant more or less the same thing. It could be said that the famous performing partnerships of Bernac–Poulenc and Pears–Britten reflected a similar, if rather more constant, favouritism born of a different sexual orientation, although the French duo were never lovers. Poulenc's partnership (from 1959) with the soprano Denise Duval for the last four years of his life is a kind of mirror-image of Fauré's collaboration with Panzéra.

To be fair, Fauré's preference for the female voice has never prevented a legion of male singers from taking up his songs and performing them very successfully – and the vast majority of the poems are actually more suitable for men to sing if one takes into account the textual content of the poems themselves. Nevertheless, I feel that in saluting the very different, the unexpectedly different, mood of *L'Horizon chimérique*, musicologists have not given enough credit to the effect on Fauré of a new and unexpected inspiration – the red-blooded male voice of Panzéra. Whether or not he could have heard it clearly is difficult to say; if not, why did the composer look on this singer with such favour? Perhaps Panzéra's voice had a timbre capable of penetrating the aural fog that surrounded the ailing composer.

Fauré was now too old to be chasing women, although his letters to Madeleine Grey, as old and infirm as he was, had still struck a flirtatious and amorous note. He could now look on the whole matter of composing songs with something approaching a disinterested equanimity. Panzéra had a wife who accompanied him, and one senses that Fauré did not *need* to accompany Panzéra as he had needed and longed to accompany his female singers. One is reminded of how very unusual it was for Fauré to hear any of his songs at one remove (that is if he could hear them at all), without him being at the piano as their accompanist. If the composer had been a close friend of such a male singer earlier in his career (the great tenor Ernest van Dyck had been an intimate colleague of Chabrier, for example), Fauré's catalogue of songs might well have looked, and sounded, rather different.

Had Fauré's health permitted it, we cannot doubt that his musical mind would have continued to evolve – the Piano Trio (written in 1922–23, at the same time as T.S. Eliot published *The Waste Land*) and String Quartet (1923–24) are proof of this. But this was his last completed song, so it is here that we must leave the composer of *mélodies*. Peering into distant horizons he slips from sight without a fuss; distrusting bombastic endings, he softens his final bold cadence with a decrescendo. On leaving his desk for the war, Jean de La Ville de Mirmont had left a line that now applied to the venerable old collaborator he was never to meet: 'Cette fois, mon cœur, c'est le grand voyage.'

As we bid farewell to Fauré's songs, we shall not immediately lose sight of a man still grappling with his loss of health with bravery and fortitude, and still determined to compose. Indeed, it is a terrible irony that for the first time in his life, at the age of seventy-seven, the composer had nothing else to do in his life *but* compose. Only his illnesses and his state of mind could now prevent him from dedicating himself entirely to composition – no teaching, no conservatoire duties, no salon networking, no travelling abroad to play his music.

There was, however, one last duty. In January 1922 from the warmth of Nice, Fauré wrote a valedictory article on Saint-Saëns for the *Revue musicale*, as moving a tribute from one composer to another as has ever been penned, and made more poignant by the fact that the former pupil knew that before long he would follow his teacher to the grave.

It is difficult to believe that the public did not also sense valediction in the air. The concert at the SNM on 13 May that offered and featured the first performance of *L'Horizon chimérique* also featured first performance of the Second Cello Sonata, played by Gérard

Camille Saint-Saëns

Hekking and Alfred Cortot. On 20 June there was a huge all-Fauré concert at the Sorbonne, nothing less than an *hommage national*. The list of artists was an extraordinary line-up of all the composer's favourite interpreters (only Marguerite Hasselmans was missing; as always she kept a discreet distance on such occasions, and she must have found it heartbreaking to do so). Present were the singers Croiza, Panzéra and Raunay, the pianists Cortot and Lortat, the cellist Casals. The conductors, from an earlier generation, were among his oldest friends – D'Indy, who had always refused to become Fauré's enemy, whatever their aesthetic differences, and Fauré's old flatmate, André Messager, who had become one of the greatest of all operetta composers. The violinist Hélène Jourdan-Mourhange informs us that this concert raised 100,000 francs for Fauré; thus, as she brusquely puts it, 'Fauré was able to finish his existence without too much bitterness.'[21]

Illness in the summer stopped the customary productivity, but Fauré embarked on the *Andante* of a new piano trio in September 1922. He remained engaged with it in the winter (the idea for the work had come from Jacques Durand and, most unusually, Fauré had obediently taken it up). A letter to Marie Fauré reveals that at first the composer had envisaged the work for clarinet, cello and piano.

In 1923 the composer received the *grand Croix* of the Légion d'Honneur, an exalted rank of honour usually reserved for politicians and normally beyond the reach of even the most distinguished of artists. There was a revival of *Pénélope* at the Opéra-Comique, and a new production in Strasbourg.

The completed Piano Trio was given its first performance at the SNM to mark the composer's seventy-eighth birthday, but he was too ill to attend the concert.

He recovered sufficiently by late June to travel down to his favourite retreat in the south, where he secretly began work on a string quartet, ever mindful that this difficult medium had been rendered sacred by Beethoven, and that the late Saint-Saëns had never succeeded in writing one. Indeed, one has the feeling that Fauré would have never attempted such a work in Saint-Saëns's lifetime for fear of hurting the older composer's feelings. In that summer he wrote to his wife from Annecy-le-Vieux:

> I do not think I have ever seen Nature looking so beautiful, so resplendent. In the evening around six o'clock there is here a lighting effect which spreads over an immense area and is deeply moving in its beauty. Why is it necessary to live in cities, in noise and for a good third of the year in darkness!'[22]

It is interesting that the composer spoke of noise. A few yards away from the gateway to the house where he was staying stands the 'Clocher roman', one of the architectural jewels of this charming little town. From this imposing Romanesque tower emanates a stentorian peal (unlike the distant bell that merely 'doucement tint' in Verlaine's 'Prison') that would have disturbed the work of most composers. We have to remind ourselves that Fauré at this stage would either have been incapable of hearing it or would have been grateful for any sound capable of penetrating the aural fog. The visit of Arthur Honegger to Annecy (unlike Poulenc, his co-member of 'Les Six', Honegger was a warm admirer of Fauré's work) was occasioned by a performance of the *Requiem* with extracts from Honegger's *Le Roi David*.

Fauré was too ill to attend a performance of the *Requiem* conducted by Mengelberg in Paris in May 1924, but he rallied sufficiently to travel to Divonne, where in June and July he worked on his String Quartet. This was finished on 11 September – one suspects that this was a final act of professional will-power that cost the composer dearly. A few days later Fauré lay seriously ill with bronchial pneumonia. In early October he wrote to his wife that his eyesight had deteriorated terribly. Nevertheless, he summoned all his energies on 14 October to write his last, and perhaps most remarkable, letter to her. After reminding her of the joy the he felt about the fact that a statue had been erected recently of her father, Emmanuel Frémiet, in the Jardins des Plantes, he asks her whether she can also find it in her heart to rejoice in the pure beauty of the works of her husband whose career had been as 'nobly disinterested' as that of her father:

> Your life has been a sad one, and perhaps what was missing for you most of all was the means to achieve your desire to be someone yourself! But does there not remain this profound happiness to which you can add that of having brought up our sons? In these troubled times, *which are so tainted by unscrupulousness and ambition*, does all that count for nothing? … Do not look for anything here which is no more than the truth, pure and simple.[23]

Four days later (18 October) the composer was taken back to Paris. On 4 November 1924 Gabriel Urbain Fauré died in Paris, at 32 rue des Vignes. At his bedside were his wife, his two sons and his doctor. The other person who must have ached to be there was Marguerite Hasselmans; but this cruel exclusion was the time-honoured punishment exacted by society, and more specifically Marie Fauré, on the mistress. At the age of forty-eight Marguerite suddenly found herself in financial difficulty

Gabriel Fauré at the end of his life

The Ronsard cover of La Revue musicale *(1924) and the first page of Ravel's* Ronsard à son âme

for the first time in her life. Her conscientious reticence during the composer's lifetime meant that few people understood her artistic importance in relation to Fauré's piano music. Her canny rival Marguerite Long eventually produced a book (*At the Piano with Fauré*) that is a fascinating account of a successful career but which tells us precious little of depth about Fauré's music; such insight would almost certainly have been provided by Marguerite Hasselmans.

Both of Fauré's sons married, but neither had children of their own. One wonders if this was a matter of choice; growing up must have been far from easy in a household that was dominated by their mother's almost hysterical possessiveness, and clouded by their father's frequent extended absences. It is to their credit that Fauré's sons did not permit Madame Hasselmans, this faithful companion of the last quarter-century of their father's life, to live in utter penury, but helped her with discretion and kindness. She lived on until 1947, an inspiration to all those who took the trouble to seek her out; Vladimir Jankélévitch visited her in the 1930s in her shabby little flat surrounded by the autographed musical scores of her past life, and she talked about Fauré and his times with charm, perception and enviable inside knowledge. She had probably known him better than almost anyone else. If one realises how much she had meant to Fauré, and how constantly she was with him, it seems inexplicable that until relatively recently she has been written out of the composer's life, as if she were invisible.

Four days after the composer's death there was a state funeral at the Madeleine. At the time, Alice Tully, later to be one of New York City's great musical patrons, was a singing student in Paris, and she was among the crowds who came to pay tribute to Fauré. She described the occasion to me more

369

than once as being incredibly moving. The whole of musical France knew that the nation had lost one of its greatest sons. Fauré was buried in Passy cemetery; Marie Fauré died in March 1926, less than eighteen months after her husband.

∾   ∾   ∾   ∾

At the end of 1921 Henri Prunières had asked Fauré to write a song for a supplement of the *Revue musicale*, a *Tombeau de Ronsard* which would honour the 400th anniversary of the poet Ronsard's birth in 1924. This is a handsome little booklet with contributions from Dukas, Roussel (a song with flute), Louis Aubert, André Caplet (a song with harp), Honegger (a *chanson* dedicated to Panzéra), Roland-Manuel and Delage. But it is the final song of Ravel that is the reason for Fauré's absence from this line-up. The ailing composer had chosen a poem very carefully for inclusion in this *recueil*; if he was proud of anything in his life one has the impression that he could truly say that his philosophy had always been one of 'scorning fame and riches'. As luck would have it, Ravel had chosen the same poem and had already set the text to music. Ever the gentleman, and ever concerned to place his pupils' interests before his own, Fauré destroyed his own sketch.

This commentary ends with the text of what might have been, what should have been, Fauré's last song. The spare and austere Ravel setting composed thirteen years before that composer's death – the accompaniment largely on a single piano stave – seems inadequate compensation for the loss of a song by Fauré, a work that might have stood beside the String Quartet as the composer's farewell both to music and to life.

Ronsard à son âme (*Ronsard to his soul*)

Âmelette Ronsardelette,	*Dear little Ronsardian soul,*
Mignonnellette, doucelette,	*Little sweet one, little soft one,*
Très chère hôtesse de mon corps,	*My body's dearest denizen,*
Tu descends là-bas faiblelette,	*You go weakly down to the depths,*
Pâle, maigrelette, seulette,	*So pale, so meagre, so lonely,*
Dans le froid Royaume des morts:	*To the pale kingdom of the dead:*
Toutefois simple, sans remords	*Simple withal, unburdened by remorse*
De meutre, poison et rancune,	*For murder, poison, and bitterness,*
Méprisant faveurs et trésors	*Scorning favours and riches,*
Tant enviés par la commune.	*So greatly envied by the common man.*
Passant, j'ai dit, suis ta fortune,	*Passer-by, I have done: follow your fortune,*
Ne trouble pas mon repos, je dors.	*Do not disturb my rest, I sleep.*

1   The last verse of Thomas Hardy's 'I Look into my Glass', in *Wessex Poems* (London: Macmillan, 1898), pp. 227–8.

2   *Gabriel Fauré: A Life in Letters*, trans. and ed. Barrie Jones (London : B.T. Batsford, 1989), letter 254, p. 182.

3   Ibid., letter 257, p. 183.

4   Ibid., letter 263, p. 185.

5   *Mirages*: Aspects of this cycle's interpretation are discussed in Chapter 16, pp. 424–5.

6   Jean-Michel Nectoux, *Gabriel Fauré: A Musical Life*, trans. Roger Nichols (Cambridge: Cambridge University Press, 1991), p. 446.

7   Recounted by Léon Vallas in his *Claude Debussy: His Life and Works*, trans. Maire and Grace O'Brien (New York: Dover, 1973), p. 69.

8	The disc is remastered in a set of CDs entitled *The Essential Pierre Bernac* (Testament Records).

9	Nectoux, *Gabriel Fauré: A Musical Life*, p. 447.

10	Claude Rostand, *L'Œuvre de Gabriel Fauré* (Paris: J.B. Janin, 'La Flûte de Pan', 1945), p. 182.

11	Norman Suckling, *Fauré* (London: Dent, 1946), p. 86.

12	Vladimir Jankélévitch, *De la musique au silence: Fauré et l'inexprimable* (Paris: Plon, 1974), p. 220.

13	Myriam Chimènes, *Mécènes et musiciens* (Paris: Fayard, 2004), p. 380.

14	Robert Orledge, *Gabriel Fauré* (London: Eulenburg, 1979), p. 192.

15	The poet's biographical details are unknown.

16	Nectoux, *Gabriel Fauré: A Musical Life*, p. 404.

17	Philippe Fauré-Fremiet, *Gabriel Fauré* (Paris: Les Éditions Rieder, 1929), p. 122.

18	Ibid.

19	*L'Horizon chimérique*: Aspects of this cycle's interpretation are discussed in Chapter 16, pp. 425–8.

20	Quoted in Nectoux, *Gabriel Fauré: A Musical Life*, p. 4; originally from Roland Barthes's essay trans. into English as 'The Grain of the Voice', in *The Responsibility of Forms: Critical Essays on Art, Music, and Representation*, trans. Richard Howard (Berkeley: University of California Press, 1985), pp. 267–77.

21	Hélène Jourdan-Morhange, *Mes amis musiciens* (Paris: Les Éditeurs Français Réunis, 1955), p. 30.

22	*Gabriel Fauré: A Life in Letters*, letter 299, p. 202.

23	Ibid., letter 312, p. 206.

Voilà ! Je suis parti, plus loin que les Antilles,
Vers des pays nouveaux, lumineux et subtils.
Je n'emporte avec moi, pour toute pacotille,
Que mon cœur… Mais les sauvages, en voudront-ils ?

Chapter Fifteen

Some Notes on the Performance of Fauré's Songs

The more clarity, correctness, precision, even concision there is in a piece of music, the more it moves me
Gabriel Fauré

The Practical Musician

Some would say that there is little point in discussing the interpretation of Fauré's music with performers unless they are already on their professional way.[2] It used to annoy Fauré no end that ignoramuses said of his songs that one did not need a voice to sing them. The truth is that one needs both a good voice and a good brain. The child musician is almost certainly bound to be bewildered by much (though not all) of Fauré's music, and the cultivated well-to-do amateur singer (of whom the composer spoke with such affection) an influential part of musical life in the twenty-first century. The imaginary singer targeted here is an adult, relatively free of technical problems; control of intonation and breath are taken for granted, as is an evenness of vocal production with equality between the registers. An ability to sing loudly or softly at will, in all parts of the voice, is assumed, as is clarity of diction. Beauty of vocal timbre – that unaccountable gift that has been given to only a few, and maddeningly without a trace of fairness in its bestowal – is another theoretical given. Added to this, we must assume that the words will be pronounced in the correct way by someone who has worked to acquire a command of the French language, even if only for reasons of singing.

The equally imaginary pianist will also be a master of his or her instrument with ready keyboard command, and evenness and clarity of touch; the pedal will be used selectively and not as an automatic *vade mecum* and palliative. The clean negotiation of tricky passage-work and a control of colour and dynamics will all lie within the range of possibility. It will be assumed that he or she has the ability to listen to the singer, and to achieve a sensitive awareness of balance when accompanying songs. (This is a generous assumption given that this is not a skill acquired without considerable application and experience.) We must also take for granted that the actual notes written by Fauré, encompassing harmonies of a rich and rare complexity, will be accurately deciphered and played.

In the real world these sweeping attributions of gift and skill are clearly over-optimistic. But none of the accomplishments mentioned above can be improved on by merely thinking or reading about them, and they must all be acquired, in some measure at least, before the finer points of music-making can be discussed. Nothing that can be written for the edification of practising musicians will ever replace the need to master these crucial areas of performance in purely practical terms with the help of teachers and endless private preparation.

It is all very well, for example, to point out sternly that Fauré's dynamic markings are important, but those whose music-making allows their listeners to differentiate clearly between *piano* and *forte* (and all the gradings between) are likely to be artists in full control of their instruments, rather than neophytes. It is an unusual blessing if a young musician is technically proficient enough to understand what is on the printed page *and put it into practice*; a conscientious determination to obey the composer's markings can all too easily be bedevilled by physical limitations. It is hellishly difficult for some singers to sustain soft passages in the higher register of the voice, however much they may long to do so. For others, the singing of louder passages with rounded vibrancy and legato (an important requirement in the Fauré songs) is a physical impossibility. Yet another kind of singer has no trouble demonstrating passionate intensity and involvement, but the intractable voice let off the leash can all too easily jump outside the stylistic frame with a *verismo* sob that will unwittingly betray Fauré's entire aesthetic.

The pianist has likewise to 'sing' with a fullness of tone that is firm and refined; he or she has to convey passion without the need to thump the keyboard, and delicacy without retreating into a wishy-washy lack of personality and colour. 'Half-light', what Nectoux has dubbed the 'clair-obscur', is certainly part of the composer's aesthetic, but this idea misapplied can all too easily play a pretentious part in performances of Fauré's music, as he himself complained.[3] It is one thing for a young and enthusiastic pianist to have in mind something heard and admired on a recording; it is quite another to have adrenalin coursing through the veins while the uncontrollable piano, no longer a well-behaved accompanying instrument, turns into a runaway train clattering down the tracks.

A performer can only be as effective and fluent as his or her technique allows; this technical self-possession is a separate issue and a lifelong quest, something quite different from a study of a composer's music and his style. I have often encountered singers and pianists who love Fauré with all their heart, and who understand a great deal more about his music than they are presently able, or will ever be able, to put into practice. They will of course take this knowledge with them to every concert they attend as listeners. But I have also encountered the opposite many times as a listener in the audience, or as a judge in competitions – singers with fine voices and extremely serviceable techniques, who have little idea of their responsibilities to the composer's score. It is only too possible for someone with great vocal talent and sovereign breath control to massacre a Fauré song (presumably without intending to do so). This is why it is perhaps worth raising the issues discussed in this chapter. There are after all very many accomplished performers who are not yet accomplished performers of Fauré's vocal works. There is nothing shameful in this; in fact it represents a perfectly normal rite of passage. Fauré's music demands the best singers and pianists, not those of the second rank who, with whatever enthusiasm, take up the composer's cause without the technical means of bringing their enthusiasm to fruition.

There was a stage in Fauré's life when he was so discouraged by the egotism of the professional musical world that he persuaded himself to retreat to amateur singers who were personally devoted to him. This is one way of solving the problem. Another is to confront the best performers when still malleable and persuade them by whatever means to think less about themselves and their voices (or their pianism), and more about the composer and his music.

Capabilities, Negative and Otherwise

If a Sparrow comes before my Window I take part in its existence and pick about the Gravel.
John Keats[4]

The word 'interpretation' is a dangerous one in the context of Fauré's melodies. If we say a song has been 'interpreted' it usually means that performers have brought their own *viewpoint* to bear on the music, and that they have *shaped* it accordingly. A reading of the poem and an examination of the score have informed their *decisions* on mood and tempo, and after they decide what they *feel* about the song, they will decide how to *present* it. Music and text are filtered through their *emotions*, which have been roused by their subjective *reactions* to the task in hand. I would not deny that all this is appropriate enough for the preparation of a majority of the song repertoire, but Fauré's music is singularly unsuitable for this treatment.

When we perform the music of Fauré we are, or should be, taking part in his existence on his own terms. Perhaps we should try to cultivate what Keats referred to as 'Negative Capability' – to make ourselves as receptive as a blank sheet of paper that will take on his characteristics, and temporarily to forget our own. Another way of putting it is to say that in the service of his music we should be prepared to give only what is asked of us as opposed to everything we have in us. As a coach I sometimes find it quite a struggle to persuade a certain kind of singer to give less than everything, although it is more usual that the student singer is not giving enough. As performers we all have different temperaments; and the music we sing and play will not suit us equally well.

As a teenager I did not fall in love with Fauré's music at first hearing, and this was because I failed to understand where the music was coming from, in every sense. Some of my colleagues experienced the very opposite reaction. We read that whereas composers such as Honegger and Poulenc took a long time to warm to Fauré's music (Poulenc remained ambivalent), Milhaud took to it immediately. In this 'elective affinity' different musical styles will seem natural in different places, different composers will become immediate friends with different performers.

Keats believed that it was Negative Capability that enabled Shakespeare to identify completely with all his different characters; the Bard was able to depict them in an instinctive intuitive flash rather than create them laboriously. But even if Shakespeare and Keats were able to place themselves in the position of other beings, they sometimes needed help in 'taking part' in these outside existences. As Keats wrote to his brothers in December 1817, one side of him disliked 'irritable reaching after facts and reason'; and yet he remained (as Douglas Bush points out in *English Romantic Poets*, 1960) 'aware of his fluctuations – between belief in the poetic efficacy of a wise passiveness, and belief in the active pursuit of rational knowledge and philosophy'. The performer too is caught between this 'wise passiveness' and the pursuit of knowledge. There is the possibility of a leap of faith that enables him or her to form a bond with a composer that is beyond rational explication, but this leap cannot take place in the dark. Before he took part in a bird's existence, Keats needed to know something of its nesting habits, its migrations, its song; he would be able to observe and listen, but as much as he rejoiced in becoming a sparrow in his imagination, he would also need to read the words of others who knew more about sparrows than he did – or *mutatis mutandis*, French song composers.

Role-Play

All performers, whether they are conscious of the fact or not, are the composer's representatives and plenipotentiaries on the concert platform; in this position they need to feel as if they 'own' the music, and have a right to perform it – not as if they had appropriated the music for their own use, but as guardians, defenders even, of the composer's domain. In a letter to his wife Fauré wrote 'Ysaÿe comprend ma musique comme s'il l'avait composée' ('Ysaÿe understands my music as if he had composed it').[5] From here it is would be only a short but crucial step to say that this great violinist–composer *played* the music as if he had composed it. This sense of pretend-ownership (perhaps a good way of defining the 'role-play' of this paragraph's heading) brings with it an almost sacred sense of responsibility, and I have no doubt that the celebrated authority of Ysaÿe's performances of the Fauré chamber music stemmed from this loving appropriation. Of course the violinist had the incalculable advantage of a friendship with the composer, whom he addressed as 'tu'.

Almost all the great song composers wrote their piano accompaniments for themselves; it follows that every pianist is standing in for the composer when accompanying one of his songs. Thinking oneself into a composer's persona in order to play or think as he did (one feels this is how Britten achieved his miraculous Schubert playing) can be a remarkably useful game, but in order to take part in it there is much preparatory work to be done. The most brilliant instinct and intuitive talent have to be schooled and informed; the singer and accompanist who have studied their subject deeply discover that a command of the facts nourishes the musical seed, but that only a touch of something magically inexplicable will make it flower and prosper.

One might begin with first impressions of the kind that remain memorable in a personal encounter. There is a theory that composers *sound* as they *look*: for example, unkempt Beethoven, rounded Schubert, portly Brahms. Britten once remarked that composers have no choice but to write themselves into their music. From there it is a short step for the performer to incorporate into his mental pictures of composers how they might have *behaved*: an obdurate Beethoven for example, or a yielding Schubert, a mercurial Britten. All of these are of course complete (and sometimes misleading) generalisations, but they begin the painstaking process whereby we assemble identi-kits of the composers we are studying, and try to make sense of how their music sounds in the context of their lives and personalities.

How we perform Fauré similarly depends to an extent on how we perceive him. The reader of this book will realise by now that Fauré was not inclined to throw his weight around; instead he was exceedingly subtle, sometimes evasive, always mysterious, charming and somewhat distant. As a musician – if not always as a man (Fauré was no saint in his private life) – he had iron integrity and would seldom deflect from his path for the sake of fashion or easy success, but he seldom made a fuss, and on many occasions was happy to keep in the background.

Carlo Caballero refers eloquently to 'the open sea of Fauré's reticence'.[6] René Dumesnil referred to his 'modesty, or rather the disdain in which he held glory during a period when it was easier than ever for a mediocrity to raise a ruckus'.[7] Marcel Proust referred with Proustian perceptiveness to Fauré's 'disdainful indifference to success' (see Chapter 1).[8] It is clear that the composer's self-effacement, though complicated in its psychological origin, was something positive as far as his music was concerned, and not a shyness that implied weakness or lack of decision – rather it was a sign of his independence. Nadia Boulanger noted 'respect for himself, and for others … as if the very thought of influencing us had never even occurred to him'.[9] Fauré himself, in a letter to Marguerite Baugnies, wrote, 'I have no desire to intrude *my personal accents* into other people's reveries.'[10]

This is the kind of biographical background that is most useful for the performers of Fauré's songs, both singers and pianists, who should spare a thought for his personality before they embark on his music. It is undeniable that Fauré's songs are more important in themselves than anything we can learn from a reconstruction of either his personality or his life, but performers are strange beings who need every bit of help they can get, and singing and playing are not things that are entirely dependent on logic. The child cyclist who still uses stabilisers certainly drives the machine, but it is only when he finds the thread that connects balance and a complete trust in the principles of gyroscopic energy that he or she takes off into a new world of freedom. Young performers must do whatever is necessary to 'find the thread' and create the conditions with which they will 'take off', as if by magic; until they are ready to do this as if it were second nature to them, no one could blame them for reaching back into the past for help and support. Some of us need more than the score, we need a quasi-personal link. It is, after all, only an accident of history and chronology that dead composers are not our living friends and colleagues; one cannot help feeling that they have always somehow remained part of our community, and continue to live with us and through us.

The Actor-in-Music

There is of course a daunting chasm between the assimilation of biographical details about a composer and an attempt to bring his music to life on stage, but this is no more of a challenge than that faced by any actor or actress who has done background research on their allotted role, and who will do everything to bring themselves into line with the character that they are attempting to play (note that the verb 'to play' links the work of theatre and concert hall). At least recitalists do not have to make themselves *look* like Fauré: no walrus moustache is necessary, there is no need for the soft, seductive accent of the Ariège with its rolled 'r's, they do not have to peer at the world through the heavy-lidded eyelids of imperturbable insouciance, they do not have to smoke incessantly. But the performer (let us focus on the accompanist here because Fauré often appeared in this capacity) has to continue to 'play' Fauré in every sense. He must attempt to do nothing at the keyboard that is out of character – thus no superfluous flourishes, no mugging at the audience at climactic points or at changes of harmony. Jankélévitch writes that in the face of death Fauré's *Requiem* knows nothing of 'les grimaces de peur' – faces contorted by pain. In fact there is little room for grimaces of any kind in Fauré's music, and the composer's treatment of death in the *Requiem* is an indication of a temperament that contains emotion rather than allows it to overflow. It is not that his music lacks drama and grandeur, but the overwrought passion of the anguished *Gretchen am Spinnrade* (a Schubert song that Fauré accompanied in public) has a Germanic spin lacking in his music. The 'rouet' of *Dans le pénombre* from *Le Jardin clos* is of French manufacture. 'I am re-turning my wheel with a patience and resignation that I undoubtedly have from birth,' Fauré wrote to the Comtesse Greffulhe in 1887.[11]

Fauré was modest but strong, withdrawn into the music and not withdrawn in self-indulgent introspection. Everything written about him tended to describe his clarity and simplicity, his unpretentiousness and his respect for others. One must attempt to translate these qualities into vocal and pianistic terms. His disinclination to influence others marks him out as a performer who would eschew any interpretative attention-seeking antics. His indifference to success implies stillness, a certain passivity in his personality. This is of prime importance to the performers of his songs. There is nothing of the charlatan about him, the conjuror who will use any means to capture the attention of his public. If he is a charmer, it is the more often the charm of a murmured endearment rather than a passionate outpouring, and this renders the occasional eruption of passionate emotion more surprising and more meaningful, the exception that proves the rule. As an accompanist one may have thought that he had far too much courtesy to attempt to bend singers to his will, although this was precisely what he did – particularly in his later years of deafness, when he accompanied implacably in time, unable to hear, and impervious to, ill-advised rubato. He simply took it for granted that the singer would politely respect the same musical notation by which he, the composer–accompanist, was also bound.

There are certain actors who are able to play Henry V in one season, and Hamlet the next – and who learn to revel in different kinds of drama, the extrovert and the introvert. Naturally extrovert artists when performing Fauré have to rein in their energies, not suppress them entirely. One is not required to become a musical milksop with nothing to say, but rather someone who generates power by a variety of means. The challenge is to find a different vocabulary of expressiveness, to channel, to economise, to think 'thrift' rather than 'extravagance', 'exquisite manners' rather than 'arresting individuality'. This is not to become mean and parsimonious, but to redefine generosity. This is the art of containment within a form too precious to tamper with, and too fastidious to spoil with inflated rhetoric. Something like old-fashioned craftsmanship comes to mind, and the quiet pride in hard-won achievement that is not a highly visible part of our new century. There is something old-world about Fauré and his polite but firm refusal to allow his music to be coerced, rushed, retarded, deflected, flattered, used, projected or vaunted. It is simply of itself, nothing more nor less.

Other abstract nouns that can be linked to Fauré's personality, and thus to his music, include honesty, sincerity, balance, probity. And one must add patience and resignation, which were his own words to describe qualities he ascribed to himself. How boring these qualities can seem for those hot-blooded romantics who encounter Fauré for the first time, how infinitely moving for those who know how this patience and resignation has seeped into the very fabric of his work, and found its most perfect expression in the songs and chamber music of the third period. The more one reads about Fauré, the more he seems to have been at one with his music, increasingly so, until in the last twenty years of his life his music and his being seem to be of one and the same substance.

The Battle of the Books

Although many practising musicians (among them some of the most distinguished singers) can rarely be persuaded to read biographies of composers, there are countless performers who make it their business to be well informed about 'their' favourites; there is even a certain possessiveness linked with their enthusiasm, as if they had been the first to discover a composer's worth (occasionally this is indeed the case). They are more than able to hold forth about their enthusiasms at a dinner table, if not at a university lectern. When the conversation is about a composer, it almost always turns on personalities rather than musical analysis. A recent example of a great performer's knowledgeable enthusiasm is *Why Handel Waggled his Wig*, an enchanting book of composers' biographies for children by the cellist Steven Isserlis (Fauré is here one of his chosen heroes).[12] Isserlis clearly aims to lead young performers into a fascinated engagement with great musicians' lives, and this, in turn, is meant to make a difference to their music-making at an early stage of their development.

There are many who will dismiss this as a fanciful notion; some musicologists will say that only analysis of the music, probably Schenkerian, can make any difference to a performance. But this is to discount the personal enthusiasm and commitment (often engendered by reading) that powers the work of artists, both great and small. The difference between what interpreters are supposed to read (according to musicologists) and what they actually read is one of the reasons for a famously wide gulf between the worlds of performance and academe.

Of course the most informed composer's biographies are usually by musicologists, but there are musical thinkers who scorn biography, and who regard any concession to extra- musical discussion as an irrelevance. These theoreticians might be compared to distinguished generals in their ivory-tower headquarters, having little understanding of, or interest in, the travails of the common foot soldier (that is, the performer), or the conditions at the front line where battle is a daily routine. In turn, the soldiers find the generals distant and remote figures, and it is regrettable that one rank is seldom in touch with the other. On the whole, the soldier–performer is less logical and more visceral than the tactician–musicologist; he or she is temperamental, more of a fantasist and 'loose cannon'. The power of those inhabiting the ivory tower, though terrifyingly deployed in the internecine warfare of learned journals, is surprisingly limited as far as the men and women in the field are concerned; a mutual lack of respect is surely to blame.

Performers in the recital world have the musical score as their map and guide. But most of these intrepid souls need more than a set of marching orders; they need something that will engage their heart and emotions, something more tailor-made and personal than a diagram by Schenker sent from headquarters, however logical that plan of attack may be. The recalcitrant questions are: 'Why should *I* be involved in this campaign?' 'For what and for whom am I fighting?' 'Why *this* composer and not *that* one?' In this respect every combatant (if a soloist and not an orchestral player) is a one-man band, and is his own man, or her own woman. It goes without saying that the music itself is what demands to be sung and played. But after the *coup de foudre* when the performer falls in love with the score, and decides to sing or play it, to *defend* it (people sometimes forget that composers need ardent, even militant advocacy in order to retain their immortality) there are other composer-related issues that play their part in the programming decisions.

There is no denying that the desire to enlist in a particular composer's cause can be self-centred, a means to an end, a fact of life in an egocentric performing environment; but with many of the greatest artists, electing to perform a piece contains a powerful element of altruistic emotion. In the early days of a performer's career his or her curiosity may be purely musical; with increasing maturity it is likely to be supplemented by a desire to make sense of a bigger picture, and this includes the composer as almost a living part of the process behind the programme planning. It is as if the recitalist were saying: 'I want to know the person behind the music. I have made up my mind that we are friends and everything about him or her fascinates me.' In an early essay on Mahler, Schoenberg wrote:

> Nothing about a great man is irrelevant … In fact, everyone of his acts is in some way revealing, and it would thus have been a great pleasure for me to watch Mahler put on his necktie, for I would as surely have found it more interesting than observing how one of our musical big-wigs compose a 'sacred work'![13]

If the performer is indeed the composer's friend and contemporary (as were Joachim and Brahms, Ysaÿe and Fauré, or Rostropovich and Britten – not to mention the famous Pears–Britten and Bernac–Poulenc duos), the creative personality is there to be observed and learned from in real life. But most performers are not lucky enough to be in the right place at the right time for this kind of interchange, and it is here that biographical study has its place. Analysis of the music's structure has an important part to play, of course, but discussion about the person who wrote the music fulfils a separate, valuable function in terms of stimulating the imagination – it provides a different *frisson* entirely, the kind that encourages singers and players to get inside the skin of their composers. Any knowledge that can lead to this somewhat mysterious – but highly potent – assimilation is valuable, and this information can be biographical, analytical or, ideally, a combination of both.

Deconstruction and Context

There are some who think it useful and revealing to play a piece of music 'blind', ignorant of where it comes from, or how it fits in with the rest of music history. This deliberately ignores the provenance of the human being who has composed it, and the complicated personal background that intersects with the music. Taking a piece entirely on its own terms is fashionable in this age of deconstruction, but such an approach yields bizarre results that would not pass muster on a concert platform, however much they might fascinate a modern aesthetician. It has been claimed that the only meaning a work has is in the mind of its individual reader, viewer or performer, but this is of little help to the music teacher whose task it is to help a student create a musical performance of a composition (by Fauré, for example) that people will pay money to hear. All my own teaching experience confirms that performers, if one assumes their technical ability, achieve a successful realisation of a work in direct relation to their knowledge of, and empathy with, their chosen composer. When uninformed about the context of a piece, the performer is playing in the dark, a place for stumbles rather than revelations. This is glaringly obvious, particularly for those teachers who work with pupils who really do play pieces 'blind' because they have not bothered to do their homework.

In order to play music convincingly we need to discover a context; this was exactly what was lacking for me when I first heard Fauré's music. In most cases a good deal of information will be already in place, particularly for more experienced players. There will be no need to ask, for example, the nationality of the composer, and whether he or she is a historical or contemporary figure. Perhaps we will have played or sung other pieces by the same composer; this is always a help, but in the case of Fauré, with a long career embracing subtly different styles, it is no guarantee of success. Perhaps we already know something of the composer's historical parameters, something about his or her language (both verbal and musical), teachers, friends and colleagues. This is the beginning of a lifelong study. There is a phrase in Fauré's song *Reflets dans l'eau* (from *Mirages*) where the poet imagines herself slipping into the lake; she describes the effect of rings of water, ever broadening, spreading over the surface: 'Un rond fluide … un autre rond … un autre à peine …'; these ever-widening circles exactly mirror a process of investigation where one ripple of interest leads to another, each of them prompting a new discovery that is related to the original research at an ever-increasing distance, and yet still part of the overall picture.

Unknown Ancestry

After a lifetime of collecting it is sometimes difficult for a musical magpie to tell the difference between information that is useful and that which is merely diverting. For example the shadowy figure of Elisabeth Vietz, Franz Schubert's mother, seems irrelevant to the performer at first, but the fact that she was born and brought up in Silesia adds an important Eastern European tinge to the composer's background: the first folksongs and lullabies sung into the ear of the infant Schubert were not Viennese in origin. The fact that she died early in the composer's life adds a poignancy to this musical legacy. If one has ever had to play that composer's *Divertissement à l'hongroise*, or any of the other music by Schubert that seems to herald Dvořák's, there is some resonance in this information, in itself no more than a tiny chip, albeit rather an exotic one, of the Schubertian mosaic.

Discussing Fauré's distant genealogical background, the pianist Marguerite Long wrote that 'some trace of Arab blood must have run in Fauré's veins, and this unknown ancestry showed itself not just in his bronzed complexion but also in his tender eyes which often seemed to catch sight of mirages'.[14] This may explain the many photographs of the composer, who always seems sun-tanned, but for performers about to embark on that exotic evocation *Les Roses d'Ispahan* it is one of those tiny fragments of information that can kick-start the imagination. For those we love, and composers come into this category after all, these snippets are seldom completely inconsequential.

Here is another snippet to know that Fauré's name is the English equivalent of 'Faber' (and thus related to the names Smith and Wright) merely raises a smile as we fancifully connect a great composer's name with an English publishing house. But to realise that the name Fauré (with an accent) is a rare variation of the more common Fabre, Favre or Faure (without an accent – the presence of the *aigu* betokens a regional difference of pronunciation of the normally silent final 'e') can indeed be useful. There was a Felix Faure who was president of the Republic between 1895 and 1899; there was also a composer, Gabriel Fabre, who was a friend of the composer, not to mention a Gabriel Faure (no *aigu*) who wrote a monograph on his friend the composer with almost exactly the same name. A cause of greater confusion was Jean Baptiste Faure (1830–1914), composer of the once-famous song *Les Rameaux* (not to be confused with Fauré's *Le Ramier*), whose more popular songs were attributed to Fauré (and vice versa) for the entire length of both composers' careers. In Charles Van Lerberghe's last book *Lettres à une jeune fille*, the poet wrongly ascribed a song he liked, entitled *Barque d'or*, to Fauré (whom he had never met). This confusion was compounded by the copyist of Van Lerberghe's manuscript, who got himself into a fine mess by confusing Fauré with both Gabriel Fabre and J.B. Faure.

Being aware of these pitfalls has recently spared me the expense of ordering a copy of (Jean-Baptiste) Faure's *Vingt-cinq mélodies*, advertised on the internet as being (Gabriel) Fauré's rare second *recueil* of 1897. The vendor, blind to the lack of a tiny *aigu* accent, had blithely assumed it was by the more famous composer (a hundred years ago the mistake would have been the other way around). In short, we can never know too much about the people whose music we play – even the most peripheral details about them help us to navigate our way through the complicated task of coming to grips with their music, and with *them*.

L'École française

The French are perhaps the most highly schooled musicians in the Western world when it comes to singers and their pianists. Musical education in France is different from that in Germany, the UK or the USA, in all of which countries the State plays a smaller role in regulating and standardising the kind of teaching available and the subjects of the curriculum. In Britain, for example, musical training varies greatly from place to place, with a certain haphazard tailoring to individual needs and talents; in the USA there is a huge difference between the music schools in different states, although it may be fair to say that in terms of vocal evaluation, a great deal is usually forgiven to anyone with a big voice.

In France the voice, whether it belongs to an opera star of the future or to an oboe player, is subjected in its student years to the *solfège* class, a compulsory part of all conservatoire life. This accounts for a high standard of sight-reading and aural training, part of a musical culture where the study of harmony and the inner workings of music is not the sole preserve of academics and theorists.

Fauré spent years travelling up and down the country as an inspector: it was drudgery and it affected the time he had left for composing, but he played his part in ensuring that all the conservatoires in the provincial towns were doing their duty and turning out well-trained students in something of a consistent manner. These were not necessarily great musicians (only a few would be singled out for the great honour of being promoted for further study at the Conservatoire in Paris), but those who passed the requisite examinations could sight-read and sing in time, and they understood the rudiments of harmony instilled in an almost mathematical way. Of course they did not have Fauré's extraordinary musical training, but the best of them were fitted to sing the music that he produced. The beneficiaries of this education had not yet been pampered and coaxed into a position of musical individuality, but they were able to sing or play what was on the printed score. They would not have been presumptuous enough to believe that the addition of their individual emotion to the music as they sang it constituted a priceless gift to a grateful composer. They might even have been perspicacious enough to realise that their emotional contribution might have represented an encumbrance.

The French students in accompaniment and most of the singers the author has encountered in a postgraduate capacity have usually arrived at London's Guildhall School of Music in a very disciplined frame of mind with regard to their work and with a high level of aural training. At this stage of their lives any inherent inclination to a 'star' temperament has been left in abeyance, perhaps to emerge at a later time. Their playing is usually accurate, sometimes polished, but they largely seem to regard self-searching individuality in their work as a kind of irrelevance. This detachment does not go hand in hand with a lack of self-confidence and self-esteem on the personal level; on the contrary. But as young professional musicians they are seldom easily able to cope with the probing demands of German romanticism; indeed, in this respect they are still at the quasi-amateur stage that Fauré, as we will see, found so attractive in those who performed his songs.

Amateur versus Professional

In a letter of November 1902, Fauré wrote to the Comtesse Greffulhe: 'I dream of having you hear them [the three Op. 85 songs] with perfect interpreters, and I know of none among the professionals. It is amateurs who express me and understand me the best.'

This is a fascinating observation. At this stage of his life Fauré preferred to work with singers who were not of the experienced, professional type; perhaps this was because 'hardened' professionals were inclined to resist the simplicity of his requirements – they had ideas of their own that got in the way of what he had written. He was more than willing to work with singers who were unknown, probably second-best if judged in terms of vocal timbre, because they possessed a quality that can only be described as 'unspoiled' in musical terms. (In the composer's time, and in the context of the salon, singers who did not need to work for a living were also likely to have been well educated and cultivated.) Fauré preferred able singers, of good taste and musical background, who were not yet grand and self-regarding. Singers of this kind were thrilled to work on his music, without making him feel that they were doing him a massive favour by doing so. The conflict between amateur singers and the famous professionals is illustrated by an entry in the journal of Marguerite de Saint-Marceaux (amateur singer and dedicatee of *Après un rêve*) for 6 June 1908 – she refers here to Félia Litvinne, one of the most famous opera sopranos of the epoch: 'Litvinne chante du Wagner de cette voix impériale et sans émotion.'[15] Litvinne's quality of voice was indisputable, but her engagement with the material, her vivacity, perhaps even her intelligence, were found wanting by her acutely informed (if not entirely impartial) amateur critic.

The word 'professional' when discussed in this way seems to encompass rather negative qualities such as 'choosy', 'fussy', 'touchy', also 'expensive', 'blasé' and 'spoiled'. The composer clearly had no time for the diva temperament, and he must have come across various opera singers of this kind who were paid to appear in the salons. But Fauré's comment to the Comtesse Greffulhe about amateurs and professionals was made in the early 1900s, when he was not yet director of the Conservatoire, not himself yet a real celebrity. On the other side of this watershed in the composer's life, from 1905 until 1921, Fauré worked with professional singers, indeed with only the very best – Jeanne Raunay, Claire Croiza, Madeleine Grey, Charles Panzéra, all of them more than satisfactory for his purposes. In the last period of his creative life he was working with a new breed of singer, the specialist in song performance, which had evolved with the coming of age of the *mélodie*. It was a tradition that was to continue to flower with the careers of Pierre Bernac, Hugues Cuénod, Camille Maurane and Gérard Souzay among many others.

The amateurs who sang Fauré's music at an earlier stage of his life were interested in his songs simply because they enjoyed singing them; Emma Bardac both loved Fauré's music and profoundly understood it. There is a great deal to be said for this purity of motive, and we cannot blame the composer for feeling far more at home in working with singers of this ilk. But what kind of artist do we require to sing Fauré in the modern age? Should only singers who are not reliant on being paid for their living be encouraged to sing the Fauré song, singers who are 'unspoiled' by success? Has Fauré's music remained the domain of the amateur?

The answer must be no, if only because Fauré's music is on the whole too hard for the present-day amateur. The best Fauré singers of our own time are the minority among the very best, the *crème de la crème* who deeply understand issues of style and rhythm, and have a quiet strength of musical personality that enables them to retain a sense of individuality while obeying the composer's instructions. But it could equally be said that the aspiring Fauré singer of today must learn the obedience and selflessness of the turn-of-the-century amateur. Perhaps the ideal person is the professional who has not lost the passion for music, who is still unashamed by the sense of wonder that characterises the dedicated amateur and who is prepared to surrender to Keats's idea of Negative Capability and place himself or herself at the disposal of Fauré's music.

The critic Émile Vuillermoz knew how important it was for performers of Fauré to be gifted and musically aware:

To love and understand Fauré, it is absolutely necessary to have a musical nature. Fauré is pure music in the strictest, acoustic sense of the word. You don't have to be a musician to love Beethoven and Berlioz. But it's not the same with Fauré. If you cannot feel the physical voluptuousness of certain modulations, if you cannot taste the disturbing poignancy of certain chords, if you are not interested in the subtle laws that govern the grouping of notes around a tonic, a dominant or a leading note, you will understand nothing of the disconcerting style and its apparent simplicity.[16]

The admittedly unusual case of Proust, not musically educated in this detailed way and yet a Fauré connoisseur, disproves an aspect of Vuillermoz's contention. But it is precisely because gifted and informed performers *do* understand the things listed by Vuillermoz that they will seek to give themselves up to this music without reservation. It is love for the music of Fauré that persuades the singer and pianist to do everything necessary to master themselves, and master the style, even if it goes against the 'default setting' of their own natures. I have known talented people with naturally ebullient personalities who happily submit to Fauré and regard it as an honour to do so; they offer themselves to this music in which there is little chance to shine in a conventional way. But they can aspire to reflect the music, which is, after all, a different kind of shining.

Lied versus mélodie

Fauré's music, like the dramas of Racine, is essentially French. Before its deceptive elegance an Anglo-Saxon or a German sometimes feels those moments of impatience and irritation which the music of Brahms or Mahler tends to provoke in a Frenchman.[17]
Nadia Boulanger

The teaching of singing in France, and the efficacy of its results, are too variable for unqualified praise. It might be argued that rational rigidity does not encourage the flowering of poetic feeling; it does not occur to young French musicians to emote about music in the same way as the Germans, or even the British. The whole question of French vs. German musical sensibility is touched on by Romain Rolland in his novel *Jean-Christophe* (ten volumes, completed in 1912). The eponymous hero, Jean-Christophe Krafft, is a young German composer, but his tastes and emotions are inevitably controlled by his French creator, and by the character's eventual adoption of Paris as his home. The novel was written at exactly the time when the whole currency of German song (once the preserve of geniuses such as Schubert, Schumann and Wolf) had fallen into the hands of the late romantics (Pfitzner and Reger come to mind), who were attempting to keep alive a tradition that was already doomed (*pace* Richard Strauss's durability) by Schoenberg's experiments in atonality.

Jean-Christophe was passing through that crisis of healthy disgust. His instinct was impelling him to eliminate from his life all the undigested elements which encumbered it.
First of all to go was the sickening sweet tenderness which sucked away the soul of Germany like a damp and mouldy river-bed … . A rough dry wind should sweep away the miasmas of the swamp, the musty staleness of the *Lieder, Liedchen, Liedlein*, as numerous as the drops of rain in which inexhaustibly the Germanic *Gemüt* is poured forth … the whole deluge of stale tenderness, stale emotion, stale melancholy, stale poetry … . A habit of undressing their hearts in public, a fond and foolish propensity of the honest people of Germany for plunging loudly into confidences. Would their chatter never cease? – one might as well bid frogs in the pond be silent.[18]

In time it is likely that it will be increasingly difficult to ascribe a national style to French singers, or British or German, come to that. But the parameters of the French style are still to be heard in the young artists who are educated in France – a way of thinking about music that remains a national characteristic, an objectivity that is at the heart of French painting and literature, at the heart, indeed, of the *esprit français*.

As Europe becomes more of an entity this will no doubt change with the years, but it remains true that France has provided the world with remarkably few great interpreters of the German lieder repertoire. And until recently there were few German singers who, when performing *mélodies*, were capable of reining in their interpretative faculties to avoid the drowning of the spirit of French song.

Fauré's gift for word-setting is a very particular one. He is far less interested in the 'tonal analogue' – the matching of a specific tonal illustration to a verbal image – than Schubert, Schumann and Wolf, who respond to words with the speed of litmus. This kind of illustrative element is to be found in Fauré's songs from time to time, but it occurs far less often than in the lied. As we listen to his songs, or as we perform them, we are far less aware of words and verbal ideas finding an apt musical 'translation' into tone – the kind of 'cleverness' in word-setting that seems almost uncanny in the greatest Germans and Austrians, or in a composer like Britten. Instead, Fauré selects the poem as a whole (or with careful internal cuts), and responds to it as a whole in musical terms (Brahms was also capable of this; his genius encompassed both the general and particular approaches to song composition). In Fauré's songs, dramatic story-telling is not his forte; he is no balladeer, and as Jankélévitch points out 'Fauré made no speciality of the picturesque'.[19] Because the songs were composed as entities, it follows that they must be performed as entities, and interpretations that find an excuse to chop them up into different sections must be avoided.

I have heard one or two German performers of the older generation lavish on Fauré (or Debussy or Poulenc) what they clearly regarded as the incalculable benefit of their poetic perceptions; words and phrases were moulded and caressed, highlighted in a manner that was knowingly arch, but this was no triumphal arch – the results were gruesome (the younger generation of German singers is, thankfully, infinitely more flexible and aware). A positive advantage for British artists is that their own song culture (of the voice and piano variety) is a shyer and younger art than the song traditions of either Germany or France; the British are France's neighbours, and Germany's cousins, and in their schools, academies and colleges the two repertoires are treated with equal seriousness. With the right guidance there is a good chance of someone born into neither the French nor German traditions mastering the differences between them, and according to each the separate respect it deserves. The same applies to American singers, who have a well-deserved reputation in the singing of French music, but whose natural ebullience and tendency to dramatise on the platform – an underestimation of the extent to which emotion has to be controlled by form – has sometimes to be moderated by the salutary pouring of cold water on over-heated enthusiasm.

Before attempting to plumb the metaphorical depths of interpretation, that problematic word, the performer must first deal with practical matters: the tempo of the song has to be ascertained and adhered to as the primary tool of interpretation. There is no area in the entire repertoire where this task is more crucial than in the *mélodies* of Fauré, and almost no group of songs where the tiniest variations of speed can make as much difference. With some exceptions, the songs of the German composers can encompass more variety of tempo within a single workable framework than the French.

In a German lied, the performers can often subtly surge forward and pull back; in different sections of the song the meaning of the words is moulded to subtle differentiations of pulse. (This is more true of Brahms, for example, than of the classically influenced Schubert – there are obviously many stylistic variations within the lied.) Many a German song seems to be clearly divisible into sections; practised performers can give the impression of having invented the music on the spot, confronting each new set of images and emotions in the poetry with a response that can easily involve a tiny quickening of the tempo or a relaxation of tension. These may be all but imperceptible to the casual listener, but the weighing-out of tiny differentiations of this kind is what gives music of this kind its life and colour. This creative steering through a song is not only allowed in lieder performance, but is required; indeed, it is a sign of the sensitivity and imagination of both singer and pianist that they give the music a shape and direction. Such flexibility is part of the fabric of the music – it is more subtle than the overused word 'rubato' can encompass.

Lieder performers generally have this kind of hands-on relationship with their songs – they are the sounding boards for the composer's emotions, but their own emotions are also part of the picture. The song and its poem are filtered through the performers' personalities and their view of the world. The singer carries the vocal line and the words, but the pianist is always there to advise and abet, to comment and underline, to propel and restrain, and all the other things of which a creative accompanist is capable.

It is possible for a duo of singer and pianist to make their way into a German lied, to have a look around, establish their presence, and carry the day by the end of the song.

Gabriel Fauré, engraved by Georges Aubert, after Reutlinger. From La Revue musicale *(October 1922). © Bibliothèque nationale de France*

The audience is aware of a progress that has involved entering the house and taking stock, opening and shutting doors, making a decision as to whether or not to climb the stairs, and so on, before progressing to clinch the performance in musical terms, and garner the applause from the top-floor balcony. I do not refer here only to the kind of German songs that tell a story; most lieder are constructed in such a way that there are various points during the song where the performers can allow themselves to pause and survey the work already done, the work that there is yet to do. Compare this with Louis Aubert's analysis of Fauré's perfection of style, a quality he refers to as 'hermetic': 'Fauré 'seldom allows the listener to take a breath. He offers him [the listener] no concessions. There are none of those landings that would ordinarily dispel fatigue and allow the listener to relax.'[20]

In lieder performance, allowing the audience to relax at the same time as being in control of one's material (bending it, if possible, to fuse with one's own ideas and feelings) is a delight. And it *is* possible to do so without damaging the composer's integrity, without making Brahms sound like Schubert or vice versa. On the contrary, this kind of involved advocacy shines the spotlight ever stronger on the lieder composer, whose work hugely benefits from emerging through lips, eyes, fingers and bodies of performers of schooled cultivation, good judgement and emotional openness. The excitement of discovery (and there is a great deal to discover about oneself in the process), combined with an interpretative freedom that enriches one's life, becomes truly addictive, and all this without the interference of a conductor. I have often reflected on the reasons why busy opera singers are so delighted to spend an evening on the recital platform: less well paid, less well attended, but vital to their musical happiness and their sense of musical independence.

Clearly singers of Fauré, and of French music in general, feel a similar kind of happiness achieved in a totally different way. The passage from Louis Aubert quoted above makes it clear that it is a disaster if the French repertoire, and Fauré in particular, is approached in the Germanic way with all those lieder-singing faculties aching to lay siege to the music of another, less co-operative, culture. The singer and pianist who approach Fauré have to start again and learn a new language – in the sense that French is not only a different language from German, but a different language of thought and behaviour. There are also those who find the French manner much more natural, and who have to learn to be more openly expressive in the German. I have often encountered young pianists who seem content accompanying *mélodies* but who are not committed enough, deep enough, opinionated enough to be successful with lieder. Students like this are bewildered by the suggestion that they need to experience more, feel more, that they need to explore their emotions. But they do bring to French song accompaniments their obedient and well-prepared fingers, their well-ordered minds, and a capacity to serve, provided the spotlight is not turned embarrassingly on them. This is certainly not enough to make them great accompanists of French vocal music, but it is indicative of the very different mind-set that this repertoire requires as a minimum requirement.

It may be the Germans who have a reputation for authoritarianism, but in reality there can be nothing more dictatorial than a French composer. And in terms of teaching, was anyone in Germany ever more terrifying than the quiet authority of Fauré's own pupil Nadia Boulanger? If there was a tyranny here, it did not include a requirement for students to emote, to feel, to indulge in introspection. The emphasis was on clear thinking and correctness; the head is schooled remorselessly, and the heart is left to take care of itself. The heart exists, of course, but it is not normally the business of music teachers to interfere with it.

Sentiment, Sentimentality and 'the Voice'

The essence of sentimentality seems to me to lie in the derivation of a specific pleasure from the contemplation of feelings – one's own or another's – regarded as a primary material of artistic satisfaction, independently of the object or the occasion that has produced them … . Sentimental music is that which concentrates on the 'rendering' of a state of emotional excitement, so it will invite the collaboration of emotional inflexions and illustrative action in performance. The majority of our Lieder rather imply such an invitation, and most of our celebrated Lieder singers are only too well aware of the fact; but a Fauré mélodie would be ruined by treatment on such lines.[21]
Norman Suckling

These words state once again the most important point that this chapter can make: when singing or playing Fauré's *mélodies*, artists have to suppress their desire to stamp a piece of music with their own personality; they must be prepared to deliver the music that comes from the composer, and goes to the listener, almost without the intervention of the middle-man. As we shall discuss later, this does not mean a robotic and unfeeling performance, but it does mean the cultivation of an entirely different mind-set from the one that is more familiar and, let us be honest, more immediately rewarding. Singers have something individual about themselves by the very nature of opening their mouths – their timbre, the sound that is theirs alone and that is immediately identifiable for all of those with sharp ears. Nothing can take the colour of a singer's voice away, nor the feelings expressed through the sounds ranging from delight to heartbreak. But it is both remarkable and regrettable how accustomed singers have become to expressing themselves through displacements of the rhythm, and rubato in general, and how difficult it is for them to preserve their sonic individuality while remaining true to the composer's rhythmic requirements.

The biggest enemy of the Fauré songs is the 'Me-Me' singer (who is to be heard voicing his personal priorities – 'Mimi!' – in the outburst of emotion at the end of *La Bohème*, but who can be of either sex of course). Such a singer does not ask what he or she can do for a song, but rather what a song can do for him or her – it is merely something to use, *matériel*, a property for the advancement of a career, and the composer is a kind of lackey who provides the means for a living. Such singers frequently refer to 'The Voice' as a separate entity with a life and mind of its own, a minotaur to which bleeding scraps of music have to be thrown from time to time in order to keep the avaricious monster pacified. With the exception of *Après un rêve* and the occasional *Fleur jetée*, there is very little in Fauré's *mélodies* to be of interest to this kind of self-centred singer.

A more well-meaning kind of enemy, but rather more insidious than the 'Me-Me', is the 'Boo-Hoo' diva (again this can be of either sex). Such singers find many of the songs *gorgeous*, and they feel they want to *share* the songs with an audience. It is all very well for a singer to be moved by a song when listening to someone else performing it, but this is the kind of performer who, in singing to the public, cannot help imagining how moving it must be to be seated in the midst of the audience. Such singers co-opt the roles of both performer and listener, and incorporate the public's (imagined) deeply moved reaction into the emotional onslaught of their own interpretations. They frequently leave the stage in floods of tears while those in the hall remain mysteriously dry-eyed. Singers of this kind, often kind and sincere people, have little idea of how this appropriation of both roles on either side of the footlights comes across as a self-regard that destroys the music they are attempting to champion. Performances of this kind will almost certainly have been too loud, and liberties will almost inevitably have been taken with the rhythm in the interests of so-called expressivity.

It is fortunate that accomplished singers are very seldom lost causes, even if they incline to self-indulgence. Fauré's style can be learned, and that is what teachers and coaches are for. And, after all, it is always necessary to sing with a certain awareness of self-worth; it is simply a question of ensuring that healthy confidence does not slide into vanity. A singer may have a strong opinion of how music should sound and how it should 'go' – it is just that this opinion must not be formed from personal caprice alone. The composer's wishes are laid down in a score that will be full of detailed requirements and directions. As for the poem, although the singer has every right to register a reaction to it as a work of art in its own right, it is the *composer's* response to the poem that has to be the lynch-pin of the conception in performance. (Singers who delve into the background of poetry often forget this.) It is the singer's task to marry word and tone in as close a way as possible to what the composer intended.

Seeing the Wood, not the Trees

(Fauré's) music makes the poem its environment, drinks up all its syllables, impregnates them to the point of silence – and has no need to spell them out note for note and word by word; and as a result fragments of music do not at all correspond to fragments of poetry.
Vladimir Jankélévitch[22]

An analysis of Fauré's output shows it to be one long essay on the principle of continuity ... One has to try ... to capture the overall meaning and the general atmosphere of the poem, and not to be seduced momentarily by details or attach too much importance to them.
Jean-Michel Nectoux[23]

Let us imagine we have been invited to perform that great Fauré song, *Dans la forêt de septembre* (see p. 277). The text by Catulle Mendès describes a forest in autumn with certain resonances for the composer in the autumn of his own life. Fauré's music is in 'madrigal' style with touches of modal harmony, which suggests the courtly self-effacement of the sixteenth century. He has not invited the performers to go into a wood in order to make an inventory of the trees, and this despite the details in the poem that single out fir tree and birch; he is not interested in an emotive commentary on their beauty, or our reactions to the melancholy metaphors of autumn. He has conjured an entire forest, and we must accept his word for it. He allows us a bird's-eye view; there is no time allowed for leisurely contemplation and the taking of fascinating side-paths. The overall configuration of a much broader vista is Fauré's concern. It is not for us, the performers on the ground, to improvise our route through the forest: indeed, we have to follow the composer's directions and rise above the tree line so that we can see the horizon. We have to encompass this Fauré song as a totality, and in a way in which we do not need to encompass a lied; we have to see the end of it as we begin, as if the whole were part of a continuous loop. And at the end of our explorations we have arrived where we started (as T.S. Eliot put it).

If we were to descend to the level of the forest itself we would be lost in a subjective *Waldeinsamkeit* – essentially the subject (and title, with sundry variations) of many famous German lieder to many different texts. And we would be in danger of getting stuck in the mud – for Romain Rolland's thoughts on this matter in the novel *Jean-Christophe* see p. 384. When we are performing *Dans la forêt de septembre*, we sing of the musical homogeneity of the forest, rather than of its constituent parts. The words must be perfectly enunciated rather than delivered in a meaningful or sentimental manner, and the music unfolds within a strict time-frame laid down by the composer. The sense of accomplishment felt at the end of the journey is in having left behind a perfect musical shape, undisturbed by a backward glance during the journey itself – like an aeroplane leaving behind an elegantly traced figure that is smoke-suspended in the skies. Only once the intrepid acrobatic manoeuvre is completed (Orpheus failed in his rescue mission because he looked back prematurely at Eurydice) can the totality of the pattern be appreciated – by the pilot or anyone else – by which time the aeroplane is already far away. I have often had to wait for the end of a Fauré song, some time after the reverberation of the final chord, to have any idea as to whether or not any sign or sound of a meaningful performance lingers in the air.

The Composer is Always Right

French music seems to require submission on the part of its performers, a yielding to a higher power. In my youth, when I accompanied Elisabeth Schwarzkopf for a few concerts, I was schooled for a very memorable week by her and her husband Walter Legge. His merciless, but highly perspicacious, coaching sessions were based on the premise that 'the composer is always right', something particularly relevant to Legge's passionate partiality for the lieder of Hugo Wolf. Fauré has no resemblance to Wolf except that they both wrote exactly what they wanted on the page – no more, no less – and that they both require obedience from their performers. Composers of this kind seem to say: 'I require the singer's voice and timbre, the pianist's hands and feet, but I am in control of this song in all other respects.' Legge liked to coach the songs of Wolf's *Italienisches Liederbuch* with a cigar in one hand and a metronome in the other. Working with Wolf's metronome markings I learned a valuable lesson: they are not to be obeyed simply because the composer has inscribed these at the head of each song; the truth is that the songs actually sound better when they are sung and played at exactly the tempi Wolf laid down for them, and when all his dynamic and articulation markings are rigorously observed.

In Fauré's case it is the idea of working with a metronome that is even more important than the individual markings themselves. In a letter of 1888 he once wrote of himself (ironically) as someone 'devoid of common sense when it comes to deciding on a speed'.[24] Nevertheless, it follows that once a speed has been settled on, the music should be subject to tight control.

The Pitiless Beat

Fauré was a walking metronome … . Above all it is slowing him down that distorts him, Fauré had a drive that bore no relation either to expression or shading.
Claire Croiza

It was the soprano who created *Le Jardin clos* and who was a great Pénélope, who spoke these words – they were taken down verbatim from masterclasses given in the 1930s.[25] In teaching the song *Clair de lune* Croiza observed: 'Fauré must be practised with the metronome: it is what he would have wanted – an absolute fidelity to the indicated marking. Work on the words by saying them in time, without singing them. Only sing them later.'[26] And then during a session on *Les Berceaux*:

In our modern French music what is needed is a pitiless beat with a rhythm that never changes. In foreign music, in Schumann, in Schubert, in Brahms, there is rubato. In French music one must sing to the metronome and never change anything further. Debussy, Duparc, the same thing with a few little rallentandi. Nevertheless Duparc said to me one day 'If I had known what singers would make of them, I would never have put in these rallentandi'. As a result of singing this modern French music I would no longer be able to sing with rubato. I would not be able to sing Brahms.'

Croiza is no doubt referring here to the tiny rallentandos indicated at expressive moments, and almost always exaggerated, in Duparc songs such as *Chanson triste* and *L'Invitation au voyage*.

She expanded on the theme of fidelity to the composer's markings while teaching Fauré's *Chanson de pêcheur*:

Claire Croiza (1882–1946)

390

Accents are not to be put where the composer did not mark them. The modern French masters, coming after an epoch where everything had been permitted to interpreters have, as a reaction, become distrustful of the interpretation of singers. They have indicated all that should be done: nuance, tempo, time signature, it is not permitted to deviate from what has been written ... . The interpreter is there to serve the musician as he wishes to be served.[27]

The violinist Hélène Jourdan-Morhange remembers an incident when the composer accompanied her in his *Berceuse*; on the same programme there was a group of *mélodies*:

The poor singer! She was used to stretching the cadences and dying with ease at the ends of phrases. She was horrified to be pulled by the piano down an unbending road ... the motorway of the future [*l'auto-strade futur*]. And Fauré, furious with this self-indulgent interpreter left the piano running, took his hat and disappeared on to the street without even having bowed to the public at the side of the mortified woman.[28]

      ∽   ∽   ∽   ∽

A word must be written about a pianist practising with the metronome – something which every student of Fauré is well advised to do. Anyone can demonstrate the potential tyranny of the metronome, its destructive side, by playing in a stilted and mechanical way as the machine ticks on imperiously. This can all too easily demonstrate that metronome work is an arid exercise. There is, however, a way of playing with the metronome which concentrates on beautifying everything within the player's control that is *not* to do with the tempo – the actual sound produced on the piano, and its expressivity within a context *not* influenced by rubato or interfering with the rhythm, the articulation of the phrase – whether legato, staccato, or mezzo-staccato – as marked by Fauré – and the control of dynamics, also as marked by the composer. Practising with a metronome does more than highlight where the danger spots are in terms of a performer dragging, or hurrying, the beat. It is also the best possible exercise for a musician to make something convincingly musical out of a phrase where only the tempo is governed by the tick-tock of the metronome, and where everything else remains within the creative control of the performer. If people find playing, or singing, with the metronome impossibly constricting, it is a sign that their entire expressive apparatus is geared to rhythmic displacement, something that can all too easily turn into an involuntary habit.

In the final stages of song preparation, it goes without saying that the metronome will be put to one side in favour of the inner metronome of the artists, both singer and pianist, something that will have been gradually developed, deep in the body and mind.

Expressiveness in music-making has so often been connected (in the German tradition above all) with displacement of the rhythm through rubati that it is nothing less than a revelation to realise how much the artists are in control of the music from *other* angles when they surrender the control of rhythm to the implacable will of the composer.

Once the tempo for a song has been found, it is necessary, except where specifically bidden by Fauré to do something different, to keep this tempo to the end; one must not slow down except where asked to do so. But it must be remembered that this is not an exercise in rigid inflexibility. Once we have understood this principle, the rule is to be administered with humanity and imagination. Singers have to breathe (and one singer's breath control will always differ from another's), and music must sound like music, not like the whirrings of an automaton. Words, and their intelligibility, will always be a benchmark for a final decision regarding tempo. Those tiny, almost imperceptible hesitations on the bar line that register a modulation or a musical change of direction (or even an emphasised consonant) will still be there, but in homoeopathic quantities; the inflections will be far smaller and more subtle than in the case of German music – almost, but not quite, imperceptible. And there is a kind of rubato within the pronunciation of a word that is practised by some French singers (I think here, in my own experience as an accompanist, of the incomparable Hugues Cuenod) where the fluidity of the rhythm of the *music* is somehow unimpaired by a freedom within the *words*. I have never encountered an English-speaking singer able to do this in the same way as those who are born to the French tradition.

The aim is not to produce a performance that is self-consciously cold and reserved, denuded of emotion and feeling. The almost mechanical and hieratic detachment of the Stravinsky neo-classical school is not our model; a self-consciously clockwork mechanism is *not* required in the performance of the Fauré songs. They eschew sentimentality, but they require humanity and a sensual response to life, and there is a great deal of scope for sensibility and feeling within the confines of their form. The pages of this book have attempted to show that Fauré was as fully human as the rest of us, with a number of human failings; it is a mistake to sing his music as if he were saint-like – this is a standard fault among certain performers, who can drain his music of emotion and passion in the interests of an anodyne authenticity that can seem almost 'holy'. It should not be forgotten that Fauré himself once remarked that 'Art has every reason to be voluptuous.' But when quoting that phrase, itself a quote from Saint-Évremond, Nadia Boulanger reminded us in effect that we should not necessarily ascribe to this powerful word 'voluptuous' the slightly decadent overtones that might suggest licence. Thus, after confirming the voluptuousness of Fauré's art, she continued: 'Here was his glory: to have discovered new sound-forms which set free our hearts and our senses, and do not debase them.' Boulanger also described Fauré as being someone who 'was guided by his feelings themselves to set reason on his altar'. By this I think she meant to underline the paradox that it was the subtlety of Fauré's emotional responses that guided him to suppress those same emotions in favour of 'reason' – rational and controlled musical behaviour. In later life Boulanger also put forward the fascinating idea that for composers there are two ways of being national: by thought and by costume. 'With Fauré it is by thought – thought so profound and passionate on the one hand, so detached and chaste on the other. It reminds me of Socrates … .'[29] We should remember that Socrates yearned for the famously beautiful Alcibiades, but when offered the opportunity (as recounted in Plato's *Symposium*) he refused to go to bed with him. Any portrait of Socrates, and of Fauré, would have to include both his propensity to passion as well as his supreme ability to control it.

All performers of Fauré's music must play their part in this refusal to be instrumental in the debasement of the senses; they must guide their feelings with reason, they must be willing to contain feelings with form. The struggle to do this is a noble one, and all the more noble (because more difficult) if one's own temperament inclines to an overflow of emotion that is the result of contact with beautiful music. The struggle to master ourselves contributes powerfully to the sense of elation that performers experience in the wake of a successful performance of a Fauré song. I have played music by hundreds of composers in my career, but among the various subjective emotions aroused on the concert platform there is nothing quite like this feeling.

If the author were asked to describe in few words the state of mind that we should find ourselves in when performing this music, I would name that condition of 'complete simplicity' (T.S. Eliot

Nadia Boulanger (1887–1979)

again). And the cost for the present-day performer is the same as it was for Eliot, as it was for Fauré himself – 'not less than everything'. This exacting cost ('not less than everything') is of course payable for music other than by Fauré; it is payable in subtly different ways by a performer in his or her every confrontation with a masterpiece. It is salutary to remind ourselves at the end of this chapter that whatever the differences in performing practice, Fauré belongs as of right to the jewelled heritage of European civilisation that includes the music of many other great composers.

Or does he? Fauré is not excluded by anyone else, but he sometimes seems to exclude himself by posthumous decree. It is as if he continues to insist on the ambiguity of his position, a reticence that places it at one remove, *à côté*, optional. He was ever the outsider and so he remains, by choice and inclination; the reader is referred to the thoughts concerning Fauré's childhood at the close of Chapter 1. There was a side of him, the secretive and solitary young dreamer from the Ariège, that would prefer to stand deferentially to one side, even at the risk of marginalisation, rather than be counted among the front-runners jostling immodestly for a place in immortality. We know, however, that his position in the grown-up world of great composers is assured, and in his heart of hearts he knew it too.

1   Gabriel Fauré in a letter to Theodore Dubois, 5 September 1896.

2   Interesting the young musician in the biographical aspects of Fauré's life is a priority for a performer like Steven Isserlis; see the reference to his writing later in this chapter.

3   Marguerite Long, *At the Piano with Fauré*, trans. Oliver Senior-Ellis (London: Kahn & Averil, 1981), p. 65.

4   Letter to Benjamin Bailey, 22 November 1817, *The Letters of John Keats 1814–1821* (Volume 1), ed. Hyder Edward Rollins, Cambridge University Press, 1958, p. 186.

5   Letter to Marie Fauré, 27 October 1900, in Gabriel Fauré, *Letters intimes*, ed. Philippe Fauré-Fremiet (Paris: La Colombe, 1951), p. 55.

6   Carlo Caballero, *Fauré and French Musical Aesthetics* (Cambridge: Cambridge University Press, 2001), p. 1.

7   Quoted in Robert Orledge, *Gabriel Fauré* (London: Eulenburg, 1979), p. 42.

8   Quoted in *Gabriel Fauré: A Life in Letters*, trans. and ed. Barrie Jones (London: B.T. Batsford, 1989), letter 75, p. 86.

9   Quoted in Caballero, *Fauré and French Musical Aesthetics*, p. 17.

10 Jean-Michel Nectoux, *Gabriel Fauré: A Musical Life* (Cambridge: Cambridge University Press, 1991), p. 178.

11 *Gabriel Fauré: His Life through his Letters*, ed. Jean-Michel Nectoux, trans. Underwood (London and New York: Marion Boyars, 1984), letter 64, p. 135.

12 Steven Isserlis, *Why Handel Waggled his Wig* (London: Faber, 2006).

13 From Arnold Schoenberg, *Style and Idea* (London: Williams & Norgate, 1950), p. 26.

14 Long, *At the Piano with Fauré*, p. 18.

15 Myriam Chimènes, *Mécènes et musiciens* (Paris: Fayard, 2004), p. 451, footnote.

16 Quoted in Long, *At the Piano with Fauré*, p. 11.

17 Quoted in a lecture given at the Rice Institute in 1925 by Nadia Boulanger, transcribed in Don G. Campbell, *Master Teacher – Nadia Boulanger* (Washington DC: The Pastoral Press, 1984), p. 106.

18 Romain Rolland: *Jean-Christophe* Part IV ('Revolt') translated by Gilbert Cannan, Heinemann, London Melbourne, Toronto 1961. Volume 2 of the English edition (*Storm and Stress*) pp. 172–3.

19 Vladimir Jankélévitch, *Music and the Ineffable*, trans. Caroline Abbate (Princeton, NJ: Princeton University Press, 2003), p. 75.

20 Quoted in Caballero, *Fauré and French Musical Aesthetics*, p. 9.

21 Norman Suckling, *Fauré* (London: Dent, 1946), p. 46.

22 Jankélévitch, *Music and the Ineffable*, p. 53.

23 Nectoux, *Gabriel Fauré: A Musical Life*, pp. 242 and 363.

24 Gabriel Fauré, *Correspondance*, ed. Jean-Michel Nectoux (Paris: Flammarion, 1980), letter 72.

25 Hélène Abraham, *Un art de l'interpretation: Claire Croiza – Les cahiers d'une auditrice* (Paris: Ars Musicae, 1954), p. 15 (masterclass on 3 June 1924). The English translation of these 'cahiers' is *The Singer as Interpreter: Claire Croiza's Master Classes*, ed. and trans. Betty Bannerman (London: Victor Gollancz, 1989).

26 Abraham, *Un art de l'interpretation*, pp. 35–6 (masterclass on 23 April 1931).

27 Ibid., p. 46 (masterclass on 18 June 1931).

28 Hélène Jourdan-Morhange, *Mes amis musiciens* (Paris: Les Éditeurs Français Réunis, 1955). p. 23.

29 Bruno Monsaingeon, *Mademoiselle: Conversations with Nadia Boulanger* (Manchester: Carcanet, 1985), p. 26.

Chapter Sixteen

The Pianist's Workshop (wherein Singers are Always Welcome)

Fauré as a Pianist

What was so overpowering about his playing lay below the surface, in the areas of thought and emotion where teaching is helpless to guide you.
Philippe Fauré-Fremiet[1]

As a pupil of Niedermeyer and Saint-Saëns, Fauré the pianist had more in common with Ignaz Moscheles and Camille Stamaty (teacher of Saint-Saëns, and himself a pupil of Kalkbrenner) than with Chopin and Liszt, with their insistence on flexible wrists and arm weight. Fauré had been schooled in Bach's *48 Preludes and Fugues* and his inventions, and he continued to be a sought-after, if unwilling, piano teacher until about 1900. He had, by all accounts, small, strong hands and short fingers. One of his protégés admired his rounded sonority, and described his striking of the keys as 'heavy, but at the same time supple, which gave his playing that precise accentuation and wonderfully tender strength his music needs'.[2] The same pianist said that the two sayings that Fauré was most fond of when he was coaching young pianists were 'Nuances without changing the speed' and 'Let's hear the bass!' He came out with these words of wisdom 'every ten minutes or so'. The composer confessed to the singer Emilie Girette in 1902 that many professional pianists had failed to come to terms with the playing he required. This is all the more remarkable in that, by this time, Fauré's piano music had been taken up by such big names as Alfred Cortot, Edouard Risler (Girette's husband-to-be, in fact), Ricardo Viñes and Raoul Pugno.

According to the composer's son Philippe Fauré-Fremiet, he kept his hands close to the keys and hardly raised them in performance, having a 'horror of virtuosity, of rubato and effects aimed at making the music swoon'[3] This tendency to keep close to the keys may have been fostered by years of careful legato fingering on organ manuals; the organ was an instrument that Fauré was not fond of – he had to play it professionally – but staying close to the keys at the piano also emphasised an aspect of non-showiness in his playing. The pianist and composer Stephen Hough makes the observation that 'Fauré's time at the organ was an additional influence on his harmony – the physical need for fingers to cling to keys for legato, and for feet on the narrow Cavaillé-Coll pedalboards to slither and shuffle rather than dart'[4]. From his organ teacher at the École Niedermeyer, Clément Loret, Fauré acquired the habit of changing his fingers on the same piano key when he moved carefully from one note to the next. This suggests the attentive care of the accompanist rather than the nervous energy of the soloist, and in time Fauré's playing became very different from that of his mentor Saint-Saëns. It was inevitable that other pianists of the time, particularly those who played the romantic piano repertoire, should have found Fauré's performances of his own music 'cold'. This was the opinion of Louis Diémer (1843–1919), a pianist-composer disinclined to over-expressiveness, whereas Marguerite Long said that Fauré's playing lacked the brilliance that she alone, naturally, brought to his works.[5]

Long patronises Fauré at the same time as attempting to own him, but the most damning comments about the composer's pianism come from that brilliant but quixotic pianist, Alfred Cortot. Cortot played many of Fauré's works, including several first premières, but as the dedicatee of the piano *Fantaisie*, Op. 111, he seldom programmed the work, much to the composer's bitter disappointment. Fauré wrote Cortot a stinging letter, which Cortot probably never forgave. In an interview with Bernard Gavoty in 1955 he said that Fauré's 'dry' playing was at odds with his sensitivity as a poetic spirit: 'his playing was percussive, without much body to it, and he never used the pedals'. He went on to talk of the composer's 'inflexible style', blaming the regimentation of the École Niedermeyer.[6]

Cortot has given us a great deal to think about. As the reader will note, I often question how much pedal is appropriate in a Fauré accompaniment. It is no surprise that Fauré did not favour a piano texture that was swimming in pedal. This would have been an affront to the clarity of texture that was his ideal. As for his insistence on the clarity of the bass (again, a subject raised in the notes below), it is helpful to be reminded by J.-M. Nectoux that the composer was ambidextrous and that many a passage he wrote (as the song accompanist will discover in *La Bonne chanson*, for example) was devilishly difficult as a result of this facility.[7] Lastly, when damning the style of Fauré's piano playing as 'archaic', Cortot might not have been amused to realise that his own performing style would one day be branded as such in turn. It must be admitted, however, that Fauré tended to be something of a 'speed merchant' when it came to performing his own works. Adrian Boult was amazed to discover that the famous *Pavane*, performed so languidly on many occasions, was played by the composer himself at a tempo not less than ♩ = 100. This music was adopted some years ago as a theme tune for the World Cup, but a tempo such as this, while matching something of the impetus of the football pitch, would have rather diminished the grandeur of the overall event.

The Conductor and the Accompanist

Metronome markings are always controversial. Many musicians have been brought up to disregard them as pedantic and useless. In reality, they are among the few things that can instantly connect us the wishes of a long-dead composer. I sometimes ask my accompaniment students to tell me who they think are the best-paid of all musicians. The immediate response (perhaps tinged with understandable envy) is usually 'singers', but after a while they come back with the correct answer: 'conductors'. It is conductors who have to determine ensemble and correct balance in an orchestra, but their most important work remains the setting of tempi, the choosing of a pulse for which they alone must bear responsibility, and which will have an incalculable effect on the music in hand. Without this fine-tuning in terms of tempo, an entire orchestral work would be heard as a generality, something that may as well be conducted by anyone, or no one.

Conductors do not have to play the notes as instrumentalists do; hapless members of the orchestra practise frantically, sometimes until the last moment, when their lord and master will sweep on to the stage, baton in hand. For a conductor, all music, as far as practical performance is concerned, is in C major: a flick of the wrist, and the most difficult passages bristling with accidentals appear as if by magic. Unless they are faced with a concerto soloist, conductors do not even have to follow and listen to others – they set the agenda. But they have to launch a piece (as do accompanists with almost every song they play) at *exactly* the right tempo to release the full power and effect of the music. If this is not the case, what is the point of having a highly paid conductor at all? (It is well known that the ensemble of most orchestras can be held together by their leaders.) Renowned conductors are famous for their skilful judgement of minute differences of pulse. They realise that a few calibrations on the metronome, one way or the other, can make a huge difference to an entire world of musical feeling.

Song pianists need to be reminded of this fact when it comes to a minute discussion of tempo differences. For some reason it is insufficiently realised that the accompanist must face exactly the same responsibility as a conductor on a daily basis, but on a smaller scale of course, and for a fraction of the financial reward. Of course the tempo will have been arrived at by discussion and rehearsal with the singer, but when it comes to the battle conditions of performance, the establishment of that tempo lies almost always entirely in the pianist's hands – unless, as occasionally happens, open warfare breaks out between the performers, and the singer embarks on a different tempo from the one given in the introduction.

A Modest Metronome Disclaimer

The Fauré metronome markings are an important part of the composer's legacy, but a performer has the right to make a careful and informed decision as to whether or not to obey them. Everyone has a different singing voice, and a different breathing capacity; in the real world students will wish to sing many a song before they are able completely to master its length of phrase, and its demands for poise. Fauré's is very 'grown-up' music, and it is very rare for younger people to be able to master all its demands, both technical and spiritual.

This composer would have been horrified by the concept of a dictatorship by metronome: the marking is always a suggestion rather than a ukase. In the performance notes below I have occasionally given reasons for preferring other markings than those given by Fauré himself; and it goes without saying that the suggestions I make below with regard to tempi should be treated only as suggestions. Singers and pianists must be able to respond subjectively to the mood of a poem, and to attempt to relate it to the setting in hand; if this were not the case, there would be no need for performers, nor for the unique package of humanity and understanding that is each musician.

The above remarks of a liberal disposition are followed by a less liberal warning. In this music it is completely unacceptable for the performers not to have done their utmost to make Fauré's markings work before deciding to differ and plan their own route. When I hear an unconvincing performance of a song where the tempo is not the one laid down by the composer, in at least nine out of ten cases it is because the metronome has not been consulted *at all*. Singers and pianists have always had a way of launching into the music and hoping for the best. Their confidence in their own ability and flair is almost comic. Working over the years with a metronome in this music is simply to cultivate one's own inner metronome. The resulting 'feel' for tempo stands students in good stead, no matter what music they are performing. Whether a piece is performed, say, at ♩ = 60 or ♩ = 66 (and even if it is not performed at Fauré's suggested marking at all) is far less important than the fact that it is being sung and played at a tempo that has been *chosen with care* (rather than one that has been arrived at by chance). In Fauré's songs, this tempo, once settled on, must be scrupulously adhered to.

The pianist may find it difficult to insist that the singer should follow the composer's markings, but he or she is entitled to await with keen interest the reasons given by the singer for alternative suggestions. If these are due to technical difficulties the pianist must accept that every song performance is 'work in progress'; young singers, for example, will grow into a song gradually, finding many phrases easier to sing ten years later than when they first learned the music. If it is a question of mood and musical effect, let the discussion begin – and the discussion should include the possibility of deferring the song to a later point of the singer's career. But unless the performers have a very cogent reason to argue otherwise, the composer really does know best.

I will not even dignify with discussion the scenario where a student singer's arbitrary tempo is autocratically defended solely on the grounds of 'feeling it that way'. (The instinctive response that might justify that kind of remark develops slowly, and it is to be taken seriously only from someone with many years of performing behind them.) A pianist will always respect a singer who says something along the lines of 'I know my tempo is not the one marked, but I am simply not able to sing it that slowly!' This is an entirely respectable statement from a musician living in the real world, and as I have already said, among the topics thus raised for discussion should be a change of repertoire choice. What is not defensible in the already over-complicated contract between singer and pianist is the disguising and rationalising of vocal inadequacy or technical limitation as artistic conviction.

Marguerite Long, the celebrated solo pianist, makes the breezy observation that one should not attach too much importance to Fauré's metronome markings; she didn't, she informs us. Her grounds for this remark were that Fauré

> almost never had the opportunity of hearing his piano pieces played by a virtuoso before they were published, and we know well the influence that hearing a piece can have on its composer … all composers are inclined to re-think their works and their tempi (even when they might not want to admit it).[8]

Whatever the truth of this observation (which scarcely hides Long's typically self-confident conviction that she, the virtuoso, believed herself a better judge of tempo than the composer), it is worth pointing out that Fauré ensured that he himself was the accompanist of his own songs, and that there was no need for a 'virtuoso' to play them so that he could change his mind about their correct tempi. A singer might well have changed the composer's mind, but it was not hard to find performers for the songs well before they were published, and we must assume that the majority of Fauré's songs received an airing or two before publication.

The important thing is that whatever the speed chosen by the performers, whether Fauré's own marking or a conscious variation of it, it is more important that the song should be prepared and practised with the controlling influence of the metronome in mind than that the composer's specific marking should be obeyed at all costs. It is right that tempo should be a subject of discussion and consideration. Once a decision about tempo is made, every fibre of the musicians' musical sensibilities should struggle, almost as a matter of honour, to conserve that tempo throughout the song. The actual speed at which the Fauré songs should be performed will always remain elusive. Many of them fall into that fascinating no-man's land of *Andante quasi allegretto*, and one will discover songs with exactly the same metronome markings with widely different tempi in performance. The most important thing is to realise that, as in the following observations, the composer's markings should at least be the starting point for a discussion about the music.

A Word about Discography

Recordings are historical documents. I began this chapter with the intention of mentioning only the Fauré recordings of Claire Croiza and Charles Panzéra because these artists had both worked with the composer. It then seemed desirable that the opinions of that great teacher and singer of the *mélodie*, Pierre Bernac, who has written the most famous book about *mélodie* interpretation,[9] should also be cited. These parameters were subsequently broadened to include the recorded performances of Ninon Vallin, whose 78 rpm records made in the inter-war years were of incomparable importance in spreading the fame of Fauré's songs throughout the world. The almost forgotten Noëmie Pérugia was also one of the greatest Fauré interpreters. This is a vast discography capable of furnishing countless vintage surprises – Reynaldo Hahn's crooned and wayward *Le Parfum impérissable* for example (as haunting as a fading sepia photograph), or John McCormack's *Automne*, or Povla Frijsh's enchanting *Dans les ruines d'une abbaye*. Archival *introuvables* by such early artists as Félia Litvinne, Edmond Clément, Gabrielle Gils, Germaine Lubin and so on require a separate study. Once we reach the second half of the twentieth century the list of singers is endless; that *impérissable* tenor and stylist Hugues Cuenod, Camille Maurane, a Fauré singer *par excellence*, the incomparable Gérard Souzay who inherited the Bernac mantle, and that more recent indefatigible champion of the *mélodie*, François Le Roux. While Schwarzkopf was recording Wolf in the 1960s, Victoria de los Angeles was working on Fauré – a reminder that it is has often been the non-French (and non-German) sopranos and mezzos – the Belgian Suzanne Danco, Elly Ameling from Holland, the Greek Irma Kolassi, the English Felicity Palmer and Sarah Walker, who have contributed most generously to this composer's discography. Ameling, Souzay and the pianist Dalton Baldwin recorded an intégrale in 1974. Since then there have been several other complete editions; over thirty years later the author of this book accompanied a 4 CD set of Fauré songs for Hyperion Records with Felicity Lott, Geraldine McGreevy, Jennifer Smith, Jean-Paul Fouchécourt, Stephen Varcoe and Christopher Maltman. It is clear that the demands and rewards of singing and playing Fauré's music have changed not at all over the years, and each generation must continue to offer resourceful yet faithful solutions to the challenges posed by this incomparable repertoire.[10]

The Songs: Rehearsal Notes and Metronome Markings

In the song commentaries below, different tempo marking are given on occasion for the same song; this is because the markings in the high – and medium-voice Hamelle editions of the songs sometimes differ. Fauré's second (and presumably definitive) thoughts about markings are sometimes to be found in songs that are not printed in the original key – the later printing of an alternative tonality presumably having given him the chance to revise his original thoughts.

(1) *Le Papillon et la fleur* (Hugo) *1861*

No printed metronome marking; suggested tempo ♩. = 72–76. *Allegretto* (Hamelle high-voice volume), *Allegro non troppo* (Hamelle medium-voice volume)

Too often we hear this song as something bumpy and breathless. A moderate tempo in the first two strophes (the song is marked *Allegro non troppo* in the original key, and it may be argued that Fauré came to prefer *Allegretto* by the time when the upper transposition was published) will allow for the *più animato* marking at the beginning of the third; it will also allow for the clarity of the words, which are too often gabbled as an incoherent patter song resulting in a mood of glittering superficiality or, even worse, comedy. Even, gracious fingerwork is required here, but nothing that shows off dexterity for its own sake. 'Oh pianists, pianists, pianists,' wrote Fauré, 'when will you consent to hold back your implacable virtuosity!!!!'[11] An unwitting accelerando should be avoided in the opening scales. The left-hand leaps in bars 2 and 4 are treacherous and have to become second nature, pianistically. In the interludes the pianist should enjoy, and slightly emphasise, the suspensions in the alto tessitura as each thumbed dotted crotchet falls to the quaver below. The vocal line is sometimes uncomfortably low, even in the higher transposition, and the right-hand quavers have to be light to avoid balance problems with the voice. Although the pedal must be used in the *ritornelli* of the song, there is no need for it in accompanying the vocal line. The left-hand rests here should be observed here to give some life and spring to the texture, which can easily sound muddy.

(2) *Mai* (Hugo) **1862?**
No printed metronome marking; suggested tempo ♩= 100–112. *Allegretto*
Fauré is unsually specific about the pedalling he requires here: once in every bar where the harmony does not change on the third beat. The gently swooning cadential ritardandos required in this song should not become a habit in other Fauré songs – they are completely untypical of this composer. These bars are accompanied by mezzo-staccato chords in the piano, which should sound as such.

(3) *Puisque j'ai mis ma lèvre* (Hugo) **1862, unpublished**
No printed metronome marking; suggested tempo ♩ = 66
This piece is much easier to play with a lavish use of the pedal, but this must be avoided because the left-hand staccatos will be lost entirely. In this madrigal one should aim for a lute effect that is achieved only with a sparing use of pedal. As Peter Pears used to say to the pianist when he was confronted with playing that was too solid and insufficiently transparent: 'Can't you half-pedal?' (This was a futile attempt to make a student accompanist sound like Benjamin Britten, master of half-pedalling technique.)

(4) *Rêve d'amour* (Hugo) **1864**
No printed metronome marking; suggested tempo ♩. = 96–104, last verse 84–88
This song is an early example of Fauré's ability to write a strong bass line that supports and underpins the melody. Without banging the bass insensitively, pianists should find a warmth and firmness for this as a support and counterbalance for the vocal line, and Fauré insisted on this 'living' or 'singing' bass in his piano lessons. If this is achieved it will stand the pianist in good stead for his or her entire career as a Fauré accompanist.

The last verse is slower ('beaucoup plus lent') than the others: this is a unique change of gear for a Fauré song, and of a kind that is to be found in the early *mélodies* rather than the later.

(5) *Tristesse d'Olympio* (Hugo) **c.1865, unpublished**
No printed metronome marking, no tempo marking; suggested tempo ♩ = 84–88 (first section), *Allegro non troppo alla breve* ♩ = 104–108
This is one of the most difficult of all the songs to bring off because Fauré left it unrevised and in rather a raw state. The composer was not yet experienced in the matter of vocal ranges (at least not adult ones). The key of E minor is strangely uncomfortable for baritones, and a transposition into E♭ minor seems to make a huge difference with a number of voices. The relatively fast suggested tempo of the second section (where the time signature is *alla breve*) saves the music from sounding hope-

lessly awkward and vocally unmanageable, although François Le Roux, in his book *Le Chant intime*, prefers a more cautious tempo of ♩ = 88–92 for the second section.

(6) *Dans les ruines d'une abbaye* (Hugo) *c.1865*

No printed metronome marking; suggested tempo ♩. = 100–116. *Allegretto* (high-voice volume), *Allegro non troppo* (medium-voice volume)

The rhythmic ebb and flow of this song is highly usual for Fauré, being necessitated partially by the metrical arrangement of the poem's alternating lines. The first two bars of each strophe gambol forward, and there is an almost imperceptible pulling back on the third and forth lines as the singer clinches the cadence and snatches a breath for the next phrase, which begins in a re-energised manner. This must be disguised so that there is the impression of a constant tempo, without reducing the words to a gabble. The accompanist has to be attached to the singer's line with the tenacity of a limpet without hectoring or rigidity – something that takes a good deal more practice than one might think. At whatever tempo this song is sung, it should be performed in four-bar phrases. If good singers find themselves needing to breathe after only two bars, the tempo is too slow.

(7) *L'Aurore* (Hugo) *c.1870*

No printed metronome marking; suggested tempo ♩ = 58–63

This charming song has the air of being in old-fashioned *romance* style while having the architectural characteristics of the *mélodie*. Nevertheless we are decades away from reaching that plateau in Fauré's music where the niceties of the salon have been completely eschewed. The rise and fall of the vocal line require a small amount of judicious shaping, especially in allowing the singer to breathe. The piece is an exercise in finger legato and a sparing use of the pedal, so that the textures of the song suggest the transparent aspects of dawn, rather than of its more opaque counterpart, dusk.

(8) *Les Matelots* (Gautier) *c.1870*

No printed metronome marking; suggested tempo ♩ = 116–138. *Tempo animato* (high-voice volume), *Tempo animato quasi allegro* (medium-voice volume)

This is a song that is all of a piece, its shifting and implacable accompaniment a forerunner of *Nell*. As in *Mai*, the composer asks the pianist to pedal 'à chaque mesure' thus once in a bar. The smoothness and evenness required of this early Fauréan water music is a piano étude in itself, but the pianist does not have the luxury of simply performing this song as such without regard to the singer. The boat must be steered carefully, even in songs with a recurring pattern like this where the pianist is tempted to think that the singer should simply fit in with the repetitive patterns of the accompaniment. The wide range of the metronome recommendation is on account of the fact that the tempo of this song, as so often, will depend on the weight and flexibility of the individual voice. A light soprano will need to sing the song faster than a more substantial baritone.

(9) *Lydia* (Leconte de Lisle) *c.1870*

No printed metronome marking; suggested tempo ♩ = 72–76. *Andante*

Choosing the correct tempo for this song with great care, and then keeping to it in the manner of the mature Fauré songs, requires much experience. Bernac opts for ♩ =76 (as does Panzéra in his recording), but a singer with good breath control can manage it slightly slower to ravishing effect. For the pianist the details to watch are the mezzo-staccato, which should register as such without a pedantic dryness, the hairpin dynamics with their gentle swells and diminuendos and the translucent part-writing – without undue emphasis on the soprano line of the accompaniment, which doubles the vocal line throughout. Most unusually for him, the composer twice calls for a ritenuto in mid-phrase. This must be managed delicately, without a trace of exaggeration or sentimentality.

(10) *Hymne* (Baudelaire) *c.1870*
No printed metronome marking; suggested tempo ♩. = 69–76. *Allegretto vivo*
The pedal markings are punctiliously printed. Whether the composer meant 'simile' for the bars that are not given pedal markings, or whether he meant there to be no pedal in the intervening bars, is something that is open to question. The right-hand semiquavers in the song's middle section (before and during 'Elle se répand') should not degenerate into an unmeasured tremolo. The 'rall. e dim.' before the song's last verse is something of an indication of Fauré's discomfort with the setting. He normally avoids such liederish signposts. The tiny 'colla voce' that appears six bars from the end is the composer's permission to approach the final cadence in something of the expansive spirit of the Italian *canzone*.

(11) *Seule!* (Gautier) *1871*
No printed metronome marking; suggested tempo ♩ = 84–92. *Andante*
The left-hand writing here has an independence and intensity of its own that must not be swamped by the bell-like right hand. The note of grandeur that exists in this song strikes a new mood in Fauré's output, and both singer and pianist must rise to the occasion, filling out the long note-values with tone of quiet intensity. As in *Dans les ruines d'une abbaye* a long line of text is followed by a short one, something that Fauré manages better here than in the earlier song. The observations made in the commentary on *Dans les ruines d'une abbaye* (above) concerning four-bar phrases to be sung in one breath also apply here. The extent of the singer's breath control will determine the tempo of the song.

(12) *L'Absent* (Hugo) *1871*
No printed metronome marking; suggested tempo ♩ = 60–69. *Andante sostenuto*
This is Fauré's most ambitious song so far. The pedal is sparingly marked – not before the song's seventh bar does it make an appearance. There is much that can be done here with finger legato; the piano's sound can, and should, be made to sound expressive without the pedal, although the look of the writing on the page seems to mirror Fauré's experience as an organist. The explosion of a more virtuoso kind of pianism after the evocative word 'L'absent' (triplets first in the right hand, and then in the left as tolling octaves in minims and semibreves ring out in the piano's treble register) must not be allowed to get out of hand. Pianists tend to go hell for leather here and crash through the sonic frame or sound barrier that should and must contain any song; the *forte* and *fortissimo* markings have to be matched to the singer's abilities, and these should never approach the *verismo* sense of drama often heard in overwrought performances of this *mélodie*. However, it must be admitted that Fauré's marking of *un poco più mosso* is rather misleading. In order to generate the tension necessary in this song the pianist will have to set a second tempo in the region of ♩ = 104 or so.

(13) *La Rançon* (Baudelaire) *1871*
No printed metronome marking; suggested tempo ♩ = 80–84. *Andante non troppo*
This song has the same portentous quality of *Seule!* with its bare, but significant, left hand as two-part counterpoint to the vocal line. This engenders a severity where the composer tries his best to

frame Baudelaire's lines, uplifting (though somewhat stagey) as declaimed poetry, leaden as song text. The song's second section (*Un poco più mosso* – about ♩ = 96) has a Schumannian feel, and is best pedalled as such without the rubato of Schumann, which by this time is already inappropriate to Fauré's style.

(14) *Chant d'automne* (Baudelaire) *1871?*

No printed metronome marking; suggested tempo *Andante* ♩. = 72–80, *Lento ma non troppo* ♩. = 56–60

There is a broody, Brahmsian grandeur to this setting which suggests, most unusually with Fauré, a lieder-like intensity of subjective expression. Providing that the pianist avoids speeding up involuntarily in the third bar of the introduction, there is a gravity here that will always be impressive. The pedal markings suggest that Fauré was prepared to countenance a quasi-impressionistic blurring of harmonies, although the lighter pedalling sonorities of French pianos should not be confused with those of a Steinway.

The second section of the song is marked *Lento non troppo*. Fauré directs that the semiquaver of this new section must be equal to a quaver of the preceding section. This is not his happiest marking. If we accept that ♩. = 80 is a reasonable tempo for the *Andante* of the first section (or ♪ = 240), this would make the *Lento ma non troppo* 40 to the dotted crotchet (six semiquavers) – very *Lento*, rather than *non troppo*. I suppose that some iron-lunged singer of magnificent breath control might make this work, but it is simply not practical for most singing mortals – and it is extremely difficult for both pianist and singer to make the long-breathed melody hang together convincingly. The suggested tempo of ♩. = 56–60 for this second section is one of those occasions when a departure from the composer's own suggested relationship of tempi may be made after a great deal of deliberation. The other option for the performers is to consider playing the first section of the song a good deal faster, but this would hardly sound like an *Andante* and would detract from the magnificent gravity of the first section.

(15) *Chanson du pêcheur* (Lamento) (Gautier) *1872?*

No printed metronome marking; suggested tempo ♩. = 58–63. *Moderato*

This is a powerful song where the piano writing, sparse at first, insinuates itself gradually into the texture. At first glance, the song appears to be a recitative, but it should be sung rigorously in time. It is all too easy to produce a loose and undisciplined performance if the piano's triplets are reduced to the role of merely accommodating the vicissitudes of an *ad libitum* vocal line. Actually, the opposite is the case: the triplet accompaniment is what gives the song its rhythmic tautness and concentration. One thinks of Ravel's Greek folksong *Chanson des cueilleuses de lentisques*, where rather similar triplets in the accompaniment are implacable and retain the rhythm of a disciplined work song, which never wavers from first to last. *Chanson du pêcheur* is similarly a work song. The recommended tempo here, if implemented, would suggest the feeling of an oar plying the water (see also *Accompagnement* from many years later). In his book Bernac preferred ♩ = 69, which is more or less the tempo of Panzéra's recording of 1935. Such a swift conception risks robbing the music of both its sadness and grandeur, and Pauline Viardot would not have thrown away its drama in so reckless a fashion. On the other hand, the doubtlessly histrionic nature of that imagined performance, and what we can safely assume to have been the use of dramatic rubato, would have made the composer restive – his usual reaction to any trace of lingering sentimentality.

(16) *Aubade* (Pomey) *c.1873*

No printed metronome marking; suggested tempo ♩. = 60–63. *Allegretto moderato, quasi andante*
This is an exercise in the Massenet style (it is astonishingly like that composer's duet of 1872 *Rêvons, c'est l'heure*). It requires a touch of emollient pedal, but perhaps underneath the legato line of the voice one should be able to hear the rests between the chords grouped in duplets – a fresher and slightly breathless effect (more dawn-like, surely) in contrast to the crepuscular complacency of simply pedalling through the bar entirely. On the other hand, a tempo must be found that avoids making the throbbing quavers of dawn, pinpricks of light, sound like convulsive electric shocks. The pianist must be aware that the singer's breath is challenged by a succession of long phrases.

(17) *Tristesse* (Gautier) *c.1873*

No printed metronome marking; suggested tempo ♩. = 42–46. *Andante*
This is an example of a song where not a single pedal marking is printed, and yet where it is clear from the phrasing of the piano part that the pedal must be used throughout. If the singer is tempted to the more casual rhythms of a *chansonnier* (a slight thing this, which imparts the swagger of the *boulevard* to the teetering semiquavers of the vocal line), it is essential for the pianist to remain in time. Perhaps the most persuasive performance of this song is that of Noëmie Pérugia.

(18) *Barcarolle* (Monnier) *1873*

Metronome marking ♩. = 60; suggested adaptation of Fauré's metronome marking ♩. = 44–48.
Andante (Hamelle high-voice volume), *Andante con moto* (Hamelle medium-voice volume)
It is almost ever singer's instinct to perform this song, on first acquaintance, a good deal more slowly than Fauré envisaged it. And no wonder! Here is an example where the composer's marking seems impossibly hurried, hardly giving the singer any chance to encompass the coloratura of the vocal line. One of the questions that the forthcoming Complete Edition will have to settle is whether this metronome marking was perhaps hurriedly added by the publisher, Hamelle (all the other second *recueil* songs already had metronome markings), when he decided to incorporate the song into the second *recueil* of 1908 against Fauré's wishes.

Even at the tempo suggested here (just think of the tempo of Chopin's *Barcarolle*, or of the dotted crotchet of Fauré's many piano pieces of the same name) there is an element of coloratura to the triplets of the gondolier's vocal line that does not always come easily to the more lugubrious of male singers. Nevertheless, the glide of the music is implacable, and instead of the gondolier emerging as a doleful but rather ingratiating character (as he sometimes does in performances where the dotted crotchet is less than 40), we sense the glint of menace reminiscent of the mysterious gondolier in Britten's (and Mann's) *Death in Venice*. This gondolier is an entirely pragmatic realist.

(19) *Puisqu'ici-bas toute âme* (Hugo) *c.1863–73*

No printed metronome marking; suggested tempo ♩ = 66–76
This duet recalls the pianist of *Les Matelots* in terms of its pianism. It has the same inevitability; a gentle hum of arpeggios, not exactly hurried, not exactly leisurely either; the tempo, perhaps, of a benign sewing machine (a Singer for a singer), and similarly implacable – also a good fifteen years before the advent of Winnaretta Singer in the composer's life. Perhaps Fauré knew Schumann's *Widmung*, of which this song is a distant relation, with its arpeggios interlocking between the hands. The need for discreet pedalling here is paramount: too heavy a foot, and one could create a dense

weave of sound inappropriate to the lightly perfumed text. In such cases it is the lower voice that is in danger of being drowned by too dense a pianistic texture.

(20) *Tarentelle* (Monnier) *1873*

No printed metronome marking; suggested tempo ♩. = 120–138

There is no other song like this in all Fauré in terms of its vocal demands. There are other songs infinitely more difficult to interpret of course, but this duet was meant to show off the Viardot sisters as a team, and the vocal triplets in tandem, particularly at the racy and quasi-contrapuntal finale, need to be practised slowly and carefully with regard to tuning. It is the accompanist's role here to keep the song held at the same tempo throughout (apart from the speedier tempo indicated on the last page). The pianist, who also has tricky triplets, is also in danger of hurrying; if this song falls apart, which it can do all too easily, it is because the rushed panic of two singers and of a pianist never occur at a concerted tempo and simultaneously.

(21) *Ici-bas!* (Sully Prudhomme) *1874?*

No printed metronome marking; suggested tempo ♩ = 44–48. *Andante* (high-voice volume), *Adagio* (medium-voice volume)

The pedalling here is carefully marked throughout. It would be a brave but correct pianist who did not use the pedal anywhere other than marked, particularly for the music supporting the vocal line at the beginning of the first and second strophes. Learning to take full responsibility for the quality of one's piano sound, without the crutch of the pedal as colourant or amplifier, seems to me a Fauréan necessity – thrifty housekeeping in musical terms – and infinitely useful everywhere else in this repertoire, as it is in the songs of Schubert. The alternative marking of *Adagio* for this song is scarcely practical for most singers, but it is a useful interpretative indication that the composer required a woebegone atmosphere for the song.

(22) *Au bord de l'eau* (Sully Prudhomme) *1875*

No printed metronome marking; suggested tempo ♩ = 52–56. *Andante quasi allegretto*

In terms of tempo, much depends here on the individual singer and his or her strength of diaphragm and length of breath. Bernac, kinder than I am in this respect, recommends ♩ = 58. On the other hand, in an early recording Ninon Vallin opts luxuriously for something between ♩. = 46 and 50, and she brings it off. The quavers that wend their way down the stave in triplets have to be of perfect smoothness and expressiveness, but the music must still suggest 'water under the bridge'. The amount of sound and 'meaning' generated in the accompaniment is a perfect test of Fauréan style: too much 'feeling' interferes with the gently implacable flow of the song, too little sounds mechanical and robotic. Noëmie Pérugia, normally the perfect Fauré stylist, here sounds rather overwrought for my taste. If pianists learn how to make a beautiful and expressive sound fluidly moving within the tempo (practise with a metronome), they will have mastered one of this composer's most crucial challenges.

(23) *Après un rêve* (Bussine) *1877*

No printed metronome marking; suggested tempo ♩ = 60–63. *Andantino*

Bernac, in *The Interpretation of French Song*, recommends ♩ = 60 for this song, but his own eloquent 1940 performance with Poulenc at the piano takes a slightly more urgent view. Panzéra sings it, in his

1937 recording, at an astonishingly fleet $\bullet$ = 76 – as if he is terrified of dragging, because he was aware (as Croiza informs us) how much Fauré disliked indulgent performances of this song. She herself, in a ravishing performance, one of only a handful of songs by this composer sung by her on disc, performs it at a seraphic $\bullet$ = 56, which is also more or less the tempo adopted by Ninon Vallin. As at least two of these artists knew Fauré personally (and we know that Croiza discussed the song with the composer), it seems that it is one of those pieces that can be played at different tempi according to the mood and time of day. Whatever the tempo, the important thing is that the music should not drag once the song has begun.

Tempo is not the problem in the famous recording of this song by the celebrated Georges Thill (accompanied by that veteran accompanist, Maurice Faure). This is a good illustration of a 'celebrity' performance, and how a Fauré song must not be sung. Of course the great Thill is in handsome voice, but it is clear that he is listening to, and enjoying, the sound of it as he sings. That audible trace of self-satisfied pride mars the purity of the interpretation. The rhythm of those crucial triplets slackens, sentimentality creeps in, particularly towards the end of the song, and the music takes on a false sense of grandeur, although Thill at least avoids the *verismo* sob to be heard in recordings by certain more modern Italian and Spanish singers. His performance is difficult to appraise because it is beautifully sung, and it has given pleasure, no doubt, to many more people than records of the same song by Croiza or even Vallin. Nevertheless, the tenor fails the composer in an essential aspect of style. One can only think of how very much more beautiful it might have been (with these wonderful vocal chords) if the singer had been encouraged to think of the music in a different, less self-indulgent, way.

To accompany this song is much harder than it seems. It calls for gentle chordal repetitions pulsing within the key (by this I mean that it is not necessary fully to depress the piano keys to sound these chords if the repeating action of the modern grand piano is best understood). This is essential to avoid a choppy succession of quavers (as in the playing of G. Andolfi on the early Vallin recording) that will overemphasise the beats and the bar lines. The accompaniment has to be something of a magic carpet with an aerial dream-like quality, notwithstanding a certain richness in the bass line that must nourish the voice and support it in its flights of fancy. A portentous mood is to be avoided at all costs, although the noble and elegiac quality of the melody is a temptation to rhetoric.

(24) *Sérénade toscane* (Bussine) 1878?
No printed metronome marking; suggested tempo $\bullet$ = 52–56. *Andante con moto quasi allegretto*
The twists and turns in the vocal line of this song, and its technical challenges, will have a bearing on the tempo – too slow and the breathing becomes impossible, too fast and a seductive serenade is easily turned into a peremptory wake-up call. A test is whether the opening bars of the accompaniment, with their unusual off-beat syncopations, sound charming rather than peremptory. Of course, at too slow a tempo there is no sense of the rhythm being off the beat, and in writing a syncopation a composer requires the music to sound displaced and at odds with the main down-beat – in this case to charming and whimsical effect.

(25) *Sylvie* (Choudens) 1878
No printed metronome marking; suggested tempo $\bullet$ = 92–100. *Allegretto moderato*
Determining the correct tempo for this song is marvellous practice for the pursuit of a mastery of the Fauréan style. Enthusiasm must be tempered by poise; gracefulness takes precedence over excite-

ment. Every semiquaver must be evenly spaced, with none of that involuntary rushing of arpeggios under the hand that all too often makes a shambles out of this music on the concert platform. It is actually one of those songs that is possibly easier to play a little faster than the best or wisest tempo, and it is certainly technically easier to sing this song faster than is comfortable for the words or the feeling behind them. This is an especially dangerous piece for those singers, tenors especially, who are inclined to depress the *vox humana* button in an ill-advised attempt to display their sincere immersion in the music – *Sylvie* is a song that can all too easily sound vulgar.

❧   ❧   ❧   ❧

With the songs of the second *recueil* we encounter Fauré's own metronome markings for the first time in his songs. Some of the earlier of these are discussable, although as we reach the third *recueil*, and particularly for the four song cycles of the last period, they seem advisable in a majority of cases.

Poëme d'un jour (Grandmougin) **1878**

(26) (i) **Rencontre** (Grandmougin) **1878**
Metronome marking ♩ = 72. *Andante*
This is a lovely marking if the singer's breath can cope with it. On the concert platform, however, and certainly in the conservatoire, it is usual to hear the song less under control, and at a slightly faster tempo. The challenge for the pianist is to do justice to the almost Bach-like requirements of Fauré's part-writing. From bar 5 onwards the left hand moves in crotchets in downward stalks, in semiquavers in terms of the upper voices. Actually holding these notes under the fingers is what is required, instead of merely hoping that the pedal will do the job. From bar 12 there is also the trace of a countermelody, reaching a climax of complexity in bars 16–17. For the first time we catch a glimpse of the kind of layered piano writing we will later encounter in *La Bonne chanson*.

(27) (ii) **Toujours** (Grandmougin) **1878**
Metronome marking ♩ = 152. *Allegro con fuoco*
Fauré invents, very ingeniously, a *moto perpetuo* of triplets that makes use of a simple, yet new, pattern of distribution between the hands. The metronome marking is that of Schubert's *Rastlose Liebe* and *Erlkönig*. The left hand (often required to stretch a tenth) must become accustomed to playing just two notes before the last of its triplets, and the first two of the next set are taken over by the right hand. This kind of inventive legerdemain will reach its apogee in *La Fleur qui va sur l'eau*. Practising this piece is a reminder that one of the most difficult things in playing the piano is an equality of agility and nimbleness in each of the hands. Fauré's own ambidextrous pianism was clearly an advantage here.

(28) **Adieu** (iii) (Grandmougin) **1878**
Metronome marking ♩ = 76. *Moderato*
Singers almost invariably attempt to sing this song at a slower, more sentimental, tempo. They should be discouraged from doing so, but the tradition that a song of farewell should also be something of a tearful elegy dies hard, whatever the textual arguments for it not being so in this case. Even if the song is started in the correct tempo, the middle section of the song, with its shades of *Chanson du pêcheur*, presents, for some, a dangerous temptation to slow down.

(29) *Nell* *(Leconte de Lisle)* **1878**

Metronome marking ♩ = 66. *Andante, quasi allegretto*

This slow marking is one of the most controversial of all the composer's metronome indications, and I have never heard a public performance that obeys it. Bernac recommends ♩ = 76, but *Nell* can sometimes be heard in performance at something approaching ♩ = 108! So great is the discrepancy between Fauré's written marking and normal performing practice that one suspects a mistake, or at least a misprint. Something like ♩ = 92–96 is much easier (too easy perhaps) to sing – was 66 possibly a misprint for 96? It could equally have been a misprint for 76, and Bernac's suggestion seems the best, given that it is nearer the printed marking. The crotchet countermelody in the left hand (bars 17–21, 27–8), and in the right (bars 20–22), requires a good deal of practice and pianistic security.

Ninon Vallin in an extraordinary performance recorded with Maurice Faure in 1943 opts for a core tempo of ♩ = 84, with sections of the song slower than this (judged thus by the metronome rather than the ear), without any sense of dislocation. Vallin cannot resist allowing herself a sense of closure, a ritenuto at the end of the song, something normally inimical to the composer's style, but here accomplished with rare charm. Pérugia's beautiful performance of the song also clocks in at about ♩ = 84. Elsewhere I have commented on the ability of Hugues Cuénod, who, in my own experience of accompanying him, somehow retained the core beat, and wove around it via the words. Vallin's is a performance born of a lifetime of Fauré singing, and this is one of her last recorded performances. Whatever licence she takes has been earned and is not abused. It would however be catastrophic for a student to copy this performance from its external characteristics, were it not in any case impossible for anyone at all to do so.

(30) *Le Voyageur* *(Silvestre)* **1878?**

Metronome marking ♩ = 112. *Allegro moderato*

This marking is one of the few that seem rather over-geared to the amateur salon artist. Any such singer would need to take this song at this fast tempo in order to encompass the long opening phrase in one breath. For singers with greater breath control it seems rather too rushed for the weight of the words, and not *moderato* at all. The danger is of a loss of the majesty and spaciousness that the poem seems to require. The alternative tempo suggestion here is for an experienced professional singer: ♩ = 96–100. It is curious that the tempo of journeying or travelling seems always to be difficult to determine: the opening song of Schubert's *Winterreise*, sometimes sung impossibly slowly, sometimes far too fast, poses similar problems. Schubert, like Fauré, opts for a *moderato* (*mässig*) in his marking, but the speed of his *Gute Nacht* (never given a metronome marking) remains an open question.

(31) *Automne* *(Silvestre)* **1878**

Metronome marking ♩ = 66. *Andante moderato*

Panzéra more or less adheres to this marking in his recording of 1937. Bernac prefers a rather more spacious ♩ = 60; in a recording from the 1930s Ninon Vallin opts for a tempo between ♩ = 50 and ♩ = 56, which sacrifices a sense of autumnal windiness in the music, not that this aspect should be exaggerated. This is one of the Fauré songs that regularly suffers from over-dramatisation, both vocal and pianistic (not, may it be said, from the famous baritones mentioned above). Both singers and pianists of less experience tend to let rip with this song and lose all sense of proportion. The *forte* markings should implode, rather than explode. The landscape is as much internal as external; a windy autumn day is no excuse for a wild operatic outburst underscored with left-hand trombones! Fauré, when in a quasi-dramatic mood of this kind, never shatters the frame of the *mélodie* or abuses a civilised means of expressing emotion within the four walls of the salon. The depressive nature of the text should be a corrective to the over-externalisation of emotion. Sheerly on colouristic grounds the original key of B minor seems infinitely preferable to the higher key of C♯ minor, which brings with it a likelihood of shrillness at the climax.

(32) *Les Berceaux* (Sully Prudhomme) **1879**

Metronome marking ♩ = 58. *Andante*

Like *L'Automne*, this is a song where unity between the sections is more important than the contrast between them; Fauré songs of this kind are meant to sound all of a piece. The gentle tones, both played and voiced, of the opening bars need to progress to the great climax of the second page without a change of cast; this is to say that the *piano* and *forte* dynamics must sound as if they are being delivered by the same voice, and the same pair of hands. The standard problem is that bigger voices tend to over-dramatise the opening, smaller ones to squawk above their punching weight at the climax. The vast range of a thirteenth in the vocal line, the largest in Fauré's songs, causes real difficulties. This matching of presences – perhaps making the softer passages more vibrant, while toning down the rawness of the louder – is an essential aspect of interpreting Fauré's song repertoire in a civilised manner. The critic J. Saint-Jean observed of Fauré in 1910 that 'out of a sensitive regard for beauty and dignity of sound, he moderates the force of his lyric transports and moulds them into graceful form'.[12] This useful observation should be remembered by all would-be performers. In terms of weight and gravity the original key of B♭ minor seems vastly superior to the upward transposition into C minor.

The great classic recording of this song is that of Ninon Vallin accompanied by Marguerite Long (1933). It more or less adheres to Fauré's marking, and it achieves the necessary unity necessary between the sections. The actual timbre of Vallin's voice is wonderfully suited to the mood of the song and the poem, and this is one of the occasions when her performance seems preferable to that of Claire Croiza (recording of 1927), whose tempo at ♩ = 54 (and slower) makes rather heavy weather of it. After practising this piece, the pianist will realise that it takes quite a lot of control to set those undulating triplets at the correct tempo – slightly faster, and slightly slower, are both a great deal easier to accomplish!

There is a filmed version of this song made in the 1930s where Vallin, dressed up in rustic costume, was required to rock a cradle at the side of the piano while cinematic vistas of ocean waves projected behind her were visible through a false window on the set. The few facial shots that we get of this great singer at work (albeit in uncomfortable, contrived circumstances) are unforgettable.

(33) *Notre amour* (Silvestre) *c.1879*

Metronome marking ♪= 126. *Allegretto*

In my opinion, this is an ideal tempo marking if we are to make sense of the words, but it is very rare, if ever, that singer and pianist have the courage to obey. Fear about the high note at the end of the song has a way of propelling the tempo forward (many singers feel they need a fast speed as a kind of launching pad for the climactic top note), and arpeggios of this kind sometimes encourage the pianist to turn on a kind of rollicking auto-pilot. It is quite common to hear *Notre amour* at something like ♪= 168. A compromise will usually have to be found that should veer towards the composer's marking as much as is practicable. Although the song is clearly written in two, it is significant that the composer has indicated a marking in six – that is, measured by the quaver beat. One should perhaps play the music in two, but count it in a rapid six to avoid speeding up involuntarily. The *ossia* high note at the end (a B in the song's original key) should be avoided.

(34) *Le Secret* (Silvestre) *1880–81*

Metronome marking ♪ = 69. *Adagio*

There are few singers who can cope with a tempo quite this *Adagio*. ♪ = 76 retains the mood, and makes breath control much easier for most singers. In the beautiful performance recorded by Pierre Bernac, the accompanist, Francis Poulenc, starts slightly more slowly than the composer's metronome marking, but it is not long before the line moves forward to establish a core tempo of something like ♪ = 72. Once again, as in *Notre amour*, we note that Fauré has written a metronome marking per quaver, not per crotchet. When it comes to fixing the tempo, it is probably better to count in 4/8, but the song's musical glide is better *thought* of in two. It is in songs like this that singers and pianists reveal their musical qualities; there should be an exactness of rhythm here, particularly with regard to how meticulously and evenly the semiquavers are apportioned within the beat.

(36) *Chanson d'amour* (Silvestre) *1882*

Metronome marking ♩ = 116. *Allegro moderato*

 This is one of the songs of the second *recueil* that gives us a prophetic glimpse into the musical economy of the last period. The piano writing is relatively *dépouillé*, but the strength of the part-writing between the vocal line and the bass, moving in minims, is a small masterclass in two-part harmony. Too much pedal here is inimical to the charm of the madrigal style; one should be able to hear the quaver rests that begin each group of notes of the broken chord. With the bars marked 'senza rigore' Fauré parodies expressive rubato (the thought of kissing his beloved makes the singer seem to lose his poise, and his heart skips a beat). The composer, however, rigorously controls the application of this licence.

(37) *La Fée aux chansons* (Silvestre) *1882*

Metronome marking ♩ = 160. *Allegretto vivo*

The very speedy metronome marking, a very definite *Allegro* in this 2/4 time signature, does not seem to fit the more moderate implication of the *Allegretto vivo* direction. For the lightest and brightest of soprano voices this may indeed work; but for voices of greater weight, ♩ = 144 is infinitely more manageable and sufficiently fleet of foot. This is a song that is in danger of being twittered.

(39) *Aurore* (Silvestre) *1884*

Metronome marking: ♩ = 76. *Andante*

In practice, few modern singers are happy in moving this song to a tempo beyond ♩ = 72. It has a danger of sounding slightly hectic at the printed marking. Ninon Vallin keeps to the marking in her recording of 1943, and Panzéra in his performance is even rather swifter than that. Bernac also sings much of the song at ♩ = 82, although Poulenc at least begins the accompaniment at the composer's marking. It is clear from these examples that we should avoid sentimentalising this song, and that dawn is a wake-up call rather than an excuse to go back to sleep! It is a Fauréan requirement to maintain smoothness and elegance, avoiding bumpiness, in relatively fast tempi.

(40) *Fleur jetée* (Silvestre) 1884
Metronome marking dotted ♩ = 72. *Allegro energico*
The marking seems an ideal tempo; many performers tend to rush this song and hector the words unnecessarily. The usual comparison with Schubert's *Erlkönig* is unhelpful for the pianist, principally because the sound of a horse's hoof thundering through a forest is entirely different from that of a gust of wind described here; in *Fleur jetée* there is no connection of horseshoes with a hard surface. Everything is a matter of touch, and of the pianist's ability to rustle rather than hammer. The singer can be too easily pushed by an insistent pianist into a type of rhetorical hysteria which emphasises the rather banal nature of the poem, where both performers' reactions seem out of proportion, and rather hysterical. The song can be exciting and vivid, and really quite loud, without releasing the singer's and pianist's energies at absolutely full throttle.

(41) *Le Pays des rêves* (Silvestre) 1884
Metronome marking ♩ = 84. *Andante quasi allegretto*
This is a realistic marking in view of the considerable challenges posed for the breath by the long notes at the end of each phrase (as at bar 5 on the word 'main'). But a technically superb singer can manage ♩ = 76, which suits the dreamy atmosphere of the poem rather better. The main advantage in taking the songs a little more slowly than Fauré's markings is that it allows a little extra time for the words, and the ever-shifting harmonies, to register on the listener's ear.

(42) *Les Roses d'Ispahan* (Leconte de Lisle) 6 June 1884
Metronome marking ♩ = 60. *Andantino*
Most singers are unwilling to sing this song *quite* as fast as this; a certain sultriness and languid atmosphere is lost with speed. The composer's marking works, however, particularly with a lighter voice. ♩ = 56 is the more usual tempo, and is still suitable for the mood of the poem. Whatever tempo is chosen, the even movement of the quavers throughout is of prime importance; the pianist should avoid speeding up in bars 4–5 and in 14–15. There is a hypnotic element to this oriental music that is prophetic of Ravel's *Bolero*. Pérugia's performance of this song is surprisingly histrionic, and seems to break any number of rules. But she is such a mistress of Fauré's style, and she knows how his music works so well, that she suffuses the song with any number of remarkable and memorable colours. Not to be imitated!

(43) *Noël* (Wilder) 1885
High-voice volume: no metronome marking, *Andante quasi allegretto*; medium-voice volume: metronome marking ♩ = 66
Almost any singer would be taxed by this rather lugubrious marking. ♩ = 76–80 is more realistic.

(44) *Nocturne* (Villiers de L'Isle-Adam) 1886
Metronome marking ♩ = 76 (missing from medium-voice volume). *Andante*
The speed suggested by this metronome marking is ideal for a good singer to perform the opening four bars of the vocal line (with upbeat) in one breath. There are no specific pedal markings here, but the mood of the song – slightly Debussy-esque – requires the pedal throughout. Although the music is written in 3/4 it should be phrased as a very slow one in a bar. Panzéra, in his recording of 1937, chooses a tempo of ♩ = 66, and it does not sound one whit too slow.

(45) *Les Présents* (*Villiers de L'Isle-Adam*) *1887*

Metronome marking ♩ = 52. *Andante*

The opening phrase of this song is four bars long, without any breathing point. The slow metronome marking is fine for a singer with good breath control, but a slightly more fluid tempo might be envisaged for others. The important thing is that, once established, the tempo is implacable, apart from the bar of the beautifully placed *poco rit.* that unaccountably brings so much poetry to the phrase 'Je t'apporterai des colombes'.

(46) *Au cimetière* (*Richepin*) *1888*

Metronome marking ♩ = 66. *Andante*

Panzéra, in his recording of 1933 (one of his earliest recordings, and one of the most beautiful), does his best to adhere to this marking, but he finds it far from easy. Bernac prefers ♩ = 60. One senses, as in the rather similar *Le Voyageur*, that Fauré foresaw a tendency towards performers being sentimental with a text of this kind. Perhaps he upped the metronome marking in an attempt to avoid this pitfall; this seems to have been his way of handling any potential portentousness where a singer might be tempted to treat a song in the grand manner. The grand manner is, however, built into any setting of Richepin's poetry; it takes more than a change of tempo to avoid this in *Au cimetière* – particularly in its opening and closing verses.

Although the date of composition suggests a song towards the end of the second period, *Au cimetière* resembles *L'Absent* from the first. Like *L'Absent*, it has a contrasting middle section of such storminess that the stamina of almost any singer is tested. A slightly faster overall tempo might in the circumstances be a blessing.

Not every singer can match the seriousness and stamina of Noëmie Pérugia in this song – a marvellously vivid performance in which she manages to adhere to the composer's markings.

(47) *Larmes* (*Richepin*) *1888*

Metronome marking ♩ = 69. *Molto moderato*

This is a song where Fauré's piano writing is particularly inventive. In the inner voices of the accompaniment there is a legato line in quavers and crotchets; this is surrounded by jabbing semiquavers punctuated by snatched rests. The pianist must avoid the pedal entirely in order for this unusual texture to be heard as intended – the fingers clinging to the inner melody in crotchets and quavers, and letting go of the semiquavers very quickly, in order to leave the bare bones of the melody resounding like a skeleton swinging in mid-air.

Shylock (*Haraucourt*) *1889*

(48) *Chanson from Shylock* (*Haraucourt*) *1889*

No metronome marking in Hamelle; ♩ = 96 in *Shylock* full orchestral score. *Allegretto*

(49) *Madrigal from Shylock* (*Haraucourt*) *1889*

Metronome marking ♩ = 106 in Hamelle; no metronome marking in *Shylock* full score. *Allegretto*
Like *Nocturne*, this piece works best if the 3/4 time signature is felt as a slow one in a bar.

(50) *La Rose* *(Leconte de Lisle)* **1890**

Metronome marking ♩ = 66. *Andante*

The vocal demands of this song make it very difficult to maintain this tempo, particularly on the closing page. In practical terms, the song usually defies the efforts of its well-meaning interpreters and gathers momentum, so that the climactic passage at the end is nearer ♩ = 72, if not faster. It usually sounds convincing as a peroration, nevertheless. But a technically superb singer can maintain the tempo throughout, as Ninon Vallin proves in her magnificent 1935 recording with Maurice Faure; she achieves a gentle but Olympian grandeur by conserving the steadiness of the composer's metronome marking from beginning to end. The performance is marred only by a strange misreading or accident by the pianist in the chord under the word 'la', the penultimate word of the poem. Perhaps this was a momentary slip on Maurice Faure's part that was deliberately overlooked because Vallin was pleased with her own take. In earlier times accompanists understood that they had to make sacrifices of this kind in the recording studio.

(51) *En prière* *(Bordèse)* **1890**

No metronome marking; suggested tempo ♩ = 88 (for lighter, more childlike voices), although a voice of greater weight (as in the recording of Noëmie Pérugia) can get away with a much slower ♩ = 72. *Moderato*

(52) *Clair de lune* *(Menuet) (Verlaine)* **1887**

Metronome marking ♩ = 78. *Andantino quasi allegretto*

Oh, to have heard Fauré himself accompany this song! The marking seems slightly fast, and Bernac thought so too. One is reminded of what Claire Croiza said about Fauré's fondness for fast tempi: her pianist opts for an astonishingly fast ♩ = 82 here (recording of 1927), but the tempo gradually slows down; at 'au calme clair de lune triste et beau' it has settled to about ♩ = 72. The whole performance eschews the soothingly exquisite in favour of a rueful sense of *ennui* – something that is certainly at the heart of Verlaine's *Fêtes galantes* poems. Jankélévitch offers superb advice for a song of this type, which he calls the ' bergamasque comedy': 'One needs infinite tact to get it right, this peaceful speed, just as one needs infinite tact to capture the anapaests of strolling with friends, a pace that is neither dragging nor hurrying, and to play them without jostling or rushing.' He goes on to bracket other Fauré works with *Clair de lune* in this regard: the *Agnus Dei* of the *Requiem*, the *Sérénade* for cello Op. 98, the *Jardin de Dolly* for piano duet, and the flute player interlude from Act I of *Pénélope*.[13]

A singer with wonderful breath control can sing this song at ♩ = 66 and still make a ravishing and stylish impression. Indeed, Ginette Guillamat in her rare recording manages to spin magic out of this song with the marking of ♩ = 58 (naughtily making a rallentando at the end of the vocal line, but in such a way that one does not mind it as much as in many other singers guilty of the same indulgence). Moreover this tempo, seems more evocative of the 'Menuet' that is this song's subtitle.

Between 69 and 72 to the crotchet would be an ideal compromise – the latter marking is Bernac's choice, as well, more or less, as that of Panzéra and Vallin.

The listener is so used to hearing this accompaniment bathed in pedal that it might seem odd to advocate its opening without pedal, or with a much reduced amount. And yet I do long to hear the beautiful melody of the right hand with the quasi-strummed left-hand arpeggios, as if on a lute, separated by their semiquaver rests, whereby the piano writing takes on the transparency of moonlight. From what we know, via Cortot, of Fauré's disinclination to use the pedal, we might have heard this effect from under his own fingers. Where the composer actually requires touches of pedal – for example on the off-beat in the song's second verse ('Jouant de luth et dansant') – he notates this very clearly. Before the beginning of the last strophe (at 'Au calme clair de lune') he allows three bars of G♭ major arpeggios to be bathed in pedal – one of the most luxurious moments in his songs. It is here that almost every singer wants to slow up – they almost all seem to lose the pulse with the dotted crotchet on 'calme' – but the *espressivo and dolce* marking is really no excuse to do so. It goes without saying that the pianist should not slow down before this section as if to usher the singer into a new section – something that is heard in far too many performances.

The singer is left unaccompanied at the end for 'parmi les [marbres]'. This is not a free bar of cadential self-indulgence (as in the early Vallin recording, for example), and there should not be a rallentando there on any account; in this passage Croiza is exemplary. Like *Les Berceaux* this song was conceived in B♭ minor. It is a real pity if sopranos with a good middle register find themselves singing it in C minor without finding out first if the original tonality is possible for their voices.

(53) *Spleen* (Verlaine) 1888
Metronome marking ♩ = 76. *Andante quasi allegretto*
This tempo can seem fractionally too fast, depending on the voice. On the other hand, Bernac, not normally a speed-merchant, does not mind the tempo going as fast as ♩ = 80. For those who prefer a slower feel, ♩ = 72 is an alternative worth considering. The performance of Noëmie Pérugia is a master-class in performing the song at precisely the composer's marking. Panzéra also recorded the song more or less at the printed marking. The faster the tempo, the greater a sense of bitterness; the slower the tempo, the more there is a sense of depressive inaction. I suppose that all performers are unconsciously influenced by the spacious lassitude of Debussy's setting, which inclines towards the latter mood.

Cinq mélodies 'de Vénise' (Verlaine) 1891

(54) *(i) Mandoline* (Verlaine) 1891
Metronome marking ♩ = 84. *Allegretto moderato*
The composer's elegant, restrained marking – on the slow side – is very seldom heard in the concert hall. It is much more common to hear performances as fast as ♩ = 100 (influenced perhaps by the singer and pianist having in mind Debussy's setting of the same words with its abundant *joie de vivre*). Bernac recommends ♩ = 92, which seems a sensible compromise. Fauré's moderate marking can sound ever so slightly lacklustre and down in the mouth, as if the 'donneurs de sérénades' lack energy and are having no fun at all. On the other hand, at this very measured tempo there is no need for the pianist to allow for the singer's tricky coloratura that begins at 'chan*teuses*'. This is an accom-modation that one has become almost accustomed to, so common is it to hear the piece played at a pace that suggests a cheeky two in a bar, rather than four, and then slowing down when the singer is faced with these difficult melismas. It is a joy to hear a singer able to deliver this passage-work in a clean and articulated manner, and exactly in time. The overall challenge here is to find a tempo that is lively, with piquant staccatos, and yet not lacking in courtly poise.

(55) *(ii) En sourdine* (Verlaine) 1891
Metronome marking ♩ = 63. *Andante moderato*
Many singers not quite capable of sustaining the song at this tempo will have to settle for ♩ = 69.

414

This is one of the songs (*Soir* is another) where the pianist must put in a great deal of practice to ensure the evenness of the semiquavers arpeggios in both hands. Each of these semiquavers must be equidistant from its neighbours, and they must not be bunched closer together by the involuntary reflexes of hands that might be more accustomed to treating broken chords as ornamental flourishes. These perfectly placed strands of sound are the fabric of the music itself. Panzéra's recording of 1933 is sung with a beautiful voice and rather more slowly than Fauré's marking, a deviation that matters far less than the fact that within its chosen tempo the singing is unrhythmical and surprisingly self-indulgent. As so often, the *version de référence* is that of Noëmie Pérugia.

(56) *(iii)* **Green** *(Verlaine)* **1891**
Metronome marking ♩ = 69 (high-voice volume); ♩ = 72 (medium-voice volume). *Andante con moto*
This is perhaps the only song whose tempo Fauré discussed in a letter. He told the Princesse de Polignac that he required a breathless enthusiasm in *Green*, an effect which will not be produced by the rather sober metronome marking (♩ = 69) in the higher transposition of the third Hamelle collection, where the song is marked *Andante con moto*. In the medium-voice Hamelle volume (where the song's original key of G♭ major is printed) the metronome marking is ♩ = 72 (also Bernac's suggested tempo) and the tempo marking is *Allegretto con moto*. Fauré had clearly changed his mind about the metronome marking, and it is interesting (and entirely typical) that a mere three calibrated points will make all the difference. The *allegretto* tempo at ♩ = 72 provides the necessary frisson of excitement. This song can, however, sound dangerously mechanical if performed too relentlessly. A mistress of French song such as Felicity Lott can make something wonderful of the last phrase by gently caressing the word 'puisque' in passing (in the phrase 'puisque vois reposez').

Exactly this kind of freedom can be found within an essential *pudeur* in Claire Croiza's recorded performance of *Soir* with Jean Doyen. Sensuality of this kind, more a way of articulating the words lovingly than of employing actual rubato, is at the heart of subtle Fauré interpretation, if only one knows how – something that acknowledges the metronome without being coldly ruled by it. It is a kind of 'making space for the music to speak' without interfering to any discernible degree with the basic tempo – and it is possible only after you have sung the music strictly in time in many a rehearsal.

(57) *(iv)* **A Clymène** *(Verlaine)* **1891**
Metronome marking ♩. = 92. *Andantino*
The marking seems just a little fast and peremptory for a quasi-Venetian *Andantino*; perhaps this is another one of those instances when the composer marks the tempo up because he fears that the performers would otherwise languish to a self-indulgent degree. There are so many twists and turns of harmony that ♩. = 80–84 seems more judicious in order to avoid a collision of gondolas. As a matter of fact, ♩. = 92 seems a suitable tempo for the passage marked *Un poco più mosso* on the song's second page. This momentary acceleration represents a squall of wind passing over the lagoon; it is an unusual effect unique in Fauré's songs, and most ingeniously engineered. The return to the equilibrium of Tempo I is equally original in its effect.

(58) *(v)* **C'est l'extase** *(Verlaine)* **1891**
Metronome marking: ♪ = 120. *Adagio non troppo*
The tempo marking *Adagio non troppo* is deceptive because in performance the song sounds anything but *adagio*. If all the semiquavers are taken away and only the minims and crotchets in the

3/4 bar are played, the tempo will appear a great deal slower. But once the semiquavers are added, the song teems, throbs and bristles with life; it is the pianist's challenge to suggest these frissons of nature at the same time as keeping the movement of the parts infinitely smooth, the many changes of harmony suave and insinuating. The opening three bars of the song are bathed in pedal – it is clear that in this case Fauré requires the throbbing mezzo-staccato semiquavers to be softened in a haze of sound.

La Bonne chanson (Verlaine) *1892–94*

Pianists will find this cycle to be one of the great challenges of their performing careers. The notes are much harder to play than almost anything else in the standard French song repertoire (although Debussy's *Proses lyriques* offer stiff competition) but the notes themselves are only the beginning of the difficulties. A highly developed sense of rhythm is essential for both performers. The singer faces the daunting task of singing nine happy songs, one after the other, and each capping its predecessor in terms of optimism, confidence and radiant ecstasy. This is especially difficult for baritones who prefer music of the *Winterreise* variety that allows them the pleasant luxury of glowering emotional pain and spleen. I always remember Pierre Bernac's comment on the exquisite but overly restrained recording of *La Bonne chanson* by Fischer-Dieskau: 'Why so *sad*?!!' The answer is that the male voice finds it infinitely easier to enter the emotional world of someone wounded and grieving than of someone endlessly exultant. There is only so much smiling that any male artist can effect on the platform without crossing into the realm of discomfort. Women seem better equipped to use the charming or radiant side of their personalities than men, particularly when it comes to classi-cally trained singers. It is perhaps for this reason that many lovers of Fauré's music prefer *La Bonne chanson* sung by the female voice, and there have been no end of such interpreters (Sophie Wyss, Suzanne Danco, Anna Reynolds, Felicity Palmer, Sarah Walker) since Emma Bardac sight-read the composer's first sketches for this work.

(59) *(i)* **Une Sainte en son auréole** (Verlaine) *17 September 1892*
Metronome marking ♩ = 138. *Allegretto con moto*
This is one of Fauré's most perfect metronome markings. Only by strictly finding this tempo, and no other, is the correct mood of calm happiness achieved. The tendency is to rush the crotchets, which means that the seraphic quality of the music is easily lost. The secret is *not* to think of the music with the 'swing' of one in a bar (whereby alternate bar lines are lost and the music is heard as if it were in 6/4), but to count in a relatively quick, but still judicious, three.

(60) *(ii)* **Puisque l'aube grandit** (Verlaine) *1893*
Metronome marking ♩ = 112. *Allegro*
Bernac writes that the tempo can be even faster than this. Admittedly this makes the last two pages of the song (accompanied in triplets) easier for the singer in terms of encompassing long phrases. But think of the poor pianist, who has a great many notes to fit in evenly, and audibly, under rotating wrists! Fauré's marking is surely fast enough.

(61) *(iii)* **La Lune blanche** (Verlaine) *20 July 1893*
Metronome marking ♩. = 76. *Andantino*
It is very easy, on seeing this song for the first time, to imagine it a great deal slower, luxuriating in its

calmness. Maggie Teyte's recording with Gerald Moore makes this cardinal error to a self-indulgent degree. The song's secret is that its repose is created not over a single phrase, but over the entire piece. I beg the student to believe in this marking, and to practise it until it becomes second nature. Bernac rightly observes that it 'discourages dragging and languishing singers'.

(62) *(iv) J'allais par des chemins perfides (Verlaine)* **1892**
Metronome marking ♩ = 112. *Allegretto quasi andante*
For the second section of this song (*un poco più mosso*), Bernac advises a tempo of ♩ = 144, but a change to ♩ = 126 is certainly sufficient (the composer himself does not give us an indication of what he regards as 'un poco').

(63) *(v) J'ai presque peur, en vérité (Verlaine)* **4 December 1893**
Metronome marking ♩ = 152. *Allegro molto*
This is the fastest marking in the cycle, but the song does not sound the quickest. The experienced Fauré pianist will be used to the texture of mezzo-staccato quavers surrounded by slower note values in both treble and bass (see *C'est l'extase*). There is a judicious use of the pedal here, but pianists must practise holding the left-hand minims for as long as their stretch allows.

(64) *(vi)* **Avant que tu ne t'en ailles** *(Verlaine)* **1892**
Metronome marking: *Quasi adagio* ♩ = 68, *Allegro moderato* ♩ = 96
The vital thing here is the tightness of rhythm in the *Allegro moderato* section. This metronome marking (96 and no faster) will allow the pianist to play the dotted figure of the bird-song with crisp intelligibility and exactitude, after getting the left-hand triplet deftly out of the way. The switching between two very exact rhythms of the song (slow and fast) requires a keen cultivation of the player's inner metronome. The *espressivo* (at the change of key that herald's the song's third strophe) is a good example of the eloquence and warmth of feeling that Fauré expects in these right-hand octaves *within* the tempo, and without any deviation from the metronome marking. For those pianists with small hands the left-hand writing on last page of this song and the stretches in the next song present one of the biggest challenges of the cycle.

(65) *(vii)* **Donc, ce sera par un clair jour d'été** *(Verlaine),* **9 August 1892**
Metronome marking: *Allegro non troppo* ♩ = 92, *Molto più lento* ♩ = 72
There is a tendency to play this song in arpeggiated sextuplets in the same tempo (♩ = 112) as the cycle's second song, *Puisque l'aube grandit*. However, the steadier tempo here, *considerably* steadier, is a real necessity: the pianist has to get a grip on this song and stop it running away, not least because of the number of notes there are to fit in. Finding exactly the right tempo for the second section is sometimes a problem – this section is never as slow as one expects it to be.

(66) *(viii)* **N'est-ce pas?** *(Verlaine)* **25 May 1893**
Metronome marking ♩ = 92. *Allegretto moderato*
It is an indication of the inconsistency of Fauré's description of his tempi that ♩ = 92 is described as *Allegro non troppo* in the previous song, and as *Allegretto moderato* here. Or perhaps it is simply an indication of how certain tempi can feel completely different under different circumstances and in different contexts. The pianist can find it useful, however, to recall the pulse of the previous song's

opening, and match it here. It is rare *not* to set off in this song at too hasty a tempo. The singing of the 'lune blanche' theme to oneself in crotchets beforehand, spacious without being sentimental, is another means of recapturing the correct momentum.

(67) *(ix) L'Hiver a cessé* (Verlaine) *February 1894*

Metronome marking ♩ = 96. *Allegro*

The necessary rhythmic exactitude of the bird-song, and of the attendant triplets, is similar to that of the similar figure in *Avant que tu ne t'en ailles*. It is astonishing that, in this wonderful song, Fauré gathers together the strands from the other songs in the cycle, and combines them within the same tempo. Even if the pianist were to return involuntarily to the ♩ = 92 of *Donc, ce sera* (when that song is quoted on the third page), the margin of difference is too small to notice. The composer does not give a marking for the *Andante moderato* in 9/8 on the last page. It seems clear that this reminiscence of *Une Sainte en son auréole* should be ♪ = 138. After four bars the time signature changes to 3/4 (marked *L'istesso tempo*); there is no change of tempo; quaver equals quaver – a delicious effect, although the performers may find it easier to think of these two remarkable bars as ♩ = 69, before the return to 9/8 in the four bars of postlude.

(68) *Prison* (Verlaine) *4 December 1894*

Metronome marking ♩ = 60. *Quasi Adagio*

Once again, the speed of Fauré's metronome marking seems to be a comment on the poem: a corrective, perhaps, against the many lachrymose performances it must have received in the composer's lifetime. It is seldom, if ever, performed at this matter-of-fact tempo where there seems no trace of an *adagio* mood, only of a rather over-speedy *andante*. A singer surely needs more time than this to put these great words across. My recommendation is ♩ = 52–54, which still sounds far from dragged. Bernac, who recorded *Prison* with Poulenc, was unafraid to recommend ♩ = 46 for this song. This is supported by the beautiful recording of 1936 in exactly this slower tempo; one has the impression that he had listened to the fine recording of the song made in 1927 by Claire Croiza, or even studied the song with her. That ♩ = 60 is certainly one of Fauré most questionable markings; one imagines that on the day of inscribing it in the score he was in the mood to pour cold water on an endless future of self-indulgent interpreters. It is surely up to us to heed this warning, while encompassing the song's *gravitas*.

(69) *Sérénade du Bourgeois gentilhomme* (Molière) *1893*

No metronome marking, no tempo marking; suggested tempo ♩. = 72

Because of this song's remarkable similarity to *Arpège*, I have suggested the same marking that Fauré has given that song, but a slightly steadier tempo than this is also feasible.

(70) *Soir* (Samain) *1894*

Metronome marking (in Hamelle medium-voice volume only) ♩ = 63; *Andante molto moderato*

The accompaniment to this song is a cross between that of *En sourdine* (the same infinitely even semiquavers) and *C'est l'extase*. The Bernac recording with Poulenc of 1947 is exactly within the parameters described in his book – ♩ = 60–63. Poulenc is the best of all the accompanists here; his rather exaggeratedly expressed antipathy to Fauré's music did not prevent him from understanding the style better than almost anyone else – the calm equidistant semiquavers provide a ravishing background for Bernac's extraordinary range of vocal and verbal colour. Pérugia too keeps her performance (for both her recordings) within the parameters of the composer's markings, a luscious ritardando for the final phrase notwithstanding.

Depending on the breath control of the singer, this song can work wonderfully well at a slightly slower marking, ♩ = 58, for example. The Panzéra recording of 1937 is even slower than this. Astonishingly, Claire Croiza's performance with Jean Doyen is the slowest of all, ♩ = 42, and it gets slower towards the end! What makes it so beautiful, despite the liberties and rallentandos, is the singer's complete lack of self-regard or self-absorption. Nothing here serves her voice or ego, only the beauties of the poem. This is a true one-off, not a performance to emulate perhaps, but one to admire in that it breaks all the rules and nevertheless retains its stylistic integrity. Nearer Fauré's marking than Croiza's performance is Ninon Vallin's recording (accompanied by Pierre Darck) of 1935. This is also a more vocally sumptuous performance than Croiza's, but similar indulgences with regard to rallentandos sound more self-conscious and 'singery'; the interpretation as a whole lacks Croiza's interiority.

(71) *Pleurs d'or* (Samain) *1896*

No printed metronome marking; suggested tempo ♩. = 58–63. *Andante quasi allegretto*
The accompaniment must suggest the tolling of bells, even if they are metaphorical; the mood of this song (and also the composure that derives from its speed) depends on the interpreters. With great singers this work, one of Fauré's most sumptuous creations, can make time stand still although the tempo is by no means slow.

(72) *Le Parfum impérissable* (Leconte de Lisle) *1897*

Metronome marking: ♩ = 60. *Andante molto moderato*
The tempo marking here seems, like *Prison*, to be a corrective against sentimentality. We know that Fauré had a way of playing down his masterpieces, of refusing to talk of them as such. And speeding them up comes across as his way of dealing with the embarrassment he feels in having created something immortal. In any case, few singers with a voice of any size could manage this song convincingly at this implacable tempo, which seems to march though the myriad harmony changes with too little time for them to register on the ear. ♩ = 56 is my recommendation; a mere four notches on the metronome can make all the difference.

Panzéra in his 1935 recording sings it even more slowly than this. Bernac does not suggest an alternative metronome marking, but he agrees that ♩ = 60 is 'on the fast side'. A fascinating performance is the radiant one that Ninon Vallin (a singer praised by Debussy in her youth) recorded with

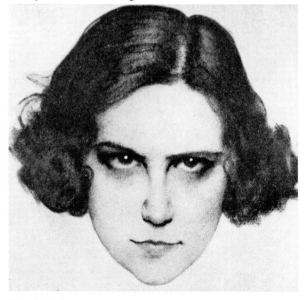

Ninon Vallin (1886–1961)

Maurice Faure in 1943. She is at her most experienced here. The core tempo of the performance is about ♩ = 52, but it begins at about ♩ = 44, and the music is made between these boundaries. This is also true of the magisterial and moving performance of this song by Noëmie Pérugia. Because we do not listen to a disc with a judgemental metronome in hand, we do not notice this flexibility: these performances have the effect of a song sung in a single tempo. The reason for this is that the vocal line is moved slightly forward, or it is slightly restrained, never for reasons of musical expression alone, but clearly to accommodate what might be termed the inner rhythm of the words.

The reader is referred to the seven-page masterclass on this song, almost entirely devoted to the placement of breaths during its performance, in Reynaldo Hahn's *Du chant* (English language edition, *On Singers and Singing*).[14]

(73) *Arpège* (Samain) **1897**
Metronome marking (medium-voice volume only) ♩. = 72. *Andante quasi allegretto*

Bernac here prefers ♩ = 66. The adoption of his tempo makes this exquisite but insubstantial song sound less 'thrown away', slightly more 'considered'.

(74) *Mélisande's Song* (Maeterlinck) **1898**
No metronome marking; suggested tempo ♩ = 48. *Lento*

The song *Crépuscule* from *La Chanson d'Ève* is marked ♩ = 72. It might seem obvious that this music, which began life as *Mélisande's Song*, should be at the same tempo. But this faster tempo applied to the setting in English sounds unnecessarily hurried, perfunctory and unmysterious.

(75) *Accompagnement* (Samain) **1902**
Metronome marking ♩ = 50. *Adagio*

This is another one of those *Adagio* markings, like *C'est l'extase*, where a basically slow pulse is disguised by a great deal of musical activity within the bar. The variety of events in this song ensures that it is one of the most difficult of all Fauré songs to unite into a whole and to bring off successfully.

(76) *La Fleur qui va sur l'eau* (Mendès) **1902**
Metronome marking ♩ = 60. *Allegro molto moderato*

This is a *tour de force* of pianism (the mastering of a devilishly ingenious pattern in the accompaniment) and of counting for dear life on the part of the singer. *La Fleur qui va sur l'eau* is among the last moments of complicated density in Fauré's *mélodies*, where the style is soon to give way to something more transparent and more simple. Sticking to this metronome marking will bring the best results.

(77) *Dans la forêt de septembre* (Mendès) **1902**
Metronome marking ♩ = 50. *Adagio*

It is worth the great effort and control needed to perform this song at the written marking, and not to get faster as it progresses; almost everyone does. It is notable that all three of the accompaniments for the Op. 85 songs contain 'wall-to-wall' piano writing; there is no moment in any of them where the texture clears, comes to a halt, or takes a breath – every bar is packed with music from the beginning to the end. This gives a certain fullness and autumnal ripeness to the texture of the song, which suit the poem extremely well. Noëmie Pérugia in her beautiful performance respects the composer's metronome marking, but she, like everyone else, gets faster as the song progresses on its way.

420

(78) *Le Plus doux chemin* (Madrigal) (Silvestre) **1904**
Metronome marking ♩ = 58. *Moderato*
This is *Chanson d'amour* for grown-ups – and, as in that song, the vibrancy of the bass and its support for the vocal line are a special feature of the music. It seems unnecessary to point out that the less music there is in the left hand (here there are mainly minims), the harder it is to play in terms of giving the bass a requisite significance. In this case the piano's left hand must be like a cello having a conversation with the vocal line. The tempo can be slightly faster than this without destroying the song's atmosphere.

(79) *Le Ramier* (Madrigal) (Silvestre) **1904**
Metronome marking ♩ = 60. *Andantino*
The coo of the pigeon has a slightly rasping quality to it which the composer has brilliantly caught in the staccato of the inner voices, together with the strangely syncopated rhythm whereby a semiquaver at the end of the first beat is tied to a minim (cf. the use of both syncopation and staccato in Schubert's pigeon song, *Die Taubenpost*). For that reason, this staccato articulation should perhaps be heard as such, without being smudged by pedal.

(80) *Le Don silencieux* (Dominique) **1906**
Metronome marking ♩=58. *Andante molto moderato*
This is a perfect tempo for a perfect song. The recorded performance by Noëmie Pérugia has my vote, together with Pierre Bernac's *Jardin nocturne*, for one of the greatest Fauré song recordings of all time. The accompaniment with the right-hand semiquavers taking over from the left hand on the second and third semiquavers of the beat are harder to play correctly, and naturally, than one ever thinks. The exactitude of the rhythm for the vocal line is a supreme test for a singer, who, at the same time as conserving the song's equilibrium in this respect, has to pronounce a great many words deftly, delicately, in time.

(81) *Chanson* (Régnier) **1906**
Metronome marking ♩ = 76 *Andante quasi allegretto*
The last of the Fauré madrigals, and the last of these lute accompaniments. This is a great deal more piquant than, for example *Le Plus doux chemin*. I can see no reason to employ any pedal here, from the beginning of the song to the end.

(82) *Vocalise-étude* (1906)
Metronome marking ♩ = 60

La Chanson d'Ève (Van Lerberghe) **1906–10**
In playing all the Fauré songs that lead up to the last great cycles, the pianist has taken part in the only masterclass that can be a suitable preparation for these ineffable masterpieces. From the performer's point of view, everything that has been learned and practised now comes into a heightened state of play: the control of rhythm, dynamics, pedalling, articulation. There is a lucidity and inevitability about almost all of these metronome markings. One has the impression that they have been thought through from the beginning, and not merely applied to the songs, like some of the others, at the last minute before publication. The composer has got over his tendency in earlier years to mark

some of his songs up to faster tempi, even if these do not quite suit the mood of the text; this had clearly been a ploy to hurry past his more lyrical moments, as if, in chivvying the performer along, he had believed speed to be an all-purpose antidote to sentimentality.

In this work Fauré is unembarrassed by his own profundity at last; everything is clear, and lucid and considered. When the pedal is used, it is sparingly, and the piano writing, confined on the whole to the middle of the keyboard, unfolds in a way that seems entirely natural and inevitable. As for the piano, everything that can be caressed and held under the fingers without pedal is to be played without pedal. Otherwise, in some of the songs the composer's inspiration seems to have been the short score of a string quartet. There is here a new purity and economy, a type of neo-classicism long before Stravinsky in that retrospective mode, a sense of balance and proportion that recalls the great French *clavecinistes*.

(83) *(i)* **Paradis** *(Van Lerberghe)* **8 September 1906, Heugel**
Metronome marking: *Andante molto moderato* 𝅗𝅥 = 69, *Andante* 𝅗𝅥 = 58, *Più mosso* ♩ = 104, *Meno mosso* ♩ = 96, *Andante* (a return to the first tempo) 𝅗𝅥 = 69
This is Fauré's longest song by far, and there is no other song with more than two metronome markings. It is clear that the composer took great pains with these tempi, which should be strictly adhered to.

(84) *(ii)* **Prima verba** *(Van Lerberghe)* **28 September 1906, Heugel**
Metronome marking ♩ = 48. *Adagio molto*
Those performers who favour a slow tempo for *Le Parfum impérissable*, one much slower than the composer's marking, might look to the tempo marking of this song (so much in the same spirit) for a justification. In terms of recordings, the *version de référence* for this entire cycle is that of Irma Kolassi, who rigorously adheres to the metromone markings without sounding as if she is constrict-ed in the slightest by the discipline of doing so.

(85) *(iii)* **Roses ardentes** *(Van Lerberghe)* **June 1908, Heugel**
Metronome marking ♩ = 72. *Andante*

(86) *(iv)* **Comme Dieu rayonne** *(Van Lerberghe)* **1909, Heugel**
Metronome marking ♩ = 56. *Quasi adagio*

(87) *(v)* **L'Aube blanche** *(Van Lerberghe)* **June 1908, Heugel**
Metronome marking ♩ = 76. *Andante*

(88) *(vi)* **Eau vivante** *(Van Lerberghe)* **1909, Heugel**
Metronome marking ♩ = 76. *Allegretto moderato*
In *(v)* and *(vi)* the matching of two tempi in one song after the other in the cycle seems significant. Both songs are in 3/4. In *L'Aube blanche* the tempo indication is *Andante*, and in *Eau vivante* it is *Allegretto moderato*; and yet the metronome marking for both songs is the same: ♩ = 76. The tempo for the spring-like bubblings of this song are difficult to get right; this problem is solved if the pianist simply continues in the same tempo as the ending of the previous song. The part-writing here is of a Bachian lucidity and complexity, requiring a remarkable kind of ambidextrous pianism.

(89) *(vii)* **Veilles-tu, ma senteur de soleil?** *(Van Lerberghe)* **January 1910, Heugel**
Metronome marking ♩ = 84. *Allegretto con moto*
This kind of joyous and life-giving two-part piano writing – occasionally filling out into three parts, and into four parts only for the chords of the last three bars – is something new in the Fauré *mélodies*. Pianists studying this music feel that they are playing something as logical (yet inscrutable, because almost unfathomable in its mastery) as a three-part invention by Bach.

(90) *(viii)* **Dans un parfum de roses blanches** *(Van Lerberghe)* **1909, Heugel**
Metronome marking ♩ = 72. *Andantino*

(91) *(ix)* **Crépuscule** *(Van Lerberghe)* **4 June 1906, Heugel**
Metronome marking ♩ = 72. *Adagio non troppo*
The matching of these two tempi in one song after the other in the cycle seems significant.

(92) *(x)* **Ô mort, poussière d'étoiles** *(Van Lerberghe)* **January 1910, Heugel**
Metronome marking ♩ = 63. *Andante molto moderato*

Le Jardin clos *(Van Lerberghe)* 1914

It is not everyone's view, but this for me is the most perfect of Fauré's song cycles, almost certainly because it benefits from everything Fauré has learned in composing his opera *Pénélope*, a work he regarded as his masterpiece. There is less novelty here than in *La Chanson d'Ève* perhaps, but from the pianist's point of view several types of Fauré songs achieve their apotheosis in this cycle. We could not tackle those descending arpeggios of *Exaucement* without having studied *En sourdine*; *Quand tu plonges tes yeux* looks back to all the throbbing, off-beat emotion of *J'ai presque peur, en vérité*. *Dans la nymphéé* is the most profound of a genre that owes its existence to *Le Parfum impérissable*, and before that to *Le Secret*. *Il m'est cher, Amour, le bandeau* is another exercise in the energy of *Veilles-tu, ma senteur de soleil?*, and *Inscription sur la sable* would have been impossible had *Ô Mort, poussière d'étoiles* not been written first. The trumpet-like fanfares of *La Messagère* are something new and bracing in the songs, owing to the influence of *Pénélope* surely. The same may be said of *Dans la pénombre*, where the presence of the spinning wheel inspires one of the most gently illustrative of all Fauré's accompaniments, and where the character of 'elle' (busy at her spinning wheel, just as Penelope is busy at her loom) has something of the gravity and radiance of Fauré's operatic heroine. Perhaps greatest of all is *Je me poserai sur ton cœur*, which is a kind of apotheosis of syncopation in Fauré's song writing, its effect dependent on the most exquisite control of time and motion. It is difficult to think of what songs might have prepared us for this masterpiece, although any singer and pianist who can give us an exquisite *Le Don silencieux* will be able to master *Je me poserai sur ton cœur*.

(93) *(i)* **Exaucement** *(Van Lerberghe)* **July–November 1914**
Metronome marking ♩ = 104. *Allegretto*
Noëmie Pérugia, in a remarkably eloquent yet idiosyncratic performance, opts for a tempo much slower than the metronome marking: about ♩ = 80. A lighter voice like Croiza's would no doubt have been more comfortable in a faster tempo.

(94) *(ii)* **Quand tu plonges tes yeux** *(Van Lerberghe)* **July–November 1914**
Metronome marking ♩ = 88. *Andante moderato*
Once again, Pérugia's tempo is slower: ♩ = c.76

(95) *(iii)* **La Messagère** *(Van Lerberghe)* **July–November 1914**
Metronome marking ♩ = 120. *Allegro*
This is more or less Pérugia's tempo.

(96) *(iv)* **Je me poserai sur ton cœur** *(Van Lerberghe)* **July–November 1914**
Metronome marking ♩ = 76. *Allegro moderato*
 In a beautiful performance Pérugia opts for a slightly slower tempo. Her closing ritardando on the concluding 'sur la mer' is a pity and does not work musically.

(97) *(v)* **Dans la nymphée** *(Van Lerberghe)* **July–November 1914**
Metronome marking ♩ = 48. *Andante molto moderato*
Pérugia adopts a slightly slower tempo to convey the grandeur of this song: ♩ = c.42. The Swiss tenor Hughes Cuénod was, in my experience, the master of this kind of Fauré song.

(98) *(vi)* **Dans la pénombre, le bandeau** *(Van Lerberghe)* **July–November 1914**
Metronome marking ♩ = 88. *Allegretto moderato*

(99) *(vii)* **Il m'est cher, amour, le bandeau** *(Van Lerberghe)* **July–November 1914**
Metronome marking ♩ = 112. *Allegro*

(100) *(viii)* **Inscription sur le sable** *(Van Lerberghe)* **July–November 1914**
Metronome marking ♩ = 56. *Andante quasi adagio*
 As is her tendency in the whole of the cycle, Pérugia's tempo is slightly slower than the markings: ♩ = c.48.

Mirages *(Brimont)* **1919**

In every other set of songs he wrote Fauré opts for contrasts of tempi between the various songs. In this case he writes four songs more or less of the same speed, certainly within the same tempo range. For those attuned to the style there is not a moment of dullness; in any case, a cycle of four songs can sustain this kind of single mood, something impossible in a longer work. The listener is drawn into the world of mirages and reflections, as if he or she has entered that world through the looking glass, and stays there until the end of the cycle. The performers of these songs must address themselves to the difference between the ♩ = 66 of the first song (with the movement of the swan through the water) and the more static ♩ = 60 of the second song, even if the listener perceives them as being similar. The identical pulses of *Jardin nocturne* and *Danseuse* (both marked *Andantino*) make for a marvellous juxtaposition. (In the otherwise beautiful recording of this cycle by Irma Kolassi, these two songs are inexplicably performed faster than their metronome markings.) Fauré has clearly planned a unity of contrasts here: the mood of the two songs is as clearly different as is their subject-matter, but the identical pulse is the thread that holds them within the same emotional dimension. If pianists are scrupulous about differentiating the sound world of Debussy and Fauré – a matter of pedal, articulation, differing approaches to word-setting and the expression of sensuality – they can perhaps afford to be *less* conscious of the differences between the two composers in performing this particular work.

(101) *(i)* ***Cygne sur l'eau*** *(Brimont)* **1919**
Metronome marking ♩ = 66. *Andantino*

(102) *(ii)* ***Reflets dans l'eau*** *(Brimont)* **1919**
Metronome marking ♩ = 60. *Quasi adagio*

(103) *(iii)* ***Jardin nocturne*** *(Brimont)* **1919**
Metronome marking ♩ = 63. *Andantino*
The recording of this song by Pierre Bernac and Francis Poulenc in 1936 is a rare example of a perfect performance of a Fauré song. The composer's ongoing tempo is adhered to, but never at the expense of the remarkable nocturnal atmosphere spun by both singer and pianist. Within this tempo Bernac finds a wonderful succession of tonal colours and word colourings, a real demonstration of the extent to which this kind of variety is possible, while avoiding both dislocation of tempo and the woodenness of slavish adherence to it. Poulenc's gliding accompaniment is also completely idiomatic: perhaps it helped that so many of his own songs were written in exactly the same tempo range (♩ = 60–63).

Pierre Bernac (1899–1979)

(104) *(iv)* ***Danseuse*** *(Brimont)* **1919**
Metronome marking ♩ = 63. *Andantino*

(105) ***C'est la paix*** *(Debladis)* **1919**
Metronome marking ♩ = 112. *Allegretto giocoso*

L'Horizon chimérique *(Jean de la Ville)* **1921**
The baritone Charles Panzéra recorded these songs for the second time with his wife, Madeleine Panzéra-Baillot, in 1936. In the absence here of a Fauré song discography, this recording must be discussed because it is one of the few performances preserved of Fauré's songs by someone who was actually a member of the composer's circle (Claire Croiza is the other artist). Of all his cycles, this was the one that the composer was never to accompany himself, at least not in public. The first performance was given by the same duo, Panzéra and his wife Madeleine, that recorded it fourteen years later. Fauré sent the manuscript of the cycle to the singer as a gift after the première.

Panzéra had one of the most remarkable voices among the singers of his generation, but he was no match for Pierre Bernac, three years his junior, when it came to the incisiveness and depth of interpretation. The idiosyncratic voice of Bernac never raised the enthusiastic response of the listening public enjoyed by Panzéra, who was born Swiss but decided to live in France. He was also appointed

Charles Panzéra (1896–1976)

a professor at the Paris Conservatoire. A post of this kind was denied to Bernac, who always stood outside the French singing establishment, no matter how highly he was admired in the United Kingdom and America, where his book *The Interpretation of French Song* influenced two generations of English-speaking *mélodie* singers.[15]

Roland Barthes, a great man of letters and an amateur singer and musician, ascribed almost god-like qualities to Panzéra, his former singing teacher and friend. Singers with difficulties regarding rhythmic exactitude and dynamics, common faults in even the most famous, cannot usually make their weaknesses appear their strong points with the philosophical elegance summoned on behalf of Panzera by someone as distinguished as Barthes. It is interesting how love of a voice with 'vocal radiance and power' (in Barthes's words) arouses such powerful emotions as to make the listener credit the possessor of such an instrument with the very intellectual qualities that are possessed by the writer of the eulogy, rather than by its subject.[16]

In listening to Panzéra's records today, the impartial listener will hear a possessor of a fine voice who (like very many singers of both his *Fach* and his period) had a sense of rhythm that frequently lost its way, not helped by an element of self-indulgence. It is notable that Milhaud, when writing to Claudel in March 1935 concerning the possible casting of Panzéra in one of his works, *Les Coëphores*, refers to the singer's 'côté assez cabotin (il donne un sort à chaque syllable)' ('his rather histrionic ham-actor side; he emphasises each syllable').[17] Perhaps this accounts for the singer's relatively modest career in the opera house. In matters of rhythm the singer on shellac is often chivvied along to return to the 'straight and narrow' by his wife and partner at the piano, but in the 1936 recording of *L'Horizon chimérique* there are many approximations of ensemble between them, musical accidents that would not pass muster in any recording studio today. The dragging behind the beat of some passages is hardly a compensation for the hurrying of others, and the dislocation of musical poise is a pity.

This does not mean that these performances are not of enormous historical value – Panzéra represents a significant departure for Fauré from the type of 'careful' and cultivated artist with whom he usually collaborated – singers such as Emma Bardac, Jeanne Raunay and Claire Croiza. But nothing that Barthes writes about his idol can convince me that the singer's inexactitudes are the result of sublime and deliberate interpretative choices.

Barthes believes that what he calls Panzéra's 'skating over his consonants', common to many singers, is a clever ploy in favour of the consonant being a 'launching pad for the admirable vowel', whereby 'the truth of the language is superior to the truth of what it expresses'.[18] My reply to this is that the vowels of Croiza, Pérugia and Bernac are also 'admirable' and that they are all more in con-

426

trol of their musical material. Barthes explains away on behalf of Panzéra the most common fault in all singers, even some of the greatest of names – a difficulty when it comes to singing in time and a concentration on the vocal production of vowels at the expense of the text.

As if in reply to any such stricture, Barthes talks about 'the extra physical dimension which organises, surpasses and overturns the whole cultural part of the art of music'.[19] This is to bow before Panzéra as a Titan of art, and it is touching that Barthes, who understands aesthetics so well, should venerate a singer with an indulgence that he would probably refuse to other musicians. The influence of a voice on its listeners is a mystery of a kind that one associates with the illogical and almost chemical imperatives of romantic attraction. Barthes seems to be saying that singers with the finest voices and visceral instincts should be *permitted* to break the rules of music – however shocking this may be to the sensibilities of over-refined musical pundits. It is all justified, Barthes might claim, because it is a kind of communication at some higher level that overturns all the normal expectations. The attribution of sovereign musical powers to people with big and noble voices is as old as time itself. It is why opera house stars are worshipped and it is seldom to the advantage of the singers' artistic progress, particularly as they get older and achieve cult status. As it happens, those who work the most closely with divas and 'divos' are seldom the ones to subscribe to their fan-clubs.

Panzéra was a fine singer by the standards of his time who enjoyed a huge success from his youth (Fauré's approbation having been one of the most important factors in his status) and who found a special place in the history of the *mélodie* at a time when he had few such vocally gifted rivals. As for the enthusiasm of the fans, one should not forget that few male singers got the chance to record *mélodies* in the 1930s, and the listener's admiration for the song itself is inevitably confused with an admiration for the performance, which becomes, in fact, one and the same thing on a record played again and again until it achieves almost a magical status. In the absence of competition from other singers, recordings of certain songs became nothing less than iconic; and it is human nature to love a song best as one heard it first.

(106) (i) *La Mer est infinie* (Jean de la Ville) **1921**

Metronome marking ♩ = 72. *Andante quasi allegretto*
This metronome marking seems perfect. The tempo is considerably faster than expected from a first glance at the song.

(107) (ii) *Je me suis embarqué* (Jean de la Ville) **1921**

Metronome marking ♩ = 63. *Andante moderato*
The pianist should avoid at all costs the trap into which Madeleine Panzéra-Baillot fell when playing this song: this is the incorrect double-dotting of the left-hand accompanying figure so that the short note after the dotted quaver is a demi-semiquaver each time, rather than a properly measured semiquaver.

(108) (iii) *Diane, Séléné* (Jean de la Ville) **1921**

Metronome marking ♩ = 52. *Lento ma non troppo*
Panzéra's recorded performance is more or less at the written marking. Once again, as in the first song of the cycle, the performer is astonished at the speed of the metronome marking. It should be possible for a fine singer to take this song at a slightly slower tempo (say, ♩ = 48) while still preserving its chaste lack of sentimentality.

(109) *(iv)* ***Vaisseaux, nous vous aurons aimés*** *(Jean de la Ville)* **1921**

Metronome marking ♩ = 66. *Andante quasi allegretto*

In his book *50 mélodies françaises* (1964) Panzéra justifies the rather big (unmarked) ritardando he makes at the end of this song in his recording: 'A slight letting up at "grands départs inassouvis" The composer advised it. However, he refused to mark it on the manuscript so afraid was he – and with good reason – that once printed, the indication would be immediately exaggerated.'[20] Fauré had reasonable grounds for his fears. The Panzéras' ritardando at the end of the cycle, on the last vocal cadence, seems to me to be a rather more extended affair than the composer would have wished. It introduces into the cycle that note of knowing portentousness, an awareness of the tragedy of the cycle (its dying composer, its poet who died far too young), that should have been avoided at all costs.

1   Philippe Fauré-Fremiet, *Gabriel Fauré* (Paris: Les Éditions Rieder, 1929), p. 76.

2   Marguerite Long, *At the Piano with Fauré*, trans. Olive Senior-Ellis (London: Kahn & Averill, 1981), p. 66.

3   Quoted in Jean-Michel Nectoux, *Gabriel Fauré: A Musical Life*, trans. Roger Nichols (Cambridge: Cambridge University Press, 1991), p. 43.

4   Stephen Hough, in private correspondence with the author.

5   Long, *At the Piano with Fauré*, p. 72.

6   Nectoux, *Gabriel Fauré: A Musical Life*, p. 45.

7   Ibid., p. 45.

8   Quoted in ibid., p. 72.

9   Pierre Bernac, *The Interpretation of French Song* (London: Cassell, 1970).

10   The major work of reference about the earlier Fauré discography is Jean-Michel Nectoux, *Phonographies: Gabriel Fauré 1900–1977*. Bibliothèque Nationale Département de la Phonothèque Nationale et de l'Audiovisuel, Paris 1979.

11   Unpublished letter to Robert Lortat, 12 March 1919, quoted in Jean-Michel Nectoux, *Gabriel Fauré: A Musical Life*, trans. Roger Nichols (Cambridge: Cambridge University Press, 1991), p. 471.

12   Norman Suckling, *Gabriel Fauré* (London: Dent, 1946), p. 6. Saint-Jean was the pseudonym of the critic Joseph de Marliave, husband of Marguerite Long.

13   Vladimir Jankélévitch, *Music and the Ineffable*, trans. Caroline Abbate (Princeton, NJ: Princeton University Press, 2003), pp. 112–13.

14   Reynaldo Hahn, *On Singers and Singing: Lectures and an Essay*, trans. Léopold Simoneau (London: Christopher Helm, 1990).

15   Bernac, *The Interpretation of French Song*.

16   Barthes, 'The Grain of the Voice', quoted in Nectoux, *Gabriel Fauré: A Musical Life*, p. 442.

17   Paul Collaer, *Correspondance avec des amis musiciens*, ed. Robert Wangermée (Liège: Mardaga, 1996), p. 340, n. 1.

18   Quoted in Nectoux, *Gabriel Fauré: A Musical Life*, p. 442.

19   Quoted in ibid., p. 442.

20   Charles Panzéra, *50 mélodies françaises: Leçons de style et d'interprétation* (Brussels: Schott Frères, 1964).

The Songs of Fauré in their Opus Number Groupings

As is the case with the lieder of Schubert, the opus number groupings of Fauré are not at all useful in terms of establishing the chronology of songs (the earlier songs, Opp. 1–8, where the convenience of the publisher was of prime importance, are particularly unreliable from this point of view). A glance at the listings below will immediately show the reader how different the opus numbering is from the actual chronology that has been almost always followed in the rest of this book. The juxtaposition of songs within these opus numbers is also, more often than not, an inaccurate indication of the composer's own programme-making impulses. Performers in search of repertoire for recitals are warned against the temptation of trying to make research easier by opting to programme an entire opus number without investigating other more creative possibilities based on subject-matter, mood, the constructive contrast of tonality and tempo, and so on. Nevertheless, in certain cases songs by Fauré on a recital programme can be usefully grouped together according to their opus numbers. This applies obviously to the cycles most of all, but there are also other groupings that work in performance (marked here with one asterisk if worth considering, and with two if particularly successful on the platform).

Op. 1
No. 1 *Le Papillon et la fleur* [Hugo, first published in 1869]; No. 2 *Mai* [Hugo, first published in 1871]

Op. 2
No. 1 *Dans les ruines d'une abbaye* [Hugo, first published in 1869]; No. 2 *Les Matelots* [Gautier, first published in 1876]

Op. 3
No. 1 *Seule!* [Gautier, first published in 1871]; No. 2 *Sérénade toscane* [Bussine, first published in 1879]

Op. 4

No. 1 *Chanson du pêcheur* [Gautier, first published in 1877]; No. 2 *Lydia* [Leconte de Lisle, first published in 1871]

Op. 5

No. 1 *Chant d'automne* [Baudelaire, first published 1879]; No. 2 *Rêve d'amour* [Hugo, first published in 1875]; No. 3 *L'Absent* [Hugo, first published in 1879]

Op. 6

No. 1 *Aubade* [Pomey, first published in 1879] No. 2 *Tristesse* [Gautier, first published in 1876]; No. 3 *Sylvie* [Choudens, first published in 1879]

Op. 7

No. 1 *Après un rêve* [Bussine, first published in 1878]; No. 2 *Hymne* [Baudelaire, first published in 1871]; No. 3 *Barcarolle* [Monnier, first published in 1877]

Op. 8

No. 1 *Au bord de l'eau* [Sully Prudhomme, first published in 1877]; No. 2 *La Rançon* [Baudelaire, first published in 1879]; No. 3 *Ici-bas!* [Sully Prudhomme, first published in 1877]

*Op. 10 (Duets)

No. 1 *Puisqu'ici bas* [Hugo, first published in 1879]; No. 2 *Tarantelle* [Monnier, first published in 1879]

These two contrasting pieces would make a charming small group in a duet recital.

*Op. 18

No. 1 *Nell* [Leconte de Lisle, first published in 1880]; *Le voyageur* [Silvestre, first published in 1880]; *Automne* [Silvestre, first published in 1880]

This grouping will only suit singers of heavier voice who can encompass the passion of *Le Voyageur* at the same time as the delicacy of *Nell*.

**Op. 21

Nos 1–3 *Poëme d'un jour* cycle [Durand, first published in 1880]

*Op. 23

No. 1 *Les Berceaux* [Sully Prudhomme, first published in 1881]; No. 2 *Notre amour* [Silvestre, first published in 1882]; No. 3 *Le Secret* [Silvestre, first published in 1881]

Not every voice will find *Les Berceaux* and *Notre amour* equally suitable for performance. For recital purposes in the concert hall, it may be better to perform this with *Notre amour* at the end of the group, and *Le Secret* in second place.

Op. 27

No. 1 *Chanson d'amour* [Silvestre, first published in 1882]; No. 2 *La Fée aux chansons* [Silvestre, first published in 1883]

*Op. 39

No. 1 *Aurore* [Silvestre, first published in 1885]; No. 2 *Fleur jetée* [Silvestre, first published in 1885]; No. 3 *Le Pays des rêves* [Silvestre, first published in 1885] No. 4 *Les Roses d'Ispahan* [Leconte de Lisle, first published in 1885]

For performance purposes in the concert hall, an all-Silvestre extract from this opus number (Op. 39 Nos 1–3) could well be appropriate; it may be better to perform *Fleur jetée* at the end of the group, and *Le Pays des rêves* and *Aurore* in first and second places.

Op. 43

No. 1 *Noël* [Wilder, first published in 1886]; No. 2 *Nocturne* [Villiers de L'Isle Adam]

*Op. 46

No. 1 *Les Présents* [Villiers de L'Isle Adam, first published in 1888]; No. 2 *Clair de lune* [Verlaine, first published in 1888]

Despite the fact that this set offers two different poets (and there are other Verlaine settings that could go with *Clair de lune*), the actual juxtaposition of these two songs is by no means unpleasant, the two *mélodies* being 'moonstruck' in different ways.

*Op. 51

No. 1 *Larmes* [Richepin, first published in 1888]; No. 2 *Au cimetière* [Richepin, first published in 1888]; *Spleen* [Verlaine, first published in 1888]; No. 4 *La Rose* [Leconte de Lisle, first published in 1890]

This first three of this set of songs (without *La Rose*) would be a particularly effective way to begin a second half of a programme planned to conclude with a substantial group of Wolf's Mörike lieder, also composed in 1888. One can imagine Wolf's *Der Genesene an die Hoffnung* as being the first of the Wolf group and an upbeat riposte to the depressive illness of Fauré's *Spleen*.

Op. 57 (from Shylock)

No. 1 *Chanson* [Haraucourt]; No. 3 *Madrigal* [Haraucourt, first published in 1897]

**Op. 58

Nos 1–5 *Cinq Mélodies 'de Venise'* cycle [Verlaine, first published in 1891]

**Op. 61

Nos 1–9 *La Bonne chanson* cycle [Verlaine, first published in 1894]

*Op. 76

No. 1 *Le Parfum impérissable* [Leconte de Lisle, first published in 1897]; *Arpège* [Samain, first published in 1897]

Although opus numbers with two songs (rather than three) are seldom suitable for recital purposes, the link between these two songs with, broadly speaking, perfume connotations could make a useful pairing in a thematic programme devoted, say, to the senses.

Op. 83

No. 1 *Prison* [Verlaine, first published in 1896]; No. 2 *Soir* [Samain, first published in 1896]

*Op. 85

No 1 *Dans la forêt de septembre* [Mendès, first published in 1902]; No. 2 *La Fleur qui va sur l'eau* [Mendès, first published in 1902]; No. 3 *Accompagnement* [Samain, first published in 1902]
These songs could work in a group in recital, but probably not in this order; suggestions would be Nos 1, 3 and 2 or Nos 3, 1 and 2 (the latter keeping the Mendès settings together).

*Op. 87

No. 1 *Le Plus doux chemin* [Silvestre, first published in 1907]; No. 2 *Le Ramier* [Silvestre, first published in 1904]

Op. 92

Le Don silencieux [Dominique, first published in 1906]

Op. 94

Chanson [Régnier, first published in 1907]

**Op. 95

Nos 1–10 *La Chanson d'Ève* cycle [Van Lerberghe, first published as a cycle in 1911]

**Op. 106

Nos 1–8 *Le Jardin clos* cycle [Van Lerberghe, first published in 1915]

**Op. 113

Nos 1–4 *Mirages* cycle [Brimont, first published in 1919]

Op. 114

C'est la paix [Debladis, first published in 1920]

**Op. 118

Nos 1–4 *L'Horizon chimérique* cycle [Jean de La Ville de Mirmont, first published in 1922]

The Tonalities of Fauré's *mélodies*

Singers are often unaware of the original keys of Fauré's songs. Sopranos who own the three Hamelle *recueils* for higher voice may sleepwalk into singing *Clair de lune* in C minor, although they are often perfectly capable of singing it in the much more beautiful original key of B♭ minor. Another Verlaine song of which this is true is *Green*, where the original is G♭ major, printed as the lower key, rather than A♭. *Automne* is a song that is infinitely more powerful in B minor rather than the shrill transposed version of C♯ minor, a tonality that should be preserved for *Au bord de l'eau*. Sometimes the transpositions are necessary for vocal comfort, but it is often merely the volume of printed music easily to hand (where all aspects of the soprano or tenor voice are termed 'high', and all aspects of the mezzo and baritone voices are termed 'middle') that decides a subtle and crucial aspect of performance.

Pianists and coaches can guide the singer to consider the possibility of singing songs in different available keys. Although the average listener is not often attuned to differences in a song's chosen key, pianists, by the very nature of their work, develop a feel for a composer's use of tonality. A list such as the one printed below can be useful for this very purpose and for linking various subjects and ideas that seemed to Fauré to require a musical treatment in the same key. Few accompanists are acquainted with Fauré's solo music; the non-vocal music listed here with the same tonalities may tempt them to investigate further.

C major
… the floating of celestial spirits in the ease of infinite embrace, the flowing of water as it bubbles up from its source, Van Lerberghe's simplicity of 'delight and peace of mind', the freedom of youth, the uncluttered sagacity of old age …

Puisqu'ici-bas (Hugo), Op. 10 No. 1
Chanson (Haraucourt) from *Shylock*, Op. 57 No. 1
Eau vivante (Van Lerberghe) (*La Chanson d'Ève*), Op. 95 No. 6
Exaucement (Van Lerberghe) (*Le Jardin clos*), Op. 106 No. 1

Barcarolle No. 13, Op. 116 (1921)

C minor

… solitary and sometimes noble sadness (capable too of reaching dramatic and anguished heights, as with Richepin), the disappointment of loss, Baudelaire's 'salt tears of an ashen brow' and 'the terrible day of strict judgement' …

Tristesse (Gautier), Op. 6 No. 2
Après un rêve (Bussine, after an anonymous Tuscan poem), Op. 7 No. 1
La Rançon (Baudelaire), Op. 8 No. 2
Larmes (Richepin), Op. 51 No. 1
Comme Dieu rayonne (Van Lerberghe) (*La Chanson d'Ève*), Op. 95 No. 4. The radiance of this song has more in common with the characteristics of C major, the key in which it ends.

Piano Quartet No. 1, Op. 15 (1879)
Elégie for cello, Op. 24 (1880)
Piano Quintet No. 2, Op. 115 (1921)

C♯ minor

… meandering melancholy, calm reflection …

Au bord de l'eau (Sully Prudhomme), Op. 8 No. 1

Improvisation, Op. 84 No. 5 (part of *Huit pièces brèves*, 1899–1902)

D♭ major

… intense intimacy, eroticism controlled yet ardent, veiled sexual adventure bristling with harmonic promise, nocturnal trysts and the awakening of love, the ecstatic adventures of death and renewal …

Le Papillon et la fleur (Hugo), Op. 1 No. 1 (original key before publication)
Rencontre (Grandmougin) (*Poème d'un jour*), Op. 21 No. 1
Le Secret (Silvestre), Op. 23 No. 3
C'est l'extase (Verlaine) (*Cinq mélodies 'de Vénise'*), Op. 58 No. 5
Avant que tu ne t'en ailles (Verlaine) (*La Bonne chanson*), Op. 61 No. 6
Soir (Samain), Op. 83 No. 2
L'Aube blanche (Van Lerberghe) (*La Chanson d'Ève*), Op. 95 No. 5
Ô Mort, poussière d'étoiles (Van Lerberghe) (*La Chanson d'Ève*), Op. 95 No. 10
Dans la nymphée (Van Lerberghe) (*Le Jardin clos*), Op. 106 No. 5
Je me suis embarqué (de la Ville de Mirmont) (*L'Horizon chimérique*), Op. 118 No. 2

Nocturne No. 6, Op. 63 (1894)
Nocturne No. 8, Op. 84 No. 8 (part of *Huit pièces brèves*, 1899–1902)
Barcarolle No. 8, Op. 96 (1906)

D major

… physicality and bracing reality, vistas of sea and distant garden oases, the flowerings of nature and the humming of bees, the warmth and radiance of the sun …

Les Roses d'Ispahan (Leconte de Lisle), Op. 39 No. 4
Veilles-tu ma senteur de soleil? (Van Lerberghe) (*La Chanson d'Ève*), Op. 95 No. 4
La Mer est infinie (de la Ville de Mirmont) (*L'Horizon chimérique*), Op. 118 No. 1
Vaisseaux, nous vous aurons aimé (de la Ville de Mirmont) (*L'Horizon chimérique*), Op. 118 No. 4

Berceuse for violin and piano, Op. 16
In Paradisum from the *Requiem*, Op. 48

D minor

… world-weary cynicism, twilight and depression, jaded eroticism, despair that fails to find a voice, the wordless expression of grief in a dancer, the cry of a wounded bird that penetrates the veil of happiness …

Madrigal (Silvestre), Op. 35
Spleen (Verlaine), Op. 51 No. 3
Mélisande's Song (Maeterlinck) (from *Pelléas et Mélisande*, Op. 80)
Crépuscule (Van Lerberghe) (*La Chanson d'Ève*), Op. 95 No. 9
Danseuse (Brimont) (*Mirages*), Op. 113 No. 4

Barcarolle No. 7, Op. 90 (1905)
Cello Sonata No. 1, Op. 109 (1917)

E♭ major

… comfort and calm intimacy, the trust and reciprocation between man and woman, between man and nature, or man and God, the guidance of nature and the celestial movement of the moon in the sky …

Rêve d'amour (Hugo), Op. 5 No. 2
Nocturne (Villiers de L'Isle Adam), Op. 43 No. 2
En prière (Bordèse) (1890)
En sourdine (Verlaine) (*Cinq mélodies 'de Venise'*), Op. 58 No. 2
Pleurs d'or (Samain), Op. 72
Je me poserai sur ton cœur (Van Lerberghe) (*Le Jardin clos*), Op. 106 No. 4
Jardin nocturne (Van Lerberghe) (*Le Jardin clos*), Op. 106 No. 3
Diane, Séléné (de la Ville Mirmont) (*L'Horizon chimérique*), Op. 118 No. 4

Nocturne No. 4, Op. 36 (1884)
Barcarolle No. 6, Op. 70 (1895?)
Sanctus from the *Requiem*, Op. 48
Barcarolle No. 12, Op. 106bis (1915)

E♭ minor

… resignation and renunciation, loneliness and regret, bitter rue …

Prison (Verlaine), Op. 83 No. 1

Nocturne No. 1, Op. 33 (*c.*1875)
Prélude No. 6, Op. 103 (1909–10)
-

E major

… unconditional devotion and quiet tenacity, emotional depth, a capacity for suffering and infinite patience …

Notre amour (Silvestre), Op. 23 No. 2
La Parfum impérissable (Leconte de Lisle), Op. 76 No. 1
Le Don silencieux (Jean Dominique), Op. 92
Roses ardentes (Van Lerberghe) (*La Chanson d'Ève*), Op. 95 No. 3
Dans la pénombre (Van Lerberghe) (*Le Jardin clos*), Op. 106 No. 6

Tantum ergo, Op. 65 No. 2 (1894)

E minor

… an emptiness both internal and external, tragic bereavement (Gautier), of bleak nothingness, of insubstantiality or haunted doubt, a Venetian mystery (Verlaine), the soul of a dying flute (Samain), noble resignation in love (Régnier), the void of Chaos before the Creation, and of a return to nescience (Van Lerberghe), a tonality fitted to the mood of the piano and chamber music of the third period …

Tristesse d'Olympio (Hugo)
Seule! (Gautier), Op. 3, No. 1
Au cimetière (Richepin), Op. 51 (later published by Hamelle in D minor)
À Clymène (Verlaine) (*Cinq mélodies 'de Venise'*), Op. 58 No. 4
J'ai presque peur, en vérité (Verlaine) (*La Bonne chanson*), Op. 61 No. 5
Arpège (Samain), Op. 76 No. 2
Le Ramier (Silvestre), Op. 87 No. 2
Chanson (Régnier), Op. 94
Vocalise
Paradis (Van Lerberghe) (*La Chanson d'Ève*), Op. 95 No. 1
Inscription sur la sable (Van Lerberghe) (*Le Jardin clos*), Op. 106 No. 8

Prélude No. 9, Op. 103 (1909–10)
Nocturne No. 12, Op. 107 (1915)
Violin Sonata No. 2, Op. 108 (1916–17)
String Quartet, Op. 121 (1923–24)

F major

… the 'doux refrain' of an 'existence sublime' (Gautier), the serenading suitor who plights his troth (successfully – Leconte de Lisle, Silvestre) or even comically (Haraucourt), a glow of health and fulfilment and enchantment (Silvestre), the lineaments of gratified desire, an ardency that encompasses both discretion and open ecstasy (Van Lerberghe) …

Les Matelots (Gautier), Op. 2 No. 2 (original key before publication)
Lydia (Leconte de Lisle), Op. 4 No. 2
Aubade (Pomey), Op. 6 No. 1
La Fée aux chansons (Silvestre), Op. 27 No. 2
Chanson d'amour (Silvestre), Op. 27 No. 1
Les Présents (Villiers de l'Isle Adam), Op. 46 No. 1
La Rose (Leconte de Lisle), Op. 51 No. 4
Madrigal (Haraucourt) from *Shylock*, Op. 57 No. 3
Quand tu plonges tes yeux (Van Lerberghe) (*Le Jardin clos*), Op. 106 No. 2
Il m'est cher, Amour, le bandeau (Van Lerberghe) (*Le Jardin clos*) Op. 106 No. 7
Cygne sur l'eau (Brimont) (*Mirages*), Op. 113 No. 1

Agnus Dei from the *Requiem*, Op. 48
Salve Regina, Op. 67 No. 1 (1895)
Prélude No. 4, Op. 103 (1909–10)

F minor

… the suppressed desperation of being abandoned or bereaved (Gautier), a glint of menace in sexual abandon (Monnier) sometimes spiced with more than a touch of anger (Silvestre), all of this under control to encompass the pain of rejection transmuted into the pain of a courtly masochism (Silvestre in a more resigned mood) …

Chanson du pêcheur (Gautier), Op. 4 No. 1
Tarentelle (Monnier), Op. 10 No. 2
Fleur jetée (Silvestre), Op. 39 No. 1
Sérénade (Molière) from *Le Bourgeois gentilhomme*
Le Plus doux chemin (Silvestre), Op. 87 No. 1

Impromptu No. 2, Op. 31 (1883)

F♯ major

… a tonality only used once in a song-writing career for the 'heure exquise' with Emma Bardac, … related to the ardour and devotion of *Nell* (in G♭ major) but spelled differently to make it even more rarefied and radiant … When the pianist Marguerite Long played Fauré's *Ballade* for piano she wore a white muslin dress with golden flowers. The composer complimented her for wearing a dress 'in F sharp major'.

La Lune blanche (Verlaine) (*La Bonne chanson*), Op. 61 No. 3
Ballade, Op. 19, for piano and orchestra (1881)

F♯ minor

… the tonality of deception and insecurity, envy for the couples who achieve a constant togetherness (Sully Prudhomme), the grandiloquent bluster of heart-on-sleeve devotion (Grandmougin), the unsettled fear of reversion to a former state of unhappiness (Verlaine) …

Ici-bas! (Sully Prudhomme), Op. 8 No. 3
Toujours (Grandmougin) (*Poëme d'un jour*), Op. 21 No. 2, later printed in Hamelle in F minor
J'allais par les chemins perfides (Verlaine) (*La Bonne chanson*), Op. 61 No. 3

Barcarolle No. 5, Op. 66 (1894)
Impromptu No. 5, Op. 102 (1908–09)
Nocturne No. 11, Op. 104 No. 1 (1913)

G♭ major

… together with D♭ major, but to a more marked degree, the tonality of seraphic calm and assured control combined with sensual pleasure; in a song like *Nell* the music glows with rapture, and there is a quiet yet radiant throb to *Green* that is unique, the diplomacy of *Adieu* holds sentimentality or embarrassment masterfully at bay, and the Samain and Mendès settings, as well as that of Van Lerberghe, create (in the midst of myriad notes and harmony shifts) a 'deep and blissful silence' …

Nell (Leconte de Lisle), Op. 18 No. 1
Adieu (Grandmougin) (*Poëme d'un jour*), Op. 21 (later published in Hamelle in F major)
Green (Verlaine) (*Cinq mélodies 'de Venise'*), Op. 58 No. 3
Accompagnement (Samain), Op. 85 No. 3
Dans la forêt de Septembre (Mendès), Op. 85 No. 1
Prima verba (Van Lerberghe) (*La Chanson d'Ève*), Op. 95 No. 2

Barcarolle No. 3, Op. 42 (1885)

G major

… the most breezy and open-aired of keys, ideal for the *Fêtes galantes* frolics of Watteau, the impossibly bold declaration of love by Baudelaire and the optimism and grandeur of dawn in various dew-bejewelled manifestations; in Verlaine's *N'est-ce pas?* passing doubts expect affirmative answers, and *La Messagère* of Van Lerberghe has a boldness and confidence that overflows. An exceptionally bright and happy tonality …

Hymne (Baudelaire), Op. 7 No. 2
Aurore (Silvestre), Op. 39 No. 1
Mandoline (Verlaine) (*Cinq mélodies 'de Venise'*), Op. 58 No. 1
Puisque l'aube (Verlaine) (*La Bonne chanson*), Op. 61 No. 2
N'est-ce pas? (Verlaine) (*La Bonne chanson*), Op. 61 No. 8
Dans un parfum de roses blanches (Van Lerberghe) (*La Chanson d'Ève*), Op. 95 No. 8
La Messagère (Van Lerberghe) (*Le Jardin clos*), Op. 106 No. 3

Barcarolle No. 2, Op. 41 (1885)
Fantaisie for piano and orchestra, Op. 111 (1918)

G minor

… a key found only once in the songs, a colour capable of darkness and anger, above all a tonality of enigma and mystery suitable for the Venetian barcarolle …

Barcarolle (Monnier), Op. 7 No. 3

Piano Quartet No. 2, Op. 45 (1885–86?)
Barcarolle No. 11, Op. 105 (1913)
Cello Sonata No. 2, Op. 117 (1921)

A♭ major

… rarified and idealistic, an elevated tonality for myths, dreams and fairy-tale fantasies in praise of beautiful lovers, madonnas and chatelaines …

Mai (Hugo), Op. 1 No. 2 (original key before publication)
L'Aurore (Hugo)
Sylvie (Choudens), Op. 6 No. 3
Le Pays de rêves (Silvestre), Op. 39 No. 3
Noël (Wilder), Op. 43 No. 1
Une Sainte en son auréole (Verlaine) (*La Bonne chanson*), Op. 61 No. 1

Nocturne No. 3, Op. 33 (1883)
Barcarolle No. 4, Op. 44 (1886)
Ave Maria, Op. 67 No. 2 (1894)

A major

… celebration and high spirits, a tonality of energy and élan …

Dans les ruines d'une abbaye (Hugo), Op. 2 No. 1
C'est la paix (Debladis), Op. 114

Violin Sonata No. 1, Op. 13 (1875–6)
Valse-caprice No. 1, Op. 30 (1882?)
Tantum ergo, Op. 55 (1890?)

A minor

… loneliness and alienation, exile and exclusion, both political and self-imposed, the drama of the *comédie humaine* …

Chant d'automne (Baudelaire), Op. 5 No. 1
L'Absent (Hugo), Op. 5 No. 3
Le Voyageur (Silvestre), Op. 18 No. 2 (later printed in Hamelle in G minor)

Barcarolle No. 1, Op. 26 (1881?)
Barcarolle No. 9, Op. 101 (1908–09)
Barcarolle No. 10, Op. 104 No. 2 (1913)

B♭ major

… a visionary tonality of optimism and idealism, music 'on a high', a belief, whether justified or not, in something better to come …

Donc ce sera (Verlaine) (*La Bonne chanson*), Op. 61 No. 6
L'Hiver a cessé (Verlaine) (*La Bonne chanson*), Op. 61 No. 9
Reflets dans l'eau (Brimont) (*Mirages*), Op. 113 No. 2

Nocturne No. 5, Op. 37 (1884)
Pie Jesu from the *Requiem*, Op. 48

B♭ minor

… the mournfulness of the endlessly rocking cradle matched with the rocking of the ocean waves (Sully Prudhomme), sensuality at one remove, a magic colouring reserved for vocal music in the shadow of moon-struck melancholy (a tonality important in *Pénélope*, but avoided in the solo piano music) …

Après un rêve (Bussine, after an anonymous Tuscan poem), Op. 3 No. 2
Les Berceaux (Sully Prudhomme), Op. 23 No. 1
Clair de lune (Verlaine), Op. 46 No. 2

B minor

… the nearest thing in Fauré's songs to a tonality of noble declamation and *verismo* gestures, bitter regret and social disgrace, a key for big emotions and wind-swept landscapes and seascapes … farewells

Automne (Silvestre), Op. 18 No. 3
La Fleur qui va sur l'eau (Mendès), Op. 85 No. 2

Nocturne No. 10, Op. 99 (1908)
Nocturne No. 13, Op. 119 (1921)

The General Index includes entries for composers within which are listed works referred to in the text. If the work is a setting of a poem or other literary piece, the author's name (if also mentioned in the text) is given in brackets.

The Index of Poets and Settings includes not only those poets whose works have been set by Fauré, but a number other poets also referred to in the text. Entries for each poet include general references to the poet, settings of their work by Fauré, settings of their work by other composers (with the composers' names given in brackets) and other works by the poet (including individual poems as well as books of poetry and so on).

The Index of Song Titles lists only those songs that are settings by Fauré. Bold page locators indicate where the main entry for each song or song cycle is to be found in the book.

General Index

Alphonse Lemerre (book publishing firm) 58, 189, 195

Ameling, Elly 399

Bach, Johann Sebastian 146

Bagès de Trigny, Maurice 177, 179, 183, 215, 246, 272, 365

Baldwin, Dalton 291

Bardac, Emma (Mme Sigismond Bardac, née Emma Moÿse, later Mme Claude Debussy) 232, 249, 253, 254, 256, 257, 264, 265, 270

    and Ravel 244

    relationship with Debussy 243–4, 256, 351

    relationship with Fauré 118, 119, 220–22, 230, 237, 238, 242–6, 249, 253, 256

    singing *La Bonne chanson* 109, 140, 222, 242, 365, 416

Bardac, Hélène (nickname Dolly) 243, 246

Bardac, Raoul 221, 242–3, 244, 246

Barthès, Roland 426–7

Bathori, Jane 262, 292, 294, 300

Baugnies, Marguerite 111, 113, 120, 130, 135, 143, 151–2, 160, 161, 164, 173, 270

Beethoven, Ludwig van, songs

    Der Wachtelschlag (The Quail) (WoO 129) (Sauter) 239

Berlioz, Hector 4, 6, 41, 50, 85

    songs and song sets

        Irlande (song set) (Thomas Moore) 6, 287

        Les Nuits d'été (song set) (Gautier) 58, 61, 80, 91

        Sur les lagunes 80

Bernac, Pierre 353, 365, 399, 416, 419, 421, 425, 426, 427

Bispham, David 260

Bizet, Georges 15, 16, 50, 65

    works

        Carmen (opera) 15, 16

        Djamileh (opera) 15

Bodin, Thierry 42

Boëllmann, Léon 163

    Shylock (Haraucourt) 175

Boissonnet, Alice 130, 132, 136

Boulanger, Nadia 3, 295, 387, 392, 393

Bourgault-Ducoudray, Louis-Albert 14

Brahms, Johannes, songs and other works

    Auf dem Kirchhofe (Op. 105, No. 4) (Liliencron) 172–3

    Rhapodie für eine Altstimme, Männerchor und Orchester (Alto Rhapsody) (Op. 53) (choral work) (Goethe) 86

Breitkopf & Härtel (music publishing firm) 87

Bréval, Lucienne 301, 325

Bréville, Pierre de 159, 183

Britten, Benjamin 30, 140, 150, 193, 222, 365, 376, 379, 385, 400

    songs and other works

        Antique (Rimbaud) from *Les Illuminations* 354

        Billy Budd (opera) (libretto by Crozier and Forster after Melville) 228

        Canticle I (Quarles) 333

        Canticle II (Chester Miracle play) 308

        Death in Venice (opera) (libretto by Piper after Mann) 404

        War Requiem (Latin Mass, Owen) 270

        Winter Words (Hardy) 210

Bussine, Prosper-Alphonse 101

Campbell, Mrs Patrick 266–7

Caraman Chimay, Elisabeth de, *see* Greffulhe, Comtesse Henri

Casals, Pau (Pablo) 102, 366

Index of Poets and Settings

456

Index of Song Titles

Bold page locators indicate where the main entry for each song or song cycle is to be found in the book.